The Christian Century in Japan

ST. FRANCIS XAVIER, 1506–1552

The Christian Century
in Japan
1549-1650

by C. R. Boxer

University of California Press

Berkeley and Los Angeles   1967

UNIVERSITY OF CALIFORNIA PRESS
BERKELEY AND LOS ANGELES, CALIFORNIA

*

CAMBRIDGE UNIVERSITY PRESS
LONDON, ENGLAND

PRINTED IN THE UNITED STATES OF AMERICA

FOR

OKAMOTO YOSHITOMO

The design shown on the cover and title page is a crest known as the Gion-mamori. Originally from the amulet of the Gion shrine, it was adopted by Japanese Christians as their crest after the suppression of Christianity by the Tokugawa shogunate.

Preface

The four hundredth anniversary of the formal introduction of Christianity into Japan with the landing of Francis Xavier at Kagoshima in August, 1549, affords an excuse for the appearance of the present work at this juncture. The period of Japanese history known as the Christian century was decisive for the development of Japan's relations with the West. But for the introduction, growth, and forcible suppression of militant Christianity in the sixteenth and seventeenth centuries, it seems probable that Tokugawa Japan would not have retired into its isolationist shell. This in turn implies that Japan's overseas expansion in that period would not have proved abortive. The Japanese, whether peacefully or otherwise, would have established themselves in the Philippines, Indo-China, and in parts of Indonesia by the turn of the seventeenth century; and they would, in all probability, have been able to share in the fruits of Europe's industrial revolution, for several decades before they actually did.

Be this as it may, the story of Japan's Christian century has proved a perennial fascination for students of the relations between East and West. Professor James Murdoch dealt with this theme in masterly fashion in his History of Japan during the Century of Early Foreign Intercourse (1542–1651), *first published at Kobe in 1903. But although Murdoch's book thus covers the same ground as mine, I can claim to have contributed a good deal of new material. Apart from the amount of water which has flowed under the historical bridge since 1903, Professor Murdoch wrote his book in Japan, where he naturally had access to none but printed European sources. I, on the contrary, have been able to use original Jesuit secret and confidential reports and relations, preserved among the Marsden manuscripts in the British Museum, and in the Ajuda Library at Lisbon. The consultation of these original sources does not make any revolutionary change in Murdoch's work,*

vii

yet it corrects or amplifies it in several important particulars.

Another point worth noting is that historians who have dealt with this topic hitherto have for the most part relied mainly on secondary, if conscientious, authorities such as Charlevoix, Bartoli, and Pagés, whose French or Italian origin was likely to blind them to the predominant part played by the Portuguese in the old Japan mission field. The Jesuit mission in feudal Japan was staffed mainly by Portuguese; it came within the sphere of the Portuguese padroado or crown patronage; it depended almost entirely on the Portuguese colony of Macao for its temporal sustenance, and it collapsed with the disappearance of Portuguese hegemony in Far Eastern waters. Portuguese sources have therefore been used more than others in the compilation of this work; although they have been checked and supplemented by reference to other material, particularly Spanish, where this was necessary.

Japanese scholars have given a great deal of attention to the Christian century in the last twenty-five years, and even during the recent war produced a number of excellent works on this topic. Due attention has been paid to their efforts, as a glance at the bibliography will show; but since, with the exception of Professor Anesaki's narratives of the activities of the Christian "underground" after 1633, they have necessarily depended almost entirely on European material, owing to the paucity of Japanese sources, I have preferred to go to the original material direct. Basil Hall Chamberlain's observation that if we had to depend solely on Japanese sources we would know next to nothing of the Catholic episode in Japan's history, is still as true today as when it was written fifty years ago. So much is clear from a perusal of the works of the principal Japanese scholars in this field, Anesaki, Shimmura, Murakami, Koda, Okamoto, Ebizawa, and Doi. This does not mean that Japanese scholars or the Japanese viewpoint have been ignored in the present work. Far from it. The distinguished Dutch scholar, J. C. Van Leur (unhappily lost in the Houston in 1942) rightly observed that there is a tendency among European colonial historians to view the relations of their ancestors with Asiatic peoples too much from the deck of an East-Indiaman, from the wall of a fortress, or from the veranda of a trading-post. I hope that I have avoided this fault, despite my inevitable reliance on primary European sources in the absence of equally copious or reliable Asiatic material. A residence of three years in Japan (1930–1933) and a somewhat longer captivity in Japanese hands a decade later, has enabled me to see something of "the other side of the hill."

Thanks are due to the following for facilities afforded me in various ways: Dr. Robert Hall, of the Department of Japanese at the University of Michigan, Ann Arbor; Dr. Lewis Hanke and Dr. W. Hummel of the Library of Congress, Washington, D.C.; Dr. Manuel Cardoso and Fr. Antonio Sisto Rosso, O.F.M., of the Catholic University of America, Washington, D.C.; Fr. A. Demko of the Franciscan Monastery, Washington, D.C.

Mr. Hasegawa (Shinzo) of Tokyo and Mr. A. Kuroda of the Library of Congress kindly assisted me with the translations of the Japanese State Papers printed in the Appendices, but should not be blamed for any errors therein. The Directors of the British Museum (MSS Dept.); Bodleian Library, Oxford; Biblioteca da Ajuda, Lisbon; Arquivo Historico Colonial, Lisbon; afforded the facilities of their respective institutions. Father Georg Schurhammer was good enough to send me from Rome various books, photographs, and extracts from the Jesuit archives, which otherwise I could not have obtained. The Council of the Hakluyt Society gave permission to quote extracts from the edition of John Saris' journal and other works published under its imprint. Thanks are due Messrs. Kegan Paul of London who courteously gave permission to reproduce the portraits of Oda Nobunaga, Toyotomi Hideyoshi, and Tokugawa Ieyasu from Dening's Life of Hideyoshi.

Mr. Mark Dinely was kind enough to lend me his interesting and valuable manuscript album of the Tokugawa period from which three of the illustrations are reproduced with his permission.

C. R. B.

London–Ann Arbor–Washington, D.C. (1948).

Contents

xi

Contents

Illustrations

Chapter I. FROM MARCO POLO TO MENDES PINTO

MARCO POLO'S graphic if scrappy account of his sojourn in Mongol China marks a new era in European knowledge of the Far East, which from Classical times had never been more than fleeting and tenuous. It was the Venetian traveler's book (widely circulated in manuscript) which first made known in Europe the existence of Japan under the name Chipangu or variations thereof, derived in their turn from the Chinese *Jihpenkuo*, "Land of the Rising Sun." The *Pax Tartarica*, which had given Cathay a common boundary with Europe for a brief span, collapsed with the rise of the native Ming dynasty in 1368, when the Italian traders and Franciscan friars were swept out by the Chinese nationalist reaction against the Great Khan who protected the Europeans. But the seed sown by *Il Milione* was to bear fruit, for, after some preliminary hesitation, his entrancing account of the wonders of the Far East was generally accepted by those thinkers and students in Europe who were groping their way toward the Renaissance.[1]

Italy was for long the fountainhead of geographical knowledge, thanks to Venetian and Genoese commercial enterprise, but interest in the mysterious Orient was fostered elsewhere in due time. In 1428 Prince Pedro of Portugal, a brother of Henry the Navigator, brought home from Venice a copy of Marco Polo's book together with a map, "with all parts of the earth described, whereby Prince Henry was much furthered." It is true that ever since the conquest of Ceuta in 1415, the Navigator was more concerned with finding the realm of Prester John (a potential ally to turn the flank of Islam) than in seeking the Great Khan of Cathay or the Golden Pal-

[1] For notes to chapter i, see pages 451–456.

ace of Chipangu, but these latter identifications might well result from the discovery of the former, since Marco made these two fabulous potentates near neighbors. Portuguese naval power and maritime enterprise were greatly fostered by Prince Henry's careful culling of all the available sources of knowledge. Italian navigators, Catalan cartographers, Majorcan mathematicians, and Jewish astronomers aided his researches. Thanks to his organizing ability and far-sighted genius, the Portuguese soon outstripped their Mediterranean teachers to become the finest pilots and seamen in the world, and soon the idea of rounding Africa to reach India took definite shape. Admiral Ballard, writing with a wealth of practical experience, declares that Vasco da Gama's direct voyage to the Cape in 1497 has a strong claim to rank as the finest feat of pure navigation ever accomplished. G. F. Hudson pertinently adds that if it has a rival, it is surely the voyage of Magellan, who was likewise a Portuguese.[2]

Although they remained for long in the van of maritime exploration, the Portuguese were not without rivals, the majority of whom were trying to compete on the West African coast, while a chosen few were looking in another direction. Whereas the Portuguese first focused their eyes on the profitable slaves and gold in Guinea and later on the alluring prospect of potential "Christians and Spices" in India, to the exclusion of Cathay and Chipangu from their immediate plans, it was far otherwise with Christopher Columbus and his vision of Marco Polo's brave new world.

About 1470, the Florentine astronomer, Toscanelli, suggested to King Affonso V of Portugal, that Cathay, Chipangu, and the Spice Islands could be reached quicker by sailing due west from Portugal than by attempting to find a sea route to Asia round Africa. Toscanelli illustrated his proposal with a map on which was marked the island of Chipangu, where "they cover the temples and the royal palaces with solid gold." This map, like his proposal, was obviously based on his reading of Marco Polo. For one reason or another, Affonso—who was anyway primarily interested in the Dark Continent as his sobriquet of "the African" implies—rejected the proposal but it was later adopted and elaborated by Christopher Columbus. By shrouding his proposals in an air of mystery which he alone could penetrate, Columbus eventually persuaded Ferdinand and Isabella to back his scheme. He himself was not unduly disconcerted by his discovery of the Antilles instead of the Spice Islands in 1492, since he identified Hispaniola (Haiti) with Chipangu. Traces of this belief survive in sixteenth-century maps as late as 1510.[3]

Although the tendency of some modern writers to dismiss Columbus as a half-crazy religious visionary who did not know whither he was bound, may be deprecated, it must be admitted that wisdom is justified of her modern American school children who, according to the *New Yorker,* express a decided preference for Vasco da Gama, on the grounds that he knew where he was going and why. Put less crudely, the Portuguese voyages of discovery were far better planned and organized than their Spanish counterparts,—aside from the fact that they were greatly facilitated by the overland journeys of Pero de Covilham and other emissaries dispatched by "The Perfect Prince," João II, to Abyssinia, India, and the Middle East. Thus, although the Spaniards finally reached China from across the Pacific, virtually a century after Toscanelli had made his suggestion of a westward approach to Marco Polo's Cathay, it was the Portuguese who reached the Spice Islands and China, within fifteen years of Vasco da Gama dropping anchor in Calicut harbor on May 20, 1498.

For the first decade after their arrival on the Malabar coast, the Portuguese were too busy struggling with the Moslems for the supremacy of the Indian Ocean to sail east of Ceylon. By 1509 their position was sufficiently firmly established to enable them to expand their activities eastward, and they turned their attention to Malacca as the key to the coveted spice trade of Indonesia. Professor Armando Cortesão has argued cogently that King João II when he concluded the Treaty of Tordesillas with Spain in 1494 (whereby the Iberian monarchs divided the world between them with the papal blessing), already knew of the approximate location of the Moluccas, from the maps and information sent home by Covilham and his colleagues. It is also likely that Malacca and the Moluccas, possibly even China, were depicted on the charts shown by the Arab pilot Ibn Mahjid to Vasco da Gama at Malindi three years later. In any event, the Portuguese were early aware of the commercial and strategic importance of Malacca. In April, 1508, a squadron of four sail left Lisbon with categorical orders to visit Madagascar and Ceylon, "and thence to take your course in search of Malacca." Once in Malacca, the commander, Diogo Lopes de Sequeira, was ordered to make careful inquiries about the whereabouts of some people called *Chijns*. A Portuguese version of Marco Polo's *Travels* had been printed at Lisbon in 1502, but King Manoel does not seem to have suspected the connection between the mediaeval traveler's Cathay and the Chinese about whom he was now receiving reports from India. So much may be inferred from the wording of the relevant paragraph of the royal instructions which reads in translation as follows:

Item:—You shall ask after *Chijns* and from what part they come, and from how far, and at what times they come to Malacca, or to the places at which they trade, and the merchandise they bring, and how many ships of them come each year, and regarding the build of their ships, and if they return in the years in which they come, and if they have factors or houses in Malacca, or in any other country, and if they are weak men, or warriors, and if they have arms or artillery, and what clothes they wear, and if they are men great in body, and all other information concerning them, and if they are Christians or heathens, or if their country is a great one, and if they have more than one king amongst them, and if there live amongst them Moors or any other people that do not live in their law or faith; and, if they are not Christians, in what they believe or what they adore, and what customs they observe, and toward what part their country extends, and with whom they confine.

It is further worth noting that another paragraph of these instructions specifically ordered Sequeira to refrain from any unprovoked offensive action against the natives. "We further forbid and enjoin you, that in the whole course of your voyage, you will take no prizes by sea or land, since thus it seems good to us, save only if you are first attacked, for then you may fight as best you can." Another paragraph stressed the value of a friendly approach to the raja of Malacca and other native rulers, and the importance of establishing mutual trust and good faith, thus facilitating reciprocal trade. "And this principle is to be the mainspring of your actions." There is more to the same effect, and this document goes far to prove that the conquistador mentality was not always so dominating a motive in Portuguese overseas expansion as is commonly supposed.[4]

Sequeira reached Malacca on September 11, 1509, where he found some Chinese junks in the harbor. Before narrating this portentous meeting between farthest East and farthest West, it may be well to take a rapid survey of the situation in East Asia at this time.

When the Portuguese reached India, Chinese junks no longer traded westward of Malacca and Siam, but the memory of their Indian voyages under the celebrated eunuch, Chengho, was still green in Ceylon and at Calicut, where the Europeans heard the first reports of the Chijns. Just why the Ming emperors suddenly stopped the dispatch of tribute-levying fleets to the Indian Ocean has never been satisfactorily explained. They were admittedly extremely costly ventures, but expense in itself never deterred China's rulers from following their settled policies or from gratifying their costly whims. Admiral Ballard has suggested that the Chinese junks could not compete economically with the Arab dhow, since that vessel, although less handy than the junk when beating to windward is swifter when running free—an important consideration in seas where all commerce swung alternately east and west with the prevailing monsoon winds. This may have been a contributory reason but can hardly have been the main cause, for the maritime trade of Asia afforded sufficient scope for all comers, and in any event Chengho's expeditions were primarily political and not commercial enterprises. G. F. Hudson points out that the removal of the capital from Nanking to Peking in 1421 may have helped to turn attention from overseas enterprise to the growing menace of the nomad barbarians from the north. Professor Duyvendak has argued that court intrigues, originating from the jealousy of senior government officials for the palace eunuchs who organized the expeditions, played no small part in preventing their resumption after Chengho's death. He also points out that Confucian mentality probably had something to do with China's voluntary retirement into her isolationist shell. "The desire for closer [foreign] intercourse was felt to be unworthy of a Confucian official; such a desire was identified with luxury and eunuch rule, it was extravagant and wasteful, and China, being economically sufficient unto herself, could very well do without the curiosities produced by foreign countries."

True enough, and probably all these motives played their part, but I cannot help feeling that there must have been some other reasons as well. Perhaps the necessity for retaining fleets and armies (the junks often carried expeditionary corps) at home for defending the China coast against the ravages of Japanese pirates, who were then at their worst, may have had something to do with it,—although I admit this is nowhere stated to my knowledge. Whatever the reasons, it is interesting, if bootless, to reflect on the course which history might have taken if Yunglo's forward policy had been continued after 1433. For then, sixty years later, the Portuguese would have met, not a few stray Fukienese smugglers at Malacca, but large and well-found Chinese fleets at Ormuz, Aden, and Mogadishu.[5]

Mention of Japanese piratical ravages on the China coast during the Ming dynasty requires a brief consideration of their scope. These piratical attacks have been loosely compared to the Elizabethan English raids on the Spanish Main in that while plunder was their main objective, the freebooters were by no means averse to a little peaceful trading when it suited them, or when the potential opposition was too strong. The Japanese raids began in the Yuan (Mongol) dynasty after the defeat of Kublai Khan's attempt to invade Nippon in 1281. They increased in scope and intensity during the early Ming period, extending from the Liaotung Peninsula in the north to Hainan Island in the south, and as far inland as the environs of Nanking on occasion. These pirates, who were ostensibly disavowed by the decaying Ashikaga shogunate, were mostly recruited from the feudal fiefs of Kyushu, although the chronic civil wars then devastating the country supplied adventurers from all over the island empire. The Chinese gave these marauding bands the name of "dwarf (or robber) slaves," whence the Sino-Japanese word *Wako* by which they were usually known, an alternative designation being *Bahan* or *Pahan*, derived from the banners inscribed to Hachiman, the God of War, which they flaunted. They were frequently joined by Chinese pirates and malcontents in their expeditions, and thus never lacked guides with local knowledge for their forays inland. Their raids were often accompanied with every circumstance of atrocity, such as ripping open pregnant women in order to decide wagers on the sex of the unborn child. The tales told of them in this respect resemble eyewitness reports of the Japanese Rape of Nanking in December, 1937.

The maritime provinces of Chekiang and Fukien were the principal sufferers from the depredations of the Wako, and the work of fortifying the coast between the mouths of the Yangtze and the Pearl rivers was compared by contemporary Chinese historians to the building of the Great Wall against the Tartar invaders from the north. This was an obvious exaggeration, but the necessity of maintaining costly coast defenses to cope with these chronic incursions was undoubtedly a severe strain on the Ming exchequer, and may, as suggested above, have contributed to the abandonment of the great Chinese maritime expeditions to the Indian Ocean.

One undoubted result of these raids was that the Ming emperors forbade all intercourse with Japan on pain of death, thereby affording the Portuguese a unique oppor-

tunity to act as middlemen, of which they were not slow to
avail themselves after their discovery of Japan. The Wako
ravages continued throughout the first half of the sixteenth
century, but gradually diminished in intensity as the Chinese
coast defense units gained experience and the technical
superiority of Chinese shipping over the undecked Japanese
craft was utilized. Their cessation in the second half of that
century coincided with the establishment of a strong central government in Japan by Nobunaga and Hideyoshi,
but the Ming prohibition of intercourse with the island empire remained on the statute book for many years.[6]

Although Chinese and Japanese junks were the most familiar ships on the South China Sea at the turn of the fifteenth
century, there were other vessels which frequented these
waters. Korean ships are occasionally recorded as voyaging in
this area, but more frequent references are made to junks
from the Ryukyu (Luchu) Islands. This group was then
as later in a state of nominal dependence on China, but virtually independent for practical purposes. These vessels traded
to Indo-China and Malaya on a wide scale, with Japanese
and Korean sailors forming no inconsiderable number among
their crews. Formosa was still largely a *terra incognita* to
the sailors of the two great Far Eastern empires, but the
hardy mariners from Fukien and Kwangtung voyaged annually, if illegally, to Luzon and the Philippines.

Chinese trading junks also visited the islands of the Malayan
archipelago as far east as Timor, but in Java and the Moluccas
they were being displaced by Arab and Gujarati traders who
accompanied their commercial activities with a steady if
unostentatious religious propaganda, thus facilitating the
conversion of many of these islands (as far as Mindanao)
to Islam. It was these Moslem traders who brought the spices
of Insulinde to the Indian ports whence they were exported
via the Persian Gulf and Red Sea to the Venetian traders
in the Levant, before this traffic was disrupted, although not
altogether stopped, as is sometimes asserted, by the arrival
of the Portuguese on the scene. The Indo-Chinese states

which acknowledged the nominal overlordship of China, do not seem to have indulged in any maritime activities worth recording; but the Javanese were capable of fitting out respectable fleets, and the Malay sultanate of Malacca was, according to the unanimous testimony of contemporary travelers, a highly prosperous commercial mart, if a half-savage town. Such in barest outline was the state of maritime trade in East Asia when Diogo Lopes de Sequeira dropped anchor off Malacca in September, 1509.

Sequeira found three Chinese junks in the harbor, probably Cantonese or Fukienese vessels, under the command of an elderly skipper whose name the Portuguese transcribed as *Cheilata*. Sequeira's visit proved a fiasco and he was forced to leave the harbor hurriedly in order to avoid capture by the Malays. During his brief stay the Chinese had shown a distinctly friendly attitude which contrasted strongly with the natural dislike and suspicion manifested by the local Moslems. These amicable relations between the representatives of farthest East and farthest West were renewed and strengthened when Affonso de Albuquerque captured Malacca two years later. On this occasion the skippers of the Chinese junks lying in the roadstead were hospitably entertained by the great conquistador, who, wrote João de Barros, "was delighted to speak with them, because of the reputed power of their king, vastness of their country, and the government and riches thereof, which reports he could verify to some extent from their manner and behavior." This favorable impression was evidently reciprocated, for the Chinese captains offered to assist Albuquerque in his attack on the city, because they had a grudge against the ruler. Their proposal was politely declined, save that the Chinese crews helped to row the first Portuguese landing parties ashore, but they remained on excellent terms with the conquistadores throughout the brief if hard-fought campaign. They also carried Albuquerque's envoys to and from Siam; and on returning to China they reported so favorably on the treatment they had received from the Portuguese that the Ming emperor rejected the appeal of his fugitive Malay vassal for assistance against the *Folangki* or Frankish invaders.[7]

More germane to the story than these Sino-Portuguese junketings, is the description of some mysterious people called *Guores,* concerning whose identity numerous Oriental scholars have expended much ink and ingenuity. Until recent years the main European source of information about the Guores was a passage in the *Commentaries* of Braz d'Albuquerque, natural son of the great Affonso; this work, although first printed in 1557, was clearly based on a study of his father's dispatches. Recently, however, Professor Armando Cortesão rediscovered in Paris the narrative of Tomé Pires, crown factor in Malacca from 1512 to 1515, who gives a fuller version, and one which Braz d'Albuquerque probably utilized for his own account. Since Pires also mentions Japan briefly, and is the first recorded European to use the name in this form, I quote the relevant passages from the scholarly translation edited by Professor Cortesão for the Hakluyt Society in 1944.

[LIU-CHIU OR RYUKYU]

The *Lequeos* are called *Guores*—they are known by either of these names. *Lequios* is the chief one. The King is a heathen and all the people too. He is a tributary vassal of the king of the Chinese. His island is large and has many people; they have small ships of their own type; they have three or four junks which are continuously buying in China, and they have no more. They trade in China and in Malacca, and sometimes in company with the Chinese, sometimes on their own. In China they trade in the port of *Foquem* [Fukien] which is in the land of China near Canton—a day and a night's sail away. The Malays say to the people of Malacca that there is no difference between Portuguese and *Lequjos,* except that the Portuguese buy women, which the *Lequjos* do not.

The *Lequjos* have only wheat in their country, and rice and wines after their fashion, meat, and fish in great abundance. They are great draftsmen and armourers. They make gilt coffers, very rich and well-made fans, swords, many arms of all kinds after their fashion. Just as we in our kingdoms speak of Milan, so do the Chinese and all other races speak of the *Lequjos.* They are very truthful men. They do not buy slaves, nor would they sell one of their own men for the whole world, and they would die over this.

The *Lequjos* are idolaters; if they are sailing and find themselves in danger, they say that if they escape they buy a beautiful maiden to be sacrificed and behead her on the prow of the junk, and other things like these. They are white men, well dressed, better than the Chinese, more dignified. They sail to China and take the merchandise that goes from Malacca to China, and go to Japan, which is an island seven or eight days' sail distant, and take the gold and copper in the said island in exchange for their merchandise. The *Lequjos* are men who sell their merchandise freely for credit, and if they are lied to when they collect payment, they collect it sword in hand.

The chief [merchandise] is gold, copper, and arms of all kinds, coffers, boxes with gold-leaf veneer, fans, wheat, and their things are well made. They bring a great deal of gold. They are truthful men—more so than the Chinese—and feared. They bring a great store of paper and silk in colours. They bring musk, porcelain, damask; they bring onions and many vegetables.

They take the same merchandise as the Chinese take. They leave here in [*blank*], and one, two, or three junks come to Malacca every year, and they take a great deal of Bengal clothing. Among the *Lequjos* Malacca wine is greatly esteemed. They load large quantities of one kind which is like brandy, with which the Malays make themselves [run] amuck. The *Lequjos* bring swords worth thirty *cruzados* each, and many of these.

[JAPAN]

The island of Japan (*Jampon*), according to what all the Chinese say, is larger than that of the *Lequjos*, and the king is more powerful and greater, and is not given to trading, nor [are] his subjects. He is a heathen king, a vassal of the king of China. They do not often trade in China because it is far off and they have no junks, nor are they seafaring men.

The *Lequjos* go to Japan in seven or eight days and take the said merchandise, and trade it for gold and copper. All that comes from the *Lequjos* is brought by them from Japan. And the *Lequjos* trade with the people of Japan in cloths, fishing nets, and other merchandise.[8]

This curious account of Tomé Pires, together with Braz d'Albuquerque's narrative in his *Commentaries*, wherein he stresses the soldierly characteristics of the Guores, should surely settle the vexed question of their identification, if these two Portuguese accounts are read in conjunction with

the excerpts from Ryukyu historical records given by Akiyama, Okamoto, and other Japanese historians. Scholars are
divided on whether the Guores were Japanese, Luchuans, or
Koreans settled in the Ryukyu Islands, but Pires seems to
me to supply the missing key to the puzzle. He draws a clear
distinction between the Ryukyu Islands and Japan, but all
the products he lists as exports from the former, (swords,
copper, gold, and lacquer wares) come in fact from Japan,
as he himself implies in the brief paragraph relating to that
island, whereas the silk, musk, porcelain, and damask come
from China, leaving only the onions and vegetables from
the Ryukyu.

These islands were then, as now, poor in natural resources,
and their inhabitants only grew rich temporarily by acting
as middlemen between China, Korea, and Japan. From the
Okinawa records published by Akiyama, it is known that
there were large Japanese, Korean, and Chinese colonies at
Naha, which were engaged in the island's maritime enterprise. The warlike characteristics given the Guores by the
Portuguese writers ill accord with the mild and gentle nature
of the Luchuans, so attractively portrayed by Captain Basil
Hall and other early nineteenth-century visitors. It is true
that four centuries might have made some change in the
bellicose nature of the inhabitants, but contemporary Chinese, Korean, or Japanese records do not imply that the
Luchuans were much more of a martial race in Hideyoshi's
century than in Napoleon's. They have never been renowned as swordsmiths or armorers, any more than their
country has ever produced gold and copper. These characteristics were and are applicable to Japan and the Japanese,
rather than to either Ryukyu and the Luchuans, or to Korea
and the Koreans. In the light of Pires' description and
Akiyama's records, the obvious conclusion is that the ships
were indeed sent out by the ruler of the Ryukyu group from
the port of Naha in Okinawa, but that their crews were
mainly composed of Japanese, since their cargoes consisted
almost entirely of Japanese and Chinese products.[9]

The fact that the Japanese were not known as such is not particularly surprising. The king of the Ryukyu was a vassal of China—and to a lesser extent of Korea—and the Chinese government had forbidden Japanese to visit the Middle Flowery Kingdom on pain of death. It is known from both Portuguese and Luchuan accounts that the junks from Okinawa normally *did* call at Fukien ports en route to Malacca, so that any Japanese on board would naturally not give themselves out as such, particularly at a time when the Wako were wasting the China coast with fire and sword. Malacca likewise was a Chinese vassal state since Chengho's first voyage of 1405–1407, and although this allegiance obviously lay lightly on her at best, and not at all after the Portuguese conquest, yet the Japanese in these junks may well have thought it wise to be reticent about their real identity. The only flaw in this argument is that Pires' Chinese informants, who carefully distinguished between the Ryukyu Islands and Japan, should not have been equally accurate about the composition of the motley crews on board the Luchuan junks. But these Chinese maritime traders were regarded askance in their own country, which they had no legal right to leave. At any rate they were not above deceiving the Portuguese when it suited them to do so, since they told Pires that Japan was far distant from China, nor (apparently) did they make any reference to the ravages of the Wako.

If Pires' concise description of the Guores' national characteristics helps to decide that they—or at any rate many of them—were Japanese hailing from Okinawa, it is not so easy to decide the origin of the word which the Portuguese and Malays used to describe them. Some Japanese scholars have sought its root in the Korean dynasty of *Ko-ryo* or *Kao-li* which gave its name to the country and which had fairly close relations with Okinawa, where a Korean seafaring community was settled. This solution has something to commend it, since Korean sailors from Naha doubtless served on board these junks with the Japanese. But whatever the remote

origin of the name, the Portuguese clearly took it over from
their Malay and Arab predecessors in Malacca, since Arab
nautical treatises of 1462 and 1489, quoted by Gabriel
Ferrand, expressly identify the Ryukyu with the island(s)
of *Ghur* or *Al-Ghur*. As for the name Japan, which with
Pires enters European history for the first time in this form,
it is generally agreed to be derived, through the Malay *Japun*
or *Japang* from the Chinese *Jihpenkuo* in one or other of
its coastal dialect forms, probably Fukienese or Ningpo. The
meaning is literally "sun's origin country," whence Marco
Polo derived his *Chipangu* that so fired the imagination of
Columbus and led him to the discovery of the New World.[10]

II

It is rather surprising that although the Portuguese met junks
from Okinawa with Japanese aboard them at Malacca in
1511, more than thirty years were to pass before they set foot
on the Land of the Rising Sun. More astonishing still, although they intermittently frequented the China coast between the Yangtze estuary and the Pearl River from 1513
onward, there is hardly a mention of their having encountered any Japanese, yet throughout those years the Wako were
plundering and trading in this very area. On the contrary,
Portuguese knowledge of the Luchuans and their mysterious northern neighbors diminished rather than improved as
they worked their way up the coast from Canton to Ningpo.
Tomé Pires gave a fairly full account of the Ryukyu, coupled
with a briefer but withal intriguing mention of Japan. But
his report was not published in full for more than four
centuries, and the chroniclers (Barros, Goes, Albuquerque)
who utilized his manuscripts, either ignored or did not appreciate the significance of his reference to Japan, still less
its connection with Polo's Chipangu.

Oriental records are scarcely more helpful. The paucity
of Japanese sources on the Wako is not surprising, for it is

understandable that there was a reluctance to recount their discreditable buccaneering. Nor do they mention the (at times) hardly more reputable activities of the Folangki merchant adventurers in the China Sea. The reticence of the Chinese records is probably because these piratical and commercial exploits were profoundly uninteresting to Chinese historians and men of letters, who saw no point in recording the doings of foreign or local banditti save in the most general terms. But if they are not prolix neither are they wholly silent. From them it is learned that, as might have been expected, Japanese corsairs, Portuguese adventurers, and Fukienese smugglers all combined to trade how, when, and where they could, in defiance of the edicts issued from the Dragon Throne.[11]

The pioneer Portuguese voyages to the Kwangtung coast were made in junks, most of them native-owned, but some freighted in Malacca by Portuguese. In 1517, with the arrival of eight sail under Fernão Peres de Andrade, the first European ships appeared in Chinese waters. Peres was a model of tact and decorum. By complying with the letter and spirit of King Manoel's standing orders to avoid aggressive action, he succeeded in overcoming the scruples of the officers commanding the coastal defenses, and was allowed to proceed up the Pearl River to Canton. Here his fair dealing and firm maintenance of discipline among his crews, enabled him to drive an exceedingly profitable trade during his three-month stay. On his departure, he left the best impression of the Franks among the officials and merchants of the City of Rams, and he, in his turn, returned to Malacca with an equally favorable opinion of the Chinese. This fact is worth noting, because after the first good impressions formed by Sequeira and Albuquerque, a slightly sour note is discernible in the 1513 report of Tomé Pires, who adverts more than once to alleged Chinese commercial dishonesty. He was admittedly writing mainly from hearsay evidence gathered from traders' gossip on the Malacca water front; but even had he spoken from direct knowledge, this report would not have been conclusive since only traders of the smuggler or adventurer type were normally able to leave China.[12]

Fernão Peres found not only Chinese shipping in the Pearl River estuary, but numerous junks manned by Luchuans, Guores, and Japanese, as Damião de Goes states in his *Chronica del Rey dom Manoel* (Lisbon, 1563). Since these islanders had "a great quantity of gold," the Portuguese commander detached a squadron under Jorge Mascarenhas, provided with local pilots, to find the Ryukyu Islands. Mascarenhas was detained en route by contrary winds in the Fukienese port of Ch'uan-chow, whence he was recalled by Peres to Namtau before he could continue his voyage, lest he might miss the monsoon for Malacca. He had likewise driven a very profitable trade in Fukien, where he found a ready welcome from the local officials and merchants; but although he brought back further encouraging, if vague, reports of the fabulously wealthy Ryukyu Islands, this abortive voyage of discovery was not followed up next year.

The reason for this was the outrageous behavior of Fernão Peres' brother and successor, Simão de Andrade, who headed the China expedition of 1519. He was hot-tempered and arrogant where his brother was patient and accommodating. Although he probably received some provocation from the turbulent Tanka boatmen who infested the Pearl River estuary, his reaction was unnecessarily violent, and is thus described in a typical Chinese text translated by S. F. Balfour from the local *District Topography*. "Some time near the end of Ching-Tê's reign (1506–1522) a people not recognised as tributary to China known as the Feringhis [Folangki], together with a crowd of riff-raff, filtered into the harbours between T'un Mun and Kwai Ch'ung and set up barracks and a fort, mounted many cannon to make war, captured islands, killed people, robbed ships and terrorised the population by their fierce dominion over the coast. Their ambition being to annex territory they made a survey and set up boundary stones and tried to administer the various other

foreign traders in this area." The boundary stones referred
to were merely the *padrões* or commemorative pillars carved
with the royal arms, which the Portuguese were accustomed
to erect in newly discovered lands, irrespective of whether
territorial occupation was intended or not. King Manoel's
orders to Diogo Lopes de Sequeira in 1508, enjoined the erection of these pillars wherever he went; and the Portuguese
pioneer in China, Rafael Perestrello, erected one (probably
on Lintin Island in the Pearl River estuary) six years later.
In modern times they have been rediscovered from West
Africa to the Banda Islands, but the Chinese knew nothing of
this custom, and naturally regarded it as a provocative act
when coupled with Andrade's other and more drastic proceedings.

Simão de Andrade left T'unmun for Malacca unmolested
in 1520, despite his provocative behavior, but his sins were
visited on the innocent heads of the next Portuguese who
visited China with Diogo Calvo in 1521. This fleet was attacked in September and driven away after a sharp fight.
Another and much larger Portuguese fleet came to Kwangtung in 1522, but this was likewise forced to retire with considerable loss after some confused fighting. Although Tomé
Pires' Malay and Javanese informants had stressed the alleged cowardice of the Chinese, and this allegation was repeated (somewhat incongruously) by the Portuguese prisoners taken by the Cantonese in these battles, it was not borne
out by the results of the naval actions of 1520–1522, in all
of which the Chinese were victorious. Their success was
largely due to a skillful use of fireships, this idea originating with a local official named Wanghung. His exploits
achieved legendary fame among the populace of the T'unmun (or Castle Peak) district in Hongkong, where he received minor canonization and is worshipped to this day.
These Chinese naval tactics formed an interesting anticipa-
tion of their similar successes against the Hollanders off the
Fukien coast a little more than a century later.[13]

After their repulse on the Kwangtung coast, the Portu-

guese transferred their efforts, although on a more modest
scale, to the neighboring maritime provinces of Fukien and
Chekiang. Curiously enough, they seem to have made no further efforts to find the Ryukyu Islands after the narrowly
abortive attempt in 1517; and this despite the fact that they
often met with Ryukyu junks in Siam as is known from
both Portuguese and Luchuan records. The story of Portuguese activities on the China coast in the third and fourth
decades of the sixteenth century is largely a matter of guesswork, for European and Asiatic histories alike are disappointingly meager in this respect. Enough is known, however, from reliable Chinese provincial records and from the
honest if tantalizingly brief *Tractado* of Frei Gaspar da
Cruz, O.P., (Evora, 1569–1570), to prove that Fernão
Mendes Pinto's stories of flourishing Portuguese colonies
drowned in blood by the infuriated Chinese, are part and
parcel of his romantic fabrications. That the Portuguese had
a furtive trade with local smugglers at various isolated localities in the coastal provinces is an established fact. But this is
something quite different from the tall tales with which
Pinto solaced his old age and immortalized his *Peregrinaçam*
[*Peregrination*].

Mention of this celebrated traveler brings me to the point
where I must briefly consider the question of his reliability,
since he is the earliest and best-known claimant for the honor
—if that is the right word—of being one of the European
discoverers of Japan. Ever since the posthumous publication of his book in 1614, he has lacked neither detractors
nor defenders, and the controversy still rages unabated in the
learned world. Even in seventeenth-century England people
took sides, for the taunt of Congreve's clownish Foresight
in *Love for Love*, "Ferdinand Mendes Pinto was but a type
of thee, thou liar of the first magnitude," is balanced by
Dorothy Osborne's charming commendation of his *Peregrinaçam* as "englished" by Henry Cogan *Gent*, in 1653,
" 'Tis as diverting a book of the kind as ever I read and is
as handsomely written. You must allow him the privilege

of a traveller, and he does not abuse it. His lies are as pleasant harmless ones, as lies can be, and in no great number considering the scope he has for them. There is one in Dublin now, that ne'er saw much farther, has told me twice as many (I dare swear) of Ireland." Much may be forgiven the traveler who helped Dorothy Osborne to while away her idle hours thus pleasantly; but I for one fear that Foresight was nearer the mark, and that Pinto's lies, though harmless enough, were colossal.[14]

Among the modern protagonists in this perennial dispute, Professor Armando Cortesão has inherited the mantle of Dorothy Osborne, and the erudite Jesuit, Father Schurhammer, is the *advocatus diaboli* of Congreve's viewpoint. An interesting if not altogether convincing attempt to reconcile the two, has been made by Professor Le Gentil in his *Fernão Mendes Pinto. Un Précurseur de l'exotisme au XVIᵉ siècle.* His conclusion, that the *Peregrinaçam* is primarily a romance and not a serious autobiography, surely supports Father Schurhammer's thesis. To recapitulate all the arguments for and against Pinto's veracity would be as tedious as unprofitable, and I preface consideration of his claim by giving a brief outline of his career, confining myself, so far as possible, to the relatively few undisputed facts of his biography.

Even the date of his birth is uncertain, being variously placed between 1509 and 1514 inclusive. Nothing is known of his origin save that he was, in all probability, born at Montemôr-o-Velho near Coimbra. "As to his father's occupation, creed, colour, character or nation, on which the rumours vary," it has been stated by some authorities, and denied by others, that he was of Jewish parentage. No proof of this has been adduced either way, and until the relevant baptismal or Inquisition records are forthcoming, the verdict must be one of "not proven." He is generally admitted to have left for India in 1537, and he then served in the Red Sea area, where he suffered the first of his allegedly numerous shipwreck and slavery experiences. Two or three years later he was apparently trading and buccaneering between Siam,

Malacca, and the China coast as far north as Ningpo; but his
stories of a lengthy sojourn in the interior of China are singularly unconvincing. In 1541–1543, he was almost certainly in
Burma, where he says he was an eyewitness of the fall of Prome
in 1542, of which he certainly gives a graphic account. This
alone, incidentally, should suffice to dispose of his claim to be
one of the discoverers of Japan, since it was precisely during
those years that the discovery took place.

Pinto left Pegu for Goa in 1543, proceeding thence to Malacca, whence he sailed for the China coast the next year. In
1544, he was, in all probability, in Japan for the first time;
and he seems to have visited the Ryukyu Islands before leaving
for Ternate. His movements during the next decade are impossible to unravel in their correct sequence, but he apparently roved around the Moluccas, Java, Indo-China, Burma,
and the China coast, in addition to visiting Japan at least twice.
At this period he became acquainted with Francisco Xavier,
and it is an established fact from Xavier's own correspondence
that in 1551, Pinto lent him 300 *cruzados* to build a church in
Yamaguchi, and that he was then a rich man. This sum, incidentally, Xavier later repaid him at Malacca, as the researches
of Jordão de Freitas have shown. Pinto was a devoted admirer
of Xavier and several years after the latter's death he was received (with all his worldly wealth) into the Company of
Jesus at Goa in 1554. His volatile and restless spirit was ill-
fitted to bear the iron discipline and rigid self-control demanded from the sons of Loyola, and during his fourth and
last visit to Japan in 1556, he voluntarily left the Society. The
Jesuits raised no objection, and "with the same ease with
which he entered it when rich, he left it when poor," as Cortesão ironically comments. This taunt is perhaps not altogether deserved, but it is less easy to excuse the vindictive
reaction of leading members of the Society who deliberately
erased, altered, or omitted his name from their written or
printed works which alluded to his temporary participation
in the Company of Jesus. Disillusioned by his experiences,
though evidently still not without a modicum of worldly

wealth, he returned to Portugal in September, 1558, after twenty-one years' absence, during which he claims to have been made "thirteen times a prisoner and seventeen a slave, in the regions of India, Ethiopia, Arabia Felix, China, Tartary, Macassar, Sumatra, and many other provinces of that eastern archipelago on the bounds of Asia, which the Chinese, Siamese, Guores, and Luchuan writers term in their geographies the edge of the world." For some twenty years after his return he was engaged in writing his *Peregrinaçam*, which he composed, as he himself admits, more for the diversion of his family circle than with the idea of publication. The Jesuit historian, Maffei, had an interview with him at his country retreat near Almada, across the Tagus from Lisbon, in October, 1582, when he repeated his claim to be one of the original discoverers of Japan. He was granted a small pension by King Felipe II a few months later, just before his death in July 1583.[15]

Although the first draft of the *Peregrinaçam* was ready in 1569, it was not published till 1614, and in criticizing its contents, it is only fair to remember that it is hard to tell how far Pinto's editors rather than himself are responsible for some of the more palpable blunders. There was obviously no careful revision of the proofs, and the book is full of misprints and self-contradictory dates, many of which might have been corrected by the author had he lived. The Portuguese chronicler, Andrade, and his Spanish editor, Maldonado, both confessedly tampered with the text, and translators of four nationalities have helped to make the existing confusion worse. However, there is no need to follow Whiteway and Ferguson in accusing the Jesuits of having concocted the work, either in whole or in part, for the purpose of glorifying St. Francis Xavier. On the contrary, recent research has conclusively proved that after he left the Society in 1556, Pinto's name was anathema to his erstwhile fathers in God, who, while keeping his money, deleted his name from all available texts. They evidently persuaded João de Barros, who had originally relied on Pinto for his information about Japan to turn to their letters instead. It is equally true that in later years, when the recollection of Pinto's brief career as a budding lay brother had been forgotten, some of the Society (Fernão de Queiroz writing in 1680 and Francisco de Sousa in 1690) showed themselves favorable to his claims, as the historian Faria y Sousa had done before them. But they were not so well placed to judge of his reliability as was that veteran of the Japan mission, Padre João Rodriguez Tçuzzu (interpreter), who, writing in 1633, from a wealth of practical experience, anticipated Congreve by contemptuously dismissing the *Peregrinaçam* as a book of "figments."

Pinto's own narrative of his "discovery" of Japan in the *Peregrinaçam* is too prolix to reproduce here, and I therefore append his more concise version as recorded by Father Maffei and his companions during their interview with the aged traveler at Valderosal in October, 1582.

Fernão Mendez took part in the first discovery of Japan with two or three Portuguese in a junk of Chinese [pirates] who had to flee from a fleet which the Chinese coastguards were preparing against them. In their flight they endured much toil and moil by sea, especially great want of water, to such an extent that the hundred odd persons aboard the junk only drank two cupfuls of water daily. Their manner of drinking was to dip a napkin in the water, and as soon as a man had taken a suck at the wet napkin, to push him away, thus making room for the next in line; albeit they treated the Portuguese better, giving them half a pint of water daily. Enduring these hardships, they finally sighted the shore of Japan, and reached the port of Tanegashima on Saint John's day [June 24] in the year of forty-one. Here Fernão Mendez ran grave risk of being killed through an accident for which he was blameless. For once while he was asleep, a son of the king or lord [*Tono*] of the soil came and primed an arquebus of Fernão Mendez, whom he had previously seen prime it, but as he was not yet expert in the handling thereof, the arquebus burst when he fired it, so badly injuring his hand that he was unconscious for some time. The news spread quickly, and the lad's mother and father rushed up, accompanied by a great crowd of people, all infuriated against Fernão Mendez and resolved to kill him. But the Lord controlled them until such time as he could prove his innocence, and he volunteered to cure the lad, as he did, thus securing the friendship of the king or *Tono* of that realm. And this was the beginning of the trade and intercourse with the Japanese, "et qui iacebant in regione umbrae mortis, lux orta est eis."

From here Fernão Mendez and his companions returned to the port of *Liampo* [Ningpo] in China, where the Portuguese then traded, giving them tidings of this most lucrative commerce. And thus they forthwith fitted out some merchant ships for Japan, but as they mistook the monsoon, they were nearly all lost, and the said Fernão Mendez escaped from the wreck, cast ashore on some islands, whence he was finally delivered. They returned subsequently and then brought back Angero [Yajiro] who later went there together with padre Master Francisco.[16]

This succinct narrative is considerably more convincing than the romantic tale of Pinto's pioneer adventures in Kyushu as related in the *Peregrinaçam*, but it is still open to the same fundamental objections which have been pointed out by Haas, Murdoch, Schurhammer, and other acknowledged authorities on Japanese history. There is also the problem of dates. In the *Peregrinaçam* the date of the discovery is variously given (or implied) as being 1544, 1543, and 1545. These discrepancies are admittedly of no great importance, since they might be due to either a faulty memory or to the carelessness of compositors and editors. But it is certain that the first recorded visit of the Portuguese to Japan did take place in 1542–1543, whereas Pinto claims to have participated in the Burma campaigns culminating in the fall and sack of Prome, after which he went to Goa before returning to the Far East. Prome fell in 1542 (not 1545 as stated in the *Peregrinaçam*) as is known from independent records. *Ergo,* either Pinto's Burmese exploits or his Japanese discoveries are fictitious. His defenders really cannot have it both ways; for ubiquitous traveler as he undoubtedly was, he cannot have been in Burma, Tartary, inland China, and Japan at one and the same time in 1542–1543, which is what the claims made in the *Peregrinaçam* amount to.

However, even if Pinto is given the benefit of the doubt and all the dates are juggled to fit his tortuous sequence of events, his reliability still leaves a lot to be desired. He retails what purport to be long and fluent conversations with the local inhabitants in the interior of China, but there is nothing to prove that he knew any Chinese. On the contrary, his

"Chinese" nomenclature is a hopeless jumble of Japanese, Siamese, bazaar Malay, and pure gibberish. His descriptions of Chinese religion and customs are fantastic where they are not clearly derived from other sources such as Galeote Pereira and Gaspar da Cruz. In Japan he is more reliable, as I shall show, but few scholars can swallow what he has to say about his wanderings in the interior of China in 1542–1544; it is far more likely that he was then, as he claims or implies elsewhere, swashbuckling in Burma and Pegu.[17] One final point in connection with his "discovery" of Japan. His story of the "gold rush" from Ningpo to Kyushu is obviously fantastic. The Chinese were perfectly aware of the existence of Japan for centuries before Pinto "discovered" it for them. Even though official trade was forbidden under the Ming, it is known from contemporary Sino-Japanese records that a contraband trade never entirely ceased, and this alone knocks the bottom out of his story.

But if Pinto was not one of the actual European discoverers of Japan, it is equally certain that he was one of the earliest Portuguese travelers to that country, which he visited three or four times between 1544 and 1556. He had plenty of opportunity to know the real discoverers, and pass off their adventures (with suitable additions) as his own, when entertaining his growing family at Almada thirty years later. That this is precisely what he did do, should be evident to anyone who compares his account carefully with the versions given by Antonio Galvão (1563), Diogo do Couto (1597), and Padre João Rodriguez (1633). Diogo do Couto was the official historian of Portuguese India, where he lived and worked between 1559 and 1616, hence he was in a good position to ascertain the facts; here, then, is his version.

There being in the year 1542, of which we are treating, three Portuguese companions, named Antonio da Mota, Francisco Zeimoto, and Antonio Peixoto, in the port of Siam, with their junk, carrying on their trade, they resolved to go to China, because of its being then a voyage of much profit. And loading the junk with hides and other commodities, they set sail, and with fair weather crossed the great Gulf of Hainan, and gave a wide berth to the city of Canton, in order to go and seek the port of Chincheo [Ch'uan-chow], since they could not enter the former city: because after that in the year 1515 Fernão Peres de Andrade, being in China as ambassador, flogged a mandarin (who are those that administer justice, which among those heathen is much venerated), the Portuguese became so detested and ab-horred, that the king commanded by a general edict: "That the men with beards and large eyes should no more be permitted within his realms," which was inscribed in large letters of gold, and affixed to the gates of the city of Canton. And thus no Portuguese had dared to go to its port; and some ships at various times afterwards went to some islands off that coast to ex-change their commodities, whence, however, they likewise expelled them. Afterwards they proceeded to Chincheo [Ch'uanchow], whither these were going, and where they allowed them because of the profits derived from this commerce; but they transacted their business out at sea, because they did not trust them. As this junk was making for the port of Chincheo [Ch'uanchow], it ran into a fearful storm of the kind the natives call typhoon, [*tuffão*], which is fierce and appalling, and makes such bravado and quaking, that it seems as if all the spirits of Hell are whirling the waves and the sea, whose fury seems to cause flashes of fire in the sky, whilst in the space of an hour-glass, the wind boxes all the points of the compass, and seems to blow stronger in each one of them. . . .

This tempest lasted these men four and twenty hours, and at the end thereof the junk stopped pitching and tossing; but it was left in such a state and so unmanageable, that there was nothing for it but to let the wind blow it where it listed, which at the end of fifteen days drove it between some islands where they anchored, without knowing where they were. From the land, small boats at once put out to meet them, in which came men whiter than the Chinese, but with small eyes and short beards. From them, they learned that these islands were called *Nipongi* [or Nipponjin, i.e., Japanese people], the one which we commonly term Japan. And finding that these people were kind, they mingled with them, by whom they were very hospitably received. Here they repaired and fitted the junk, and exchanged their merchandise for silver, since there is none other; and as it was then the season, they returned to Malacca.

Although Couto gives a rather bowdlerized version of the misdeeds of Simão de Andrade, whom he confuses with his innocent brother, his succinct account of the Sino-Portuguese contraband trade off the Fukien coast is perfectly correct so far as it goes. There seems no reason to doubt the essential truth of his story, which does not vary in any important par-ticular from the shorter accounts given by Antonio Galvão in his well-known treatise on the history of maritime discovery, 1563 and by Padre João de Lucena in his life of Xavier (1600). When the narratives of Couto and Galvão are compared with the very similar but more detailed report of the Spaniard, Garcia de Escalante Alvarado (Lisbon, 1548), it seems probable that all three refer to the same event. Galvão and Escalante both got their information in Tidore from Diogo de Freitas, who had previously been in Siam and personally knew the men whose junk had been blown off its course from Fukien. The only difference is that Couto and Galvão state that the storm-battered junk reached Japan, whereas Escalante says that the island in question was one of the Ryukyu group.[18]

Japanese accounts help to decide this point; the most trustworthy is apparently the *Teppo-ki* or history of the introduction of firearms into Japan. It was first printed in 1649, but was written during the Keicho period (1596–1614), and is thus contemporaneous with Couto's account. The author was connected with the feudal lords of Tanegashima, and lived and wrote in the neighboring province of Satsuma, where he had good opportunities of ascertaining the facts and of meeting people who remembered the arrival of the first Portuguese in Kyushu. He places their arrival in Tanegashima on the Japanese date corresponding to September 23, 1543, adding that the vessel had about one hundred men on board, including Chinese. His transcription in Sino-Japanese characters of the names of the two (? or three) principal Portuguese can be read phonetically in more ways than one, but definitely contains the name Mota, who was one of those mentioned by Couto. However, this does not prove anything, for Mota is the Portuguese equivalent of Robinson or Smith.[19]

Escalante's description of the Ryukyu men whom Diogo de Freitas and his companions met in Siam in 1542, sounds (cf. the Pires-Albuquerque account of the Guores in 1511–1513) far more like the warrior Wako than the gentle and inoffensive Luchuans. It is also (perhaps) significant that though Freitas claimed to be their exceptionally good friend, they would never tell him where their country was situated. This again sounds more like Japanese than Luchuans. All in all, after a comparison of the available European and Japanese accounts, I am inclined to agree with the German scholars Haas and Schurhammer that the first voyage of the Portuguese to Tanegashima took place in 1543, and that if the 1542 voyage was made, it may have been to the Ryukyu Islands.

Finally, it is worth recalling Dahlgren's suggestion that the word "discovery" is possibly a misnomer for the events of 1542–1543. The Portuguese frequented the Fukien and Chekiang coasts in company (or at least in occasional contact) with the Wako for ten or fifteen years previously, and there would have been nothing strange in a few sailors having reached the Ryukyu Islands or Japan on board Wako or Luchuan junks at any time in that period. A Portuguese report written at Ternate in February, 1544, refers to a Scots pilot in their service going to "China and the Lequeos." It is interesting that the ubiquitous Scots should be represented thus early on the Far Eastern stage where they have loomed so large since. But whether or not stray mariners of this type reached Japan before 1544, it is fairly certain that Fernão Mendes Pinto was not of their number, though he was not far behind. It is equally probable that he met Mota *et sociis* and heard of their adventures at firsthand, since he evidently got the story of the arquebus accident from Diogo Vaz de Aragão, to whom something of the kind did happen. Despite the certificates of veracity accorded him by Samuel Purchas, Dorothy Osborne, and Armando Cortesão, I feel that he merits the criticism leveled at him by the Interpreter-Padre João Rodriguez, in 1633.

Fernão Mendes Pinto in his book of Figments tries to make out that he was one of these three [discoverers], and that he was aboard their junk, but it is false, as are many other things in his book, which he seems to have composed more as a pastime than to tell truths; for there is not a kingdom nor event in which he does not pretend to have been.[20]

III

Although much of Pinto's *Peregrinaçam* was clearly written "rather to fit his listener's humor than agree with the truth indeed," as he himself said of the tall tales he told Tanegashima Naotoki, yet the general accuracy of his description of Japan and the Japanese is a refreshing contrast to the arrant non-sense he wrote about China and the Chinese. Both his own account and otherwise discordant Japanese sources are agreed that it was primarily to the novelty of their firearms that the Portuguese owed their cordial reception in Japan, for the popularity attained by these new-fangled weapons was im-mediate and striking. Pinto, indeed, says that within six months of his first arrival more than six hundred arquebuses had been made by local armorers in imitation of the Portu-guese model. Like others of his contemporaries, he evidently considered it a sign of disrespect to the multiplication table to let it rest unused, and the more modest estimate in the *Teppo-ki* of ten arquebuses within a twelvemonth is probably nearer the mark. Pinto is on safer ground when he explains the great popularity of the new weapon as owing to the Japanese being "naturally addicted to the wars, wherein they take more de-light than any other nation that we know." The civil strife then endemic in Japan supplied a ready market for these guns, and for many years all firearms of this type were known as *tanegashima* after their original place of manufacture. This word was applied to pistols and carbines down to the nine-teenth century, although gradually superseded by the word *teppo* for matchlocks and muskets in the meantime.[21]

In the course of three visits to Kyushu within the next dozen years, Pinto certainly attained a better knowledge of the Japanese than his imaginary travels in the interior of China had given him of their neighbors. He noted that "these Japanese are much more ambitious of honour than any other nation on earth." He also remarked that they were usually "very fond of hunting and fishing," besides being "greatly given to joking and punning." In one of the earliest European observations on the use of chopsticks, he describes how, at a banquet given by Otomo, daimyo of Bungo, in 1556, the serving maids made fun of the Western barbarians who took the food with their fingers, "for as all their people are accustomed to eat with two [chop] sticks, they think it very dirty to eat with the hands as we are wont to do." They did indeed, and this natural reaction of the Far East to its Far Western visitors is evident from the remarks of the Chinese who acted as impromptu interpreter to the first Portuguese party on Tanegashima, as recorded in the Japanese chronicle *Yaita-ki*.

These men are traders of *Seinamban* [Southwest Barbary]. They understand to a certain degree the distinction between Superior and Inferior, but I do not know whether they have a proper system of ceremonial etiquette. They eat with their fingers instead of with chopsticks such as we use. They show their feelings without any self-control. They cannot understand the meaning of written characters. They are people who spend their lives roving hither and yon. They have no fixed abode and barter things which they have for those they do not, but withal they are a harmless sort of people.[22]

Although this record is not exactly contemporaneous with the arrival of the Portuguese, it bears the unmistakable stamp of truth. This is just the way that an educated Chinese or Japanese would have reacted to sixteenth-century Europeans. The rigid self-control enjoined on both Confucian Chinese scholars and spartan Japanese *bushi* must have made them all the more surprised at the relatively volatile temperament of the "Southwest Barbarians." I say "relatively" because there was an at any rate superficial resemblance between Portuguese *pundonor* and Japanese pride, as Engelbert Kaempfer noted one hundred and fifty years later, when he commented on that "serious and pleasing gravity" common to both nations. But although the *fidalgo's* temperament was on the reserved and phlegmatic side in comparison with French and Italians, the sailors and traders who first came to Japan were doubtless of the more lively meridional type.

Both Japanese and Chinese were accustomed to a rigid class society with a clearly defined code of ceremonial etiquette which they regarded as the hallmark of civilization, although the Chinese social system placed the scholar at the summit and the Japanese, the warrior. In this last point, the samurai had spiritually more in common with the fidalgos than with the Confucian literati, since in contemporary Europe arms were decidedly preferred above letters. Nevertheless in the outward forms of rigid etiquette, there was naturally more resemblance between the two Far Eastern races, and it was to this all-important point in Oriental eyes that the Chinese go-between referred. Yet even though traders were ostensibly relegated to the bottom of the social system in Japan and China, it may be doubted whether this affected the prestige of the newcomers very adversely. Kyushu was the home ground of the Wako, who were often as ready to trade as to fight; and Portuguese dexterity in the use of firearms doubtless placed them from the beginning above the level of mere hucksters in the eyes of the Japanese. For the rest, although the feudal nobility professed a great contempt for traders and all their works, in practice they displayed a frantic eagerness to attract the foreign merchants to their fiefs on any pretext whatsoever. The reasons will be discussed later.

In any event, the Japanese from the first showed themselves avid not only for commercial but also for social and intellectual intercourse with the Southern Barbarians. The Portuguese found this attitude a welcome contrast to their previous experiences in China, though it is only fair to remember that their earliest contacts with the Chinese, before Simão de Andrade's maladroit behavior, had been promising enough. Nor should it be forgotten that some of the Portuguese captives who spent long years of durance vile in the inland provinces, sometimes experienced kindly hospitality, or underwent lengthy interrogations inspired by disinterested curiosity. On the whole, however, it is probably not an oversimplification to say that the Portuguese met with a far readier and more spontaneous welcome in Japan than they ever did or could have done in China. The Confucian philosophical mold had not yet fixed the Japanese social structure as hard as it had the corresponding Chinese framework, nor did its mentality command the universal acceptance which it was to attain under the Tokugawa a century later. Consequently the Japanese—who were uneasily aware that the Chinese looked down even on them as barbarians—were not so instinctively disposed to despise foreigners, nor was their national superiority complex so firmly developed as with their neighbors.

Reverting to the earliest European accounts of Japan, it is worth glancing at those of Garcia de Escalante and Jorge Alvares, both of which date from 1548 or thereabouts. The Spaniard's account is hearsay, based on what he was told by a Galician named Pero Diez who said he had been there in 1544—probably at the same time as Pinto. Although Escalante's account contains some obvious errors, such as the extraordinary assertion that the Japanese possessed neither swords nor lances, it is of interest as the oldest known report on Japan by a European who had actually visited that country. Even if Pinto was there at the same time, he did not write down his recollections until twenty years later. Escalante reports Diez as follows:

It is a very cold country; the villages which they saw on the coast are small and on each island there is a chief, but he could not say where the King over them resides. The inhabitants of these islands are good-looking, white, and bearded, with shaved heads. They are heathens; their weapon is the bow and arrow, but the latter is not poisoned as in the Philippine Islands. They fight with rods with pointed spikes but they possess neither swords nor lances [*sic!*]. They read and write in the same manner as do the Chinese; their language is similar to German. They keep many horses, on which they ride; the saddles lack saddle bows behind and their stirrups are of copper. The working people dress in woollen clothes which are similar to those which Francisco Vazquez found in the country he visited [the Zuñi Indians in New Mexico]. The superior classes are dressed in silk, brocade, satin, and taffeta; the women have mostly very white complexions and are very beautiful; they are dressed in the same manner as the women of Castile, in wool or silk according to their station. The houses are built of stone and clay, the interior is plastered and the roofs are covered with tiles in the same manner as in our country, and they have upper floors, windows and galleries. Necessaries of life such as cattle and fruits of all kinds are to be found, just as on the mainland. There is also a quantity of sugar. They keep hawks and falcons for hunting purposes, but they do not use the meat of cattle for food. The country enjoys a wealth of fruits, especially melons. They cultivate the ground with oxen and ploughs; they use shoes of leather and small hats of horsehair similar to those used by the Albanians. They bid each other farewell with ceremonious courtesy. There is an abundance of fishing. The wealth they possess consists of silver which is found in small ingots of which a sample was sent to Your Worship.[23]

The report of the Portuguese captain Jorge Alvares (December, 1547) is more valuable, because he was clearly a much better educated and more observant man than the Galician sailor. It is also of interest as being the last report available by a layman, for after the arrival of Francis Xavier Japan is seen only through missionary spectacles until the coming of the heretic Hollanders half a century later. His report is too long for reproduction here but the gist of it is as follows.

Alvares states frankly that he had never been more than nine miles inland, so that his direct observation was limited to the vicinity of the only port he had actually visited, Yamagawa, at the southern tip of Satsuma. All the terrain he had seen was cultivated and hilly, but he was told there was open rolling country inland. He comments on the beautiful scenery and fine woods of pine, cedar, laurel, chestnut, oak, and so on. He mentions various fruits and vegetables and alludes to the sweet-smelling roses, pinks, and other flowers, proving in this respect a better observer than the nineteenth-century English diplomat who fatuously remarked that Japan was a country where the flowers had no scent and the birds no song. He comments on the intensive cultivation of the soil and use of horse manure as fertilizer, listing the main crops as wheat, barley, turnips, radishes, and beets sown in November; millet, pulse, beans, cucumbers, and melons in March; rice, yams, and onions in July. He noticed that Japanese horses were small but hardy; comments on the paucity of cattle, pigs, goats, and sheep, and (what is more surprising) poultry, which he states were few and stringy.

He observed the abundance of deer, rabbits [he means hares], pheasants, turtle-doves, and so on, and, like Pinto, remarks on the Japanese fondness for fowling and hawking which was the favorite sport of the nobility. Nor did the numerous varieties of fish and mollusks with which the Japanese waters are so plentifully stocked escape his observation.

He duly notes the hot springs and volcanic nature of the country, apropos of which, he comments on the fondness of the inhabitants of both sexes for bathing and washing in the hot springs and rivers—something new and strange to a European. He also alludes with real or assumed prudery to their shamelessness (or naturalness) in so doing, careless whether passers-by see their privy parts. He mentions the frequent earthquakes and prevalance of active volcanoes, as well as the stormy seas and dangerous typhoons which multiply the hazards of navigation in those waters. During his stay in Kyushu, sixty Chinese junks and a Portuguese ship were stranded by a typhoon, and he assures his readers that it was no uncommon thing for ships to be thrown up some distance ashore in these storms and then refloated by the resultant tidal waves. He states that the Japanese usually built their houses low to withstand these periodic windstorms, and large stones were often placed on the roof to prevent its being bodily blown away.

The excessive formality and punctilio which characterizes Japanese social behavior naturally did not escape his observation; nor did he fail to remark the self-contained nature of the average household, with the women doing all the domestic work and weaving their own clothes from homespun material. Each substantial household had its own well, and an orchard or kitchen garden. Altogether he gives a distinctly idyllic picture of rural life and contentment.

The proud and martial nature of the people naturally impressed him, and he noted that males customarily carried swords from the tender age of eight years.[24] He makes an interesting comparison between the large Japanese bow and the English longbow. He praises the generous and open-

handed nature of the average Japanese, and notes that they
freely and hospitably invited the Portuguese to their homes,
not only to eat and drink, but to pass the night as well—
something quite new in Oriental hospitality as far as they
were concerned. He adds that they were very inquisitive and
most desirous to find out all they could about Europe and
its inhabitants, nor were they in the least bigoted or narrow-
minded. He pointed out that they expected to be treated
similarly, and when asked aboard the Portuguese ships liked
to be dined and wined liberally, and to be shown everything
of interest.

Theft was very severely punished, and it was not only
regarded as no crime to kill a thief, even for the equivalent
of a few pence, but, on the contrary, an honor. If it was
noised abroad that a thief was in hiding or on the road, hunting parties were organized to beat the countryside, and the
thief, if caught, was killed like a beast of the chase. He
noted the uncommon frugality of the Japanese in eating,
both in quantity and quality of the food they ate. They
were, for the most part, vegetarians and rice eaters who seldom touched meat. He makes the rather surprising observation that he never saw anyone much the worse for liquor,
since, when a man had had enough rice wine (saké) he
lay down and slept it off. The accuracy of this statement
may be doubted, since nowadays the Japanese get intoxicated
with surprising ease and frequency, in great contrast to the
Chinese, who are usually heavier drinkers but hold their
liquor very much better. He duly noted that they never drank
cold water, either in summer or winter, but barley water
in the summer season and an infusion of some herb, which
he could not identify, during winter. This last beverage was
evidently tea, although Alvares might have been expected
to identify it from his previous experience in China.

He states that the Japanese were monogamous, although
rich people often had slave girls in their household. Adultery
on the wife's part was punished with death, for it was not
thought a crime to kill an adulterous spouse. There were no

prisons or penal establishments, "for each man does justice on those of his household." Slaves were relatively few, most of them being debtors, and if dissatisfied with their master, they could compel him to sell them to another. The Japanese were greatly intrigued by colored people, the Negro slaves of the Portuguese particularly arousing their utmost curiosity. They would often come thirty or forty miles to see them, and entertain them honorably for three or four days at a time. This is interesting, for the *Kurombojin,* or blackamoor, is frequently depicted in popular Japanese glyptic and applied art (*netsuké, inro*).

Japanese were normally loyal to their feudal superiors (whom he misterms "kings") and prided themselves on their iron discipline and self-control, tending to despise the Portuguese for giving away so easily to their emotions. He mentions (rather oddly) their fondness for music and hatred of gambling,[25] and notes they had theatrical comedies (*autos de folgar*). He commends their manner of building castles and fortified towns on the summits of hills, often thus rendering them impregnable by nature and art. His account of Japanese religion is confined to its outward observances, such as the Buddhist ceremonies, (telling of beads and so on), which had a certain superficial resemblance to Catholic Christianity, but he makes the correct observation that it was clearly derived from China. That Alvares was no uncommon observer, is seen from his remark that, despite the nominally inferior position of women, the gray mare was frequently the better horse. He alludes wonderingly to the relative freedom of movement enjoyed by women who could go out unaccompanied by their menfolk or chaperons— something very daring to an Iberian, for as the result of centuries of Mohammedan rule, Moslem ideas on the seclusion of women were much stronger in the Peninsula than elsewhere in Europe. Like all his compatriots, he was horrified by the prevalence of sodomy, especially in the precincts of Buddhist temples. He highly commended the pleasant location of the temples, and duly noted that, although Chinese and Japanese could read each other's writing, they could not understand each other's speech. All in all, it is obvious that Captain Jorge Alvares had used his eyes and ears to good purpose when he was in the country, and many of his observations still hold good today.[26]

This report was given by Alvares to Francis Xavier at Malacca, toward the end of December, 1547, when the future saint stopped there for a few days on his way from the Moluccas to Goa. Alvares was accompanied by a Japanese refugee named Yajiro, who already spoke a little pidgin Portuguese and whom he introduced to the Apostle of the Indies. Xavier was entranced with what he heard of the newly discovered land, and a glorious vista of missionary activity opened up before him. Here was a rich and populous country, inhabited by a highly cultivated society, something like the Chinese but without their xenophobia, and on a much higher level than the fisherfolk of Malabar or the headhunters of the Moluccas among whom the Apostle had hitherto labored. Here was a chance to sow the Gospel seed on more promising soil, and Xavier was not the man to let slip the opportunity.

Yajiro, his servant, and another compatriot were received into the Catholic faith on Whitsunday, 1548, soon after their arrival at Goa, and all three Japanese made speedy progress in studying Portuguese at the Jesuit College of St. Paul. Preparations for the expedition were pushed on throughout that year and in April, 1549, Xavier, accompanied by the Jesuits, Torres and Fernandez, three Japanese, and two body servants (a Chinese and a Malabari) left the Indo-Portuguese capital for Malacca on the first stage of their voyage to Japan. At Malacca they transshipped to a Chinese pirate junk, which was the only craft wherein they could book a passage, since the Portuguese voyages to Japan started from the island-studded Fukien and Kwangtung coast where their ships wintered. Dom Pedro da Silva, the captain of Malacca, provided money and supplies with a lavish hand, and it was chiefly due to his enthusiastic coöperation that Xavier's party

was enabled to leave on Midsummer Day, 1549. The voyage
was a relatively speedy one. On August 15, Feast Day of Our
Lady of the Assumption, the junk dropped anchor off Yajiro's
home town in Kagoshima harbor, and Xavier stepped ashore
on his promised land.[27]

Xavier landed with high hopes, nor were his early ex-
pectations disappointed. Hard experience eventually caused
some modification of his plans, and he ended by advocating
the conversion of China as an essential preliminary to that of
Japan. But he never lost his liking for the Japanese, and it is
interesting to reread his letter of November 5, 1549, written when the first flush of enthusiasm had been strengthened
rather than weakened by what he had seen, heard, and done
during his ten-week sojourn in Satsuma. It will be noticed
from the opening paragraphs that Xavier still had much of
the Spanish (or Basque) hidalgo beneath the Jesuit's soutane.

By the experience which we have had of this land of Japan, I can inform
you thereof as follows,—Firstly the people whom we have met so far, are
the best who have as yet been discovered, and it seems to me that we shall
never find among heathens another race to equal the Japanese. They are a
people of very good manners, good in general, and not malicious; they are
men of honor to a marvel, and prize honor above all else in the world. They
are a poor people in general, but their poverty whether among the gentry or
those who are not so, is not considered a shame. They have one quality which
I cannot recall in any people of Christendom; this is that their gentry howsoever poor they be, and the commoners howsoever rich they be, render as
much honor to a poor gentleman as if he were passing rich. On no account
would a poverty-stricken gentleman marry someone outside his class, even
if he were given great sums to do so; and this they do because they consider
that they would lose their honor by marrying into a lower class. Whence it
can clearly be seen that they esteem honor more than riches. They are very
courteous in their dealings one with another; they highly regard arms and
trust much therein; always carrying sword and dirk, both high and low
alike, from the age of fourteen onwards. They are a people who will not
submit to any insults or contemptuous words. Those who are not of gentle
birth give much honor to the gentry, who in their turn pride themselves on
faithfully serving their feudal lord to whom they are very obedient. It seems
to me that they act thus more because they think that they would lose their
honor if they acted contrarily, rather than for fear of the punishment they
would receive if disobedient. They are small eaters albeit somewhat heavy

drinkers, and they drink rice wine since there are no ordinary wines in these parts. They are men who never gamble, because they consider it a great dishonor, since those who gamble desire what is not theirs and hence tend to become thieves.[28] They swear but little, and when they do it is by the Sun. There are many who can read and write, which is a great help to their learning quickly prayers and religious matters. It is a land where there are but few thieves in some kingdoms, and this by the strict justice which is executed against those that are, for their lives are never spared. They abhor beyond measure this vice of theft. They are a people of very good will, very sociable, and very desirous of knowledge; they are very fond of hearing about things of God, chiefly when they understand them. Of all the lands which I have seen in my life, whether of Christians or of heathens, never yet did I see a people so honest in not thieving. Most of them believe in the men of old, who were (so far as I understand) persons who lived like philosophers; many of them adore the sun and others the moon. They like to hear things propounded according to reason; and granted that there are sins and vices among them, when one reasons with them pointing out that what they do is evil, they are convinced by this reasoning. I discovered fewer sins in the laity and found them more obedient to reason, than those whom they regard as fathers and priests, whom they call bonzes.[29]

Xavier harps continually on the alleged shortcomings of the local Buddhist priesthood, although he confesses to a rather reluctant admiration of Ninjitsu, the elderly abbot of the Fukushoji temple, whom he describes as follows: "I spoke many times with some of the wiser, chiefly with one who is highly esteemed by all in these parts, both for learning, life, and dignity, as for his great age, he being eighty years old, and called Ningit, which is to say in Japanese 'truthful heart.' He is as a bishop amongst them and if the term could be applied to him, might well be called 'blessed.' In many talks which I had with him, I found him doubtful, and unable to decide whether our soul is immortal, or whether it dies with the body; sometimes he told me yes, at others no, and I fear that the other wise men are all alike. This Ningit is so great a friend of mine that it is a marvel to see."

Xavier admits, however, that the old abbot was not the only one to give them a friendly welcome, for everyone from the daimyo, Shimadzu Takahisa, down showed himself eager to meet and to hear the foreigner. The Japanese freely confessed their surprise and admiration at the Jesuits traveling six thousand leagues solely for the purpose of preaching the Gospel to strange peoples.

In view of what some of Xavier's more uncritical panegyrists state about his gift of tongues, it is worth noting that he himself makes no such claim. On the contrary, he emphasizes the hindrance to evangelical work imposed by the Europeans' ignorance of the language. "Now we are like so many statues amongst them, for they speak and talk to us about many things, whilst we, not understanding the language, hold our peace. And now we have to be as little children learning the language."

Xavier gives information similar to that of Alvares concerning the relative poverty of natural resources and the frugality of the Japanese in eating, adding, "This people live wonderfully healthy lives and there are many aged. The Japanese are a convincing proof of how our nature can subsist on little, even if it is not a pleasing sustenance. We live in this land very healthy in body, God grant that we may be likewise in our souls." He concludes this very long and interesting letter by describing his plan of going inland to Kyoto, the imperial capital, and to the "university of Bando," by which he meant the Ashikaga-gakko, a celebrated monastic school of that name, then controlled by priests of the Zen sect, and famous as a center for the study of Chinese literature and Confucian philosophy. He mentions that two Buddhist priests from this "university" were on the point of leaving for Portuguese India "together with many other Japanese to learn the things of our Law." Shimadzu Takahisa had received him kindly and given leave for any of his vassals to become Christians who might wish to do so.

When Xavier quitted Japan in November, 1551, he left behind him a promising Christian community of a thousand souls, whose conversion had been achieved despite the handicaps imposed by his own admitted linguistic deficiency and by Yajiro's ignorance of the finer points of Buddhist philosophy evidenced during doctrinal disputations. Small wonder that Xavier termed the Japanese "the delight of his heart," and freely avowed to his colleagues their superiority over Europeans in many respects.[30]

Chapter II. JAPAN THROUGH JESUIT SPECTACLES

THE Land of Promise which unfolded before Xavier's eager eyes in August, 1549 was, as he very soon found out, likewise a land of strife and turmoil. Satsuma itself was not just then distracted by civil wars, but in this respect it was almost unique among the sixty-six provinces into which Japan was nominally divided. Even so, the Shimadzu clan was engaged in intermittent hostilities with its neighbors, and the chaotic feudal anarchy which prevailed throughout the rest of Kyushu was merely a reflection of the state of affairs in the other main islands of Honshu and Shikohu. Ever since the collapse first of the imperial authority (exercised through the Fujiwara) and later of the Minamoto shogunate (1200), the provincial war lords had been fighting among themselves for dominance, in a bewildering series of ever-changing combinations. These endemic civil wars had only ceased for brief spans under the strongest of the Hojo regents or Ashikaga shoguns, as when the whole nation combined to repel the Mongol invasions of 1276–1281, but at the time of the Portuguese discovery, Japan was quite literally *Sengoku* or the "Country at War." During this period, the transition from a patrician to a feudal social and economic order, begun under the Kamakura shogunate, was completed. "It was in these years that there was built up the fighting habit, the military caste, and the so-called warrior's code known to us as *Bushido*." (Sansom.)

So far as the Jesuits and their propagation of Christianity were concerned, this chaotic condition of the country had its advantages and disadvantages. On the one hand it meant that the missionaries were not placed at the mercy of a strong central government, which could effectively decree their exclusion, as in China; if one daimyo showed himself hostile to their preaching, they were fairly certain of a welcome from his neighbors, and when expelled from one fief, they could move on to the next. On the other hand, the lack of political and administrative stability, resulting from the kaleidoscopic changes of fortune in the civil wars, exposed their establishments to destruction overnight, if the fief wherein they labored was overrun by hostile forces. It is, however, a remarkable fact, and one to which they themselves bear witness, that there is no recorded instance of a European Jesuit losing his life in these civil broils, although they were often threatened and sometimes ill-treated.

The emperor at Kyoto still had much of his former moral prestige, but not even the shadow of his temporal power. He was usually referred to by the missionaries as the *Dairi*, a palace title meaning "Inner Sanctum," and applied by extension to its occupant in much the same way as the term Sublime Porte was used to designate the Sultan of Turkey. To such a parlous plight was the once magnificent court of Kyoto reduced, that the Lord of Heaven (*Tenno*) and his attendant nobles (*Kugé*) were forced to supplement their meager incomes by selling autographed verses or precious household utensils. Gone were the glittering days of colorful splendor with their endless round of ceremonious amusements so vividly described by Lady Murasaki in the *Genji-Monogatari,* and a contemporary Japanese record (*Rojin Zatsuwa*) states that the imperial palace was hardly distinguishable from a peasant's hut. This is doubtless an exaggeration, but it is a historical fact that the reigning monarch, Go-Nara Tenno (1527–1557), was forced to postpone his enthronement ceremony for several years, owing to lack of funds to defray the expenses. These were eventually paid by the daimyo of Suwo, Ouchi Yoshitaka, who received a court title in return. This form of reward for services rendered was one of the precarious sources of the Tenno's scanty income, since however low his temporal estate, the Heavenly

Lord still remained the acknowledged fountainhead of all titular honors.[1]

Since it fared so ill with the nominal liege lord of the land, it is not surprising to find that the condition of his deputy, the shogun or generalissimo, was little better. The powerful military dictatorship established in 1192 by Minamoto Yoritomo, after his defeat of the rival Taira clan, had by now shrunk to an empty shell. The Ashikaga shogun, whom the Jesuits usually designated by his popular title *Kubosama,* exercised only a tenuous authority throughout the *Gokinai,* or five home provinces around Kyoto, and none at all elsewhere. However, in one respect the shogunate was better off than the imperial house, since the Ashikaga still possessed considerable landed property, from which they derived a fairly substantial income, though they spent it freely on their lavish patronage of the arts. The pleasure-loving Ashikaga had delegated many of their administrative functions to provincial constables (*shugo*) who, in the course of time, had either become practically autonomous, or had delegated their authority to others who had. The warring daimyo, whether owning a nominal allegiance to the shogun or not, were thus virtually independent of both him and the emperor, ruling their own fiefs as they saw fit. The only political maxim which held good throughout the land was

> The good old rule, the simple plan,
> that they should take who have the power,
> and they should keep who can.

Another important factor in the political and cultural life of the country was the Buddhist priesthood. The most interesting branch of this community was the Zen sect, which was particularly favored by the Ashikaga shogunate to whom their prelates acted not only as spiritual but also as temporal advisers. They are known to have drafted diplomatic dispatches to the Ming court, and to have supervised the official

[1] For notes to chapter ii, see pages 456–461.

commercial intercourse with China, which still continued
sporadically despite its formal abrogation by the Ming. This
combination of trade with religion may have prepared the
minds of the Japanese for that close connection between
God and Mammon later evinced by the Jesuit's share in the
silk cargo of the "Great Ship from Amacon." Although
the Zen creed was the favored one of the feudal aristocracy,
the Hokke (Lotus), Jodo (Pure Land), and other forms of
popular Buddhism were the sects in which the great mass
of the tradesmen, peasants, and small samurai put their trust.
But although commerce and war respectively may have lured
many of the monks from leading an austerely devout and
holy life, it was likewise the Buddhist clergy who kept the
torch of culture alight during this time, in a manner somewhat reminiscent of their Christian counterparts during
Europe's dark ages. Largely thanks to their efforts, pictorial,
glyptic, and applied art all flourished in despite of—or perhaps in some respects thanks to the stimulus of—the unend-
ing turmoil of civil war. The celebrated Ashikaga college
(Xavier's "university of Bando") sheltered some three thousand students drawn from all over the country, forming a
center of Chinese classical learning which was visited by
scholars from the Middle Flowery Kingdom itself. Moreover, the little temple kindergarten schools known as *terakoya* flourished under the direction of the Zen priests, and
the Jesuits are found referring to their work in this connection with reluctant admiration.

The fortunes of Shinto are unimportant here, since
throughout the sixteenth century it was completely overshadowed by Buddhism, and possibly owed its survival to
compromising with the latter, under its dual (Ryobu) form.
Nevertheless the ancient cult was preserved in relatively
pristine purity at the great national shrines of Ise and Idzumo
—the former even extended its influence through organizing pilgrimages on the Buddhist model. It was some time
before the Jesuits grasped the difference between Shinto and

Buddhism, their early references to the former being both brief and confused.[2]

Other aspects of Japanese culture may be mentioned in passing. The theater, in the form of the *No* lyric drama, painting, mainly inspired by the Sung masters of China, and poetry, all flourished in varying degrees. The Zen-fostered tea ceremony (*Chanoyu*) attained the dimensions of a fashionable craze carried to ridiculous lengths. Many of the military feudal aristocracy, often enough upstarts brought to power by the fortune of war, were anxious not to appear culturally inferior to the kuge of Kyoto, and this in itself gave a considerable stimulus to the arts, so long as the capital was not involved in the internecine fighting.

Before turning to the Jesuit accounts which describe the reaction of intelligent European observers to this scene, it may be well to give the briefest possible outline of the Order itself, to assist in understanding something of their viewpoint.[3]

When Xavier stepped ashore in Satsuma, August, 1549, the Society was not quite a decade old, but it had already given ample promise of the missionary greatness it was to attain with the powerful backing of the kings of Portugal. Formally founded by the Bull *Regimini militantis Ecclesiae* (September, 1540), the institution from the first reflected that military character which was stamped on its organization by its founder, Xavier's friend and compatriot, Iñigo Loyola. In the Latin translation of the original constitutions, approved by the pope, the Spanish word *compañia* was translated by *Societas,* and thus the Jesuit body was called indifferently *Company,* or *Society,* by the Portuguese and Spaniards. Pope Paul III is said to have exclaimed on perusing Loyola's proposals for its establishment, "the finger of God is here"; but whatever the part played by the deity in its erection, the influence of Loyola's military instincts and training is obvious. Rigid discipline and blind obedience were inculcated as the cardinal virtues in members of the

Society whose whole organization reflected the soldierly spirit.

The older monastic and mendicant orders (Benedictines, Dominicans, Franciscans, and others) had a distinctly democratic and republican cast, in that their superiors were elected by ballot and served for a limited period only, and their powers were closely circumscribed and chapter meetings were frequent. Moreover, novices were admitted relatively easily after a short period of probation; the parent house seldom retained much control over its offshoots. The Jesuit "General" on the other hand, was a commander in chief in fact as well as in name. He was indeed elected; but once appointed, it was for life, and he exercised virtually unchecked and undisputed control over all the manifold activities and ramifications of the Company from his headquarters at Rome. He alone nominated to every office in the Society, and he could appoint or remove at his pleasure the provincials, vice-provincials, superiors, and rectors, in the same way as a military commander in chief could appoint or dismiss his subordinates in time of war. Whereas the monks of the monastic orders tended to pass their lives vegetating within or near their convent walls, mobility and missionary activity were of the essence of the Society of Jesus, whose founder extolled his institution as the cavalry of the Church, ready to go anywhere or to do anything at a moment's notice.

The personnel of the Society and its aspirants were organized into eight categories. Novices or probationers were classified as either *scholastics* or *temporal coadjutors,* according to whether their destination was the priesthood or the lay brotherhood. They first underwent a strict retreat for a month, virtually amounting to solitary confinement, during which they studied Loyola's *Spiritual Exercises* as their basic training manual. They then entered on their novitiate of two years, spent partly in daily study, partly in hospital work, and partly in catechizing the children and the poor. If they made good in this rigorous novitiate (small wonder that Mendes Pinto fell by the wayside!) they were advanced to the grade of either *approved scholastics* or *approved tem-*

poral coadjutors, after having taken the three "simple" as distinct from the three "solemn" religious vows. The training and education of a Jesuit in the sixteenth century was not, in some respects, so lengthy and rigorous as it subsequently became. But even then the approved scholastics or would-be spiritual coadjutors had to study grammar, the humanities, and rhetoric for two years or more before they could take the four-year course of philosophy which included the natural sciences, metaphysics, and ethics. This in itself was merely the preliminary, together with some practical experience in the teaching of junior classes, to the four- or six-year course of theology which formed the crown of the potential spiritual coadjutor's academic career. The training of approved temporal coadjutors was not so rigorous, since they were only destined to discharge the functions of a lay brother (artisan and technical avocations generally), but even they normally had to work ten years for the Society before they could be admitted to its ranks as *formed temporal coadjutors.* They were not admitted to Holy Orders which were reserved for the *formed spiritual coadjutors,* some of whom could, in the course of time, aspire to the grade of *professed of the three solemn vows,* and, fewer and later still, to the highest grade of the *professed of the four solemn vows.* The last-named group constituted the real core of the Society. The fourth vow which they took was one of special allegiance to the pope, promising to go, for missionary purposes, whenever and wherever he ordered—a pledge qualified in practice by the power conferred on the General of sending out or recalling any missionary. Thus, once the Society had got into its stride, the final grade normally could not be attained by a Jesuit before his forty-fifth year, even for those who had entered the novitiate at the earliest legal age of fourteen. This was in marked contrast to the other religious orders, wherein the three solemn vows were taken after a preliminary year's novitiate.

Territorially, the Company was organized into provinces and vice-provinces, of which Portugal was founded in 1540,

Goa in 1542, Japan in 1549, and the vice-province of China in 1583. Both provincials and vice-provincials were directly subordinated to the general at Rome, who, in addition, exercised control over the provinces and vice-provinces by the periodic dispatch of specially appointed visitors. The efficient functioning of this rigid hierarchy was facilitated by a very comprehensive system of periodical confidential reports, covering not only the provinces and vice-provinces but the activities of the "professed houses" and of each individual member of the Society. Small wonder that this new and well-organized branch of the Church Militant stopped the advance of Protestantism in its tracks, and rolled back the wave of heresy from the foot of the Alps to the shores of the Baltic (to borrow a phrase from Macaulay).[4]

Such was the ubiquity and enthusiasm displayed by the devoted members of the Company of Jesus that their inspiring leadership of the Counter Reformation in Europe did not distract either their attention or their efforts from the expansion of their missionary activities overseas. The Society, then, was not ten years old when Xavier stepped ashore at Kagoshima, but within another three decades, the Jesuits had high hopes that the complete conversion of the island empire would counterbalance the defection of England from the comity of Catholic nations. Xavier's instinctive liking for the Japanese was clearly reciprocated; and perhaps part of the preliminary successes of the Jesuits in Japan can be explained by a certain similarity of training between these soldiers of the Cross and the samurai nurtured in the spartan precepts of the Warriors' Way. The parallel must not be pushed too far; but the following quotation from the *Spiritual Exercises* might have come equally well from either the stoical *Meditations* of Marcus Aurelius or the *Legacy* of Tokugawa Ieyasu: "We must make ourselves indifferent in regard to all created things, so that we shall not wish for health rather than sickness, for riches rather than poverty, for honor rather than reproach, for a long life rather than a short one." I have said the parallel must not be pushed too far, for this detachment from and indifference to worldly things, did not signify with Loyola an end in itself, as did the *ataraxia* of the ancient Stoics. With the Jesuit, it was an essential condition for the mind to free itself from all earthly attachments in order that it could act solely in accordance with the Divine will. The samurai was satisfied with sacrificing everything for the sake of his feudal superior.[5]

The American historian Richard Hildreth in his still readable *Japan As It Was And Is,* has stigmatized the Portuguese Jesuits as "poor observers," but in this he was grossly unfair. It can be pleaded in his extenuation that most of their works were not available to him in their original Portuguese dress, but only in truncated and bowdlerized Italian, Latin, or French translations. The Jesuits themselves are partly to blame for this, since the researches of Father Schurhammer have established that some of the original editors at Rome strongly objected to what they termed the "prolix and detailed" nature of these reports, and the censors wielded the scissors and blue pencil most ruthlessly. Moreover, it was precisely to the lengthy descriptions of the temples of Nara and Kyoto, and to the detailed analysis of the various Buddhist sects—in which the Portuguese Jesuits Almeida and Frois showed themselves particularly interested—that the editors objected. It was these "unedifying" accounts of Japanese Buddhism which they cut so ruthlessly, whence the garbled and truncated versions which appeared in print. The censors of the Portuguese edition of the *Cartas* of 1570 and 1598, do not seem to have been so drastic, and it is from them that my translations are taken. Moreover, the discovery and partial publication within recent years of the voluminous histories of Japan by Luis Frois and João Rodriguez Tçuzzu, together with the masterly reports of Alessandro Valignano, have disposed once for all of Hildreth's charge. Their publication has served to place these Portuguese Jesuits on a par with their French and Flemish colleagues of the China mission whose full and methodical *Lettres édifiantes et curieuses* on the Middle Kingdom did so much to popularize China in Europe. True it is, that the

Japan Jesuits are not always very clear or concise in their
descriptions of esoteric Buddhism; but much may be forgiven them in this respect, when consideration is given, on
the one hand, to their inherent prejudices, and on the other
to the fact that scholars of the standing of Sir George Sansom have been accused of similar superficiality by native
Zen professors.[6]

Whatever their shortcomings as expositors of the mysti-
cal profundities of Zen, the missionaries were certainly keen
and intelligent observers of the mundane life that went on
around them. They were, of course, first and foremost
sowers of the Gospel seed, true to their motto of working
"ad majorem Dei gloriam," hence the carping critic should
remember that in their "edifying and curious" letters, the
emphasis is necessarily on the edifying rather than on the
curious. Nevertheless the student of Old Japan will find a
wealth of interesting material if he knows where to look,
and it is significant that leading Japanese historians (Anesaki,
Murakami, Koda, and others) rate their correspondence very
highly. The best and most voluminous printed source for
this period is the collection of Jesuit Letters printed by order
of the Portuguese Archbishop Dom Theotonio de Braganza
at Evora in 1598, comprising a stout folio volume of 750
pages. For reasons already explained, these collected *Cartas*
are mostly preferable to the Italian and Latin translations,
apart from the fact that many of them were not printed
either before or since their publication in 1598.

Naturally, wars and rumors of wars occupy much space
in these reports written during the turmoil of the "Country
at War," but the more peaceful and unchanging aspects of
the national scene are by no means neglected. By way of illus-
trating their value, I select three extracts which give an
interesting glimpse of Japanese life during the *Sengoku-jidai*.
The first is a description of the popular Buddhist festival of
O-Bon, corresponding roughly to the Christian All Soul's
Eve, taken from a letter of Padre Gaspar Vilela written at
Sakai on August 17, 1561. The second extract is from an

extremely interesting and lengthy epistle written by Luis d'Almeida at Fukuda, near Nagasaki, on October 25, 1565, in which he gives the earliest account of the formal tea ceremony or chanoyu, and one which Luis Frois, who evidently helped draft the letter, later embodied in his *History* of the Church in Japan. The third and last extract is another from the same letter of Almeida, describing Matsunaga Hisahide's great castle at Nara. Almeida also describes the famous Buddhist temple of the Daibutsu, and the Shinto Kasuga shrine, in the course of this letter; but I have selected the description of the castle for translation, since that typical example of Japanese feudal architecture was destroyed shortly afterward, leaving not a wrack behind, whereas the Daibutsu and the colorful Kasuga shrine still stand in Nara's leafy park and may be visited by any tourist today.

Vilela begins his letter of August 17, 1561 with a brief description of his journey from Sakai to Kyoto via the famous Tendai temples on Hieizan, which he was told had been reduced in number from 3,300 to about 500 by the wars. After giving an account of the Shinto festival of Gion, celebrated annually in July, he proceeds with his description of the Buddhist festival of the dead.

They have another festival called *Bon,* held each year in the memory of the souls of their forebears in the month of August, on the fifteenth day of the moon thereof, beginning on the evening of the fourteenth. Everybody sets lighted lamps in the streets, decorated as best he can, and all night long the streets are thronged with people, some out of devotion to the dead, and others out of curiosity to see what is going on. On the evening of this day of All Souls, many people go outside the city, to receive the souls of their ancestors, and reaching a place where they imagine that they can meet the souls they have come in quest of, they begin to converse with them. Some offer them rice, others vermicelli, whilst those who are very poor proffer hot water, together with many offerings, saying unto them "come and welcome! We have not met for a long time; you must be tired, pray be seated and eat a little," and suchlike words. They then place what they have brought on the ground, and wait for about an hour, as if to give their unseen guests time to rest and eat. This done, they ask them to come home, and say they will go on ahead to make ready for them. Returning to the house, they arrange a table after the fashion of an altar, whereon they place rice and other foodstuffs sufficient to last for the two days which the festival endures. On the evening of the second day, many people roam through the hills and fields with torches and lights, saying that they are showing the souls their way back, lest they should miss their way; there they take leave of them, and returning home they throw many stones on the roof, saying they do this lest some souls should have stayed on the roof not wishing to leave, and they will drive them away for fear that if they stay, they might do them some harm; albeit they are sorry for them, saying that the souls are very small, and if it should rain on the way, some of them would die. They are so convinced of the truth of these things about souls, through their celebration of these and similar festivals, that they cannot be persuaded to think otherwise about them. If they are asked why they give these souls to eat, they reply that they are going to their paradise, which is ten thousand million leagues away and takes three years to reach, so that becoming weary on the way, they come to get that help which enables them to renew their journey once more. During these days they clean all their tombs, and the Bonzes dominate over them on account of the great sacrifices which are made to the souls. For no matter how poor they may be, everybody offers what he can to the souls of his forebears, and whosoever does not, is regarded as beyond the pale.[7]

After Vilela's graphic description of a popular Buddhist festival, which anticipates by more than three centuries the moving accounts of Lafcadio Hearn and Wenceslau de Moraes, I turn to his colleague, Luis d'Almeida, for a succinct version of the cultured aristocratic pastime of chanoyu. On the eve of Almeida's departure to join Vilela at Nara castle, his host, a Christian convert, introduced him to this unique form of entertainment, which the Jesuit describes in his letter of October, 1565.

It is customary with the noble and wealthy Japanese, when they have an honored guest who is on the point of leaving, to show him their treasures as a sign of esteem. These treasures consist of the utensils they use in drinking a certain powdered herb called *cha*, which is very pleasant to those who are accustomed to drink it. Their way of doing so, is to grind half a handful of the leaves of this herb in a porcelain bowl, after which they drink them infused with very hot water. For this purpose they use some very old iron kettles, as also the vessel wherein they put the water to rinse the porcelain bowl, and a little tripod whereon they put the lid of the iron kettle so as to avoid placing it on the mats. The caddy in which they place the cha leaves, the spoon with which they scoop them, the ladle with which they take the water from the kettle, and the stove—all these utensils form the jewelry of Japan, in the same way as rings, necklaces, and ornaments of magnificent rubies and diamonds do with us. And they have experts who appraise these utensils, and who act as brokers in selling or buying them. Thus they give parties to drink this herb (of which the best sort costs about nine or ten ducats a pound) and to display these utensils, each one as best as his wealth and rank will allow. These parties are given in special houses, only used on such occasions, which are marvels of cleanliness.

On the next day at nine o'clock they sent a message for me, and a Japanese Brother, and another man who looks after all our affairs in Japan, [Cosme Kozen] a rich man and a very good Christian. They led me behind some of his apartments, through a small door by which a man could just enter comfortably; and passing along a narrow corridor, we ascended a cedarwood staircase, of such exceptional cleanliness that it seemed as if it had never yet been trodden upon by human feet. We emerged into a court-yard measuring a few square yards, and passing along a verandah, entered the house where we were to eat. This place was a little larger than the court-yard, and appeared to have been built by the hands of angels rather than of mortal men. On one side was a sort of cupboard such as is usual here, and right in front a hearth of black earthenware about a yard in circumference, that shone like the most highly-polished mirror, strange to say, in spite of its jet-black hue. Upon it there stood a pleasingly fashioned kettle, placed on a very curiously wrought tripod. The ashes on which the glowing char-coal lay, looked like finely ground and sifted eggshells. Everything was ex-quisitely clean and set out with such order as to be beyond description; and this is not perhaps so remarkable seeing that on these occasions they con-centrate their attention only on such things. My companion informed me that the kettle had been bought by Sancho, as a great bargain, for six hundred ducats, but that it was worth much more.

When we had taken our places, they began to serve the repast. I do not praise the food, for Japan is but poorly provided in this respect; but as regards the service, order, cleanliness, and utensils, I can confidently affirm that nowhere in the whole wide world would it be possible to find a meal better served and appointed than in Japan. Even if there should be a thou-sand men eating, one never hears a single word spoken by any of those who serve it, everything being carried out in an incredibly orderly manner. When dinner was over, we all said grace upon our knees, for such is the good custom among the Japanese Christians. Sancho with his own hands made and served the *cha,* which is the powdered leaves I spoke of. After-wards he showed me, among many others of his treasures, a small iron tripod, little more than a span round, on which they put the lid of the kettle when it is taken off. I took this in my hand, and it was so worn with age in parts, that it was soldered in two places where it had broken through sheer decay. He told me that this was one of the most valuable of its kind in all Japan, and that it had cost him 1,030 ducats, although he personally considered that it was worth much more. All these things were kept in fine damask and silk bags, each in its valuable little box. He told me that he had more of these treasures, but could not show them just then for they were stored away in a place where it was not easy to get at them, but that he would show us them if we came again. Nor is the worth of these things to be wondered at, since here in Kyoto there is a man who has an earthenware caddy for the cha leaves valued at thirty thousand ducats. I don't say it would necessarily be sold for so much, but it is quite likely that many princes would give ten thousand for it. These kind of vessels frequently fetch between three and five thousand ducats apiece and are often bought and sold. Some of their swords likewise fetch similar prices.[8]

Although this account may sound a trifle exaggerated it was the sober truth. The tea caddy referred to in the concluding sentence was the famous *Tsukuno-gami* or "Dishevelled Hair," which was later presented by Matsunaga Danjo Hisahide to Oda Nobunaga. Matsunaga was an enthusiastic connoisseur of Chanoyu, who, before committing suicide, smashed to pieces another priceless teakettle rather than let it fall into the hands of a rival collector. Almeida, in this same letter of 1565, gives an interesting account of his visit to Matsunaga's new (and short-lived) castle of Tamon at Nara, which he visited at the end of April.

This Lord being, as I said, so powerful in wealth and lands, and strictly obeyed, resolved to build a fortress in this city, as is customary with them. For this purpose he occupied a hill and excavated it, the stone being very soft, and made many towers of the same material. In the middle thereof was a large space, about one third of the circuit of the city of Goa, wherein he sank many wells, since much water was found three fathoms down. He then invited his chiefest and wealthiest noblemen and those of their retainers whom he trusted, to build their houses within this circuit, for which purpose he partitioned out their sites. He began this five years ago, and they all being envious of each other, built the richest and most sumptuous storied houses that can be imagined, with very good lattices after our manner. All these, as likewise the circuit of the castle and its towers are built with whiter and smoother walls than ever yet I saw in Christendom. For they mix no sand with the lime, but only knead it with a special kind of very white paper which they make for this purpose.

All the houses and towers are roofed with the finest tiles I have ever seen. These were all black in color and of various shapes, being about two fingers thick. Once they are made, they last four or five hundred years unchanged, as I myself have seen in many temples six or seven hundred years old. To enter in this town (for so I may call it) and to walk about its streets seems to be like entering Paradise. It is so clean and white that it looks as if all the buildings had been finished that very day.

I think there can scarcely be a more beautiful sight in the world than this fortress seen from the outside, for it is a sheer joy to look on it. I went inside to see its palatial buildings, and to describe them I would need reams of paper, since it does not appear to be the work of human hands. For not only are they all constructed of cedarwood, whose delicious odor delights the senses of all those who enter, but all the verandahs are built of single beams about seven feet long. The walls are all decorated with paintings of ancient stories on a background of gold leaf. The pillars are sheathed with lead for about a span at the top and bottom respectively, and gilded and carved in such a way that everything looks as if it was covered with gold. In the center of the pillars are large and beautiful bosses decorated in the same manner. The ceiling of these buildings looks like a single piece of wood, since no join is visible even if you look very closely. I cannot write of the other decorations, for words fail me.

Among the many houses I saw in this palace, there was one room even fairer than all the rest, measuring about thirty feet square, built of a wave-grained yellow wood with the most beautiful and pleasing waves that can possibly be imagined. This wood was so highly polished that it shone like gleaming mirrors, but I thought that no wood could shine like that unless it had been treated with some kind of lacquer. As for the gardens and artificially shaped trees which I saw in the palace grounds, I cannot imagine anything more delightfully cool and fresh. For I have seen in Kyoto many things worth seeing but they are as nothing in comparison with all this. I am sure that in the whole world it would be impossible to find anything more splendid and attractive than this fortress, and in fact people come from all over Japan just to see it.[9]

Some writers have maintained that this famous castle of Tamonjo was the first built in Japan which owed something to Portuguese ideas of military architecture, but there is nothing in Almeida's exhaustive description to indicate this. On the contrary, he expressly states that he had seen nothing like it in Europe, and it is understandable that this lyrical account was probably one of the items that the bigoted censors at Rome had in mind when they criticized these Jesuit reports from Japan as being too prolix and full of unedifying comparisons. Similar invidious comparisons between things Chinese and European to the advantage of the former during the eighteenth century were later to invite carping criticism of the *Lettres édifiantes et curieuses* for the same reason. Nara castle was not destined to stand for long in its glory. In the same summer that Almeida set his wondering eyes on it, Matsunaga and his confederate Miyoshi, murdered the fourteenth Ashikaga shogun, Yoshiteru, thus starting a series of wars which culminated in his own defeat and death by Hideyoshi twelve years later, and the reduction of his castle to a heap of ashes. No trace now remains of this structure and the modern visitor to the site can repeat the famous lines of Basho:

> The Summer Grasses!
> All that is left of the Warriors' dream! [10]

II

The importance of the sixteenth century as the starting point of modern Japanese history is well known. One authority has stated that a Japanese wishing to study his civilization in the light of its own history, need go no farther back than the beginning of the *Sengoku-jidai* (1467), since all previous national history might as well be that of a foreign country. This is a palpable exaggeration, but it is generally admitted that the foundations of the modern militarized Japan which burst its bounds in 1941 were laid some four centuries earlier. It is likewise common knowledge that the three main architects of the political unification of the country under military rule were Oda Nobunaga, Toyotomi Hideyoshi, and Tokugawa Ieyasu. Their respective shares in this task are defined in the well-known saying that Nobunaga mixed the dough, Hideyoshi baked the cake, but Ieyasu ate it. Perhaps Dr. Hara's definition expressed the same idea rather more accurately when he wrote that Nobunaga quarried the stones for New Japan, Hideyoshi rough-hewed them, and Ieyasu set them finally in their proper place.

The Jesuits were the only Europeans who from first to last had a good front-seat view of this process; and the ac-

counts of these intelligent and (up to a point) trained observers are all the more welcome because of the silence or un-
trustworthiness of many of the native records on crucial
points. Thus Frois and Organtino were on such familiar
terms with Nobunaga, that it recalls at times the Manchu
Emperor Kanghsi's warm personal friendship for the elderly
Flemish Jesuit, Ferdinand Verbiest, a century later. The
Taiko Hideyoshi only occasionally admitted foreigners to
such real familiarity, but nevertheless both he and his successor, the less temperamental Tokugawa Ieyasu, showed great
confidence in their astute Jesuit interpreter, the Portuguese
João Rodriguez Tçuzzu, even at times when they were pub-
lishing admonitory decrees against the practice of Christianity. Rodriguez was in fact only superseded by Will Adams
as Ieyasu's confidential if unofficial foreign adviser; and thus
it is hardly too much to say that from 1570 to 1614, the
Jesuits held a peculiarly favorable position as observers at the
court of the Bakufu—quite apart from what their relatively
numerous and influential converts in high places were willing to tell them. This is probably the reason why modern
historical research has shown that the Jesuit accounts of some
disputed facts of Japanese history are perfectly correct,
where the popular native historians are sadly astray. The
glimpses which the Portuguese Jesuits afford of Kyoto, Nara,
and Adzuchi, are comparable in value and interest to the
better-known relations of their colleagues concerning the
tawdry splendors of Moghul Delhi or the more austere attrac-
tions of the Manchu court at Peking. I therefore give in this
section some extracts from their letters depicting various
aspects of men and things in Nobunaga's day, particularly in
the region around Kyoto, where the decisive struggle for
political supremacy was centered.[11]

The warring daimyo were virtually autonomous princes,
ruling their own lands as they saw fit, while nominally profes-
sing loyalty to the throne and (to a lesser extent), to the
decaying Ashikaga shogunate. Obviously this was a state of
affairs which could not continue indefinitely and it was only

a question of time before some powerful personality or group emerged to bring order out of feudal chaos by dint of *force majeure*. By 1569, the struggle had come to a point where the principal contestants for political supremacy were narrowed down to less than half a dozen, of whom the most centrally placed was Oda Nobunaga, who in that year had occupied Kyoto on behalf of his puppet, Yoshiaki, the nominal Ashikaga shogun. It was at this juncture that fate, in the person of Wada, Iga-no-kami Koremasa intervened on behalf of the Jesuits. This feudal lord, one of Nobunaga's most trusted lieutenants before Hideyoshi and Ieyasu came to the fore, took an extraordinary fancy to Father Luis Frois, and arranged to present him to Nobunaga, which he accordingly did in April, 1569, after a previous attempt had proved abortive.

At the time of what turned out to be a momentous meeting, Nobunaga controlled only about a dozen provinces out of the sixty-six into which Japan was divided, but he was clearly recognized as a coming man, and evidently inspired no little awe among his subordinates. Frois' account of his appearance on their first meeting is therefore worth quoting in full.

He would be about thirty-seven years old, a tall man, lean, scantly bearded, with a clear voice, greatly addicted to military exercises, hardy, disposed to temper justice with mercy, proud, a great stickler for honor, very secretive in his plans, most expert in the wiles of warfare, little or nothing disposed to accept reproof or advice from his subordinates, but greatly feared and respected by everyone. He does not drink wine, he is rough mannered, contemptuous of all the other kings and nobles of Japan whom he addresses brusquely over his shoulder as if they were inferiors, while he is punctiliously obeyed by all as their complete master. He is of good understanding and clear judgment, despising both Shinto and Buddhist deities and all other forms of idolatry and superstition. He is a nominal adherent of the Hokke [Lotus] sect but he openly proclaims that there are no such things as a Creator of the Universe nor immortality of the soul, nor any life after death. Extremely refined and clean in his dress and in the nobility of his actions; annoyed at anybody who addresses him hesitantly or with circumlocution; not even a prince dare appear before him with a sword; he is always attended by a train of at least two thousand pages on horseback. Whereas his father was merely Lord of Owari, he, by his masterful skill, has conquered seventeen or eighteen fiefs within the last four years;

and the eight principal ones, including Yamashiro, Kyoto, and the neighboring provinces, he subjected within seven or eight days.

Although Frois slightly exaggerates the extent of Nobunaga's conquests, for he was as yet by no means the unchallenged master of the five metropolitan provinces, where the militant monks of Hieizan and Osaka declined to acknowledge his authority, yet there is no reason to doubt the Jesuit's eyewitness description of Nijo castle. This castle was being built as a residence for the puppet Ashikaga shogun, and Frois says gleefully that stone images from the neighboring temples were being freely used to supply the material, for lack of suitable quarries in the neighborhood. From fifteen to twenty-five thousand workmen were normally employed on this building, the construction of which progressed so rapidly that work which might have been expected to last four or five years was accomplished in seventy days. The furnishings were provided with a similar disregard for local religious susceptibilities, since Nobunaga took the priceless gold-leaf picture screens (*byobu*) from one of the leading Nichiren temples (the Rokujo Honkoku-ji) for this purpose, despite the pleas of the Hokke devotees and the offers of large bribes to desist from his intention. The Jesuits record this incident with malicious satisfaction since it was popularly believed that the Nichiren monks had bribed Matsunaga to kill Vilela and Frois in the same way as he had killed the Shogun Ashikaga Yoshiteru.

Frois was kindly received at this first interview by Nobunaga, who was seated on a drawbridge according to his usual custom, clad in a tigerskin thrown over his rough clothes, superintending the constructional work in the presence of a crowd of six or seven thousand onlookers. He talked familiarly with the Jesuit for nearly two hours, partly directly, and partly through his Japanese interpreter, Brother Lourenço. Frois was then shown over the uncompleted Nijo castle by Wada Koremasa at Nobunaga's special behest. He was extremely impressed by what he saw, comparing it to Solomon's construction of the Temple at Jerusalem and Dido's building

of Carthage. He and Nobunaga then parted with many pro-
fessions of mutual esteem which left the Jesuit with high and
justified hopes for the future.[12]

This memorable meeting swiftly yielded concrete results
for the mission, chiefly through the good offices of Wada Iga-
no-kami, who though never actually converted likewise never
wearied in well-doing on behalf of the missionaries, and took
endless trouble to get their position formally recognized by
Nobunaga and the shogun. As a result of his efforts and
Nobunaga's intervention, Frois was soon after kindly received
in audience by Ashikaga Yoshiaki, who liberally plied the
Jesuit with wine, and on his departure came and peeped after
him curiously from behind the sliding doors. Matsunaga Hisahide, after killing Yoshiaki's predecessor, had subsequently
patched up a peace with Nobunaga, and he attempted to
deter the latter from receiving Frois on the grounds that the
Jesuit was a potential disturber of the public peace. Nobunaga
scornfully rejected his advice, adding that he must be a very
mean-spirited and narrow-minded man to imagine that a
single unarmed foreigner could pervert the peace of the empire in a populous city like Kyoto. This was the end of any
opposition from those of Nobunaga's immediate entourage,
but considerable hostility was encountered in another and
more august quarter.

The reigning emperor, Ogimachi Tenno, had already
banned the foreigners from the capital five years previously,
on the prompting of the Tendai monks of Hieizan. This
was one of the reasons why Vilela and Frois took refuge in
the "free city" of Sakai, until the patronage of Nobunaga
and Wada enabled the latter to come to Kyoto in 1569. In
order to obviate future trouble of this kind, Frois asked for
and obtained from both Nobunaga and the shogun formal
letters patent under their respective seals, authorizing him
to stay unmolested in the district. These documents were likewise owing to the untiring efforts of Wada Koremasa who
importuned his superiors until they were granted. As Frois
observed in forwarding the translation of Nobunaga's patent

(*Shuinjo*) to Goa, the wording of these official documents is brief in the extreme but their meaning conversely very wide, and I therefore give his version of the original (drafted by Wada) dated April, 1569.

I hereby authorize the padre to stay in Kyoto. Nobody may be billeted in his house, nor will he be expected to share in the customary ward and street duties, since I exempt him from them all. He will not be molested throughout any of my provinces. If by any chance anybody does him any wrong, I will see that thorough justice is done and punish most severely whosoever harms him.

[Endorsed at the foot]—For the Padre of Christendom in the hermitage called The True Doctrine.

It will be observed that neither this nor (apparently) the shogunal license gave Frois a specific authorization to preach the Gospel unmolested, but this privilege was most certainly implied, and both documents were undoubtedly meant to be understood in that sense. This unprecedented concession roused the opposition to fury. Their spokesman was a Hokke zealot named Nichijo Shonin who persuaded the emperor to issue another and more emphatic edict, decreeing the death of the Jesuit and prohibiting the propagation of his faith. Nobunaga merely ignored this decree; but Yoshiaki, on the prompting of Wada, reacted more violently and informed the emperor categorically that he (the shogun) would be personally responsible for the Jesuit's safety, and that anyone trying to enforce the imperial mandate would get the shortest of shrifts. Ogimachi's reply is not recorded, but may perhaps be guessed from Nichijo's reaction. The infuriated monk did not mince his words either and in an indignant letter to Wada, upbraided him for thus unprecedently flouting the imperial edict which, like the sweat from the body once it had gone out from the pores of the skin, could not be recalled. These fulminations were disregarded by all concerned, although later when Wada tried to get some of the Kuge to obtain the formal recall of the imperial edict, he was equally unsuccessful in his turn.[13]

Meanwhile Frois, on Wada's advice, thought it advisable

to pay a visit to Nobunaga at his castle at Gifu, in order to ensure the continuance of his support in despite of Nichijo's intrigues at court, for the latter was still in Nobunaga's if not in Yoshiaki's good graces. Wada gave Frois a letter of introduction to his friend Shibata Katsuie who was at that time Nobunaga's right-hand man. The Jesuit was more kindly received than he had dared hope, and during his eight-day stay at Gifu had several long and confidential talks with Nobunaga and Shibata, the former of whom gave him written and verbal assurances of support, couched in as emphatic terms as could be desired. Nobunaga told him, on the eve of his departure, in front of a vast concourse of Kyoto nobility, "Do not worry about either the emperor or the shogun, because I am in complete control of everything. Only do what I tell you, and you can go where you like." This incident has been gone into at some length because it proves what certain Japanese historians are inclined to forget, that the Heavenly Lord (Tenno) was treated in the most summary fashion by his nominal subordinates, without even a pretense of politeness when it suited them.

Frois had many opportunities of looking over Gifu castle before he left, Nobunaga himself acting as cicerone on one occasion. Despite his previous enthusiasm with the sights of Nara and Kyoto, the Jesuit was evidently unprepared for the splendors of Gifu which he described to his superior, Melchior Barreto, in terms of unqualified rapture, prefacing his description in these words:

I wish I was a good architect, or had the gift of being able to describe places well, because I assure you most emphatically, that among all the palaces and houses which I have seen in Portugal, India, and Japan, I never yet saw anything comparable to this in freshness, elegance, sumptuousness and cleanliness; as Your Reverence may readily guess when I tell you that since Nobunaga is no believer in the life to come, nor in anything which he cannot see, and being as he is extremely wealthy, and desirous not only of being unrivaled by any other ruler but of surpassing them all,—by way of displaying his magnificence and consumating the enjoyment of his pleasures, he decided to build this for his earthly paradise, for thus it is called by the people of Mino, wherein he has expended vast sums of money. As soon as I entered the palace gates, I tried to memorize their appearance and shape, so that I could subsequently describe them in this letter. But so many and such varied things did I see, that no sooner did I memorize the grandeur and perfection of some, than similar qualities in others made me forget the first.

Frois' frankness is engaging and he does himself less than justice in this respect, for his pen picture of Gifu castle brings this vanished structure vividly before the eyes of the reader. His account, although interesting in the extreme, is too long to quote here, and I can only allude to his principal points. He noticed the superb stonework of the outer wall, where the gigantic blocks were fitted together without the use of lime. The spaciousness of the entrance hall and its graceful proportions impressed him greatly, but he was still more entranced with the interior rooms, the ground plan of which he compared to the labyrinth of Crete. Like most visitors to Japanese temples and palaces, he much admired the artistic gold-leaf screens, which formed the principal furnishing of the rooms; and he was much struck by the beautiful polish attained on the fine-grained floor boards which shone like glass. The formal gardens, including those of the ceremonial tea cult, with their surface of "white sand-like snow," aroused his unstinted admiration, as did the skillful use made of running mountain water in streams, pools, and ornamental ponds throughout the grounds. From the reception rooms on the first floor, Nobunaga took him up to the richly-furnished women's apartments on the second, which had entrancing views over the city and countryside, "with all the music and beauty of birds which could be wished for in Japan." Thence the wondering Jesuit was led to the third floor, where the neatness, cleanliness, and absolute perfection of the rooms destined for chanoyu left him quite speechless: "truly I have no words wherewith adequately to praise them, since I have never seen their like." By the time they reached the donjon keep with its superb vistas over city, hill, and dale, Frois had exhausted his supply of superlatives. He was clearly relieved when Nobunaga took his party downstairs, and afforded a welcome change from the sublime to the ridiculous by entertaining them with the spectacle of a dancing dwarf, "very small, with a huge head and voice," who was brought out of a basket for the occasion.[14]

This was by no means the only occasion on which Nobunaga treated Frois with the greatest familiarity, laying himself out to please the Southern Barbarian in a manner which astounded his Japanese retainers, who went in the greatest awe of his capricious, haughty, and despotic temper. For the remaining thirteen years of his life, Nobunaga displayed a consistent liking and admiration for the strangers from the West, of which he gave practical proof many times. The reasons for this have often been discussed by Japanese historians, and his motives were doubtless rather mixed. But it seems to me that Sansom has put his finger on the principal one, when he points out that Nobunaga was an autocrat who could not afford any intimacy with his vassals, and would thus probably enjoy relaxing in the company of men of strong character and high attainments from whom he had nothing to fear. The Jesuits, whether by instinct or by training, had many characteristics which appealed to the military cast of mind, but they evidently fascinated Nobunaga in much the same way as they later attracted such different personalities as Akbar and Kanghsi.

There was also another bond between them in their common hatred of Buddhism, although the reasons for their common dislike were grounded on very different principles. Nobunaga was a militant agnostic—if not an atheist—and his hatred of the bonzes sprang from purely political motives, since they had shown an annoying tendency to support his opponents. With the Jesuits, of course, it was an instance of *odium theologicum;* and the bitterness of their dislike was sharpened by the fact that they had frequently been taken for a Buddhist subsect in their early days, as was understandable in view of certain striking if superficial outward resemblances between the two creeds. The Jesuit view of Buddhist sects and institutions in the neighborhood of Kyoto, Nara, and Koyasan appears in Gaspar Vilela's lengthy report on the subject addressed to his compatriots of the Benedictine convent of Aviz, on October 6, 1571. Vilela wrote from Goa, but he had only just left Japan after a residence of seventeen years, nine of which had been spent in Kyoto. During this time he had attained a considerable mastery of the language and a clearer notion than had some of his colleagues of the ramifications of the various Buddhist sects, although it would be illogical to expect from him an impartial exposition of esoteric Buddhism.[15]

He begins his letter with a general description of Kyoto, which according to him then contained about three hundred monasteries and sixty thousand houses, out of the three hundred thousand it had reputedly numbered in its heyday. Although this estimate is considerably lower than some other ones (96,000 houses) it can be accepted, since Vilela had lived there so long. Even this figure would indicate a population of nearly half a million, larger than that of any contemporary European city, save Paris. Despite his abhorrence of the bonzes and all their ways—he is markedly more vituperative than his better balanced colleague Luis Frois—Vilela could not repress his wholehearted admiration of the cleanliness and neatness of their persons and surroundings, which he noted as forming a glaring contrast to "the filthiness of their consciences." The elegant and finely proportioned temple buildings with their remarkably simple but effective architectural style impressed him; nor could he forbear to dilate on the skill of the Japanese carpenters and the excellence of their woodwork. His enthusiastic praise of the beauty, order, and taste of the temple gardens, recalls Frois' transports over Nobunaga's "earthly paradise" at Gifu, and, like him, he considered the perfect touch was provided by the impromptu music of numerous songbirds. He frankly confessed that the quiet peace of these monastery gardens was singularly conducive to leading men's thoughts insensibly to higher things.

The shrine which most intrigued him was apparently the Rokujo or Hongoku-ji, one of the four principal temples of

the Nichiren Hokke or Lotus sect. It originally stood at Kamakura, but was removed to its present site in 1345, since when
it has been repeatedly damaged by fires. Vilela was therefore
guilty of exaggeration, though doubtless unwittingly, when
he observed that although this temple was four centuries old,
it looked as if it was only ten years. He noted the great hall
where the monks were wont to say "matins, tierce, vespers
and complines, for the Devil wished them to imitate the things
of Our Lord in everything." He waxed positively lyrical over
the artistic beauty of the folding screens he was shown, being
particularly struck by one which depicted snow on bamboos
so realistically that it could easily have been mistaken for an
actual view of nature in winter. He explains the wonderful
beauty of the miniature gardens by stating that the monks
lavished such loving care on them because they did not believe in a future life, and thus sought to make an earthly paradise of their mundane temples.[16]

The other temples which he describes include the Tofukuji,
where he duly noted the celebrated wooden statues of Buddha
and his sixteen disciples enshrined there, and the picturesquely
situated Kiyomizu-dera, from which a magnificent pano-
ramic view over Kyoto and the neighborhood may be obtained. His descriptions of these Buddhist temples and their
enchanting gardens might have come out of a modern guide-
book, but he is a good deal less accurate in his summary account of their inmates. He does, it is true, distinguish (up to a
point) between the Buddhist and Shinto faiths, but he is inclined to overrate the nihilistic tendency in Buddhist philosophical thought and to dismiss the devotees of the "Three
Treasures" (Buddha, the Law, and the priesthood) as a bunch
of pederastic hypocrites. Not all of his colleagues were so
bigoted, as will be seen from the summary of Valignano's
views in the next chapter.

Vilela gives a curious account of the Tendai monasteries
on Hieizan, where he had stayed for a short time when he
first came to Kyoto. He is not sparing in retailing the alleged
vices of the occupants, particularly their addiction to sodomy,

but he gives them credit for some things such as the careful husbandry with which they tilled the mountain valleys, thus making the place virtually self-supporting with its rice, and other natural resources. He states that there were only about eight hundred temples left by the ravages of war out of the original five thousand, but admits that the surviving buildings were well worth seeing. He is eloquent about the technical perfection of their construction and the beauty of the local woods used therein; stating that although they were naturally somewhat weather-beaten on the outside, the interiors were so superb that "nothing finer could possibly be wrought from wood." The temple gardens likewise claimed his reluctant admiration, especially in the skillful use which was made of the mountain streams and springs in their layout. I will mention only his description of the famous Miidera temple overlooking Lake Otsu, which he states in his time still had about two thousand priests, though sadly fallen from its former high estate, with many of its buildings in ruin and its gardens overgrown. Of more value is his description of Nara and its neighborhood.

Vilela give his itinerary in the ancient capital of Japan, and it is interesting to note that then as now the three principal sights shown to the tourist were the Kofukuji temple with its neighboring Sarusawa Pond, traditionally connected with a beautiful court lady who drowned herself because of unrequited love for an emperor; the Daibutsuden or "Hall of the Great Buddha," containing the celebrated image more than fifty feet high, inside the largest wooden building under one roof in the world; and the Shinto shrine of Kasuga, with its beautiful cryptomeria grove and herds of sacred deer. I once lived in Nara for a year or more and hence appreciate Vilela's succinct account. I cannot resist quoting an extract from his description of the Kasuga shrine.

This temple is very large and attracts many pilgrims of the Zen sect. When I visited it, I approached it along a path like a broad highway which had in the middle a row of stone columns about three hundred in number. Their use is in having lamps placed on top at night, which as I say, are lighted every evening and kept burning. They have been presented by several rulers and powerful people who have made endowments for lighting the lamps and keeping them burning perpetually. The temple was all richly gilded. It had a very large close wherein were more than four hundred men robed in white and having something like bishops' miters on their heads. These are the people who serve the temple, and from its revenues they derive their food, clothing, footwear, and maintenance. It further possessed a very large house in which were women, something like sorceresses who, when required, dance in front of the temple. For the first thing visitors do on their arrival is to offer this dance to the temple. These reminded me of the priests of Baal and of his temple, which must have been something very like this. I was longing to have had a second Elias there to do to them what he did to those who served Baal at the behest of Jezabel. This temple has great revenues and is held in great veneration by the heathen. Lying within the bounds of the estate is a mountain thickly covered with many and diverse giant trees, which nobody has felled for the space of the last six hundred years, since the people say that they are sacred to the temple. There are more than five thousand deer in the park and these roam about the streets like the dogs in Spain.[17]

Shaking the dust of Nara off his feet, the truculent Jesuit proceeded to the famous stronghold of the Ikko or Monto sect, known as the Hongwanji at Ishiyama near Osaka, whither these turbulent monks had removed after the destruction of their parent foundation at Kyoto in 1465. Vilela did not mince his words in his description of their worldly living, but with more reason than usual, since these militant monks kept no rule, did not fast, and were more mercenary soldiers than anything else. He noted that they each made seven arrows daily, held weekly musketry and archery competitions, and spent all their time in practicing rigorous military exercises. He observed that their weapons were correspondingly efficient, for their great swords could cut through a man in armor "as easily as a sharp knife cleaves a very tender rump," and they were well provided with offensive and defensive arms of every kind. They believed (so he says) in a short life if a gay one, for they readily hired themselves out as mercenaries to warring daimyo, and atoned for the resultant heavy casualty rate by eating, drinking, and making merry generally in their heavily fortified "monastery of the Original Vow."

After reading Vilela's description of Ishiyama, it is easier to understand how its inmates for many years baffled all Nobunaga's efforts to reduce them.

Vilela also gives a short account of the great Shingon monastery of Koyasan, one of the most sacred places in all Japan and a great resort of pilgrims since its foundation in A.D. 816. He was told that this institution then harbored about ten thousand monks. Its founder is revered throughout the empire as the inventor of many of the adjuncts of Japanese civilization, including the native syllabary known as *hiragana;* but Vilela likewise credits (or rather discredits) him with the invention of the *peccado nefando,* or "accursed sin" of sodomy in this country. Since the Jesuit has now reached a point where his bigotry has got the better of his common sense, I take leave of him for a consideration of Nobunaga's massacre of the monks of Hieizan. This event took place in the year of Vilela's departure from Japan and must have rejoiced his heart exceedingly when he heard of it.[18]

Allusion has already been made to the political power wielded by the turbulent Tendai monks of the Enryaku-ji, and their constant armed interference in the struggles which frequently convulsed Kyoto. Nobunaga had long had his eye on them, and in 1571 they definitely overstepped the mark by supporting his enemies, Asakura and Asai. This same year, incidentally, saw the defeat and death of Wada Iga-no-kami Koremasa, who was, it will be remembered, a staunch and effective patron of the Jesuits. Frois was very upset—and understandably so—when he heard of Wada's heroic end in battle, of which he has left a graphic account. He was, therefore, all the more delighted when a few days later he received the glad tidings that this paragon's death had been amply counterbalanced by the holocaust which Nobunaga had made of the Tendai stronghold on Hieizan. On receiving the news, Frois wrote a brief narrative of this campaign for the information of the Jesuit provincial of India, the gist of which follows.[19]

The buildings of the Enryaku-ji at one time numbered

3,800 (or so he was informed) covering an area of three square leagues and extending over sixteen valleys and ridges on the slopes of Hieizan. The war of Onin and subsequent fighting had reduced the number to a mere four hundred or so in Frois' time; but it is known from both his own and Vilela's description, that the Enryaku-ji was still a political as well as a religious power in the land. The monastery was chiefly revered as the place where the Shinto deity, Okuninishi, was worshipped under the name of Sanno on the summit of the mountain. He was further enshrined in the cluster of temples at Sakamoto, at the foot of the eastern slopes of Hieizan, where a festival was annually celebrated in his honor. This cult was closely connected with the famous Gion festival at Kyoto, which Frois complains was the Devil's attempt to imitate the Feast of Corpus Christi, and it was generally considered that the sacredness of the spot would give even that militant agnostic, Nobunaga, pause.

In this, general opinion was mistaken. After a preliminary feint in another direction, Nobunaga swung round and closed in on Hieizan with a force of 30,000 men. In vain some of his own subordinates remonstrated with him on the sanctity of the Enryaku-ji, and in vain the threatened monks offered him a huge bribe to forego his design. To the former he replied that the monks had abandoned their rule and led dissolute lives, and to the latter he retorted that he had not come to enrich himself with their gold but to punish them with the utmost rigor for their misdeeds. Somewhat foolishly, in view of his reply, the bonzes abandoned all the buildings on the lower slopes of the hills to concentrate in the sacred Sanno temple on the summit, whither they were followed by all the men, women, and children from the Sakamoto villages in the foothills.

Nobunaga began his operations on September 29, 1571, the Feast of the Archangel Michael, as Frois jubilantly noted. He first destroyed the abandoned villages with fire and sword, killing any stragglers he found, and burning the *Mikoshi* or sacred cars in which the deities were wont to be carried during the festival. He then spread his troops out around the foothills of Hieizan and ordered them to advance fanwise and converge on the summit. Seeing this, the monks advanced to resist, but their decision was too late to be effective, and they only succeeded in inflicting about one hundred and fifty casualties on the attacking troops, if Frois' account is to be credited. All the villagers of both sexes were likewise killed in the ensuing massacre. On the following day (September 30, the Feast of St. Jerome), Nobunaga organized a battue in which all the surviving monks and villagers were hunted down and killed on the wooded mountainside, no regard being paid either to age or to sex. Frois estimates the total number killed at three thousand, about half of whom were the hapless villagers. On the same day all the temples were fired and reduced to ashes, and then and only then was Nobunaga's thirst for vengeance slaked and Frois satisfied.

This summary procedure with the Tendai monks spread consternation throughout the land, although it does not seem to have adversely affected the fighting spirit of the Monto (Ikko) monks of Ishiyama who successfully defied Nobunaga to the end. But although these doughty warriors could hold out more or less indefinitely on the defensive, they were never in a position to operate far from their base, and could never conduct offensive operations save in conjunction with daimyo hostile to Nobunaga. They were, therefore, more of a nuisance than a serious threat to his power, and the drastic lesson of September, 1571, was not lost on the other Buddhist sects. The massacre of Hieizan proved conclusively that the military leaders of Japan would tolerate no further interference with their political designs by the Buddhist clergy.

Nobunaga continued his campaigns to consolidate and extend his dominion for the remaining decade of his life, and by 1582 he was a master of more than half the provinces of Japan, including the key districts around the capital. Nor were his ambitions limited to the island empire, for he confided to his Jesuit friends that after completing the unification of the country, he intended to invade and conquer

China. But fate had disposed otherwise, and his career of conquest was cut short by the rebellion of Akechi Mitsuhide,
who treacherously attacked and killed him at Kyoto on June
21, 1582.[20] His death coincided with the opening of a new era
in the Jesuit Japan mission with the report of Father
Valignano.

III

One of the reproaches often leveled at the Jesuits of the
old Japan mission is their alleged reluctance to ordain Japanese as priests of the Society, or to have anything to do with
the organization of a native clergy. It will be of interest,
then, to examine how far, if at all, this allegation is justified,
particularly since the problem of a native clergy has long
been a bone of contention among Christian missionaries of
all varieties. The Jesuits approached it at the time of their
greatest success against the Counter Reformation in Europe,
which in itself was largely owing to their superior educational technique. It is appropriate, here, to consider the
proposals of the chief protagonist of the formation of a
native clergy in Japan, the Italian Jesuit Alessandro
Valignano.

Scion of a noble Neapolitan family, Valignano studied
law at Padua before being received into the Company by
Francis Borgia in 1566, at the age of twenty-seven. He was
destined for great things from the start, since the general,
Everard Mercurian, made him take his fourth vow as early
as 1573, before sending him next year to the East, in the
capacity of vicar-general and visitor of the Orient. Very few
of his colleagues could boast of such rapid promotion, and
even the most distinguished of his successors in the Far East,
men of the caliber of Longobardi, Rodriguez, and Verbiest,
had to wait twenty years or more from the time of their admission to that of their profession of the fourth vow.
Valignano lost no time in getting to work at Goa and
elsewhere, but I can allude here only to his connection

with Japan, where he arrived for the first time in July, 1579.

From the beginning he realized the importance of providing the mission with a native clergy, and since the then superior, Francisco Cabral, did not share his views on this matter, Cabral was in due course sent packing to Macao. Valignano arranged for the establishment of training seminaries in Arima and Adzuchi, a novitiate in Usuki, and a college in Funai (Oita). He traveled extensively through his province and was received in audience by Nobunaga, on whom he made a great impression, thanks to his imposing appearance (he was more than six feet tall) and striking personality. On his return to Kyushu, he arranged at very short notice for the dispatch of some youthful samurai as envoys to King Felipe and the Pope from the Christian daimyo of Bungo, Arima, and Omura. This embassy fulfilled his double intention of attracting the attention of Christendom to the splendid progress the Jesuits were making in Japan, and of impressing the Japanese with the power and civilization of Catholic Europe. Valignano left Nagasaki with the envoys in February, 1582, but went no further than Goa, where he remained as provincial for a number of years.

He came back to Japan with the returning samurai and during his second sojourn (July, 1590–October, 1592) he was as kindly received by Toyotomi Hideyoshi as he had been by Nobunaga in the previous decade. For the next six years he worked at Macao, where he transformed the Jesuit College of Madre de Deus (popularly, but incorrectly, called St. Paul) into the headquarters of missionary work in Japan and China. After another trip to Goa, he paid his last and longest visit to Japan, from August, 1598 to January, 1603, during which time he had the satisfaction of seeing the first fruits of his 1580 policy, with the ordination of two Japanese as priests of the Society. His tactful handling of the mission during the critical years following the death of Hideyoshi and Ieyasu's seizure of power after the battle of Sekigahara was largely responsible for the relative peace and quiet it enjoyed. He died in harness at Macao, January 20,

1606, working with his last breath like his predecessor, St. Francis Xavier, for the conversion of Japan and the opening of the "Rock" of China. The views of such a man, with his background, training, and experience on Japan and the Japanese, must command respect. His "Sumario" of August, 1580, shows his first reaction to the problems posed by the progress of the Japan mission.[21]

His report can be best considered in three sections: one, the raw material with which he had to deal, that is, the Japanese of the *Sengoku-jidai;* two, the tools he had to work with, that is, the caliber of the Jesuit missionaries themselves; and three, his plan of action. At the time he wrote, Nobunaga controlled some two dozen of Japan's sixty-six provinces, the Mori family based on Yamaguchi another dozen or so, and Otomo of Bungo, five. It was with their vassals that he was chiefly concerned, since the northeast or Tohoku area was still virtually *terra incognita* to himself and his colleagues. Nevertheless his description of the national character was probably of fairly general application; it reads in part as follows.

The people are all white, courteous and highly civilized, so much so that they surpass all the other known races of the world. They are naturally very intelligent, although they have no knowledge of sciences, because they are the most warlike and bellicose race yet discovered on the earth. From the age of fifteen onwards, all youths and men, rich and poor, in all walks of life, wear a sword and dagger at their side. Moreover, every man, whether a gentleman or common fellow, has such complete control over his sons, servants, and others of his household, that he can kill any of them on the smallest pretext at any time he likes, and seize their land or goods. They are absolute lords of their land, although the chiefest among them frequently league together for defense against their suzerains, who are thus often prevented from doing as they wish. They think nothing more of killing a man than they do an animal; so that they will kill a man not only on the smallest excuse but merely to try the edge of their swords. Since a man can kill anybody of his own household and wars are so frequent, it seems that the majority of them perish by the sword. Such is their cruelty that often the very mothers when they have brought forth a child will put their foot on its chest and kill it, simply because they cannot nurture them. Similarly many men kill themselves by cutting their intestines with a dagger.

On the one hand, they are the most affable people and a race more given to outward marks of affection than any yet known. They have such control over their anger and impatience that it is almost a miracle to witness any quarrel or insulting words in Japan, whether with one another or with foreigners; in such wise that even if they are killed, they do not revile thereat, neither do they ever complain or grumble about bad luck. On the other hand, they are the most false and treacherous people of any known in the world; for from childhood they are taught never to reveal their hearts, and they regard this as prudence and the contrary as folly, to such a degree that those who lightly reveal their mind are looked upon as nitwits, and are contemptuously termed single-hearted men. Even fathers and sons never reveal their true thoughts to each other, because there can be no mutual confidence between them in word or deed; for when they are most determined to do evil to someone, the more outward compliments they pay him. Thus when they wish to kill somebody, just when they are about to do so, they show him more politeness and kind words, in order the better to effect their intention; and in truth they cannot live with one another in any other way. For this reason, and because Japan is divided between so many lords and fiefs, it is continually torn by civil wars and treasons, nor is there any lord who is secure in his domain. This is why Japan is never a firm whole, but is always revolving like a wheel; for he who today is a great lord, may be a penniless nobody tomorrow. Every individual acts in such wise that he will take any chance of increasing his income or rank by deserting his natural lord and taking service with another or betraying him, even to their own fathers on occasion. These latter, to safeguard themselves from their sons, have no other recourse but to make over to them their household and income when they grow up, retiring to live modestly on some small portion which they have retained for themselves, and this is the universal custom in Japan.

They are likewise so poor that it is an amazing thing to see with how little even kings and lords can sustain themselves. These commonly have their lands parceled out among their vassals in such a way that even though the latter serve them free of charge, yet withal the former usually have very little income. On the other hand, everyone in general and the nobles in particular are served and treated so cleanly and honorably, that it is a marvel to see how despite so much poverty they can keep such cleanliness and good breeding; although their dress, food, ceremonies, and all else they have or do, are so different from those of Europe and all other known races, that it seems as if they purposely contrive to do everything clean contrary to everyone else. Thus we who come hither from Europe find ourselves as veritable children who have to learn how to eat, sit, converse, dress, act politely, and so on. This is the reason why it is impossible either in India or in Europe, to evaluate or to decide the problems of Japan; nor can one even understand or imagine how things occur there, because it is another world, another way of life, other customs, and other laws. Many things which are regarded as courteous and honorable in Europe, are here resented as great insults and injuries. Contrariwise, many things which are here regarded as the common usages of daily life, and without which no social intercourse is possible with the Japanese, are despised in Europe as base and unworthy, especially in a religious community.

They are a people universally accustomed to living as they wish, for both men and women are brought up in such freedom from childhood that they are allowed to behave as they please, without their fathers checking them in the smallest degree, for they neither whip nor scold them. This is particularly so with the nobility and gentry, who are so wedded to their own ideas, that nobody, however much a servant or a friend he may be, dares to contradict them, whether they want to do good or ill; on the contrary, they try to divine their master's wish and to give their advice and counsel in conformity therewith.

Among other things, they are accustomed never to discuss affairs of moment face to face, but always through an intermediary; so much so, that even fathers and sons never ask nor discuss any question of importance with each other, nor counsel nor warn each other save through a third person; all of which renders very slow and difficult the dispatch of any weighty business with them. They hold some horrible sins to be positive virtues and they are taught as such by their bonzes and priests, particularly as regards the accursed sin [of sodomy] which is allowed free rein to an extent that is as unspeakable as unbelievable. Likewise they have many iniquitous customs and laws so unjust and contrary to natural reason, that it is an exceedingly difficult thing to persuade them to live in conformity with our law. Withal, when they do become Christians, they leave off cultivating these vices and are much addicted to religion and the celebration of the divine cult. Thus they frequent the churches and the sacraments and treat holy things with great reverence and outward humility. This is particularly so with the middle classes and peasantry, for the nobility and gentry, even though they show the same outward reverence only with great difficulty attain an equal inward virtue. Finally, since this people is the best and most civilized of all the East, with the exception of the Chinese, so it is likewise the most apt to be taught and to adopt our holy law, and to produce the finest Christianity in all the East, as in fact it already is.[22]

Valignano did not fail to note the numerous instances of topsy-turveydom which Western visitors to Japan still encounter today. Thus in his later and fuller report, written from Cochin on October 28, 1583, he cites the following instances of mutual contrariness between the European and Japanese ways of life.

White, which with us is a festive and cheerful color, is a sign of mourning and sadness with them, whereas they like black and mulberry as gay colors. Our vocal and instrumental music wounds their ears, and they delight in their own music which truly tortures our hearing. They cannot stand the smell of incense, benzoin and such like things. We remove our hats and stand up as a sign of politeness; contrariwise they remove their sandals and squat down, for to receive guests standing up would be the height of rudeness. We admire golden hair and white teeth, whereas they paint theirs black. We mount a horse with the left foot first, they with the right. They put tripods on their braziers, with the feet in the air and the circular ring at the bottom. They think it an unhealthy thing to give hens, chickens, sweets to sick people, and almost everything which we do; they give them salted or raw fish, limes, sea snails, and such like bitter or salty things, and they have found by experience that these are in fact good for them. They never bleed the sick, and the purges they give them are all sweet smelling and mild, and in this way they have much the advantage of us, since ours are very harsh and bitter. Their women before they conceive go very loosely girt about the waist in a flowing dress, whereas when they conceive they tie themselves so tightly round the waist, that it looks as if they would burst; so that when they are on the point of giving birth, they look smaller and less big-bellied than they did before they conceived. If they do not bind themselves round so tightly, they often miscarry or abort.[23]

Valignano was not the first nor the last European to complain bitterly of the inadequacy and unappetizing nature of Japanese food in comparison with European, although he could not refrain from highly commending the fastidious cleanliness and neatness with which it was cooked and served. The Japanese mode of squatting on the heels was likewise a physical torture to him, particularly since he was a veritable giant among men. Finally, he noted the Japanese contempt for jewelry and precious stones, and their corresponding craze for ceremonial tea utensils (*chadogu*), as instanced by a little jar which Otomo Sorin, daimyo of Bungo, proudly showed him, and for which he had paid 9,000 *taels* in silver. Valignano observed acidly that it was only fit for a water jar in a bird's cage, and that he personally would not have given three farthings for it.

So much for Valignano's opinion of the Japanese national character in general, and I now turn to his estimate of the worth of the converts in particular. At the time he wrote

his second report (October, 1583) he estimated that there
were about 600,000 native Christian converts throughout
Asia, of whom about 150,000 were in Japan. It will be remembered that the Jesuits claimed a thousand converts in
Japan at the time of Xavier's departure, but many of these
can hardly have been more than nominal. At any rate, Gaspar Vilela says that when he arrived three years later, in 1554,
he found only 500 Christians, which number had increased to
30,000 by the time he left the country in 1571. The real increase came later, following the conversion of the Kyushu
daimyo of Omura, Arima, and Bungo, whose example was
followed by many of their retainers. These numbers may
not sound very impressive, but they are truly remarkable
when it is considered how very few Jesuits there were in
Japan (never more than nine before 1563). Ricci complained in 1596 that only a hundred Chinese had been converted after fifteen years of missionary effort in Kwangtung.
The Japanese Christians were undoubtedly the flower of the
flock, and the comparison which Valignano drew between
them and their Indian counterparts was anything but flattering to the latter. He stated roundly that whereas in the rest
of Asia, low-class "rice Christians" were the only converts
whom the missionaries had to show for their pains, in Japan
they numbered many of the nobility and gentry among their
flock.

Moreover, only the Japanese showed a readiness to accept
Christianity from disinterested motives, moved by arguments appealing to reason or to faith alone. They were not
merely receptive to the Jesuits' religious propaganda, but
very interested to learn anything the Europeans had to teach
them. They were disposed to respect the missionaries owing
to the veneration they normally felt for their own Buddhist
priesthood, whereas in China the bonzes were commonly regarded with contempt and aversion. Most important of all,
they alone of all the Asiatic peoples (save the Chinese, who
were virtually *incommunicado*) were capable of being ordained as priests and clergy, and of leading a devout and

holy life. Furthermore, converts were subsequently held in great respect by their heathen compatriots, which was quite contrary to the attitude of other Asiatics. Finally, the missionaries had free access to all parts of Japan, which was not true in India and still less so in China; and the spread of religious propaganda was further facilitated by the fact that one language was understood and spoken throughout the entire country.[24]

Of course there were some admitted drawbacks to this picture. In the first place, there were considerable differences in quality between the Japanese Christians themselves. Those from the Gokinai were very much better and more sincere than the majority of the Kyushu converts, many of whom had simply followed the lead of their local daimyo, who were likely to display a regard for the Faith in direct proportion to their hopes of attracting Portuguese traders to their fiefs. Valignano was seriously to modify his views on this point a decade later, but at the time of his visit it was undoubtedly true that the majority of the converts in the home provinces around Kyoto were of a better type than the Kyushu converts whose motives were frequently more mixed. Another difficulty was that the proud and bellicose character of the Japanese made it quite impossible to treat them like the Indian Christians, "for we have no jurisdiction whatsoever in Japan, nor can we compel them to do anything which they do not wish to do, other than by pure persuasion and force of argument; they will not suffer being slapped or beaten, nor imprisonment, nor any similar methods commonly used with other Asiatic Christians, for they are so punctilious that they will not brook even a single harsh or impolite word." They therefore had to be handled with the greatest tact and care; their national customs and idiosyncrasies being scrupulously respected wherever and whenever they did not openly conflict with the rules of Holy Mother Church. They had to be guided with a loving and fatherly hand, and not a stern or rigorous one, "because if we press them too hard, they will not tolerate it, especially if they are of the nobility or gentry."

They could likewise be controlled through their daimyo, if this latter happened to be a Christian; but this cut both ways, since if the daimyo turned sour he was likely to force all his vassals and dependents to do likewise. Nevertheless, when all was said and done, Valignano claimed that the inate good qualities of the Japanese Christians far outweighed their defects. The results already achieved in this field gave the brightest promise for the future; and Japan was the only Asiatic mission which held any prospect of soon becoming a healthy and self-supporting Christian realm with a trustworthy native clergy of its own.

After what is set forth in the foregoing paragraphs, the reader will probably not be surprised to learn that Japan was by far the most popular Asiatic mission field with the sons of Loyola. Valignano admitted roundly that the Jesuits would rather work in Japan than elsewhere, since they could see and reap the reward of their proselytizing labors with relative ease and frequency, whereas their years of arduous effort in India brought tardy and meager results at the best. Living with Japanese on the one hand and with Indians on the other, was like "living with cultivated and intelligent people in the former instance, and with base and bestial people in the latter." There was consequently no lack of apostolic ardor or want of willing recruits for Japan, but it was essential that only the very best men should be sent thither, and this was something more difficult to ensure.

In reporting on the possible sources of recruits in Asia, Valignano classified these as Portuguese born in Europe; those born in India of pure European parentage, who were very few and far between; those born of a European father and Eurasian mother (*castiços*) ; half-castes or *mestiços;* and native Indians with little or no European blood in their veins. He regarded all these as unsuitable and the majority as definitely beyond the pale. The pure Portuguese were mostly illiterate pages or soldiers who would have to be taught to read and write during their novitiate. Those born in India were soft and effeminate, brought up by slave women in every kind of vice, and inherently unfitted for the austerities of a religious life. The *mestiços* or Eurasians were even more despicable characters and none of them were fit to be admitted into the Society of Jesus, apart from the fact that they were despised by pure-bred Europeans and by Asiatics alike. As for the natives, they were beneath contempt, and none should ever be received into the Company, "because all these dusky races are very stupid and vicious, and of the basest spirits, and likewise because the Portuguese treat them with the greatest contempt." Valignano expressly excepted the Japanese from his sweeping strictures, and stated emphatically that he regarded them as on an absolute level with Europeans.

Turning to this latter category, the visitor was most insistent that on no account should any Europeans be admitted who had any trace of Jewish blood "even if they should possess all the other talents and qualifications which could possibly be desired." The reason for this was the profound loathing felt for the despised and hated "New Christians" or crypto-Jews by the Portuguese in general, and the consequent disrepute into which the Society would fall if it admitted anyone with the slightest taint of Jewish blood. Finally, Valignano rounded off this chapter of his report, by relating the difficulties caused through the reluctance of Portuguese to enlist in sufficient numbers as temporal coadjutors, since they nearly all aspired to the far more coveted and honorable, if difficult, grade of spiritual coadjutor.

It is interesting to note that Valignano's recommendations were adopted *in toto* by the Jesuit general. The Society made it a strict rule not to admit any Asiatics or Eurasians other than Japanese—this solitary exception later being extended to include Chinese and, in 1608, Koreans. Moreover, although the Jesuit record with respect to persons of real or suspected Jewish origin had been previously an enlightened one, at any rate in comparison with that of the Dominicans and other orders, the most stringent instructions were now issued by general headquarters at Rome to prevent the admission of persons "tainted" (however, remotely) with Jewish blood, and to expel any who might be found to have this stain in the future. Even the aid of the Inquisition, with which the Society was not normally on the best or closest of terms, was invoked on this occasion; and all the methods of deceit and dissimulation usually, if unjustly, associated with the adjective "Jesuitical," were endorsed by the general as being licit and proper in ascertaining the "purity" of an aspirant's blood. The effect of these decisions, which were certainly enforced during the existence of the Japan mission proper, was to limit the Jesuits working in Japan to pureblood Europeans and Japanese.[25]

Apart from this blatant racial discrimination, Valignano made some other interesting recommendations about the qualifications required of a potential missionary for the Japan mission field. Some of the comparisons he makes between the European and Asiatic character still hold good today. Thus he notes that "the Japanese are slow and deliberate in their dealings, and similarly they never display outward resentment or impatience, even when they are inwardly much upset. They do not lightly murmur or complain, nor do they speak evil of one another. They are very secretive in their hearts. They are greatly addicted to formal manners and empty compliments, but know how to bide their time in silence very patiently. Whereas we on the contrary are usually quite the reverse. For we are hasty, choleric, free and easy in our speech, and straightway disclose our thoughts and minds, and we have no fondness for these formal manners and empty compliments." It is amusing to find a Jesuit— traditionally the embodiment of reticence and guile—writing thus, but the celebrated French Jesuit, Jean de Fontaney, wrote in a similar strain about the contrast between Chinese and Europeans more than a century later.

A European is naturally lively, passionate, eager, and inquisitive; but when such a one arrives in China, he must become a quite different man. He must form a resolution to conduct himself, his whole lifetime, with calmness, complaisance, patience, and seriousness. He must receive all visitants with the highest civility; must discover a satisfaction at seeing them; and listen to whatever they shall say with the greatest patience. He must propose his reasons with all imaginable mildness; with a soft tone of voice, and few gestures; the Chinese being very much offended, whenever they see a missionary of a sour temper, and hard to please. If such a one should be passionate and fiery, this would be still worse, for then even his own servants would be the first to despise and inveigh against him.[26]

There is not space to enumerate all the other qualifications listed by Padre Valignano as essential for a Far Eastern missionary in 1580, but it is worth noting his insistence on the necessity for the European missionaries to conform and adapt themselves, so far as they possibly and legitimately could, to Japanese social customs and way of life. He advocated that new arrivals should not only be learned and virtuous, but dignified in their behavior, "since the bonzes of Japan are distinguished by their dignity and gravity." It is worth noting that (unlike Vilela, Frois, and most of his confreres) Valignano frequently held up the Buddhist priests as models to be followed in deportment and general behavior. He added that Japanese had often told him that they would make allowances for foreigners' eccentricities for two years; but that if after that the Jesuits were still unable or unwilling to accommodate themselves to Japanese standards, they would be despised as "ignorant louts." The great importance of language study was also stressed, and this was one of the reasons why he arranged some years later for the installation of a Jesuit mission press, where not only theological works of devotion were printed, but Japanese grammars and dictionaries. He frankly recognized, however, that no European who had not been brought up among the Japanese from childhood, could ever hope to attain a mastery of the language comparable to that of an educated native; this was one of the reasons why he never ceased to urge that Japanese should be admitted to the Society, and the formation of a native clergy taken seriously in hand. Valignano did not fail to note that cleanliness emphatically came next to godliness in Japanese eyes and he stressed the vital importance of a spick

and span house. As a good sixteenth-century European, however, even he was unable to accommodate himself to the
Japanese custom of a daily hot bath; and in his "Obediencias"
of 1592, he laid down that none but the very sick or aged
were to be allowed the frequent use of a *furo,* and all other
personnel, European and Japanese alike, could only take a
proper bath once in eight days. To such ridiculous lengths
had the mediaeval Christian reaction against Roman cleanliness and personal hygiene carried the men of the Renaissance.

Given the assumption that only the cream of the Society
of Jesus was good enough to work in Japan, and Valignano's
emphasis that Japanese were as good (or better) than Europeans, it necessarily followed that the only possible method
of finding sufficient workers for this particular vineyard of
the Lord was to employ Japanese themselves as laborers. This
is precisely what the visitor did urge time and again upon
his superiors at Rome, for he advocated that Japanese be
received into the Society of Jesus, with a view to their becoming, not merely lay brothers or temporal coadjutors, but
full-fledged priests. He likewise proclaimed the necessity of
forming a native clergy in order to ensure a constant supply
of parish priests, and to relieve the Jesuits of much of the
burdensome routine work which they had to shoulder in
default of a secular clergy. Although the majority of his colleagues agreed with him in both points, there was some local
opposition to his views, and he foresaw there would be a great
deal more at Rome.

The principal local difficulty was (so he said) the attitude
of the Portuguese, who treated all Asiatic races with contempt, and termed even highly cultivated peoples like the
Chinese and Japanese, "niggers." This is rather surprising,
for modern Portuguese writers are never tired of extolling
their compatriots' disregard of the color bar, and they point
proudly to Brazil as the classic example of what can be
achieved by an enlightened policy in this respect. There is
obviously a great deal of truth in this; but a long study of
Portuguese colonial history has enabled me to appreciate that

Valignano's charges were by no means unfounded, if care is taken to distinguish between the enlightened official policy of the Portuguese monarchs and the more or less instinctive racial reactions of many of their subjects.

From the time of the "Fortunate" King Manoel onward, the kings of the dynasty of Aviz, and their successors of Hapsburg and Braganza, issued repeated injunctions to their viceroys and governors in India, that there was to be no distinction on grounds of color in the Portuguese Asiatic colonies, but only on the ground of religion,—or with crypto-Jews, of blood. This was the official attitude, but the viceroys themselves often protested against it; and everyone who cares to read through the correspondence, for example, of the Count of Vidigueira (1596–1628), the Count of Linhares (1629–1635), or the Count of São Vicente (1666–1668), will find innumerable slighting references to Eurasians and "niggers," on the same lines as later Anglo-Saxon sneers at "wogs" and "wops." True it is, that the Portuguese had not the smallest objection to cohabiting with native women, but their English successors were no more abstemious in this respect down to the end of the eighteenth century at least. The offspring of these mixed unions were not usually respected by pure-blooded fidalgos. Even the broad-minded Diogo do Couto is found writing scornfully (*ca.* 1600) about half-caste captains who "had more relatives in Gujarat than in Tras-os-Montes." Many other instances of this color-conscious attitude could be given, but it will suffice to quote the Jesuit chronicler Padre Francisco de Sousa's remark on Father Cabral's opposition to Valignano's advocacy of equality between Europeans and Japanese: "And he has an excuse in the Portuguese character which naturally despises all these Asiatic races." [27]

Despite his sweeping denunciations of Indians and all their ways, Valignano included them in his recommendation for the formation of a native clergy in Asia, although he set his face against their admission to the Society. He advanced the rather peculiar argument that although the vast majority of

Indian or mestiço clergy led unedifying and dissolute lives, it was better to have immoral pastors preaching sound doctrine, than no pastors and consequently no doctrine. Moreover, he grudgingly admitted that even some Indians and Eurasians, if caught and trained sufficiently young, eventually grew up to be no discredit to their cloth, "as experience has shown with some who were ordained clergy, and lived devoutly and without scandal even amongst the Portuguese." These, however, were the few exceptions, and he turned with relief to advocating the formation of a native clergy in Japan, where the national character gave him so much less cause for misgiving.

The first essential was the foundation of training seminaries and colleges where the Japanese could be trained from childhood in the articles of the Faith. It was essential to "catch them young," for their minds could be easily molded at that age and they were by nature most receptive to what they were taught, absorbing knowledge far more quickly, eagerly and thoroughly, than children of corresponding age in Europe. But although Valignano and his colleagues were unanimous in their decision to establish training seminaries for the education of native clergy, there was more argument about the curriculum to be taught therein. It was agreed that pupils should be admitted from a very early age, although provision was likewise made for older youths of sixteen to eighteen, but the die-hard Father Cabral jibbed at the idea of teaching them anything more than Latin and cases of conscience: "for once they became expert theologians, being of a proud disposition, and still young in the Faith, they would be readily prone to divide the Law of Christ into heresies as numerous as the sects which their ancestors had evolved from the false doctrine of Buddha." Cabral further maintained that it was essential for Europeans to keep the whip hand of the Japanese and to treat them as inferiors, since once their fundamentally proud, arrogant, and sensual nature was allowed to get the upper hand, they would prove quite unamenable to the discipline of their erstwhile mentors, and intolerant of all restraints whether human or divine. Valignano, on the other hand, advocated that the Japanese should be taught all that it was in the power of the Company of Jesus to teach them, since they had mental aptitude enough for everything, and they possessed a linguistic skill which Europeans who came to Japan as adults could never hope to attain. Valignano's viewpoint prevailed, and, since Cabral showed himself uncoöperative, he was later removed to Macao, being replaced by the more pliable Gaspar Coelho.

The visitor advocated the establishment of three seminaries, one for youths over eighteen, and two for boys under that age, the pupils to be drawn exclusively from the sons of the nobility and gentry. The curriculum was to include reading and writing in Japanese and Latin, "with the humanities and other sciences," virtue, deportment, and good manners "which is the chiefest of all," including the Japanese social code. The textbooks used should be specially compiled for the occasion, and the Jesuits could edit and compose them exactly as they chose, since the Japanese had no other contact with educated Europeans, nor were they in a position to check anything they were told but had to take it on trust ("han de tomar a ciegos"). The cynical reader may recall Macaulay's observation that the Jesuits "appear to have discovered the precise point to which intellectual culture can be carried without risk of intellectual emancipation." This was indeed the whole burden of Valignano's proposals, and he adverts over and over again to the fact that here in Japan they had a clear field and no competitors (provided they kept out the friars from the Philippines), so they could limit their teaching to books of their own selection or composition, free from any interference, doubt, or criticism. These three seminaries were intended for aspirants to the native clergy, but he likewise advocated the establishment of kindergarten schools to give elementary education to the children of Christian converts, thus forming an alternative or a substitute to the elementary education given by the Buddhist temple schools or terakoya. The visitor did not fail to stress the importance of keeping a tight control over the native clergy, even after they had been ordained. He pressed the general to secure from the Pope permission for the local Jesuit superior to ordain, suspend, excommunicate, or arrest them as he thought fit, and to limit their authority and control their movements in every way. However, he did envisage the prospect that in some dim and distant future, Japan would have its own native bishop to control its own clergy; for he admitted that Japanese national pride would not tolerate their being controlled by foreigners indefinitely.[28]

Valignano's arguments for the establishment of a native clergy were repeated with still more force in his advocacy of the unqualified admission of Japanese to the Society. His chief argument was the language one, because God had not (contrary to what might have been expected of Him) given the missionaries the gift of tongues or miracles, and their best linguists were virtually tongue-tied and halting in comparison with their Japanese lay brothers. Moreover, their coöperation was essential in the composition of native books and polemical tracts, and their compatriots trusted and confided in them more than they ever could or would in Europeans. The relatively few Japanese brothers were responsible for all the treatises hitherto translated, but they were too old now to learn Latin and it was essential to train a new generation who could be taught Latin when young.

The only possible source of recruits for the Society was the *dojuku,* or *doshuku* who formed the catechists, acolytes, sacristans, and so on, of the missionaries, and who (as Valignano frankly admitted) really bore the burden and heat of the day. The term and the idea had been taken over by the Jesuits from their Buddhist opponents, for the dojuku were the disciples or aspirant monks who performed the household and routine duties in the monasteries. Although they knew no Latin, and sometimes only the rudiments of catechizing, they were the most promising material, and if given proper training in one of the seminaries, would make excellent recruits. Many of them were being brought up on this understanding, and if they were disappointed in their hopes of being able to enter the Society in due course, they would probably become embittered, and might even apostasize. The chief difficulty was their ignorance of Latin, for it was virtually impossible for adult Japanese to cope with this language, and only those dojuku who were taught it from childhood could hope to reach the standard normally demanded by the Company of Jesus from its members.[29]

When he first left the country in 1582, Valignano felt sanguine that, despite the acknowledged difficulties with which the mission had to contend, Japan would become the best and biggest Christian community in the world, if his advice was followed at Rome. For the most part it was; but on his next visit ten years later, doubts had evidently crept into his mind. His correspondence of 1590–1596, does not show quite the same missionary *élan* as that of 1580–1583. He still has high hopes of the ultimate conversion of Japan, but the immediate difficulties are seen to be greater than anticipated. After the snub he had administered to the old diehard Cabral, it is amusing to find that he was perturbed at Cabral's successor, Coelho, having received so many Japanese novices into the Society, that there were seventy budding native Jesuits on his return in 1590. He promptly applied the brake, and was careful to admit only five newcomers (the samurai who had been to Rome and one of their relatives) within the next two years—and even this accession was offset by his dismissal of five unsatisfactory native novices. He also now realized that the prospect of the few Jesuits in Japan being able simultaneously to train novices for the Society, form an embryo native clergy, and continue the consolidation and expansion of the mission in general, was something beyond even the remarkable capabilities of the sons of Loyola. He compromised to some extent by sanctioning the admission of a few aspirants who knew little or no Latin; but the dojuku, once they had attained the age of twenty years, tended to become disgruntled or dispirited if they were not admitted without further ado.

Headquarters at Rome had meanwhile undergone some

change of heart as well. Valignano's opposition to the appointment of a bishop was overruled, although the rebuff was mitigated by the selection of a Jesuit. The scheme for the formation of a native clergy had been approved, but nothing effectual was done to implement it, since the promised financial assistance was not forthcoming. The Jesuit General, Claudio Aquaviva, wrote, somewhat grudgingly, in January, 1610, that Japanese brothers could and should be ordained priests of the Society, since otherwise they and the dojuku grumbled. But only a select few should be admitted at infrequent intervals, and not before they had attained the age of forty. They were not to be sent to the college at Macao to complete their studies, but were to remain in Japan. Valignano's high hopes must have already begun to fade; by the time this decision was taken he was in his grave. The years of bloody persecution which opened in 1614 put an end to all further discussion; but many Japanese Jesuits and dojuku have written their names with their blood in the long roll of martyrs which enobles the Church in Japan.[30]

Chapter III. CHRISTIANITY
AND THE KUROFUNE

AT the time the Portuguese discovered Japan, they had, as already seen, no firm footing or official trade with China. They drove, however, a contraband trade at different times and places along the China coast, principally in the neighborhood of Ningpo (Liampo) and Ch'uanchow (Chincheo). When driven away by the Chinese coast-guard squadrons from these coastal areas about 1550, they moved back to their old haunts in Kwangtung Province, first to the island of Sanchuan or St. John; and thence, after making a semiofficial agreement with the local *Haitao* in 1554, to the neighboring island of Lampacau. Three years later they acquired what proved to be a more permanent base in the bay of the Goddess Ama, the local dialectal pronunciation of which they slurred into Amacao, whence some years later evolved the word Macao.

The discovery of Japan opened a new and most welcome market to them, for despite the ravages of civil war, there was a keen demand for foreign goods, and particularly for the Chinese silk yarn which the daimyo and samurai preferred to the native product, in much the same way as English cloth was valued in Spain and Portugal above the indigenous make. Since both Japanese and Portuguese were forbidden to trade, or indeed to visit, the ports of the Middle Flowery Kingdom on pain of death, it was not an easy matter for either of them to secure the coveted China silks. Nevertheless, the Wako had made themselves so feared and hated, that the Folangki seemed relatively innocuous by comparison; and since they were able to supply Japanese silver, which the Chinese coveted as much as the Japanese did Chinese silk, the Portuguese, despite periodic setbacks, were enabled to drive a highly profitable if precarious commerce. The agreement made by Leonel de Sousa with the Haitao of Kwangtung in 1554, followed as it was by the acquisition of Macao three years later, virtually placed Portuguese-Chinese relations on an official basis, and withdrew the foreign devils from the outlawed category of the dwarf slaves. The trade increased in a most astonishing way, forming an interesting example of how commercial enterprise in alliance with official graft can overcome all kinds of political and geographical handicaps.[1]

The stormy China Sea was not as yet very familiar to the Portuguese pilots, the dangerous Chinese coast virtually uncharted, and the Japanese coast unknown. But this handicap did not deter the descendants of the mariners who had rounded the Cape of Good Hope, and within a few years their own ships, or Chinese junks freighted by them, had visited all the harbors on the coast of Kyushu, from Yamagawa, at the southern tip of Satsuma, to Usuki in Bungo, and Hirado in Hizen. The voyages were apparently at first free for all, and any captain who could secure a ship, cargo, and pilot could make the voyage to Japan. But after the viceroy at Goa had got wind of this new Eldorado, the voyage was placed on the usual monopoly footing under the control of a captain-major, who acquired his position by royal grant or by purchase. It was coupled with the captaincy of the China voyage from 1550, after which date the annual voyage was usually limited to one or two ships, whereas in the previous years three or four had often come at a time.

Since the essence of the transaction was the exchange of Chinese silk for Japanese silver, the voyages were based from the beginning on the precarious settlements (if such they could be called) secured by the Portuguese in Fukien and Kwangtung, and not on Malacca. Thus Xavier's friend, Duarte da Gama, made half a dozen voyages between Kyushu and Kwangtung in as many years before returning to India. The informant on this point, the Jesuit Belchior Gago, writing from Hirado in September, 1555, adds that he had only

---

[1] For notes to chapter iii, see pages 461–468.

received one letter from Goa in the last six years. This fact shows how tenuous communications between India and Japan were before the establishment of Macao; for although there was a fair amount of Portuguese shipping engaged in the China-Japan trade by this time, these vessels seldom went west of Malacca. The ships used in this trade were mainly of the type called *Nao* or Great Ship, which Elizabethan sailors designated as "carracks," and they ranged in size from 600 to 1,600 tons. The Japanese called them *Kurofune* or Black Ships, presumably from the color of their hulls.

Father Gago in his letter highly commended the generosity and kindness which the aged Captain-Major Duarte da Gama had shown to the Jesuits in general and to Xavier in particular; adding that the marked deference which he paid to Xavier and his fellow missionaries had greatly impressed the Japanese and redounded to the credit of Christianity. This was indeed true, and the close connection between God and Mammon which characterized missionary work in Kyushu for the remainder of the Christian century is strikingly attested by the following extract from Valignano's oft-quoted "Sumario" of 1580.

Your Reverence must understand that after the grace and favor of God, the greatest help that we have had hitherto in securing Christians is that of the Great Ship. This applies in the lower Kyushu region which was all that I had seen when this treatise was drafted, but it does not apply in Bungo nor in the Kyoto district, for the Great Ship does not go thither. The same distinction is applicable when the interests of the various lords are under discussion, since these interests only apply in lower Kyushu, whither Portuguese ships and junks come yearly from China. For as the lords of Japan are very poor, as has been said, and the benefits they derive when the ships come to their ports are very great, they try hard to entice them to their fiefs. And since they have convinced themselves that they will come to where there are Christians and churches, and whither the padres wish them to come, it therefore follows that many of them, even though they are heathen, seek to get the padres to come thither and to secure churches and converts, thinking that by this means the ships will [in their turn] secure other favors they wish to obtain from the padres. And since the Japanese are so much at the disposal of their lords, they readily become converted when told to do so by their lords and they think it is their wish. This is the door by which entered most of those who were baptized in the beginning; and in this way we began to be welcomed in Japan and to convert Christians in diverse places. Whereby it can be said, as it has been said of the Indian Christians, that here likewise few of the Japanese came honestly to receive our Law, except in the Kyoto district where there is no question of any benefits deriving from the Great Ship. Withal there is this difference between the Indian and Japanese Christians, which in itself proves that there is really no room for comparison between them, for each one of the former was converted from some individual ulterior motive, and since they are blacks, and of small sense, they are subsequently very difficult to improve and turn into good Christians; whereas the Japanese usually become converted, not on some whimsical individual ulterior motive (since it is their suzerains who expect to benefit thereby and not they themselves) but only in obedience to their lord's command; and since they are white and of good understanding and behavior, and greatly given to outward show, they readily frequent the churches and sermons, and when they are instructed they become very good Christians, albeit the lords who have an eye on the main chance and are so preoccupied with warfare are usually the worst.

In the Kyoto region where these commercial considerations do not apply, those lords who have been converted hitherto, have been so mainly because having heard the things of our Law they seemed good to them. And although their vassals likewise followed suit in order to please their lords, yet since these latter entered by a straighter and narrower way than those of Kyushu, they have a better understanding of our faith and are better Christians. . . . But they all have this in common, that after they become Christians they pay no regard whatsoever to their idols, and in this point they far surpass those of India, who even after their conversion to Christianity are greatly prone to hanker after their idols. Hence the Christian community in Japan is beyond comparison better than any other and easier to maintain, despite its great extent and the lack of workers. . . . and this is why it is more necessary for us to employ the help of natives in Japan than elsewhere.[2]

Valignano was not blind to the fact that many of these Christians, whether from the Gokinai or from Kyushu, who became converts on the orders of their feudal superiors, likewise apostatized with equal facility when ordered to do so. But he considered that, even making allowance for this (so to speak) "floating vote," there remained a goodly residue who once converted stayed that way, and preferred death or exile to recantation.

The visitor elsewhere explains succinctly that although the Christian community in the Kyoto district was superior in quality to that of Kyushu, the Jesuits had to concentrate their efforts in the southern island rather than in the capital, since in Kyushu, "the Company had greater strength and prestige because of the Portuguese ships which came there annually." It is true that (as I shall show later) Valignano recommended a change of policy in this respect, urging that the maximum missionary effort should be made in the Gokinai and not in Kyushu. Experience proved to him that this policy was impracticable, for the influence exercised by the Jesuits was so closely connected with the Great Ship, that their headquarters had to be situated in the latter's terminal port. Of this more anon, and I return to a consideration of the factors affecting the Japanese attitude toward Christianity and toward foreign trade during the first forty years of the Christian century.

It is known from Japanese sources that, as Valignano explains, desire for foreign trade was the primary impulse which drove the Kyushu daimyo to welcome the padres to their fiefs, even though some of them, such as Otomo Yoshishige, became loyal converts in due course. The Japanese, like the Athenians of old, have always hankered after some new thing, and quite apart from the Chinese silks which formed an indispensable part of the dress of all who could afford them, European and Indian curiosities and *objets d'art* commanded a ready sale and market. There is an interesting glimpse of this in Frois' previously quoted letter of 1569, relating his historic meeting with Oda Nobunaga. Frois writes, apropos of Nobunaga's immense personal fortune:

As soon as the nobles, bonzes, citizens, and merchants who had dealings with him, realized that Nobunaga wanted dresses and objects from India and Portugal, truly such an amazing amount of material was presented to him, that I was left quite astounded and beside myself. For I could not imagine whence came such a great variety of goods to these so distant regions, nor how the Japanese could have got them from the Portuguese, namely, all the scarlet capes and *cabaias* [Malay "shifts"], velvet caps with their feathers and medallions of Our Lady of Grace, many pieces of crimson satin, Cordova leather skins, hourglasses and sundials, candlesticks and tapers, Chinese furred robes and furbelows, the finest glassware, every kind of rich damask, and many other different kinds of things which I do not remember. All this in such abundance, that he has twelve or fifteen chests, like those of Portugal, filled with these things during the last three or four months, so that I cannot for the life of me imagine what can be brought thence that will still be a novelty for him.

Some of these Chinese silks and furbelows were probably a by-product of the piratical ravages of the Wako, but Frois was doubtless correct in supposing that the greater part of this material, whether European or Asiatic, was brought by the Kurofune or Black Ship.[3]

Needless to say, so bellicose a race as the Japanese eagerly welcomed the muskets and other weapons brought by the Southern Barbarians, and the Portuguese, in their turn, were keen collectors of Japanese swords and partisans. Both these weapons were speedily naturalized in Portuguese under their original etymology of *katana* and *naginata* respectively. In 1561–1562, the daimyo of Bungo, Otomo Sorin, sent "a fine new dirk with its scabbard entwined with a golden snake, very artistically mounted, as a present for our lord the king, since he knew he was but a little child." Dom Sebastião was indeed only five or six years old, but this *wakizashi* probably gave him great pleasure if it ever arrived (it was damaged in a typhoon in the China Sea and sent back to Japan for repair) since this ill-fated monarch was a visionary crusader, greatly addicted to the practice of arms from his earliest youth. On the same occasion, Otomo Sorin sent the viceroy of India a magnificent suit of armor together with two massive silver-hafted *naginata* which gave great pleasure to their recipient. Another Portuguese viceroy later sent to the Taiko Hideyoshi a present of a European stand of armor and a campaign tent in 1588, through the returning Father Valignano; the finely illuminated address on vellum accompanying this gift is still preserved in Japan.[4]

What with their anxiety to secure Chinese silks, Indian stuffs, and European gewgaws, it is understandable that there was the greatest competition among the Kyushu daimyo to attract Portuguese traders to their ports. Many modern writers list European firearms as the main attraction, but this was only true in the very early days of the trade, since the Japanese learned how to imitate and make them within a twelvemonth, and the national production was speedily sufficient to supply the demand. Cannon seem to have played virtually no part in the civil struggles of the sixteenth century, and either the Portuguese refrained from importing them or, more probably, the Japanese were not particularly interested. This is rather surprising, for there is no reason why the Japanese should not have become as good gun founders as they did gunsmiths or armorers, but this branch of the "noble art of military" was neglected by them for many years.

The Jesuits were not slow in utilizing the facilities of the Great Ship, and Valignano complains more than once that the later captain-majors were not always so ready to comply with ecclesiastical suggestions as had been Xavier's friend, Duarte da Gama. He wrote in the "Sumario" of 1583, when dealing with the prospects of Christianity in Kyushu,

If the Portuguese would pay more consideration to the service of Our Lord and less to their own purely selfish interests, and would go one year to one port and the next to another, in conformity with the decision of the local Jesuit superior, the whole of that Christianity could be controlled very easily and smoothly, whilst good progress would be made in Satsuma and elsewhere. For all the lords are moved solely by the prospect of gain, and with this and the fear of losing their profits they would compound very readily with the padres, doing what the padres want them to do. But since the Portuguese are unwilling to do this, and they often go to places against the padres' wishes, there is always much jealousy and rivalry between these lords, from which follow in turn great toil and moil to the padres and to Christianity. And, moreover, it sometimes happens that the Portuguese go with their ships to the fiefs of heathen lords who bitterly persecute the padres and Christianity, wrecking churches and burning images, which causes great scandal and contempt of the Christian religion. Since we cannot now force the captain-majors to go into the ports that we wish, it seems both necessary and expedient that we should obtain a brief from His Holiness, forbidding the Portuguese, on pain of excommunication, to enter the ports of lords who persecute Christianity or who are reluctant to allow their vassals to be converted. For the Portuguese would lose none of their profits thereby, whereas we could raise up or pull down the daimyo. Padre Melchior Carneiro always did this so long as he was bishop of China, but with the change of the new bishop and in view of what might happen in future, it would be better to have this order of His Holiness, albeit if he made the local Jesuit superior his representative in Japan, this of itself would suffice.[5]

The reader will see from this extract that not only were the things of God and Caesar getting inextricably mixed in sixteenth-century Japan, but that Professor Murdoch's observation that it needed no very lusty blast on the Jesuit whistle to bring the Portuguese laity humbly and crouchingly to heel, requires serious modification. As usual, there is something to be said on both sides. It is quite true, as the experience of 1543–1580 showed, and as Japanese records attest, that the Kyushu daimyo would go to almost any lengths to attract the Kurofune to their ports, and were always prepared to stomach the Jesuits provided that they could get the Namban traders as well. Even the redoubtable Shimadzu of Satsuma was no exception in this respect, and he more than once wrote asking for Jesuits to come to his fief on the implicit condition that the Great Ship would not be far behind. Moreover, as Valignano pointed out, the Portuguese were pretty sure of making a handsome profit wherever they went, and, from the ecclesiastical point of view, no doubt one port was as good as another.[6]

This, however, was something which the Jesuit forgot or ignored. The rugged Kyushu coast and stormy China Sea was not the ideal fairway for the clumsy carracks with their cargoes of silk and silver valued at more than a million in gold. One reason why the Portuguese frequented so many ports in the early years was because they were looking for a safe harbor with easy access to the hinterland, and landward communications not unduly exposed to political interference. In the absence of any reliable charts, or indeed of any large-scale charts at all, they were far more at the mercy of wind and weather than it is easy to visualize today. They could not do without a good landlocked harbor. Furthermore, a certain degree of stability and confidence is essential for the healthy growth of trade; and if the Portuguese were to chop and change their terminal port annually at the passing whim of the Jesuits, they could not have built up a reliable commercial clientele—to say nothing of the inconvenience thus caused to the merchants who came from all over Japan to bid for their silks. Finally, this business of taking sides in local feudal squabbles was to prove a two-edged weapon.

Valignano himself wrote some years later, when his views had been somewhat changed by bitter experience, that the Jesuits could not fathom the rights and wrongs of Japanese civil wars, and their intervention therein had nearly always proved disastrous to themselves in the end. He therefore categorically forbade the practice, even if it was merely advising a Christian daimyo against a heathen one, save under the most rigid safeguards. As an instance of misplaced intervention, he cited a war between the two Christian daimyo of Omura and Arima, in which the local padres had taken the side of the daimyo in whose fief they then happened to be working. This ridiculous situation was of course a logical result of the interference advocated by Valignano in local Kyushu politics in 1580. It may pertinently be asked what the captain-major of that year would have been expected to do, if one group of Jesuits had told him to take his ship to Arima's fief, and another group to Omura's.

On the whole, the Jesuits' early attitude must be pronounced a mischievous one, and it was in any event impracticable; for with only one annual carrack at their disposal (as was the rule after 1550) the Portuguese could not possibly comply with a request to visit various fiefs at frequent intervals. Incidentally, there is another minor point which may have made some of the captain-majors boggle at acceding to every request of this kind. The Jesuits had no better friend and protector than Otomo Yoshishige (Sorin) the daimyo of Bungo, whose ports were often visited by the Kurofune in the early years of Christian propaganda in Kyushu. Father Gago, in his letter of September, 1562, after extolling Otomo's many benefactions to the missionaries adds, "When one of our captain-majors, who are fidalgos, comes to trade in his port and invites him on board the Great Ship to entertain him, the Portuguese merchants crowd around

him and he laughs and jokes with them and gives them things
to eat, but the captain-major stands cap in hand and is treated
with scant respect for a long while." It will be seen that the
admiration rightly felt by the Jesuits for their princely patron was not necessarily shared by a fidalgo who prided himself on his *pundonor* and *primor*.[7]

In the year 1569, or thereabouts, that old missionary war
horse, Gaspar Vilela, was invited by one of Omura Sumitada's
(*alias* Dom Bartholomew) Christian vassals to visit him at a
picturesque little fishing village known as Nagasaki. Vilela
accepted the invitation, and, after some preliminary palaver,
converted all the lord's retainers to the number of fifteen hundred. He then burned the empty Buddhist temple in which his
patron had lodged him and erected a Christian church on the
site, which, in the course of time, became a cathedral under
its original invocation of All Saints (Todos os Sanctos). The
Great Ship from Amacao was at this period frequenting the
neighboring harbors of Shiki in Amakusa and Fukuda in
Nagasaki fjord; but because these places were rendered in-
secure by the progress of a widespread rebellion against
Omura, the Great Ship came to Nagasaki for the first time
in the monsoon of 1571, under the Captain-Major Tristão
Vaz de Veiga. This splendid harbor proved to be the ideal for
which the Portuguese had been seeking so long; and since
the peripatetic Jesuits were likewise looking for a base which
could serve as a safe refuge in time of trouble, and Omura
was anxious to secure a profitable source of revenue, matters were speedily arranged to the satisfaction of all concerned.
It is fitting, at this point, to reproduce Valignano's version
of this momentous event, as embodied in chapter xvii of his
preliminary "Sumario" of August, 1580.[8]

The lives and property of our missionaries in Japan are continually exposed to imminent hazard and risk owing to the constant warfare and ups
and downs of fortune which prevail; and this not for the love of God or his
glory, nor for the defense of his holy Law, but merely because it is the custom of the Japanese to destroy everything they take, whether temples of
their own sects or those of others, without paying the smallest respect to

the very idols they worship. For this reason, all of us who have experience of these parts, considered it very necessary, both for our own sakes as for the spread of Christianity, that we should take charge of the port of Nagasaki which is in the fief of Dom Bartholomew, and whither the Great Ship normally comes. This place is a natural stronghold, and one which no Japanese lord could take by force. Moreover, since it is the port whither the Great Ship comes, anyone who is lord of the soil will be delighted to have the padres there, in order to ensure that the ship does likewise. Altogether it seemed a very desirable place, and one very suitable for the preservation of our property, as also a refuge for personnel when necessary. Moreover, another fortress called Mogi, which lies a league from this place, is the natural gateway between the fief of Dom Bartholomew and that of Arima. It, therefore, seemed beneficial for both their sakes that we should likewise take charge of this fortress of Mogi. Accordingly, these two places were willingly given us by Dom Bartholomew, both because he thought that he would secure his fief in this way, as because he considered that he would thus ensure always having the Great Ship in that port, which would bring him great renown and make him a great lord through the duties and profits he would derive therefrom. He, therefore, gave it to us on the sole condition that the ship would pay him an annual due of 1,000 ducats, part to be expended on the maintenance of the padres who live in that port and on the fortification of the two said places, and part to be divided amongst the Christian lords. And albeit this may well appear a strange thing in Europe, and something foreign to our institution, withal it seems absolutely vital and necessary to those of us here in Japan who have had local experience. But since the whirligig of time and change may show that it might be advisable in the future, either to return them to their original lord, or to hand them over to the Church if a bishopric is formed later, the Company has received these two places on the condition that they can hand them over even before an answer is received from the father general, if the superior in India should see fit and there is no time to await a written reply from Rome. Nevertheless the lord of the soil gave them to us in perpetuity and virtually unconditionally as regards the Company.

This cession of Japanese soil to foreigners was something quite unprecedented, and Valignano further elaborated on it in his fuller report of October, 1583. After dilating on the natural advantages of Nagasaki, which was then a fortified town of more than four hundred houses with a strongly-built Jesuit residence, Valignano stated that they had not derived quite so much benefit as they had originally expected from occupying Nagasaki and Mogi, since they could not inflict summary capital punishment on the local inhabitants (who incidentally were nearly all Christians) : "if we could govern these places with true Japanese severity, killing whenever necessary, they would be much more useful to us than they are now; but since we cannot order people to be killed, and the Japanese do as they please unless they go in fear of the headsman, we do not derive so much benefit from it as did its former lord." Nevertheless despite their inability (though clearly not their unwillingness) to inflict summary capital punishment, the Jesuits found the place very useful; and Valignano advocated its retention on the grounds that the port revenues (which the complacent Sumitada handed over to them *en bloc*) not only paid for the upkeep of their local establishment but for that of Omura as well.⁹

The Jesuit General, Claudio Aquaviva, professed to be taken somewhat aback by this unusual example of temporal ambition; but after duly considering the matter with prayerful deliberation, he came round to Valignano's point of view. He stressed that the cession should be regarded as a temporary one, and only binding so long as the Society's possession of these two places was considered essential to the progress of Christianity in Kyushu, and not merely for the protection of Jesuit life and property. Despite this piece of casuistry, there is every reason to suppose that the Jesuits retained the virtual overlordship of Nagasaki, if not of Mogi, until Toyotomi Hideyoshi brought them under the direct control of the central government seven years later.

Meanwhile Nagasaki continued to grow and prosper exceedingly, for its harbor became the recognized terminal port of the Kurofune from Macao, which from 1571 onward only very occasionally went elsewhere. It is interesting to follow Valignano's vacillations concerning the exact nature of the debt which God (as personified by the Jesuits) owed to Mammon (represented by the Great Ship) in connection with the Kurofune and Christianity. It has been seen that in 1580, he had no doubts of the superiority of the Kyoto Christians, who were not influenced by mundane commercial considerations when adopting their new faith, as were their coreligionists in Kyushu. He also complained bitterly that the Portuguese would not coöperate with the Jesuits by sending the Great Ship to the ports of the different daimyo in turn, so that the latter would want the Jesuits to be established in their respective fiefs. But three years later he wrote that, although the Society in Japan had now progressed to a point where it had no need to truckle to the local daimyo, it lacked sufficient workers to establish Christian communities in all the local seaports, even if asked to do so. He admitted (what he might have realized sooner) that the Portuguese, having only one annual carrack at their disposal, could not cater for everyone. Finally, he acknowledged that the places where Christianity was originally planted "with this eye on the Great Ship, are less fruitful and more expensive, as experience has shown."

A dozen years more were to show him something else. Nobunaga was dead, and Japan effectively unified for the first time in centuries under the iron hand of Toyotomi Hideyoshi. This political unification of the empire cut both ways as far as the Jesuits were concerned. On the one hand the country was quieter and more settled, but on the other hand the former disinterestedness of the Gokinai daimyo was a thing of the past. The political and financial policy followed first by Nobunaga and then by the Taiko, had resulted in a great increase in the demand for gold and foreign goods among the various daimyo, whether for the purpose of saving up for a rainy day, or for placating their jealous and greedy suzerain with costly gifts in kind and bullion. Moreover, communications were greatly improved, trade circulated far more freely than during the civil wars, and the artistic standards of the Adzuchi-Momoyama periods demanded a profusion of wealth and show. The daimyo were frequently changed from one fief to another, regardless of their territorial origin or family connections.

For all these reasons, Chinese silks and other goods brought by the Kurofune were in general demand over the whole country, and in the Kyoto district as much as or more than elsewhere. Consequently, the motives of the Gokinai daimyo were no longer so pure, with the result that there was no longer the same necessity as formerly to concentrate mission- ary efforts in that area. Last but by no means least, Hideyoshi's anti-Christian edict of 1587 (of which more later) was not enforced in the Christian fiefs of Kyushu where the Jesuits were allowed to propagate their faith openly, if unobtru- sively. In view of all these reasons, Valignano, in 1592, no longer felt the same way about the relative importance of Kyoto and Kyushu as he had done a dozen years earlier. But irrespective of where the Jesuit missionary effort was con- centrated, one fact becomes clear from a perusal of Vali- gnano's reports and the reaction thereto at Rome, namely, that Christianity in Japan depended first, last and all the time on the Great Ship from Amacao. It was in the Great Ship that the Jesuits came to Japan; it was mainly from their share in the sale of its cargoes that they supported their promising mission field; it was the wish for the Great Ship which induced otherwise hostile or indifferent daimyo to welcome them to their fiefs and to permit the conversion of their retainers; it was the fear that the Great Ship would no longer come, if the Jesuits were driven away, which repeat- edly caused Hideyoshi and Ieyasu to hold their hands when they were on the point of expelling the missionaries. In short, it was the Great Ship which was the temporal mainstay of the Japan mission; and it is typical of their close connection that the disappearance of the one should virtually coincide with the collapse of the other.[10]

II

The allusion in the last section to Jesuit participation in the Macao-Japan trade makes it necessary to explain further this singular combination of God and Mammon. In order to do this, it must be placed in its proper setting as a part of

the Portuguese interport trade in Asia. After the decisive
defeat of their Moslem rivals in the first quarter of the sixteenth century, the Portuguese dominated (where they did
not monopolize) the maritime trade of Asia for the best part
of a hundred years. Their naval supremacy was greatly facilitated by the fact that their potential Indian, Chinese, and
Japanese rivals all had their attention concentrated on their
respective internal affairs for varying reasons; and the seafaring races of Indonesia had not made sufficient progress in
the technique of naval architecture to be a serious menace to
the *Feringis*. The Great Ships could thus ply the Indian
Ocean and the China Sea without being effectively challenged
by Arab dhows, Malay prows, or Sino-Japanese junks, and
were, consequently, in great demand as safe carriers of valuable cargo from the Yellow Sea to the Persian Gulf. If, in some
areas, they indulged in piratical acts themselves, they at least
prevented others from doing so; and though the *Pax Lusi-
tanica* had its seamy side, it indubitably contributed to the
advancement of commercial technique and prosperity in this
quarter of the globe.

Of all the aspects of the interport trade of sixteenth-
century Portuguese Asia, few are more interesting and none
were more prosperous than the trade between India, China,
and Japan, which was epitomized in the annual voyage of the
Great Ship from Golden Goa (*Goa Dourado*) to Macao and
the Long Cape, to give Nagasaki its literal translation. The
classic account of this voyage, as it was in its heyday during
the last quarter of the century, is that given by the English
merchant-adventurer, Ralph Fitch, who visited the East Indies in 1585–1591, and whose report can be read in the pages
of Hakluyt and Purchas.

When the Portugales goe from Macao in China to Japan, they carrie much
white Silke, Gold, Muske, and Porcelanes; and they bring from thence nothing but Silver. They have a great Carake which goeth thither every yeere,
and shee bringeth from thence every yeere above six hundred thousand crusadoes [ducats]; and all this silver of Japan, and two hundred thousand

crusadoes more in silver which they bring yeerly out of India, they imploy
to their great advantage in China; and they bring from thence Gold, Muske,
Silke, Copper, Porcelanes, and many other things very costly, and gilded.

The captaincy of this annual carrack was at first awarded
(and later sold) by the crown to a deserving or wealthy
fidalgo. Apart from other obvious perquisites, this Captain-
Major of the Voyage of China and Japan, as he was grandiloquently entitled, acted as governor of Macao during his ship's
ten- or eleven-month stay in that port. In both China and
Japan, he was the senior Portuguese authority vis-à-vis the
native officials. In addition to his own investment in the
voyage, he apparently collected ten per cent on the freight
of that part of the cargo which consisted of silk, and this was
precisely the most valuable and bulky. He was also vested
with wide executive and judicial powers over all of his compatriots in the China Sea and along the China coast. Thanks
to these prerogatives, perquisites, and pickings, he was in the
enviable position of being able to make his fortune on one
voyage, as did several of John Company's captains trading to Canton two centuries later. Small wonder that Valignano wrote, a trifle acrimoniously, about people who grumbled over the money spent by the Jesuits in the service of
God, when a fidalgo, who had spent only half a dozen years
in India, "often enough merely passing the time and amusing himself," was granted a Japan voyage which brought him
in a clear profit of as much as 50,000 ducats! [11]

Honest Ralph Fitch's succinct account of the Macao-
Nagasaki trade in 1590, though accurate in outline, requires
more clarification in detail to understand the why and the
wherefore of the Jesuits' participation therein. In this connection, it must be remembered that the virtual Portuguese
monopoly of this richest of all interport trades was influenced
by two main factors. First was the political tension between
Ming China and Adzuchi-Momoyama Japan which made
direct official commerce between the two empires impossible;
second, the different (and fluctuating) ratio of value between
gold and silver which prevailed in China, Japan, and the

Iberian colonial empire. Further enlightenment on the subject comes from an anonymous Spanish report on the interport trade of the Portuguese in Asia. Its author had visited Japan, Goa, and Macao and wrote from personal observation of commodities and prices as he found them at the turn of the sixteenth century.

When the Great Ship left Goa in April or May on her voyage to Macao and Nagasaki, the principal items in her cargo were: two or three hundred thousand silver coins; ivory; cloth of grain; one hundred and fifty or two hundred pipes of wine; supplies of olives and olive oil for the Portuguese of Macao, and odds and ends of lesser value. The anonymous Spaniard was astonished at the cheapness of European products in Macao, since the wine was priced almost as cheaply there as in Lisbon. "The Portuguese say that they are only interested in laying out their capital in China, for it is in the investment that they make their profits." The Portuguese alone, he adds, invested more than a million cruzados annually in the purchase of Chinese goods at Canton for sale in Japan and India. The bulk of this capital came not from Goa, as is obvious from the scanty list, but from Japanese silver.

This same report lists eighteen principal commodities bought by the Portuguese in China for sale in Japan, with their cost and sale prices, and it is these that reveal where the money went. The writer explains that all the silver from Japan, India, and Europe went into China, but none came out, since the Chinese never paid for their purchases in coin but only in goods. The prices he gives must be understood in this sense, since the monetary standard used was expressed in *taels, mace, condorins,* and *cash,* only the last of which had any real existence as a coin, being a small coin of base metal. The *tael* (Chinese *liang*) was the Chinese money of weight and account, and was theoretically subdivided into 10 mace or 100 condorins, or 1,000 cash. For purposes of calculation it was normally equated with 7½ silver *tangas,* an Indo-Portuguese silver coin of which five made up the cruzado;

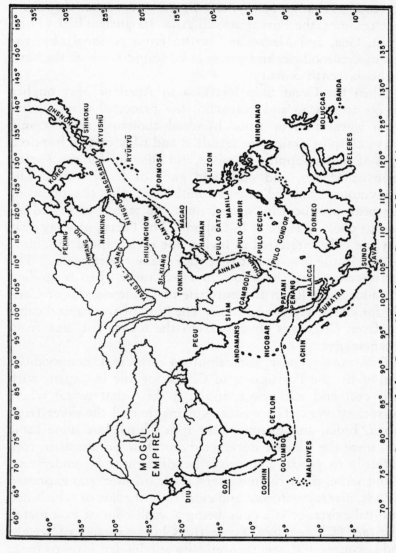

Course of the Great Ship from Goa to Nagasaki, *ca.* 1600

but in Japan, according to Padre João Rodriguez' *Grammar* of 1604, it was regarded as the equivalent of the cruzado. It is hoped that the reader will not become too confused if he is reminded that the tael was likewise the trade name of the Chinese ounce; 16 taels made up a *catty* (or *kin*), and 100 catties made a *picul* which is nowadays reckoned as 133½ pounds avoirdupois weight (61.1999 kg.). With this in mind, let the reader take a deep breath and follow the sixteenth-century Spanish guide into the welter of taels, catties, and piculs, all Javanese or Malay terms.

The principal commodities purchased by the Portuguese at Canton for loading in the Great Ship at Macao on her way to Nagasaki were as follows. Five or six hundred piculs of white silk floss, costing 80 taels the picul at Canton for delivery in Macao; they sold in Japan for 140 to 150 taels the picul. Four or five hundred piculs of colored silk stuffs, costing from 40 to 140 taels the picul, according to quality; these sold in Japan for 100 to 400 taels the picul, respectively. Seventeen hundred to two thousand bundles of "painted silks," which likewise sold at Nagasaki for two or three times their purchase price at Canton and Macao. Three to four thousand taels of unrefined gold, costing a little under 5½ taels each at Canton, which sold for a little more than 7½ taels each at Nagasaki. Refined gold cost the equivalent of 6 taels 6 maces the tael (of weight) at Canton, and sold for 8 taels 3 maces the tael at Nagasaki.

There is no need to inflict more of these figures on the reader. It is enough to know that practically all the other items listed have the laconic notation *doblase el dinero* after their prices; those that did not fetch double their cost price, usually tripled or quadrupled it. These other goods included cotton cloth and textiles of various kinds, quicksilver, rouge (much prized by Japanese women), lead, tin, rhubarb, boxwood, sugar, and, rather surprisingly, about 2,000 packages of porcelain. Most of the other items were on a rather modest scale, but even the rhubarb fetched double its cost price.[12]

The return cargo of the Great Ship from Nagasaki was

principally silver bullion. The bulk of this bullion was invested at Canton in the purchase of the silk floss and other commodities listed above, which were then disposed of at a profit in Japan; and so on in rotation. A proportion of these Chinese goods were, however, re-exported to India, whence a few items such as camphor, lacquered furniture, and some of the silks and porcelain, found their way from Goa to Europe. On the gold bullion alone, a profit of eighty or ninety per cent was not uncommon in India, apart from the considerable amount which was smuggled in, according to the Spanish informant.

The gauntlet of customs duties, taxes, and imposts which the Great Ship had to run on the course of its round trip was onerous only in Portuguese territory. A duty of eight and a half per cent was levied at Goa on all imports and exports, and another of seven and a half per cent at Malacca, although (after about 1570) the China carrack seldom landed or disposed of any of her return cargo there. If the Great Ship was unwise enough to call at Columbo, the local captain exacted a payment of two or three thousand cruzados as an (apparently) unauthorized contribution to the upkeep of the Ceylon garrison. At Macao, the Portuguese had to pay a duty on each ship to the Kwangtung customs commissioners; but the measurement was made in a most peculiar way, and the payment could usually be adjusted to a mere bagatelle by judicious bribery. In Japan, an anchorage tax of 1,000 ducats was originally paid at Nagasaki to the local Jesuits at Omura's instigation; but I am not certain whether Hideyoshi's representatives received this sum after the Taiko's seizure of the port. In any event, handsome presents were expected by the local daimyo, and later by Hideyoshi and Ieyasu in succession. Actually these taxes did not take much of the sugar coating off the gingerbread; and the profits derived from the Macao carrack were only rivaled by those of her more celebrated contemporary, the Manila galleon.

One of the principal items brought by the Great Ship to Nagasaki was gold, although this precious metal had at one time been exported from Japan to China in the Ashikaga period. New gold and silver mines were discovered and worked in various parts of Japan during the sixteenth century, the best known being those of Kai, Idzu, Iwami provinces, and Sado Island. It was, however, as a potential Potosí that Japan chiefly aroused the interest of both European and Chinese traders. Gold is mentioned as one of the most coveted products brought by the mysterious Guores to Malacca in Albuquerque's time; but when Japan was formally discovered thirty years later, it was as the *Ilhas Argentarias*, or *Ilhas Platerias* (Silver Islands) that they achieved their immediate fame. Francis Xavier alludes to them in this connection as early as 1552, and Luis de Camões sang in his *Lusiadas* of "Iapão, onde naçe a prata fina." The subject is a complicated one, since reliable information about the output of the Japanese mines was often concealed by the local daimyo, who were doubtless afraid of drawing the unwelcome attentions of Nobunaga and Hideyoshi to this source of revenue. Both these potentates followed a deliberate policy of amassing gold, and were far from scrupulous in the methods they used to collect it. Nobunaga was a pioneer in this respect and introduced the flat oval-shaped gold coin known as *oban*. In any event, by about 1570, the differing ratio of gold to silver, as between China and Japan, rendered it profitable to send silver from Japan to China for the purchase of gold.[13]

Valignano explains in his supplementary report ("Addiciones") of 1592, that one of the major tribulations of the Jesuits in Japan was the importunity with which numerous daimyo besought them to act as bullion brokers in this business. He observes that this pernicious practice first started in a small way with petty Christian daimyo, such as Omura and Arima, sending modest amounts of silver to be exchanged in China for gold. The padres had perforce to act as intermediaries and raised no great objections to doing so, since this little favor laid the Christian daimyo under greater obligations to them. Otomo Sorin of Bungo did the same thing, but on a rather larger scale, for his annual investment amounted to 3,000 ducats before his conversion to Christianity in 1578.

This trickle of silver soon became a spate, since the political and financial policies followed by Nobunaga and Hideyoshi gave a great impetus to the demand for gold. Valignano explains that not only did these dictators collect all their dues, rents, and taxes in gold wherever and whenever practicable, but that all the daimyo were likewise stimulated to collect gold for two reasons. First, because with the frequent changes of fiefs and fortune, gold was the handiest and most compact form in which to keep capital. Second, (writing in 1592) everyone expected a fearful civil war to break out immediately after Hideyoshi's death, which could not be very distant, and then gold would be needed more than ever. Finally, nothing was so calculated to assuage the wrath of either Nobunaga or Hideyoshi as the presentation of a substantial slug of gold, and hence gold was a good thing to have handy. The result of these activities was that not only Christian but heathen daimyo constantly importuned the padres to act as bullion brokers between Canton, Macao, and Nagasaki. To a lesser degree they invested their silver in the purchase of Chinese silk, "aunque comunmente no quieren mas que oro" (although as a rule they want nothing but gold).

This unwanted increase in their broker business, embarrassed the Jesuits considerably. The Macaonese merchants looked somewhat askance at it, and Valignano had difficulty in persuading them to agree to the Jesuits handling a maximum annual sum of 6,000 ducats, although this was less than half the sum that the daimyo wanted to send yearly. More serious was the attitude of the Christian daimyo. When the Jesuits expressed their distaste for acting as bullion brokers, Arima, Omura, and the rest became furious, pointing out that it was most ungrateful of the padres to quibble at doing the daimyo a favor which cost them nothing, when the said daimyo were daily risking their fiefs, honors, and lives through their profession of Christianity. They also alleged that they could not keep pace with the Taiko's exactions without the profits they derived from this investment; without the Chinese gold they would be ruined, their fiefs abandoned to the heathen, and all hopes of the spread of Christianity stultified. There was obviously much truth in this, nor could the Jesuits possibly refuse to take the silver investments of heathen daimyo when asked to do so; since these men, from being friendly or indifferent, would then become actively hostile, with dire results for their Christian vassals. All that the Jesuits could do in the circumstances was to keep the volume of silver exported to within reasonable proportions, and hope that Hideyoshi's expected death would plunge the land into the civil strife of the *Sengoku-jidai*, when the value of gold might reasonably be expected to fall.[14]

This involuntary and distasteful business of bullion brokerage, although unbecoming to their clerical cloth, did not put the Jesuits to any expense, but only to trouble and inconvenience. The same could not be said of other activities in which they were compelled to participate, the chief of these being the interminable present-giving. In accordance with Japanese (or for that matter Asiatic) social etiquette, it was *de rigeur* to present a gift to anyone from whom a favor was (or might be at some future date) solicited. Presents must be offered to all high-ranking individuals whenever they were visited, apart from the New Year and other periodical occasions. All endeavors of the Jesuits to evade or modify this long-standing custom not only failed, but brought obloquy on their heads, even from the Christian daimyo, whom they vainly tried to persuade to abrogate this expensive national custom. Nor could these costly gifts be limited to friends or neutrals. They had to be offered to declared opponents, although this was mitigated by the fact that if they accepted them (as they often did) then they invariably modified or restrained their anti-Christian attitude. Moreover, the Jesuits, as cultured *Nambanjin* who could speak Japanese, had a never-ending stream of visitors of all classes, inspired by motives varying from mere curiosity to the desire to hear the Catholic faith expounded. Whatever their motives, none could be refused, but all must be politely received, entertained, and dismissed with a parting gift of some kind. This meant a colossal expenditure, which could not by any means be reduced, but on the contrary tended to increase automatically with the growth and spread of the Christian missions throughout the empire.[15]

Apart from this perennial drain, the Jesuits had many and heavy calls on their scanty monetary resources. By 1580, they had to help maintain an expanding Christian community of 150,000 souls, served by 200 churches with 85 Jesuits, including 20 Japanese brothers, apart from 100 acolytes or dojuku. Ten years later, there were 136 Jesuits in Japan, and the number of dojuku had increased to 170, and the caretaking and menial staff to 300, making a total of more than 600 persons who were entirely dependent for their support on the mission funds. The cost of maintaining the churches, schools, training seminaries, and the functioning of the already active Jesuit mission press, fell almost entirely on the Jesuits; although the Christian daimyo helped where they could, and even heathen feudal lords, such as Hosokawa Tadaoki, gave occasional donations in land or in kind. Moreover, many of the local Christians were very poor, apart from that increasingly numerous category of penniless refugees who had been exiled for their faith from anti-Christian fiefs. All these people had to be supported by charity, as did some aged but deserving dojuku, too old for further evangelical work. Obviously Valignano was not guilty of exaggeration when he estimated the cost of running the Japan mission at between 10,000 and 12,000 cruzados annually; nor did he forbear to point out that this sum compared very favorably with the cost of maintaining a single Jesuit college in Europe, which usually had a smaller personnel, but where maintenance costs were far more.

It might be asked (and Valignano in fact was asked) why

the Christian daimyo and community could not support their Jesuit pastors and churches in the same way as the Buddhist temples were supported by their devotees, but the father-visitor had no difficulty in showing that the analogy was a false one. The majority of the daimyo were very poor in this world's goods. Their only extensive source of income was rice, most of which they had to dole out again to their samurai as their stipend in lieu of money. Thus a daimyo with an income of 500,000 *koku* of rice would in practice only have 40,000 or 50,000 koku left for himself, after doling out what was required to ensure his samurai a living wage, and this last was often enough on the level of bare subsistence. An ordinary samurai had to maintain himself, his wife, and their eight or ten servants out of an annual allowance of 150 or 200 koku which meant that the whole household was living on a precarious diet of vegetables, fruit, and radishes (*daikon*) for part of the year. This was the general condition in Kyushu, although the bushi of the agriculturally richer Gokinai district were somewhat better off in this respect. Consequently, even generous benefactors such as Otomo Sorin seldom had much money at short notice.

The poverty of the daimyo was aggravated by their custom of formal retirement (*inkyo*) at a comparatively early age, which might, as with Otomo, result in the direction of affairs passing from a pro-Christian father to an anti-Christian son and successor. It was true that all the daimyo kept great state and large establishments, and even poor samurai had eight or ten servants for a household of two. But these swarms of male and female retainers were not maintained with money, but out of the meager rice allowance, which was the only thing they received in return for their services. The Jesuits, not being feudal lords or warriors, had to pay their household personnel on a more liberal scale. Finally, Christianity being a young and tender foreign plant, the Japanese could not be expected to support its priests with the same readiness and facility as the Buddhist institutions of their own compatriots.[16]

Valignano further pointed out that the parallel with the bonzes was misleading because Buddhism was introduced into Japan at a time of peace and plenty, when the land was effectively united under the rule of a single emperor. Once the imperial house was converted, it could, and did, lavishly endow monastic foundations with large, fixed landed incomes, something impossible for the best-disposed Christian daimyo to do during the turmoil of the "country at war." Many of these monasteries still had the means to maintain themselves, despite all the hardships they suffered at the hands of Nobunaga and Hideyoshi. Another advantage held by the bonzes was that they had numerous Japanese relatives, some in high places, who naturally supported members of their families; whereas the Southern Barbarians could only expect personal support on purely religious grounds, and not from any claims on flesh and blood. Another advantage held by the Buddhist priests was the popularity derived from their temple kindergarten schools or terakoya, where the "young idea" was given a free primary education. These two last-named considerations were to lose much of their validity with that progressive increase in the numbers of Japanese Jesuits and the formation of a native clergy for which Valignano kept pressing, but at this time they were adverse factors to be reckoned with. Even so, the visitor ended by drawing a consoling parallel between the rapid progress made by the Jesuit mission in Japan, despite all these handicaps, and the slow progress made by the primitive Church for centuries under persecution.

Since it was clearly impossible for the Japan mission to be self-supporting for some time to come, reliance on outside help was meanwhile indispensable. The original means for this were extremely exiguous, being limited to gifts made by friendly fidalgos, such as the captain of Malacca who helped Xavier so lavishly in 1549, or by rich novices, such as Fernão Mendes Pinto and Luis d'Almeida, who brought their worldly goods with them on their entry into the Society. Contrary to popular belief, wealthy novices were rare in the Society, and recourse was necessarily had to royal and papal bounty. Before 1574, the sole official allotment was an annual endowment of 500 cruzados charged against the crown revenue from the customs at Malacca. This was increased to 1,000 cruzados a year, by King Sebastião in that year, but the payment was irregular and tardy, apart from the fact that thirty per cent was lost on the exchange when the money was remitted (as it had to be) via China. King Felipe of Spain later made an additional annual grant of 1,000 ducats, which was subject to the same discount on remittance, as was another yearly payment of 4,000 ducats given by Pope Gregory XIII in 1583. Finally there was an allotment of 1,200 ducats earmarked for the Japan mission from the revenues of the Jesuits' landed property in India. These sums produced a maximum annual income of 7,700 ducats, at a time when the minimum expenses of the Japan mission oscillated between 10,000 and 12,000 cruzados.[17]

In these circumstances, how was it possible for them to make both ends meet? Only, as Valignano proved, and as the Pope and King reluctantly agreed, by the help of Mammon. Not to put too fine a point on it, the Jesuits in the Far East inevitably became traders on a considerable scale. The practice must have started very early, although Luis d'Almeida's generous donation of all his worldly wealth to the local coffers of the Society in 1555 may have kept the Jesuits in Japan going for a few years. But in 1567, General Francis Borgia wrote to the provincial at Goa that he heartily disliked the methods used by the Japan missionaries to finance their operations, and earnestly hoped that they would soon find a safe and more edifying alternative. They certainly found a safer if not a more edifying one, when, in 1578, Father-Visitor Valignano concluded a contract with the mercantile community at Macao, for the formal participation of the Japan Jesuits in the Macao-Nagasaki silk trade on the following basis.

The maximum cargo of white silk floss shipped annually to Japan at that period was 1,600 piculs. This cargo was made up by each local merchant contributing proportionately in accordance with his means, as laid down in an agreed sliding scale. The total of 1,600 piculs was handled and marketed as a single shipment at Nagasaki by the Macao municipal factor, and the profits were then distributed *pro rata* to the individual shippers on the carrack's return to Macao. Since the whole cargo was seldom disposed of in the first seasonal sales, the balance was left at Nagasaki for sale after the carrack's return. By the terms of the 1578 agreement, the Japan Jesuits were allotted a share of 50 piculs (bought with the interest on d'Almeida's legacy), the proceeds of the sale of which at Nagasaki were automatically credited to them at the highest ruling prices. Similarly, another 50 piculs were allotted them on the same terms in the balance of the silk left behind for sale at the end of the season. Thus their whole share amounted to 100 piculs per annum, and their profits from 4,000 to 6,000 ducats a year. This sum was the most stable source from which their income was drawn, and, when added to the less reliable proceeds from Malacca, India, and Europe, produced the total of 12,000 cruzados or ducats, under the most favorable circumstances. Since, however, the remaining contributions were almost invariably in arrears, either in whole or in great part, the Jesuits' difficulty in making two ends meet was such that Valignano compared their ability to do so to the Gospel miracle of the loaves and fishes.

This agreement with the Macao mercantile ring was formally ratified by the viceroy of India in April, 1584; by the senate of the newly-created City of the Name of God in China five years later; and by the Jesuit general, the King of Spain (and Portugal), and the Pope in 1582–1583. Despite the formal papal ban on ecclesiastical trading, Pope Gregory XIII ruled that this was an instance of charity rather than of commerce; "and he told me clearly that he thought this could not properly be termed trade, since it was done out of pure necessity," so Claudio Aquaviva reported to Valignano in February, 1582. Nevertheless, the Holy See evidently was not without misgivings, for complaints began to come in from Macao via Lisbon; although Valignano assured his superiors that the

1578 agreement had been purely voluntary on the part of the Macao citizens, who fully realized that the mission had no other means of adequately financing its evangelistic work. These complaints eventually became so strong that, in 1585, the Pope canceled the concession and ordered its immediate cessation. He and King Felipe promised greatly increased annual subsidies to cover the resultant deficit.[18]

"Socorro de España ó llega tarde ó nunca." Help from Spain comes late or never, runs an old proverb which was verified on this occasion, nor were the promised subsidies from the papacy much more regular in their remittance. Valignano therefore carried on with the silk trade, pending an appeal to Rome, with the result that once more the Jesuit general formally authorized its continuance, which likewise was connived at by the King and the Pope, even if they did not again specifically authorize it. Aquaviva urged Valignano to keep the trade within its original limits and to conduct the business as unobtrusively as possible. It is clear from subsequent correspondence between Jesuit headquarters at Rome and their college at Macao, that these last injunctions were not always strictly observed. The scope and extent of the trading operations of the Japan province led to the Society incurring a good deal of unmerited odium.

Meanwhile the China-Japan silk trade underwent an important change during the last decade of the sixteenth century; whereas the bulk of the Great Ship's cargo had hitherto consisted of silk floss, an increasingly large proportion was now taken up by manufactured damask and silk textiles. Moreover, the mercantile silk ring at Macao was reorganized, and individual traders could ship as much as they desired. For these and other reasons, the 1578 agreement fell through, but the Japan province still retained the acknowledged right to a share of 100 piculs in the cargo for sale at the highest ruling prices. In 1598, Valignano side-stepped the terms of the original understanding with the Macaonese, by secretly sending some gold for investment in India. He was reprimanded by the general for this unethical behavior, which was indeed not only a crime but a blunder, since the viceroy had got wind of the whole transaction and it put the Society in an exceedingly awkward position. Aquaviva reminded his overzealous subordinate that the Jesuits' share in the Macao-Nagasaki silk trade had been authorized by Pope and King on the specific condition that it was to be carried on in silk and in Japan alone. He had given a formal written oath to this effect; and if the Roman Curia and the Court of Madrid heard that Valignano was exceeding his instructions, the worst possible impression would be created in both places.[19]

Opposition to this combination of God and Mammon was not confined to the Macaonese merchants. The Jesuits of the China mission looked askance at the extent and scope of the commerce of their Japan colleagues, although they indulged in similar activities on a more modest scale themselves. Their Franciscan rivals and Protestant enemies made great play with it in Europe; but the practice inevitably continued because the necessary funds were not forthcoming from elsewhere. Replying to the exaggerated accusations of his Franciscan critics, Valignano expressed the Jesuits' willingness to drop all participation in the silk trade, just as soon as the 12,000 ducats required to meet their minimum expenses in Japan were forthcoming from another and more reputable source. He pointed out that the abandonment of the silk trade would be equivalent to abandoning the Japan mission, in the circumstances. Contrariwise, as the mission prospered and expanded, either King and Pope must provide it with a fixed and adequate annual income, or else the Jesuits must be allowed a still greater share of the silk trade. He deprecated this last course, since there was already sufficient opposition among the Macao merchants, and any further increase in the Jesuits' profit could only result in the diminution of their own. He suggested that either the Pope or the King should settle a good landed income on the Japan province somewhere, or enable it to buy land in Japan, which would have the additional advantage of making the Jesuits self-supporting as regards rice, at least in some areas. The province could use all the money it could get, for there was urgent need to expand the existing seminaries and to found new hospitals and elementary schools.

To anticipate matters somewhat, it may be noted that although the Jesuit practice of trading in Asia was periodically prohibited by the crown and the papacy, it continued in practice to grow and expand, since only in this way could the provinces of China and Japan meet their ever increasing expenses. This, however, is not to say that they grew rich on the proceeds, for all their profits were immediately spent on good works in the mission, and not infrequently they suffered from "bad debts" and commercial losses. Thus, in 1664, the Japan province (operating in Indo-China since 1640) had a debt of 22,000 dollars; the China vice-province had no capital whatever; and the annual expenses of the Macao college alone amounted to more than 4,000 dollars. Small wonder that the emissaries of Pombal found little beyond their breviaries on the Jesuits whom they so brutally seized in 1762, and no trace whatever of the gold and silver allegedly hoarded in the vaults of St. Paul.

"Our Trade is only that of souls" wrote Padre Antonio Vieira, greatest of Portuguese Jesuits, from Brazil in 1688. Although his Far Eastern colleagues could hardly claim to conform entirely with that proud boast, they found an adequate apologist in Protestant Peter Mundy, who, after duly noting that they were forced to engage in trade from Peking to Pnompenh in order to find the wherewithal for their missions, added fairly enough, "And to speak truly, they neither spare cost nor labour, diligence nor danger, to attain their purpose," to the Greater Glory of God.[20]

III

Since the whole existence of the Jesuit mission in Japan hinged upon the safe arrival at Nagasaki of the annual Macao carrack, something must be said about how this clumsy vessel navigated such "dangerous and stormy seas as are those of China and Japan," to quote Valignano once more. The Náo do Trato or

Kurofune as she was respectively termed by Portuguese and Japanese, was a large lubberly carrack, often of 1,200 or 1,600 tons. As such, she corresponded to the giant Cunarders of our day; for the Portuguese East-India carracks were, by common consent, the largest ships then afloat on the seven seas. Their stupendous size alone accounts for the great impression they made in Japan, where they were regarded as one of the seven wonders of the world. Their form is familiar to all connoisseurs of Japanese art as the central motif of the so-called *Namban-byobu*, or Southern Barbarian picture screens, which reached the height of their splendor during the Keicho period (1596–1614) at the hands of the masters of the Kano, Tosa, and Sumiyoshi schools.

Nevertheless they were not altogether without competitors even as regards mere size. Some of the Manila galleons, or silver ships on the Luzon-Mexico run, so eagerly pursued by English and Dutch sailors from Thomas Cavendish to Commodore Anson, attained a comparable tonnage. If Marco Polo and the Chinese chronicles can be believed (and there is independent proof of their reliability in this connection) the Kwangtung and Fukien ocean-going junks likewise presented an imposing appearance. Ming records refer to war junks of three decks carrying a crew of two thousand men, and it is said some of the trading junks were still larger. Even Japanese ships, though usually regarded as being far behind Chinese in design and construction at that epoch, boasted some comparative leviathans. Thus the Italian Jesuit, Organtino, writing from Usuki (in Bungo) in September, 1578, waxes eloquent over seven gigantic *fune* which Nobunaga had built in Ise Province, and which he was then using for blockading the warlike Monto monks in their stronghold of Osaka. Organtino went thither purposely to see them, and says that they carried heavy artillery (a thing hitherto unknown in Japan) and were comparable in size to Portuguese carracks. This is probably an exaggeration, but even if taken literally, might indicate not more than 450 tons, since that was the official limit for the tonnage of Portuguese East-Indiamen during the last decade of the reign of King Sebastião. Mention must be made, too, of the celebrated Korean "turtle ships," which gave such a good account of themselves in frustrating Hideyoshi's invasion of Korea, although they do not seem to have exceeded 300 tons.[21]

The large if lubberly vessel, in which the Japan Jesuits perforce placed all their eggs, usually left Goa about April or May. After wintering at Macao, where the silk cargo from Canton was taken aboard, she left for Nagasaki with the southwest monsoon in June or July. With fair weather, the voyage did not take more than twelve or fifteen days, but since departure coincided with the beginning of the typhoon season, the length of time for the run depended upon the weather. The return voyage took place during the northeast monsoon winds between November and March inclusive, the length of time spent by the carrack at Nagasaki depending on local political and commercial conditions rather than on wind and weather.

The navigation of the Great Ship was in charge of a pilot, or pilot-major (*piloto-mór*), if there was more than one of them, as was sometimes true. He was a personage of considerably more authority and importance than his Dutch or English counterpart; perhaps because Portuguese ships' captains were usually blue-blooded fidalgos rather than weather-beaten seamen. These pilots usually more than atoned for any technical deficiencies in their superiors. Their devotion to duty is strikingly attested by the English navigator, Richard Hawkins, who noted in his *Observations* of 1622:

In this point of Steeridge, the *Spaniards* and *Portingalls* doe exceede all that I have seene, I meane for their care, which is chiefest in Navigation. And I wish in this, and in all their workes of discipline and reformation, we should follow their examples. . . . In every ship of moment, upon the halfe decke, or quarter decke, they have a chayre, or seat; out of which whilst they navigate, the Pilot, or his *Adjutants* (which are the same officers which in our Shippes we terme, the Master and his Mates) never depart day nor night, from the sight of the Compasse; and have another before them; whereby they see what they doe, and are ever witnesses of the good or bad steeridge of all men that do take the Helme.

Nautical instruments were few and simple, being virtually limited to the compass, astrolabe, and Jacob's staff, for there was no sextant or telescope. In default of hydrographic charts and large-scale maps, the mariner's chief reliance was inevitably placed on local knowledge, supplemented (or when necessary substituted) by written sailing directions. These seaman's manuals were termed *roteiros* by the Portuguese, whence the French *routier* and the English *rutter*. They contained, in addition to a series of elementary stereotyped navigational rules and tables, a description of the coastline, with notes on anchorages, shallows, and depths, together with observations (often very detailed) on the prevailing winds, currents, and other natural phenomena which might help the mariner to identify his position off a given stretch of coast.

The first European roteiros were of Mediterranean origin, and probably date from the time of the earliest Phoenician navigators. They achieved their highest standard under the stimulus of the great Portuguese maritime discoveries, inspired and organized by Prince Henry the Navigator. The excellence which they attained in the second half of the sixteenth century is obvious from the examples given in Appendix II (pp. 406–414). But although brought to a high perfection by the Portuguese pilots, this type of seaman's manual was not, of course, the exclusive property of European navigators. The Arab dhow and Chinese junk masters were likewise well provided with similar navigational aids. A good idea of those used by the Arabs, Persians, and Turks can be derived from a perusal of the works of Moslem seamen and geographers so carefully edited by Gabriel Ferrand in 1913–1928; it is known that Vasco da Gama and his successors derived much of their information from the nautical lore of Ibn Mahjid and other Indian Ocean pilots. The seafaring abilities of the Chinese mariners of Kwangtung and Fukien are amply attested by their voyages to places as far distant as Timor and the Moluccas in the east, and to the Persian Gulf and Somaliland in the west. The surprising accuracy of their sailing directions for Singapore Straits has recently been demonstrated by a comparison of early Ming sea manuals with modern charts and practice.[22]

The artistic beauty of many of the old European portulans should not blind the reader to the fact that in the sixteenth century and for long afterwards, it was not charts but written rutters, on which pilots placed their chief reliance in default of detailed local knowledge. As the late Captain Warnsinck pointed out in his scholarly introduction to the reprint of Jan Huyghen Van Linschoten's *Itinerario,* whereas nowadays, thanks to mathematical and technical progress, the chart is the mainstay of navigation, and the pilot merely consults the printed sailing directions at infrequent intervals, the exact reverse was formerly true. For centuries it was the roteiros and rutters which formed the pilot's standby, with his compass, lead, log, and astrolabe. Hydrographic charts in the modern sense of the word did not exist, although some of Dom João de Castro's charts of Indian harbors came very close to being so. But the vast majority of maps and portulans, over whose origin and development such rivers of ink have been expended by learned investigators, were on too small a scale to be of the slightest use to the practical mariner; and even the larger ones, owing to faulty projection and other defects, must ofttimes have been more of a hindrance than a help to navigation. But at this point I cannot do better than quote Warnsinck himself.

In contrast with the description of a fairwater or of a coast, wherein the author can easily omit anything of which he is uncertain, the delineation of a map imperceptibly leads the cartographer to indulge in a little guesswork, the better to conceal his lack of knowledge. It is easy to express in written words that there is a bank some miles off shore which may be dangerous to navigation; the map maker, on the contrary, is virtually forced to give this bank a fixed location, thereby giving his work a misleading appearance of accuracy. If the compiler of a seaman's manual is uncertain about the configuration of a particular stretch of coast, then he need not attempt to describe it; the cartographer, on the other hand, has a strong inducement to continue his delineation of the coastline (if only to maintain his reputation) and sometimes misleads the navigator thereby. Only since the evolution of mathematically accurate maps, drawn from triangulation and base measurement, has the navigator learned fully to trust his charts. Only when charts, through the innovation of conventional signs and abbreviations, recorded virtually all the necessary navigational details, could they supersede sailing directions as one of the main essentials of navigation.

Since it was on their sixteenth-century sailing directions that the Portuguese pilots chiefly depended, to enable them to navigate the Great Ship in safety from Golden Goa to the Long Cape, an examination of their rutters for the sea south of Japan is in order here. Several of the relevant roteiros have been preserved for posterity in the pages of Linschoten's *Itinerario.* Although he never went east of Cape Comorin, the industrious Hollander utilized his position as secretary to the Archbishop of Goa in 1583–1589, to gather full descriptions of "all the courses, Havens, islands, depthes, shallowes, sands, droughts, riffes and cliffes, with their situations, also the times of the yeares when the winds blow, with the true tokens and knowledge of the tides and the weather, water, and streams in all the Orientall coasts and Havens, as they are observed and set downe by the Kings Pilots, in their continuall and dayly Voyages," as his English translator of 1598 somewhat breathlessly informs the reader. How successful he was in his self-imposed task, can be read by all who turn to his *Discours of Voyages.* Taking Linschoten as guide and his learned compatriot Warnsinck as commentator, I shall consider some of the Portuguese roteiros which these two Hollanders have respectively preserved and annotated.[23]

Twelve chapters of varying length reproduce Portuguese pilots' roteiros of their voyages to and from the southern islands of Japan, between 1550 and 1585. The majority of these voyages were made between Kwangtung and Kyushu; but the first and fullest chapter records the observations of a Portuguese pilot who sailed from Ningpo in a Chinese junk to Tanegashima, and thence up the coast of Kyushu, round Shikoku to Sakai and the Inland Sea. The voyage from Ningpo to Tanegashima began Wednesday, June 30, and ended Thursday, July 8, in some unspecified year. Warnsinck suggested 1588, since those dates and days coincide for that year according to the Gregorian calendar introduced in 1582. On the other hand, it would seem from the context that the voyage was made at a time when feudal anarchy and the Wako were still rife, when Otomo of Bungo was a power in the land, and before Hideyoshi's pacification of Kyushu in 1587. I, therefore, suggest that this voyage belongs to the early period of Portuguese intercourse with Japan, and probably before 1560. This date would also account for the presence of a Portuguese pilot at Ningpo, something decidely unlikely, if not impossible, in 1588, and would imply the use of the Julian calendar.

The eight-day voyage from Chekiang to southern Kyushu is graphically described with the pilot's daily observations and estimates of his position. He was not very enamored of his Chinese shipmates, animadverting on their fright at the expected approach of a typhoon (July 1), and on the ineptitude of his Fukienese co-pilot who failed to hold the proper course one night. Nevertheless, by good luck or good judgment,—or more probably a combination of both—he made a perfect landfall off Tanegashima at dawn on July 8, at the exact time and place he had calculated the previous midnight. "This island reacheth North and South, being long and low ground, having white sandy strands, with a very green country of valleys; it hath many pine trees, but they stand scattering from each other, and very open: it is about seven or eight miles long, having in the middle way on the East side close by the land, an island of stony cliff, which far off showeth like a foist under sail. This island lyeth under 30½ degrees right in the middle; it is all fair and clear ground." So must the island have appeared to Pinto and to his predecessors in the discovery of Japan, which is my excuse for this quotation.

The rest of his roteiro is not in the form of a daily journal, but of a rutter of the coast of Kyushu, Shikoku, and the Inland Sea. Sakai was the principal point of call; but in the instructions for negotiating the Kii Channel, due warning is given against the piratical proclivities of the local inhabitants, this region being a breeding ground of the Wako. Thus, "all the people of this land (on the N. side) are not in any sort to be trusted." Fukura, in Awaji, is noted as "a good harbour for all winds, but not for Rovers, for there they have many foists wherewith they rove and steal." Awa, the eastern province of Shikoku, "is inhabited by a very fierce and stout people. There is always a great army of foists prepared for the wars, wherewith they rob and spoil all the coast along." Sakai is described as having a shallow, open roadstead, which may have been one of the reasons for its commercial decline in later years. This anonymous pilot is particularly careful in describing the sea marks for the Bungo harbors of Usuki, Hiji, and Oita, which is another indication that his rutter was written in the halcyon days of Portuguese trade with Otomo before 1560.

It may be noted in passing that he refers to the observations of Indian as well as of Portuguese pilots in Kyushu ports, presumably meaning Gujarati navigators in Portuguese service. He concludes his able and conscientious survey with the note that "two Japan miles make just a Portugal mile: which is found to be true by the Portugal pilots, that have therein taken the height of the sun, and made their account after the Japan mile." This last observation is of considerable interest, in connection with the knotty problem of the true length of the old Portuguese nautical mile, commonly estimated at 17½ to a degree.[24]

Chapter 32 describes the course from Lampacau to Hirado, and therefore in all probability antedates the foundation of Macao in 1557, although there were still a few hundred Portuguese on Lampacau three years later. This pilot does not confine himself entirely to the Lampacau-Hirado run, but gives additional details of various ports in Amakusa and Arima. Nagasaki is not mentioned, another indication that the roteiro is older than 1569. This anonymous author extols Shiki on Amakusa Island as one of the best natural harbors in Japan, adding "but in this Haven three or four Portugals were slain." The Calvinist in Linschoten here got the better of his seaman's admiration for the technical skill of the Portuguese pilots, as evidenced by one of his rare personal interpolations, "I think it happened by their filthy pride and presumptuousness, for in all places they will be lords and masters, to the contempt and embasing of the inhabitants, which in all places will not be endured, namely in Japan, being a stubborn and obstinate people." This rutter alludes to the large number of Chinese trading junks which frequented Omura Bay and Hirado Island. This is interesting in view of the contemporary Ming prohibition of trade with Japan and the ravages of the China coast by the Wako. The sailing directions for entering Hirado harbor may be quoted as an example of Portuguese pilots at their best.

If you desire to sail into this haven, do so when it is almost high water, then it helpeth to bring you in: then you shall run in such manner along by the island as I said before: and being past the creek of Kochi to the first point of land that you shall come unto, that sticketh out from the same island (from the which point northward there jutteth two stony cliffs) you shall go near the stony cliffs, the better to get into the haven, and you shall presently see before you on the side of Hirado, a great and high island, full of trees and when you see it, take your course right upon the West point of the same island, until the said island lyeth wholly uncovered to leeward from you, whereby presently you shall see inward the point or end of the town: and when you begin to see the houses, then put somewhat nearer to it, right over against the aforesaid island on the south side and the left hand, and there the island hath a small low point of land comming from a high hill, and stretcheth into the sea, from the which point there runneth a sand or bank, therefore you shall put towards the side of the houses or end of the town to keep out of the stream, and when you are out being in calm water, if the wind be not good then anchor, and from thence be rowed in, either with foists, barques, or your own boat, West and West-South-West into the Haven.

Although the clarity of these instructions has suffered somewhat from the 1598 English version being a translation at one remove, yet it remains obvious that this rutter is the work of an exceptionally able, experienced, and observant pilot.[25]

Chapters 33 and 34 contain further roteiros from Macao and its neighborhod to Tanegashima, Kuchinotsu, Hirado, and other ports in Kyushu. No mention being made therein of Nagasaki, it is justifiable in assuming that the roteiros likewise date from the period 1550–1570. These rutters occasionally allude to Formosa, sometimes under the sobriquet of Lequeo Pequeno (Little Luchu), since the distinction be-

tween the Ryukyu Islands and Formosa was not always clear
to the early navigators, and sometimes under its more modern
name. The Portuguese, although they coasted the green-clad
shore of the "Beautiful Isle" often enough, never seem to have
felt the urge to explore its beauty at close quarters. At any
rate, their first recorded visit was an involuntary one, occasioned by the shipwreck of André Feio's junk on the western
shore in July, 1582.

Chapter 35 contains "a declaration of the winds called
Tuffon, by an expert Pilot." This succinct but vivid account
is also of interest to lexicographers, since its author assured his
readers that ". . . to understand the meaning of this word
Tuffon, it is a Chinish word, which the Portugals also do hold
without altering the same, and signifieth a storm or tempest,
which you commonly find in those voyages from China to
Japan." This explicit declaration of the Chinese origin of the
word had evidently escaped the attention of the learned Yule
and Burnell, when they poured scorn on the later suggestions
of Barrow and Hirth to this effect. It must be admitted, however, that the Arabic word for a sudden and violent storm,
tūfān, is a closer approximation to the original Portuguese
form; and the Chinese mariners might in point of fact have
picked it up from the Arabs or Portuguese, instead of the
other way round.[26]

Chapters 36 and 41 give the roteiros for the round trip from
Macao to Nagasaki, as sailed by the Great Ship *Santa Cruz*,
Captain-Major Francisco Paes, in July, 1585–March, 1586.
Since these two journals give an excellent idea of the China-
Japan voyage under normal conditions in those days—the
Santa Cruz weathered a typhoon on the outward voyage and
had an uneventful return passage—they are reproduced in
full in Appendix II; they are too long for inclusion here, despite their great nautical interest. Linschoten obviously got the
original journals through one of his compatriots, Dirck Gerritszoon Pomp, *alias* "China," who served as the carrack's
master gunner on these two voyages. Their compiler was not,
of course, the Dutch gunner, but the anonymous Portuguese

pilot, whose meticulous accuracy has earned the unstinted praise of so competent an authority as J. C. M. Warnsinck, himself a practical hydrographer of extensive experience in the eastern seas.

Further detailed consideration of the remaining rutters in the *Discours of Voyages* is unnecessary since although each one of them is interesting in itself, they are all on the lines of those roteiros discussed already, or reproduced in Appendix II. Chapter 37 contains sailing directions for the approaches to Nagasaki harbor from Meshima Island, a prominent mark for Japan-bound vessels at the present day. I cannot forbear to quote the pilot's instructions for anchoring in the harbor, since they sound more applicable to a European than an Asiatic port. ". . . In the entry of Nagasaki there is nothing else to do, than only to run in through the middle thereof, till you be in the road, where you must anchor, having 4½ fathom, and 5 fathom water, which is when a tree that is right over against the great and principalest Church is even with the top of the Church, and you over against it, then you are at the right place, and it is a very good place to anchor in; but when you are hard by the point of land that commeth right from the Church, you must take care to keep on the left hand, thereby to shunne a reef of sand that commeth from the same point, and so anchor as aforesaid."

Chapter 38 gives another rutter for southwest Kyushu, chiefly for the harbors of Kuchinotsu and Fukuda, which were the ones favored by the Portuguese during the years immediately preceding their occupation of Nagasaki. Chapters 39 and 40 give the return course from Nagasaki to Macao, the last of these being a ship's journal for March, 1584, narrating an awkward encounter with the fisherfolk of the Goto Islands. Chapter 42, with which the Japan section proper of the *Itinerario* concludes, gives an alternative course from Hirado to Macao, with better instructions for sailing along the China coast than those in any of the other roteiros. Linschoten did not forget to supplement his rutters of the China-Japan seas, with six chapters on the winds, weather, and tides prevailing between Malacca and Nagasaki, as recorded in the observations of contemporary Portuguese pilots. Warnsinck notes that Chapter 46, entitled "Of the tides both for ebb and flood by the days and hours of the moon, in the haven of Macau in China, with the height of the same haven, found by experience of an expert pilot," could hardly be bettered at the present day.[27]

Whoever has had the patience to read thus far, or, better still, to peruse the journal of the *Santa Cruz* as reproduced in Appendix II (pp. 406–414), can scarcely doubt the professional competence of the Portuguese pilots, or be surprised at their ability to navigate the Great Ship through the stormy waters of the China Sea. It will also be clear that they relied mainly on their local knowledge and roteiros, for there is no indication that they possessed any charts worthy of the name. Linschoten's publisher boasts that the picturesque maps which adorn his *Itinerario* were carefully copied from the most accurate "sea cardes" and portulans used by the Portuguese pilots in Asia. There is no reason to doubt this statement; but, since Linschoten's reproductions are on a scale of 1:12.5 million, they were completely useless as practical charts, quite apart from other glaring defects, and it is unlikely that the Portuguese originals were very much better. None of the maps of the Far East reproduced in Armando Cortesão's monumental work on sixteenth-century Portuguese cartography could have been of any use to the practical mariner in the China Sea; and although a large proportion of the original maps and charts have been lost, the surviving copies probably give a good idea of their standard as a whole. Some of Dom João de Castro's charts of 1548, were, as already noted, worthy to be ranked with the productions of d'Après de Mannvillette and Alexander Dalrymple, more than two centuries later; but Castro was a genius far in advance of his time in this respect. So much will become evident from a brief survey of the evolution of the cartography of sixteenth-century Japan.[28]

The origin of Japanese cartography is generally ascribed to Gyogi-Bosatsu, a Buddhist priest of Korean origin who became patriarch of the Hosso sect, and who shares with Kobo Daishi the credit of inventing many of the adjuncts of Japanese civilization. Be this as it may, the cadastral surveys and sketch maps which formed the basis of Japanese cartography are known as Gyogi-type maps. The oldest original map of this kind is one, dated A.D. 1305, in a Shinto temple at Kyoto; but copies of an earlier one, dated A.D. 805, are in existence. Although differing in unimportant details, their essential features remained stereotyped for eight hundred years. They are characterized by the round or oval form given to each of the sixty-six provinces, with scant regard to their relative proportions, and they normally list the names of the provinces, main highways, and provincial subdivisions in marginal explanatory notes, after the style of a concise gazetteer. Several of these maps have been reproduced by Japanese scholars, notably that belonging to the Tosho-daiji temple at Nara; and a comparison of these *Gyogi-zu* with sixteenth-century European maps of Japan derived from Fernão Vaz Dourado, Luis Teixeira, and other Portuguese cartographers leaves no doubt that the latter type were derived from the former.

This assumption, which was formerly contested by European authorities such as Dahlgren and Crino, has recently been proved conclusively by Professor H. Nakamura. The Japanese savant identified a sketch map of Japan, dated 1585, in the archives at Florence, as being a Portuguese transcription or draft of a Gyogi-type map, as evidenced by the regional circuit designations of Tokaido, Tosando, Sanyodo, and so on, which do not occur again in European maps of Japan until the middle of the eighteenth century. Professor Nakamura likewise examined at Madrid an original report on Japan drawn up by the Archbishop of Manila, Fr. Domingo de Salazar, O.P., in July–September, 1587, with the aid of eleven Japanese Christians. This curious survey is accompanied by the draft of a Gyogi-type map of Japan, evidently sketched from memory by one of the Japanese. Although so carelessly drawn as to resemble a cluster of eggs or a bunch of balloons at first glance, further examination clearly reveals its origin, which, for the rest, is explained in Archbishop Salazar's covering note.

Professor Nakamura has compared some thirty or forty of the so-called Vaz Dourado type of maps with a corresponding number of Gyogi-zu and suggests that the originals of the former type were compiled at Goa, from sketches or drafts of the Gyogi maps, similar to that sent to Madrid by Archbishop Salazar. He points out that the main difference between the Portuguese and Japanese delineations was that the nomenclature of the sixty-six provinces was omitted in the former type, where the interest was naturally concentrated on southwest Japan, the nomenclature of Kyushu and the Inland Sea area being relatively abundant. These last details were presumably added from the pilots' roteiros and the Jesuits' *Letters;* but part at least of the nomenclature of Honshu was derived directly from Japanese sources. The silver mines (*minas de prata*) which figure so prominently on many of the maps, are no fevered creation of the cartographer's brain, but derived from the silver mines of Omori in Iwami Province, then at the height of their production under the wealthy daimyo Mori Terumoto.[29]

It is sometimes forgotten how much sixteenth-century European cartographers owed to their Far Eastern colleagues. The Portuguese historian, João de Barros, procured Chinese maps as early as 1540, and even bought a Chinese slave to translate the cosmographical material that he collected, part of which he utilized in his *Decadas* (1552–1563), although the greater part has perished with his lost *Geografía*. Moreover he forwarded some of this material to Rome, at the request of the Italian chronicler Paolo Jovio, who seems to have used it without due acknowledgment. Matteo Ricci procured a wood-block map of China dated 1555, during his stay in the Kwangtung provincial capital in 1584. This map was sent home by the Spanish factor at Macao next year and may still be seen in the Seville Archives. Clearly this map, or another like it, was utilized by contemporary Iberian cartographers, for the shape of Korea in their works is obviously modeled on the representation of the peninsula in Ming maps. Ricci later utilized Chinese as well as European material for his famous mappemondes of 1584–1602.

Valignano, in his instructions to the Jesuit mentor of the Kyushu emissaries to Pope Gregory XIII in 1583, alludes to a map of China which he had ordered to be painted on a folding screen for presentation to King Felipe. The reverse process was also in operation. Professor Nakamura has unearthed a curious sketch copied from a Portuguese mappemonde by the Japanese Buddhist priest Sosetsu at Hangchow in 1525, and sent home to the Ouchi daimyo nearly three decades before the arrival of the Southern Barbarians in Japan. Valignano, in forwarding his picture screens depicting Adzuchi and China to Europe, specially asked that similar screens should be painted in Rome (with European motifs) for presentation to Japanese magnificoes. That this request was carried out is evident from a number of *Sekai-byobu* or "world-map picture-screens," possibly modeled on the *Theatrum Orbis Terrarum* of Ortelius, which date from the Keicho period (1596–1614) and are still extant in Japan. These were presumably copied or adapted from the originals ordered by Valignano; but in their delineation of Japan they were clearly modified by the Gyogi-zu concept of the country, and sometimes contain additional details such as the mysterious Gold and Silver islands (Kinjima and Ginjima).

Although the earliest European cartographers apparently depended largely on Japanese sketch maps for their basic material, a more systematic and scientific attempt to survey the country was made at the time of Valignano's return to Japan with the Kyushu embassy in 1590. He was accompanied by "an honorable Portuguese, and one very curious in making such descriptions of new-found lands," named Inacio Monteiro. This cosmographer, for such he seems to have been, as Valignano implies elsewhere, went to Kyoto with the father-visitor and spent two years in Japan collecting all the cartographical and cosmographical material which he could, whether by personal observation or by diligent interrogation of the natives. Monteiro estimated that Japan extended between 30½° and 39° of latitude, which was a remarkable improvement on all previous calculations, and one which was not surpassed until the publication of Father Antonio Cardim's map in 1646. This map, as is evident from its accompanying annotations, was originally compiled before 1614, and certainly owed something to Monteiro's observations.

It is likewise possible that the first approximately correct delineation of Japan in European cartography, Luis Teixeira's map published by Ortelius in 1595, owes its great improvement over the monstrous "hair-pin" distortions of the Vaz Dourado type, to material supplied by Monteiro, although this is admittedly pure guesswork. It is a great pity that Monteiro's own map has not survived; but however good it may have been, it could not, in the nature of things, have provided a really adequate representation even of the Kyushu coast which had been frequented by the Portuguese for nearly half a century. The science of cartography was still in its infancy during the sixteenth century, nor was the standard of mathematical knowledge sufficient to permit the construction of proper hydrographical charts. The tried and tested mariner's manuals were inevitably the main standby in the circumstances; and that the hand of the Portuguese pilot had lost nothing of its cunning is formally attested by Captain John Saris, who noted in his journal of the first English voyage to Japan: "We found John Huyghen Van Linschoten's book to be very true, for thereby we directed ourselves from our setting-forth from Hirado." [30]

Chapter IV. JESUITS AND FRIARS

FATHER-VISITOR VALIGNANO in his oft-quoted "Sumario" of 1583, found occasion to moralize on the inscrutable ways of God to Man, as revealed by a brief review of the progress of Christianity in the island empire to that date. For whereas, sighed Valignano, it might reasonably have been expected that in such a remote, virgin, and utterly strange mission field, "Our Lord would help us, as He did the primitive Church, by granting the gift of tongues and miracles, the better to induce the Japanese to receive our holy Faith," yet God in His divine wisdom decided otherwise. Not only so, but He apparently "even wished to show that to some extent He wanted to unmake what the fathers were busy making," by ordaining repeatedly that just when everything seemed to be progressing smoothly, disaster and persecution should overtake the mission out of a clear sky, and cause much backsliding among the new converts. Valignano suggested that God acted thus to show that He had more than one method of saving souls, and to demonstrate that the Faith could not only flourish without miracles and supernatural works, but thrive on humiliation and persecution. For contrariwise, when time and again the padres saw their best efforts brought to nought, and the mission on the brink of ruin without the smallest prospect, humanly speaking, of a successful outcome, then, with equal suddenness and for no apparent reason, the persecution ceased, conversions came thick and fast, and all previous losses were more than redeemed.

The great Italian Jesuit proceeded to prove his argument with chapter and verse. He tells of the conversion of Omura Sumitada, who, immediately after his baptism, indulged in

an orgy of idol burning and temple wrecking, thus provoking from his vassals a violent reaction, which threw him from
power and forced him to lead the life of a hunted fugitive
for three years. Then, when everything seemed irretrievably
lost, and the Buddhist bonzes were exulting over the humiliation of the Jesuits and their protégés as the cogent revenge
of the native deities, fortune changed once more. "God gave
such a strength to the padres that . . . they destroyed and
burned all the monasteries and temples of the bonzes, and
converted within a few months all the heathen of those lands,
without leaving a single gentile or trace of a bonze, so that
our Law and the padres now acquired greater power and
prestige than they had done previously."

Another striking instance was afforded by events in the
neighboring fief of Arima, where the old daimyo died a sudden and painful death from cancer, contracted (as it was
believed) on a final visit to the padres before accepting baptism. This untoward event resulted in a local persecution of
the Christians and Jesuits for three years, when Valignano's
arrival in Japan changed everything for no apparent reason. The young daimyo became a staunch convert and mass
conversions of his vassals took place, accompanied by the
destruction of all Buddhist buildings. Elsewhere, in Tosa, the
padres were given local Shinto and Buddhist temples by a
friendly daimyo, only to be expelled shortly afterward by
a popular revolt. In Bungo, Otomo Sorin at the height of
his power burned and wrecked the temples, whereupon the
bonzes clamorously prophesied the revenge of the gods,
which occurred almost at once with his crushing defeat at
the hands of Shimadzu of Satsuma. There is no need to continue Valignano's recital of the vicissitudes of Christianity
in Kyushu, but it will suffice to add that his thesis was still
more strikingly endorsed five years later by the *volte-face* of
Toyotomi Hideyoshi.[1]

Hideyoshi's attitude to Christianity has often been discussed, but it is still far from being explained in many par-

[1] For notes to chapter iv, see pages 468–475.

ticulars, nor do I pretend to have the key to his puzzling behavior. But although there is considerable doubt about his motives, there is none about the consequences which ensued from his apparently wayward actions. The masterful dictator who had succeeded to Nobunaga's position and policy, at first made no change in his predecessor's favorable attitude toward Christianity. Some of his most trusted adherents, such as Takayama Ukon, Kuroda Josui, and Konishi Yukinaga, were practicing Christians, whereas others, such as Hosokawa Tadaoki and Gamo Ujisato were sympathetically inclined to the Faith. The conversion of his court physician, Manase Dosan, widely regarded as one of the most learned men of his time, caused a great sensation, and gave no umbrage whatever to Hideyoshi.

If Valignano is to be believed, and he was certainly in a position to know, Hideyoshi chastised the Buddhist priests with scorpions where his predecessor had used whips. Writing in 1592, the father-visitor stated that the regent's (*Kwambaku*) drastic methods had resulted in such a decline of the Buddhist priesthood's power, that in many places where there were formerly a hundred or so monks, there were then only four or five. Although not quite such an avowed iconoclast of Buddhist images as Nobunaga, Hideyoshi was not above destroying them on occasion. When the Buddhist priests from Takayama's new fief at Akashi in Harima appealed to the Kwambaku for the protection of their temples against the expected iconoclasm of this Christian daimyo, Hideyoshi not only flatly declined to intervene on their behalf (despite the expostulations of his consort), but ordered that the sacred images which they had brought with them should be burned for firewood at Kyoto. On one occasion, during Holy Week of 1586, he paid an informal call on the Jesuits in their church at Osaka, and after contrasting the padres and their creed very favorably with the bonzes and their beliefs, informed the presiding padre that the only thing which prevented him becoming a Christian, then and there, was the prohibition against having many

women, "and if you will stretch a point in this, I will likewise become a convert."

All things considered, Vice-Provincial Gaspar Coelho, who
came to pay his respects to Hideyoshi at Osaka castle in
May, 1586, had no reason to expect anything but a favorable welcome from the virtual ruler of Japan; although the
Jesuits expressed some doubts on whether Hideyoshi would
prove really affable, in view of the arrogance with which he
ordinarily treated even powerful daimyo. But Coelho's reception recalled the very friendly interviews accorded the
Jesuits by Nobunaga at Gifu and Adzuchi, as may be seen
from the account given in Frois' long and exceedingly interesting letter of October 17, 1586. The calculated reticence
of certain passages in the printed version of this missive (in
the 1598 edition of the *Cartas*) is atoned for by an unpublished letter of Valignano preserved in the Jesuit Archives
at Rome.

Coelho's first interview took place on May 4, Feast Day of
St. Monica, when he was accompanied by more than thirty
people, including Jesuit padres, Japanese brothers, and
dojuku, as well as some youthful pupils from the seminary
founded by Valignano. The formal reception was held in a
room beautifully decorated with paintings of some birds and
trees on a background of gold leaf—evidently *fusuma* painted
by one of the masters of the Kano school. Punctilio having
been satisfied, Hideyoshi left the dais on which he was
seated and came over to sit (or rather squat) near Coelho,
to whom he spoke in an even more frank and friendly manner than ever had Nobunaga to Valignano. He laughed and
joked over old times with Frois, who was acting as interpreter,
and praised the disinterestedness of the Jesuits in coming so
far for the sole purpose of preaching the Gospel. He told
them of his intention to conquer Kyushu and reduce the
obstreperous Shimadzu of Satsuma to obedience. He added
that his sole ambition was to leave a great name behind him
after his death, for which reason he had resolved to entrust
the government of Japan to his brother, and to cross the sea

at the head of a vast expeditionary force with the object of conquering Korea and China. In this connection, he would like the padres to make arrangements for him to charter two large Portuguese carracks, whose captains and crews he would lavishly recompense while serving as his auxiliaries. He concluded this surprising harangue by informing the Jesuits that in the event of his campaign proving successful, he would have churches built throughout the length and breadth of China, and order the populace to become converted *en masse*.

The vice-provincial now made a most unfortunate blunder—one of those errors of judgment characterized by Talleyrand as being worse than a crime. Disregarding Valignano's standing orders against any interference in local politics by the missionaries, Coelho not only agreed with everything that Hideyoshi said, but promised that he would secure the help of the Christian daimyo of Kyushu against Satsuma and Ryuzoji Masaie. Moreover, thinking that the expedition to China would never materialize, and that Hideyoshi was merely suffering from delusions of grandeur, the vice-provincial promised the Kwambaku that he would provide the two Portuguese ships, in addition to proferring other help from Portuguese India, for which Hideyoshi had never asked. The latter professed himself delighted with Coelho's coöperation; but Valignano commented that he must have thought in his heart, "this father-provincial is very rich and influential. One day he will make war against me as did the abbot of the Ishiyama Hongwanji against Nobunaga." Otomo and the other Christian daimyo were aghast when they heard of Coelho's rashness, but he remained convinced that he had acted rightly.[2]

Hideyoshi then showed Coelho and his suite of Jesuits and dojuku all over Osaka castle, acting himself as cicerone in the same way as Nobunaga with Frois at Gifu eighteen years before. Indeed the years must have rolled back as far as the latter was concerned, for his letter of October, 1586, recounting the splendors of Osaka-jo, reads very like that of

July, 1569, in which he narrated so naïvely and vividly the
wonders of Gifu. Just as Nobunaga had done, Hideyoshi
guided the party up the keep from floor to floor, opening
doors and windows with his own hand, "as if he was an
ordinary householder," drawing the Jesuits' attention to anything which he wished to emphasize: "here you see this room
full of gold, this of silver, that of silk and damask, that of
clothing, that of swords and rich weapons." No wonder that
the Jesuits were much impressed, "looking at each other in
amazement." A peculiarly intimate touch is provided by
Frois' observation that "along all these floors and stairways,
[the] Kwambaku-dono was preceded by a richly dressed
young girl who carried his sword on her shoulder, and with
whom he joked from time to time."

From the top of the donjon keep, Hideyoshi showed the
Jesuits the magnificent view over Osaka and the surrounding countryside, at the same time telling them of his intended
redistribution of fiefs in Kyushu as between the Otomo,
Satsuma, and Omura clans. Frois, with all his memories of
Gifu and Adzuchi, considered that the gardens and rooms
of Osaka castle were the finest he had seen in Japan, and
added that Hideyoshi's demeanor was so frank and friendly
throughout this three-hour interview, that "it seemed in-
dubitable that he was completely straightforward with us."
Following Hideyoshi's example, his brother and all the feudal
nobility then at Osaka vied with one another in paying
flattering attentions to the Jesuits, whose prestige reached
unprecedented heights. His consort, O-Yae, although a fervent Buddhist and hitherto inclined to be hostile to the missionaries, now showed herself friendly and gracious in the
extreme.

Coelho's main purpose in visiting the Kwambaku had
been to obtain his formal written assent to three requests.
First, license to preach the Gospel throughout all the provinces
controlled by him. Second, to have the Jesuits exempted
from the prevailing street and ward duties, automatically
incumbent on all residents in accordance with Japanese mu-

nicipal organization, and from which the Buddhist priest-hood was *not* exempt. These privileges had, in effect, been granted by Nobunaga and the Ashikaga shogun's patent (shuinjo) of April, 1569, but either they had lapsed with the former's death, or were regarded as inoperative outside of the Gokinai district to which alone they had originally applied. At any rate, the Jesuits were anxious to secure Hideyoshi's shuinjo since he controlled more of Japan than Nobunaga had ever done, and they induced O-Yae, who at this time was equally ready to intercede on behalf of either Buddhists or Christians, to act as intermediary.

Hideyoshi not only accorded these letters patent, which naturally placed the Christian missionaries in a more privi-leged position than the native Buddhist clergy (somewhat analogous to the position of the Protestant English in Portu-gal from the time of Oliver Cromwell to that of the Marquis of Pombal) but even drafted the patent in more emphatic terms than originally asked, and sent a copy to the viceroy at Goa as proof of his friendly feeling for foreigners. Coelho rounded off his highly successful trip to Osaka with another visit of thanks to the Kwambaku, who showed himself even more gracious and condescending on this occasion than he had been on the first.[3]

While things were thus progressing favorably for Christi-anity in central Japan, what was happening in the southern island of Kyushu was just as important for the Jesuits, since the very existence of their mission depended on the men and money brought by the Great Ship from Macao to Nagasaki. With the decisive defeat of Otomo of Bungo by Shimadzu of Satsuma in 1579, the struggle for the hegemony of Kyushu had resolved itself into a duel between the latter clan and the Ryuzoji of Hizen. The result was for some time in doubt, but was finally decided in favor of Satsuma by a decisive bat-tle at Shimabara (April 24, 1584) which resulted in the de-feat and death of Ryuzoji Takanobu. The victorious army now lorded it over the fiefs of their petty Christian allies, Arima and Omura, occupying Nagasaki, where they caused the Jesuits a good deal of disquiet and annoyance. Shimadzu's occupation of Nagasaki was doubtless the main reason why the Great Ship commanded by Domingos Monteiro in 1586, went to Hirado instead of to Nagasaki, despite the pleas of the Jesuits who vainly tried to persuade the captain-major to visit one of Omura's ports.

Meanwhile, Shimadzu Yoshihisa decided to complete his subjugation of Kyushu by the capture of Bungo, which was speedily reduced to such straits that old Otomo Sorin posted off to Osaka to solicit the intervention of Hideyoshi, arriving at the Kwambaku's headquarters just about the time that the latter was junketing with Coelho. Needless to say, the regent had already decided to intervene, and ordered Mori and Sengoku to dispatch immediate aid to the hard-pressed Otomo, while he himself followed with an expeditionary corps of 130,000 men early in 1587. Shimadzu thought it no shame to retreat before such overwhelming odds, and accordingly his samurai evacuated Nagasaki and other conquered districts in western Kyushu, to fall back upon Kagoshima where they made a final but unsuccessful stand.[4]

During the brief Kyushu campaign of February–May 1587, Hideyoshi had received the Jesuit vice-provincial in audience at his field headquarters at Yatsushiro in Higo, on which occasion his kindness and familiarity surpassed his gracious reception of the Jesuit at Osaka the previous May. On the victorious conclusion of the campaign, the regent made a sort of triumphal progress on his return journey, during which he stopped at Hakata (the modern Fukuoka) in Hizen. Here he again accorded another friendly interview to Coelho, visiting the vice-provincial on board a Portuguese *fusta* (foist) which the latter had brought to help in the campaign, and partaking of a picnic lunch and some Portuguese wine with every appearance of enjoyment. He likewise gave a valuable plot of ground in Hakata to the Jesuits, and generally showed himself friendly in extreme to the foreigners. Hearing that Domingos Monteiro's carrack still lay in Hirado roads, he told Coelho that he would like the captain-major to bring his ship round to Hakata harbor, since he very much wished to see this leviathan. Monteiro declared his inability to comply with this order, but when he came round in the foist to make his apologies in person, Hideyoshi accepted his excuses in good part and dismissed him with a handsome present on July 24, Vigil of the Feast of St. James.

Nothing could have been fairer than the prospect for Christianity in Kyushu on the eve of the feast day of the patron saint of Spain and Portugal, then combined in a dual monarchy under the rule of King Felipe II, "the devil of the south." Not only did Hideyoshi's personal attitude leave nothing to be desired, but in the redistribution of fiefs which followed from the subjugation of Satsuma, the Christian daimyo and their sympathizers had come off exceedingly well. It is true that old Otomo Sorin, staunchest pillar of the Japan Church, had rejected the regent's offer of the fief of Hyuga for himself, and had died (in something approaching the odor of sanctity, if his Jesuit panegyrists are to be taken at their face value)in June, 1587. Omura Sumitada, another staunch protagonist, had died the previous May: but these losses were more than atoned for by the greatly increased power of Konishi Yukinaga, Kuroda Josui, and Arima Harunobu, all of whom received additional land; the two first-named stood high in Hideyoshi's favor. All the more unexpected and crushing, therefore, was the blow which fell out of a clear sky on July 24.[5]

On that night, after his courteous dismissal of Captain-Major Domingos Monteiro, Hideyoshi was carousing (or at any rate drinking) with some of his intimates, among whom was his physician, Seiyakuin Hoin (Tokuun) who, for all his politeness to Coelho during the vice-provincial's visit to Osaka, was a bitter opponent of Christianity and its adherents. As Hideyoshi was regaling himself with some Portuguese wine which Coelho had sent him at the regent's own request, Hoin brought the conversation round to the subjection to the Jesuits of the Christian daimyo in general, and of Takayama Ukon in particular. He further criticized the destruction of Shinto and Buddhist temples by zealous Christian converts, and the forcible conversion of their vassals to the Roman Catholic Faith. As the discussion of this topic progressed, Hideyoshi became (or affected to become) more and more enraged, until he finally dispatched a messenger to Takayama Ukon, ordering him either to renounce his faith forthwith or to submit to the confiscation of his fief and rigorous exile therefrom. Takayama did not hesitate, and rejecting the pleas of his friends that he would at any rate feign submission while remaining a Christian at heart, he returned a reply to the effect that he could never renounce his religion, and for the rest would gladly go into exile. On receiving this sturdy answer, Hideyoshi flew into a real or simulated passion (it is impossible to say which) and stripped Takayama of his fief. He then dispatched two couriers one after another, to awaken the unsuspecting Coelho from his peaceful slumber in the foist, and to ask him four questions.

1. Why are the padres so desirous of making converts, and why do they even use force on occasion?

2. Why do they destroy Shinto and Buddhist temples, and persecute the bonzes, instead of compromising with them?

3. Why do they eat useful and valuable animals like horses and cows?

4. Why do the Portuguese buy many Japanese and export them from their native land as slaves?

Coelho was so staggered by this completely unexpected verbal onslaught, that it was some time before he could reply. When he had pulled himself together, he answered to the following effect:

1. The only reason the padres come from such distant regions to Japan is their desire to save souls, but they only use peaceful means to persuade their converts.

2. Since the padres are on Japanese soil, where they have no political power whatever, they cannot use forceful methods against the wish of the local inhabitants, even if they want to do so. The destruction of Buddhist and Shinto temples is therefore the work of their converts, who are inspired thereto by spontaneous religious zeal.

3. Neither the padres nor the Portuguese ever eat horseflesh, and although

they occasionally eat veal, as is customary in Europe, they will certainly refrain from doing so in the future if the regent wishes it.

4. Although the padres deprecate the Portuguese slave trade in Japanese ports, they cannot in practice forbid it, since it takes place on Japanese soil and the sellers are Japanese. Hideyoshi can end this practice himself by expressly forbidding it in all ports of the empire.

No immediate reply was returned by Hideyoshi to this memorandum, but he sent another courier to notify the vice-provincial of the sentence of exile decreed against Takayama Ukon, which brought the doings of this momentous night to a close.[6]

Next morning (July 25, St. James's Day) Hideyoshi showed himself bitterer than ever against the Jesuits, telling his entourage that the padres were deceitful propagandists of a devilish and subversive creed, and their smooth and specious arguments had deceived many daimyo and samurai. They might even have deceived him, had he not been clever enough to see through their plausible conversation. He went on to compare them to the ambitious and worldly Monto or Ikko monks of Osaka, but added that the Jesuits were far more dangerous; since the Ikko devotees were mostly mere ignorant canaille, whereas the padres had taken care to concentrate their efforts on the cream of the Japanese feudal aristocracy. Not only had they achieved a large measure of success in this aim, but their converts were so submissive and obedient to their spiritual pastors that they were wholly at the beck and call of the Jesuits and formed a potential "fifth column" (as it is termed nowadays) of a most dangerous kind.

Needless to say, all his listeners loudly proclaimed their entire agreement with these sentiments; and those who, following Hideyoshi's cue, had previously fawned upon the Jesuits, now excelled themselves in denouncing them as spies and traitors. This tirade concluded with Hideyoshi sending two more successive couriers to notify the vice-provincial of his decree of banishment against the Jesuits, a copy of which was likewise sent to Captain-Major Domingos Monteiro. The literal translation is given by Luis Frois as follows.

1. Japan is a country of the Kami [Gods] and for the padres to come hither and preach a devilish law, is a most reprehensible and evil thing.

2. For the padres to come to Japan and convert people to their creed, destroying Shinto and Buddhist temples to this end, is a hitherto unseen and unheard-of thing. When the Lord of the Tenka gives fiefs, cities, towns, or income to anybody, it is purely temporarily, and the recipients are obliged to observe inviolably the laws and ordinances of Japan; but to stir up the canaille to commit outrages of this sort is something deserving of severe punishment.

3. If the Lord of the Tenka allowed the padres to propagate their sect, as the Christians wish and intend, this is contrary to the laws of Japan, as previously stated. Since such a thing is intolerable, I am resolved that the padres should not stay on Japanese soil. I therefore order that having settled their affairs within twenty days, they must return to their own country. If anyone should harm them within this period, the culprit will be punished.

4. As the Great Ship comes to trade, and this is something quite different, the Portuguese can carry on their commerce unmolested.

5. Henceforward not only merchants, but anyone else coming from India, who does not interfere with the laws of the Shinto and Buddhist deities may come freely to Japan, and thus let them take due note of this. On the nineteenth day of the sixth month of the fifteenth year of Tensho [July 25, 1587].

When Coelho was notified of this edict of banishment, he replied to the effect that it was impossible to obey it, since the Great Ship was not due to leave for Macao for another six months, and no other means of maritime transport were available. Hideyoshi accepted this excuse, but ordered all Jesuits concentrated in Hirado pending their embarkation; and to prove that he was in earnest, he promulgated a further series of anti-Christian regulations. These included the stipulation that not only the European but all Japanese Jesuits were to quit Japan on pain of death, and the Portuguese were expressly forbidden to bring any more missionaries in their annual carrack. Public notices were put up in Hakata and elsewhere, notifying the populace that the padres were being expelled for propagating an evil creed and for destroying Shinto and Buddhist temples. Another edict ordered the removal of all crosses, rosaries, and other outward signs of Christianity from the dress or equipment of samurai in his army. The Jesuits' property at Hakata, Osaka, Sakai, and elsewhere was confiscated and their churches seized or closed. All Christian converts were ordered to recant, or to take the alternative of exile or death, although no attempt whatever was made to enforce this particular injunction. Finally, the Jesuits' strongholds of Nagasaki, Mogi, and Urakami were taken over by Hideyoshi's emissaries, and the inhabitants of Nagasaki condemned to pay a large fine.

The flustered Coelho now went to the other extreme of his former complaisance to Hideyoshi. He endeavored to get Arima to induce the other Christian daimyo to unite in armed resistance against the expulsion edict. In this he failed, so he fell back on a more temporizing policy. But he still had not learned his lesson entirely, since he wrote to Manila, Macao, and Goa begging for two or three hundred soldiers and fire-arms wherewith to stiffen the Christian daimyo. The Spanish authorities contented themselves with referring his request to Madrid, and the Jesuit superior at Manila sent him a severe reprimand for his imprudence. The Portuguese sent him some weapons but no troops. Valignano was furious when he heard of Coelho's extraordinary behavior, which he charac-terized as the ravings of an afflicted mind driven to despair by Hideyoshi's unexpected action. Father Valignano wrote in October, 1590, that only the vice-provincial's death in the previous May had saved him from severe punishment at his hands. It should be added that Coelho's bellicose suggestions were opposed by the great majority of his colleagues in Japan (Belchior de Moura was one of the few exceptions) as well as by the Christian daimyo themselves. Valignano's sole consolation was that he did not believe that everything had come to the ears of Hideyoshi. In this he was probably mistaken, as the latter had many informers in Kyushu, and the gunrunning from Macao to Nagasaki can hardly have been kept secret. Valignano sent these compromising weap-ons back to Macao on his arrival in 1590.[7]

To what extent was Hideyoshi in earnest in making this amazing *volte-face*? Were his drastic actions part of a long-premeditated plan (as he himself averred at the time), or

were they mainly due to a drunken whim? The Jesuits themselves were very puzzled and oscillated between the two
opinions, for both of which, indeed, convincing evidence
can be produced. On the one hand, as Frois pointed out, it
could be argued that the expulsion edict was mainly inspired by an unpremeditated drunken fury, since there was
no need whatever for the all-powerful Hideyoshi to have
gone to such lengths to maintain friendly relations with the
Jesuits before St. James's Day, 1587, nor to place Christian
daimyo like Konishi and Kuroda in positions of great trust
and power. The dictator who changed three and twenty
daimyo from their fiefs in a single day, without arousing
the slightest opposition, certainly had no need to truckle to
petty lordlings like Omura or Arima. The only territorially
important Christian daimyo were those of his own make
and choice within the last few years. Similar instances of
impulsive behavior were instanced by Frois, who further
pointed out that Hideyoshi, in common with all untrammeled
Oriental despots, suffered from megalomania and delusions
of grandeur, such as had inspired the Egyptian Pharaohs and
Babylonian Kings to similar excesses recorded in Holy Writ.

Finally, Hideyoshi made no attempt to enforce the letter
of his anti-Christian law, as he easily could have done, had he
been so disposed. Although nearly a hundred and twenty
Jesuits assembled at Hirado, only three actually left the
country when the Great Ship finally sailed for Macao, and
the remainder dispersed to the territories of the neighboring
Christian daimyo, where they continued their work steadily
if unobtrusively,—a fact which could not have failed to come
to the ears of Hideyoshi. The Kwambaku did not even trouble to order the anti-Christian daimyo of Hirado to supervise
their departure, as was the obvious course if he was wholly in
earnest. Although Hideyoshi's emissaries formally took over
the Jesuit-owned districts of Nagasaki, Mogi, and Urakami,
they contented themselves with exacting the fine levied on
the populace, and with closing the churches temporarily instead of destroying them permanently. Not only so, but when

Arima and Omura represented to Hideyoshi that these districts had been originally in their fiefs, and should therefore revert to them, the regent at once gave his consent, and the Jesuits (as they themselves admit) were soon as effectively the real masters of Nagasaki as they had been before July 25; although the port was nominally administered by Arima, Omura, or Ryuzoji as the Kwambaku's successive local representatives.

Against this viewpoint that Hideyoshi's anti-Christian fulminations were rather the result of caprice than of considered deliberation, the following arguments can be advanced. First, his previous excessive friendliness may have been nothing more than a "blind"; for as Valignano stressed in his "Sumario" of 1583, the Japanese were never more fair-spoken than when they were on the point of making a sudden and unexpected attack—as the start of the wars of 1904 and 1941 go to show. Second, the idea of the Christian converts being used as a "fifth column" was nothing new, and Hideyoshi must often have heard this possibility suggested, apart from Coelho's harebrained schemes in 1587. To take one instance among many, Frois' letter of October 16, 1578, cites the widely-believed report in Bungo that the padres were merely waiting till they had a sufficient number of converts to act as auxiliaries, when a Portuguese armada would come from India to complete their spiritual conquest with a temporal one. Old Otomo and Nobunaga had laughed these suggestions to scorn, but Hideyoshi may have taken them more seriously, particularly when he noticed the subservience of the Christian daimyo to their mentors. Although the Jesuits sometimes complain that their flock was not always so obedient as they could wish, Takayama was clearly their pliable tool, and Frois records approvingly that Arima "is very docile and submissive to the fathers." [8]

On the other hand, if Hideyoshi was seriously concerned about the loyalty of the Christian daimyo, it is very odd that he should have limited his action to deposing Takayama, and not only let the others go unscathed, but even transferred some of the most enthusiastic (Kuroda and Konishi) to districts of western Kyushu, where they were more favorably placed for assisting the Jesuits than anywhere else in Japan. Nor did he take any notice of the conversion of Hosokawa Tadaoki's wife, Gracia, which occurred at this time and cannot have remained secret for long. Of nearly two hundred and fifty Jesuit establishments, only sixty were actually destroyed. Most of the remainder were brought into practical if unobtrusive use during the next decade.[9]

Nor did Hideyoshi's complaisance or indifference to this systematic violation of his St. James's Day edict stop here. When he heard that his old acquaintance, the venerable Japanese Brother Lourenço, was not sailing in the Great Ship, he merely shrugged his shoulders and observed it was only right that the veteran should spend the evening of his days in Japan. When the captain-major's emissary, in 1588, told him that Father Alessandro Valignano, in his capacity of envoy from the viceroy at Goa, was awaiting his permission at Macao before returning to Japan with the four young Kyushu samurai who had gone to Rome in 1583, the regent at once replied that Valignano was more than welcome to return in his diplomatic (as distinct from his ecclesiastical) capacity. Furthermore, he later gave official permission for the Jesuits to leave a dozen of their number at Nagasaki to serve as go-betweens and interpreters. Here, perhaps, is the crux of the matter; but the way in which Mammon proved of timely assistance, is best related in Valignano's own words in his "Addiciones" of 1592.

After explaining that the Jesuits often acted as intermediaries for the purchase of Chinese gold and silks from the carrack's cargo by Japanese grandees, Valignano adds, "with this Great Ship, and with our doing them these little favors, they deceive themselves, and they are nearly all of them convinced that if the padres were not here, the Japanese could not deal with the Portuguese, which opinion is of no small help to us at this juncture. For whereas this matter was sometimes argued before the Kwambaku and the bugyo or governors whom he sent to this port last year [1591], these latter, even though they were our enemies and gave us a lot of trouble, because they wanted to obtain the impossible from the Portuguese, yet withal even they were convinced that there was no trading with the Portuguese in Japan unless the padres acted as intermediaries."

On the receipt of Hideyoshi's safe-conduct, Valignano decided to risk going to Japan. He disembarked at Nagasaki in July, 1590, together with the four returning Kyushu envoys to the Pope, and a magnificent assortment of presents from Rome, Lisbon, "Golden Goa," and other parts of the Gorgeous East then held in fee by the Portuguese. After some preliminary misunderstanding and delay, Valignano proceeded to the capital with a splendid suite, the very Negro slaves being dressed in velvet liveries and chains of gold. Hideyoshi gave the envoy a solemn audience at his palace of Juraku at Kyoto (March 3, 1591). His familiarity with various members of the embassy during the subsequent dinner party, recalled his friendly attitude at Osaka castle in 1586. He made it quite clear in confidential conversation that he was prepared to connive at the nonenforcement of his anti-Christian edicts, provided the Jesuits continued to act with modesty and discretion, and indulged in no overt anti-Buddhist or iconoclastic acts. Thanks to Valignano's exemplary tact, aided by the exceptional linguistic skill of the Portuguese Jesuit, João Rodriguez, nicknamed "Tçuzzu," or interpreter, to distinguish him from other colleagues of the same name, everything passed off as merrily as the proverbial marriage bell.

Valignano's philosophical wheel had thus come full circle again, within four short years of the formal order for the Jesuits' total expulsion in 1587, with a community of more than 200,000 converts increasing daily, and Hideyoshi defying his own prohibition by strolling through the gilded halls of Juraku palace wearing a rosary and Portuguese dress. Yet the wheel revolved once more, and disaster again struck the mission just when its barometer read "Set Fair." This time the blow was not so unforeseen as the thunderbolt of St. James's

Day, 1587, since it came from a quarter which Valignano had long regarded with a wary eye, but to understand its genesis it is necessary to consider the activities of the friars from the Philippines.[10]

II

It is one of the commonplaces of history that there are no feuds so bitter as those engendered by the *odium theologicum* which seems to be inseparable from all doctrinal disputes, and not least in religions like Christianity and Buddhism which theoretically lay such stress on peace and goodwill. The record of the Christian Church in this respect is even blacker than that of the followers of the Enlightened One, and the mutual calumny to which the rival Roman Catholic orders descended in the Far East was one of the main causes of the relative failure of their China and Japan missions. As Professor Murdoch has observed, "The simple truth of the matter is that, from 1594 down to 1614 at least, between Jesuits and Franciscans in Japan it was all but war to the knife, just as it was in Paraguay a few years later on. No amount of Church historianizing will suffice to conceal that truth from anyone who takes the trouble to spend some little time over the respective letters sent by the rival Order and Society to their respective head-quarters."

I am not quite sure whom Professor Murdoch had in mind when he used the term "Church historianizing"; for the original participants in these unedifying disputes made no more attempt to conceal what they conceived to be the truth than did the Jesuit and Dominican protagonists in the equally bitter strife over the Chinese rites which convulsed the Catholic Church during the next century. On the contrary, the candor and plain speaking of their respective spokesmen leave not the smallest doubt of their sincerity, whatever is thought of the motives (often paltry enough) which inspired these outbursts of envy, hatred, malice, and uncharitableness. *Frailes idiotas* ("crazy friars") was a term of opprobrium used by the Jesuits long before it became a battle cry of anticlerical Spaniards in the nineteenth century. To what extent this contemptuous epithet was justified, the reader of Valignano's and Cerqueira's reports, summarized in the following pages, can decide for himself, after squaring them with the Franciscan versions given in Appendix III.[11]

The forceful Italian Jesuit, Valignano, was never a man to mince his words, and from the time of his first arrival in Japan he voiced his mistrust of possible complications from the presence of Spanish friars in the Philippines. The reader will probably not need reminding that at this period Spain and Portugal had just (1580) been united in a dual monarchy (after the style of England and Scotland in 1603) under the scepter of King Felipe II. One of the express conditions of this union was that the two colonial empires should continue to be separately administered and completely independent of each other as hitherto. Moreover, the privileges of the Portuguese *padroado* or religious patronage in the Orient, deriving from a series of papal briefs and bulls solemnly affirming the right of the Crown of Portugal to the exclusive supervision of missionary activity in Asia, were likewise formally recognized by the Spanish monarch.

His older subjects did not, however, display the same complacent attitude to the sweeping claims of their new fellow vassals; and the ecclesiastical and secular authorities at Manila were (with the significant exception of the Jesuits) unanimous in declining to recognize the validity of the claims of the Portuguese Crown to the exercise of its padroado east of Malacca. Soon after the consolidation of the Spanish conquest of Luzon with the defeat of Limahon in 1575, the mendicant orders established at Manila made several attempts to gain a foothold in the provinces of Fukien and Kwangtung on the Chinese mainland, which were explicitly recognized by the papacy as within the spiritual jurisdiction of the Portuguese bishop of China and Japan with his headquarters at Macao. These attempts all ended in failure in view of Chinese intransigeance, but they went to show that the friars paid no heed to the claims of the Portuguese padroado where these conflicted with those of the parallel *patronazgo* of the Spanish Crown in the Philippines and the countries bordering on the China Sea.[12]

Valignano had therefore good reason to expect that eventually the Spaniards would switch their efforts from China to Japan; especially since this ecclesiastical jealousy was acerbated by a political and economic Luso-Spanish rivalry, deriving from the natural Castilian dislike of the Macao Portuguese monopolizing the fabulously wealthy China-Japan trade. Since God and Mammon, as represented respectively by the Jesuits and the Great Ship, worked hand in hand at Nagasaki, it was obvious that the friars would likewise have to work through or with the merchants at Manila in order to get a satisfactory footing in Japan. Hence traders and priests of both nations stood shoulder to shoulder, the Portuguese and Jesuits in their efforts to keep the intruding Spaniards and friars out, whereas the *conquistadores* and *frailes* were no less united in their determination to get in. All the elements for a head-on clash of Portuguese and Spanish interests were therefore present. It was with a view to forestalling such a blow, with its inevitable untoward consequences for the Jesuit Japan mission, that Valignano gave a whole chapter in his 1583 "Sumario" to proving "Why it is not convenient that other religious orders should come to Japan." [13]

He began his indictment by pointing out that one of the main reasons for the Jesuits' success was the dissatisfaction felt by many Japanese at the numerous "splinter sects" into which Buddhism tended to disintegrate, whereas the uniformity of the Jesuits' teaching in itself impressed them as indicative of its divine origin. This impression would be destroyed if the friars came to Japan, since the diversity in dress and habits of various religious orders would lead the Japanese to believe that Christianity, like Buddhism, though nominally acknowledging a supreme god and with one sacred text, was in reality composed of many different subsects.

Second, the Japanese Christian community was a new and

tender plant which needed the most careful handling and uniformity of instruction, not merely in religious but in secular teaching, "because they have not got, nor can they get, any books other than those which we give them." This uniformity of doctrinal instruction would disappear if the friars were admitted, since they might give dispensations in instances where the Jesuits would deny them, or vice versa— "and if suchlike controversies occurred among those of the primitive Church, where there was such holiness and doctrine, being so close to the Supreme Pontiff . . . it can easily be imagined what will happen here in Japan which is so distant and isolated."

Previous experience in Portuguese Asia showed only too clearly that the admission of the friars to the Japan mission field would inevitably result in bitter disputes between them and the Jesuits, since all the mendicant orders, "whether it be through pure zeal or whether through something else," invariably combined their forces against the Jesuits in India. Things would be even worse in Japan, where there was no viceroy or archbishop to interpose a restraining authority as at Goa.

The Jesuit visitor further pointed out that Japanese manners and customs being so contrary to those of Europeans, the new arrivals would inevitably commit many of the mistakes which the Jesuits had only learned to avoid by bitter experience, thus damaging or destroying the work of the latter. "Japan is not a place which can be controlled by foreigners, for the Japanese are neither so weak nor so stupid a race as to permit this, and the King of Spain neither has nor ever could have any power or jurisdiction here. Therefore there is no alternative to relying on training the natives in the way they should go and subsequently leaving them to manage their churches themselves. For this, a single religious order will suffice . . . and this is conclusively proved by the great difficulty we have experienced in uniting the hearts of our people with those of the Japanese and theirs with ours, owing to the mutual contrariness of our respective national customs, and wherein they are so determined that on no single point will they adjust themselves to our usages, but on the contrary, we have to accommodate ourselves to their ways in everything. This is very difficult for us, but if we did not do so, we would lose face, and do no good at all." Valignano obviously considered that the friars from Mexico and the Philippines, who were accustomed to use conquistador methods with their half-savage Aztec and Filipino neophytes, would not compromise with Japanese social usages in the way that the more pliable and intelligent Jesuits had done.

He also pointed out that if the friars came, it would be in either large or small numbers. If the latter, then they would be too few to be of any practical use; if the former, from where, he pertinently asked, would they get their financial support? He deprecated the suggestion that the mendicant orders should subsist on local charity, since Japan was a poor country; their endeavoring to do so would lend point to the bonzes' favorite accusation that the European missionaries really came to Japan to get a living, under the pretext of proselytizing. The Jesuits could hardly make two ends meet as it was, and neither King nor Pope could be expected to find vast additional sums to maintain the friars.

His last reason is the most interesting of all, and, in view of subsequent developments, it certainly has a prophetic ring about it. "Hitherto many of the Japanese lords had a great fear that we [Jesuits] were concocting some evil in Japan, and that if they allowed the conversion of Christians in their fiefs, we could afterwards use them to raise a rebellion on behalf of the [Spanish] King who supports us; for they could not understand why these monarchs should spend such vast sums on the mission, if it was not with the ultimate intention of seizing their lands. Several lords have told us this openly on many occasions, for this is one of the principal allegations of the bonzes against us. And now that they know that the kingdoms of Spain and Portugal are united, this existing suspicion would be vastly strengthened by the arrival of new foreign religious, and might easily induce them to wreak some harm on the local Christians and on ourselves."

For all of these reasons, Valignano strongly urged the Jesuit General at Rome to obtain forthwith a papal bull categorically forbidding any religious order except the Jesuits to go to Japan. This bull, he stressed, should be published in Macao and in Luzon, whence many friars were desirous of going to Japan, "because they have to do with inferior races where they are," and the local authorities should be ordered to forbid the departure of friars under pain of excommunication. "And Our Lord knows that I say this purely for his glory and from my personal experience in Japan, and I would say this same were I in *articulo mortis*."

This considered opinion of Valignano was evidently a hardening of his previous attitude; for at an earlier date he had stated that if Capuchin friars came to Japan, they should be lodged in the Jesuits' houses for ten or twelve days, and given (against a written receipt) the charge of a Christian community "of so many thousand souls." The only hostile stipulation was that Jesuits should not be seen in the company of Capuchins when they went to visit daimyo. This relatively tolerant attitude did not last long; for in 1585, Valignano ordered that stray Capuchins coming to Japan should not receive Jesuit hospitality for more than three days, and that the friars should not be entrusted with the care of any existing Christian community, but left to found their own in the "hard way," as the Jesuits had done before them. These categorical prohibitions were rendered necessary by the fact that the Jesuit visitor had caught some of his subordinates clandestinely corresponding with the Spanish authorities in the Philippines, urging them to send friars to help reap the increasing harvest of souls in Japan, particularly in Bungo, where old Otomo Sorin, as an ardent devotee of St. Francis, would give them a warm welcome. This attitude Valignano maintained for the remainder of his life.[14]

The Jesuit's request for a papal bull forbidding any change

in the existing status of the Japan mission field as a Jesuit monopoly was warmly pressed by the general of the Society, and speedily granted by the promulgation of the brief *Ex Pastoralis Officio* by Pope Gregory XIII on January 23, 1585. Meanwhile, King Felipe, who had likewise been approached by the Jesuits, gave similar orders to the secular authorities in Portuguese India, after first referring the matter to the viceroy and archbishop for their opinion of the Jesuits' pretensions. On the arrival of the papal brief at Goa, Viceroy Dom Duarte de Menezes gave categorical instructions to Domingos Monteiro, captain-major of the Japan voyage, on April 12, 1586, to ensure that no friars from the Philippines or elsewhere entered Japan, authorizing him to deport summarily to Macao any that he might find there. The bishop of Macao was instructed to the same effect, having already been told three years earlier that he was not to disturb the Jesuits by carrying out a projected episcopal visit to Japan, although this island was then within the limits of his nominal diocese.

But although the Jesuits had thus apparently triumphed all along the line, and the Spanish King had sacrificed the interests of his own subjects to placate the Portuguese, the struggle had in reality only begun. The friars made no secret of their intention to ignore the papal brief, which they claimed had been obtained through false information and backstairs intrigue; and the secular authorities at Manila were anxious to second their efforts from political and commercial jealousy of the Portuguese at Macao.

Although a few stray Franciscans reached Japan before 1590, they left virtually no traces of their fugitive passage, and the first real chance of breaking the Jesuit-Portuguese monopoly in the island empire occurred in 1592. In the previous year, a Japanese adventurer named Harada Magoshichiro exploited the growing megalomania of Hideyoshi, which had just found vent in the unprovoked invasion of Korea, by inducing him to send an emissary to the governor of the Philippines with a demand for the submission of the Spanish colony to the Lord of the Land of the Rising Sun. The emissary, who was Harada's cousin, explained confidentially to the governor that what Hideyoshi really wanted was the establishment of mutually profitable commercial relations between Japan and the Philippines, and that reinforcements of friars for the Jesuit mission would be welcomed. The Spanish authorities were rightly suspicious of the self-styled ambassador's credentials, but this gave them the opportunity of sending an envoy to ask for explanation and clarification of the Taiko Hideyoshi's demands, and the Dominican friar, Juan Cobo, was selected for the post. Cobo was the most accomplished Sinologue among the Europeans in the Philippines, for he knew more than three thousand Chinese ideographs and was the real or reputed author of several translations from and into Chinese, despite the fact that he had only come to Manila from Mexico in 1588.

He landed in Satsuma in June, 1592, and after joining forces with a disgruntled Peruvian merchant who had (so he said) been defrauded by the Portuguese mercantile community of Nagasaki, proceeded to Hideyoshi's field headquarters at Nagoya in Hizen. Nothing much came of his interview with the regent, although the complaints lodged by the two Spaniards against the Nagasaki Portuguese had unfavorable if temporary repercussions there. Hideyoshi had Cobo explain to him by means of a globe the position and extent of the Spanish colonial empire (an incident possibly not without significance in view of what happened four years later). The Dominican was dismissed with a reply to the governor of Manila, but was shipwrecked on the return voyage, and perished at the hands of the head-hunters of Formosa.

Harada was encouraged rather than daunted at this mishap, and himself headed a second "embassy" to Manila, which resulted in the dispatch of another pseudo-diplomatic Spanish mission, this time led by a Franciscan, Pedro Bautista, who with his three companions was cordially received by Hideyoshi in 1593. The sole reason for Hideyoshi's cordiality was that he saw in the Spaniards not merely potential subjects, but future commercial competitors of the Portuguese. He would thus be enabled to acquire the coveted Chinese silks and gold at cheaper prices than he had to pay the Macao monopolists of the Nagasaki trade, whose profits were now more desirable than ever with the expense of the costly Korean expedition. Hideyoshi therefore permitted the four Franciscans to remain at Kyoto, in the hope that they would prove a bait for the Manila traders in the same way as the Jesuits were considered to be part and parcel of the trade driven by the Great Ship from Macao.[15]

The Franciscans were overjoyed by the all-powerful dictator's apparent friendliness, which they took at its face value and promptly exploited to the utmost, celebrating Mass openly and behaving generally as if they were in Rome rather than in a country where the letter if not the spirit of the law expressly prohibited the practice of Christianity. The Jesuits and such local Japanese officials as were friendly to Christianity were naturally aghast at this intemperate zeal. They more than once remonstrated with the friars over their reckless behavior, advising them to tread delicately like Agag, and to dress as Buddhist priests as the Jesuits did. The infatuated friars not only laughed these warnings to scorn, but boasted that they basked in the sunshine of Hideyoshi's favor, accusing the Jesuits of cowardice for going about their work in disguise, "as we do in England," wrote Bishop Pedro Martins.

A modern Jesuit writer, who can afford to take a more tolerant view of the Franciscans' actions than could (or did) his sixteenth-century colleagues, points out that there is something to be said in their favor. The methods they employed were merely those which had met with such success in Mexico, Peru, and the Philippines, or for that matter in Portuguese Brazil, where the comparatively backward native cultures could be largely ignored, and a clean sweep made of all existing beliefs and prejudices, in order to sow the Gospel seed. Such drastic methods were doomed to failure when applied to the inhabitants of Japan, China, and Hindustan, the culture of which was in all cases older, and in many ways superior, to that of the West. The Jesuits had realized this fact earlier than their colleagues as a whole; although the Franciscan Bernardino de Sahagún in Mexico ably defended this viewpoint of adapting rather than destroying the indigenous civilizations, and it was implicit in the courageous stand of the Dominican Bishop, Bartolomé de Las Casas, on behalf of the Amerindians. This was also one of the reasons why such converts as the Franciscans made were mostly from "the ignorant and the forgotten" lower classes; whereas the Jesuits concentrated their efforts primarily on the upper strata of society whose example would be followed automatically by their inferiors.[16]

Be this as it may, the Franciscans had some excuse for believing that Hideyoshi's 1587 prohibition of Christianity was by now a dead letter, in fact if not in theory. He had received them, as he had previously received Valignano, in solemn official audience and set his own edict at nought by allowing his courtiers to wear Christian rosaries and crosses, and by conniving at Konishi Yukinaga's mass conversions in Higo Province. Moreover, the Jesuits were quietly but steadily continuing their work in Kyushu. They had installed a printing press at Amakusa which printed books in both European letters and in Sino-Japanese characters, and the religious plays staged at their training seminary in Arima's fief, included representations of Buddhist priests being driven away by Christian angels. Finally, the newly arrived Jesuit Bishop of Japan, Pedro Martins, was kindly received by Hideyoshi when this prelate made what virtually amounted to a triumphal tour of the Christian communities in the Kyoto district, although the regent told him half-jokingly that he ought to go back to Macao. With Hideyoshi thus conniving at the flouting of his own edicts, whether openly by the Franciscans, or less obtrusively by the Jesuits, the Spanish friars may perhaps be excused for not realizing that his tolerance of Christian propaganda was in direct proportion to the profits he hoped to gain from the Iberian traders. At this point, the wreck of the great galleon *San Felipe* off the coast of Shikoku, set in motion a train of events which roughly disillusioned the friars from the Philippines, and justified Valignano's Cassandra-like forebodings on their coming.

This richly-laden vessel had left Manila for Acapulco in July with a cargo valued at more than a million and a half silver pesos. Forced off her course by a typhoon, she made a landfall off the Tosa coast on October 19, 1596. If the sworn testimony of Bishop Pedro Martins on the *San Felipe* affair is to be credited, the pilot offered to take the ship round to Nagasaki despite her battered condition; but the commander (or "general" as the Spaniards termed him) declined this offer on the promptings of Fray Juan Pobre, who had visited Japan in the previous year and who assured him that Hideyoshi was a virtual father to the Kyoto Franciscans. A couple of days later the ship broke her back on the bar and the passengers and cargo were only disembarked with difficulty. The local daimyo showed himself anything but friendly, and since the Shikoku samurai appropriated most of the cargo—for that matter the coastal inhabitants of any European country would have done the same—the Spaniards sent a delegation to Kyoto to solicit Hideyoshi's intervention in their favor.

The resident Franciscan commissary, Pedro Bautista, not only gave them every hope of success, but (again if Bishop Martins is to be relied on) induced them brusquely to reject the Jesuits' offer to act as intermediaries, since he had everything well in hand. The same authority states that the Franciscans were so maladroit that they likewise rejected the suggestion to employ the friendly Governor of Kyoto, Maeda Genni Hoin Munehisa, to intercede with the regent, and selected instead Masuda Nagamori, the minister of works and Hideyoshi's special commissioner of investigation, who "double-crossed" them. When Konishi Yukinaga suggested that Masuda should take a good interpreter with him on his trip of investigation, the latter retorted brusquely "if I was going with the intention of reaching an agreement, I would need a good tongue; but as I am only going to collect the swag, hands are all that I need." This was no happy augury, but worse was to come.[17]

Hideyoshi was at this time in a somewhat critical financial position. Although by the unanimous testimony of contemporary European and Japanese authors he had amassed a great personal fortune, by means which were not always above reproach, his expenditure was likewise on the most lavish scale. The Korean war was a drain on his exchequer in much the same way as Napoleon's Peninsula campaign proved a running sore to him. The fighting had bogged down after the first swift Japanese successes on land had been more than offset by crushing reverses at sea at the hands of the great Korean admiral Yi Sunsin, one of the outstanding naval leaders of all time. The Chinese had intervened tardily but effectively, and an attempt to reach an agreement with them at the expense of the luckless Koreans, had just broken down ignominiously with Hideyoshi's indignant refusal to accept the Ming emperor's condescending offer to invest him formally as King of Japan (October 20, 1596).

He was, therefore, faced with the necessity of renewing the war on a larger scale than ever, shortly after a series of disastrous earthquakes in central Japan during the previous September had devastated large areas of the Gokinai, including his costly new palace at Fushimi. In these circumstances, even his own very considerable resources were strained to the utmost, and he therefore gave an attentive ear to the joint proposals of Masuda, and the Jesuits' old enemy, the court physician (and pimp) Seyakuin Hoin, that now was the time to recoup his losses by confiscating the *San Felipe*'s cargo which represented obviously a gift from the gods. If the Jesuits are to be believed, he hesitated for some time before doing so. As Bishop Martins frankly recognized, Hideyoshi was a statesman whose considered policy was to favor and not to rob foreign traders; nor had he any desire to imperil the prospect of trade with the Philippines by arbitrarily seizing the Spanish treasureship.

While he was thus hesitating, and assuring the Jesuits with apparent sincerity that he would return the confiscated cargo if they humbly asked him for it, an unfortunate incident occurred which swung his volatile mind round to the anti-Christian views of Masuda, Seyakuin, and other cronies. The Spanish Pilot-Major, Francisco de Olandia, in an ill-judged effort to impress the Taiko Hideyoshi's commissioners with the power of the Spanish King, incautiously admitted to Masuda that the Spanish overseas conquests had been greatly facilitated by the Christian "fifth column" (to use modern jargon) formed by the missionary friars before the arrival of the conquistadores themselves. This observation coincided exactly with what the bonzes had been telling anyone who would listen to them, since 1570 at least. Coming from, as it were, the horse's mouth, it could hardly be ignored by even a confessed anti-Buddhist like Hideyoshi. This allegation either gave him the pretext for which he was seeking, or else (more likely) decided him that Masuda and Seyakuin were right in their denunciation of the political menace of Christianity.

In either event, his reaction was swift and decisive. He forthwith sentenced the Franciscans to death by crucifixion at Nagasaki, as violators of the law of the realm and disturbers of the public peace. At first Hideyoshi threatened to include all the missionaries in his condemnation, but he soon thought better of this—mainly because the Jesuits were still regarded as essential intermediaries for the Macao trade—and in the end only a mixed party of six Franciscans, seventeen of their Japanese neophytes, three Japanese Jesuit lay brothers (these last included by mistake) or twenty-six persons in all, were crucified in Japanese fashion at Nagasaki on a cold winter's morning, February 5, 1597, after having been paraded overland from Kyoto via Sakai and exposed to the derision of the populace.

The foregoing, be it noted, is substantially the Portuguese and Jesuit account of the matter; for the Spaniards and surviving Franciscans roundly declared that it was the Portuguese who denounced the Spaniards as conquistadores, and who instigated the Japanese to confiscate the *San Felipe*'s cargo. Fray Juan Pobre (an eyewitness and passenger in the great galleon), expressly states that Hideyoshi's decision to confiscate the cargo was taken *before* the pilot's interview with Masuda, and not after it as the Jesuit accounts imply. The Spaniards further alleged that the Jesuits not only de-

clined to intervene on behalf of the Franciscans when asked
to do so, but went so far as to entertain the judge who pre-
sided at the execution. Bishop Martins and his compatriots, it
is perhaps needless to add, formally denied on oath these and
similar accusations; but they were nevertheless widely believed and repeated throughout the Spanish colonial empire,
and did a great deal to foster the ill-feeling between Spaniards
and Portuguese which was never very far below the surface.[18]

It may be asked what justification did the Japanese have for
their suspicions of European aggression by or through the
missionaries? The answer is that they had more excuse than
reason. Christian religious propaganda was (and is) in the nature of things difficult, if not impossible, to disentangle from
the political affiliations of those who support it. Thus Charlevoix, the Jesuit historian of the Society's activities in Canada
as well as in Japan, pays his colleagues the somewhat dubious
compliment that they taught their Red Indian converts to
mingle Christ and France together in their affections. Without suggesting that they proceeded on exactly parallel lines in
Japan, it is worth noting that the Jesuit padre, Balthazar
Gago, writing from Hirado to his patron King João III of
Portugal in September, 1555, claims credit for teaching his
neophytes to pray for the Lusitanian monarch as their potential protector. This king, it will be remembered, was responsible not only for the admission of the Society of Jesus into
Portugal and its dominions, but also for that of the Inquisition
and the *auto-da-fé*, and this in despite of extreme reluctance
on the part of the papacy.

Valignano, in his *Historia* of the Society in India, written in
1601, refers approvingly to Francis Xavier having realized
"with his spirit and prudence, how rude and incapable these
people are by nature in the things of God, and that reason is
not so effective with them as is force." It is true that he was
thinking of a Konkani and not of a Far Eastern race, as was
Lord Elgin when he characterized the Chinese as yielding
nothing to reason and everything to force; but the sentiment
of racial superiority which inspired the Renaissance Italian

and the Victorian Englishman was essentially the same. The proud Neapolitan nobleman would doubtless have agreed with William Cobbett, who sneered at the "sooty slaves of Hindoostan," in the course of a public debate in the House of Commons. Quite a number of Japanese had visited the Spanish Asiatic colonies on one occasion or another, and their reports on the European attitude toward their colonial subjects were doubtless not so favorable as the rose-colored impressions of the Kyushu envoys who had been so carefully shepherded during their memorable trip to Goa, Lisbon, Madrid, and Rome. Responsible clerics, such as Bishop Domingo de Salazar, O.P. (often termed the Las Casas of the Philippines), and the restless intriguing Jesuit, Alonso Sánchez, repeatedly advocated the conquest of China by force of arms, on the grounds that such a war was thoroughly justified in view of the Ming emperor's refusal to allow the presence of Gospel preachers in his empire.

It is true that experience of the warlike nature of the Japanese speedily disillusioned the vast majority of the Jesuits from any notions they might ever have harbored about the feasibility of the conquest of Japan by the Catholic King, and Valignano was at pains to stress repeatedly the vital necessity of respecting Japanese national independence. But it was the father-superior, Gaspar Coelho, a responsible and withal avowedly pro-Japanese Jesuit, who admitted more native novices into the Society than any of his predecessors or successors, who had warmly advocated the conversion of Nagasaki into a strongly fortified Portuguese *point d'appui,* and even suggested Spanish military aid for the Christian daimyo of Kyushu. It is true that Valignano sharply rejected these dangerous suggestions. But he and Bishop Martins were both at one in urging King Felipe to order the cancellation of the Great Ship's annual voyage from Macao to Nagasaki, after the martyrdom of 1597, in order to cause an economic crisis and general unrest in Japan. They considered that this situation would bring about either the overthrow of Hideyoshi, or induce him to accord official recognition to Christianity in his domains. Bishop Martins pointed out that the regent was particularly vulnerable to this form of economic sanctions, since he was at war with China, and had deliberately broken with his only other overseas market in the Philippines. The advice was not taken, and Hideyoshi's death the next year rendered it unnecessary; but it is interesting as showing how inextricably mixed were religious, political, and economic motives in the Jesuit Japan mission.

That the Japanese were by no means so ignorant of the state of affairs in Europe, as the Jesuits sometimes seem to have imagined, can be seen from Hideyoshi's correspondence with the Governor of the Philippines, Don Francisco Tello. The governor had sent an envoy, Don Luis Navarrete, to claim the confiscated cargo of the *San Felipe,* and to ask why the Franciscans had been executed. Hideyoshi in his reply, drafted in a spirit more of sorrow than of anger, explained that Shinto (there is no mention of Buddhism, be it noted) was the pith and core of the Japanese social structure. He went on to point out that the friars threatened to upset the whole national fabric with their subversive Christian propaganda, "and if perchance, either religious or secular Japanese proceeded to your kingdoms and preached the law of Shinto therein, disquieting and disturbing the public peace and tranquillity thereby, would you, as lord of the soil, be pleased thereat? Certainly not; and therefore by this you can judge what I have done." The logic of this retort is indeed unanswerable; although there is no need to suppose that it carried the slightest conviction to the closed mind of a Roman Catholic conquistador, who naturally considered that the activities of the Franciscans were inspired by God, and therefore above human interference, whereas those of the Shinto priests were motivated by the Devil, and as such entitled to be forcibly suppressed.

It may be added that, as usual, there was something to be said on both sides. For although the close connection between politics and religion exemplified by the Portuguese and Spanish padroados in their respective colonial empires gave every excuse for Japanese apprehensions, the Europeans in their turn had cause to fear the aggressive tendencies of Hideyoshi's megalomania as evidenced by his declared policy of invading China, Korea, and the Philippines.[19]

After this lengthy digression it is more than time to return to the immediate consequences of the martyrdom of February 5, 1597. These were not nearly so drastic as at first seemed likely. For one reason or another the Taiko Hideyoshi held his hand. Although the local repercussions were more severe than in 1587, only some hundred and twenty churches out of a total of several hundred were destroyed, and only eleven Jesuits out of a hundred and twenty-five actually left the country (as against three in 1587). Hideyoshi's death in 1598 gave the Christian community a further breathing space, but the Jesuits were strictly enjoined by Konishi and Arima not to display any sign of rejoicing at the regent's demise nor did they endeavor to do so. Ieyasu, his virtual if not theoretical successor, displayed an unexpectedly tolerant attitude; but what shook them to the core was the reappearance of friars from the Philippines in the unwelcome person of Fray Jerónimo de Jesús, one of the survivors of the previous year's tragedy, in very transparent disguise in June, 1598.

Bishop Martins had left for Macao and India in March, 1597, largely with the object of convincing the authorities at Goa of the urgent necessity of stopping the infiltration of friars into Japan. He died on the voyage off Malacca, but his successor, Dom Luis Cerqueira, likewise a Jesuit, reached Nagasaki on August 5, 1598, and remained at the head of the Catholic Church in Japan for more than fifteen eventful years until his death in 1614. During all this time the friars were virtually the bane of his existence, as they had been that of Valignano according to the father-visitor's own confession. Both these Jesuits as well as a succession of viceroys, archbishops, and other civil and ecclesiastical dignitaries of Portuguese India, wrote repeatedly to the King and the Pope, complaining bitterly of the unwanted and unauthorized intrusion of the friars on their cherished preserves, but all in vain. Fray Jerónimo de Jesús publicly proclaimed in 1598 that he and his colleagues would stay in Japan in spite of Pope, King, prelate or governor; and Bishop Cerqueira, writing to the Archbishop of Goa in November, 1604, ruefully admitted that the Franciscan had made good his boast.

The friars were supported in their contumacious stand by the ecclesiastical and secular authorities at Manila. The Jesuit Bishop complained, "they have all of them been most earnest to help this passage, and they aspire, it is to be feared, to subordinate the spiritual [jurisdiction] of Japan to the archbishopric of Manila, and to make this commerce common to both Spaniards and Portuguese." That was indeed the long and the short of it; and this international rivalry was the main reason for the Spanish friars retaining their foothold in Japan, despite all the efforts of the Portuguese Jesuits to dislodge them.[20]

III

It was remarked in the penultimate section that Hideyoshi's fundamental attitude to Christianity is exceedingly difficult to fathom, since his avowed distrust of the foreign religion was usually far from squaring with his actions toward its adherents. If he really regarded Christianity as a potential menace to national security, it is odd that he should have gone out of his way to put avowed Christian daimyo, such as Konishi Yukinaga and Gamo Ujisato, into positions of peculiar trust and influence. That he was under no obligation to favor any particular daimyo, becomes clearly apparent in considering the structure of feudal Japan during Hideyoshi's heyday, as sketched by those close and keen observers, the Portuguese father, Luis Frois, and the Italian visitor, Alessandro Valignano.

Writing in 1588, Frois explains that the Kwambaku (as he then was) could and did distribute the feudal fiefs among the daimyo as he saw fit. These lands were then subdivided among their relatives, retainers, and samurai, who, in return, were obliged to furnish certain services to their liege lord, both in peace and war, at their own cost. Although the land was thus nominally distributed among the bushi or samurai class, in practice this ownership was the right of tax collection, the true owners being, in spite of several and increasing restrictions, the peasant cultivators of the soil. The tax usually took the form of a percentage of the total crop (rice being, of course, the staple) and this was fixed by Hideyoshi in 1589 or thereabouts, at the ratio of "one third to the cultivator and two thirds to the lord." He ordered a nationwide cadastral survey to be made, in order to ensure that all available arable land was being both cultivated and taxed, thus ending the chaos into which the demarcation of landed property had fallen during the centuries of feudal anarchy. By this and other methods he increased the cultivated area by ten per cent.

Although he simultaneously abolished many other local, vexatious or redundant taxes, the net result of his drastic land-tax reform, when taken in conjunction with other measures designed to stabilize the existing feudal society, was to increase the burden on the peasant class. His enactments included the prohibition of farmers leaving their land or avocation without the permission of their feudal lord, and the confiscation of all weapons which belonged to persons other than samurai. These edicts stultified the growth of a yeoman or peasant-warrior class, which, in some districts at least, was one of the by-products of the civil wars. Hideyoshi himself was the son of such a peasant soldier, but he evidently had no love for the class from which he had sprung. Once he had attained the supreme power, his policy, like that of most despots, inevitably tended to try to stabilize the existing social structure on the basis of

> God bless the squire and his relations
> and keep us in our proper stations.

But although he tried to ossify (as it were) the social hierarchy as a whole, he had as little compunction about moving individuals as pawns on a chessboard. After the subjugation of the Odawara Hojo in 1590, Hideyoshi was the undisputed

master of Japan from the Straits of Tsugaru to the tip of
Tanegashima, and the first ruler for five hundred years whose
writ ran unquestioned throughout the length and breadth
of the land. Frois says that he used three principal methods
to consolidate his hold on the country, which may be briefly
summarized at this point.[21]

First was his policy of rearranging the distribution of fiefs
periodically in order to ensure the maintenance of his strategic ascendency. Nobunaga had done the same thing on a
smaller scale; but neither he nor the Ashikaga shoguns had
ever wielded such effective power over so wide an area, and,
consequently, could not do it with equal thoroughness. Frois
points out that these moves gave no trouble to Hideyoshi.
He merely promulgated a brief edict with a list of fief changes,
specifying that by a certain day daimyo A would exchange
fiefs with daimyo B, whereas daimyo C would be stripped
of his and exiled, and so on. On one occasion, twenty-three
fiefs changed hands in a day. These changes or depositions
did not involve merely the daimyo and their families, but
their retainers and samurai as well, all of whom "must needs
pack up and leave with what they could carry, without
speaking or saying a word, and if they did not bestir themselves speedily, those who came in with the incoming daimyo
would as likely as not seize their goods and let them lump it."
However unequal the exchange, the daimyo must not only
show no sign whatsoever of resentment, but make the dictator
a costly gift of "thanks" to boot.

By manipulating the daimyo and samurai in this way,
Hideyoshi could station those whom he trusted in strategic
centers around the capital and elsewhere, or displace territorial lords of long standing to make room for men of his
own creation, such as the Christian daimyo, Konishi Yukinaga and Kuroda Josui, both of whom he raised from ob-
scurity to affluence. Local ties were thus broken, and potential centers of disaffection could be painlessly "purged"
in this manner, or by placing mutually hostile daimyo, such
as Konishi and Kato Kiyomasa, in neighboring fiefs to keep

watch on one another. Frois states, further, that (contrary to what Professor Murdoch has stated) Hideyoshi did employ on a large scale William the Conqueror's favorite device for weakening his feudatories, namely, by giving a daimyo different areas of land in widely separate parts of the country, thus preventing the formation of too many homogeneous territorial fiefs. Finally, in making these periodic redistributions of land, Hideyoshi was prone to detach particularly valuable sites or areas for his own use. He thus acquired private domains bringing him an annual income of more than two million in gold, "which seems incredible for a Japanese feudal lord" as Gaspar Coelho noted. The modern historian, Takekoshi, gives Hideyoshi's income from his private landed property as a little more than two million koku of rice, which is probably what Coelho meant, and which amounted apparently to about an eighth of the total production.

One untoward result of these periodic mass migrations of samurai, was the breakup of their families and the consequent commonness of divorce. Valignano, writing in 1592, explains that although all samurai had to follow their liege lord to his new fief or to exile, as the case might be, very few wanted to take their wives with them, nor did the vast majority of the women wish to leave. Since every samurai was compelled by law to live with a woman and could not lead a bachelor existence, both spouses divorced and remarried with the utmost facility, although the father-visitor does not explain what became of the children by the first marriage. Evidently, in the Keicho period at least, the samurai merely swapped wives when their respective daimyo exchanged fiefs, but this "general post" attitude toward matrimony naturally did not meet with the approval of those who had been nurtured on the precepts of the Council of Trent.

Valignano wrote that the Church's reluctance to grant divorce or to recognize the validity of a new marriage on such occasions was one of the greatest obstacles to conversion among the bushi. Quite apart from this, he added, the Japanese cannot for the life of them understand the Christian doctrine of one man one wife, for better or for worse; since they considered it utterly unreasonable to expect a person to remain tied for life to a bad or intolerable spouse of either sex. He therefore pressed the Jesuit general at Rome to obtain some temporary relaxation of the Church's Tridentine rulings on lawful matrimony; but I am not aware that he got any satisfaction, except on a few minor points, such as a waiving of the provision that the marriage ceremony must be performed by a parish priest in the presence of witnesses.[22]

Hideyoshi's second device for increasing his own power at the expense of his feudatories was to amass wealth by every possible means. Here again his policy was not, in its broad outline, new of itself; but he was able to apply it more sweepingly and thoroughly than his predecessors, and he invented new pretexts to secure his ends. All daimyo had to make him costly gifts twice yearly (January 1, and August 1), silver and gold coin or bullion being preferred. Similar presents were expected whenever a daimyo changed his fief, whether he benefited or the reverse by the exchange. Confiscations and foreign trade proved another useful source of income, although Hideyoshi never showed himself disposed to kill the goose that laid the golden egg by imposing crippling taxes on the Portuguese traders. Indeed, his policy was the free and enlightened one of encouraging them, as some, at least, had the grace to recognize.

If he was greedy about amassing money, he was certainly no niggard in spending it, as his lavish entertainments, such as the gigantic ceremonial tea party at Kitano (1587) and the flower-viewing party at the Sambo temple (1598) attest, apart from the magnificent structures he reared at Osaka, Kyoto, and Fushimi. Osaka owes its rise as one of the great commercial centers of the Far East entirely to him, and it is a more enduring monument to his megalomania than the vanished beauties of the Jurakudai or "Palace of Pleasures" and Momoyama palace. He also made lavish distributions of gold and silver coins to deserving samurai on occasion, in this

respect resembling rather his predecessor, the open-handed
Nobunaga, than his successor, the miserly Ieyasu. Mention
of Hideyoshi's grandiose building projects brings me to the
third and last of his measures to achieve power and popularity, and this was his indulgence of the popular fancy by
lavish display, pomp, and ceremony.

His actions in this respect include the erection of the
Daibutsu at Kyoto. The Jesuits stress that he had no pro-
Buddhist sympathies; and indeed, Valignano considered that
Hideyoshi had done more to break the political power of the
Buddhist church than had Nobunaga. But he knew that such
a move would be popular with the mass of the people and so
it proved. He further contrived to make the best of both
worlds by making the construction of the image a pretext for
confiscating all weapons of the non-samurai class, for beating not into ploughshares but nails and bolts, which he assured the naïve owners would bring them felicity in the next
world as well as in this.

Another astute and popular move in this direction, was
his attitude to the Tenno whose court, income, and outward
standing he improved and enriched on a scale undreamed of
since the golden days of the *Genji Monogatari*. The kuge or
court nobility likewise shared in the new prosperity of the
imperial court, and were consequently well-disposed toward
Hideyoshi, who likewise derived both honor and profit from
a lavish distribution of the (as always) coveted court titles
among upstart daimyo. The grateful emperor was induced to
pay a state visit to Hideyoshi in 1588, being lavishly entertained for five days, after which he returned to his own palace,
"leaving Hideyoshi with the lordship and control of all Japan,
with all the wealth and resources he could extract therefrom,
and in great repute and glory with the people, whereas the
poor Tenno was left with only the shadow of the name as
hitherto," the Jesuit vice-provincial sourly noted.[23]

I have no space to deal here with Hideyoshi's other innovations, such as the erection of prisons, nor to follow the vicissitudes of that ill-starred adventure into which his growing

megalomania led him, the sorry story of the *Chosen Seibatsu* or expedition to Korea. This inexcusable and wasteful enterprise apart, the Taiko Hideyoshi's measures were in the main salutary and beneficial to the nation as a whole. The rise in the general standard of living is apparent from the Jesuit *Letters,* as is the gradual diffusion of wealth and culture over the whole country. This process was presumably accelerated by the frequent changes of daimyo and their samurai from one fief to another, since the culture of the Kyoto district was thereby carried to the remoter parts of the empire, which, in the earlier Nara and Heian periods, had been hardly affected by the high cultural level of the capital. The regent's lavish, if admittedly somewhat uncritical patronage of the arts, was also responsible for the flowering of the Kano school of screen painters, and the one good result of the wasteful Korean expedition was the introduction of new and improved methods of making porcelain by captive Korean potters.

So far as Christianity was concerned, it is clear from the Jesuits' correspondence that Hideyoshi connived not merely at their presence in Kyushu, despite the terms of his expulsion edict, but at Konishi's ardent propagation of the Faith, by methods which at times came perilously close to those which had been the ostensible cause of Takayama Ukon's undoing. Valignano in his "Obediencias" of 1592, went on record as stating that Hideyoshi had on the whole done more to foster Christianity than to suppress it, since his exclusion edict was more than outweighed by his keeping the Buddhist church in its place and by his support of the Christian daimyo. His motives in this policy of toleration were undoubtedly somewhat mixed, but that Mammon was his lodestar rather than God is clear not only from what was set forth in the last chapter, but from a more detailed consideration of his attitude to the town and traders of Nagasaki.[24]

It will be remembered that after a brief occupation by Shimadzu of Satsuma in 1586, Nagasaki had been taken over by Hideyoshi during his Kyushu campaign of 1587; but the municipal government was left in the hands of a locally elected number of elders, who were, to all intents and purposes, nominees of the Jesuits. Hideyoshi's visiting commissioners (bugyo and daikwan) seem to have limited their activities to buying for their master a good portion of the best silks in the cargo annually brought by the Great Ship from Macao, a business in which, as noted, the Jesuits were likewise closely interested. Nagasaki was still virtually Portuguese territory, and this fact was pointed out to Hideyoshi by the Dominican friar, Juan Cobo, and by his disgruntled Spanish companions in 1592, or so the Jesuits professed to believe. Father Frois, who, after all, was in a position to know, further assures his readers that the Spaniards alleged that the obstructive attitude of their Portuguese fellow subjects at Macao and Nagasaki was the main reason why no Spanish trading ships had come to Japan hitherto. Hideyoshi flew into one of his real or simulated rages on hearing this, and sent commissioners posting down to Nagasaki with orders to tell the Portuguese to stop behaving as if they had taken the place by force of arms, and to destroy all the local churches and ecclesiastical establishments forthwith, sending the wood to his field headquarters at Nagoya in Hizen. The bugyo, Terazawa Hirotaka, was entrusted with investigating the complaints of the defrauded Peruvian merchant, de Solis, and others against the Portuguese (August, 1592).

Things looked very awkward, but, as with the 1597 edict, they petered out rather inconclusively in the end. One church and a few houses were dismantled, but Terezawa accepted a not very princely gift of twenty-five ducats to spare the remainder, which indicates that Hideyoshi could hardly have been in earnest. Terazawa and his colleague the daikwan, Murayama Toan, reported that the Portuguese had been maligned by the Spaniards; and since Hideyoshi was mainly preoccupied by the progress of the Korean expedition, the whole business subsided as suddenly as it had arisen. The Jesuits were left in peace and quiet once more, although they had lost one of their churches thanks to the Philippine emissaries, as Frois dolefully observed.

The point is that Hideyoshi was satisfied with bringing the foreign community to a sense of their obligations on Japanese soil, and had no intention of pushing matters to extremities. A year later he gave formal permission for a few Jesuits to stay permanently in Nagasaki, for the express purpose of assisting in the Portuguese-Japanese commercial negotiations connected with the disposal of the Great Ship's cargo. Not even the *San Felipe* affair shook his confidence in his interpreter, Father João Rodriguez, who was with him when he died, and who has left on record his sorrow at seeing a man of such undoubted genius destined for hell-fire.[25]

Valignano, writing his annual report in October, 1599, a year after Hideyoshi's death, does not conceal his admiration for the statesmanship which the latter had displayed in arranging for the undisputed succession of his infant son Hideyori. He describes how he entrusted the chief power to a board of five ministers (*tairo*), namely, the leading daimyo Tokugawa Ieyasu, Maeda Toshiie, Mori Terumoto, Ukita Hideie, and Uesugi Kagekatsu, with the first-named as chief. As a check on these territorial magnates, he associated five commissioners (bugyo), namely his own trusted officials, Ishida Kazushige (Mitsunari), Asano Nagamasa, Masuda Nagamori, Nagatsuka Masaie, and Maeda Genni Hoin, with the ministers in the government, cementing their connection with solemn oaths, matrimonial alliances, and a judicious distribution of the sweets of office and money. The expeditionary forces were also recalled from Korea, in accordance with the Taiko Hideyoshi's last will and testament. Although rival cliques were being formed among the returning daimyo, no fighting had broken out hitherto, and some preliminary misunderstanding between Ieyasu on the one hand, and Ishida and Konishi on the other, had been settled to the satisfaction of both parties.

Valignano reported that Ieyasu was indubitably the *primus inter pares*, showing himself tolerant and forbearing not only to potential rivals like Ishida, but to the nominally prescribed foreign religious as well. He followed his predecessor's example in being particularly gracious to Padre João Rodriguez, and wrote to the daikwan of Nagasaki, telling this official to seek the coöperation of the local padres in the management of the port and to ensue it. Encouraged by this unexpected display of benevolence, Rodriguez sounded Ieyasu on the possibility of his promulgating an edict formally revoking Hideyoshi's anti-Christian laws of 1587 and 1597. Ieyasu replied that it was too early then to flout the memory of the illustrious dead by giving official recognition to Christianity, "but that everything would come to pass in good time." A few months later (February, 1600), Valignano wrote jubilantly that Ieyasu had said that everyone was free to choose what faith he preferred, and, more specifically, that the padres and Christians of Nagasaki could live unmolested as such. This intimation was naturally regarded as being virtually the same as a formal edict of restitution, so that Christianity was increasing by leaps and bounds, 30,000 converts being baptized in six months in Konishi's fief of Higo alone.[26]

Although Valignano was full of admiration for Ieyasu's adroit diplomacy whereby the *kubo* had secured the virtual dictatorship of Japan without unsheathing his sword, a trial of strength was inevitable. Earlier forecasts of the outbreak of war after the return of the disgruntled daimyo from Korea proved correct. The story of the Sekigahara campaign is too well known for repetition here. It suffices to say that after the confederates had outmaneuvered Ieyasu in the opening round, they were decisively defeated on the Moor of the Barrier (October 20, 1600), mainly owing to the treachery of Kobayakawa and the cowardice of Mori Terumoto. The Jesuits pay frank tribute to Ieyasu's statesmanlike moderation after the victory, his revengeful measures being virtually limited to the execution of the three curiously-assorted ringleaders; the intriguing official Ishida Mitsunari, the militant Buddhist monk, Ankokuji Ekei, and the chivalrous Christian daimyo, Konishi Yukinaga.

Ieyasu had previously made great efforts to attach the latter to his side, even betrothing his granddaughter to Konishi's young son; but Konishi refused his blandishments, considering himself in honor bound to support Toyotomi Hideyori, to whose father he owed everything, as he frankly admitted. It was widely believed—by the Franciscan friars among others —that the Jesuits had either egged on Konishi to oppose Ieyasu, or at any rate refrained from dissuading him, as they easily could have done, "for he was very obedient to the padres." The Jesuits deny this charge emphatically, and certainly there is nothing in their correspondence of 1599–1600 to support it. Nevertheless, Konishi was the outstanding Christian daimyo, and they naturally feared, immediately after the battle, that Ieyasu would suspect them of inciting Konishi against him, and they were correspondingly ill at ease.

From this anxiety they were speedily and pleasantly disillusioned. If Ieyasu had any rancor against them he dissembled it, but his actions tend to show that he had none. He accepted the aged Father Organtino's congratulations kindly, and was so pleased with the commercial exertions of Father João Rodriguez (whom he had taken over from Hideyoshi as interpreter and trading agent) at Nagasaki, that he signed three letters patent allowing the padres and Christians the use of their cult and churches in Nagasaki, Kyoto, and Osaka. This was an immense step forward, virtually amounting to the formal annulment of Hideyoshi's expulsion edict of 1587, since all previous concessions had been merely verbal "gentlemen's agreements," or unspoken understandings. This benevolence was likewise reflected in the attitude of the majority of daimyo and of the Nagasaki officials. Altogether, far from the Battle of Sekigahara and Ieyasu's accession to power marking the beginning of the decline of Christianity, as is usually asserted, on the contrary it ushered in a period of expansion, fruitful if shortlived.[27]

This much is apparent from an examination of the original letters of the Japan Jesuits for the years 1600–1604. They state therein that had Hideyori's partisans won, respect for his father's memory would have prevented his champions from abrogating Hideyoshi's anti-Christian decree, apart from the

fact that, except for Konishi, few of them had any love
for Christianity, and they would have been divided in their
views. Ieyasu, on the contrary, was now the unchallenged
military dictator of the country, and under no obligation to
obey the late-lamented Hideyoshi's injunctions if they did
not suit him. The majority of the Christian daimyo had sided
with Ieyasu and not with Konishi; and in the redistribution
of fiefs after Sekigahara, the Christian daimyo and Christian sympathizers were handsomely rewarded by the victor.
Konishi's death was indeed a great loss, the more so since his
Higo fief was inherited by the fervent Buddhist, Kato
Kiyomasa; but this disaster was more than offset by the greatly
increased power and prestige of such staunch supporters as
Kuroda Nagamasa (Fukuoka), Asano Yukinaga (Wakayama), and Hosokawa Tadaoki (Buzen), all of whom summoned padres to work in their expanded fiefs. Kuroda
promised the Jesuits that he would take Konishi's place as
their protector and advocate at court.

Nor were these the limits of Ieyasu's direct and indirect
toleration of Christianity. So delighted was he with the commercial acumen of his astute priest-interpreter that, after a
brief misunderstanding over some unsatisfactory purchases
made on his behalf by others from the cargo of the Great
Ship in 1602, he appointed Padre João Rodriguez as his commercial agent at Nagasaki, directly responsible to himself.
Not only so, but he dismissed the (latterly) unfriendly bugyo,
Terazawa Shinano-no-kami, and entrusted the municipal
government of the port to a council of four headmen, local
Christians or their sympathizers, under the chairmanship of
a glib-tongued convert known as Murayama Toan or Antonio, enjoining them to work in close coöperation with the
Jesuits. Moreover, when he heard the next year that the padres
were practically penniless, owing to the loss of their annual
silk investment in the Macao carrack which had been captured
by the Hollanders (July, 1603), he spontaneously offered the
Jesuits a donation equivalent to 350 cruzados,—"whereat

the whole court was amazed, since the shogun did not usually give anything to anybody."

At the same time, the Jesuits were under no illusion about the motives for Ieyasu's unwonted benevolence. They realized that, unlike Hideyoshi, he was a practicing Buddhist, and as such either hostile or indifferent to the claims of militant Christianity. But they further recognized his great desire to foster foreign trade; and since, like his predecessor, he regarded Jesuits as essential intermediaries in this matter, he was prepared to tolerate their missionary activities, provided always that they restricted their efforts to the middle and lower classes, and did not try to convert any of the daimyo. It may be added that he was not altogether wrong in his assumption that the presence of the Jesuits was essential for the smooth progress of Portuguese-Japanese trading, since they were the only well-educated linguists available; and their mediation, if not always absolutely necessary, at any rate indubitably facilitated matters and lessened the chances of mutual misunderstandings. So delighted were the Japan Jesuits with the shogun's mild government of the country in general and his toleration of Christianity in particular, that they regarded the discovery of new gold mines on Sado Island, which brought him in nearly a million and a half of gold a year, as a direct reward from God. He was consolidating his temporal power with the erection of a colossal castle at Yedo (modern Tokyo). The Jesuits estimated that more than 300,000 men were employed on these *corvées*, all furnished and fed by different daimyo in rotation, "the shogun not giving them anything beyond a little rice now and again as extra rations." [28]

Encouraged unduly by this toleration, the Kyoto Jesuits ventured on a rather tactless step at the funeral service for one of their flock, a Christian daughter of the noble Kyogoku family. This was celebrated with a full choral service in great splendor, and rounded off by an eloquent sermon by the Japanese brother, Fabian, who proved the falsity of all Buddhist teaching with a wealth of polemical arguments. This ill-timed display of zeal was duly reported with suitable embellishments by local Buddhist dignitaries to Ieyasu, who was at first understandably annoyed thereat. However, he soon calmed down, and observed sarcastically that priests of all creeds were alike in their desire to obtain converts by traducing the tenets of their theological opponents. He added that he did not care what converts Christianity made among the lower classes, provided that the daimyo were unaffected, and that "the conversion of merchants was all to the good, since this would foster trade with the Portuguese and with the Spaniards of the Philippines." No clearer indication could be given of Ieyasu's idea of the relative importance of God and Mammon in the scheme of things. It is true that at the request of Yodogimi, Hideyori's mother, the shogun published a very mild and rather vague anti-Christian edict at Osaka in 1604, but this was intended, as he clearly let it be understood, for strictly local consumption. It was more than offset by his reception of Padre Morejon, rector of the Kyoto seminary, whom he had refused to see hitherto, and by the audience which he gave to the Bishop of Japan, Luis de Cerqueira, at Kyoto in 1606.

This audience was regarded as a great triumph for Christianity, since Cerqueira was received in his avowed capacity as Jesuit bishop of Japan; whereas Valignano had only been received by Hideyoshi at Kyoto in his role of secular envoy from the viceroy of India. It was largely the work of Padre João Rodriguez, who had once more won the old man's heart with a present of a magnificent clock "which likewise showed the movements of the sun and moon and indicated the days of the week," ably abetted by one of Ieyasu's most trusted retainers, Honda Kodzuke-no-suké. Bishop Cerqueira's reception left nothing to be desired, since he was received with the same protocol as would have been given to a prince of the blood, "which was an outstanding honor." It was followed up next year with a similar trip by Vice-Provincial Francisco Pasio, who visited both Ieyasu at Shidzuoka, and his son Hidetada, to whom he had just handed over the shogunate, at Yedo. The ubiquitous Honda was also much to the fore on this occasion, when the vice-provincial gave him a treatise specially composed to prove that the Christian commandments inculcated full obedience to feudal lords, and that Christianity was not a subversive religion, as Ieyasu had supposed when he forbade the conversion of daimyo.

On his return to Nagasaki, Pasio ventured on the rather questionable step (as Professor Murdoch observes) of visiting the Tokugawa's potential rival, Toyotomi Hideyori, at Osaka. The youthful Hideyori and his anti-Christian mother, Yodogimi, received the Jesuit very cordially; but this visit probably did him more harm than good in the eyes of the jealous Tokugawa. Both Bishop Cerqueira and Vice-Provincial Pasio rounded off their respective journeys by visiting Hosokawa Tadaoki, who had shown himself increasingly friendly to the Faith ever since the heroic death of his Christian wife, Gracia, at Osaka in 1600. Tadaoki gave generous hospitality and new homes in his fief at Buzen (Kokura) to hundreds of Christian refugees from Hirado, whose daimyo was one of the few persecutors in Japan. He told the Jesuits that he would become a Christian at once, were it not for the Catholic Sixth Commandment which he felt constitutionally incapable of observing in good faith.[29]

Cerqueira's satisfaction at the unexpected success of his episcopal visit was tempered by some unfortunate developments which had occurred at Nagasaki. This place, it will be remembered, had originally been given to the Jesuits, and taken over from them by the central government after Hideyoshi's edict of 1587, although they still retained a large if indirect share in the municipal administration. The city had long outgrown its original bounds, but only that part within the area actually ceded by Omura Sumitada in 1570, was regarded as being the city proper and administered by a local self-governing municipal council, periodically supervized by shogunal commissioners of the rank of bugyo and daikwan. The remainder of the town area was regarded as being within Omura's fief, and this unsatisfactory duality led to constant disputes and quarrels, and malefactors escaped arrest by slipping from one area into the other. The inhabitants of the inner town depended on the surrounding country for all their food, fuel, timber, cattle, and even drinking and laundry water, nor did Omura's minions lose any chance of deriving a substantial "rake-off" from the supply of these daily necessities. The municipal council had often tried to buy out Omura, or otherwise to arrange the amalgamation of the two zones, but he had always declined to come to terms.

In 1605, one of Ieyasu's cronies named Ogasawara, came to Nagasaki on official business for his lord, and the municipal councilors complained to him of the anomalous situation with its resultant denigration to Ieyasu's power and prestige as lord of only a limited area of the town. Ogasawara agreed with their representations, and on his return to court, he took a map of the situation with him, proposing to Ieyasu that Omura's land in and around Nagasaki should be incorporated within the city limits, he being given additional land in compensation elsewhere. The shogun agreed, but the arrangement was carried out in such a way that the value of Omura's new lands was much less than the valuable property he had lost in the growing port. Knowing Padre João Rodriguez' great influence at court, Omura suspected him of having engineered the whole business, particularly as Rodriguez and some of the city fathers were at court when Ogasawara returned with his report. So furious was he with what he believed to be the Jesuit's ungrateful treachery, that he apostatized from the Faith and forthwith expelled all the padres from his fief, becoming a persecutor instead of a protector of Christians. When Ogasawara returned next year, the Jesuits persuaded him to visit Omura and tell him that the shogun's action had been taken on his (Ogasawara's) recommendation, and that the padres were blameless in the matter. But Omura proved obdurate, and he and his family were lost to the Church for good.

Apart from this unfortunate imbroglio, and a few local persecutions in the fiefs of Matsura (Hirado), Kato (Higo), and Mori (Yamaguchi), Christianity in Japan was never more prosperous than during the first half-dozen years of Tokugawa rule. In 1606, the Jesuits could claim a Christian community of about 750,000 believers, with an average annual increase of five or six thousand, and Nagasaki could vie with Manila and Macao for the title of the "Rome of the Far East." [30]

Chapter V. CHRISTIAN CULTURE AND MISSIONARY LIFE

I T can be argued, in a general way, that a nation which has attained a high degree of culture of its own cannot be profoundly affected by that of another race, unless afforded the opportunity for the interchange (or at least the importation) of ideas over a considerable period of time. Commercial and political intercourse are not of themselves sufficient to bring about far-reaching changes in the national way of life or outlook; although either commerce or diplomacy may act as the vehicle for the importation of ideas, religion, or philosophy. Thus Buddhism was originally introduced into Japan through the medium of Korean diplomatic missions; and the spread of Islam through Indonesia, from Malaya to Mindanao, seems to have been more the work of Arab and Gujarati traders in the first instance than the calculated religious propaganda of the missionary caste known as the Hadramaut Sayyids. By the time that the Portuguese reached Japan, the island empire had already developed a deeply rooted culture of its own and had absorbed what it had originally derived from China and Korea.

Despite the early sanguine prognostications of the Jesuits, it is evident that they could only hope for lasting success if they could continue their religious propaganda for a sufficient length of time to get their ideas across and let them sink in. The paucity of their numbers rendered this an exceedingly difficult task from the first, since they could hardly rely on their lay compatriots and co-religionists to exercise any great influence on Japanese life and thought. Valignano limned the situation with his usual accuracy when he pointed out, in 1583, that owing to the geographical and political isolation of Japan, it was only the Jesuits who could introduce new ideas. He explained that the average Japanese felt no urge for foreign travel ("ni ellos son curiosos de salir de su tierra para yr ver otras"), and the Spaniards were forbidden to come to Japan by Pope and King alike. The merchants from Macao did not attempt to go further inland than the Kyushu ports, "and because of the great difference in language, manners, and customs, the Japanese think very little of them, and they still less of the Japanese." Their mutual intercourse was therefore confined to indispensable commercial negotiations, and even in these matters they often had to have the help of Jesuit interpreters. From all of this it followed that the Jesuits were the only Europeans able to inaugurate an interchange of ideas involving religion, philosophy, literature, and art.[1]

The printed word is of course one of the most potent factors in the propagation of ideas, and the Japanese were familiar with wood-block or xylographic engraving for centuries before the arrival of the Jesuits. Curiously enough, the latter do not seem to have exploited this technique to any appreciable extent. This is all the more surprising, since their colleagues of the neighboring China mission made the most extensive use of this process; the first of their many xylographic productions being the Chinese catechism printed by Fathers Ruggieri and Ricci in Kwangtung in 1584. Contrariwise, the Japan Jesuits made great use of a press with movable metal types from 1590 to 1614; whereas their colleagues in China did not utilize this method, but clung to their wood blocks even for works published at Canton, Peking, and Heungshan in European languages.

As early as 1549, Francis Xavier was endeavoring to compose devotional treatises in Japanese for circulation among potential neophytes; but these works, like the dictionary and grammar ascribed to Father Duarte de Silva (who worked in Japan from 1552–1564) in 1564, were evidently circulated in manuscript. The work of copying and distributing these religious and linguistic treatises was both burdensome

---

[1] For notes to chapter v, see pages 475–483.

and slow, as the older missionaries often complained; but nothing seems to have been done about it, until the arrival of the indefatigable Valignano, who was soon busy with schemes for the introduction of more modern methods. The origin of the celebrated Jesuit mission press in Japan is to be found in a letter written by the father-visitor from Goa to Theotonio de Braganza, Archbishop of Evora, on December 1, 1587, which also throws an interesting sidelight on the Jesuits' educational methods. Valignano wrote:

As regards your Lordship's opinion that heretical books should not be introduced into Japan, nor those which contain heathen mythology, this is so fit and proper that it would be a great mistake to do otherwise. This is why not only have we forbidden such things, but further ordained that the youths in all the seminaries should only study from very holy and Catholic works, whence they will learn Latin in such a way as to imbibe simultaneously Christian precepts and virtue and to abhor vices. Even as regards the philosophy and theology which we are to teach them, we must omit all mention of differences of opinion, erroneous viewpoints, and controversial topics, for a long time at least, and we must confine ourselves to teaching them only tried and tested true Catholic doctrine. Not even our holy books should be introduced indiscriminately into Japan, especially those which confute heresies and other abuses which are sometimes prevalent in European Christendom. For this reason I have ordered a printing press which I am taking with me to Japan, so that we can print there such books as are fit for circulation in Japan after having been previously censored and purified.

Acting on this principle, not merely the *Fables* of the heathen Aesop, but even the *Sinner's Guide* (*Guia do Pecador*) of the great Spanish devotional writer, Fray Luis de Granada, O.P., were recast by the Jesuits before publication in Japan.[2]

It will be observed that in his letter of 1587, Valignano speaks of only one press, which it is clear from his previous letters was one equipped with a font of movable Latin type, and from which a few works were printed at Goa and Macao in 1588–1590, before the arrival of the press in Japan with Valignano in July of this last year. From Valignano's correspondence and from some rather ambiguous entries in the minutes of the Kazusa missionary conference in August, 1590, it seems probable that the visitor brought with him some metal matrices for the *katakana* syllabary, besides others for the commonest Sino-Japanese characters, which he had previously suggested ordering from Italy or Flanders. However this may be, they do not seem to have been used, since the earliest recorded productions of the Jesuit mission press are in Roman type. True enough, the press was soon expanded to include works in *kana* (chiefly *hiragana*) and characters, but these were cast first from wooden and later from metal types. From 1591 to 1614, this press produced a remarkable series of devotional and linguistic works in Latin and Japanese. These have nowadays attained a bibliographical rarity and interest comparable to those of the Gutenberg Bible or the Shakespeare First Folio.

The works published by the Jesuit mission press in its heyday, which roughly coincided with the Keicho period (1596–1614), can be divided into three main groups. First, those translated from a European language into Japanese. With the solitary exception of Aesop's *Fables,* these all seem to have been devotional or religious catechisms, calendars, and the like. Second, works adapted from Japanese originals, such as the *Heike Monogatari.* Third, and most interesting to the modern student, were the linguistic works, grammars, and dictionaries which reflect the greatest credit on their originators and mark the beginning of the serious study of the Japanese language. Since the titles of the works published by the Jesuit mission press in Japan are readily available to the interested reader in the standard bibliographies of Satow, Cordier, Koda, and Laures, to mention only a few of the writers on this topic, I shall confine myself to a brief consideration of some typical examples of each class.[3]

The earliest recorded volume, *Sanctos no Gosagyo,* printed at Kazusa in 1591, is a compendium of the Lives of the Saints, adapted from the *Flos Sanctorum,* and other sources. It includes a section on martyrdom, dealing with examples taken from Roman times, and the translation of a part of a treatise on martyrdom by Fray Luis de Granada. These translations are the work of Paulo Yoho and his son Vicente, according to Professor M. Anesaki. The same authority says that the style and quality of the Kirishitan literature of the Keicho period, as evinced in these *romaji* versions and in the later hiragana versions compiled by Japanese dojuku and brothers, do not fall below the standard of the best Buddhist literature of the preceding century, and far surpass that of the Keicho era. Fray Luis de Granada, was evidently a popular writer with the Jesuits, who requited the affection which he, unlike most other Dominicans, showed to the Society. Thus his version of the *Imitatio Christi* of Thomas à Kempis was used by them in their preparation of the Japanese edition published under the title *Contemptus Mundi* at Amakusa in 1596. The *Fides no doxi,* printed at the same place and abridged in 1592, is likewise a translation of Granada's *El Sumario de la Introducción del Símbolo de la Fé* (Salamanca, 1582), with some sections, such as that on the martyrdom of Father Campion in England, omitted. This was presumably in line with Valignano's policy of 1587, to suppress all mention of contemporary heresy, in order to avoid giving the Japanese neophytes "dangerous thoughts." What is perhaps the most celebrated literary production of this press, the *Guia do Pecador* or *Sinner's Guide,* printed in two volumes at Nagasaki in 1599–1600, is likewise an abridged translation of one of Fray Luis de Granada's most popular masterpieces, which has been frequently translated into the majority of European languages. It had a second edition in 1606.

I need not specify the Church calendars, manuals, and catechisms which offer no particular points of interest to the lay reader, but will conclude this first section with mention of the *Esopu no Fabulas* or *Fables of Aesop,* printed at Amakusa in 1593, together with an abridgement of the *Heike Monogatari.* This translation of the *Fables* is interesting as being (to my knowledge) the only surviving non-religious literary work translated or adapted by the Jesuits into Japanese. It was probably the work of Fabian Fukansai, for long a pillar of the Church and in later years one of its most formidable opponents as an apostate. Cicero's *Speeches* (in Latin) were printed between 1590 and 1593, but no copy has hitherto come to light.

The preface to the *Heike Monogatari* is dated December 10, 1593, and signed by Fucan Fabian. He explains that his romaji version of this feudal Japanese classic was compiled for the benefit of European Jesuits who were studying the language, and it was accordingly somewhat abridged and simplified by him from the long-winded original. Although this is the only work of its kind extant (it was printed at Amakusa in 1592–1593 together with the *Esopu no Fabulas*), it is known from the *Grammar* of Padre João Rodriguez that many other *monogatari* and *mai* in a mixture of the classical and colloquial styles were edited for the use of European language students. Whether they were all printed at the Jesuit press, or whether they circulated in manuscript or xylographic form is uncertain; but it seems probable that others beside the *Heike* were printed from movable types, since they are quoted by Rodriguez in marginal references to his *Arte* of 1604–1608, in the same way as Aesop's *Fables* are cited. Their titles include the *Kurofune no Monogatari,* which, from the brief extracts given evidently dealt with the arrival of the Portuguese in Japan, the *Bungo no Monogatari,* and the mystery plays or *mai,* fragments of which were identified by Padre Humbertclaude in 1941.[4]

The third and last category of Jesuit press publications is linguistic and grammatical works, which here as in Brazil, Paraguay, Angola, the Philippines, and elsewhere have shed such luster on the labors of the Society. The bitterest critics of the Jesuits have never ventured to deny the value of their pioneer labors in this field, and many language students owe them a lasting debt.

The early Jesuit letters speak in glowing terms of the linguistic attainments of Brother Juan Hernandez, one of Xavier's companions. Padre Luis Frois says in a letter of 1564, that his Spanish colleague had composed a Japanese grammar, "with its conjugations, syntax, and other necessary rules together with two vocabularies in alphabetical order, one in

Portuguese and the other in Japanese." Since, however, the
same informant adds that Hernandez only spent six or seven
months in compiling these works "taking no time off from his
usual prayers and religious exercises," they must have been
rather rough and ready productions, to say the least. There is
little to indicate that either these drafts, or a previous dictionary and grammar compiled by Padre Duarte de Silva were
ever printed xylographically, although the possibility cannot
be altogether excluded. At any rate, when the Spanish friars
from the Philippines settled at Kyoto in 1593, Valignano
states categorically that the local Jesuits gave their unwelcome
colleagues a printed grammar and dictionary, to enable them
to learn the language. He further complained of their base in-
gratitude in stating that these works were so superficial as to
be virtually uselesss; but if they were indeed based on those
compiled by Hernandez in 1564, it is to be feared that the
friars' acidulous criticism was probably not wholly unjustified.

Be this as it may, the earliest linguistic works which have
survived in print are those alluded to in a letter of Francisco
Pasio dated September, 1594, as follows. "The press has been
enriched with a font of *letra grifa* which the natives made at
very little cost, since they are very fine and excellent workmen, and it was beautifully done. We are now printing the
grammar of Father Manuel Alvarez in both the Portuguese
and Japanese tongues, and when this is finished, we will proceed with a Calepin in Portuguese and Japanese, in order that
the Japanese may learn Latin and we of Europe, Japanese."

The first work mentioned by Pasio is the Latin grammar of
Padre Manuel Alvarez, *De Institutione Grammatica,* for many
years a textbook in the Jesuit schools of Europe. The Japanese
version printed at Amakusa in 1594, was mainly intended for
the use of Japanese students of Latin—a language as "pere-
grina" for them as was Japanese for Europeans. Besides conjugations in Latin, Japanese, and Portuguese it gives a number of examples of Japanese sentences in illustration of the
Latin rule of construction, the dialect of which is reminiscent
of the *kyogen* or farces of feudal Japan, according to Satow.

There are also a few quotations from the Confucian Analects and some monogatari. The "Calepin" mentioned by Pasio was the *Dictionarum Latino Lusitanicum ac Iaponicum,* which came off the press next year (1595). Based on the Latin dictionary of Ambrògio Calepío, it was the first printed dictionary of the Japanese language, since native scholars did not begin to study their own tongue scientifically until much later, and as such it is a landmark in Japanese lexicography.

It was closely followed by the *Racuyoxu* (*Rakuyoshu*), a dictionary of Chinese characters with Sino-Japanese readings, printed by the Jesuits at Nagasaki in 1598–1599, which was mainly the work of Japanese brothers and dojuku. It contains several important innovations in Japanese printing which survive to this day, and which may have been suggested by some of the European collaborators. One of these is the printing of the kana alongside the Chinese characters, so as to enable beginners to read the latter easily, a universal custom in modern popular literature. The other is the addition of *handakuon,* or pronunciation marks to certain kana syllables, in order to denote the changes in pronunciation known as *nigori.*[5]

In 1603, appeared the *Vocabulario da Lingoa de Japam com a declaração em Portugues,* with a supplement thereto the following year. This Japanese-Portuguese dictionary is a masterpiece of its kind, containing some thirty thousand words on a great variety of subjects. It includes the technical terms of Buddhism and of Japanese literature, gives copious examples of colloquial expressions, and makes a careful distinction between the dialect of central Japan and that of Kyushu. One of the editors of this vocabulary was the priest-interpreter, João Rodriguez (Tçuzzu or Tsuji), confidant of Hideyoshi and Ieyasu, who had been in Japan since he was a lad of fifteen in the service of old Otomo of Bungo, and who by common consent was the most fluent Japanese scholar of all the Europeans in the country.

Father Rodriguez was the author of the *Arte da Lingoa de Iapam,* printed at Nagasaki between the years 1604 and 1608. This work, the starting point of the scientific study of

Japanese as a language, is divided into three parts. The first
section deals with the rudiments of the language, and is copiously (perhaps too much so) illustrated with examples from
colloquial and classic texts. It is amusing to note in passing
that Rodriguez, in explaining the use of the plural suffix -ra
in its derogatory sense, selects as an illustration the Jews
(*Iudeura, os Judeos*)—surely a rather unexpected note of
anti-Semitism in an out of the way spot. It contains meticulous explanations on the correct pronunciation of Japanese
words, and it is clear from the examples he gives that the pronunciation of colloquial Japanese has remained virtually unchanged for the last three hundred and fifty years.

The second part deals with syntax, and explains the difference between the various provincial dialects and that of the
capital (Kyoto) which Rodriguez inculcates as being the
best and purest spoken in Japan. The third section contains a
treatise on Japanese poetry, with numerous examples, historical information on the imperial dynasty and Japanese chron-
ology, followed by a wealth of commercial information on
prices, weights, coins, and measures, and so on. This last information is not perhaps what the reader would expect to find
recorded so fully in a work primarily intended, like all others
of this series, *ad majorem Dei gloriam;* but it is explained by
Father Rodriguez' position as the official intermediary between the Portuguese merchants at Nagasaki and Ieyasu, a
position which aroused a lot of unfavorable criticism, and one
which even the Bishop of Japan regarded with a good deal of
misgiving. The author rounds off this remarkable work with
a dissertation on the descent of the Chinese from the Lost Ten
Tribes of Israel, of whom he regards the philosophers Lao-
Tse and Confucius as the last surviving exponents.

Admirable as the *Arte da Lingoa de Iapam* indubitably is,
it suffers from a certain prolixity and overelaboration of
which its author was clearly conscious. He apologizes for it in
his preface, "as this is a strange and wandering tongue." He
promised the jaded reader a concise compendium containing
the gist of the whole grammar, which, however, did not see

the light of day until sixteen years later, when Rodriguez had been exiled to Macao. This was the *Arte Breve da Lingoa Japoa* printed at Macao in a very limited edition (100 copies) in 1620. Though much shorter than the *Arte Grande* (as Rodriguez called it) of 1604–1608, it is technically a much better work. The dross and prolixity have been pruned away, and the author formulates his method more concisely and clearly. It is interesting to note that in the 1620 edition, Rodriguez stresses that no amount of book learning or study can ever replace living in a country and participating in the daily life of its inhabitants as the only really satisfactory way of learning the language.

In this second edition of the *Arte,* Rodriguez reverses his earlier stand on learning Japanese with the aid of the monogatari and mai prepared for the use of Europeans by Japanese dojuku, and advocates reading the unadulterated native texts. In this he was perhaps unduly severe. According to the eminent scholar, Professor M. Anesaki, the native Jesuits wrote a singularly mellifluous colloquial Japanese, and the literature they produced was of a higher standard than that of contemporary Buddhists.

From the writings of both Rodriguez and Valignano, it is clear that the Japanese members of the Society, whether brothers or dojuku, took a far greater part in the editing and composition of the works of the Jesuit mission press than many European writers have given them credit for. As with the more numerous xylographic publications of their colleagues in China, although the ideas and the basis of the work are nearly always of European origin, the native dress in which it appears, the style and literary expressions, is almost entirely the work of their native collaborators, whose names for the most part remain unknown. Nor in the nature of things could it have been otherwise; for it may be doubted whether an adult Westerner has ever succeeded in mastering either Chinse or Japanese well enough to compose unaided in either of those languages, a single work of any great extent. This may seem incredible when it is well known how faultlessly many Orientals can write in a European language, but it is, I think, true.

Apart from help given in other directions, one branch of the Jesuit mission press was placed entirely in the hands of Japanese about 1610. This was a natural development, as by this time the Jesuits were evidently dropping the habit of printing vernacular works in romaji, in favor of printing them in hiragana and characters. From Pasio's letter of 1594, it is apparent that Japanese printers could already make matrices at that time, and there were two Japanese printers (trained in Europe) attached to the press from its origin in 1588. Consequently, it is not surprising to find that in 1610–1611, the Jesuits were leaving virtually all the work to the Japanese. In those years books were printed at Kyoto (where a separate press had been established) and at Nagasaki, by Antonio Harada and Thomas Goto Soin, respectively. Although the Nagasaki imprint of 1611 is the last surviving publication of the Jesuit mission press hitherto discovered, it is virtually certain that both the Kyoto publisher and the Nagasaki office were functioning up to the promulgation of Ieyasu's edict of banishment in 1614, when the Nagasaki press at all events was packed up and sent (via Manila) to Macao. Here, except for the *Arte Breve* of 1620, it seems to have been left to rust unused in the godowns; since for one reason or another the art of printing from movable types never found favor in China until the nineteenth century, and the local Jesuits were satisfied with engraving from wood blocks as of old.[6]

Closely connected with the Jesuit mission press was the introduction of copper-plate engraving and oil painting into Japan by the Jesuits. The Portuguese took with them to Japan, as elsewhere in Asia, *retablos*, votive and altar pictures painted in the Flemish school style which was then in vogue in Portugal. Konishi Yukinaga was very proud of a votive picture which had been sent him by the Dowager Queen Catarina of Portugal. Some of these were doubtless copied by Japanese Christians of an artistic turn, if only out of curiosity. The real founder of the Jesuit school of painting was the choleric Italian, Giovanni Nicolo, who, although stigmatized by his superiors as of "less than medium intelligence" in his judgment, knowledge, prudence, and so forth, conducted an atelier which operated successively at Shiki, Arima, Nagasaki (1603–1613), and Macao, (1614–1623). The Japanese proved apt pupils, and the alumni of this atelier produced many paintings for the churches of Kyushu and for those of the China mission.

The works of Jacobo Niwa (son of a Japanese mother and Chinese father) were particularly admired at Peking, where he stayed for some time as assistant to Matteo Ricci. Pasio's above-quoted letter of September, 1594, pays a warm tribute to the great progress made by the pupils of the seminary in copying the paintings and engravings which had been brought from Rome by the Kyushu envoys who returned with Valignano in 1590. Visitors to the same place in 1596 were likewise much impressed by the skill of the Japanese painters in oils. These paintings, like the vast majority of the books printed by the Jesuit mission press, were given away to actual and potential converts, hence they had a wide distribution.

The arts of copper-plate engraving, and engraving from wood blocks, were also taught by the Jesuits in addition to painting in oils and water colors. Here again European prototypes brought from Rome by the envoys of 1582–1590 served as models, as can be seen from an examination of the engravings on the title pages of some of the Jesuit mission press publications, and such few other examples as have survived. Among these last is a copper-plate engraving of the famous picture of "Nuestra Señora de L'Antigua" in Seville Cathedral, which was reproduced in 1597. The Portuguese party which visited the seminary with Bishop Pedro Martins in 1596 was much impressed by seeing the Japanese pupils strike off these engravings which they then distributed to the interested onlookers.

So far as known, these forms of art (painting and engraving) were confined to copies or close adaptations of European originals, chiefly Italian and Spanish. The outbreak of persecution in 1614, and the resultant destruction of all outward evidences of Christianity, not only destroyed almost all of the existing works in Japan, but effectively prevented what might perhaps have developed into something more genuinely Japanese. Among the few survivals may be mentioned three oil paintings in the Professed House of Al Gesù at Rome representing the martyrdoms of 1597–1633, 1619, and 1622, respectively. All three were apparently painted by a Japanese Jesuit (perhaps Niwa) at Macao about 1632. A water-color picture of Xavier and Loyola, together with paintings of the fifteen mysteries of the Virgin were found in the house of a former crypto-Christian family at Takatsuki (in Takayama Ukon's old fief) in 1923. Since these saints were only canonized in 1622, these pictures may have been painted at Macao about 1623, and smuggled secretly into Japan, as were doubtless many others.[7]

Apart from the foregoing more or less slavish copies of European art, Western influence can be discerned in other directions. Chief among the artistic productions of the Keicho era (1594–1618) were the so-called Namban-byobu or Southern Barbarian picture screens, painted by masters of the Kano, Tosa, and Sumiyoshi schools. They owed nothing to Western inspiration in their technique, distinguished by a lavish use of gold leaf, paints made from powdered malachite, lapis-lazuli, and so on, but the motifs were directly inspired by European objects. The favorite theme of these Namban-byobu, is the arrival of a Portuguese carrack and the disembarkation of the captain-major, attended by a suite of richly-dressed fidalgos, followed by a crowd of Negro slaves and coolies bearing presents of Arabian horses, Bengal tigers, peacocks, and other exotic fauna. This scene usually takes up half the picture screen, the other half being occupied by a counterbalancing procession of Japanese officials and townsmen, occasionally intermingled with resident Jesuits and friars advancing to receive the newcomers. Sometimes these screens are in pairs; one screen shows the Black Ship or Kurofune, setting out from her home port of Goa, with the viceroy, archbishop, and other dignitaries speeding the parting vessel; the other screen depicts the arrival at Nagasaki with the disembarkation of fidalgos and their welcome by residents.

Aside from these Namban-byobu proper, there are also picture screens depicting world maps after the style of those in the *Theatrum Orbis Terrarum* of Abraham Ortelius, a copy of which was brought from Rome in 1590, and which was probably the prototype of some of them. For eastern Asia at least, they were no mere slavish copies of the Flemish cartographer's maps, since their depiction of Japan, China, and Korea is far more accurate, and was clearly corrected from native sources. The mysterious Gold and Silver islands (Kinjima and Ginjima), also known as Rica de Oro and Rica de Plata, are likewise depicted on some of these maps. Whether this innovation is of European or Japanese origin it is difficult to say, for these legendary islands were a popular topic among the seamen and navigators of both races.

The byobu form of art became very popular among Europeans also. Valignano was delighted with some beautiful picture screens of Adzuchi which he had received from Nobunaga, and presented them to the Pope. He also ordered a geographical representation of China to be made on a byobu at Macao, which was likewise destined as a gift for the Sovereign Pontiff. He further asked that some picture screens be made at Rome, depicting the Eternal City and other European capitals after the style of the Adzuchi-byobu. Judging by the fact that Namban-byobu depicting Rome, Madrid, Lisbon, and Constantinople have come to light in recent years, it is possible that his request was complied with; although it is equally possible that they were taken from the illustrations of a book such as Braun's *Civitates Orbis Terrarum*. According to the Jesuit "Obediencias" of 1612, the padres were prohibited from decorating their cells with byobu unnecessarily—an interesting indication of their popularity. Mention may also be made of Peter Mundy's enthusiastic description of their beauty and utility as household furnishings at Macao in 1637.

Shah Abbas the Great of Persia was delighted with a pair of gold-leaf byobu which were presented to him by the Portuguese in 1608.

Although Portuguese shipping and personalities at Nagasaki formed a favorite theme with the painters of Namban-byobu, the majority of these screens were not painted there, but by artists of the Kano school at Kyoto and elsewhere. A curious sidelight on this is afforded by one of the perennial quarrels between the Franciscans and Jesuits during the Keicho period. On this particular occasion, four Japanese painters of the Kano school at Kyoto wrote a letter at the instigation of the local Franciscans (or so the Jesuits professed to believe) which contained various vile and baseless insinuations against the Jesuits. This letter was addressed to the heads of the Franciscan, Dominican, and Augustinian orders at Manila, in 1602, and was naturally used to the disadvantage of the Jesuits. Next year the chief culprit, Pedro Kano, came to Nagasaki en route to Manila, and the Jesuits obtained from him a formal retraction on oath of the evidence which he and his companions had given in 1602, as being inspired by malice aforethought and at the instigation of the Franciscan commissary, Fray Jerónimo de Jesús. This otherwise unedifying storm in a teacup serves to show that there was close (if not always very correct) contact between the European missionaries and the painters of the Kano school.[8]

Although medical and surgical science in Renaissance Europe was at an exceedingly low ebb, and sixteenth-century doctors and surgeons probably killed or maimed as many patients as they cured, the Portuguese won some renown in the Far East as healers. How justified this was, it is difficult to say. From a perusal of Garcia d'Orta's *Coloquios*, printed at Goa in 1563, it seems obvious that the native Indian physicians were on the whole decidedly more advanced than their European colleagues. It is also significant that the local viceroys preferred Hindus as their medical attendants, rather than trust themselves to the tender mercies of the European Physico-Mór, and this despite the frequent promulgation of decrees condemning the practice. Bad as European standards were, however, Japanese were probably not much better, save perhaps in the important matter of cleanliness. In any event, medical treatment of the poor and needy classes in Japan was conspicuous by its absence, and it was here that the Jesuits (initially) stepped into the breach.

The chief figure in the early stages of this work was that of Padre Luis d'Almeida, of "New Christian" origin, who had so generously endowed the mission on his entry into the Company. With the cordial support of Otomo of Bungo, he had founded a hospital at Oita (Funai) for the care of lepers and syphilitics, together with an orphanage for the care of destitute children. Almeida also established a pharmacy which he stocked with herbs and medicines ordered from Macao, and his organization seems to have been remarkably efficient. In 1559, two years after its foundation, there were sixty seriously ill patients, besides another hundred and forty who were convalescing from internal and external disease of one kind or another. This hospital was the first of its kind ever erected in Japan, and patients flocked to it from far and wide. It did not, however, operate for more than a few years on this truly democratic basis, as can be seen from Valignano's oft-quoted "Sumario" of 1583.

In the concluding chapter of this report, Valignano puts forward a plea for papal authorization enabling the Jesuits to lend money at interest at the rate of ten per cent. He explains that the local usurers charged as high as seventy or eighty per cent per annum, and that if the Jesuits were allowed to lend money at ten per cent, this would not only satisfy the Christians who were continually pleading for this concession, but would help to boost the conversion rate as well, and give "great luster to our Religion." Loans would be limited to a maximum of six cruzados, and the profits would be expended on the construction of three foundling hospitals and some *Montes de Piedade*, where the Christian poor could obtain financial help on easy terms. These institutions, like the hospitals, were to be limited to Christians, and the hospitals would receive only samurai and nobles as patients. Lepers and sufferers from venereal disease were on no account to be admitted, since they were so repulsive to the Japanese ("que son tan asquerosos a los Japones"). The visitor explained that they could not help everyone; and if they admitted low-class patients, it gave the hospital and the missionaries a bad name. This was indeed a startling change of policy from the truly Christian charity of Luis Almeida's day, but it was evidently sanctioned by headquarters at Rome. It is true that in 1600, there was a Jesuit hospital at Nagasaki which included an isolation ward for lepers. The *Annual Letter* for 1604 alludes to the spiritual and corporal assistance given to the lepers and sick poor of Nagasaki by the local Jesuit dojuku. But the definitive "Obediencias" of 1612, emphatically reaffirm Valignano's standpoint. The relevant paragraph reads in translation as follows.

"Nobody of the Company will be allowed to learn medicine or surgery, nor to practice anything of these two arts which he may already know, nor to have books which treat of these subjects, and the same prohibitions apply to the dojuku."

Nothing could be more categorical. Thus we can understand the criticisms of Fray Juan Pobre, O.F.M., who contrasted the generous care so freely given to the "asquerosos" lepers and syphilitics in the Franciscan hospitals at Kyoto in 1595, with the local Jesuits' studied neglect of the poor and needy. Moreover, such care as they did give was not entirely disinterested. Valignano pointed out (in 1583) that the proposed foundling homes would assure the Jesuits a good supply of servants besides a harvest of souls. Modern writers, who are blissfully unaware of Valignano's reports, often dilate on the debt owed by Japanese medicine to the Jesuit founders of the *Namban-ryu* or Southern Barbarian school of medicine and surgery. Apart from the fact that sixteenth-century Europeans had very little of value to teach in either branch of the art of healing, the foregoing quotations will suffice to show that the claims made on behalf of the Jesuits in this respect are grossly exaggerated.[9]

Valignano's far-reaching plans of 1583, for the establishment of a number of seminaries for the training of theological students destined to form the nucleus of a native clergy, did not materialize in their original form. But a number of training centers for the education of the dojuku, chiefly with a view to their becoming brothers (*irmãos*) of the Company, were established at different times and places. I need allude here only to the seminary at Adzuchi, patronized by Nobunaga, and those later established at Shiki, Arima, Nagasaki, and so on, in Kyushu, and a small but select center at Kyoto. Valignano, writing in 1583, extolled the natural studiousness of the Japanese youth, stating that the lads in the seminary would sit studying earnestly for three or four hours at a time, without moving in their seats. Francisco Pasio's letter of September 16, 1594, describing the Arima seminary, gives a good idea of the way in which they functioned.

There were this year in the seminary about one hundred pupils divided into three classes of Latin, written and oral, of writing Japanese and Latin, and of chanting and playing musical instruments. Those of the first class can already compose and recite therein, reading some lessons in a masterly manner, and they can perform some dialogue plays in Latin. Twenty students will graduate this year . . . The painters and those who engrave on copper plates become daily more skillful, and their works are but little inferior to those which are brought from Rome.

One of the visitors to this institution in 1596 describes two of these dialogue plays; in one the devil and Buddhist priests were triumphantly vanquished by Christian angels and converts,—this, be it noted, at a time when the propagation of Christianity was ostensibly strictly forbidden! The same eyewitness tells that one of the Japanese youths spoke such perfect Portuguese that he could hardly believe the scholar was not a Lusitanian. These plays were of the kind staged by the Jesuits for their youthful pupils in their schools from the Maranhão to Macao. Although popular enough in their way, it is unfortunate that they ousted the more genuinely national and spontaneous *autos de folgar* in vogue in Gil Vicente's day.

The earlier Jesuits, from Francis Xavier in 1549 to Gaspar Coelho in 1582, had claimed that Japanese children were nat-

urally more intelligent and studious than those of the corresponding age in Europe, and consequently made greater
progress in their studies, even in purely European subjects
such as Latin. Valignano, although giving implicit support
to this viewpoint in his preliminary report of 1580, later
changed his mind. Writing in 1601, he disclaimed the accuracy of reports that the Japanese children were cleverer for
their age than Europeans, save possibly in brush and pen work.
They might, he wrote, learn to form the letters quicker than
European children; but he stated emphatically that otherwise they were no more advanced, nor did they learn Latin and
the arts more rapidly. On the contrary, the difficulty experienced by Japanese youths in grappling with Latin, and the
strong distaste they evinced for the study of this language,
was one of the chief stumbling blocks for the admission of
dojuku and brothers as ordained priests, and for the formation
of a native clergy. Whenever they could, the pupils chose to
learn Japanese classics rather than Latin, and had practically
to be forced to study this last language. These complaints of
Valignano were echoed by Padre João Rodriguez and others.
They must have caused Francisco Cabral to smile sarcastically,
when he read or heard them. There were exceptions, of course,
and several fluent Latin scholars were numbered among the
Japanese Jesuits of the seventeenth century; but generally
speaking Valignano's contentions were doubtless correct, since
the Japanese, like the English, certainly do not have the gift of
tongues.

In view of the warlike characteristics of the Japanese, and
the avidity with which they adopted Western military and
naval technical innovations from 1868 to 1941, it is rather
surprising that there was no comparable development in the
sixteenth and seventeenth centuries. The musket was, it is
true, taken over lock, stock, and barrel, and cannon were also
taken into use, although on a smaller scale. The Japanese, although skillful enough gun founders in early days (Richard
Cocks wrote that the Hirado founders "made as formal ord-

nance as we do in Christendom") told the Westerners that they "would rather have one of those cast in Europe than ten of such as were ever cast in Japan." Artillery was used by Ieyasu both at Sekigahara and in the Osaka campaign, but neither then, nor later at Shimabara, did it play a decisive or even an important part.

In naval and maritime technique the Japanese began to copy Portuguese charts and navigational methods during the Keicho period. At the same time, European methods of shipbuilding were introduced both by Will Adams and by the Spaniards. These promising but abortive beginnings will be referred to in a later chapter. It is sufficient to note here that apart from the introduction of firearms, the Portuguese neither imparted nor left any important innovations in "the noble Art Military" as practiced in feudal Japan. Scholars have suggested that the architecture of some strongholds, such as Nobunaga's castle at Adzuchiyama, were influenced by Portuguese or Jesuit theories of military architecture; but, as noted elsewhere, the Jesuits gave no hint of this in any of their letters, and the supposition must be dismissed as purely gratuitous.

The picture screens of Kano Yeitoku and other artists of the Keicho period, show that the Japanese gentry often aped contemporary Indo-Portuguese dress, and one famous screen depicting a *kyogen* actor shows him wearing a rosary. This fashionable craze is reflected in Padre Pasio's oft-quoted letter of September, 1594, which proves that not only native converts but ordinary samurai followed the prevailing whim.

Quambacudono [i.e., the Kwambaku, Toyotomi Hideyoshi] has become so enamored of Portuguese dress and costume that he and his retainers frequently wear this apparel, as do all the other lords of Japan, even the gentiles, with rosaries of driftwood on the breast above all their clothing, and with a crucifix at their side, or hanging from the waist, and sometimes even with kerchiefs in their hands; some of them are so curious that they learn by rote the litanies of *Pater Noster* and *Ave Maria* and go along praying in the streets, not in mockery or scorn of the Christians, but simply for gallantry, or because they think it is a good thing and one which will help them to achieve prosperity in worldly things. In this way they order oval-shaped pendants to be made containing reliques of the images of Our Lord and Our Lady painted on glass at great cost. . . .

This attitude, which coincided with Hideyoshi's formal prohibition of Christianity, was merely a passing fashionable craze. It was no more permanent in its effects than the abortive effort of King Charles II to array the courtiers of Whitehall in Persian costumes, in an attempt to wean them from the prevailing French fashions inspired by the court of *Le Roi Soleil* at Versailles. In another respect, the Keicho craze for things Portuguese left more permanent traces. Apart from what Pasio states in his above-quoted letter, Sansom says that a contemporary Japanese grammarian noted the habit (which he much disliked) of interlarding one's conversation with scraps of Portuguese. A similar craze for the use of English words followed after the Meiji restoration of 1868. Of Portuguese words which have survived in the vernacular to this day, the best known are *tabako* (tobacco): *kappa* (*capa*, a straw raincoat); *karuta* (*carta*, playing card); *kompeito* (*confeito*, confits, sweets, or jam), and *biidro* (*vidro*, glass), but there were many others which are now obsolete. Nor was this influence entirely one-sided, for a few Japanese words like *katana* (sword) and *byobu* were taken over by the Portuguese, and the rapidly disappearing Macao dialect had many more.

The cross-cultural influences briefly outlined in this chapter proved largely abortive, owing to the prohibition of Christianity and the expulsion of the missionaries in 1614. But the brief flowering of Kirishitan culture in the Keicho period foreshadowed the more permanent effects of the Westernization of Japan in the Meiji era. It is also interesting to compare the popular appeal of Western ways and ideas in Japan with their strictly limited reception in contemporary China. Despite the active patronage of enlightened emperors such as Kanghsi and Ch'ienlung, Western art and science never aroused the same widespread interest in China as they did in Japan, and of social influence there was virtually none. On the contrary, thanks to the *Lettres édifiantes et curieuses* of the French

Jesuits, and to the interest taken by Leibniz, Voltaire, and others in their description of Chinese civilization, China exerted, if only indirectly, far more influence on eighteenth-century Europe than the reverse.

But the indications are that if the spread of Namban and Kirishitan culture had not been artificially but effectively arrested by the Tokugawa government in 1614, Japan might have adopted, or rather adapted, a measure of Western civilization. It has been noted that Jorge Alvarez in 1547 expressed his wonder at the fact that ordinary householders in Satsuma frequently asked the Portuguese to their homes. This was in strong contrast to the experiences of the Europeans elsewhere in Asia, since neither Hindu nor Moslem Indians could be expected to afford similar opportunities for social intercourse, owing to the religious barrier; and the Portuguese were of course equally hidebound in their attitude to them. The same was true of the Malays and other races with whom the Portuguese might have consorted on equal terms. The Chinese and Koreans were too encrusted in their Confucian mental shell to feel any deep interest in or regard for an alien civilization. Alone among the civilized Asiatic peoples, the Japanese were in a position to give and take as between acknowledged equals. A study of the Kirishitan culture of the Keicho period inclines me to the belief that but for the arbitrary action of the Tokugawa, Japan might have achieved a considerable degree of Westernization and started on a policy of overseas expansion about two and a half centuries before she did.[10]

II

The Company of Jesus has often been termed the most militant and uncompromising of all the Roman Catholic religious orders, but, like most generalizations, this verdict is only partly correct. The controversy over the Confucian rites in China, and the Jesuit tolerance of many Hindu practices in Malabar, showed to what lengths they were prepared to go when they thought that the end justified the means. Their active participation in the Macao-Nagasaki silk trade was another instance of their malleability, which they justified on the grounds that necessity knew no law ("uno de aquellos casos en el qual la necessidade dispensa sobre toda Ley"). Similarly, Valignano's suggestion of conniving at Japanese matrimonial peccadilloes under certain circumstances, was regarded askance by a papacy which had outlived its Renaissance reputation for profligacy.

The truth is (or was) that the Company, although fundamentally militant, was by no means equally uncompromising. The manner in which the sons of Loyola adapted themselves to the Japanese way of life is another instance of their genius for compromise. It also affords an interesting indication of the mutual reactions of intelligent but prejudiced Europeans and Asiatics when confronted with another civilization, equal in most ways and superior in some, to their own. A study of "the daily round, the common task," of the Jesuit missionaries in Japan is particularly enlightening in this respect; since for reasons which I need not go into, their colleagues of the China mission did not mix quite so freely with the different grades of society in the Middle Flowery Kingdom.

The adaptability of the Jesuits was evinced by the founder of the Japan mission, the apostolic Francis Xavier. After Xavier's preliminary and Franciscan-like humility had failed to produce any impression on the haughty daimyo, the Jesuit made a more fruitful use of pomp and ceremony with the aid of his seafaring friend, Duarte da Gama. But the attitude of the Jesuits toward Japanese culture and civilization was really clarified by Valignano, who, in this matter as in so many others, clearly laid down the policy and methods to be followed. He decided, probably at the suggestion of Luis Frois and other veteran missionaries, that the Jesuits should arrogate to themselves the status and standing of the Zen priests, as the most potent, intelligent, and respected members of the Buddhist clergy. Comparisons are supposed to be odious, but the reader may be reminded at this point of Ricci's adoption of the dress and manners of the Confucian literati as the ideal to be aimed at in China, and Nobili's imitation of the high-caste Brahmins of Madura. The three great Italian Jesuits were merely carrying out, as Valignano explicitly stated of his own methods, the Pauline maxim of *Omnibus Omnia*, all things to all men.

The Jesuits in Japan could be divided into three groups. First came the fathers (padres) with whom the real authority was vested, and who, up to Valignano's time, were all Europeans. Next came the brothers (irmãos), most of whom were Europeans, but who included about seventy Japanese in 1592. Lastly came the dojuku or native acolytes and catechists, of whom there were about a hundred in 1582, and two hundred and sixty in 1604. Strictly speaking, these last were not members of the Company, but for practical purposes they can be considered as such, since Valignano repeatedly stressed that they were an essential part of the mission organization. There were also the household servants and caretakers ("moços e gente de serviço") who performed menial but useful tasks. They were not Jesuits, but were a charge on the Company's pay roll. The Japanese commonly termed the fathers *bateren* and the brothers *iruman* from a corruption of the corresponding Portuguese words. Perhaps the best way to understand the working of the Jesuit mission during its heyday in the Keicho period, is to consider each of these categories in turn before looking at the picture as a whole.[11]

Although Cabral's policy of "keeping the Japanese in their place," was overruled by Valignano in favor of one of racial equality, the fact that no Japanese brothers were ordained as priests in the Society for many years, automatically ensured that the control of the mission remained with the European padres. Since the Jesuit mission in Japan came in the sphere of the Portuguese padroado or Crown Patronage in the East, the majority of these missionaries were Portuguese. Even those who were not, acknowledged the validity of the Portuguese claims, and since the mission largely depended for its existence on the resources and facilities furnished by Goa, Macao, and Malacca, Portuguese influence was naturally predominant.

Portuguese was the lingua franca of the missionaries themselves, and most of their official correspondence with Goa, Lisbon, and Rome was written in this language. The rivalry with the Spanish friars from the Philippines tended to strengthen the Lusitanian cast of the Japan mission, which it retained throughout the whole time that it functioned in the island empire. The fact that its founder, Xavier, was a Basque, and its great organizer, Valignano, was an Italian, does not affect the general accuracy of this statement. The local chroniclers of the mission, Luis Frois and João Rodriguez Tçuzzu were both Portuguese, as was Padre Diogo de Mesquita, the "bear leader" of the Kyushu envoys to Rome in 1582–1590. From the beginning to the end, Portugal contributed more in men and money to the Japan Jesuit mission than did any other country.

The chief native protectors of the padres, old Otomo of Bungo, and the daimyo of Arima and Omura, had always been insistent on the advisability of the European Jesuits conforming to the Japanese way of life so far as they possibly could. Valignano accepted and enforced this principle, which was laid down in the local Jesuit code of behavior, as instanced by the "Advertimentos" of 1583, the "Addiciones" and "Obediencias" of 1592, and Pasio's final revision of the "Obediencias" in 1612. These sources give a clear idea of the way the mission functioned during the Keicho period, and of the motives which supplied the main springs for many of its actions.

Valignano stated that nowhere was the proverb of "When in Rome, do as the Romans do" more applicable than in Japan. He insisted that the padres make a detailed study of the minutiae of Japanese etiquette, and conform closely to Japanese customs in this respect. He stressed the vital necessity of understanding the delicately graded differences and the subtle distinctions between the various classes of society in Japan. He insisted on the correct use of honorifics in the colloquial and written languages. He ruled that the padres should exact the deference that was due to them as priests on a level with those of Zen sect, but added that they should not allow overzealous

Christians to give them more than their due. Padres were to be addressed by the term *sama* (lord) as a sign of respect, and were always to be treated as social superiors by the brothers and dojuku.

Similarly, he stressed the importance of the European padres addressing daimyo and samurai with due deference and politeness, but warned them against overdoing this, for excessive politeness was likewise taken amiss in Japan, and did the speaker more harm than good. He continually reiterated the importance of Europeans always keeping their tempers, even under insult and provocation, since nothing was so demeaning in the eyes of Japanese as lack of self-control or any outward display of feeling. Boisterous laughter and gesticulation were also to be carefully avoided; and any rudeness from a daimyo or noble was not to be openly resented, but met with a display of mingled politeness and firmness in order to shame the offender. Japanese etiquette in the serving of *saké* to guests and casual callers was also adopted, as was the formal tea ceremony, chanoyu. The implements for this social rite were always kept on hand in the larger Jesuit establishments which were also provided with a *chashitsu,* or ceremonial tea room, for the entertainment of guests.

The complicated code of present giving, formal calls on New Year's Day, and similar national customs were also adopted by the Jesuits, although they were directed to exercise due economy wherever practicable in the selection of gifts. Buddhist or Shinto holidays were to be ignored by the missionaries. Intensive language study was decreed for all newcomers from Europe, a year and a half being usually allowed for this purpose. Owing to shortage of personnel (there were less than fifty ordained priests in Japan in 1598), this study was not always done. Padre João Rodriguez complained in 1598 that several of the padres had only a rudimentary grasp of the language, and that other new arrivals were too old to make more than very slow and unsatisfactory progress in this difficult tongue. Xavier had asked for Basques and Flemings to be sent out to Japan, since he thought that they would become acclimatized more readily than would southern Europeans. This suggestion was not carried out and the mission continued to be predominantly staffed by Portuguese. Incidentally, it is amusing to find Rodriguez further complaining that some of the local superiors and rectors had become too bureaucratic and set in their ways. He added slyly that once these reverend gentlemen had given up office, they were likely to display a reluctance for the daily drudgery of ordinary missionary work, and their religious ardor noticeably cooled. Rodriguez was a decidedly carping critic and there is no need to take his strictures too seriously, but they are not without significance in the light of later Franciscan and Dominican accusations that the Jesuits were liable to neglect the end for the means.[12]

The influence of the Japanese code of behavior is also evident in Valignano's rule that erring sinners of good social standing should not be admonished directly by a padre, but through a third person, preferably a Japanese brother or senior native convert of the same social standing as the offender. Likewise the padres were to be very careful in fault finding or in reproving their Japanese inferiors, for the latter were prone to react violently if admonished in other than a kindly paternal fashion.

Unlike contemporary Europe, cleanliness emphatically came next to godliness in Japan, and of this the Jesuits were early aware. Physical dirt and religious poverty tended to be closely associated in Catholic Europe, where lice were regarded as the inseparable companions of monks and soldiers. The Japanese craze for fastidious cleanliness formed a sharp contrast. The Jesuits soon realized that in this they had something to learn from the Buddhist bonzes; and Valignano repeatedly stresses the importance of scrupulous cleanliness in the dress and housing of Jesuits in Japan. He could not shake off his inherent European prejudice against washing, and approve of the Japanese custom of a daily hot bath, but in other respects he insisted that Jesuits conform to local standards of cleanliness.

Their houses were built and furnished in Japanese style, from plans drawn by native architects in consultation with the Jesuit superiors. Guest chambers were included for the reception of distinguished travelers, but the "Obediencias" of 1612 contain a warning against indiscriminate hospitality, and the abuse thereof by *itazura-mono,* or idlers who were merely bent on cadging a free meal and bed. Since women were not so secluded in Japan as they were in most Asiatic countries (or in sixteenth-century Spain and Portugal for that matter), the Jesuits were permitted to receive female visitors, although in a *zashiki* or a room with sliding doors ajar so that the occupants were visible to those elsewhere in the building.

These standing orders of 1612, also contain the curious injunction that on no account were European (as distinct from Japanese) laymen to stay at a Jesuit establishment overnight. Contrary to the practice of the mendicant orders, the Jesuits made a point of never begging alms from anyone, whether European or Japanese, and aimed at being financially self-supporting. Conversely, the practice of indiscriminate charity was deprecated, and it was forbidden to give alms to indigent Europeans without leave of the local superior. Similarly, although the padres were permitted to have some cash in hand for distribution as alms to the local poor at the discretion of the rector, the brothers (an increasing number of whom were Japanese) were not permitted to keep any money whatsoever, "nem ainda para esmolas."

The Jesuit residences in Japan were plainly but adequately furnished. Each padre normally had a room or cell to himself, provided with a bedding roll, chair, table, and candle. Cells were to be cleaned twice weekly by the occupying padre, but on the remaining five days this work could be done by one of the dojuku associated with the padre. One of the regulations promulgated in 1612 forbade the practice of decorating these rooms with picture screens, limiting the use thereof to plain two-leaf screens. It was forbidden to keep any food in the cell. Sobriety in dress was required by these same regulations of 1612, which forbade the use of silk in dress material. Padres and irmãos alike had to wear the Jesuit *roupeta* in winter and summer, but during the hot weather they could sleep in their shirts and drawers, with the window open. The dojuku, unlike their older colleagues, could wear the native *katabira,* instead of the European type of shirt which was obligatory for the latter. Both Jesuits and dojuku normally wore Japanese sandals and *tabi* (socks).

The padres were evidently provided with something more than an "elegant sufficiency" in food and drink. The regulations of 1612 stipulated that the ordinary meal should consist of rice, soup (*shiru*), together with a "substantial dish" of fish or meat, cooked in either European or Japanese style, besides a side dish of vegetables, fruit, or herbs, and cake (*kashi*) "when there is any." On Wednesdays and Sundays something extra was provided. All Europeans were served a small pot of wine at each meal, "if anyone needs more he can have it," and high days and holidays were celebrated with an additional large pot or two of wine, as well as an extra dish of meat. An amusing instance of the attention paid by the Jesuits to the welfare of the inner man was the concession that although married servants were normally not allowed in Jesuit houses, an exception was made for those Japanese cooks who were well versed in the arts of *Namban-ryori,* or Southern Barbarian cooking.

These meals were clearly no Lucullan repasts, yet it is equally certain that they involved no mortification of the flesh. In this respect, the reader is inclined to see the point of the Society's contemporary critic who complained that the Jesuits gave a misleading impression of self-inflicted austerity in their printed *Cartas.* He sneered that they wrote about the dried radish leaves which they consumed for their nourishment, but made no mention of the very delectable chicken which followed. When first reading this acidulous observation, I dismissed it as mere Dominican *má-lingua,* but subsequent research has made me realize that the allegation was not completely gratuitous. Fernandez Navarrete likewise complained fifty years later that the Jesuits of the China mission lived far better than their colleagues of the mendicant orders. Here again, there is evidence from Padre Luis da Gama's letter of December, 1664, that this allegation was not altogether unfounded. There is no need to go to the other extreme and accuse the Jesuits of being *bon viveurs,* but obviously the implications of unrelieved austerity in the *Cartas* of 1598, are something in the nature of *suggestio falsi.*[13]

Nor were the bodily needs of the Jesuit missionaries in Japan unduly neglected in other ways. A Franciscan allegation that the Jesuits were customarily surrounded with a bevy of servants, one priest going about in a litter accompanied by sixty horsemen, is obviously exaggerated. But it is significant that the regulations of 1612 stipulated that a padre visiting the country districts ("correrem as Inacas") should not take with him more than a brother, a dojuku, and two or three servants, "even if he goes on horseback." These same regulations also stressed that walking was considered no disgrace in Japan, and that padres going on short journeys should naturally go on foot, rather than ahorse or in a litter. This was not true in China, where social stigma attached to any senior official making a journey afoot.

No brother could have a servant without special permission of the rector, but each padre had his own servant. When a father moved from one post to another, he could take two servants with him to his new station. Those servants who were bought as slaves, and the validity of whose status as slaves was open to doubt, had their slavery commuted to a fixed period of years, varying in accordance with the circumstances of each individual case. Married servants were not permitted, except for the skilled cooks, bakers, and so on, already alluded to. Youths less than eighteen years of age were not to be employed for the indoor staff of Jesuit establishments. Other prohibitions included the breeding of specially fine horses, the keeping or training of dogs, and the playing of *go,* or *shogi* (Japanese draughts and chess). The mere fact of these prohibitions being made indicates that these pastimes must have been indulged in at one time or another.

Valignano saw clearly enough that the progress of the

Jesuit mission in Japan was directly dependent on the admission of Japanese into the Society of Jesus, and on the maintenance of brotherly love between the European missionaries and their Japanese colleagues. The vital importance of this uniformity was stressed in all the rules and regulations promulgated for the guidance and instruction of missionaries from 1580 to 1612. Nevertheless, it was not until 1601, that a Japanese brother was ordained as a priest of the Society, so that for many years the native Jesuits were uniformly subordinated to the wishes and commands of the European padres.

It is obvious that so proud and high-spirited a race as the Japanese would not be content with this inferior role for long, nor were they. They grumbled repeatedly at not being permitted to become ordained priests, and several of them left the Society because of this prohibition. Some of these embittered men even apostatized from the Faith, the best-known instance being that of Fabian Fukansai. Fabian left the Company in 1607, disgusted at his slow promotion and the reluctance of his superiors to ordain him. His defection was a great loss, since he had been one of the pillars of the Jesuits' polemical attacks on Buddhism, and was one of their best apologists with tongue and brush. As late as 1627, the Japanese Jesuits are found complaining that they were passed over for promotion in favor of their European colleagues.

Although Valignano had transferred Francisco Cabral from Japan to Macao, in consequence of the latter's outspoken mistrust of the religious capabilities of the Japanese brothers and their unfitness for ordination, Cabral was not alone in his views. Padre João Rodriguez Tçuzzu, the acknowledged Japanese language expert among the missionaries, gave vent to similar anti-Japanese sentiments in 1598. In a confidential letter to General Aquaviva, he advised that great care should be taken in admitting any of the dojuku as brothers into the Company. He termed the Japanese a wayward and volatile race ("gente flaca y inconstante"). He considered that they could not really understand the profound truths and fundamentals of Christianity, as shown by the relative ease with which they apostatized under temptation. He deplored the fact that the Jesuits had no "secular arm" in Japan, wherewith to arrest and punish such apostates, some of whom had added insult to injury by subsequently marrying, "which is a very great discredit to our Company." He stated flatly that of the hundred-odd Japanese brothers, there was not a single one fit to be ordained. As with Cabral, he thought that once they were admitted in large numbers, they would swamp the mentally superior Europeans and drag the Society down to their own level. He rounded off this denunciation of his Japanese colleagues by stating that their modest and decorous exterior captivated all newcomers, but that this fair outward appearance concealed a guileful and unreliable character.[14]

Rodriguez added that he had held these views for many years; it is possible that he was partly responsible for Valignano reversing his former stand, and deliberately slowing-up the admission of Japanese to the Society of Jesus. At any rate this is what Valignano did do, although he had the satisfaction of seeing several Japanese ordained as priests shortly before his death in 1606. The general at Rome also adopted a "go-slow" policy, and, writing to Valignano in the year of his death, he stated that only a few Japanese should be ordained, rejecting the Chinese as being still too young in the Faith. This comparison is interesting, for seven years later one of the China Jesuits wrote to Aquaviva that although the Japanese Jesuits are virtuous, "they are not so Portugueseified (*Aportuguesados*) as these Chinese brothers." One of the principal stumbling blocks to their admission as fully fledged members of the Society was their inability to learn Latin, fluency in that tongue being essential for the fathers of the Society. Eventually, insistence on this point had to be tacitly abandoned, and some Orientals who possessed only a rudimentary knowledge of Latin were admitted to the priesthood.

The Japanese brothers were recruited almost exclusively from the ranks of the dojuku, and were, therefore, nearly all of gentle birth, since admission thereto was normally dependent on this. European histories of Japan all seem to assume that the Jesuit mission was almost entirely the work of the Western padres, but a perusal of the Jesuits' own correspondence during the years 1580–1614, makes it abundantly clear that it was really the native brothers and dojuku who bore the burden and heat of the day. Valignano explicitly states as much, adding that it was the Japanese brothers who compiled all the political literature against the Buddhist sects. Even the most fluent European speaker of Japanese sounded awkward and tongue-tied in preaching, when compared to his Japanese colleagues. It was the iruman and dojuku who went out preaching and catechizing into the highways and byways. It was they who carried on theological arguments with the Buddhist priests, and it was they who searched the Buddhist scriptures for texts wherewith to refute the bonzes' own arguments. Rodriguez was clearly blinded by prejudice when he penned his anti-Japanese tirade in 1598, and the facts all go to prove the accuracy of Valignano's earlier assertion that the native members of the Company formed its sheet-anchor in Japan.[15]

The general method of indoctrinating converts is drawn from Valignano's report of 1583. First of all, the catechism was explained in great detail in about seven teaching sessions. Next the "falsities and errors" of the Buddhist and Shinto creeds were pointed out, and it was proved that there was only one universal God who distributed rewards and punishments to the soul, the immortality of which was likewise demonstrated. The coming of Our Lord was then explained, after which the converts were taught the Creed, Pater Noster, Ave Maria, and the Ten Commandments in Japanese, besides some other few prayers. The father-visitor said that those who progressed this far, seldom or never returned to their idols, but they were naturally not yet firmly grounded in the principles and fundamentals of Christianity, which followed after further intensive indoctrination. Only after they had attended church and confessions, and heard sermons and Mass for a good number of times, were converts admitted to communion. Naturally enough, it was the Japanese brothers and dojuku who bore the brunt of this work, although it was, of course, organized and directed by the European Jesuits. Further evidence of the vital part played by the native members of the Company appears in the Annual Letter for 1604, written by Padre João Rodriguez Girão.

Padre Rodriguez Girão explains that a special course had been organized in the Jesuit college at Nagasaki, for selected Japanese iruman and dojuku, who were being trained in anti-Buddhist polemics. The teacher of this course was a Japanese brother from Kyoto, who had visited many of the most famous temples in Japan, not as an avowed Christian, but as a seeker after knowledge. He had thus heard the Buddhist texts expounded by their most qualified exponents, and he brought with him to Nagasaki copies of the most authoritative Buddhist scriptures and philosophical works. The students were taught to confute the bonzes from their own texts, and Rodriguez Girão assures his readers that this method of propaganda was expected to prove a most effective one. The *Myotei-Mondo,* one of the best-known Christian apologetics, also dates from this period.

Apparently, then, the course at Nagasaki was the first in which the study of Buddhism was seriously undertaken by the Jesuits, who had hitherto been content to denounce it in terms of sweeping condemnation as the work of the Devil, and let it go at that. Naturally, such an attitude could hardly be expected to commend itself to well-educated people; and this new line of attack, which was initiated by Vice-Provincial Francisco Pasio, was also paralleled by the Jesuits' study of Buddhism and Confucianism in China. Incidentally, it is interesting to note that Fabian after his apostasy, stated that Buddhist anti-Christian propaganda was not very effective, since the bonzes likewise had not troubled to study the fundamentals of Christianity and, consequently, their polemical attacks were too vague and sweeping to be convincing.

Although the brothers were not so privileged as the padres, Valignano and his successors stressed the importance of the European priests going out of their way to treat the senior Japanese brothers with great consideration, thus offsetting to some extent the natural disappointment of the latter at not yet being ordained priests. The native brothers had the privilege of visiting their own families and of corresponding with their friends (other than women). They also seem to have been permitted to indulge on occasion in their national love of a hot bath. A European padre traveling in the interior was invariably accompanied by a Japanese iruman, which affords another indication of the degree to which the Society relied on the native element in Japan. Nevertheless, Valignano wrote to Macao in 1599, begging that some European temporal coadjutors (lay brothers) be sent to him without delay, since there were some administrative posts which could not be satisfactorily filled by Japanese, and for which a European personnel was essential.

Aquaviva finally ruled (on New Year's Day, 1610) that a few Japanese brothers could be ordained at infrequent intervals, if only to prevent the remainder from becoming discouraged. He added that they should be selected from individuals about forty years old, and stipulated that they should not go to Macao to complete their studies. Perhaps he considered that the cosmopolitan character of the colony would give them "dangerous thoughts." In any event, the exodus of 1614, rendered this stipulation pointless. Despite their difficulties, and the outspoken bias of Padre João Rodriguez Tçuzzu, the history of the Japan mission showed clearly enough that Valignano was right when he wrote in 1583 that it could never rest on a secure basis unless an increasingly large proportion of native brothers were admitted, "for they are the principal ministers of this work, both in respect of the language as for other reasons." [16]

The term dojuku, usually corrupted to *dogico* by the Portuguese, meant "fellow lodger" or "fellow guest." It was taken over by the Jesuits from the Buddhists and applied to their lay acolytes. Their duties are clearly explained in Valignano's report of 1592.

In Japan the word *dogico* is used to describe a class of men who, whether young or old, shave their heads and renounce the world by entering the service of the Church. Some study with a view to becoming eventually religious and clergy, whereas others render various household services which cannot be performed in Japan save by shaven acolytes of this kind, such as the office of sacristan, server of chanoyu, messenger, helper at Mass, or burial services, at baptisms, and in other like solemnities of the Church, and in accompanying the padres. Those of them who are capable thereof, likewise help in catechizing, in preaching, and in converting the Christians. These dogicos are respected in Japan and looked upon as churchmen, and they wear cassocks of a different fashion from those worn by the padres and brothers. Everyone is aware that they are not really religious but either are resolved to become so or to help the religious in their ministerings. Some of these are occupied in studying Latin, like those who are in the seminaries, and our brothers are drawn from their class. Others are divided among the other houses and residences, and employed in the aforesaid duties. The total number of these dogicos in Japan at this time is one hundred and eighty, to which if we add the other servants and acolytes who are distributed among the various houses in the service of the Church, we get a total of more than six hundred and seventy persons, including the padres and brothers, who are at present maintained at the cost of the Company in Japan.

The importance of the dojuku in the Jesuit organization is evident from the following statistics. In 1582, there were about a hundred of them; ten years later, there were one hundred and eighty; and in February, 1604, this number had increased to two hundred and sixty, out of a total of nine hundred persons maintained by the Company in Japan. In addition to the occupations listed by Valignano in 1592, most of the painters, printers, and engravers for the Jesuit mission during the Keicho period were dojuku. In accordance with the policy laid down by Valignano in 1582, and reaffirmed in the regulations of 1592 and 1612, the dojuku were recruited almost exclusively from the sons of the nobility and samurai, children of tradesmen or farmers being only very occasionally accepted. The Jesuits hoped in this way to maintain the social prestige of the Company, and to ensure that its native members would not be despised by their compatriots as social inferiors, which was likely to happen with the native clergy in India.

Needless to say, the dojuku were strictly supervised by their spiritual fathers, although some concessions were made to Japanese standards of behavior. Thus, Valignano stated that they undoubtedly would desert en masse if they were not permitted to live in Japanese-style houses, and if Japanese standards of cleanliness were not maintained in all Jesuit establishments. A certain number of dojuku were allotted to each padre, who supervised their spiritual welfare and religious education, although they were not normally permitted to confess to the padre to whom they were attached. They had half an hour of prayer every morning and an "examination of the conscience" every evening. They had to confess once a month, and could receive communion at the discretion of their father confessor.

Particular attention was paid to the preacher dojuku and catechists who received special favors. They wore long black cassocks, and some of them had permission to eat at the padres' own table. This was doubtless a valued concession, since the dojuku's ordinary ration was not so substantial as that of their spiritual fathers. It was normally limited to rice, shiru, and a side dish of vegetables, save on feast days, when they were given something extra. In the smaller establishments, where it would have been inconvenient to cook three different kinds of rice, that is to say, the best quality for the padres and brothers, the next best for the dojuku, and a third grade for the household servants, it was stipulated that the dojuku could partake of the same quality of rice as their superiors.

When the dojuku were ill, the padres were told to treat them with loving care, but not to spoil them by giving them chickens and poultry (which sick European Jesuits were given in such circumstances) but native Japanese dishes only. Dojuku who had grown old in the service of the Church were likewise to be treated with special favor and consideration, although no dojuku could be received into or dismissed from the service of the Company without permission of the provincial. These acolytes normally slept altogether in a large dormitory; but in the residences each youth was given a cubicle of his own. In accordance with the Jesuit rule, the shoji or sliding door of their cubicle had always to be kept ajar, transgression of this rule being punished by withdrawal of the privilege of having one's own cubicle. Under no circumstances could a dojuku sleep in the same room as a padre or brother.

The dojuku had to treat the padres, and to a lesser degree the brothers, with the greatest respect and veneration. Thus they could never wear any headgear when speaking with their superiors, except some old and favored catechists who were given this privilege. When a dojuku spoke with a padre in the street, he had to remove his sandals, and speak in a humble posture with his hands on his knees. This custom and other rules and regulations for the behavior of the dojuku toward the padres were evidently taken over from the corresponding procedure among the bonzes of the Zen sect, where the *jisha* or temple acolytes held an analogous position to that of the Jesuit dojuku. The chronicler Antonio Bocarro, writing in 1635, alleges that this exaggerated respect which the Jesuit padres exacted from their converts was one of the most bitterly criticized aspects of their behavior when Christianity was finally proscribed in 1614. It was certainly implied in Hasegawa Sahioye's anti-Christian memorial of 1613, when he criticized the missionaries for inculcating obedience to themselves as more important than loyalty to feudal and temporal superiors.

It was originally intended that the dojuku should furnish recruits for the native clergy as well as for the Society of Jesus, but this scheme largely broke down in practice. There were not enough teachers to staff the training seminaries on the necessary scale, and inevitably the majority of the dojuku automatically gravitated into the Company itself. Disgruntled dojuku showed a distressing tendency to desert to the more easy-going mendicant orders, as Provincial Carvalho complained in 1617.

The first two Japanese Jesuit priests were ordained in 1601, and the first of the native secular clergy three years later. By 1606, there were three Japanese serving as parish priests in Nagasaki. This was the year in which Valignano died at Macao, and perhaps he could not help feeling disappointed at the slow and meager results of his earlier grandiose ambitions. Six years later, there were only ten native clergy in Japan, half of whom were ordained priests, and the other five were in minor orders. Bishop Cerqueira still professed optimism for the future and believed that the Nagasaki seminary would slowly but surely provide the Christian community of Japan with pastors of their own race. The expulsion of the Jesuits and definitive prohibition of Christianity in 1614 put an abrupt stop to any such development, the possibility of which had always seemed doubtful.

Cerqueira was satisfied with the behavior of his native clergy, and stated that the Japanese in general greatly appreciated the honor of their nationals being enabled to take holy orders. These parish priests were all brought up by the Company as dojuku, and it must have been the unkindest cut of all when they formally repudiated Bishop Cerqueira's Jesuit successor, and went over to the hostile Dominicans and Franciscans in the Nagasaki schism of 1614. All Valignano's forethought, and all Cerqueira's watchful care, thus ended in the ignominious denouement of tragicomedy.[17]

Both free and bond servants were represented on the domestic staff of the Jesuits in Japan, the majority of the former being Japanese, whereas the slaves included Negroes, Indians, Malays, and other Asiatic and African races. The Regulations of 1612 stipulated that fugitive slaves or servants who sought refuge with the Jesuits from their masters should be treated "charitably," but withal good care should be taken to avoid losing the friendship of the master by helping the servant. It was stated that the best course in these circumstances was to get rid of the unwanted refugee, and ask some local native Christian to arrange an amicable solution between master and man.

The same Regulations stressed the importance of not questioning the validity of the lawful captivity of slaves belonging to Christian owners, since the latter strongly resented any interference by the Jesuits in what they regarded as a purely domestic affair. One of Valignano's difficulties in this respect was the problem of the status of the numerous Korean slaves taken as a result of Hideyoshi's "unjust war" in the peninsula in 1592–1598. Altogether, the Jesuit attitude toward these oppressed classes in Japan was definitely on the side of the "haves" as against the "have-nots." It forms a strong contrast to their more liberal policy in Brazil, where they opposed the enslavement of the Amerindians by all the means in their power. Even their denunciation of the holding of Japanese and Chinese slaves by the Portuguese was not so much inspired by disinterested motives as by the realization that this practice was disliked by the two great Far Eastern governments, and was a bar to the progress of Christianity.[18]

Having thus briefly reviewed the organization of the Church militant in Japan, let us consider its outlook and influence. The principle of "Japanization" having once been accepted (though with misgivings by some members of the Company) no trouble or effort was spared by the Jesuits to accommodate themselves to the Japanese way of life. They were ready at all times to receive and welcome visitors of either sex, and Valignano was insistent on the necessity for them to play the part of perfect hosts, even when they were secretly bored or physically exhausted. Their strict adherence to native social etiquette, their adoption of the fashionable craze for chanoyu were all done with the deliberate design of gaining the friendly confidence of the Japanese, as an essential preliminary to their ultimate conversion. That their tactics in this respect were fundamentally sound is shown by the long list of distinguished converts, including a number of daimyo renowned for their aesthetic tastes and high culture (Otomo Sorin, Gamo Ujisato, and Takayama Ukon).

More questionable, perhaps, was their relative neglect of the poorer classes in their eagerness to attract the powerful and influential. Admission to the Company itself, so far as the Japanese were concerned, was virtually dependent on their being well-born. The Regulations of 1612 explicitly stated that no particular care was to be taken to convert the peasantry, since they were too dependent on the local daimyo and likely to renounce the Faith when ordered to do so by their feudal suzerains. This is all the more surprising, since this order was made at a time when the conversion of daimyo had become a virtual impossibility, and that of samurai exceedingly difficult, owing to Tokugawa Ieyasu's increasingly anti-Christian stand. In any event, aside from Nagasaki, which had an almost exclusively Christian population, the majority of converts were farmers or peasants.

The Jesuits' earlier temple-wrecking and idol-burning propensities had really done them more harm than good in the long run. They evidently realized this themselves, since the Regulations of 1612 are much more moderate and prudent on this point than was the general behavior of the Jesuits as mirrored in the iconoclastic activities of their zealous converts before Hideyoshi's outburst in 1587. It was ordered that even in the territory of Christian daimyo, no aggressive proselytizing or temple burning would be permitted. The missionaries were told to walk delicately and warily like Agag. Buddhist temples were not to be destroyed outright, but gradually to be taken over for Christian churches or secular dwellings. This marks a *volte-face* from such acts as Vilela's burning of the local temple at Nagasaki to make room for a Christian church in 1569. Heathen vassals of Christian daimyo were to be converted by appeals to reason and not by force —a marked change from the forcible conversion of Takayama Ukon's fief of Akashi in 1582.

Great care was to be taken to avoid provoking heathen daimyo by staging ostentatious religious propaganda, processions, burials, or ceremonies in their fiefs. Even in Christian fiefs, the padres were forbidden to erect crosses without leave of the local rector. At this time (1612) converts were normally intensively catechized for a week before being baptized. Finally (and this is very important) the Regulations of 1612 expressly stated that the Gospel should be preached in such a way that European manners and customs should not be introduced with it. On the contrary, Japanese mores were not to be interfered with, save only when they were in direct conflict with Christian morality. As with the primitive Church in Roman times, the Catholic Church in Japan gradually introduced the celebration of Christian saints' days to displace those of the popular Buddhist and Shinto feast days. One of the most significant of these changes was the Feast of Our Lady of Protection, which Bishop Cerqueira introduced at the beginning of the native lunar year, in order to compete with that greatest of all Japanese festivals.[19]

Another interesting evidence of Jesuit adaptability is to be found in their attitude toward the warring daimyo. It was noticed that Valignano soon reversed his early viewpoint on the advisability of the Jesuits interfering in local politics, and that he was furious with Gaspar Coelho for trying to stir up the Kyushu Christian daimyo to defy Hideyoshi's expulsion edict by force of arms. His "Obediencias" of 1592 are most explicit on this point. He laid down that on no account were the Jesuits to encourage or forment any fighting among the Japanese, even if it was in support of a Christian daimyo against a heathen, or Christian vassals oppressed by a heathen overlord. Similarly, he reversed his early stand on the advisability of the Jesuits holding Nagasaki and Mogi as strongholds, and categorically forbade the Company in Japan to hold any fortresses or to possess firearms and artillery, either on their own account or for others. The Jesuits were warned against interference in local disputes and cautioned against giving any advice or council on matters of state or war, even if asked to do so by Christian daimyo. Experience had shown that such advice was usually wrong, and that the untoward results were then blamed on the Jesuits.

Padres and brothers were strictly forbidden to act as military intelligence agents, or to pass on news of the progress of a campaign, even if it was in the interests of a Christian daimyo against a heathen. Scrupulous neutrality in word and deed was inculcated as the cardinal principle in nearly all circumstances. Only if intervention seemed absolutely essential in order to save a Christian fief from extinction, could help be given with the permission of the provincial, and then "rather with money than with material." The padres should try to avoid being involved in sieges, and were to maintain strict neutrality as between warring Christian daimyo, "being Fathers in God to all Christians." They were further to refrain from encouraging Christian soldiers in battle, "since this is of little avail in Japan," but were to confine themselves to praying to God for the success of Christian arms. Even in the event of a daimyo starting an unjust war, the padres were not to try to dissuade his Christian samurai from supporting him, "since this never avails, and can cause grave scandals, so that it is better to leave them in their ignorance."

The Jesuits were clearly carrying out the maxim of *omnibus omnia* to its logical limit, nor were the concrete results of their policy disheartening. On the contrary, Christianity made steady progress throughout the Keicho period, until its final prohibition in 1614. The 150,000 converts at the time of Valignano's arrival had increased to about 300,000 thirty-four years later. No small part of this success must be attributed to the Jesuits practicing their declared policy of being all things to all men.[20]

III

Those who fancy that the Roman Catholic Church has always presented a united front in the foreign mission field, in contrast to the "splinter" tendencies of the various Protestant sects, would be rudely disillusioned if they studied the history of overseas Christian missions during their first three centuries of existence. The Company of Jesus in particular acted as a discordant as well as a unifying element in the bosom of Holy Mother Church. From the Maranhão to Macao, the Jesuits are found complaining bitterly about what Padre Antonio Vieira called their "continual and cruel war" with the friars. Needless to say, the latter were not backward with similar complaints of Jesuit hostility, and nowhere did feelings run higher in this fratricidal strife than they did in Japan. It is true that the causes of friction were not doctrinal, but they were none the less real and profound.

The mendicant orders and the Society of Jesus differed in almost every way in their methods of evangelization in China and Japan. There were exceptions of course, but broadly speaking the friars favored the clean sweep of the *Tabula Rasa* which had proved so successful in Ibero-America, whereas the Jesuits preferred to avoid any direct attack on the native cultures, except where these openly conflicted with the claims of Christian morality. This was particularly true after Hideyoshi's outburst in 1587 had taught them that temple burning and idol wrecking would no longer be tolerated in Japan. The position was further complicated by acute national rivalry and by the conflicting claims of the Portuguese padroado and the Spanish patronazgo in the Far East. Religious, political, and economic motives all contributed to widen the gulf between the Society and the mendicant orders. It will perhaps be better to consider their mutual differences under these three heads, rather than to attempt a chronological survey of the orders, counterorders, and consequent disorder which emanated from Lisbon, Madrid, and Rome, making the existing confusion worse confounded.

The differences of opinion over methods of evangelization in Japan took a very different course from what they did a little later in China. Whereas in China the struggle was primarily waged over the question of the Confucian rites, this problem did not arise in Japan, where Buddhism, rather than

either Shinto or the cult of Confucius, was the most formidable enemy. Neither Jesuits nor friars showed any disposition to tolerate relics of Buddhist or Shinto practices
among their converts. Even when Christianity was proscribed
on pain of death, the missionaries forbade their flock to wear
Buddhist rosaries, to visit either *tera* or *jinja,* or to participate in their festivals. The slightest outward observance of
any of the practices of the two native creeds was condemned
as a mortal sin.

It is true that another bone of contention between the
missionaries in China was present in Japan, although to a
lesser degree. The friars often complained that the Jesuits
deliberately avoided preaching Christ crucified in China, and
crosses in Jesuit churches were conspicuous by their absence.
Fray Juan Pobre and other Franciscans twitted the Jesuits
with a similar excess of caution in Japan. In this the friars
apparently acted unfairly, although it can be gathered from
the "Obediencias" of 1612, that the Jesuits were certainly
very careful about where, when, and how they planted
crosses, erected wayside calvaries, or displayed crucifixes,
particularly in the fiefs of heathen daimyo. In this they were
merely following the dictates of common sense; as they likewise were in making only a sparing distribution of relics,
medals, rosaries, holy water, and the like among the faithful.
The Franciscans, on the other hand, gave these symbols of
the Christian faith freely to all and sundry among their flock;
and were severely criticized by the Jesuits for distributing
amulets of dubious authenticity, such as the beads of St.
Jeronima.[21]

A more significant difference of opinion turned on the
direction in which their propaganda was directed. The Jesuits,
from the time of Xavier onward, directed their main efforts
toward winning over the samurai and daimyo, in the conviction that the lower orders would follow whither their
social superiors led. This point emerges very clearly from the
confidential correspondence of Valignano with Rome, as well
as from the tenor of his instructions to the missionaries from

1580 until his death in 1606. Hence his insistence that the dojuku should be recruited almost exclusively from the upper classes, and his orders that no time need be wasted on converting the peasants and farmers. This was also the reason for the abandonment of the Jesuits' Bungo hospital work, and the prohibition of their practice of medicine and surgery in 1612.

It cannot be denied that this policy was successful up to a point, for without the conversion of daimyo such as Otomo, Takayama, Arima, and Omura, it is difficult to see how Christianity could have progressed very far—at any rate so long as it was preached on a militant note. The Jesuits' friendship with such influential personages as Wada Koremasa and Hosokawa Tadaoki, who, although no Christians themselves, protected or favored the converts because of this friendship, was of great value to the Church. Rodriguez' relationship with Hideyoshi and Ieyasu, although based far more on the things of Caesar than on those of God, was likewise advantageous to the Catholic cause. Many other instances could be quoted to show that the calculated policy of the Jesuits of keeping on good terms with those in temporal power, was of very real benefit to the Church in more humble quarters. Nevertheless, it is easy to see the point of the Franciscan argument that the Jesuits were neglecting the end for the means.

The Franciscans, whether from necessity (as the Jesuits insinuated) or from choice (as they themselves maintained) proceeded on very different principles. They flaunted their monastic habits, rosaries, crosses, and so forth, and concentrated on "the ignorant and the forgotten" classes of the city slums and rural hamlets, rather than on their social superiors. The Jesuits freely and frequently expressed their contempt for the "poxy rabble" which the Franciscans gathered around them at Kyoto. Fray Juan Pobre alleges that the two Franciscan hospices of St. Joseph and St. Anne were full of the "blind, halt, burned, deaf, dumb, lame,—nearly all lepers," who had previously applied to the Jesuits for charitable care, but had been turned away because of the

padres' preoccupation with their worldly rank and dignity.
There was certainly a striking contrast between these un-
fortunates and the stately samurai who frequented the
chanoyu sessions of the elegant Jesuit establishment in the
same city. Fray Pobre—and he was qualified to express an
opinion on this point, being a fanatical ascetic—wrote that
the Japanese lower classes were veritably the poorest of the
poor in all the world. He stated that when the Spaniards
captured an occasional Japanese pirate ship in Philippine
waters, the conquistadores could never find a single silver
coin on board. This is a rather curious criterion of poverty;
but there is no reason to dispute his observation that the Japanese lower classes were greatly oppressed by the arrogant
daimyo and samurai, who lost no opportunity of grinding
the faces of the poor.

The Franciscans did not entirely neglect Jesuit methods
in their own work. They had, for a time at any rate, a small
kindergarten school attached to their Kyoto hospice, and
used the *Flors Sanctorum* (*Sanctos no Gosagyo*) printed in
the vernacular by the Jesuit mission press for the edification
of their neophytes. As noted in the previous chapter, they
also adopted the Jesuit system of dojuku, although they did
not apparently keep them under such strict surveillance as
did the Jesuits. The padres said roundly that the friars were
unduly lax with their converts, granting them absolution
very readily. Sinners who could not make their peace with
their Jesuit confessors thus gravitated into the Franciscan
orbit, but Carvalho insinuated that this was an instance of
good riddance of bad rubbish.[22]

The fathers were very scornful of both the methods used
and the results achieved by the Franciscans. In conversation
among themselves, they dismissed anything botched or inferior with the sarcastic observation that it was the handi-
work or method of friars ("isto he modo de frades, aquillo
he modo fradesco"). They contrasted their own flock, headed
by representatives of the cream of the Japanese feudal nobility, with the "poxy lepers" and seedy ragamuffins who fre-

quented the purlieus of the Franciscan convents. They also alleged that since the friars were sadly deficient in linguistic ability, and few of their flock knew Spanish or Portuguese, they could not hear confessions properly, so that egregious misunderstandings were inevitable. They further alleged that the Franciscans taught such unedifying subjects as fencing (Japanese style presumably) in order to attract potential converts to their Kyoto convent. Padre Valentim de Carvalho reflected the general feeling among his colleagues, when he wrote in his *Apologia* of 1617: "It is notorious in all Japan what few converts they have made, and how few of the nobility they have converted, for most of their neophytes are very poor, lepers, and people of little worth." The same authority quotes a Japanese bugyo as saying that the country could well do without such missionaries, who only served to take bread from the mouths of the poor.

Although the ranks of the Franciscans' converts did in fact include a few aristocrats such as Asano Yukinaga, daimyo of Wakayama, and intellectuals such as the four painters of the Kano school already alluded to, the friars did not attempt to deny that the vast majority of their disciples were of the poor and lowly. On the contrary they gloried in this, and claimed that although the educated Japanese were critical of their hospital activities in the first instance, that this feeling of repulsion at such close contact with poverty, disease, and dirt, later changed to whole-hearted admiration. Fray Juan Pobre says that learned bonzes, who could not be convinced by purely theological arguments, on passing by the Kyoto hospice and seeing the friars washing the lepers' feet, exclaimed, "We do not want any more arguments. This is it! There must be salvation."

The same friar wrote in 1605, that the Franciscans had made more converts in the seven years which had elapsed since the Nagasaki martyrdom of 1592, than the Jesuits had during their first fifty years in Japan. This was palpable nonsense; but there may be more truth in his assertion that the Jesuits had admitted to him that more than 30,000 of their converts had renounced the Faith as a result of Hideyoshi's edict of 1587. Fray Juan Pobre pointed out that the blood of martyrs was the seed of the Church, and that the Franciscan converts, being mostly made as a result of the 1597 crucifixion, would prove stauncher under future persecution than the Jesuits' converts who were moved by self-interest. Pobre's unkindest cut of all, was his assertion that the friars had made more than 2,000 converts among the Fukienese traders who visited Manila annually, whereas the total number of Chinese converts at Macao after nearly fifty years of Jesuit labor was four!

It will be apparent, then, how wide a rift there was between Jesuit and Franciscan men and methods. Just as the Jesuits scoffed at the ignorance and poverty of the *frailes idiotas,* so the Franciscans sneered at the sterile erudition of the Jesuits. That some of the friars were indeed a little crazy is proved by the affair of Fray Juan de Madrid. This friar was working in the Kwanto district, a few years after the arrival of Will Adams and his Dutch shipmates of the *Liefde* in 1600, and he got into a theological argument one day with the heretics at Uraga. In order to prove the validity of the Roman Catholic doctrine, he offered to perform a miracle, either by bringing the sun down from the sky, or removing a neighboring hill, or walking on the sea like St. Peter. The Protestants, who apparently regarded the whole thing as a joke, replied that the first suggestion would burn them alive, and the second would adversely affect the local landowners, and even tried to dissuade the fanatical friar from attempting to make good his third offer. He foolishly insisted on trying, and was only saved from drowning by Melchior Van Santvoort, who put off in a boat to save him. Bishop Cerqueira subsequently reported that the friar was not a bit abashed at his failure, but on the contrary stated that he had a right to expect that God would make good his boast, since he had more faith than the proverbial grain of mustard seed. Padre Carvalho says that this man was subsequently a familiar figure at Malacca and Macao, where he was popularly nick-named "the miracle-monger" (*O Milagreiro*).[23]

Something has already been said in Chapter III about the political and national rivalry between Portuguese and Spaniards. A popular Portuguese proverb has it that neither a good wind nor a good marriage can be expected from Spain, ("De Espanha nem bom vento nem bom casamento"), and certainly the "Babylonian captivity" under the dual Iberian monarchy of 1580–1640, was bitterly resented in the smaller country. For reasons which I need not go into here, the Jesuits of the Province of Portugal were by and large supporters of Portuguese autonomy, particularly in the Iberian colonial empire. It is interesting to note that even the cosmopolitan Jesuit organization in the Orient reflected this nationalist sentiment. Thus the Italians, Valignano and Pasio, were just as ardent defenders of the claims of the Portuguese padroado as were the Portuguese, Carvalho and Cerqueira. The Philippine missionaries, on the other hand, were predominantly Spanish; and most of them made no secret of their conviction that Castilians were morally superior to Portuguese.

The reader has already seen how this latent bitterness flared up over the *San Felipe* affair, whose tragic denouement at Nagasaki in February, 1597, added fuel to the flames. Twenty years later, the blame for this tragedy was still being hotly debated between Jesuit and Franciscan controversialists, and it was taken up by the protagonists of both orders for centuries. Fray Juan Pobre stated roundly that the Jesuits actively worked against recognition of his crucified comrades as martyrs; and that this was indeed true, is obvious from a perusal of the confidential reports of Valignano and Cerqueira in 1597–1600. The Jesuits laid the blame for the whole affair squarely on the shoulders of the Franciscans, whom they accused of provoking Hideyoshi by their wanton rashness and perpetual talk of the Spanish *conquistas*. There is much to be said in justification of this viewpoint, since the connection between Church and State in the Iberian dominions was of the closest, and wars and rumors of wars formed the prevalent topic at Manila.

Not that provocative talk was all on one side of the China Sea, or confined to the mendicant orders as the padres insinuated. Here, the reader need only to recall Gaspar Coelho's gun-running at Nagasaki in 1587, and Antonio Sánchez' ambitions but detailed scheme for the conquest of China two years later, to realize that the Jesuits too had their firebrands. But these latter were more under the control of their level-headed superiors, as a general rule, than were the fanatical friars in the Philippines. This "talk of conquests" was a favorite gibe hurled by the Jesuits at the mendicant orders. It crops up (usually supported by chapter and verse) in all the Jesuit apologetic literature dealing with Luso-Spanish rivalry in the Far East. They were never tired of emphasizing the contrast between peaceful, commercial Macao, which was a reassuringly open city (before 1622), with heavily fortified Manila, which was regarded as a menace by all the Asiatic races around the China Sea. Perhaps they were not far wrong, although Fray Juan Pobre thought otherwise. He claimed that Manila inspired awe, not through its scanty Spanish garrison of six hundred, but because of the numerous friars who prayed for it, "standing like a lone spiritual sentinel of Spain to give light to that New World, five thousand leagues away." [24]

The mutual dislike of Portuguese and Spaniards was evidenced in a hundred ways in Japan. The Portuguese said that the Spaniards of the *San Felipe* told the Japanese that the Portuguese were a decadent race, barely able to cope with half-naked Achinese. Similarly in 1609, some Spanish Franciscans were alleged to have told the Japanese that King Felipe regarded the Spaniards as his sons, whereas the Portuguese were only his servants whom he held in scant regard. On the other hand, the Spaniards alleged that the Macaonese merchants branded them as potential conquistadores of Japan, and disclaimed Portuguese allegiance to King Felipe, concealing the fact that the two Iberian crowns were united. Needless to say, all concerned formally denied having ever said any such thing, but the reports continued to circulate none the less. There is every reason to believe that although the Portuguese and Jesuits did not actually disown Lusitanian allegiance to King Felipe of Spain, they certainly did not stress it.

There is one point worth mentioning in connection with these mutual accusations of bad faith. That is the possibility that some of them were started, or at all events circulated, by the Japanese officials, with the deliberate object of fomenting the existing rivalry between the two peoples and turning it to their own advantage. They certainly followed this course with the squabbling Portuguese, Dutch, and English in the seventeenth century, although the rival Europeans did not need much urging to malign one another's characters. Those who have lived in Japan before 1941, will reflect that it was a favorite device of Japanese to traduce Americans while in conversation with Englishmen, and vice versa. But even if, as is probable, the Japanese acted as *agents provocateurs* in this way as far back as the sixteenth century, there is no need to take them too much to task for it. The rivalry between Portuguese and Spaniards on the one hand, and between Jesuits and friars on the other, was a very real thing. The Japanese may have added a little fuel to the flames now and then, more out of malicious humor than anything else, but they certainly did not originate this deep-rooted feeling, and it would have produced its poisoned fruit in any event.

The mendicant orders had never ceased to press for a revocation of the papal brief *Ex pastoralis officio* of 1585, by which the Japan mission field was reserved as a Jesuit monopoly within the sphere of the Portuguese padroado. The friars' representatives at court claimed that Japan really lay within the limits of the Spanish patronazgo, and Fray Juan Pobre and his Dominican colleague, Fray Diego Aduarte, spent much ink and paper in demonstrating the truth of this claim to their own satisfaction at least. The Jesuits on the other hand, used all their influence to keep the brief on the papal statute book, and (what was far more difficult) to secure its observance by the friars from the Philippines. Both sides had powerful friends at Rome and Valladolid, so the struggle was long and keen. Pope Clement VIII promulgated a compromise brief in 1600, whereby the mendicant orders were indeed allowed to proceed to Japan, but only by way of Lisbon and Portuguese India. Those friars already in Japan were ordered to leave forthwith and return to Manila, whence they could (if their superiors so desired) return to Japan by going three-quarters of the way round the world via Lisbon, Goa, and Macao.

This ruling was tantamount to maintaining the Jesuits' monopoly, since their overwhelming influence in Portuguese India would ensure that no Spanish friars who left for the Far East via Lisbon would ever reach their destination. The secular Portuguese authorities were past masters in the art of procrastination, and bureaucratic red tape would effectively enmesh any unwanted Spaniard trying to pass through the seas controlled by the lord of the "conquest, navigation, and commerce of Ethiopia, India, Arabia, and Persia." The Jesuits in Japan were delighted, and Bishop Cerqueira promptly published the papal brief at Nagasaki (August, 1604), although "without any noise or ostentation." He formally notified the resident friars in Japan that they must leave forthwith. Needless to say, none of them budged. They retorted that the Holy Father must have been misinformed, and they said they would stay where they were and await developments. Nor were these long in coming.

Fray Juan Pobre, O.F.M., Fray Diego Aduarte, O.P., and other stalwarts were in Valladolid when they heard the news, and they bombarded the king and his councils with scorching protests. Their arguments eventually convinced the slow-moving Council of State, which reported to King Felipe in December, 1607, that the mendicant orders should be allowed to proceed from the Philippines to Japan. They added that Portuguese commercial interests would be safeguarded by enjoining the friars to sail only in Japanese ships, so that the Macao-Nagasaki trade of the Great Ship would be undisturbed by any Spanish rivals. The sluggish King Felipe, who hitherto had sided with his Portuguese vassals rather than his

Spanish subjects on this point, now gave way. He instructed the council to write secretly to Rome, asking for the revocation of the brief. The Jesuits still fought hard to ward off the blow but in vain. In June, 1608, Pope Paul V promulgated the brief *Sedis Apostolicae providentia,* which opened Japan officially to the ministrations of missionaries from the mendicant orders.[25]

Closely connected with the sectarian and nationalistic rivalry which set Spaniards and Portuguese by the ears in the Far East, was their mutual commercial jealousy. The Portuguese were anxious to maintain their monopoly of the lucrative China-Japan silk trade, and the Spaniards at Manila were equally desirous of participating in it. The Jesuits were well aware of this rivalry, and one of the arguments that Valignano and Cerqueira used in their correspondence with the authorities at Goa and Lisbon was the great financial loss which the state of India would suffer if the Spaniards were allowed to drain off a great part of this wealth at its source. Spanish attempts to establish themselves on the Kwangtung seaboard were forcibly resisted by the Portuguese in 1599. Even this display of force against fellow subjects of the crown did not satisfy Bishop Cerqueira, who complained to the archbishop of Goa that the secular authorities were less alive to the danger of Spanish encroachment than were the Jesuits. The friars on the other hand roundly declared that the main reason for the Jesuits' reaction was not to maintain the purity of the Faith in Japan, as they alleged, but to prevent the mendicant orders from seeing the thriving commerce which the Society drove at Nagasaki. Pobre also claimed that the Japanese, whether Christian or heathen, were far more edified by the ascetic poverty of the Franciscans, than by what he stigmatized as the worldly wisdom of the Jesuits.

It should be noted that the inter-Iberian commercial rivalry was not quite so clear cut as were the sectarian and political differences. Although all trade between Macao and Manila was repeatedly forbidden by the Iberian kings, yet the merchants of both colonies found in each other customers as well as competitors. The Macaonese exported Chinese silks to Manila, and although the Spaniards complained that the Portuguese charged them far higher prices than did the Fukien merchants, yet they continued to buy from both. Similarly, the Spaniards often sent to Macao for the purchase of ship chandler's stores and shipping; although here again they complained that the Macaonese charged higher prices than the Cantonese would have done. Conversely, the Portuguese at Macao sometimes bought munitions and other commodities at Manila, so that a constant if ostensibly illicit trade was driven between the two colonies. It is none the less true that it was as competitors that they eyed the Japan trade.

The Dominican friar, Diego Aduarte, seriously suggested that King Felipe should order the abandonment of Macao, and the forcible deportation of its inhabitants to Portuguese India. He pointed out that this would leave Manila as the sole Iberian port for Japan, whence the Philippine Spaniards could secure silver, instead of from Mexico as at present (1618). Another authority suggested that the colonists should be transferred to Formosa; and a third school of thought proposed the scarcely less drastic step of exchanging the Philippines with the Crown of Portugal for Brazil.[26]

Fray Juan Pobre, writing in 1605, stated that from five to ten Japanese ships visited Manila every year. About half of their crews were Christians on their arrival in the colony, yet he claimed that by the time the vessels returned to Japan, nearly all the remainder had been converted by the Franciscans. Apart from this spiritual fruit, the temporal advantages of the Japan-Philippines trade were not to be denied. He wrote that these ships not only brought supplies of wheat flour, which relieved Manila's chronic food shortage, but cordage for shipping, and copper and other metals for gun founding. All these materials were supplied at very reasonable prices, and the local Japanese Christians served the Spaniards faithfully and well in a military capacity when required. The Japan Jesuits, on the other hand, insinuated that the actual Japan-Manila trade was of little value, and that the authorities merely kept it going in the hope that it would ultimately increase to the detriment of the Macao-Nagasaki commerce.

What annoyed the friars most of all about their rivals, was the vast profits allegedly made by the Jesuits from their share in the Japan silk trade. Friar Pobre brushed aside the protestations of the Society's official apologists that its earnings hardly covered its expenses in the Far East. He repeated the common assertion that the silk trade was worth at least 200,000 ducats a year to them, whereas Valignano explicitly stated that it did not amount to a twentieth of that sum. Other Franciscans drew unedifying comparisons between the Jesuit college at Nagasaki and the customs house at Seville, indicating that there was nothing to choose between them in the way of bustling commercial activity. This was a palpable exaggeration; but there was more substance in Fray Diego Aduarte's acidulous observations about the warehouse attached to the Jesuit college in Macao, where Chinese merchants chaffered over the price of silk with the presiding padre, whose reputation for commercial acumen was considerable. A letter from General Mucio Vitelleschi to the local father-visitor alludes to the numerous complaints received at Rome about this unedifying juxtaposition of God and Mammon, and orders the visitor to find another warehouse in a more secluded spot.[27]

Valignano and Carvalho in their several *Apologia* give a great deal of space to refuting the friars' allegations on the extent of the Jesuit trade at Nagasaki. Undoubtedly the figures given by the spokesmen of the mendicant orders were grossly exaggerated, but some of the Jesuits' labored denials are likewise far from convincing. Carvalho endeavors to show that most of the mercantile hustle and bustle around the college was not caused by the sale of the Jesuits' own bales of silk (which were marketed by the Great Ship's factor with the bulk of the cargo) but by secular traders who brought disputed goods to be adjudicated on. He explains that both Japanese and Portuguese merchants were anxious to do business through Jesuit interpreters, since the padres alone had sufficient command of both languages to carry through any com-

plicated negotiations. Moreover, both nationals trusted the
Jesuits in preference to one another, and hence preferred to
clinch their commercial bargains through a Jesuit father. This
involved bringing the goods to the scene of arbitration in most
instances; hence the animated commercial chaffering, "about
which the friars kick up such a dust." He adds that this activity did not last long, and that the usual cloistered calm of
the convent returned when it was all over.

This defense is convincing enough so far as it goes, but it
does not tell the whole story. As Fray Pobre said of the Jesuit
printed relations in another connection, "I do not question
what they say, but what they omit." Carvalho denies that the
Jesuits got any profit from acting as intermediaries, but he
admits that it was natural that most people should think "we
must also dip our spoon in the honey." The silk cargo of the
Great Ship at this time was annually sold in bulk, at a price
agreed between the Portuguese and the representatives of the
commercial communities of Kyoto, Yedo, Osaka, Sakai, and
Nagasaki. This system was known as the *pancada,* and the
Jesuits' share was included therein. Carvalho admits that sometimes they "sold some piculs before the ship left and at higher
prices than those of the pancada, just as everybody else did."
Aye, there's the rub! The point at issue is not so much whether
they operated on the "black market" (they obviously did),
but whether their transactions were on a large scale. It is not
easy to write with full assurance on this point; but from
Padre Luis da Gama's review of the Jesuit trade in the Far
East from its inception to 1664, it is clear that the Jesuits
traded in secret on a larger scale than they admitted to doing
in public.[28]

As to the reaction which their commercial activities caused
in Japan, it is easier to write with assurance. It certainly did
them no harm in the eyes of either Hideyoshi or Ieyasu, both
of whom placed implicit trust in their commercial agent at
Nagasaki, the astute Padre João Rodriguez Tçuzzu. Time and
again the Jesuits state—no doubt correctly—that they would
have been expelled from the country long before 1614, but for

the fact that their presence at Nagasaki was thought to be essential to the smooth conduct of the Macao trade. Although the merchant was relegated to near the bottom of the Japanese social scale, neither Hideyoshi nor Ieyasu shared this typically feudal prejudice, and both did all in their power to encourage the growth of commerce. Padre Carvalho relates an amusing anecdote in this respect. A young samurai asked his father why he had abandoned his calling as a soldier and gone into the shipping trade? The father replied that he had often vainly tried to attract Ieyasu's notice as a samurai, but no sooner did he turn trader than the old shogun became most gracious toward him. This is in striking contrast to the attitude of the second Tokugawa shogun, Hidetada. Writing to the King of Siam about the misbehavior of some local Japanese traders, he advised this monarch to put them to death, since "merchants are fond of gain and given up to greed, and abominable fellows of this kind ought not to escape punishment."

But if the rulers of Japan no more objected to the Jesuits engaging in trade with China than they did to similar activities on the part of the Zen priesthood, it was far otherwise with their underlings. Ieyasu's confidence in his interpreter Rodriguez was such, that at one time he was even directly associated with the municipal governors of Nagasaki. His non-Christian Japanese colleagues on the governing board resented his presence in this capacity, and did all they could to destroy the shogun's confidence in him. Moreover, Rodriguez' responsibility and activity over the disposal of the Great Ship's yearly cargo, could not fail to arouse animosity in the local mercantile community, and many of his colleagues considered it unbecoming to his cloth. Bishop Cerqueira admitted that Rodriguez delved into these negotiations "with less moderation and religious prudence than could be wished"; but he added that it could not be denied that "he was very expert and intelligent in this business." The bishop considered that nearly all the troubles which had come to the Jesuits in Japan in the years 1604–1607, were due to this awkward mixture of the sacred and the profane, which led the Japanese to accuse both

Rodriguez and Vice-Provincial Pasio of meddling in temporal matters which did not really concern them. He realized that Rodriguez would have to continue his commercial activities, since Ieyasu insisted on it; but he frankly admitted that he ought to do so with more prudence and moderation.

This extract from the confidential episcopal correspondence of 1607 is sufficiently revealing; and it is not surprising to read in Padre Carvalho's *Apologia* of ten years later, that Rodriguez was finally "framed" by his enemies and expelled from Japan by order of Ieyasu in 1612. Carvalho would have his readers believe that Ieyasu was subsequently convinced of his former protégé's innocence, and announced his intention of recalling him ("eu tornarey a chamar a João"). This may have been so, but it need hardly be added that the real or imaginary origin of this scandal provided plenty of grist for the Franciscans' anti-Jesuit mill. The last word has not yet been said on what was undoubtedly a shady affair.[29]

It must not be imagined that the Jesuits remained silent in face of the friars' verbal and written onslaughts. Guzman, Valignano, and Carvalho, to mention only three of their champions, replied at length and on the whole convincingly. Nor did they refrain from using the *Tu Quoque*. In reply to the friars' exaggerated accounts of Jesuit trading, they twitted the mendicant orders with holding vast landed properties in all quarters of the globe. Padre Carvalho claimed that the sacristan of a Franciscan convent at Lisbon had an annual income of between 20,000 and 30,000 cruzados, derived from the ecclesiastical dues exacted for burials, masses, and so forth. He also alleged that the sacristan of the Franciscan convent at Goa enjoyed a yearly income of 11,000 or 12,000 *xerafines*, besides regal gifts of wine, rice, and cotton. There is no doubt that several of the monasteries were very wealthy, and that their boasts of ascetic poverty were misplaced; but Carvalho in his turn probably exaggerated gossip which he had heard about the *parvoice de frades* ("friars' folly"). In any event, the friars, like the Jesuits, undoubtedly spent the greater part if not all of their income on charitable works. The bitter words which passed between the champions of the Society of Jesus and the spokesmen of the rival orders should not blind the reader to the fact that the majority of the missionaries whom they represented were working sincerely, if at times mistakenly, toward one and the same end—the greater glory of God.

It will be apparent that the rivalry between the various Roman Catholic orders in Japan was one of the prime causes of the ruin of their missions, just as it was two centuries later in China. Irrespective of the rights and wrongs of the disputants, it was inevitable that this fratricidal strife would have disastrous repercussions on the mission as a whole, as Valignano foresaw in 1583. In the bitterness of their disputes, both sides lost sight of the wood for the trees. One of the Spanish councilors of state, commenting on the Jesuits' objection to the dissimilarity of the friars' garb in Japan, remarked that "quarrels between the different religious orders will be of much greater injury and less edification than the diversity of their garb." And so it proved.

Bishop Cerqueira quotes a Japanese Christian as remarking (apropos of the friars' refusal to recognize the validity of the 1603 brief) that "those who know the pope best, obey him the least." The bishop professed his amazement that the friars should maintain that the papacy was ill-informed, after all the arguments had been thrashed out before the Holy See for the last eight years. Yet the Jesuits themselves proved equally obstinate on occasion, as witness their failure to obey the rulings of nine successive popes who condemned the Chinese rites. Even if the Jesuits were right in maintaining that the Japan mission field was best left in their hands, they surely acted unwisely in trying to exclude the friars once the latter had gained a firm footing.[30]

Chapter VI. PIRATES AND TRADERS

THE "Christian Century" (1549–1650) witnessed three important developments in the history of Japan. First, the unification of the country by Hideyoshi. Second, the molding of the Tokugawa dictatorship which in many respects laid the foundations of modern militarized Japan. Third, the short-lived but significant expansion of Japanese activities, legitimate and otherwise, in southeast Asia. The first two developments are sufficiently well known to warrant no detailed treatment here, but it may be well to consider certain aspects of the third. In order to do this, I must retrace my steps for a couple of centuries and briefly review the doings of the Wako, who will be remembered as the unedifying forerunners of this movement.

The piratical forays of the "dwarf robbers" along the China coast, had begun in Mongol times, presumably by way of reprisals for Kublai Khan's unsuccessful invasions. They did not cease with the expulsion of the Mongols from China, but on the contrary greatly increased after 1350. Hungwu, the founder of the dynasty, was no sooner seated on his throne in 1369, than he sent an envoy to Japan with the double object of notifying the Japanese government of his accession and asking them to stop these raids. No answer was returned to this last request. A second mission was more successful, so far as it arranged for the renewal of friendly official intercourse between the two empires which had been sundered since the reign of the Great Khan.

The raids still continued as merrily as ever in spite of this display of cordiality in high quarters, Shantung Province being the principal sufferer. This provoked another embassy from the Ming emperor, bringing a long-winded admonitory

248

edict, couched in that Confucian tone of *de haut en bas,* which the Chinese emperors invariably employed in addressing their subjects. This rescript demanded the immediate cessation of Japanese piratical activities, and threatened that otherwise the Chinese would send a fleet to take punitive action. The Ashikaga government now went so far as to send some envoys, headed by a Zen priest named Sorai, to proffer excuses and presents, together with seventy Chinese captives who had been taken in these *razzias.* Although the sincerity of this embassy was somewhat offset by the fact that the Wako were simultaneously raiding the China coast from Chekiang to Kwangtung, the Ming court accepted it at its face value. Hungwu had declared the cult of Confucius the state religion (or its equivalent) on his accession; but in view of the Japanese veneration for the Buddhist priesthood he sent a bonze as head of return mission. This clerical diplomat was no more successful than his predecessors in persuading the Ashikaga to take active steps to put down piracy. Piratical forays and diplomatic missions continued to be exchanged between Japan and China with monotonous regularity.[1]

The organization of the diplomatic missions was in the hands of the Zen priesthood, and more particularly in those of the abbot of the Tenryuji or Heavenly Dragon Temple at Saga village, west of Kyoto. This practice had originated with Abbot Soseki, who induced Ashikaga Takauji to build this temple to the memory of the Emperor Go-Daigo whom he had dethroned. The construction was largely financed (likewise at Soseki's suggestion) with the profits gained from the sale of the cargoes of shipping which the abbot was authorized to send to China annually. These vessels normally went to Ningpo or neighboring ports, and were known as *Tenryujibune* because of their origin. Once intercourse with China was placed on a regular footing by the first Ming emperor, these ships usually carried the official envoys from the Ashikaga shoguns to the court of Peking. The envoys were often Zen priests; these clerics were likewise prominent in all the ship-

[1] For notes to chapter vi, see pages 483–490.

ping, commercial, and political negotiations with the Chinese. As the best educated men in Japan, they had some knowledge of the Chinese classics, and were more fitted to negotiate with the celestials than were unlettered merchants or belli-cose samurai. These missions were designated by the Chinese as tribute-bearing embassies, on a level with those from Korea, Annam, and other satellite states. Shogun Ashikaga Yoshi-mitsu has incurred much odium from modern Japanese his-torians for accepting this role of vassal, and thus affronting the national pride. Yoshimitsu did not take his nominal inferi-ority very seriously, as may be seen from his correspondence with the Emperor Hungwu.

In addition to these genuine tributary missions, which from the Japanese point of view were mercantile voyages in diplo-matic guise, a large number of self-styled envoys, who were traders, adventurers, or even pirates more or less thinly dis-guised, presented themselves at Chinese ports. So frequent had these pseudo-envoys become by 1379–1380, that the irritated Hungwu exiled a number of them to the frontier provinces of Yunnan and Shensi. He also wrote to Yoshimitsu complain-ing of the affront given to Chinese imperial dignity by the shogun's failure to stop either their activities or those of the Wako. The imperial rescript was couched in the usual lofty Confucian style, but merely drew a sarcastic retort from Yoshimitsu. He pointed out that the Chinese were suffering from delusions of grandeur in considering their country as the center of the world, when it was only a mere outlying seg-ment thereof. Chinese emphasis on the superiority of Con-fucian doctrine was countered with the assertion that the teachings of the sage and his followers were equally well known and revered in Japan. A veiled Chinese threat of hos-tilities was met by open defiance.

Neither Hungwu nor any of his successors ventured to at-tack the Wako in their Kyushu bases, but contented them-selves with purely defensive (and for the most part ineffec-tive) measures, such as reorganizing the coastal defenses and building more forts. This is rather surprising, since for most of this time at any rate, China had a far more powerful and efficient sea-going fleet than the Japanese. Moreover, Japan was rent by civil broils, and no longer the united country which had repelled the Mongol invasion in Hojo Tokimune's time. Whether this attitude was due to the inherent peacefulness of the Chinese character, or to a superstitious fear of provoking the guardian gods of the island empire into sending another typhoon like those which had wrecked the Great Khan's enterprises, it is difficult to say. The Emperor Yunglo did dispatch his famous eunuch Admiral Chengho to sweep the China Sea of the corsairs on one occasion; but the latter, on the approach of the Chinese fleet of 208 ships and 28,000 men, merely retired to their island fastnesses of Goto, Tsushima, and Iki, whither the Chinese did not venture to follow them. This naval demonstration may have been an inducement for the Japanese to surrender voluntarily twenty of the Wako in 1405. These were grilled to death over a slow fire at Ningpo by their own countrymen, since the Ming emperor had left the manner of their execution to their Japanese escort. It may be added that the completion of the Grand Canal in the reign of Chengtsu was due to the desire to transport the tribute rice from the southern provinces in safety to Peking, since the Wako intercepted the bulk of it by sea.

Piratical raids and pseudo-diplomatic embassies continued throughout the fifteenth century. So frequent did the latter become that the Chinese government repeatedly tried to ensure the authenticity of their credentials. One of these methods was the presentation of a bamboo baton to the outgoing genuine envoy. This baton, with the imperial vermillion seal in the center, was cut in half, one half being retained in the chancery in Peking; the other half being taken by the returning envoy to Japan in order to give it to the next envoy. Neither this nor other less puerile measures proved of much avail; and by 1548, there were more than two hundred Chinese imperial seals in Japan, in one form or another, the return of which the Chinese vainly demanded before authorizing any new missions. Relatively few of these seals were returned by the Jap-

anese government, which cynically admitted that the Wako
had obtained many of them. Others had been sold or given by
the Zen priests to local daimyo or prominent traders, who
were thus enabled to provide their own commercial ventures
to China with diplomatic credentials.[2]

These Japanese embassies, whether genuine or otherwise,
were clearly a great source of trouble to the Court of Peking,
and it is difficult to understand why it tolerated them for so
long, especially in view of the concomitant increase in the
Wako's raiding activities. The envoys and their suites frequently numbered several hundred armed men, who did not
scruple to use force when they did not get what they wanted,
even when in the interior of China on their way to or from
court. Takekoshi gives the cargoes of ten tributary vessels in
1453, as comprising 397,500 kin of sulphur; 154,500 kin of
copper; 10,003 kin of iron; 106,000 kin of dye; 9,500 swords;
1,250 fans; 81 lances; and 630 picture scrolls. The presence of
so much copper is rather surprising, since copper was the main
article of export from China to Japan at this time. The large
number of swords is also rather odd, particularly since they
must have been meant for use against the Wako. They were
evidently highly valued by the Chinese, since the return present for 67,000 swords in 1483, consisted of a quantity of
copper, on the basis of 3,000 *mon* of copper for each sword. In
later years a little gold was included, for which the Chinese
gave silver in exchange. This is a reversal of what occured in
the sixteenth century, when the Portuguese exchanged Japanese silver for Chinese gold. It is curious that so many fans
were imported, since the Chinese can hardly have been inferior
to the Japanese in the making of these fragile articles.

A proportion of this cargo was recognized as tribute, but
in accordance with Chinese etiquette, the Ming court had to
give presents of equal value in return. The Japanese loudly
complained if they did not get what they considered a good
bargain in this exchange, and it seems obvious that the whole
transaction was far more profitable to them than to the

Chinese. The Ming emperors tried to reduce this "ramp" (for such it was) to manageable proportions, by ordaining that these embassies should only come once in ten years, and be limited to two hundred armed men in two ships, and only thirty individuals would be allowed to proceed to court. Embargoes were placed on foreign trade, sometimes wholesale, and sometimes on unlicensed trade only. All of these edicts seem to have been ignored. The Japanese cajoled, bribed, or threatened the local mandarins as occasion offered; nor did they refrain from insinuating that the Wako raids would become fiercer than ever if their demands were not met. All complaints to the Ashikaga shogunate met with evasive or non-committal answers; and indeed this decaying institution was in no condition to control its unruly subordinates after the outbreak of the Onin war (1467), even if it had wanted to do so. By this time, the Zen priesthood was no longer monopolizing the Tenryuji-bune, and trade to China was likewise being driven by powerful daimyo, such as Otomo of Bungo, Ouchi of Suwo, and Shimadzu of Satsuma, as well as by the merchants of Hakata and Sakai, and even by the agents of the Shinto shrine at Ise.

Although the Ming court derived no concrete benefit from their unwanted Japanese visitors, this evidently did not apply to the mercantile community in the seaports. At any rate, the Japanese traders and pseudo-envoys drove a flourishing trade whenever the Chinese littoral was not ravaged by the Wako. Moreover, Chinese junks visited Japan despite the ostensible bans on foreign trade, and some of the leading Chinese merchants, like their Japanese counterparts, doubled the roles of trader and pirate. Prominent among these Jekyll and Hyde characters was Wangchih, a native of Anhwei, who, after trading with Japan, Siam, and the Portuguese, amassed a gigantic fortune and settled in the Chusan Islands which he ruled as an independent principality. He was eventually enticed to the mainland by specious promises of pardon and high office, when he was promptly seized and executed as a traitor at

Hangchow in 1557. Despite his origin, he had for many years been the organizer of the worst Wako raids along the China coast.[3]

The depredations of the "dwarf robbers" increased proportionately with the unsettled condition of Japan during the *Sengoku-jidai*. By the middle of the sixteenth century, their ravages extended from Liaotung in the north to Hainan Island in the south, and they had penetrated as far inland as Anhwei and Hunan. On two occasions the ancestral tomb of the founder of the Ming dynasty narrowly escaped destruction and desecration at their hands. Chinese and Japanese records both agree that these piratical bands were not composed entirely, or even mainly of Japanese. Generally, about one-third of any given gang consisted of Japanese, whereas the remainder were Chinese with a sprinkling of Malays, Annamites, and Koreans. Doubtless a few Portuguese were sometimes included, as is explicitly stated in the Chinese records. Perhaps Pinto participated in such a foray, or at any rate spoke with someone who had. This would account for his tall tales about plundering the imperial tombs, and traversing China from north to south. The Wako raids were frequently conducted with every circumstance of atrocity. Takekoshi and other Japanese historians pour scorn on the Ming stories of scalding babies to death, ripping open pregnant women, and so forth; but in view of the behavior of the Imperial Japanese Army in China from 1937 to 1945, few writers nowadays would dream of contesting the accuracy of the Chinese chronicles in this respect.

In spite (or perhaps because) of this behavior, the Wako found no lack of helpers among the populace of the China coast. The local banditti made common cause with them, and they never lacked guides who knew the terrain and the whereabouts of the local garrisons. They were thus usually able to conduct their raids and be gone before any troops arrived to interfere with them. Many of the local gentry in Fukien were hand in glove with them, purchasing part of their booty when occasion offered. In other instances the Wako combined with the proletariat to plunder the rich; but in one way or another they could count on collaborators, guides, and "fifth-columnists" of some kind. The Ming court also gave them useful if involuntary assistance by its invariable custom of impeaching and executing capable field commanders as traitors, and at the same time promoting inefficient eunuch favorites to high command.

One of the best-known instances of this gratuitous folly was that of Chuhuan, viceroy of Chekiang and Fukien provinces, and his Admiral Lutang. These worthies had restored Chinese morale, which was at an exceedingly low ebb, by training, disciplining (and above all paying), their soldiers and sailors. Between them they inflicted a series of crushing defeats on the Wako in 1547–1549. Provincial traitors and envious court rivals combined to discredit Chuhuan with the moonstruck Ming emperor, who cashiered him in 1549, without attempting to verify the accusations made against him. Chuhuan committed suicide in order to save his family from being involved in his disgrace, and his admiral and other loyal subordinates were executed. The 140 forts and 439 ships which these two commanders had built or repaired, were allowed to lapse into ruin, and their demoralized soldiers were no match for the returning Wako. China's worst enemies were ever those of her own household.

The Wako reached their peak in the years 1552–1556, when it was estimated that more than a hundred thousand of them were ravaging the China coast and the Yangtse Valley delta. These numbers are doubtless exaggerated, even if their local adherents are included; but there can be no doubt that they were exceedingly formidable and greatly feared. In 1559, they met with several reverses, after having previously carried their depredations to the walls of Nanking. So alarmed was the sluggish government of Peking at this bravado, that they at length based a large army in Chekiang Province. The Japanese now concentrated their attacks on Fukien and Kwangtung, whose coastal districts they harried with fire and sword, although seventy Wako junks sailed a good distance up the Yangtse with impunity in 1565. Particularly heavy raids were made in Kwangtung Province in 1567–1572; but the emergence of a strong central government in Japan which was anxious for peaceful foreign trade, gradually tended to dry up the supply of recruits at its source. The attacks continued intermittently down to the end of the century, but their last formidable effort was made in 1588. This year also witnessed a not altogether unfounded scare of a general Japanese invasion of China, despite the promulgation of an edict by Hideyoshi stringently prohibiting the practice of piracy in any shape or form.

Chinese resistance had also increased in effectiveness, despite the criminal inefficiency of the Ming court. Matteo Ricci, writing in 1584, said that two or three small vessels of the Wako frequently landed pirate bands which ravaged the countryside and captured populous cities and towns with virtually no resistance, unless through treason or overconfidence they fell into an ambush. But Valignano, writing about ten years later, observed that this was no longer true. On the contrary, the Chinese had become such veteran soldiers that even large forces of Japanese could not disembark with any hope of success. Wako piracy had thus virtually ceased, despite the fact that the two empires were at war. The truth of this observation is borne out by the Korean campaign of 1592–1598, when the Chinese, once they had taken the measure of their enemy, proved themselves tough and indomitable fighters, as the Japanese freely admitted in later years to the Hollanders at Hirado. In mediaeval as in modern times, it was not the Chinese soldiery so much as the Chinese government which was responsible for disastrous defeats on the battlefield.

The close connection between the Portuguese and the Japanese, to say nothing of the former's coöperation with the Fukienese smuggler allies of the Wako, naturally aroused Chinese dislike and suspicion. An imperial decree of Emperor Wanli in 1613 chided the inhabitants of Macao for their patronage of the Japanese, who were described as "thieves, birds of prey, and rebels against the sovereign emperor of

WAKO

ODA NOBUNAGA

A PORTUGUESE CARRACK

TWO FRIARS AND A JESUIT

TOYOTOMI HIDEYOSHI

ARTE DA L'INGOA DE IA-
PAM COMPOSTA PELLO

Padre Ioão Rodriguez, Portugues da Companhia de IESV diuidida em tres

LIVROS.

COM LICENÇA DO ORDI-
NARIO, E SVPERIORES EM

Nangasaqui no Collegio de Iapão da

Companhia de IESV

Anno. 1604.

PADRE RODRIGUEZ' JAPANESE GRAMMAR

TOKUGAWA IEYASU

THE GREAT MARTYRDOM OF SEPTEMBER 10, 1622

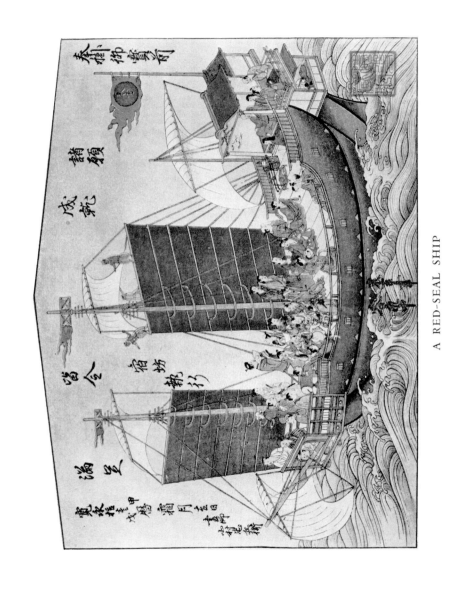

A RED-SEAL SHIP

PRISONERS ON WAY TO INTERROGATION BY A BUGYO

PRISONER ON WAY TO EXECUTION

A JAPANESE CRUCIFIXION

ATTACK ON HARA CASTLE, 1638

A PORTUGUESE FIDALGO

S. Francicus Xaanni   Iapaiqae Apoftolis.

P.ᵉ Edit:

JESUIT MARTYRS, 1597–1633

China." The Macaonese were sharply reminded that Japanese were forbidden to visit China on pain of death, whereas "the Europeans of Macao harbor Japanese and keep them as slaves, oblivious of the fact that they are rearing tigers." A stringent investigation by the Kwangtung provincial authorities had disclosed ninety-eight Japanese in Macao, who were summarily deported. It was now ordained that no more should be introduced into the colony, on pain of the offenders being banished for life. How much notice was taken of this effusion may be gathered from the fact that it had to be repeated in 1617.[4]

It was mentioned earlier that Chinese fear of a reported Japanese invasion in 1588, was not altogether unreasonable. It has been shown that Nobunaga and Hideyoshi both talked freely to the Jesuits of their projects to conquer China, and that some at least of the fathers had taken the bait. Coelho's rashness in responding to Hideyoshi's overtures in 1586 has already been discussed; but still less excusable was the project of the Spanish Jesuit, Padre Alonso Sánchez.

This report has to be read to be believed. It was a serious proposal for the conquest of China and its conversion to the Christian faith. It was supported by the governor, the bishop, and the notables of Manila assembled in council (April, 1586), not one dissenting voice being raised to point out the monstrous folly of so absurd an undertaking. On the contrary, the *junta* considered that the five hundred odd Spaniards in the Philippines would live in history as "mean-spirited cowards" if they refused to undertake "an object as important for the world, for God, for our king, for ourselves, and above all for the people of this country." An expeditionary force of 10,000 or 12,000 men was requested from Europe, including as many Biscayans as possible. It was proposed to recruit 5,000 or 6,000 Visayan Indians locally, aside from an equal number of Japanese who would be obtained through the Jesuits in Japan. The province of Cagayan was selected as the concentration area for this army, since it was only a three-day sail from China, and conveniently situated for the arrival of Japanese auxiliaries. Slaves and shipping stores were obtainable at cheap rates from Portuguese India, and many of the transports could be built locally, since the natives proved skillful shipwrights under the guidance of a few Spanish experts. It was suggested that the Portuguese should mount another attack by way of Macao and Canton, while the Spaniards would land in Fukien. Ricci and the other Jesuits in the interior of China would be recalled to Macao and Manila to act as guides and interpreters to the invading forces.

The provisions regarding the Japanese contingent are especially interesting.

> If the Japanese who are to be taken on the expedition do not wish to join the Castilians, and prefer to go in with the Portuguese, since they already know them, and likewise because they get along better, and the Portuguese treat them more as equals than is permitted here, they may do so. But if they wish to go with the Castilians, let them come to Cagayan, and this will be arranged with them and with the fathers of the Society of Jesus, who are to act as guides . . . His Majesty should procure and bring about that the general of the Society of Jesus should command and ordain to the fathers in Japan, not to hinder the bringing of this reinforcement of Japanese, and whatever may be needed therefore; and to this end he should send a father sufficiently commissioned, who should be an Italian.

Valignano's blood pressure must have risen several degrees when he heard of this extraordinary proposal; particularly since it must have come to his ears at about the same time as he heard of Gaspar Coelho's offer to obtain for Hideyoshi the use of Portuguese ships and artillery from Goa, in connection with the Kwambaku's slightly more rational scheme for the conquest of China. The Audiencia of Manila in describing this project to King Felipe, particularly commended its originator and their representative, Padre Alonso Sánchez, as "a man of the highest prudence and learning, and most excellent in Christian faith and practice." One member of the Audiencia, Pedro de Rojas, writing separately to the king in favor of the proposed expedition and its sponsor, extolled the Jesuit as being "a person of very holy life, much learning, prudence, and excellent judgment." Whatever the holiness of his life and the depth of his learning, his judgment would have disgraced a child of six; but his report may serve as a quaint example of clerical arrogance and conquistador cocksureness during the days of Spanish grandeur.[5]

Valignano, who did not share the naïve delusions of so many of his contemporaries, rejected the scheme in toto; but it probably stood little chance of being accepted at Madrid, since Sánchez and his proposal reached Spain in the year of the loss of the Invincible Armada. The kings of Spain, to their honor be it said, were usually far less anxious for the extension of their conquests and patronazgo than were their hot-headed servants in the colonies. Either because they were more enlightened, or because their attention was primarily fixed on Europe, where they had wars enough and to spare against Turks and heretics, the Felipes and their councilors almost invariably rejected such proposals out of hand.

Support, however, was forthcoming from another interested quarter. In the year following the formal elaboration of Sánchez' pet project, a number of Japanese merchants and Wako from Hirado reached Manila. They declared that both Matsura of Hirado and the Christian daimyo, Konishi Yukinaga, would willingly supply 6,000 men or more, for the invasion of China, Borneo, the Moluccas, or Indo-China, "without asking anything in return, for they only wish to serve your majesty and to gain honor." The governor, Santiago de Vera, seems to have had second (and better) thoughts about the conquest of China, since he contented himself with thanking the Japanese for their offer. He explicitly stated that he had kept this conference secret, so as to avoid alarming the Chinese, "who tremble at their name," and were a "very suspicious and timorous race." Even if he kept his mouth shut, it is unlikely that either the Manila gossips or the swashbuckling Wako did so; hence the Chinese fear of a threatened Ibero-Japanese invasion of 1588, was not so ridiculous as it would otherwise seem.

The Spanish readiness to use the Japanese as mercenary soldiers is all the more surprising, since they had already experienced their fighting qualities at Cagayan Province in 1582. Carrion's brush with some local Wako clearly showed what a potential menace the warlike Nipponese were to the sparsely garrisoned colony. The Spaniards had only overcome their opponents after a stiff fight and the use of artillery. Moreover, Limahon's second in command in the attack on Manila in 1574, was a Japanese, and there were several Wako in the celebrated Chinese corsair's force. The introduction of Japanese mercenaries was therefore the equivalent of a Trojan horse, but it was some time before the colonial government realized this obvious fact. Only the presentation of Hideyoshi's arrogant ultimatum in 1592, finally disillusioned them.

At the time of the Spaniards' arrival in the Philippines, a few stray traders and Wako visited northern Luzon; but contrary to what most modern writers state, I know of no good evidence which indicates that they had any fixed settlement in the Philippines before 1582. One of the principal objects for which they were seeking in Luzon was the Sung and Yuan ceramic ware, buried in old Philippine graves. Some specimens of this ware had an enormous value to the devotees of chanoyu, according to contemporary Iberian chroniclers.

The Spaniards started playing with fire again when they employed a number of Japanese adventurers in their expedition to Cambodia in 1595; although in this instance the desire to remove the Japanese as far as possible from Manila may have been a motive for their employment. One of the moving spirits in this enterprise was the Dominican, Fray Diego Aduarte, who in later years distinguished himself as a bitter critic of the Jesuits and their missionary methods in the Orient. The Filipino patriot and scholar, Rizal, aptly characterized the bellicose Dominican: "Fray Diego Aduarte is the type of the adventurous friar of that period, half warrior and half priest, brave and enduring; confessing, baptizing, and killing, full of faith and without any scruples." Largely because of their own truculence, the Spaniards fell foul of the Khmers, and were compelled to retreat down the Mekong

River to the coast, after reaching Phnom Penh, and killing the King of Cambodia (to say nothing of a large number of innocent Chinese) in a night attack. Both Fray Aduarte and the Japanese distinguished themselves in this buccaneering expedition by their courage; although Aduarte's friend, Fray Juan Pobre, was guilty of exaggeration when he wrote a few years later that "twenty-two Spaniards and as many Japanese were masters of the kingdom of Cambodia."

The next occasion on which the Japanese distinguished themselves in the Philippines was in the bloody suppression of the "Sangley" Chinese rebellion at Manila in October, 1603. The outbreak of this rising was due largely to the imprudent conduct of Archbishop Benavides and like-minded bigots, whose exaggerated suspicions precipitated if they did not originate the actual rebellion. Its suppression would scarcely have been possible without the aid of the local Japanese community which joined in the slaughter with a will. In accordance with the time-honored practice of the Japanese in China, they spared neither age nor sex in their favorite pastime of beheading prisoners, although it would be hard to say whether they exceeded the Spaniards in blind ferocity. Three years later, it was the turn of the Japanese to threaten to revolt at Manila, but they were pacified by the local friars after some difficulty. This was just as well, since the bulk of the scanty garrison was absent with the governor, Don Pedro de Acuña, on an expedition to the Moluccas.[6]

The Japanese were active in southeast Asia as well as in the Philippines at this time, but their activities on the mainland were more in the nature of genuine trading than in the swashbuckling reminiscent of the Wako. Their overseas maritime commerce was carried on in ships called *Go-shuin-sen* or August Red-seal ships, from the official license or letters patent granted to their owners by the Bakufu. These Red-seal ships may be regarded in a sense as the descendants of the Tenryuji-bune of Ashikaga days, although it would be difficult to state when the changeover took place. The first recorded issue of the *shuinjo* or red-seal passport for overseas navigation was made by Hideyoshi in 1592. The French Orientalist, Noël Peri, has argued cogently that this move was probably connected with the tighter control over Japan's foreign contacts evidenced in that year by the Taiko Hideyoshi's invasion of Korea, his ultimatum to the Spaniards at Manila, and the dispatch of special commissioners to Nagasaki.

Be this as it may, the system now inaugurated lasted for more than forty years. Under it, all Japanese shipping, or that belonging to foreigners resident in Japan, which was engaged in maritime commerce with foreign countries had to be provided with the shuinjo. Skippers or merchants whose voyages were not authorized by such an official document were regarded as pirates or smugglers. Such at any rate became the general practice during the second half of the Keicho period, although between 1592 and 1604, a number of Japanese ships frequented foreign ports without carrying any such passports. Once Ieyasu felt himself firmly in the saddle, he seems to have insisted on the shuinjo. Sometimes the shuinjo was given for one voyage only, but more often for several. These passports were apparently first issued through the Zen Buddhist monks of the Konji-in and other Kyoto temples, who staffed the government bureau which corresponded to the foreign office in early Tokugawa days. This was, perhaps, partly a relic of the Tenryuji-bune times, but it is not clear whether Hideyoshi employed this method in 1592, or whether he gave them directly to the individuals concerned. During Ieyasu's lifetime, his favorite, Honda Kozuke-no-suké Masazumi, acted as a foreign minister; and he apparently dealt with all applications for red-seal passports, which he then passed to the Zen monks of the chancery for drafting, in the event of their being granted. This was not an invariable practice, since sometimes passports are found endorsed by other prominent officials, such as Hasegawa Sahioye Fujihiro, bugyo of Nagasaki, or Goto Shozaburo Mitsutsugu, master of the mint at Kyoto. These documents were very simple in form, and merely gave the destination of the voyage, the date, and the owner's name.

Kawajima, in his standard work on the shuin-sen, gives a

list of passports issued for overseas trade which covers the first twenty years or so of the seventeenth century. Although based on the *Todaiki* and other original records, it is obviously not a complete list, but can be taken as giving a fair approximation of the direction and scope of Japanese maritime expansion during the Keicho period. If the facts and figures reproduced by Kawajima are analyzed and checked with those given by Noël Peri from the same sources, some interesting information appears.[7]

The eighty-two shippers who received these maritime passports during the Keicho period, can be divided as follows: daimyo, 8; bakufu officials, 4; merchants, 50; Europeans, 14; Chinese, 6. The Kyushu daimyo naturally predominated among the feudal nobility, Arima, Omura, Matsura, Hosokawa, Nabeshima, and Shimadzu comprising six out of the eight. An interesting personage who figures among the official recipients is O-Natsu, favorite concubine of Ieyasu, and younger sister of Hasegawa Sahioye, bugyo of Nagasaki. She was licensed to send one ship to Annam and another to Cochin China. The mercantile community, which in contrast to the early Tenryuji-bune days was now the best represented of all, included such great traders as the Suetsugu, Funamoto, Araki, Chaya, Sueyoshi, and Suminokura. As might be expected, most of these were of Kyushu or of Kamigata (Osaka-Kyoto) origin, and some of them were of samurai descent. The European merchant venturers included the English pilot, Will Adams, his unpopular Dutch shipmate, Jan Joosten, and several Iberian residents of Nagasaki. The Chinese were all domiciled at either Hirado or Nagasaki. Perhaps the most intriguing name of all is that of the Christian, Padre Thomas (*Krishitan Bateren Tomasu*). This was probably Thomas Araki, one of the few Japanese priests to be ordained at Rome. He was excommunicated and defrocked for unchastity after his return to Japan, and subsequently apostatized.

Although only eighty-two passports are recorded as having been issued during the period under review, there were

one hundred and eighty-two voyages listed, so it is probable that the majority of passports was not restricted to covering a single voyage. Most of these voyages were made
to countries which today comprise the territory of French
Indo-China. At that time, Annam had not emerged as the
most powerful state, and the petty kingdoms of Cambodia,
Champa, Giaochi or Kochi (Tongking), and others, had
constantly fluctuating boundaries. Eighty vessels were bound
for this area of Indo-China, including twenty-six for Kochi,
and twenty-three for Cambodia which had been a happy
hunting ground for the Japanese since their participation
in the filibustering expedition of 1595. Thirty-seven passports were endorsed for Siam, and a few stray ones for the
Malay states of Patani and Pahang.

Next to the Indo-China Peninsula, the Philippines were
the most popular destination. No fewer than thirty vessels
took out passports for Luzon between 1604 and 1616. Two
vessels are recorded as having gone to Visayas (Panay), but
otherwise Manila seems to have been the exclusive destination
of Japanese voyages to the Philippines at this time. Nineteen
vessels were destined for Macao, some of which subsequently
proceeded to Indo-China. It is interesting to note that despite the Ming ban on Japanese shipping, two ships (probably foreign or Chinese owned) received permits to go to the
Fukienese port of Ch'uanchow. Two ships went to Borneo;
the Moluccas, Siak, and Formosa (Takasago) received only
one each.

Noël Peri calculates that the number of shuinjo for 1606
was about nineteen or twenty. It rose to twenty-two or
twenty-three in 1607, to drop sharply to a beggarly three
in the next year. There were twelve in 1609, nine in 1610,
but they dropped to six in 1611, and to two in 1612. Things
then improved, and nine are found in 1613, and sixteen in
1614 and 1615. Naturally the original lists are not complete,
but these figures afford a fair indication of the extent of the
trade.

The list of goods imported and exported by these Red-seal ships varied somewhat with their destination; but Japanese products such as swords and armor, folding picture screens, lacquer ware, rice, barley, wheat flour, tunny, salted fish, and horses are mentioned by the Spanish writers in their lists of Japanese imports to the Philippines. Silver and copper bars were also included in some of the cargoes, but it does not seem that the shuin-sen exported anything like as much of the white metal as did the Great Ship from Macao in normal years. Exports from the Philippines to Japan consisted mainly of Chinese raw and manufactured silks, gold, hides, and the old Chinese ceramics so sought after by connoisseurs of chanoyu, in addition to European wares. Silk was also the principal commodity exported by the shuin-sen from Indo-China; incense and aromatic woods were other important items.[8]

Progress in navigation and shipbuilding likewise accompanied the growth of the Red-seal ships. Originally the shuin-sen were compelled by law to carry Portuguese pilots, but this edict does not seem to have been seriously enforced. The Japanese were soon able to fend for themselves, even in navigating as far as Malaya, although there can be no doubt that their high-sea pilots learned their trade from the Portuguese. A number of Portuguese-Japanese portulans dating from the first half of the seventeenth century are still preserved in Japan. These charts are all painted on vellum, and several of them are liberally decorated with typical Portuguese insignia such as the Quinas and Cruz de Christo. But although their windroses, compass lines, scale of leagues, and embellishments are taken from Portuguese sources, their Japanese manufacture is obvious from the following points. Their nomenclature is almost exclusively in kana, European letters being sparingly used. Japan and the neighboring continental coast line are far more accurately delineated than in any known European map of the period. In short, they are the work of native cartographers who learned their craft from Portuguese pilots or Jesuits.

The best of these portulan charts were but doubtful guides,

and more reliance was placed by contemporary pilots on
their written sailing directions or rutters (*roteiros*). These,
too, were translated or rather adapted by the Japanese, as
is evidenced by a remarkable manuscript of this kind preserved in the library of the Imperial University at Kyoto.
It was compiled by a Nagasaki seaman and professional diver
named Ikeda Yoyemon, about 1622. Examination of its contents discloses that it must have been compiled from a Portuguese original of the type of the *roteiros* and *Exames de
Pilotos,* published periodically by the cosmographer-major,
Manuel de Figueiredo, at Lisbon between 1608 and 1625.
The contents include directions for finding position at sea
by means of the Southern Cross; tables for finding the alti-
tude of the sun at noon; tables of declination for the years
1629–1688, explanation of nautical and astronomical terms,
as also of the Julian and Gregorian calendars, and other useful information. It contains a compass rose with the thirty-
two points of the compass transcribed from the Portuguese
in kana script. It further has a series of sailing directions
from Nagasaki to various ports of south China and Indo-
China. The work is written in a mixture of kana and kanji,
but most of the technical terms with which it is interlarded
are transliterated in *katakana,* although some are given in
manyogana or Chinese characters used phonetically.[9]

Curiously enough, shipbuilding innovations did not keep
pace with the strides made in theoretical navigation under
Portuguese tuition. Despite Padre Organtino's praise of
Nobunaga's shipping in 1578, which the Jesuit rated as equal
in tonnage to contemporary Portuguese carracks, it is clear
that the Japanese lagged behind the Europeans, the Chinese,
and the Koreans in this respect. Hideyoshi's anxiety to secure two large well-gunned Portuguese vessels for his Korean
campaign is sufficient proof of Japanese inferiority in naval
construction, which was further evinced by the victories
of Admiral Yisun. Chinese chroniclers also characterize the
Wako vessels as poorly constructed and vastly inferior to
the great Cantonese sea-going junks. Some efforts were made

to improve matters, but they do not seem to have made much headway. Small craft of the *fusta* type were built at Hirado in imitation of the Portuguese craft of that name. Pictures and descriptions of some of the Red-seal ships belonging to the great mercantile houses of Sueyoshi and Suminokura, show certain European influences in both their hull design and sail plan, but nothing very striking.

Ieyasu showed himself particularly anxious to get ship-wrights and metal miners from the Spaniards at Manila, but he only got begging friars. Will Adams built a couple of small ships for him, but since he was primarily a pilot and not a naval architect, he could not design any vessel of great burden. The Spanish friar, Luis Sotelo, had a hand in the preparation of Daté Masamune's expedition to Mexico, but his naval activities made him heartily disliked at Manila. Los Rios Coronel suggested that he should not be allowed to return to Japan, lest the Japanese should learn shipbuilding through his agency. The best proof of Japanese backwardness in naval architecture is the reply given by the Tokugawa "admiral," Mukai Shogen, to Richard Cocks, when the Englishman suggested a Japanese invasion of the Philippines in 1616: "At which speeches he seemed to make a pause, and in the end said that they wanted such ships as ours were." That was the heart of the matter; for had Ieyasu's plan succeeded, the Japanese would have conquered the Philippines in 1642, instead of three centuries later.[10]

II

It should be clear from what was said in the last section, that the Japanese had a reputation for pugnacity at the time of their first attempts at overseas expansion. That this was indeed so, may be seen from a few typical observations on Japanese national characteristics by Europeans who frequented the Far East at the time.

The governor of the Philippines, Don Pedro Bravo de Acuña, writing to King Felipe (July 7, 1605), observed that they were "all very brave men, who have little fear of death and are fond of going to the wars; their character is most cruel and ferocious, and they are bandits by nature." He expressed anxiety lest they might learn better gunnery and navigation from the Dutch; their want of skill in these two sciences being the only reasons why they had not yet invaded the Philippines. The Spaniards were not alone in their fears of Japanese aggression, and the Portuguese viceroy at Goa had expressly prohibited any Japanese from landing with arms at Macao (in 1597), irrespective of whether they were slaves or samurai, Christians or heathen.

A somewhat exaggerated reference to this last rule is to be found in Sir Edward Michelbourne's account of his privateering voyage in Far Eastern waters. "About the 27th of December 1605, I met with a Iuncke of the Japons, which had been pirating along the coast of China and Cambodia. Their pilots being dead, with ignorance and foule weather, they had cast away their ship on the sholds of the great Iland Borneo, and to enter into the countrey of Borneo they durst not; for the Japons are not suffered to land in any port in India with weapons; being accounted a people so desperate and daring, that they are feared in all places where they come." Michelbourne spoke from experience, since his pilot-major, John Davis, and several of his crew were killed in a fight with this Wako (or Go-shuin?) ship. The only Japanese prisoner taken, although seriously wounded and loaded with chains, jumped overboard and drowned himself shortly afterwards.

A couple of years later, the Dutch admiral, Cornelis Matelief de Jonge, was cruising off the Kwangtung coast and fell in with a Wako junk, whose crew he describes as follows. "These Japanese were all brave men and looked like pirates, as indeed they were. They are a very determined race, for when they see that they will be overwhelmed by the Chinese, they cut open their own bellies rather than fall alive into the hands of their enemies and be tortured to death." This was not Matelief's first experience of Japanese determination. His failure to take the Portuguese stronghold of Malacca in the previous year was due largely to the bravery of a Japanese contingent serving with the scanty garrison. Nor did the Dutch admiral exaggerate their readiness to take their own lives rather than surrender to the Chinese. The Franciscan chronicler, Domingo Martinez, relates how a Spanish missionary was wrecked on the China coast with two Japanese sailors. Thinking that they would be mistaken for Wako and killed, they prepared to commit *seppuku*. When the Franciscan tried to dissuade them from such an un-Christian act, they turned on the wretched friar and buried their swords in his belly before slitting their own.

Several of Matelief's countrymen had an opportunity of verifying his statements on the fighting qualities of the Japanese. At one time the Hollanders had a considerable number of Japanese mercenaries in their service, and they distinguished themselves at the capture of the Banda Islands, the defense of Jacatra, and elsewhere. Nevertheless, the Dutch, like the Spaniards before them, came to mistrust their bellicosity, and to doubt the wisdom of employing them on a large scale. As one of the Dutch commanders wrote (about 1615), "they are a rough and fearless people, lambs in their own country, but well-nigh devils outside of it." The Bakufu finally forbade this recruiting in 1621.

In 1606, a rumor spread throughout the Pearl River delta district that the Portuguese and Wako were about to unite in an invasion of Kwangtung Province. The Portuguese were reported to be fortifying Macao, and an auxiliary force of Japanese Christian samurai was said to be hourly expected. A preliminary panic led to open rioting at Macao, and a Chinese Christian acolyte was seized and tortured to death as a spy at Canton. The report was false, but since Padre Alonso Sánchez had proposed just such an expedition in 1586–1588, the suspicions of the Chinese were not so unreasonable as many modern historians would have their readers believe. Six large Portuguese ships arrived at Macao in 1607, under the command of Captain-Major André Pessoa, one of the heroes of the defense of Malacca, where he had been wounded fighting alongside the Japanese. Fortunately the invasion scare had subsided by this time, and Pessoa's squadron drove Matelief's ships away from the Kwangtung coast without interference from the Chinese.[11]

All these wars and rumors of wars naturally made the local populace very nervous when a Red-seal ship belonging to Arima Harunobu on the return voyage from Indo-China with a cargo of aromatic eagle wood put into Macao for the winter. The junk was in charge of two of Arima's retainers, "men of low degree but quarrelsome and presumptuous." Richard Cocks aptly termed others of this kidney a few years later, "brabbling Japons." The crew of this vessel was joined by other Japanese sailors who had been shipwrecked near by and made their way to Macao on board pirated Chinese fishing vessels. The two ringleaders now incited their compatriots to walk through the town in gangs of thirty or forty men at a time, armed to the teeth with lighted matchlocks and other weapons. This bellicose behavior naturally gave great umbrage, coming so soon after the invasion scare of 1606, and the local Chinese asked the senate to expel the intruders. They pointed out that they did not permit the heretic Dutch enemies of the Portuguese in Chinese ports, so the Portuguese should not permit their enemies the Japanese in Macao. The Portuguese were in a very difficult position, since they could not afford to antagonize either party, in view of the potential repercussions to their trade at Canton or at Nagasaki. They compromised by requesting the Japanese to moderate their truculence, and to go about in Chinese dress, since their compatriots were forbidden to land in China on pain of death.

The Japanese not only flatly declined to do as suggested, but behaved so provocatively that a serious water-front fracas occurred on November 30, 1608. When a Portuguese *ouvidor* (or magistrate) hurried to the scene to quiet the rioters, he and his posse were attacked by the infuriated Japanese. He himself was wounded and some of his men were killed. The general alarm was then sounded by ringing the church bells, and André Pessoa (who was acting governor by virtue of his captaincy of the Japan voyage), hastened to the spot with all the available armed men. On his approach, the Japanese took refuge in a couple of houses, wherein they strongly barricaded themselves and prepared to fight to the last. Pessoa offered quarter to those who would surrender, but only a few accepted his offer. He then attacked one of the two houses, and stormed it after a desperate action in which all of the Japanese defenders lost their lives. The Portuguese then prepared to tackle the other group, but at this point the bishop of Macao and the local clergy intervened. Through this clerical mediation, and on obtaining a promise of life and freedom, the remaining Japanese, who numbered about fifty, were eventually induced to surrender.

Pessoa now ventured on a very questionable step. Disregarding the promise of life and freedom, he imprisoned the suspected ringleaders and finally had one of them strangled in the jail. The others were released; but before allowing the Japanese to leave the colony, he compelled them to sign an affidavit admitting their responsibility for the outbreak, and absolving the Portuguese from all blame.

Pessoa took this affidavit with him to Japan when he made his voyage thither in the summer of 1609, narrowly escaping two Dutch ships which were cruising for him in the Formosa Channel. A providential fog enabled him to slip past them unseen and he reached Nagasaki on July 29, the disappointed Dutchmen arriving at Hirado a couple of days later. When Pessoa related his version of the Macao imbroglio to Hasegawa Sahioye, bugyo of Nagasaki, and suggested forwarding the affidavit to court, Hasegawa strongly advised him to do nothing of the kind. He pointed out that Ieyasu was well aware of the truculent behavior of some of his countrymen abroad, and that he was far from approving thereof. But if the Portuguese brought an official complaint, the matter would have to be investigated; and then the ex-

shogun might feel compelled to take the side of his compatriots out of *amour propre*. His crony at the court of
Shidzuoka, Goto Shozaburo, master of the mint, who was
well-disposed toward the Portuguese, likewise gave the same
advice when the matter was referred to him. Pessoa was not
fully convinced by these arguments, and he evidently made
some sort of a *démarche* through Honda, Kodzuke-no-suké
Masazumi. At any rate, Ieyasu authorized the following
red-seal letter (shuinjo) to be sent to the senate of Macao,
not long after Pessoa's arrival in Japan. It was given to
Pessoa's emissary, Mateo Leitão.

Since it is an undoubted fact that the going of Japanese in ships to Macao
is prejudicial to that place, this practice will be strictly prohibited for the
future. If any Japanese should go there, they may be dealt with according
to the local laws. Twenty-fifth day of the seventh month of the fourteenth
year of Keicho.

This was eminently satisfactory so far as it went, but the
Japanese survivors of the Macao affair had not yet returned
to give their version, and meanwhile other complications
cropped up for Pessoa at Nagasaki.[12]

On the very day of his arrival (July 29, 1609), Hasegawa
had tried to enforce some unwelcome innovations on the
Portuguese. Before Pessoa's ship, *Nossa Senhora da Graça*
(*Our Lady of Grace*) had dropped anchor in the harbor, a
number of boats came alongside, manned by armed guards
who were supposed to prevent any persons or goods from going ashore without leave. The irate captain-major flatly refused to let these men remain aboard his carrack and after
some argument they returned ashore. Hasegawa next tried to
station two customs inspectors on the ship in order to examine
and appraise all the cargo. This demand was likewise rejected
by Pessoa who retorted that the bugyo could do what he
liked on land but not aboard a Portuguese ship. After much
acrimonious dispute, Hasegawa dropped his demand for ship-
board control and agreed to limit his inspection of the cargo
to a superficial examination and inventory of the goods as
they were landed. No sooner were the Macaonese merchants

and their bales of silk safely ashore, than Hasegawa and his minions made a round of all the houses where the foreign traders were lodged and inspected all their wares. The best of these were bought at fixed prices, ostensibly on behalf of Tokugawa Ieyasu, then living in dignified retirement at Shidzukoa. The Jesuit chronicler would have his readers believe that they were really purchased by Hasegawa for subsequent resale at enhanced prices in the "black market."

Nor was this the only grievance of the Portuguese against the Nagasaki bugyo. He treated Pessoa and his compatriots with marked rudeness, in striking contrast to the courtesy with which Europeans were usually received in Japan. In this he was supported by his colleague, the daikwan or lieutenant-governor, Murayama Toan, whose previous career deserves a few words. Murayama was born at Nagoya of humble parents. He went to Nagasaki when a youth, where he was baptized under the name of Antonio. Here he not only displayed a commercial acumen which enabled him to amass a large fortune, but became famous as a gourmand and cook, particularly in European dishes or Namban-ryori. Wealthy, amusing, and hospitable as he was, he soon became one of the leading members of the city. He was selected as delegate from the municipal council to Hideyoshi in 1592, when the latter made his second attempt to incorporate Nagasaki in his own domains. His conversation and buffoonery so pleased the Taiko Hideyoshi, with whom he seems to have had a good deal in common, that the latter changed his name to Toan (since he could not pronounce Antonio properly) and made him the local tax farmer, in return for a fixed annual payment of 25 *kwamme* of silver.

In 1602, a large part of the Chinese silks imported by the Great Ship from Macao remained unsold, since the Japanese merchants complained that the prices asked by the Portuguese were too high. Both sides appealed to Ieyasu who ordered an investigation to be made. The Jesuits were involved in this affair, and for a time things looked awkward for them and the Portuguese. Eventually (in 1603 or 1604) the matter was settled in their favor, largely through the activities of Padre João Rodriguez Tçuzzu and Murayama Toan, who procured the dismissal of the then daikwan, Terazawa Shinano-no-kami Hirotaka, and his replacement by Murayama. From this time dates the system of bulk purchase called *pancada* by the Portuguese and *ito-wappu* by the Japanese. Under the terms of this arrangement, the bulk of the annual carrack's cargo of silk was purchased by representatives of a guild of silk merchants from the five shogunal towns of Yedo, Kyoto, Osaka, Sakai, and Nagasaki. Certain of the most valuable varieties of weave and pattern were reserved for Ieyasu's purchase at his local representative's valuation. Such at least was the theory, although it is obvious from the contemporary records that there was a good deal of elasticity in this arrangement, and that private trading and "black-market" transactions were not infrequent. Toan's connection with the Jesuits had hitherto been close and cordial, and it was further cemented by the ordination of one of his sons, Francisco, as a parish priest of Nagasaki in 1602, one of the first Japanese to receive holy orders.[13]

"But the good things of life last little, and covetousness is the root of all evil," observes our Jesuit chronicler sententiously. Murayama now began to intrigue with his colleague Hasegawa against the Portuguese, largely out of jealousy of Padre João Rodriguez Tçuzzu, who still enjoyed Ieyasu's confidence and a position of exceptional influence in municipal and court affairs. They did not venture on an open break with the Europeans, but began to treat them cavalierly, and complained to Ieyasu of Portuguese pride and arrogance. They pointed out that the Portuguese enjoyed a virtual extraterritoriality at Nagasaki, acting as if they were lords of the soil, whereas the Japanese who visited Manila and Macao were rigorously punished by the Iberian authorities for any infraction of the local laws. They further accused the Portuguese of concealing the best silk textiles, which should have been Ieyasu's pickings, in order to sell them subsequently at higher prices on the "black market." Finally, they claimed that if the ex-shogun took a stronger line with the Portuguese, they would not (as he feared) refrain from importing Chinese silks, since Macao could not exist without the importation of silver bullion from Japan. They also suggested that by this time the Red-seal ships could take care of the necessary silk imports. This last suggestion was demonstrably untrue, since the Portuguese alone had direct access to the Canton silk market; whereas Japanese, Spaniards, and Hollanders alike depended on second-hand purchases in Indo-China, or Manila—or more frequently on plundering Chinese shipping.

Mention of the Dutch calls to mind that in August of this year they founded a factory or trading station at Hirado. Their appearance forced Pessoa to choose the lesser of two evils in coming to terms with Hasegawa and Murayama, since the Portuguese could not afford the enmity of both Japanese and Dutch. An outward reconciliation was reached through the good offices of the Jesuits and a heavy monetary bribe, but Pessoa, rightly or wrongly, still mistrusted the sincerity of Hasegawa's intentions. In this he was probably mistaken, as the Jesuits pointed out, for the bugyo's interests were to a large extent bound up with the continuance of the Macao-Nagasaki trade.

Be this as it may, Hasegawa's actions left nothing to be desired in outward appearances. He arranged for Pessoa's envoy to Ieyasu to reach Shidzuoka before the arrival of the two Dutch envoys, Van den Broeck and Puick. This did not help much, it is true, since Ieyasu chose to receive the Hollanders in audience first; but he was affable enough to the Portuguese representative when he did see him, giving him the shuinjo mentioned above. An appeal for the exclusion of the Dutch as pirates was less successful. Ieyasu retorted that Japan was a free country for all merchants, whereas "at sea let each one look to himself." Meanwhile, Hasegawa kept Pessoa informed of all the Dutch and Spanish intrigues against him, and he doubtless derived a malicious satisfaction at thus setting the various European nations by the ears.

In spite of this real or assumed cordiality, the Portuguese merchants at Nagasaki were deeply suspicious of Hasegawa's intentions, and tried to persuade the captain-major to lodge a formal complaint at Shidzuoka of their grievances against the local bugyo and daikwan. This decision was kept secret from the Jesuits, who were horrified when they heard of it, and did their best to dissuade Pessoa from going. In this they were eventually successful, but meanwhile the damage had been done. For the Japanese interpreter employed to translate the Portuguese petition of grievances had shown it to the bugyo himself. Hasegawa was naturally livid with rage, and henceforth became Pessoa's mortal foe, swearing to get even with him dead or alive. This was all the more unfortunate since Hasegawa's sister, O-Natsu, was so great a favorite with Ieyasu "that if she said black was white he would believe it."

Just about this time, the Japanese survivors of the Macao imbroglio reached Japan and gave their version of the affair to Arima Shuri-no-Taiyu Harunobu. News of the incident filtered through to Ieyasu, who reprimanded Hasegawa for not divulging it before, and ordered him to make a thorough investigation. Hasegawa's report, which was drawn up in consultation with the aggrieved Arima, who had taken the loss of his men very hardly, naturally painted Pessoa's conduct in the blackest of colors. The Japanese sailors made no difficulty about disavowing their Macao affidavits which had obviously been extorted under duress. Hasegawa and his clique also pointed out to Ieyasu that Arima's ship had been provided with a shuinjo, and hence the shogunal honor was involved as much as the daimyo's. They further alleged that the Spaniards at Manila had twice inflicted capital punishment on Japanese without any protest from Ieyasu. They added that if nothing was done to stop this periodic slaughter of Japanese in Iberian colonies, it would soon spread.[14]

Ieyasu was much impressed by these arguments, but he still hesitated to take drastic action, lest this should result in the loss of the silk trade, despite all Hasegawa's assurances to the contrary. While he was hesitating, it happened that a Spanish ship bound from Manila to Mexico was wrecked off the Kwanto coast, and the survivors were brought to Shidzuoka. More fortunate than their predecessors of the *San Felipe*, they were very kindly received by Ieyasu, who was still most anxious to foster the Manila trade. Their leader, Don Rodrigo de Vivero y Velasco, who had been interim governor of the Philippines for a few months, was so enchanted with Japan that he wrote, "if I could persuade myself to renounce my God and my King, I would prefer this country to my own." When Ieyasu asked the enthusiastic Spaniard whether the Spaniards could supply the bulk of the silk imports to Japan, in default of the annual Portuguese carrack, Vivero rashly replied that they would send not merely one but two or three ships yearly. If Padre João Rodriguez Girão (writing in 1610) is to be believed, it was this provocative answer of the Spanish hidalgo which caused Ieyasu to make up his hesitant mind and to resolve on drastic measures of some kind.[15]

The same authority informs us that Ieyasu in his old age showed an increasing reluctance to consult tried and trusted advisers from the feudal nobility, especially in matters of foreign trade, and relied instead on the opinions of such upstarts as Hasegawa, Murayama, and Goto Shozaburo. Even after Don Rodrigo's brash answer, Ieyasu still hesitated for some time, "changing his views daily but always from bad to worse; for he first of all talked about mulcting the Portuguese with a large fine, then about killing the captain-major and four or five of the chief Portuguese whom he was told were mainly responsible for the death of the Japanese; but finally he decided to kill the captain with all the Portuguese and to seize the ship with all its cargo." Padre Girão is quite categorical on this point; but from what actually transpired, it is more likely that Ieyasu's intention was limited to seizing Pessoa and his ship, the passengers and crew being allowed to go free, provided that they offered no resistance. Arima was entrusted with the task of taking Pessoa, dead or alive, since he was the injured party in the original dispute.

Pessoa was warned of what was contemplated, doubtless through native Christians as the Japanese chronicles allege, and he promptly took all possible precautions to avoid being surprised. He stayed aboard his ship, not even going ashore to hear Mass, and made the *Nossa Senhora da Graça* ready for action at a moment's notice. He prepared a large quantity of hand grenades, powder, and shot, secure in the conviction that even if it should not be necessary to use them against the Japanese, they would come in handy for defense against Dutch attacks on the homeward voyage. Finally, he tried to get clear of the harbor and to coast down to the anchorage of Fukuda, but owing to the contrary winds he could not leave his moorings.

All these warlike preparations were obvious to Hasegawa, who immediately informed Ieyasu that Pessoa was unlikely to be caught napping. The old man then resolved to try guile, and got Goto Shozaburo to write to Bishop Cerqueira, Vice-Provincial Carvalho, and Padre João Rodriguez, telling them to advise Pessoa to proceed forthwith to Shidzuoka and give an account of his actions at Macao. If he was innocent, he would be absolved; and even if he was guilty, he would be pardoned as an ignorant foreigner; in this way the affair would be amicably concluded with "face" saved all round. This intimation was so artfully worded that it deceived many of the local Portuguese; but not André Pessoa, who fully realized that he had forfeited his head, and flatly declined to go. Much discussion took place among the Portuguese whether they should send a deputy in order to try and placate Ieyasu; but by the time they finally despatched an envoy, it was too late for him to effect anything for the die had been cast.

Arima Harunobu arrived at Nagasaki thirsting for vengeance, but he too resolved first to try guile rather than force. He therefore proceeded to the Jesuits' college and showed them letters from Honda and Goto, stating that he had been entrusted with fixing the price (*pancada*) for the bulk of the silk cargo, since he was a Christian daimyo and well disposed to the Portuguese, whereas the local authorities were hostile. This specious talk deceived nobody, and Pessoa politely but firmly declined to come ashore and discuss the terms of the pancada. While these farcical negotiations were proceeding, Arima assembled a force of about 1,200 samurai, who concentrated on the water front in the darkness of the small hours of Sunday, January 3, 1610.

Pessoa received warning of this concentration, but when he sent ashore to warn all stragglers to embark in the carrack forthwith, he met with but a poor response. Some men considered it a false alarm; others did not wish to leave their goods ashore; the majority of those who did try to embark were prevented from doing so by the Japanese guards, only seven or eight unarmed men succeeding in reaching the ship. The situation was serious, for the ship's complement was only a relatively small one at the best of times. The lubberly carracks of the Japan voyage normally carried less than forty Europeans among the crew, including the ship's officers, sailors, gunners, and soldiers. The fact that only a handful of the Macao merchants were able or willing to join him at the critical moment, meant that Pessoa had about forty Europeans aboard when the battle began, the remainder of the crew being lascars and Negroes. Moreover, the ship was very lightly armed for her size, mounting not more than ten or twelve cannon of all calibers.[16]

Just before the attack began, Arima, Hasegawa, and Murayama sent a joint message to the Jesuits telling them that since the captain-major was trying to set sail, the Japanese would take his ship by force of arms. This was shortly followed by a second message stating that if the Portuguese would hand over Pessoa, everything would be settled amicably. To this the Jesuits replied that their intervention would be useless, "because the Portuguese are not accustomed to give up their own captains." During this time, Arima's samurai were embarking in their flotilla, to the accompani-

ment of much noise and the light of burning torches. Some
of his officers wanted Pessoa to fire on the shouting mob, which
formed an excellent target by torchlight, but he declined to
take the responsibility of opening hostilities. The *Nossa
Senhora da Graça* remained shrouded in utter darkness, and
the work of weighing the anchor and setting the foresail was
carried out in complete silence.

As soon as the ship got under way, about thirty craft
laden with yelling samurai approached her, shooting off their
muskets and arrows for all they were worth. Pessoa ignored
the first volley, but after the second he fired two successive
broadsides of five guns apiece. These shots wrought great
havoc in the crowded Japanese flotilla; but what infuriated
the assailants most of all was that the ship's trumpets played
a derisive tune after each broadside. The carrack dropped
down the harbor with the tide, but for lack of wind could
not reach its intended anchorage at Fukuda, and, therefore,
anchored off Fukabori. Thus ended the first attack on the
Nossa Senhora da Graça. The battle was renewed with similar
results for three nights in succession, but the Japanese did
not dare to approach the carrack closely in the daytime.

On the morning of the third day (January 5), Arima sent
a message to Pessoa (how or by whom is uncertain) telling him
that he wished to renew the negotiations about the silk
pancada, and that if the captain-major was still suspicious
of the purity of his intentions he would send him some
hostages, providing that the ship stayed where she was.
Pessoa replied with protestations of friendship, but demanded
Arima's son and Murayama's son as hostages, adding that he
must sail to Fukuda as soon as the wind served, since it was the
only secure anchorage. Nothing came of this exchange, except that Hasegawa was furious when he heard of it. He sent
a message to Pessoa next morning, telling him that Arima had
no authority to make any such proposal, but on the contrary
had orders from Ieyasu to kill him. Hasegawa added that he
told him this out of the sincerity of his heart; but that if
Pessoa surrendered, and offered the whole of the carrack's

cargo to Ieyasu at a price to be fixed by the latter, he (Hasegawa) would intercede for him at court, although he could not guarantee the result. Pessoa gave a polite but noncommittal reply, declining to negotiate further so long as the Japanese continued hostilities.[17]

On the morning of January 6, Feast Day of the Magi, Pessoa succeeded in warping the carrack out of the harbor by the ship's boat, arriving near his intended anchorage of Fukuda by the evening. The Japanese, seeing their prey about to escape them, resolved to make a final effort. Previous attempts to use fireships, and to cut the carrack's cables by deep-sea divers having proved unsuccessful, Arima now tried something new. He lashed two large boats together and erected on top of them a wooden tower, about the height of the carrack's upper works, covered with wet hides to prevent the Portuguese from setting it afire, and manned by many musketeers. Arima's samurai had been continually reinforced during the last three days and eventually numbered about 3,000 men. Between eight and nine o'clock at night, the flotilla closed in for the kill. The floating tower attacked the carrack from the stern, whence only one gun could be brought to bear against it, since the other stern chaser had been transferred to the prow in order to protect the cables against Japanese attacks.

The combat now reached its height. A few Japanese succeeded in boarding the carrack, but they were either cut down forthwith or forced to leap into the sea. Pessoa killed two boarders with his own hands, according to Avila Giron's account. The Portuguese fire did little harm to the floating tower, but it wrought great havoc in the crowded boats which eventually began to sheer off, the excited Portuguese shouting *Victory! Victory!* Just at this critical moment, a chance shot hit a grenade which a Portuguese soldier was about to throw, and the blazing fragments fell on some gunpowder at his feet, whence the fire spread to the mizzen sail. From here it spread so rapidly that it was obvious the scanty crew had no chance to extinguish it and carry on the fight simultaneously. Seeing that all was lost, Pessoa ordered the master gunner to fire the magazine, since he was resolved to die rather than surrender. The ship's purser, Pedro d'Estorci, demurred at this drastic order, whereupon "Pessoa with an intrepid heart put down his sword and shield in a cabin without saying another word, and taking a crucifix in one hand and a firebrand in the other, he went below and set fire to the powder magazine." The ship blew up with two successive explosions, splitting in half and sinking in thirty-two fathoms of water.

Up till the time that the carrack caught fire, the defenders' casualties had been extraordinarily light, only four or five Portuguese having been killed in the four days' or rather nights' fighting. A good number perished in the explosion, but there were some survivors. Most of them were killed by the Japanese while swimming in the water, including a Spanish Augustinian friar, Fray Juan Damorin, the only priest on board, but a few lucky individuals reached the shore and safety. The Japanese casualties were naturally much heavier and amounted to several hundred men. The bulk of the silk cargo was still on board at the time, since no agreement had been reached over the price of the pancada. There was also a quantity of silver bullion aboard, and the total loss was estimated at more than a million in gold. Some baskets of silk were picked up while floating in the water, but repeated efforts by divers, from 1610 down to 1933, recovered only a few bars of silver, a quantity of cabin-window oyster-shell panes, a bronze cannon, and the ship's astrolabe. The Japanese had won the battle in the end; but Pessoa had shown that when he could not conquer, he knew how to die.[18]

The smoke of battle had barely died away when Hasegawa sent for the Macao merchants who had remained ashore, and told them that if they wanted their trade renewed, it would have to be on the Japanese terms. When the conditions were read out to them, the majority refused to sign, since the terms were too humiliating, and commercially disadvantageous. Some of the weaker spirits subsequently did so under duress, but this turned out to be unnecessary. Ieyasu was at first very angry over the loss of the carrack's precious cargo and threatened to kill all the Portuguese traders and to exile the Jesuits. He soon calmed down, and allowed those of the Macao merchants who had not taken part in the battle, to return to Macao in a hired junk with all their goods.

The Jesuits were also permitted to remain in Japan, nominally at the intercession of Arima, but in reality because Ieyasu was convinced that there would be no Macao silk trade without them. Hasegawa likewise shared this opinion, and he told the departing Macao merchants in March, 1610, "that they should not cut the thread of trade, but arrange for at least a small vessel to come this year, and the Great Ship the next, when all would be well." [19]

Hasegawa proved a true prophet. The Portuguese either could not or would not send a ship, large or small, in 1610; but in July of the following year, an envoy named Dom Nuno Soutomaior arrived in a small vessel. He landed in Satsuma, being uncertain of his welcome at Nagasaki, but he need not have worried. Ieyasu was by now thoroughly disillusioned about the ability of the Spaniards or Dutch to take the place of the Macaonese as suppliers of Chinese silk on a large scale, and he was ready to welcome the Great Ship on the old terms. Soutomaior met with a gracious reception at Shidzuoka, where Honda showed himself as obliging as ever and procured a go-shuinjo couched in the following terms:

An ambassador has come from Goa to request permission for the Black Ship to come again. There is no objection to this. The regulations under which trade will be conducted, shall be the same as in the past without any change.

If anyone violates them he will be punished.

Acknowledge receipt.

In the late Autumn of the sixteenth Year of Keicho and Year of the Wild Boar.

The Portuguese chronicler, Antonio Bocarro, says that "although the Japanese are a very noble-minded people, this fidalgo behaved in such a way as to leave them astounded at his nobility of soul and how he otherwise represented the Portuguese nation." Soutomaior brought the good news back to Macao, together with a sheaf of letters from Honda, Hasegawa, and Goto, urging the senate to renew the trade and promising to let bygones be bygones. The blame for the disaster was placed on Pessoa for refusing to surrender himself as Ieyasu had ordered. The Macao senate, in acknowledging receipt of this Red-seal passport, wrote (in Sino-Japanese) "Spring sunshine has come to the withered reeds, and a broad highway has been driven through the thorns and briars." Nevertheless the shuinjo given to Soutomaior was not deemed explicit enough, and the Portuguese asked for further assurances, which were given in another passport issued by order of Shogun Hidetada in 1612, to Captain-Major Pedro Martins Gaio.

Trade is permitted as previously for the Black Ship and the shipping of the Namban people at Nagasaki. If the ship should be damaged and forced by stress of weather into any Japanese port, the safety of the ship and cargo are hereby fully guaranteed. Ninth Month of the seventeenth Year of Keicho.

The voyages were thus renewed with the great galleon *São Felipe e Santiago* in 1612. An interchange of letters between the viceroy at Goa and the senate of Macao on the one hand, and Ieyasu, Hidetada, Honda, Hasegawa, and Goto on the other, tacitly agreed that the trade was resumed on the *status quo ante bellum*.

But Pessoa's heroism, though speedily forgotten by his own countrymen, lived long in the memory of the Japanese. Some of his compatriots considered that he had died "like a Roman rather than a Christian," but this spectacular suicide was just what appealed to samurai hearts. The last fight of the *Nossa Senhora da Graça* became part of the folklore of Nagasaki and was handed down in several Kyushu chronicles. The memory of it was still preserved, if a trifle inaccurately, at the time of the British frigate *Phaeton*'s unwelcome intrusion two centuries later; and diving operations on the wreck in 1930–1933 have revived it in recent years. Well might one of the Jesuit missionaries write that whatever the ethical aspect of Pessoa's deed, it had bruited his fame abroad through all Japan: "magnum animi sui nomen tota Japonia evulgarunt." [20]

III

The story of the arrival of the Dutch and English in Japan is probably familiar to every student of Japanese history. It is none the less essential briefly to recapitulate it here, since the presence of the heretics exercised a decisive influence on the course of Japan's foreign relations at a critical epoch.

The last three years of the sixteenth century saw an extraordinary outburst of Dutch maritime activity, following on the return of three out of four ships from Houtman's pioneer voyage to Sumatra and Java. Six separate companies were formed in the Netherlands for trade with the Orient, and twenty-two Dutch ships left in 1598 for the East Indies. This was thirty years after the commencement of Holland's revolt from Spain, and at a time when an average of only four or five carracks annually left Lisbon for Goa. One of these Dutch ships, Captain Jacob Quaeckernaeck and Pilot-Major William Adams, reached Japan, more by good luck than good judgment, in April, 1600, after a calamitous voyage via the Straits of Magellan.

A few days after the arrival of the *Liefde* (*Charity*) at Beppu Bay in Bungo, a Portuguese Jesuit arrived from Nagasaki to act as interpreter, "which was not to our good, our mortal enemies being our truchmen" as Will Adams wrote. Nevertheless, the local daimyo treated the castaways kindly; and Ieyasu, when he heard of their arrival, ordered Adams to be sent to him for an interview. The Jesuits and Portuguese, through Padre João Rodriguez presumably, made every effort to have the newcomers crucified as pirates, since they were doubly damned in their eyes. "The Hollanders are only good gunners, and beyond that fit for nothing save to be burned as desperate heretics," wrote the contemporary Portuguese chronicler, Coelho Barbuda. His countrymen in Japan would doubtless have agreed with him; and since the new arrivals presented a potential danger to the purity of Catholic doctrine and the monopoly of the Macao silk trade, neither missionaries nor traders spared any efforts to nip the threat in the bud.

Tokugawa Ieyasu was not the man to be pushed into taking hasty action. He had several long interviews with Will Adams, and was obviously impressed by his demeanor. He finally told the Jesuits that "we as yet had not doen to him nor to none of his lande any harme or damage; therefore against Reason and Justice to put us to death. If our countrey had warres the one with the other, that was no cause that he should put us to death; with which they were out of heart that their cruell pretence failed them. For which God be for evermore praised." The heretics had indeed reason to be grateful to both God and Caesar, for the Iberians would have given them short shrift if they could have had their way. Anyone who doubts this fact, need only recall the judicial murders of the captured sailors from Olivier Van Noort's ship at Manila in 1600, and of those from Van Neck's squadron at Macao a couple of years later; to say nothing of the fate of the crew of the *Liefde*'s consort (the *Trouw*), butchered by the Portuguese at Tidore in January, 1601.[21]

Having been saved from the clutches of their fellow Europeans, the Hollanders were allowed to settle in Japan, Adams being granted the status of a samurai and a small estate at Hemimura near Yokosuka. Indirect news of the castaways reached Holland in August, 1601, when Oliver Van Noort returned to Rotterdam after his voyage round the world. The Dutchman had met a Japanese Red-seal ship off the Borneo coast, whose Portuguese pilot had told him of the arrival of his countrymen in Japan. Direct communication with the outside world was only possible four years later, when Will Adams, after vainly endeavoring to get Ieyasu's permission to leave the country, procured it for his captain and another Hollander named Melchior Van Santvoort, who accordingly left in a Red-seal ship, provided by the daimyo of Hirado, for Patani.

While the crew of the *Liefde* were lotus eating in Japan, their countrymen had succeeded in placing their East India trade on a really firm basis. Largely through the efforts of Oldenbarneveldt, the rival companies trading to the Orient had been merged in the chartered East India Company in 1602. The capture of Amboina, Ternate, and Tidore three years later gave the Hollanders the keys to the coveted Spice Islands, and they established factories at Bantam in Java, at Patani in Malaya, in the Banda Islands, and elsewhere. A Spanish expedition from Manila recaptured Ternate and Tidore, "whence merchants bring their spicy drugs," in April, 1606; and André Furtado de Mendoça with the help of the crew of a Japanese Red-seal ship, repulsed the Dutch admiral, Cornelis Matelief de Jonge, at Malacca after a five-month siege in the same year. But these reverses were largely offset by Matelief's subsequent destruction of half of the Portuguese armada which had raised the siege of Malacca in August. The casualties in Matelief's October victory included Jacob Quaeckernaeck, who had joined the fleet from Patani on August 19. He told the Hollanders that there were still twelve survivors from the *Liefde* living in Japan, and he brought with him a passport authorizing his countrymen to trade there. Melchior van Santvoort had returned direct to Japan from Patani in the meanwhile.

After an unsuccessful attack on the surviving half of the Portuguese armada at Pulo Buton (near Kedah) in December, Matelief proceeded by way of Bantam to the Moluccas, where he retook half of the island of Ternate from the Spaniards and founded Fort Oranje. In June, 1607, he sailed to the China coast and cruised off Macao for some weeks until he was driven away by André Pessoa, who arrived in August with six of the seven sail which the Hollanders had failed to trap at Pulo Buton in the previous year. The failure to complete the destruction of the Portuguese armada was to cost the Hollanders dear, as they realized when too late. Victor Sprinckel, their factor at Patani, wrote to Will Adams in February, 1608, that the reason for their delay in sending shipping to Japan was because "our deadly enemies, the Portuguese, are so powerful at sea that we have enough to do to hold our own against them." He added that he hoped they would be able to send a ship or two to Japan within the next two years, and in this he was not disappointed.

Admiral Verhoeven, commander of the fleet that left Texel for the East Indies in December, 1607, received instructions to send at least one of his ships to Japan in order to deliver a letter from the Prince of Orange and to found a factory for regular trade. Two of Matelief's vessels had been destined for the same place in 1605; but one of them (the *Middelburgh*) was lost in the battle of Cape Rachado in August, 1606. The failure of his China voyage in the following year further prevented him from carrying out his instructions. Verhoeven, like his predecessor, found that Malacca was "not the kind of a cat to be taken without gloves," and he anchored at Bantam in April, 1609, after a futile blockade of the Portuguese stronghold. Here he learned that an exceptionally richly-laden carrack was being fitted out at Macao for the Japan voyage. He therefore sent orders to two of his ships which he had left cruising in the Straits of Singapore, to try to intercept this treasure ship in the Formosa Channel, and in the event of missing her to proceed to Japan.

Abraham Van den Broeck, commander of the two vessels concerned, *Roode Leeuw met pijlen* (*Red Lion with Arrows*) and *Griffoen* (*Griffin*), received these orders off Johore on May 4. He subsequently set sail for the China Sea, calling en route at Patani, where he took on board some "silk, pepper, and a little lead, in order that if we failed to capture the carrack, we might have some evidence that we wished to establish trade" in Japan. As stated earlier, Van den Broeck narrowly missed Pessoa and the *Nossa Senhora da Graça* in the Straits of Formosa, and being balked of his prey, anchored at Hirado on July 31. The Hollander lost no time in seeing Will Adams and Melchoir Van Santvoort, who accompanied him to the court of Ieyasu at Shidzuoka. The ex-shogun was delighted at their arrival, and gave the Dutch permission to found a trading agency wherever they pleased. They received a reply to the Prince of Orange's letter, and a shuinjo in duplicate authorizing Dutch trade to Japan. They were particularly pleased by the fact that no restrictions were placed on the sale of their merchandise, whereas the Portuguese had to sell their silk imports in bulk at fixed prices under the pancada or ito-wappu system. This last concession was probably somewhat illusory, since it is unlikely that the Japanese merchants would have given a higher price for the Dutch silks than the rate fixed by the prevailing Portuguese pancada. The *Roode Leeuw* and *Griffoen* then returned to Patani in October, leaving Jacques Specx and a skeleton staff in their newly founded factory at Hirado.[22]

Ieyasu had rejected out of hand all Portuguese and Spanish representations against the Dutch as pirates, but he was distinctly disappointed that no Dutch vessel came in 1610, as had been promised. This was due to the fact that the ships intended for Japan had been involved in Admiral Wittert's crushing defeat at the hands of Governor Juan de Silva of the Philippines, in Manila Bay during April of that year. The Iberian rivals of the Hollanders did not fail to point out to the Japanese that the Dutch were not in a position to fulfil their specious promises of 1609, and that they were nothing better than pirates, who could only trade when they had made sufficient prizes. Nor did these suggestions fall on deaf ears. Jacques Specx, writing to his employers from Nagasaki in November, 1610, noted that some Japanese "do not hesitate to say openly now what last year was murmured only in secret, namely that we come rather to waylay the Great Ship from Macao than to seek and ensure trade with Japan. They point out that because this year no ship came from Macao or Manila, and we likewise stayed away from Japan, that we must needs be concerned more with piracy than with trade."

To counteract these calumnies and in order to "show the flag" at Hirado, the Dutch factors at Patani dispatched the yacht *Braeck* to Japan in 1611. Her cargo was of small value compared to that normally brought by the Macao carrack; but the Dutch envoys, Specx and Segerszoon, were well received by Ieyasu who told the protesting Portuguese and Spaniards that the trade of Japan was open to all comers. The success was partly due to the presence of Will Adams, who acted as interpreter, and who was reported by Specx to be in high favor with the ex-shogun. This fact is confirmed from Iberian sources; and it is clear that Adams had now to a great extent supplanted Padre João Rodriguez Tçuzzu, who next year fell into disgrace and was exiled to Macao.

The expulsion of this Jesuit was a very serious loss to the Portuguese, who now had to depend on the heretic Englishman as their court interpreter, on some occasions at least. Adams claims that he recompensed evil with good, and asked and obtained favors from Ieyasu for both Spaniards and Portuguese. In this he was probably guilty of exaggeration, and it is likely that he confined his efforts on their behalf to purely minor matters. He certainly showed friendship to individual Iberian friars and sailors at times, but his general attitude remained strongly anti-Catholic to his dying day. His Japanese consort was a Catholic convert, and perhaps his children adhered to their mother's faith; but this did not prevent Adams from traducing the friars and the Jesuits whenever he had the opportunity, as I shall show in the next chapter.[23]

The English were not very far behind the Dutch in establishing themselves in Japan; in fact the latter complained that the islanders deliberately dogged their footsteps all over the East, only venturing to trade in places where the Hollanders had already broken the back of Iberian resistance. This was only partly true, and the chief reason for the appearance of the English in Japan was doubtless the same as that for the Dutch, namely the publication of Linschoten's *Itinerario* or *Discovrs of Voyages*. This work was the *vade mecum* of Hollanders, English, and Frenchmen alike, in their endeavors to poach on King Felipe's preserves. It extolled Japan as a land comparable to Mexico or Peru in its wealth of silver. Linschoten's description of the "easy money" made by the Portuguese on their China-Japan voyages had aroused the cupidity of the merchants of Amsterdam and London some years before the first letters of Will Adams reached their several destinations. But the English East India Company was not yet so well organized or so well directed as its Dutch namesake, nor did it have such strong support from the state. It was therefore thirteen years before its intention to trade with Japan materialized.

The first English ship to reach the island empire was the *Clove*, Captain (or "General" as he was grandiloquently termed after the Iberian fashion) John Saris, which reached Hirado in June, 1613. Adams and Saris took a dislike to each other from the start, and this mutual ill-will grew worse during the time of "General" Saris' stay in Japan. He could not do without Adams, who was an essential intermediary, and a great favorite of Ieyasu; but their personal relations were such that Adams flatly refused to be repatriated in the *Clove*, although the ex-shogun had given him reluctant permission to do so. Saris was not alone in his opinion, for others of his compatriots considered Adams to be "a naturalised Japanner." He was also accused of being "altogether Hollandized," and too friendly with "divers Spaniards and Portingales"; although Richard Cocks, one of his earlier critics, had the grace to write on the news of his death in May, 1620: "I cannot but be sorrowful for the loss of such a man as Captain Adams was, he having been in such favor with two Emperors of Japan as never was any Christian in these parts of the world, and might freely have entered and had speech with the Emperors [Ieyasu and Hidetada] when many Japan Kings stood without and could not be permitted." This was the truth of the matter; and it redounds to Adam's credit rather than the reverse that he did not use his influence to favor his countrymen exclusively.

Anjin-sama, or "Mr. Pilot" as the Englishman was popularly known throughout Japan, obtained for the ungrateful Saris trading privileges as extensive as those granted to the Dutch. Contrary to the dictates of common sense and to Adams' advice, Saris declined to place the English factory at Uraga, which was conveniently close to Ieyasu's rapidly expanding castle town of Yedo, but preferred to leave it at Hirado. This fishing town was not only a "wearisome way and foul" from the great commercial centers of the Kwansai and Kwanto, but was overshadowed by the thriving port of Nagasaki, whose excellent and spacious harbor contrasted strongly with Hirado's narrow and dangerous roadstead. Adams had suggested that the English company settle in the vicinity of Yedo before ever the *Clove* arrived in Japan; but his sound advice was ignored both by Saris and his successor at Hirado, Richard Cocks, as also by the directors at London. Experience proved that he was right, and the precarious position of the English company during the decade of its existence in Japan (1613–1623) was largely due to its being based on Hirado rather than in some part of the Kwanto district.[24]

Both English and Hollanders had realized from reading Linschoten's work before they reached the Far East, that direct access to the Chinese silk market was the soundest base for a lucrative trade with Japan. Adams had written to Bantam before the *Clove*'s arrival there, "can the English merchants get the handling or trade with the Chinese, then shall our country make great profit, and the Worshipful India Company of London shall not have need to send money out of England, for in Japan is gold and silver in abundance." By force of arms and otherwise, the Portuguese of Macao effectively prevented the Hollanders from establishing themselves on the Kwangtung coast in 1601–1607; and the Dutch then rashly resorted to pillaging not merely Iberian but also Chinese shipping, with a view to obtaining the coveted silks.

The ships of the English company, as distinct from privateers like Sir Edward Michelbourne, did not resort to such drastic methods, but it was widely believed that they did. The exploits of Drake and Cavendish in the Pacific were known in Japan through the intermediary of the Portuguese Jesuits, if Saris' account is to be believed.

Before our coming they [the Hollanders] passed generally under the name of Englishmen, for our English nation hath been long known by report among them, but much scandalled by the Portugal Jesuits as pirates and rovers upon the seas; so that the naturals have a song which they call the English Crofonia [*Igirisu Kurofune*], showing how the English do take the Spanish ships, which they [singing] do act likewise in gesture with their cattans by their sides, with which song and acting they terrify and scare their children, as the French sometimes did theirs with the name of Lord Talbot.

Both Dutch and English were popularly termed Red-hairs (*Komojin* in Japanese) in China and Japan, by way of distinguishing them from the Nambanjin or Southern Barbarians.

In default of captured cargoes from Macao or Manila-bound junks, Patani and Bantam were the principal ports at which the English and Hollanders obtained Chinese silks by legitimate purchase. An increasingly large quantity was also obtainable in Tongking, Annam, Champa, and Cambodia; but since the Japanese Red-seal ships frequented these ports in preference to others, they usually got the bulk of the available supplies. Apart from silks, however and wherever procured, deerskins and ray or sharkskins from Siam proved the most profitable commodity. The latter were worked up by the Japanese into a kind of shagreen, which under the name of *samé* was in great demand for the covering of sword handles and scabbards. Among the few profitable ventures of the English factory at Hirado, were two voyages made by the junk *Sea Adventure* to Siam in 1615–1618.The English were particularly chagrined by their failure to find a ready market for their broadcloth in Japan, "but as yet they are soe addicted to silks that they doe not enter into consideration of the benefitt of wearinge cloth." This was partly because the Japanese noticed that the English themselves did not wear the material which they recommended, "for, said they, you commend your cloth unto us, but you yourselves wear least thereof, the better sort of you wearing silken garments, the meaner, fustians." About the only use they had for cloth was in the lining of cases for arms and armor.

Cocks and his compatriots complained bitterly of the "brabbling Japons . . . who are so unruly that when a ship is wholly manned with them there is no dealing with them," as Will Adams found to his cost in the *Sea Adventure*. This seems to have been an instance of the pot calling the kettle black, for Jack Tar and Jan Maat were equally unruly, by their commanders' own admissions. Cocks records disgustedly on July 6, 1617: "It is strang to see the unrulynes of these Hollande mareners and souldiers, how they goe stagring drunk up and downe the streetes, slashing and cutting of each other with their knyves, like mad men." It should not have been so very strange to him, after what he had written about the ships' company of the *Hosiander*, eighteen months previously, "here doe I confess before God and the world, I never did see a more unruly company of people, and are far worse than they in the *Clove*, although they were bad enough." Time brought no improvement in this respect, for drunken brawls between English and Dutch sailors at Hirado, sometimes with fatal results, were the order of the day so long as ships of the two nations lay in the roads. Cocks suggested that the majority of the English vessels were manned by crews whose friends were anxious to be rid of them, and who had sent them out, "hoping these long voyages may make an end of them." In November, 1620, the old man is still bemoaning the unruliness of "mariners and sailors, and some not of the meanest sort, who daily lie ashore at tippling houses." Needless to add, fights between these brawling tipplers and the local populace were of frequent occurrence and also ended fatally on occasion.

In extenuation of this riotous behavior, it can be pleaded that the lot of a sailor was far harder in the seventeenth century than now, and the savage corporal punishments then in vogue (flogging, keelhauling, and the like) drove men not merely to drink but desertion. There are several complaints in Cocks' diary of disgruntled sailors seeking refuge with the Portuguese of Nagasaki. One such party was recaptured and four participants hanged at the yardarm; but it is not surprising to find one of the factors complaining that "the common sailor is grown so careless that if he could find opportunity he had rather serve the Spaniard than live under the whip or other strange punishment now in use." The Portuguese seem to have treated their own sailors (as distinct from the lascars) more humanely. At any rate, there is no mention of their deserting to their enemies, whereas desertions of English mariners to them were of frequent occurrence at Goa and Macao. Their slaves, on the other hand, did desert to the Dutch and English.

"Brabbling Japons" annoyed not only Cocks and his colleagues, who seem to have been rather testy individuals anyway, but their fellow Asiatics elsewhere. It is true that the Wako were now virtually extinct, owing to Ieyasu's firm suppression of piracy; but the crews of some of the Red-seal ships vied with the Dutch and English mariners in their addiction to women and liquor. Complaints of their unruly behavior came from Manila, Cochin China, Cambodia, and Siam. To take the last first, the following quotations from Cocks' diary are illuminating. On July 4 (O.S.), 1617, he notes that the King of Cochin China was particularly anxious to receive English traders, "but to come in our owne shipping, and not in Japons, for that he hath banished them out of his countrey, I meane the renegades enhabiting in those partes, which did all the mischiefe before." Nine days later, he notes that "serten Japon fugeties, which are thought to be of them which were formerly banished out of Cochinchina, did joine with the said Portingales, whereupon the King of Cambodia hath lykwaies banished all Japons out of his countrey."

This last report proved premature, but the King of Cambodia complained to the Bakufu of the truculent behavior of the Japanese in his realm as early as 1605. The king suggested somewhat pathetically that only one or two licensed ships should come in a year, and that the captain should keep his crew aboard in irons when in port. "It is only thus that the King of Japan can give proof of his genuine goodwill toward Cambodia and his desire to maintain cordial relations with our country." As for the ruler of Cochin China's complaint in 1618, Honda and Doi dispatched Funamoto Yashichiro thither, with full powers to restore order in the Japanese community. Funamoto had been trading to Indo-China since 1598, and the monarch had asked for him to be sent owing to the confidence he placed in him. As already noted, Hidetada gave the King of Siam carte blanche to deal with the turbulent Japanese in Cambodia—claimed by His Siamese Majesty as a vassal state—as he wished, since they were mere merchants and deserving of no consideration. This would suggest that they were licensed traders rather than Wako, although Cocks' dismissal of them as "renegades" might imply the latter.

In any event, Japanese trade with Indo-China steadily increased during this period, and became of national importance. Padre Valentim de Carvalho states that the Great Ship which renewed the Macao-Nagasaki trade in 1612, brought 1,300 quintals of silk, whereas another 5,000 quintals were imported in Red-seal ships and in shipping from China and Manila. He complains that there was no lack of Portuguese pilots to navigate the Japanese ships for good pay. This is confirmed by an examination of the votive pictures from the Suminokura and Sueyoshi families which are still preserved in the Kiyomizu temple at Kyoto. They clearly show a number of persons in Portuguese dress on board the ships, one of whom is usually sitting next to the Japanese captain and is presumably the pilot.

The extent of Japanese trade with Indo-China and further India during the first quarter of the seventeenth century is attested by the following facts. In 1626, the Portuguese Jesuits record four hundred Japanese Christians in Siam alone, with large colonies in Annam and Tongking, where

their numbers had been considerably increased by the arrival of exiled or fugitive Christians after the promulgation
of Ieyasu's edict in 1614. Other accounts speak of there being more than six hundred Japanese in Siam during the
second decade of the seventeenth century. Their principal
center was the capital of Ayuthia, and there were smaller
groups at Ligor and Patani in the Malay Peninsula. Despite
Hidetada's ban on Japanese serving as foreign mercenaries
in 1621, there is mention of a Japanese contingent in Reyer-
sen's unsuccessful attack on Macao the next year, and Japanese
soldiers were to be found in the Dutch garrisons at Amboina
and Formosa in 1624. The Japanese mercantile colony at
Batavia contained some interesting characters, including a
business associate of the famous navigator, Abel Janszoon
Tasman. The Portuguese captain of Malacca in 1610, had a
Japanese bodyguard which he was ordered to disband, since
their ferocity was a danger to the fortress; and mention is
made of individual Japanese in the Lesser Sunda Islands and
the Moluccas.

So long as Ieyasu was alive, Japanese expansion overseas
gave every promise of vigorous growth. Some of the individuals who directed this maritime activity were men who
would have made their mark in any age or nation. Such were
Suminokura Genso and his son Genshi who claimed descent
from the Minamoto Genji. The former was famous for his
great engineering works, such as the construction of a
navigable channel in the Hozu River near Kyoto, and similar
works in the capital which gave it improved river communications with Lake Biwa and with the sea. His son was likewise a famous public works contractor, and a mining engineer
to boot. He was responsible for the supply and transport of
wood from the forests of Fujiyama for Hidetada's additions
to the castle at Yedo. Nor did his many-sided activities end
here. He was a pupil of Fujiwara Seigwa and a friend of the
famous Confucianist, Hayashi Razan, who mentions him in
his works. He formed a remarkable library of Japanese and
Chinese classics, and published editions of the former (*Isé*

Monogatari, Genji Monogatari, Heike Monogatari) which are treasured by bibliographers nowadays. He was also a celebrated calligrapher and an ardent devotee of the *No* drama and chanoyu. It was this family who founded the trade with Tongking on a firm basis. They and others like them (the Araki, Chaya, and Sueyoshi) did much to atone for the damage done by the better known but more swashbuckling Suetsugu Heizo, Yamada Nagamasa, and Murayama Toan.[25]

Mention of this last bravo, recalls that he was the sponsor of an abortive Japanese attempt to conquer Formosa. Cocks, following Nagasaki gossip, alleges that Toan "is held to be the richest man in Japon, and com up of base parentage by his subtill and craftie wyt." This was an exaggeration, but he tried to outdo Shimadzu of Satsuma's recent conquest of the Ryuku Islands by his expedition to Formosa. The expeditionary force of thirteen junks filled with soldiers, under the command of one of his sons, left Nagasaki on May 15, 1616. It proved to be a reversion to the bad old Wako days; for after one junk had been ambushed in a Formosan creek and her crew had committed *seppuku* to avoid capture by the local headhunters, the remainder gave up the attempt and went "a boot-haling" on the coast of China. Here they were reported "to have killed above 1,200 Chinas, and taken all the barkes or junks they met withal, throwing the people overboard."

This was not the first time that the occupation of Formosa had been mooted. A letter from King Felipe to the Viceroy of India, dated February 17, 1610, states that Bishop Cerqueira and other persons had written that the Japanese were contemplating the occupation of the island, with the idea of establishing a center for the purchase of Chinese silks which would cut out Macao and Manila. The king ordered the viceroy to thwart this plan "by means of subtle negotiations" if it ever showed signs of maturing. Bishop Cerqueira was admittedly skeptical of its practibility, since he thought that the Chinese would oppose it by force of arms. On the other

hand, Cerqueira's original informants may have been referring to Shimadzu Iehisa's preparations for his expedition to
the Ryukyu Islands in 1609.

The juxtaposition of Chinese, Japanese, and Portuguese at
Macao was also a source of acute embarrassment to the last
named, who were confronted with another ultimatum from
the Kwangtung provincial authorities in 1613. It was presented in the name of Viceroy Chang Ming-hang, and one
of the paragraphs ran as follows: "You must not harbor Japanese. Since you are Westerners, why do you employ Japanese
when you have Negro slaves to serve you? In this way they
multiply. The Law ordains that when they are to be found
anywhere, they are to be killed out of hand; yet you persist
in harboring these people, which is like rearing tigers. I went
to the port where I saw many and ordered their immediate
expulsion to the number of ninety or more. I ordered this act
to be engraved in stone. Now that they are expelled, you may
live quietly, but I fear that though these are gone you may
bring others. When you go thither to trade, you must not
bring back any, either great or small; and whosoever does so
will be punished according to Chinese law by having his head
cut off." The viceroy, reporting his action to the Dragon
Throne in a weird and wonderful mixture of metaphors,
labeled the Macaonese "an ulcer on a person's back, and the
Japanese there are like the wings of a Portuguese tiger." The
Portuguese referred to the Pessoa affair of 1608–1610, as proof
of the mutual enmity between themselves and the Japanese,
which obviated any danger of an alliance between the "ulcer"
and "tiger" against the Middle Flowery Kingdom.

It is difficult to get a clear picture of Chinese trade in Japan
at this time. Cocks mentions the arrival of sixty or seventy
Chinese junks at Nagasaki in 1614, and this is confirmed to
some extent by a Portuguese document of the same year,
which adds that the majority of their crews were Fukienese
smugglers, "who settle down there and marry." Some of the
junks were the property of Chinese established in Japan, such
as Cocks' friends, the Li family, one of whom was chief of

the Chinese community at Nagasaki, while his brother, "Andrea Dittis," (alias Li Hankok) held a similar post at Hirado. Both Portuguese and Dutch complained increasingly of Chinese competition; although admittedly the Dutch did not begin to feel the full force of it until after the expulsion of the Portuguese from Japan and the establishment of the Manchu dynasty in China (1644).

The bad example given by Murayama Toan in going "a boot-haling" on the China coast was later followed by the Chinese themselves. Cocks wrote to his employers in December, 1620, "The Cheenas themselves robb one another at sea, thinking to lay all the fault on the Dutch and English; but some have byn intersepted in some provinces of Japon and paid dearly for it. And other China shipping, being sett out of Nangasaque by their owne countreymen to goe for Isla Fermosa (called by them Tacca Sanga) to trade for silks, are run away for China with all the money and left their countreymen in Japon in the lurch." It is clear from a perusal of Cocks' correspondence, that the Chinese only started trading with the aborigines of Formosa on a considerable scale during the first quarter of the seventeenth century. Any previous contact which they had with the island was limited to a few occasional voyages and involuntary visits by shipwrecked mariners. The Japanese called the island Takasago, and the Chinese still confused it in nomenclature at least with the Liu-Kiu (Ryukyu) Islands up to this time. Cocks did his best to procure permission to trade with China, so as to get direct access to the coveted silk market; but his artful intermediaries simply pocketed his bribes and paid him with empty promises. Cocks spent 6,636 taels throwing good money after bad in this way, and his superiors at Bantam finally wrote him, "the China Nachoda hath two long deluded you through your owne simplicite to give creditt unto him." Failure to get a footing in China was one of the main reasons for the withdrawal of the English company from Japan, since without it they could not compete effectively either with the Dutch or with the Portuguese.[26]

Spanish trade with Japan likewise fizzled out about the same time. The Spaniards had an advantage in that they had the germ of an establishment at Uraga (where Will Adams acted as their agent on occasion) but mutual suspicions between the Bakufu and the Manila authorities prevented the growth of a healthy trade. The Mexico-bound galleon *Santo Espiritu* was forced by stress of weather into the port of Urado in Tosa in 1602, and only escaped the fate of the *San Felipe* at the same place six years earlier, by fighting her way out of the harbor. Ieyasu's attitude on this occasion was in marked contrast to Hideyoshi's in 1596. He said that the Tosa pirates had got their deserts, and gave the Spaniards a permit expressly authorizing them to trade and navigate to Japan without molestation. The Manila authorities remained distrustful and continued to regard the shogun's advances with a wary eye.

A report from the Council of the Indies at Madrid in March, 1607, states that a ship was sent yearly from Manila to the Kwanto at Ieyasu's request, bringing Chinese silks and other merchandise, and exporting silver, flour, dried beef, hemp, iron, steel, gunpowder, and hafted weapons. The Council considered that this trade might be permitted to continue merely for the purpose of keeping Ieyasu in a good temper and inducing him to tolerate the presence of the friars in Japan. Another document says that the annual expenses of this voyage cost the royal treasury 6,000 pesos, but the profit (if any) is not stated. The suggestions of Fray Juan Pobre, Fray Diego Aduarte, and others, that this trade should be expanded at the expense of Macao and to the advantage of Manila were not adopted by the crown councilors. On the contrary, they suggested (in 1608) that the Philippine-Japan trade should be confined to the Red-seal ships only, and that Spanish vessels should be withdrawn therefrom as a sop to the commercial jealousy of the Portuguese at Macao.

Although this recommendation was reversed the next year, when a law was promulgated that shipping plying between the Philippines and Japan must be Spanish and not Japanese-owned, the Red-seal trade with Manila steadily increased during the first fifteen years of the century. This is evident from the figures for the Japanese population in the Philippines, who were mostly resident at Dilao, a suburb of Manila. In 1593, there were between 300 and 400 residents. At the time of the suppression of the Sangley rebellion in 1603, they numbered about 1,500; three years later they exceeded 3,000. After the abortive rebellions in 1606–1607, a number of the Japanese were deported, but this setback was only temporary, and trade continued to flourish in a modest way until Ieyasu's final prohibition of Christianity in 1614. Takayama Ukon and some 300 refugee Christians arrived at the end of this year, and these formed the nucleus of a more permanent colony, since many of the remainder were transient traders or mariners. Nevertheless, the Dilao settlement probably formed the largest group of Japanese outside of Japan, since Hernando de los Rios Coronel gives their number as 2,000 in 1619. Archbishop Serrano, writing in August, 1621, stated that there were still more than 1,800 Christian Japanese at Dilao; but Governor Fajardo wrote four months later that a large number of resident Japanese had been expelled recently, "so that for a long time there have not been so few of them here as now."

Before the Japan-Manila trade petered out in the third decade of the century, it had evidently attained respectable proportions. Duarte Gomes de Solis, a Portuguese-Jewish economist writing in 1622, complained bitterly of the harm done to Iberian interests by the tendency of Manila to expand as an entrepôt for Chinese silks at the expense of Macao. He alleged that the Spaniards were cutting off their nose to spite their face, since they had forced up the price of silk to more than double its cost when the Portuguese alone were in the market. Moreover, the Japanese came to buy it at the Philippines, where the triangular competition had raised the price from 140 to 260 pesos the picul.[27]

When all is said and done, the Great Ship from Macao was still the most important single factor in the foreign trade of

Japan during this period. Chinese silk in one form or another was the most sought-after commodity among all Japan's foreign imports, and the Portuguese alone had direct access to the Chinese silk market. Consequently there was usually keen bidding for the purchase of one of these voyages at Goa, although the successful bidder sometimes had reason to repent his bargain, as instanced by the tale of woe of João Serrão da Cunha.

This fidalgo, according to the notarial papers which contain the story of his fifteen-year suit against the crown, was one of the richest merchants at Goa when he bought a Japan voyage at the annual auction on March 9, 1610, for the sum of 27,000 *pardaos xerafines*. This was an average price at that time, when the voyage was estimated to yield a clear profit of 150,000 xerafines "rather more than less" to the captain-major. Serrão's particular voyage was sold at auction to collect funds for the fortification of the city of Cochin; and in accordance with the usual custom, he paid half the price cash down, and gave security for the payment of the remainder on his return from Japan. He then bought a fine new carrack called *Nossa Senhora da Vida*, which had just been launched from the stocks by the Raja of Cochin for whom it had been built. He paid more than 40,000 xerafines in ready money for this ship, "fitted out and ready to sail at the bar of Goa," which he says was then a fair average price for a typical Japan-bound carrack. Since his original working capital was only 50,000 xerafines, he had to raise a loan in order to pay the wages of the crew, and lay in provisions for the voyage. These two items worked out at an average of a little more than 500 xerafines a month.[28]

News of the *Nossa Senhora da Graça* disaster and of Dutch depredations in the China Sea reached Goa before he left, since he sailed in April, 1611, convoyed by five galleons commanded by Miguel de Sousa Pimental, together with a ship belonging to the captain of Malacca. His first misfortune was that the squadron missed the monsoon and was compelled to winter at Malacca, only reaching Macao in the following year.

There had been no Japan voyage in 1610 or 1611, since the Macaonese did not dare to resume regular sailings until Soutomaior brought back the shogunal Red-seal passport, together with pacific assurances from Honda, Goto, and Hasegawa. The voyage was then renewed in 1612 by Pero Martins Gayo in the great galleon *São Felipe e Santiago,* since Gayo had bought his voyage (which had been sold for the fortification of Malacca) before Serrão, and thus had priority. Another and more explicit shuinjo came from Japan in 1613; but Serrão's right to make the next voyage was challenged by two fidalgos who had bought two Japan voyages granted to the Queen of Spain for the Convent of the Incarnation at Madrid. These two voyages had precedence over all others, and although Serrão took the case to court both at Macao and Goa, the verdict went against him in both places.

The unfortunate captain-major, who was now two years overdue and more deeply indebted than ever, was forced to raise another loan on the last remnants of his credit, in order to buy out one of his rivals, so as to enable him to sail. This he did, but ill-luck still dogged him. Contrary winds and weather prevented him from making the voyage that year, so he was compelled to maintain himself, his family, and crew, in idleness for another twelvemonth. Only in July, 1614, did the unlucky Serrão see Nagasaki, but even then his troubles had barely begun. Despite Ieyasu's expulsion of the Jesuits that year, the Great Ship's trading balance showed a handsome profit, but the captain-major's share was wiped out in payments to his creditors. He was unable to get anyone to finance his next voyage, and his creditors foreclosed in September, 1616, when his ship and few remaining assets were sold. During the five and a half years which his unlucky voyage lasted, he had paid out a total of more than 50,000 xerafines in wages and running expenses alone. From being one of the richest men in Goa, "regarded and reputed as such, he was reduced to a beggar and kicked out of doors." [29]

The *Nossa Senhora da Vida* made another voyage in 1615,

under Martim da Cunha, who had bought one of those sold for the Queen of Spain. Jan Joosten informed Cocks that "she is not soe well laden as she was the yeare past, but, as it should seeme, cometh more to fetch away the lagg they left heare the last yeare than for anything else." Cocks says elsewhere that the price of Canton silk, which on this Great Ship's arrival fetched only 165 taels a picul, rose to 230 taels after her departure, whereas the superior Nanking quality fetched more than 300 a picul. The Portuguese envoys had a chilly reception at court, where they waited forty days to deliver their present, "which was at last received but none of them admitted" to the ex-shogun's sanctum.

However surly Ieyasu might show himself toward Roman Catholics, he still invested a handsome sum in the Great Ship's cargo, which is more than he ever did in the ladings of Dutch of English vessels. Padre Carvalho in his "Apologia" of 1617, complains of the trouble caused the Portuguese by Ieyasu's investments for the purchase of Chinese gold and selected silks. He alleges that their Japanese enemies more than once tried to shake the old man's confidence by substituting shoddy material for the original fine stuffs. These intrigues were evidently unsuccessful in the long run, since in the year of Ieyasu's death (1616) Hasegawa Genroku warned the English and Dutch "that they should take heed they did not meddel with the greate ship of Amacon, for that the Emperour had much adventure in her." Cocks added testily, "Yet I say I wish we might take her and then make the reconying after;" but it was as well for him that he had no opportunity of putting this theory to the test.

Cocks also complains that Hasegawa Gonroku (bugyo of Nagasaki from 1615 to 1625) and other Bakufu officials secretly or openly favored the Portuguese as against their European rivals, even after the expulsion of the missionaries in 1614. He further alleges that the big merchants of the shogunal "silk ring" likewise favored the Portuguese; but this, if true, was probably due to their being older customers and providing better goods than either Dutch or English could

normally produce. Apart from the official classes, it is clear
that there was still a lot of goodwill felt by the Christian
populace of Nagasaki for their old Namban acquaintances
and fellow Catholics. Thus Cocks, writing in 1620, about
the attitude of the townspeople in Bishop Cerqueira's days,
states: "in the time of that bishopp heare were soe many priests
and Jesuits with their partakers, that one could not passe the
streetes without being by them called Lutranos and herejos,
which now are very quiet and non of them dare open his
mouth to speake such a word." Another indication is afforded
by Saris' experience on his arrival at Hirado (June, 1613),
when the local populace were obviously not clear about the
distinction between Portuguese and English: "I gave leave to
divers sorts of women to come into my Cabinn, where the
picture of Venus did hang very lasciviously set out and in
large frame. They thinking it to bee Our Ladie, fell downe
and worshipped it, with shewes of great devotion, telling me
in a whispering manner (that some of their own companions
which were not so, might not heare) that they were *Chris-
tianos;* whereby we perceived them to be Christians, made
Papists by the Portugale Jesuits."

Moreover, many of the local Portuguese merchants were
married to Japanese women, and not merely living with
them as were the heretics at Hirado. The Portuguese sailors
were likewise better behaved than their north European
rivals, if only because of Latin abstemiousness as opposed
to Anglo-Dutch thirst for liquor. Of course, conflicts sometimes occurred; but these were usually due to the misbehavior
of Negro slaves or lascars rather than to the Portuguese
"filthie pride and lecherie" which Linschoten had denounced
so scathingly. The Portuguese were generous spenders, as
Specx shrewdly observed in 1610, and this and their sobriety
probably atoned for their "pride and lechery" in the eyes of
those who had to live cheek by jowl with them.

So envious was Cocks of the superiority of the Portuguese
position at Nagasaki, that at one time he was anxious to move
the English from the neighborhood of their quondam allies

at Hirado, and take his chance alongside those whom he had previously stigmatized as the "villanose papisticall rabble at Langasaque." He pointed out that Nagasaki harbor was "the best in all Japon, wheare there may 1,000 seale of shipps ride land lockt, and the greatest shipps or carickess in the world may goe in and out at pleasure and ride before the towne within a cables length of the shore in 7 or 8 fathom water at least, yt being a great cittie and many rich merchantes dwelling in it, where, to the contrary, Firando is a fisher towne and a very small and badd harbour, wherein not above 8 or 10 shipps can ride at a tyme without greate danger to spoile one another in stormy weather." Furthermore, whereas the daimyo of Hirado, his family, friends, and a host of flunkies had to be bribed continuously, "or else it is no living among them," the Portuguese at Nagasaki had only to grease the palm of the local bugyo. Cocks got Adams to seek the shogun's permission for the transfer of the English in 1618, but nothing came of the proposal in the upshot. Despite the natural advantages of Nagasaki, it is unlikely that he would have made this request before 1614, when the Jesuits still had a large say in the administration of the port. Since their expulsion marked a turning point in the history of Japan's foreign relations, I shall consider that episode in the next chapter.[30]

Chapter VII. THE PALM OF
CHRISTIAN FORTITUDE

AN attentive perusal of the correspondence of Bishop Cerqueira and his colleagues during the first decade of the seventeenth century shows that the Jesuits were under no illusion about the reason for Ieyasu's reluctant tolerance of their presence in Japan. It was simply and solely due to his conviction that they were indispensable intermediaries for the smooth functioning of the Macao-Nagasaki silk trade. This fact is accepted by modern historians, although they never state the exact nature of this connection between God and Mammon. It is clear from the confidential correspondence of Valignano, Cerqueira, and Carvalho, that the Jesuits were essential intermediaries for so long as they alone had sufficient knowledge of the language, manners, and customs of the country to act as satisfactory interpreters. By 1613, this state of affairs was no longer true. Father João Rodriguez Tçuzzu had been replaced at court by Will Adams, and there were a number of Portuguese merchants married to Japanese women and resident at Nagasaki, who spoke the language fluently. Moreover, numbers of Japanese in northwest Kyushu had attained a good working knowledge of Portuguese, as evidenced by the translation of Pessoa's draft petition in 1609, unbeknown to the Jesuits. There were also a number of renegade dojuku whose services could have been used in a pinch.[1]

More important still, the Great Ship was no longer so necessary to Japanese economy as of old. True, she was still the most important single factor in Japan's foreign trade; but, as seen, her import of silks in 1612 amounted to less than half the total from other sources, among which the

[1] For notes to chapter vii, see pages 490–496.

Red-seal ships figured with increasing vigor and success. The upshot of the Pessoa affair had shown that the Portuguese would probably want to trade with Japan in any event, although the resumption of trade in 1612, was partly negotiated through the Jesuits. Dutch and English competition, disappointingly meager in its early days from Ieyasu's point of view, held great promise for the future, particularly if the heretics succeeded in supplanting the Iberians at either Manila or Macao as they threatened to do. In short, although the Bakufu regarded the Macao trade as extremely desirable, it was no longer considered to be absolutely essential, if placed in the balance against a political threat to the stability of the country in general and the hegemony of the house of Tokugawa in particular.

The potential menace of the Christian "fifth column" had never been wholly absent from the minds of Japan's rulers since it had been suggested by the Buddhist priesthood in Nobunaga's day. It is true that he had scornfully rejected these insinuations, but other scarcely less influential daimyo did not. Hideyoshi's suspicions had been aroused by Coelho's compromising proposals in 1586–1587, and had been sharply rekindled by the alleged indiscretion of the *San Felipe*'s pilot ten years later. Ieyasu at first showed himself unexpectedly gracious, and even advocated the conversion of merchants as an encouragement to foreign trade; but politically he was always opposed to the Faith and he never tolerated the conversion of daimyo. The mutual accusations bandied about between Portuguese and Spaniards in Japan, particularly over the loss of the *San Felipe* and the *Nossa Senhora de Graça* respectively, did nothing to lull his suspicions of Iberian integrity. These were further strengthened by the allegations and insinuations of the Red-haired Barbarians about the character and motives of their Catholic rivals—allegations which were sometimes justified, more often not, but in either event lost nothing in the telling.

Will Adams' boast that he had returned good for evil by helping Portuguese and Spaniards in their affairs at court, can only be accepted at its face value if taken as limited to private individuals and their own concerns. Otherwise he lost no opportunity of traducing the Catholic Church and King in and out of season; nor were Richard Cocks and others of his countrymen backward in denouncing the "villanose Papisticall rabble," whether at Nagasaki or elsewhere. The following extracts from the correspondence of the English traders in Japan are typical of their attitude on this point. In October, 1615, Cocks wrote to Wickham in the Kwansai district about procuring the release of two of his agents who had been "shanghaied" aboard the *Nossa Senhora da Vida* at Nagasaki. He told Wickham to say that King Felipe had usurped Portugal by force of arms, and would do the like in Japan if he could, and the padres were fit instruments to stir the people to rebellion: "harp upon this string, but be sure they secretly do you no mischief."

Harp upon this string Cocks himself certainly did, as can be seen from the entries referring to his conversation with Honda and Doi at the shogunal court next year.

The Councell sent unto us I think above twenty tymes to know whether the English nation were Christians or no. I answered we were, and that they knew that before by our Kinges Majesty's letter sent to the Emperor his father (and hym selfe), wherein it appeared he was defender of the Christian faith. "But," said they, "are not the Jesuites and fryres Christians two?" Unto which I answered they were, but not such as we were, for that all Jesuits and fryres were banished out of England before I was borne, the English nation not houlding with the Pope nor his doctryne, whose followers these padres (as they cald them) weare. It is strange to see how often they sent to me about this matter, and in the end gave us wayning that we did not comunecate, confesse, nor baptiz with them, for then they should hold us to be all of one sect. Unto which I replied that their Honours needed not to stand in doubt of any such matter, for that was not the custom of our nation.

This observation of Cocks led to a member of the *Roju,* or great council, retorting to a Portuguese envoy who complained of the expulsion of the missionaries on the same occasion: "Hath not the Emperor of Japan as much reason to put your Jesuits and friars out of Japan and to withstand the secret entrance of them, knowing them to be stirrers up of sedition and turbulent people?" Ieyasu had made a similar remark three years earlier, after listening to Will Adams' exposition of the Jesuits as potential traitors: "If the Kings and Princes of Europe do banish the Fathers out of their countries, I shall do them no injury to send them out of mine."

The deadliest thrust of all, Cocks reserved for two Spanish ships bound from Mexico to the Philippines which had been forced into Kyushu ports by contrary winds. The Spaniards sent an envoy to court who gave out that the English and Dutch were robbing Chinese ships at sea, which was the reason that few or none had come to Japan that year. Infuriated by this story, which was probably correct for the Dutch at least, Cocks told "Oyendono" (Doi) and "Codsquin Dono" (Honda)

that if they lookt out well about those 2 Spanish ships arrived in Xaxama [Satsuma] full of men and treasure, they would fynd that they were sent of purpose by the King of Spaine haveing knowledge of the death of the ould Emperor, thinking som papisticall *tono* might rise and rebell and so draw all the papistes to flock to them and take part, by which means they might on a sudden seaz som strong place and keepe it till more succors came, they not wanting money nor men for thackomplishing such a strattagim. Which speeches of myne wrought so far that the Emperor sent to stay them, and, had not the great shipp cut her cable in the howse so to escape, she had byn arrested, yet with her haste she left som of her men behind; and the other shipp being of som 300 tons was cast away in a storme and driven on shore, but all the people saved. So in this sort I crid quittance with the Spaniards for geveing out falce reports of us, yet since verely thought to be true which I reported of them.

There is every reason to believe that this allegation of Cocks, which was neither the first nor the last of its kind, fell on particularly receptive ears. Padre Valentim Carvalho, writing in his exile at Macao just about the same time, stated that what Ieyasu (or Hideyoshi for that matter) was really afraid of, was not the prospect of the conquest of Japan by King Felipe for himself, but of Spanish military aid for a Christian daimyo who might be ambitious of seizing the supreme power. Cocks was indeed mistaken in believing—or affecting to believe—that the Spaniards lacked neither money nor men "for thackomplishing such a strattagim"; but the reader will remember that Padre Gaspar Coelho had indeed suggested the fortification of Nagasaki with Spanish help in 1587, for use as a *point d'appui* around which to rally the Christian daimyo of Kyushu against Hideyoshi. Coelho's request had been rejected by all concerned, and the central government at Madrid was equally frigid to later schemes of conquest elaborated by religious or military hotheads at Manila. Nevertheless, such projects *were* mooted from time to time; so that Cocks' allegation, although baseless in this particular instance, was therefore treated more seriously than it deserved. The Bakufu's panic was further increased by Shimadzu of Satsuma erroneously reporting that many friars had been landed secretly from the ships and were in hiding up country.[2]

This incident took place a couple of years after the formal expulsion of the missionaries, but the seeds of suspicion had been sown many years before. Apart from real or alleged Portuguese complaints of Spanish aggression at the time of the *San Felipe* incident, the doings of Sebastián Vizcaíno in 1611–1612, aroused much unfavorable comment. This Spanish navigator, famous for his surveys of the California coast, received permission from the Bakufu to survey the east coast of Japan, in order that the Mexico-bound Manila galleons might utilize the Kwanto ports with more safety than they had in 1596–1602, if driven off their course by bad weather. After granting the desired permission, the ex-shogun had some misgivings about the concession, and he asked Will Adams what he thought about it. The English pilot replied that in Europe any such action would be suspected as the preliminary reconnaissance for an invading army. Contemporary sources differ widely on whether this observation had any great effect on the Bakufu. Vizcaíno claims that Ieyasu treated Adams' warning with scorn, and he was certainly allowed to finish his surveys in peace. Irrespective of this point, it is certain that the Spaniard gave great offense by his ill-advised displays of stiff-necked pride. He refused to conform to Japanese etiquette during his interviews with Ieyasu and Hidetada, and consequently found himself scurvily treated by them later on. Vizcaíno was no admirer of the Japanese, and his Spanish sobriety was outraged by the way in which they tippled the sherry wine he offered them occasionally. He observed maliciously that the best way to convert them to the Catholic Faith would be to make St. Martín of Valdeiglesias y Xerez their patron saint.

The wide gulf between the two sides is evidenced from Ieyasu's correspondence with the viceroy of Mexico on the subject of Vizcaíno's mission. The ex-shogun observed: "The doctrine followed in your country differs entirely from ours. Therefore, I am persuaded that it would not suit us. In the Buddhist sutras it is said that it is difficult to convert those who are not disposed toward being converted. It is best, therefore, to put an end to the preaching of your doctrine on our soil. On the other hand, you can multiply the voyages of merchant ships, and thus promote mutual interests and relations. Your ships can enter Japanese ports without exception. I have given strict orders to this effect."

Vizcaíno, on the other hand, said virtually nothing about trade in his requests to the Bakufu, but confined himself to asking for the free admission of friars and the expulsion of the Dutch. He was even so tactless as to tell a daimyo in conversation, "that the King of Spain did not care about trade with Japan, nor any temporal interest, for God had given him many kingdoms and dominions. The only inducement that his Christian Majesty had [for relations with Japan] was a pious desire that all nations should be taught the Holy Catholic Faith and thus be saved." Justice compels me to add that any promises which Vizcaíno might have made about sending the galleons which Ieyasu so ardently desired to see from New Spain, would have been promptly repudiated by the Spanish colonial authorities. It was an inviolable rule that all colonial trade must be channeled exclusively to the mother country, and repeated requests from

Manila to be allowed more trade to China and Japan were always regarded askance by the government at Madrid.

When Vizcaíno finally set sail for Mexico in October, 1613, he had to carry with him (to his no little disgust) a curious combination of the sacred and the profane in the persons of Fray Luis Sotelo, O.F.M., and Hasekura Rokuemon, who were sent by Date Masamuné, the "one-eyed dragon" of Sendai, as envoys to the King of Spain and the Pope. The aims and objects of this party are best summed up by the Japanese historian, Tokutomi, who characterized it as a combination of those who wished to use the Kingdom of Heaven for trade, and those who wished to use trade for the Kingdom of Heaven. Hasekura only returned to Sendai in 1620; but since this embassy, though interesting enough in its way, exercised no effect on the development of the Bakufu's foreign policy, there is no need to record its meanderings through Mediterranean Europe.[3]

Ieyasu's patience was clearly wearing thin and was finally exhausted by three incidents. The first of these was the discovery of a court intrigue involving the Christian daimyo family of Arima, which was at this time the main prop and stay of Christianity in Japan. Arima Harunobu was anxious to obtain the reversion of some lands which had been lost to Matsura of Hirado in the civil wars of the preceding century. The better to effect this end, "he used some means not so conformable either to reason or to the law of God as might have been wished and desired," as a Jesuit chronicler put it. In other words, he married his son and heir, Naozumi (baptismal name Miguel) to an adopted granddaughter of Ieyasu, named Senhimé, oblivious of the fact that the young hopeful was already married in the face of Mother Church to Konishi's Christian niece, Martha. Old Arima was further induced to bribe a Christian secretary of Honda Kozuke-no-suké, named Paulo or Okamoto Daihachi, in the belief that the latter could arrange the restoration of the coveted lands through the mediation of his master. Arima paid over a large sum in bribes before he discovered that Okamoto neither could nor would do anything to assist him. He then called in the help of a Jesuit brother, but this latter was unable to reconcile the contending parties; and the plot was promptly given away by his son and daughter-in-law, who were apparently in league with Hasegawa Sahioye, bugyo of Nagasaki, against the head of the family. Ieyasu was furious when the matter came to his knowledge. Old Arima was promptly dispossessed of his fief in 1612, and executed the following year. The scapegrace Miguel promptly apostatized and was given his luckless father's fief as a reward. He did not enjoy it for long, since he was exiled to Hyuga in 1614. Okamoto was burned alive in the sight of his wife for forging Ieyasu's letters patent.

Since three of the participants in this sordid tragedy were Christians, Ieyasu's aversion to the Faith became greater than ever. It was further increased when a strict search among the members of his own private household revealed a number of Christians who were forced to recant or were exiled without further ado. Chief among them was one of his favorite waiting women, a Korean named Julia Ota, although the Jesuits claim that she was not actually his concubine as the Franciscans alleged. Young Arima became a reluctant persecutor, killing two of his own half-brothers; but when he had a number of Christians burned alive for refusing to deny their faith, a crowd of believers estimated at thirty thousand attended their martyrdom, singing hymns and offering prayers. This demonstration served further to infuriate the Bakufu who naturally regarded it as an indication of Christian disobedience to feudal law and order.

Ieyasu had not recovered from the shock of the Arima disclosures, when the equally unedifying Okubo scandal came to light. The ramifications of this exceedingly shady business are still far from clear, and it is by no means certain that the chief culprit was a Christian, as his accusers alleged. Okubo Nagayasu was a *No* actor who specialized in the *sarugaku* or monkey dance, before he attracted the attention

of Ieyasu with a proposal to increase the output of the gold
and silver mines. Like Murayama, Hasegawa, and others of
this ilk, he rose rapidly in the world and was finally created
daimyo of Hachioji. He evidently possessed real talents, since
he had not only increased the output of the mines on Sado
Island and in Idzu Province, but brought the posting and
pack-horse system on the Tokaido and other highroads to
a high degree of efficiency. He took advantage of his position as overseer of the mines to falsify the accounts and indulge in peculation on a grand scale. After his death in
1613, his misdeeds were discovered through the action of
his twenty-four concubines who complained that his heirs
had defrauded them of large sums of gold which their protector had promised them. The foregoing rests on ascertained
facts, but there is no convincing evidence to support the
further allegation that Okubo was plotting with the missionaries for the dispatch of an expeditionary force to aid the
native Christians against the Bakufu. But although the allegation was certainly false, Ieyasu may well have believed it.
Okubo was beyond his reach, but his sons were killed, his
fortune confiscated, and it is said that Ieyasu's sixth son,
Tadateru, was disgraced because of his connection with the
culprit.[4]

Christianity's connection with criminals and conspirators
of every degree was further cemented in the eyes of the
Bakufu with the arrest and crucifixion of a notorious coiner
named Jirobioye, who happened to be a Christian. "Many
people according to the custome of all places went to see the
execution, and when the Christian gave up the ghost, the
Christians that were present kneeled downe upon their
knees to commend his soule unto God; and thereupon some
of the Gentiles, malicious persons, tooke occasion to give out
that they did adore him that way crucified."

Hasegawa Sahioye now addressed a memorial to the Bakufu,
pointing out the dangers to the existing feudal form of
government which were inherent in the continued propagation of Christianity. Citing the Arima and Jirobioye affairs

in support of his contention, he denounced the Christians and their religion on these grounds:

1. The Christian doctrine teaches that believers should obey the padres as their spiritual pastors, rather than the daimyo as their temporal lords.

2. The Christians sacrifice everything in favor of their law, and worship criminals who have been justly condemned as evil-doers and rebels; they carry their relics as amulets.

3. In order to imitate Jesus Christ, who died crucified between two thieves, the Christians glory in dying such a death, and for such a cause; hence they are a fanatical and pernicious sect, dangerous to the Empire, and ripe for any mischief.

This memorial and the news of the spectacular (if orderly) mass demonstration at the crucifixion of the Arima martyrs, seem to have disposed of any hesitations which Ieyasu may still have felt. He decided on the expulsion of all missionaries from Japan, the closing of all churches, and the strict prohibition of the outward or secret practice of Christianity by any Japanese. The Franciscan churches in the Kwansai and Kwanto had been officially closed the year before, doubtless owing to Ieyasu's annoyance at the close connection of the friars minor with Vizcaíno's uncoöperative attitude. The Jesuits had been (after some preliminary hesitation) specifically exempted from this ruling, through the intercession of Itakura Katsushige the *shoshidai* or shogunal governor of Kyoto, whom the Jesuits describe as an "honorable, moderate and moral man, and a friend unto the Fathers." The Franciscans, although ostensibly dispossessed, were still permitted to stay on at Fushimi. The 1614 decree included all the missionaries without exception. Padre Morejon, rector of the Kyoto college, was warned of the coming blow in December, 1613, when he received a letter from Hasegawa Sahioye and another from Goto Shozaburo, telling him of what was toward, although Hasegawa did not add that he himself had been the principal instigator of Ieyasu's final decision.[5]

The text of the famous edict which was promulgated on January 27, 1614, has been variously ascribed to the Confucian scholar, Hayashi Razan, and to the Zen priest Soden (Suden) of the Konji-in at Kyoto. Probably both had a hand in it, since it is a curious medley of Buddhist and Confucian ideas, with a few passing allusions to Shinto. It begins by invoking the principles of *Yang* (male or positive) and *Yin* (female or negative) as the foundation of all life, and alludes to various Buddhist texts, before denouncing Christianity in the following terms: "the Kirishitan band have come to Japan, not only sending their merchant vessels to exchange commodities, but also longing to disseminate an evil law, to overthrow true doctrine, so that they may change the government of the country, and obtain possession of the land. This is the germ of great disaster, and must be crushed."

It extols Japan as "the country of the Gods and of Buddha," and quotes the Confucian Book of Etiquette on the five appropriate punishments (branding, noseslitting, cutting off the feet, castration, and death) for malefactors. "The faction of the bateren rebel against this dispensation. If they see a condemned fellow, they run to him with joy, bow to him, and do him reverence. This they say is the essence of their belief. If this is not an evil law, what is it? They truly are the enemies of the Gods and of Buddha." The mixture of Confucian and Buddhist ideas (so different from contemporary China where the two were sharply differentiated) is evidenced by sentences such as "Abroad we have manifested the Five Cardinal Virtues, while at home we have returned to the Doctrine of the Scriptures," Confucian and Buddhist texts being quoted alternatively. It concludes with the statement that "for the way of the Gods and the law of Buddha to prosper in spite of the degeneracy of these latter days is a mark of a good ruler. Let Heaven and the Four Seas hear this and obey."

Attached to this edict, which sounded the death knell for Christianity in Japan for two and a half centuries, were fifteen rules for the guidance of the Buddhist priesthood in securing its enforcement. These directed that everyone must become a member of one or another of the principal Buddhist sects, the head of the family being responsible for the choice thereof. The priests were to visit their parishioners at the period of the Bon (*Urabon*) Festival in the seventh lunar month, to read prayers, and to ascertain that there was no falling away on the part of members of the family. The result of this investigation was consigned to a register, which was eventually sent in to the Ecclesiastical Commissioners. These measures were ostensibly enforced up to 1868, although their actual application seems to have varied widely according to time, place, and circumstances.[6]

While this edict was being concocted, overt persecution was virtually confined to the apostate Arima's fief, and the Church elsewhere was left in that ominous calm which precedes the storm. The Jesuit writer of the *Annual Letter* for 1614, or rather his contemporary English translator at Saint-Omer, wrote of the situation elsewhere than Arima: "The Churches there stood open unto all, and Gods' Word was freely preached therein, although they were not without some fear and care to see what that tempest which threatened some greater storms to come, would prove at length. They celebrated in the yeare 1613 the Night of our Blessed Saviour his Nativity in all the places afore mentioned, with great solemnity, concourse and devotion of the Christians."

The blow fell two days after this deceptively peaceful Christmas morning, when Itakura received the order to make a nominal roll of all Christians in the Kyoto district. The local Jesuits were left in suspense until they received the letters from Hasegawa and Goto warning them that Ieyasu was contemplating the complete prohibition of Christianity. The formal notification arrived at Kyoto on February 14, 1614, when the Jesuits "were required to give up a Catalogue of the names of all the Fathers, Brethren, and *Doxucos*, or Seminaries, as also of the servantes they had, to the end that none of them should remaine behind. But because it was necessary that some should stay secretly there for the helpe of the Christians of that City, and of other townes and villages there about, of eight Fathers they put only three in the Catalogue, and of seaven Brethren only three, and of twenty Seminaristes only six."

It need hardly be added that this "pious fraud"—which was carried out on a greater or lesser scale in the vast majority of the missionary establishments throughout Japan—could never have been effected without the connivance of Itakura. The Jesuits had been for years on familiar terms with him, and it is obvious that he must have turned a blind eye to the palpable discrepancy between the number of those who went and the number who were there. The padres also bear witness to the kindness and consideration which he and his minions showed them during their arrest and their transfer to Nagasaki. This good treatment was the general though not the invariable rule; and it is clear that Ieyasu must have given orders that the missionaries were not to be personally molested or ill-treated. All missionary personnel, whether European or Japanese, was ordered to concentrate at Nagasaki, pending embarkation for Macao and Manila. A number of leading native Christians including Takayama Ukon and Naito Tokuan received the same orders.[7]

It is not easy to ascertain even the approximate number of Christians at the time when the blow fell in 1614. Some writers credit the Jesuits with a total of two million converts at this period, but there is nothing in the contemporary records to support so extravagant an estimate. Fernão Guerreiro in his *Relaçam Anual* of 1605, claims a total of 750,000 converts at that date, but it is probable that even this figure was exaggerated. Padre Valentim de Carvalho, who was the head of the Jesuit mission in Japan at the time of the expulsion, and who had been provincial at Nagasaki since 1611, states that there were nearly 300,000 Christians in Japan in January, 1614. Since Carvalho had all the annual returns at his disposal when he wrote, his estimate is certainly a reliable one. It also agrees fairly well with that of the writer of the *Annual Letter* of 1614 who notes that "there were then living more than 250,000 Christians." Since the first decade of the seventeenth century was one of steady progress in the propagation of Christianity in Japan, and there are no records of any large-scale persecutions or mass apostasies, it is certain that Guerreiro's estimate is far too high. Carvalho's figure of 300,000 should be taken as the maximum, even including the converts made by the mendicant orders, who, if the Jesuits are to be believed, were poor in numbers if proud in spirit. Even so, this is a remarkable figure considering the total number of missionaries (143) then working in Japan, and the difficulties under which they labored when deprived of the support of Konishi and Arima. The total population of the empire at that time is roughly estimated at about twenty million, but it would be difficult, if not impossible, to find another highly civilized pagan country where Christianity had made such a mark, not merely in numbers but in influence.

It is easier to speak with greater confidence about other mission statistics, since a detailed list of the Jesuit mission stations for 1612 was forwarded to the general at Rome. Reduced to tabular form, the list is here summarized.

Nagasaki and district: 1 college, 6 residencies; 28 padres and 18 irmãos.
Arima and district: 1 college, 8 residencies; 16 padres and 15 irmãos.
Hakata and district: 1 house, 2 residencies; 4 padres and 3 irmãos.
Bungo Province: 1 house, 2 residencies; 4 padres and 3 irmãos.
Kwansai and Kwanto: 1 rectory, 6 residencies; 10 padres and 13 irmãos.

A total of 2 colleges, 2 houses (*casa*), 1 rectory (*casa reitoral*), and 24 residencies, staffed by a bishop (Cerqueira), a provincial (Carvalho), 62 padres and 52 irmãos, or 116 Jesuits altogether. The seminary attached to the college at Hachirao (Arima), had fifty-eight "youths and children of the Japonians, teaching them learning and vertue, latin, musicke, and the characters of the Religions and Sectes of *Iapone,* and the manner how to confute them, which hath beene one of the best and most efficacious meanes for the conversion of those Gentiles." The exact number of Jesuit churches throughout Japan at this time is more uncertain, but there were seventy in Arima's fief alone when the local persecution broke out in 1613.

There were 250 native catechists, distributed as follows: Nagasaki and district, 103; Kwansai and Kwanto, 59; Arima Province, 58; Hakata and district, 18; Bungo Province, 12. This figure did not include "the numerous household servants who cannot be dispensed with here because of the customs of the country," nor the Christian refugees who were maintained by Jesuit charity. Exclusive of these last two categories, the Society in Japan was responsible for a total of 534 persons.

The mendicant orders made a modest showing in comparison with these figures, there being only 14 Franciscans, 9 Dominicans, and 4 Augustinians at this time. Carvalho claims that the closing of the Franciscan establishments by the Bakufu in 1612, did not amount to much, since outside of Nagasaki they merely had a straw hut at Uraga (where there was only a friar when the Spanish ships called there) and another at Yedo with a small leprosarium attached thereto. He further claims that they had relatively few converts, the majority of whom had originally been converted by the Jesuits. Even allowing for the provincial's dislike of the Franciscans, which clearly influenced his judgment (since he does not mention their house at Kyoto), it is obvious that the Friars Minor could not have had more than a few thousand converts. The Dominican and Augustinian communities were numerically insignificant, the former being established in Hizen and the latter in Bungo (Usuki), in addition to their convents at Nagasaki. Finally, mention should be made of the seven Japanese secular clergy, four of whom were parish priests at Nagasaki.

It will be obvious from a cursory glance at the foregoing facts and figures, that the overwhelming strength of the missionary enterprise in Japan was concentrated in northwest Kyushu, with Nagasaki as headquarters. The reasons are equally obvious on reflecting that, "by occasion of the traffique from the Indies and Macao, the Christian religion

found first entrance into Iapone, and how by meanes
thereof it hath hitherto also beene there conserved," as the
English translator of the *Annual Letter* of 1614 noted.
Arima, Omura, Shimabara, and Amakusa had been Christian strongholds for nearly fifty years, and neighboring Higo
still had many converts from Konishi's time. The last of
the local Christian daimyo (Arima) had only just disap-
peared from the scene, and no other part of Japan had been
subjected so long and so continuously to Christian influence
backed by the favor and patronage of the local feudal
nobility.[8]

It must not be thought that the Jesuits made no effort
to turn the tide against them at court, but in the circumstances their efforts were foredoomed to failure. Itakura received, marked, learned, and inwardly digested an apologetic tract which Padre Morejon gave him before his
departure, but neither he nor anyone else dared to offend
Ieyasu by bringing it to his notice. Bishop Cerqueira had
died in February, 1614, at the very height of the crisis, and
his successor, the Provincial Valentim Carvalho, determined
to send to court the veteran Padre Diogo de Mesquita, rector
of the college at Nagasaki, and an old friend of Hasegawa
Sahioye, to see if he could not induce the bugyo to intercede for them. "The Father went and did his best endeavours,
but Safioye himselfe being the chiefe sticler in the business,
gave him answer, that it was not possible to have audience in
the matter, because the Xogun was already fully resolved that
not so much as one of all the Fathers should remayne in all
the Country, and therewith he commanded him imediately
to returne to Nangasaqui, where all did prepare themselves
to the conflict no lesse than in other places, using to that
end all spirituall meanes they could, now that there was no
hope in humane diligence."

Nagasaki was now the scene of an outbreak of mass religious fervor which must at times have reminded the missionaries of Lisbon or Seville during Holy Week. The month
of May was almost entirely taken up with a series of religious

processions in which thousands participated, including
Murayama Toan and all his family. Flagellations and mutila-
tions were the order of the day, several penitents dying from
self-inflicted wounds. A "round robin" was also circulated
in which many of the citizens of all ages and sexes declared
their intention to remain faithful to their religion unto
death. These demonstrations were not originally sanctioned
by the Jesuits, who rightly feared that they would be regarded by the Bakufu as seditious; but the general fervor
was such that the padres finally organized one of their own
on the Feast of Corpus Christi.

These somewhat ill-timed displays of religious zeal thoroughly alarmed Hasegawa's underlings, who wrote an exaggerated account of them to the bugyo at Shidzuoka,
implying that Nagasaki was on the brink of a general revolt.
Hasegawa was on his way back to the port at this time, but
the messenger missed him on the road and handed the dispatches to his sister, O-Natsu. "She being a wicked woman,
a Gentill and an enemy to the Christian faith, went weeping
with them unto the *Xogun*, and related the matter in such
manner, as though doubtlesse her brethren were both of
them slaine already at *Nangasaqui*. Wherewithall the *Xogun*
[Ieyasu] was so moved to anger and indignation that laying
his hand upon his sword, he swore, that if *Nangasaque* were
neere at hand he would go thither himselfe in person, and
put all to sword and fire." As it was, he sent a special commissioner, Yamaguchi Suruga-no-kami Masatomo, to Nagasaki with 500 samurai to restore law and order. In point of
fact, Hasegawa Sahioye had already reached the city and
found all quiet.

Both those officials sent reassuring reports to Ieyasu, and
a few days later they notified him of the arrival of the
Great Ship from Macao with Captain-Major João Serrão
da Cunha. Ieyasu was delighted at this news, but he kept
enquiring anxiously of his advisers whether the Portuguese
would continue to trade if he expelled the padres from Japan.
The Jesuits also took heart with the arrival of the *Nossa*

Senhora da Vida, "for they hoped that upon this occasion the Gentills through the great desire they have to traffique with the Portugalls, would wincke at them, at least for a tyme; especially it being most certaine that the *Xogun* himselfe had shewed great contentment when he heard thereof, and commanded that all favour and kind usage should be showed both to the Captaine, and his Company."

Provincial Carvalho now asked Captain-Major Serrão da Cunha to take advantage of Ieyasu's complaisance and go in person to Shidzuoka in order to ask that the Portuguese be permitted to retain one church at Nagasaki for their own use, as in Hideyoshi's time. Serrão da Cunha was more than willing to do what was asked of him, "both because he greatly regretted that this Christianity would be abandoned if its pastors were exiled, as because of the inconvenience which the captains would feel if the Company was no longer there to help them in their business negotiations." This project, however, was stillborn owing to the opposition of the local authorities.

Both *Safioye* and *Surungadono* were unwilling that the Captaine of the Portugal ship should go unto the Court, saying that it would be an occasion of a greater breach if the *Xogun* should not graunt (as they thought he would not) that which the Captaine in person should aske of him, and that it were far better to send an embassage unto him with a present, the which although for this yeare perhapps it would not do much good, yet would it be a disposition for the yeare following, when his anger was once past, to get a grant of what they desired. There was no remedy but to follow their counsayle, because it was impossible that anything could have successe which was against their good liking; so thereupon foure or five Portugalls of good estimation were sent unto the Court.

Hasegawa also promised, probably with his tongue in his cheek, that he would write to his loving sister, O-Natsu, to do what she could to help the Portuguese.

This forlorn hope failed as might have been foreseen. Ieyasu "receaved the Embassaye of the *Portugalls,* and promised them all favour in such things as concerned their trade and traffique, yet as for other matters concerning the stay of some of the Fathers in *Nangasaqui*, there was no remedy; saying that by only granting or permitting them one Church there on other occasions heretofore, they had by that meanes entred againe into all the Countries of *Japone*, and that therefore now he would see if he could put them out for good and all." This news arrived at Nagasaki at the beginning of October, with the intimation that all priests and catechists, whether native or foreign, must be embarked for Macao or Manila at the end of the month.[9]

The Jesuits' cup of bitterness was not yet full. On the eve of the embarkation of the missionaries for China and Luzon, the latent rivalry between the Society and the mendicant orders burst into open flame. After the death of Bishop Cerqueira in February, Provincial Valentim Carvalho had been designated as vicar and administrator of the bishopric by a majority vote. The friars apparently acquiesced in this decision at first, but they later reversed their stand at the instigation of the Franciscan commissary, Fray Diego de Chinchon, who characterized Carvalho as an unlawful intruder. The friars' chief argument was that a Jesuit, by the rules of his own Society, could not hold any such post without the special written permission of his general and of the Pope. Even the local Japanese parish priests, who were Jesuit-trained dojuku to a man, deserted their spiritual fathers in this crisis and sided with the friars. Both parties circulated public manifestos denouncing each other, right up to the day that they were forcibly interned in a few fishermen's huts before being placed on board ship. This unedifying schism—for as such it was openly designated—naturally caused much scandal to the faithful at a time when unity was essential. Nor were its evil effects confined to Nagasaki, for the quarrel was transferred to Manila, Macao, and Goa after the deportation of the missionaries from Japan. It was only finally resolved by the fact that the archbishops of Goa and Manila (both of them friars) sided with the Jesuits and severely admonished their unruly subordinates and the recalcitrant native clergy.

The missionaries removed the pictures and other religious objects from their churches and convents before the Japanese officials took formal possession of all their establishments on October 27, 1614. They had also exhumed the bodies of their dead colleagues and those of the Japanese martyrs interred there, and reburied them secretly by night, in order to avoid the profanation of their tombs. The exiles were concentrated at Fukuda and another outlying village for some days before their embarkation, during which time they were rigorously guarded from all contact with their sorrowful flock outside. Most of the churches were pulled down forthwith, but the Misericordia and one or two other buildings were temporarily spared. There were two small ships in the harbor besides the Great Ship from Macao, and this convoy of three sail left Nagasaki on November 7–8, the *Nossa Senhora da Vida* and a junk bound for China, and the remaining vessel for Manila. "All the Fathers did desire to remayne hid and disguised in *Japone* to help the Christians and be partakers of their sufferings, but it could not be, by reason of the strict order that was taken against their stay, and the extreme difficulty in fynding meanes to keep them secret."

Nevertheless, a goodly number managed by one means or another to stay disguised in Japan, in order to show the Christians that they were not deserted, and that their pastors were willing to testify to their Faith with their blood. Of those who remained there were 27 Jesuits, 7 Franciscans, 7 Dominicans, 1 Augustinian, and 5 secular clerics, or (as Murdoch observes) another edition of the famous Forty-Seven Ronin, succeeded in going into hiding. More than a hundred dojuku (the exact number is nowhere stated to my knowledge) also remained behind, concealment for them being relatively easy.

The ship which went to Manila with Takayama, Naito, and their followers also carried 7 friars, 23 Jesuits, and 15 dojuku. The voyage proved a long and difficult one, and Takayama's health was so undermined by the exposure, that

he fell sick and died shortly after his arrival at Manila,
where the refugees were received with every mark of sympathy by the Spaniards. The Great Ship and the junk, on the
contrary, had a speedy passage to Macao, where they landed
more than 60 Jesuits and more than 50 dojuku.

Although Ieyasu's expulsion edict had not been evaded on
anything like the same scale as Hideyoshi's Hakata ultimatum had been twenty-seven years earlier, it must have
been perfectly obvious to many Japanese officials that a considerable proportion of missionaries had "gone underground."
There are a hundred and one instances of this fact, not
only in the letters of the Jesuits themselves, but in the correspondence of Richard Cocks and his colleagues. Those of
the European missionaries who had stayed, disguised themselves as Iberian traders domiciled at Nagasaki, whence they
could travel throughout the country. It was not long before
the Bakufu became aware of this fact, and this was the
reason why the English and Dutch were compelled to confine their mercantile operations to Hirado and Nagasaki,
where they could be kept under surveillance. This check
on their freedom of movement annoyed the heretics extremely, and they vainly tried to induce Hidetada to cancel
his decision. With a strange lack of "hindsight," Adams
wrote to Specx in October, 1616: "All this trouble is arising
from the Portuguese priests, as the Emperor does not suffer
foreigners to trade in the upper country for fear of the
people being made Christians. All our trouble is wholly to
be imputed to the Papists." He might have saved his breath
to cool his own porridge; he would have found it scalding
hot.[10]

II

The trial which the Japanese Christians and, in due course,
their spiritual pastors of all races, had to endure was much
more severe than any of the periodic persecutions which had
troubled the Church hitherto. Hideyoshi's so-called general

persecution of 1587–1597, was a relatively mild affair, and the wind had been tempered to the shorn lambs by the protection afforded them by Arima, Omura, and other Christian daimyo. By 1614, the Christian daimyo were no more, and there was no one left in high places to intercede with the Tokugawa on behalf of the proscribed faith. There had been local persecutions in Higo and elsewhere since the accession of Ieyasu to power, but the victims of these sporadic outbreaks could (if they were of the lower classes) seek refuge in other fiefs at a pinch, whereas the present crisis was nationwide. Even before the promulgation of the edict of 1614, the shape of things to come had been shown by the progress of events in Arima, to which I must turn attention once more.

Arima Naozumi, old Harunobu's unfilial and apostate son, had indulged in some occasional and apparently half-hearted anti-Christian measures before he was stirred up to a further display of persecuting zeal by a letter from Hasegawa Sahioye. In this missive, the Nagasaki governor warned him "that it was reported in the court that he was a Christian, and that therefore he did not only not endeavor that his subjects should be otherwise, but rather procured that the Faith of Christ should daily flourish more and more in his dominions." Hasegawa unctuously added that he would be obliged to tell the Bakufu that there was some substance in this report, unless Arima gave some striking proof to the contrary without loss of time.

On receipt of this blackmailing letter, Arima summoned eight of his principal samurai who were Christians, and, showing them Hasegawa's missive, asked them to abjure their faith, even though purely temporarily and merely to save him. When they declined to do this, he called them in separately next day and pleaded with each individually, as a contemporary chronicler describes:

My estate and honour wholy standeth at this present in your handes, for as you cannot choose but know I have many enemies who by this meanes do seeke my utter overthrowe. For the love therefore that you bare me, I beseech you make but only some kind of show before the Bonze for one day, nay but for one hour's space that you be no Christians, and afterwards do even as you please. To the rest of the Christians you shall do a great good turne in doing so, for I with this will rest satisfied and trouble no one man more, and if you do it not I shall be compelled to proceed with rigour against them all. And although perhaps it be a sinne, you are not ignorant that *Saint Peter* being an Apostle, yea the chiefe of them all, denied Christ, and yet afterwards obteyned pardon for it: much more may you who do not deny him in your hearts nor yet for fear, but only make a show to deny him, and that for a very little tyme, to conserve thereby a whole Province and the Christians thereof in peace and quietness.

Given this eloquent piece of special pleading and in view of the strong appeal of feudal loyalty, it is not surprising that five of the eight wavered, and followed St. Peter's example which Arima had so artfully adduced. The other three remained staunch, and after further appeals had failed to shake them, the daimyo reluctantly decided to let feudal justice take its course. All three were sentenced (by Hasegawa apparently) to be burned at the stake, together with their families. The sentence was duly carried out on October 7, 1613, in the presence of a vast concourse of Christian believers praying and singing hymns. Not the least remarkable feature of this incident was the fact that although four of the five pseudo-apostates forthwith recanted their apostasy both in word, deed, and writing, yet Arima flatly refused to recognize their retraction and remained deaf to their appeals to let them join the martyrs.

On the occasion of this martyrdom, the organized demonstration by thousands of the faithful, grouped in serried rows according to their respective religious confraternities, naturally served to increase the suspicion of the Bakufu that Christianity was a subversive religion. The demonstration provoked Ieyasu's wrath, but, despite the expulsion edict of January, 1614, a temporary reprieve was granted to the afflicted Christians by the outbreak of the Osaka campaign. This culminated in the fall of the fortress and the ruin of the house of Toyotomi, with the defeat and death of Hideyoshi's son and heir, Hideyori (June, 1615). The garrison of Osaka castle contained many Christian samurai and ronin; and Padre João Rodriguez Girão, writing from Nagasaki in March, 1616, admitted that "there were so many crosses, *Jesus* and *Santiagos* on the flags, tents, and other martial insignia which the Japanese use in their encampments, that this must needs have made Ieyasu sick to his stomach." By way of adding insult to injury, there were no fewer than seven religious (2 Jesuits, 3 friars and 2 native clergy) in the castle at the time of its fall. Nevertheless, although a veritable blood bath marked the capture of the fortress, in which innocent women and children perished by thousands, not one of the proscribed foreign missionaries was killed—nor was a single foreigner killed for his religion during the lifetime of Ieyasu. This fact alone should suffice to discount much of the criticism leveled against him by some Church historians; nor was Padre Rodriguez Girão alone in his opinion that in the long run the triumph of Hideyori would have been even more ruinous to Christianity than that of Ieyasu.[11]

The "terrible old man" barely survived his victory a twelvemonth, dying at Shidzuoka in June, 1616. His successor, Hidetada, proved to be a more determined persecutor than his father, nor did he have the ardent desire for foreign trade which had induced the latter to hold his hand for so long. Nevertheless even Hidetada "dissembled" (as the Jesuits phrased it) with the Christian population of Nagasaki, since an open recantation of their faith was not at first exacted. The incidence of the persecution varied widely in different provinces, since some daimyo enforced the letter of the anti-Christian laws against their vassals, whereas others connived at the presence of native Christians and of missionaries in their fiefs.

Sansom has observed that the Japanese, like the English, have a convenient if illogical habit of winking at disobedience of laws, so long as it is not too flagrant. The years 1613–1618, afford an instance of this, for, as a Jesuit chronicler expressed it, "there was a kind of silence or conveniency

touching matters of Religion; not that it was lawful to
preach or make publique profession thereof under peril of
death or banishment; but that the Magistrates did either
dissemble or neglect to looke after those who embraced Christianity." So far as the Bakufu was concerned, this "blind
eye" was applied only to the native Christians of Nagasaki,
and not to the European missionaries whom they were resolved to expel by all means. Revelation of the presence of
so many of them at Osaka in 1615, and the suspicion (correct
enough) that others might be traveling disguised as foreign
traders throughout the country, led Hidetada to tighten the
control of European merchants by confining them to the two
ports of Nagasaki and Hirado, whence they were only allowed to proceed to court once a year in closely supervised
groups for the purpose of bringing their annual presents to
the shogun. It has been seen that the machinations of the
English and Dutch against the Catholic missionaries recoiled
on their own heads in this respect.

The deceptive calm which reigned at Nagasaki even after
the death of Ieyasu, encouraged some of the fugitive friars
to come out more into the open; much to the annoyance of
the Jesuits who realized that this was no time to do anything
which might cause the smoldering embers of persecution
to burst into flame. The Jesuit Visitor, Francisco Vieira,
writing from Macao in November, 1617, complains that
this incautious behavior forced the hands of the bugyo of
Nagasaki. They felt themselves obliged to report the matter
to the Bakufu before it could come to the shogun's ears
through the numerous government spies who were stationed
in Kyushu. Hidetada had already promulgated an anti-
Christian decree on October 1, 1616, reiterating and strengthening Ieyasu's measures. There was now a fresh spurt of
persecution in which for the first time some of the foreign
missionaries forfeited their lives. A Jesuit and a Franciscan
were beheaded at Omura (April, 1617), and a Dominican
and an Augustinian friar were executed in the same fief a
few weeks later. All the four religious orders were thus evenly

represented. The two latter had deliberately courted martyrdom with a view to strengthening the spirit of their flock,
since they felt that it was distinctly invidious that hitherto
only native converts and none of their foreign pastors had
suffered for the Faith. Judging by subsequent developments
in Omura's fief, this spectacular self-sacrifice was not without its intended effect. In none of these instances was torture
used, but all the foreigners were merely decapitated.

It may be doubted whether the friars' alleged rashness
was the main reason for the subsequent increase in the tempo
of the persecution. More harm to the common cause was
probably done by the bitter dispute between Murayama
Toan and Suetsugu Heizo which came to a head in 1618.
Jorge Durões, Cocks' confidential Goanese agent at Nagasaki, wrote him in June of that year "how Feze Dono had accused Twan Dono for murthering 17 or 18 Japons without
law or justice, and amongst the rest a family, because the
parents would not consent to let hym have their daughter,
and the maid herselfe passed the same way. But the council
tould Feze Dono they would have him to take in hand matters
of leeveing and not dead people. Soe then he apeached Twan
and his children as Christians and maintayners of Jesuits and
fryres whoe were enemies to the state and hath cauced 18 or
20 to be taken. So that it is thought greate persecution will
ensue at Langasaque."

Cocks' succinct account can be amplified by reference
to contemporary Portuguese and Spanish sources, from
which it is learned that it was Toan who first accused Heizo
of concealing Jesuits. He made use of Fabian and other ex-
dojuku, "who, like thieves of the household, knew very well
how many padres there were, and in whose houses they lay
concealed." Heizo promptly retaliated by accusing Toan of
concealing his clerical sons and some Spanish friars, at the
same time formally declaring his own apostasy from Christianity. This gave him an advantage in the campaign of
mutual calumny, since Toan did not deny his faith, although
the Jesuits stigmatized him as "the principal Judas of Japan."

The Bakufu gave its decision in favor of Heizo, who was awarded the lieutenant governorship of Nagasaki, whereas Toan was condemned to death together with most of his family. His name survives in the Jesuit histories as that of an apostate, whereas the Dominican chroniclers claim him as one of their martyrs. A cynic might observe that there are grounds for both classifications; but whatever were Toan's real motives, Richard Cocks was correct in forecasting that this affair would result in the intensification of the persecution at Nagasaki.[12]

Although the churches and ecclesiastical buildings at Nagasaki had been dismantled on the departure of the missionaries in 1614, they had not been entirely destroyed, and some (like the building of the Misericordia) had been closed but not otherwise interfered with. As a result of the "witch hunt" occasioned by the Suetsugu-Murayama revelations of local crypto-Christianity, all these edifices were completely destroyed, and either streets or Buddhist temples were built on their sites. Moreover, the Christian cemeteries were desecrated and the bodies of those buried therein were exhumed. Partly as a result of this imbroglio, partly through the revelation of many of the missionaries' hiding places by the renegade Japanese Jesuit priest, Thomas Araki, (previously dismissed and excommunicated for unchastity), arrests and martyrdoms took a sharp upward turn in 1619. But the latter, as distinct from the former category, dropped even more steeply in the next two years, only to surpass previous records with the "Great Martyrdom" at Nagasaki in September, 1622. The recorded number of those who were killed, tortured to death, or died of privations suffered in prison during 1614–1622, is as follows: In 1614, 63 persons; in 1615, 13; in 1616, 13; in 1617, 20; in 1618, 68; in 1619, 88; in 1620, 17; in 1621, 20; and in 1622, 132. Of course, these figures represent the absolute minimum, and it is virtually certain that others suffered for their faith, whose names or martyrdom did not find their way into the contemporary missionary reports on which the foregoing figures are based.

Nevertheless, these reports were compiled with great care and accuracy, despite the difficulties under which their writers labored, so that it is unlikely that the real number of martyrs substantially exceeded the figures given.

Father João Rodriguez Girão writing in 1615, says that a census taken at Nagasaki in that year showed that the local population had decreased by 20,000 in comparison with the figures for two years previously. Since the total number of martyrs for those years, including the victims at Arima, was less than two hundred, and there is no record nor indication of any mass apostasies, it is obvious that the greater number of these 20,000 Christians had sought shelter elsewhere. This bears out what is known from other contemporary sources that as a result of the search for Christians in southwest Japan, many refugees sought shelter in the northeastern provinces, hitherto almost virgin soil for the foreign religion. The exclusion edict of 1614 was thus responsible not only for driving Christianity "underground," but for its spread as far northward as the island of Yezo (the modern Hokkaido).

Even before the promulgation of Ieyasu's edict, the Bakufu had unwittingly helped to foster the propagation of Christianity in the northeast by exiling thither a number of ardent Christians from central Japan. When the Jesuit, Father de Angelis, first visited the Semboku district of Dewa Province in 1615, he found a flourishing Christian community of about 200 souls, who had never seen a priest, but who had been converted and maintained in the Faith by the exemplary piety of one Pedro Hitomi Munetsugu, "an old and noble Christian from Fushimi" who had gone thither to serve the local daimyo, apparently as a riding master, some six or seven years previously. Father de Angelis made a brief trip to Matsumae in Yezo during July, 1618, and has left the first European eyewitness account of the hairy Ainu and their ways. Like later travelers, he noticed the craving for strong drink which has been the curse of this race, although he added that he had never seen any of them actually drunk, "which is something that surprised me greatly." He was also partly responsible for misleading later cartographers by stating that Yezo was not an island, "as it is depicted in our old maps," but connected with Tartary on the west, and only divided from the American continent on the east by the narrow "strait of Anian." He made no converts among the ignorant Ainu, but he heard confessions from the fifteen Japanese who comprised the local Christian community.

At this period, crypto-Christian communities of varying strength were scattered throughout Japan from the Goto Islands in the extreme south to Matsumae in the far north. The European missionaries were likewise represented throughout this range of territory, but the majority were still stationed in Kyushu, despite the fact that concealment in the remote northeast was in some respects easier. It says much for the loyalty of their flocks that some priests remained in hiding for more than twenty years; and this despite the very considerable monetary rewards which were publicly offered for their detection and arrest. These rewards were periodically renewed or adjusted and during the century from 1616 to 1716, they varied as follows:

CATEGORY	MAXIMUM REWARD	MINIMUM REWARD
Bateren	500 pieces of silver	200 pieces of silver
Iruman	300 pieces of silver	100 pieces of silver
Dojuku	100 pieces of silver	50 pieces of silver

The Jesuits were hopeful that things would prove a little easier for them on the retirement of Shogun Hidetada, and the accession of Iemitsu to power in January, 1623. In this they were grievously disappointed, for the new shogun chastised Christianity with scorpions where his father (worse in his turn than Ieyasu) had used whips. Iemitsu was a moody, cruel, and capricious, if withal an intelligent, tyrant. He soon revealed a morbid preoccupation with Christianity, closely associated in his mind with the potential menace to the Tokugawa family personified by the unemployed ronin. Neither the infamous brutality of the methods which he used to exterminate the Christians, nor the heroic constancy of the sufferers have ever been surpassed in the long and painful history of the martyrdom of man; but before relating something of these horrors, it may be as well to review the psychological aspect of persecutors and persecuted.[13]

The reaction of intelligent but hostile Japanese to Christianity can be seen from two extant anti-Christian works. These are the *Ha Deus* (*Against God*) of the renegade Jesuit dojuku, Fabian Fukansai, published in 1620; and the memoranda of the Kirishitan bugyo, Inouye Chikugo-no-kami, embodied in the *Kirishito-ki,* a confidential report drawn up for the guidance of his successor in 1658. Professor Anesaki has described the former work as based on Buddhist doctrine with a tinge of Confucian ethics. Inouye's work, being that of a government official with no particular religious leanings, contains less Buddhist philosophy and more Confucian and feudal ideas, but many of the arguments employed in both works are virtually the same. Since they give some notion of the ideas which inspired the persecutors, it is worth while briefly to recapitulate them.

Both reports take the stand that to postulate a personal creator is absurd. They both point out that the Christian doctrine of an omnipotent and merciful God is inconsistent with the teaching of the temptation of Adam and Eve, the Fall of Man, and the eternal punishment in Hell of people who may have led blameless lives but deny God. In this connection, Inouye observes that righteous but agnostic monarchs such as the Chinese model emperors, Yao and Shun, cannot go to Heaven according to Christian doctrine, even though they lived as purely as the Pope; whereas a traitorous parricide can hope for salvation provided that he believes in God. Both sources give a list of the Ten Commandments; but Fabian, although approving of all these tenets save the first, points out that these high moral principles are not peculiar to Christianity, but are universally accepted among civilized mankind. His refutation is concentrated on the First Commandment, which is stigmatized as justifying disobedience to parents and feudal overlords, besides authorizing regicide and parricide, under certain circumstances.

It is interesting to note that whereas Fabian complains of the pride and arrogance of the European missionaries and their alleged contempt for their junior Japanese colleagues, Inouye makes no allusion to this, but stresses the danger of the missionaries acting as a Christian "fifth column." Inouye also twits the Christian God with his powerlessness to stop the persecution, torture, and eventual extinction of his followers in Japan, as exemplified by the numerous martyrdoms, the bloody suppression of the Shimabara rebellion (1638), and the execution of the Macao envoys two years later. The creation of barbarous and ignorant races such as African Hottentots and cannibals (stories of whom he had heard from the Hollanders) is cited as unworthy of an allegedly all-wise and all-powerful God. Claims of miracles on the occasions of martyrdoms are also emphatically refuted.

It is obvious that the chief objection of the Bakufu to the propagation of Christianity was that the foreign religion was regarded as subversive of feudal law and order in general; and hence (in alliance with the ronin), of the hegemony of the house of Tokugawa in particular. This was likewise the feeling of the majority of the daimyo, in all probability; for the existence of the feudal structure was dependent on the loyalty of a vassal to his lord transcending any heavenly claims. In this connection, the following anecdotes will bear repetition. One of Hosokawa Tadaoki's leading retainers, Kagayama Hayato, was a fervent Christian, and nothing would induce him to recant. His master long hesitated to put him to death, and eventually only did so on specific orders from Yedo in 1619. One day, when Tadaoki was vainly trying to persuade Diogo (his baptismal name) to renounce his faith, the latter said to him, "surely you would not wish me to go to Hell?" Tadaoki, although he had a good idea of the tenets of Christianity, since his wife had been a devout Christian and Takayama Ukon one of his closest friends, replied as much in earnest as in jest,

"Why not? If I am to go there, would not you be prepared to accompany me? Do it like a loyal vassal, and for love of me!"

The attitude of Hosokawa Tadaoki is all the more significant because of the fact that five years earlier he had taken a very different view of the conflicting claims of God and Caesar. To quote a contemporary Jesuit chronicler, "When in the yeare 1614 he understood how *Don Iusto* [Takayama] his great friend had left and lost his estate for his faith and religion, he commended him very much for it, and said: 'If Don Iusto had not done in this occasion as he hath done, he should have blemished all the noble actions of his life. For a magnanimous man both in prosperity and adversity ought still to be the same without any change or mutation at all.'" This observation recalls the sentiments expressed in the *Meditations* of Marcus Aurelius; but the Japanese daimyo, no less than the Roman emperor, evidently found that it was easier to enunciate these high-flown principles than to live up to them. It is true that Tadaoki was never a Christian; but all the evidence goes to show that the vast majority of the Christian samurai, when the day of reckoning came, took the attitude which he advocated in 1619, rather than that which he had extolled in Takayama Ukon five years earlier. In the clash between feudal loyalty and Christian ethics, it was usually the latter which succumbed in the bushi's breast.

Perhaps the friars made a wiser choice than the Jesuits, in concentrating their efforts on converting the poor and lowly, rather than on the military caste with whom the padres were primarily preoccupied in Valignano's days. A much higher proportion of *heimin* (peasants, artisans, and merchants) than of samurai remained faithful unto death during the persecution. The Bakufu was particularly annoyed by the courageous obstinacy displayed by these humble folk. It evidently surprised the government as much as the fighting qualities revealed by the raw peasant conscripts in 1877, surprised the Satsuma samurai during Saigo Takamori's rebellion. The neurotic and overweening Iemitsu was infuriated by this defiance of the canons of feudal loyalty, especially as the dreaded ronin came within this category. Consequently, the methods of suppressing Christianity grew increasingly savage with each fresh discovery of crypto-Christians, and with each martyr who endured to the bitter end. It is interesting to note that Inouye observed that Korean converts were particularly staunch, especially the women. This must have annoyed the inquisitors intensely, since the Koreans were a despised race. Conversely, Korean courage in defying Japanese tormentors doubtless owed something to the inherent hatred between the two races— lasting to the present day—which dates from the time of the Wako raids and Hideyoshi's invasion.

As for the feelings and attitude of the persecuted Christians toward their oppressors, there are interesting glimpses in such works as the *Exhortations to Martyrdom,* compiled by the missionaries to encourage their flock from 1615 onwards, as well as from Inquisitor Inouye's *Kirishito-ki* of 1658, and from the clandestine correspondence of the missionaries in 1614–1634. Professor Anesaki aptly characterizes them as documents written in tears and blood.

The *Exhortations to Martyrdom* begin by explaining how and why God permits the Christians to be persecuted. The next section explains why the persecutors are not necessarily punished at once, or even in their lifetime, but may be allowed to flourish like the green bay tree. The third section explains what a grave sin it is to deny Christ, even under torture; and other parts deal with the honor and glory accruing to martyrs in this world and the next. The concluding section deals with the spiritual preparation for martyrdom and how to endure torture. Stress is naturally laid on the Christian doctrine of not fearing those who can kill the body, but only those who induce you to forfeit the salvation of your soul. Temporal tortures, however severe, are in the nature of things impermanent, whereas the sufferings of the damned in hell are eternal. The various excuses given for apostasy,—attachment to family or worldly ties; loyalty to the feudal lord; unendurable pain of torture—are discussed and refuted in turn.

The reader is reminded that "frail women and children, princesses and noble ladies rarely exposed to the wind" have endured martyrdom, not only with fortitude but delight, which suffices to prove that God must lend supernatural aid to the martyrs. Potential victims are warned that they must never cherish an evil thought toward their judge, torturer, or executioner, since it is through their actions that they will gain a martyr's crown. This instruction was evidently widely obeyed, as Inouye noted in his memoranda that Christians had been taught that they would forfeit their entrance into paradise if they died with feelings of hate toward their persecutors. Consequently they very rarely displayed any resentment, however much they suffered. He also noted that the padres claimed that God often obscured the understanding of intelligent bugyo, rendering them slow and stupid when they were cross-examining Christians. Contrariwise, He gave strength and eloquence to the latter during their ordeal. Although Inouye scouted this idea, he nevertheless advised his colleagues not to get involved in logic chopping or abstruse theological arguments with the accused.

Fidelity to death, whether by execution, torture, starvation, malnutrition in jail, or exposure to the elements, was regarded as the essential consideration for martyrdom. Forcible or armed resistance was held to disqualify any claim thereto; thus those who fell fighting in the Shimabara rebellion (1637–1638) were not regarded as martyrs. On the other hand, a child which was killed with its mother automatically became a martyr, even in the womb. The most common reasons for martyrdom were listed as:

1) Refusal to act as informer or stool pigeon against Christians.
2) Refusal to "bow the knee to Baal" in the form of the *kami* and *hotoke*.
3) Indulging in Christian propaganda.
4) Helping those who were being tortured for their faith.

5) Disposing of a martyr's corpse or venerating a martyr's relics.
6) Sheltering missionaries or their servants.
7) Refusal to reveal the whereabouts of missionaries in hiding.

One of the curious features of the first decade of the persecution inaugurated in 1614, was that the authorities often allowed mass demonstrations of the faithful when some of their co-religionists were being martyred at the stake. These demonstrations were presumably permitted under the impression that the victims' sufferings would induce the onlookers to recant their religion. But it must have been obvious after a while, that these spectacular burnings served rather to demonstrate the truth of the adage that the blood of martyrs is the seed of the Church. Far from being intimidated, the majority of the bystanders were edified by the constancy of the sufferers and became desirous of emulating them. Morever, the victims themselves doubtless derived some comfort from the fact that so many of their fellow-believers were watching and praying for them.

Reference has already been made to the spectacular demonstration of the religious confraternities at the burning of the Arima martyrs in October, 1613. On that occasion, "after they were all bound to their pillars, the Christians lifted up aloft, for the Martyrs and all the rest to looke and meditate upon, a very devout picture of our Blessed Saviour as he was bound to a pillar. Then the souldiers putting fire unto the wood and straw, the Holy Martyrs in the middest thereof with all devotion called upon the help and favour of our Blessed Saviour often tymes, to that end naming the most holy name of Jesus, and all the Christians upon their knees did sing the *Creed*, the *Pater Noster, Ave Maria*, and other praiers untill the Martyrs had given their Holy soules into the handes of God."

Similar scenes occurred at other martyrdoms during the ensuing decade, the most remarkable being that at the burning of Flores and Zuñiga with their Japanese companions in August, 1622. This ordeal was witnessed by 150,000 people, according to some writers, or 30,000 according to other and in all probability more reliable chroniclers. When the faggots were kindled, the martyrs said *sayonara* ("farewell") to the onlookers who then began to intone the *Magnificat,* followed by the psalms *Laudate pueri Dominum* and *Laudate Dominum omnes gentes,* while the Japanese judges sat on one side "in affected majesty and gravity, as is their favorite posture." Since it had rained heavily the night before, the faggots were wet and the wood burned slowly; but as long as the martyrdom lasted, the spectators continued to sing hymns and canticles. When death put an end to the victims' sufferings, the crowd intoned the *Te Deum Laudamus.*

The great martyrdom at Nagasaki was also witnessed by a large and sympathetic crowd, but the procedure was subsequently tightened. At the martyrdom of the Jesuit Navarro and his companions in November of that year, the onlookers were not permitted to invoke the name of Jesus, nor to give the slightest sign of encouragement on pain of being cut down out of hand by the guards. Yet at the martydom of de Angelis and his forty-nine companions at Yedo in December, 1623, no attempt was made to prevent the Jesuit's preaching to the crowd, and to such effect that two of the bystanders rushed forward and vainly begged the presiding judges to let them join the martyrs.

This was about the last occasion on which such demonstrations of sympathy were permitted; for the authorities had by now come to realize that the deterrent effect of these public tortures was as a rule more than offset by the admiration aroused for the heroism of the sufferers. It is perhaps worth while reminding the reader that in contemporary Europe no such evidence of sympathy for the victims would have been permitted among the onlookers at the hanging of Roman Catholic priests in London, nor at the *autos da fé* for the Jews in Lisbon. But from about 1626 onward, the captured missionaries, whether Japanese or European, were sent to the execution ground with "the hair of their heads and beards half shaven off, the shaven part being colored

red; bits were put in their mouths to hinder them from speaking; and their heads being pulled backwards with halters put about their necks and tied behind them, they were compelled to hold their faces directly upwards; and thus sitting upon a lean horse they were carried to the place designed for their martyrdom." [14]

Although the ferocity of the persecutors gradually hardened in response to the challenge presented by the calm courage of the persecuted, there were plenty of exceptions to the general rule. Both Japanese and European sources agree that the incidence of persecution varied widely in the different fiefs, some daimyo continuing to turn a blind eye on the crypto-Christians in their domains, down to the time of the accession of Iemitsu to power (1623) at least. Thus the Matsumae daimyo of Yezo soon penetrated Father de Angelis' rather transparent disguise in 1619, but told him he had nothing to fear, although the shogun had proscribed Christianity in Japan, "for Matsumae is not Japan." Even traditionally anti-Christian daimyo, such as Matsura of Hirado, sometimes behaved more charitably to the hated Catholics than those who were bound closer to them by the ties of race and religion. Richard Cocks wrote in his *Diary* on October 9, 1621:

Yistarnight I was enformed that Francisco Lopez and a semenary priest were com to towne, and lodged in the howse of the Capt. of the friggot taken the last yeare; of which I advised Torezemon Dono to tell the King thereof by Coa Jno., our *jurebasso* [interpreter], it being late, and to geve order noe strangers should pass out. And this morning I sent the same *jurebasso* to Torezemon Dono secretary, to know the kinges answere; which was, I might speake of these matters when Gonrok Dono came. Unto which I sent answer, it might be that then these pristes would be gon, and then it was to late to speake. Yet, for all this, there was noe eare nor respect geven to my speeches.

A few months later Cocks referred as irritably as erroneously to "the King of Firando, whose mother is a papisticall Jesuit [*sic*] and he and the rest of his brethren and sisters papisticall Christians."

The "Gonrok Dono" mentioned by Cocks in the foregoing quotation, was Hasegawa Gonroku, a nephew of Sahioye, who had succeeded his uncle as bugyo of Nagasaki in 1615. During the ten years in which he occupied this post, he frequently gave evidence of his desire to avoid bloodshed, and of the reluctance with which he acted as the shogunal watchdog. The Hollander, Reyer Gysbertszoon, who knew him well, states that "he was always ill or feigned to be," adding that he could not sleep at night for thinking about his distasteful duties. Moreover, an Augustinian chronicler writes that when informers came to his *yashiki* with news of the whereabouts of some missionary, he usually contrived to avoid sending a search party until after he had sent a trusty servant to the place indicated, with a message telling the fugitive to move elsewhere forthwith.

On the occasion of the martyrdom of the Portuguese, Domingos Jorge (the first European layman to die for the Faith in Japan, incidentally), the Japanese Jesuit, Leonardo Kimura, Murayama Tokuan, one of the famous Toan's sons, and two other Japanese in November, 1619, Hasegawa Gonroku gave what was almost a farewell party for them. The martyrs stopped at his house on their way to the execution ground, when Gonroku "took leave of them, and particularly of the Brother whom he knew very well, giving to and receiving from each one in turn, the *sakazuki,* or parting wine cup, in accordance with Japanese custom and not without tears on the part of some of the bystanders." The weakest member of the party was given a litter, and Hasegawa offered another to Domingos Jorge; but the brave Portuguese replied that "he would go afoot and unshod, in order to imitate Our Lord Jesus Christ, who afoot and unshod went to Calvary hill in order to die for us." The captain was as good as his word, and walked with a red bonnet on his head "so gladly that it seemed he was going to a country picnic rather than to be burned alive."

Hasegawa's most remarkable effort, however, was connected with the *cause célèbre* of Zuñiga and Flores, who were captured at sea by the English in 1621, disguised as Spanish merchants, but carrying letters from the ecclesiastical authorities at Manila which conclusively proved that they were missionaries bound for Japan. Despite the fact that Hasegawa knew Zuñiga perfectly well from his previous residence at Nagasaki (he had personally warned the friar to leave for Manila a couple of years earlier), he blandly refused to identify the Augustinian when he saw him. He turned a deaf ear to all the protestations of the Dutch and English, and flatly declined to admit the genuineness of the incriminating letters and dispatches. It was only when Flores and Zuñiga finally and voluntarily confessed that they were missionaries that he allowed Japanese justice to take its course. How odious his inquisitorial duties were to him, is evident from the fact that he repeatedly requested the Bakufu to relieve him of his post on the grounds of ill-health. He was indeed a very sick man when finally replaced in 1626.

His successor, Mizuno Kawachi, was a man of very different caliber, and resembled his master, the neurotic megalomaniac Iemitsu. Utterly intolerant of opposition, he came resolved to stamp out Christianity in Kyushu by all and every means, inaugurating a three-year reign of terror which ultimately largely succeeded in extirpating the foreign religion. Before describing the methods which he and his likeminded successor, Takenaka Uneme-no-sho, adopted to achieve their ends, it may be noted that the Nagasaki bugyo and daikwan were placed in a difficult position, between the enraged shogun on the one hand and the obstinate Christians on the other. But whereas Hasegawa Gonroku had tried to temper the wind to the shorn lamb, Kawachi and Takenaka brooked no compromise. They found an able abettor in the apostate Suetsugu Heizo, who had been daikwan since Murayama's disgrace in 1618. All three indulged heavily in bribery and corruption as well as cruelty, and Professor Anesaki remarks that this "mentality of self-indulgence, greed, and wantonness was mutually associated with hatred and cruelty toward the persecuted." It is some satisfaction to know that in one form or another they all three came to a bad end.[15]

Before relating in more detail some of the ordeals to which the Christians were subjected, it is well to remind the reader that virtually everything in this catalogue of horrors could have been paralleled in contemporary Europe. A possible exception to this, was the state of the Japanese jails; for noisesome and foul as European prisons were, they do not seem to have been quite such hells on earth as were the Japanese variety.

Valignano relates that prisons were unknown in Japan before Hideyoshi's time; but the way in which these institutions functioned in the first half of the seventeenth century has left its mark down to the present day, as inmates of Japanese jails in 1941–1945 can testify. There are several lurid descriptions of these prisons from the pens of missionaries who suffered therein. One of the most graphic is the account of Yedo jail by the Spanish Franciscan, Fray Diego de San Francisco, in 1615, but I have not confined myself to his narrative in compiling the outline of Japanese prison life which follows.

One of the peculiarities of Japanese jurisprudence was that accusers and accused were generally treated on the same footing during the preliminary investigation, both being placed on remand—samurai with their feudal lord, shogunal officials with the local magistrate, and commoners with the head of their five mutually responsible families or *gonin-gumi*. When the judicial investigation was finished and the evidence extracted (usually by torture) the accused, and sometimes the accusers, were transferred to prison. A man was emphatically regarded as guilty until he could prove his innocence.

Fray Diego de San Francisco describes his prison as a square wooden building with a central cage for the remand prisoners. The thick wooden bars of which it was constructed were so close together that daylight could hardly penetrate. There were no windows, but only a small wicket which was used for passing in food and water. The cage measured five *varas* by twelve and had a very low ceiling. It was divided into two sections by a big beam down the middle. All prisoners were stripped and searched before entering, and were not allowed to take anything in with them. They sat huddled on the floor in three rows, two of which faced each other; it was impossible for a prisoner to move his feet without inconveniencing the person opposite. There were usually between one hundred and one hundred fifty-three wretches in this confined space during the eighteen months that Fray Diego spent there. The overcrowding was such that most of the prisoners sat naked, although a few wore a *fundoshi* (breech clout); but the friar, as a special favor, was permitted to wear a very thin vest. As a foreigner, Fray Diego also received the most floor space of any individual, (three hands' breadths by four and a half). There was only one tub or bucket in which the prisoners had to perform their natural functions. The stench and filth is easier imagined than described, particularly since about thirty or forty of the prisoners were always prostrated by dysentery and had not the strength to reach the bucket but lay in their own filth. The official ration was a handful of rice daily, barely enough to sustain life for forty or fifty days, although some prisoners got nothing at all. On the other hand, the guards could sometimes be bribed to allow prisoners' friends to smuggle in a little rice, *soy*, or fish by way of supplementing the starvation diet. In some other jails (Yatsushiro in 1608, for instance) prisoners were officially allowed to receive periodic gifts of food from friends or relatives. The drinking ration was limited to a small saucer of water, at sunrise and sunset. Prisoners were not allowed to cut their hair or nails; and some missionaries had hair down to their shoulders, and beards extending to the waist, by the time that they were taken out for execution.

Deaths from dysentery, hunger, and thirst were of daily occurrence, but new arrivals supplanted the dead. The putrefying corpses were often left rotting for a week or more, before the official written authorization could be obtained for their removal. There was no wind or breeze which could penetrate the dank and dark central cage, so that the heat and stench were insupportable. The damp earth afforded additional facilities for the breeding of lice and other vermin. All the inmates were speedily covered with the most loathsome sores, and fought savagely among themselves for grains of rice or drops of water. The place resounded with the cries and screams of those driven mad by thirst or disease, but the two dozen guards who were normally on duty do not seem to have interfered in the prisoners' quarrels. Those who lay helplessly sick were often killed during the night by their neighbors, who said that they did them a favor in thus putting them out of their misery. It speaks volumes for the courage and self-sacrifice of Fray Diego, that he not only converted about seventy people in the first three months, but that after his release and voyage to Mexico, he returned once more to Japan, where he carried on a daring "underground" evangelization for about twenty years or more. His end is not recorded, unless he was one of the two Franciscans martyred in 1639, whose identity has never been established.[16]

For the first twelve or fifteen years of the general persecution, burning alive was the general punishment for most of the foreign missionaries and many of their native converts who were caught. The Japanese form of burning at the stake was slightly different from the contemporary European variety, in that the victim was not bound tightly to a post with the faggots piled around his feet. The normal practice in Japan was for the victim to be loosely tied to the stake by one wrist only, and the faggots were placed in a ring at a radius of a few feet from the stake. The idea was that the pain of the slow fire would cause the sufferer to jump and hop around in a ludicrous manner, like the proverbial cat on hot bricks, to the amusement of the crowd. In this the persecutors were generally disappointed, for the large majority of martyrs bore their fiery ordeal unflinchingly. Richard Cocks describes how he saw fifty-five persons of all ages and both sexes burnt alive on the dry bed on the Kamo River in Kyoto (October, 1619), and among them little children of five or six years old in their mothers' arms, crying out "Jesus receive their souls."

Among the very rare exceptions to this general stoicism, may be mentioned the burning witnessed by the Hollander, Reyer Gysbertszoon, on the occasion of the Italian Jesuit Spinola and his companions being roasted alive at Nagasaki (September 10, 1622). "Two others who were something nearer in the wind, and whose cords were burned by the flames, sprang through the fire, sorely burned, and begged to be allowed to renounce their faith, in order to save their lives, but were driven back into the fire with sticks and pikes by the executioners, who told them that they wished to recant not from any real inner reason but merely because they could bear the heat of the flames no longer, wherefore they should have bethought themselves earlier, there being no mercy for them now." This, incidentally, contradicts Professor Murdoch's assertion that the Japanese officials were always ready to spare the life of anyone who recanted. Admittedly, they were usually satisfied with a formal denial of the Faith. Alluding to the apostasy of four Portuguese and Spanish laymen who thus avoided being burned at the stake as concealors of missionaries in June, 1626, Fray Diego de San Francisco wrote, "I believe that these will do more harm by their bad example, if they do not repent and make amends, than all the Japanese who have recanted hitherto. God convert them in His Mercy. Brother Francisco de Santa Maria wrote them that they should reconcile themselves to God and retract their recantation, offering to go with them before the governors. Two of them answered that it was no use crying over spilt milk." One of these four renegades was Richard Cocks' old friend and correspondent, Alvaro Muñoz.

Although Cocks was justified in noting, in 1620, that the vast majority of Christians in Kyushu would die rather than recant the Faith under torture, the fiendish pertinacity of the persecutors had brought about an entirely different state of affairs ten years later. Japanese, Iberian, and Dutch accounts all agree that this was due to the methods employed by the two bugyo, Kawachi and Takenaka. The Bakufu also introduced more drastic legislation against the Nagasaki Christians. Those who would not renounce the Faith were forbidden to engage in any shipping, commercial, or other business whereby they might earn their daily bread. Christian families were thus faced with the alternatives of being reduced to beggary or seeking their livelihood elsewhere. Not many took this latter course, as Fray Diego de San Francisco (back in Japan since 1618) complained, and apostasies, whether sincere or otherwise, became increasingly numerous. The system of lavish monetary rewards for informers also began to pay off after the departure of Hasegawa Gonroku, who, as already seen, ignored or sidetracked such gentry.[17]

One of the mildest forms of torture was the so-called water torture, the principal varieties of which are described by a contemporary Portuguese source. "In the first kind, they hang the martyr upside down with his legs apart, placing his head in a bucket of water whose level is above his nostrils. After the cord attached to his feet is drawn tight, they let the body revolve slowly in the air. This is a very painful torture, through the efforts the sufferer makes to breath. In the second kind, they tie the martyr down on a board, leaving his left hand free so that he can place it on his breast if he wishes to give a sign that he will recant. His head is left hanging down a little, and the torturers do not stop pouring great quantities of water on his face [usually covered with a thin piece of cloth]. The victims make such frantic efforts to breath that they usually burst a blood-vessel." This form of torture was a favorite one in the *kempeitai* (gendarmerie) jails in 1941–1945, but the record for enduring it is still that of the seventeenth-century Italian Jesuit, Mastrilli, who is said to have withstood it for two days, and received four hundred jars of water on the second day alone.

Kawachi introduced a new and crueler form of water torture by transporting several hundred particularly obstinate victims to the sulphur hot springs of Unzen. Here the poor wretches were tortured by having incisions made in the flesh, into which the boiling water was slowly poured. If this treatment failed to make the sufferer recant, he was then suspended or thrown into the hot springs. Since Kawachi's avowed object was to get apostates rather than martyrs, he had a doctor present, who intervened when the victim appeared to be on the verge of expiring. The martyr was then carefully treated for a few days until he had recovered sufficiently to be subjected to the same round again. Despite all Kawachi's precautions, a few individuals did die under this treatment; but by these and other methods (branding, burning with red-hot pincers, sawing off limbs with a bamboo saw, etc.), he forced three hundred and seventy out of a total of four hundred to recant; these people were sent back to Nagasaki as free men.

After their arrival in the port, a public proclamation was made that anyone who did not recant within a given time limit would be similarly treated. Fray Diego de San Francisco, writing from his hiding place in November, 1629, says that about a thousand Christians now fled from the city, but that virtually all of the remainder recanted, "without their having been either rewarded or punished other than with the ordinary punishments which they had long since suffered, of confinement to the city, and not being allowed to work or trade, nor to earn their daily bread, and being burdened with imposts." He estimated that only about two hundred out of some ten thousand families had declined to recant. He admitted that the formal recantation was made only by the heads of families and did not involve their wives, children, or servants; but he foresaw that once the head of the family had recanted, it was only a question of time before the other members fell away from the Faith.

These scenes were duplicated in Omura, Arima, and elsewhere, with the result that the once flourishing Christianity of Kyushu was to all appearance vitually extinct by the end of 1630. The general success of Kawachi and Uneme's methods was offset only by the extraordinary heroism displayed by a party of five foreign missionaries and two Macaonese women, who were tortured in the sulphur springs of Unzen during the whole month of December, 1631. None of them recanted, with the possible exception of the younger of the two women, who was a mere girl. Uneme finally had to acknowledge defeat, and the party was brought back to Nagasaki, mutilated but triumphant. The missionaries were burned alive in September of the following year, and the heroic Beatriz da Costa and her daughter were exiled to Macao.

The successful resistance of this party to the worst that the sulphur springs of Unzen could do was probably responsible for the abandonment of this particular form of torment and its substitution by the *ana-tsurushi,* or hanging in the pit. This diabolical invention is variously ascribed to Takenaka Uneme and to the (later) inquisitor, Inouye, and it largely replaced burning at the stake from 1632 on. Professor Anesaki states that this method consisted in burying the body in an upright position in a pit, so that only the head protruded. In this he is completely mistaken; and it is abundantly clear from the contemporary Portuguese and Dutch eyewitness accounts that the method involved bodily suspension in a pit or hole, as the Japanese name implies. The victim was tightly bound around the body as high as the breast (one hand being left free to give the signal of recantation) and then hung head downwards from a gallows into a pit which usually contained excreta and other filth, the top of the pit being level with his knees. In order to give the blood some vent, the forehead was lightly slashed with a knife. Some of the stronger martyrs lived more than a week in this position, but the majority did not survive more than a day or two.

This innovation achieved tremendous prestige among the inquisitors when its employment induced the apostasy of the aged Jesuit Provincial, Padre Christovão Ferreira, who gave the signal for recantation after enduring six hours of agony (October, 1633). Its efficacy in inducing apostasy was testified in many other instances. The Dutch factor at Hirado, François Caron, relates how "some of those who had hung for two or three days assured me that the pains they endured were wholly unsufferable, no fire nor no torture equaling their langour and violence." Yet one young woman endured it for fourteen days before dying a martyr.

As to the spirit with which the Christians faced these and other sickening forms of torture, too numerous for repetition here, I may conclude with a quotation from one of the manuscript manuals on martyrdom which were circulated among the faithful.

> When martyrdom is imminent, you have to prepare yourself with a confession. When a formal confession is impossible, you have to repent by recalling all your offenses. Then you should ask pardon in appealing to the grace of God, making up your mind never to commit any mortal sin; also pray for valor and grace so that you can endure the pangs of martyrdom.
>
> Never cherish an evil thought toward the officer passing the sentence of death, or the executioner, but pray to God that they may be led to the way of truth, since it is their deeds that take you on the road to Paradise.
>
> While being tortured visualize the Passion of Jesus. Think intently that Santa Maria, many Angels and Blessed ones are looking upon your fight from Heaven, and the Angels are awaiting the coming of your Soul with the crown in their hands. Hope and confidence should occupy your mind, since at that moment God shall tender a special help. And if possible utter anything which would benefit the soul of the bystanders. Say, for instance, "There is no way besides the religion of Christ which can save you in the future life. I am now going to sacrifice my life as a testimony to the truth of this religion. There is no joy greater than this, because this is the way to infinite bliss." Say something like this, with "flowers of words." But never think that you are compelled to say that. God will certainly guide you as to what to do and what to say, so trust everything to his guidance.[18]

In the early years of the general persecution, when the missionaries were hopeful that it would prove but a passing storm, partly on account of the deceptive calm which reigned at Nagasaki in 1615–1619, concealment of the Faith was regarded as a deadly sin. The instructions to Christians which were clandestinely circulated among the faithful in 1614–1616, state that no denial of the Faith was permitted, even if the heart was unchanged and outward apostasy only intended. It was likewise forbidden to disguise oneself by carrying a Buddhist rosary or amulet, nor was an equivocal reply to an inquisitor permitted. "You should never say 'no' when you are asked by anyone whether you are a Kirishitan." At times when Christians were being searched for and put to death, flight to safer localities was permitted, especially for anyone who felt that he might apostatize under torture. But generally speaking, these early instructions inculcate the taking of a bold and forthright line, irrespective of the consequences. In the first decade of the persecution, missionaries from Macao and Manila also entered Japan relatively freely through the port of Nagasaki, disguised as merchants on board Portuguese and Spanish ships. More than twenty entered this way in 1615–1616 alone.

The increasing severity of the persecution after the accession of Iemitsu soon changed all that. Inquisitor Inouye noted in his memorandum that whereas Christians had originally freely avowed their faith when first questioned about it, they had long since ceased to do so, and the avowal usually had to be extracted by torture. Whereas the observance of Buddhist and Shinto high days and holidays by converts had been originally condemned as a mortal sin, Richard Cocks notes in his *Diary* (April 14, 1621), "This day being a great pagon feast called *Sanguach sanch* (sangatsu sannichi), or the therd day of the therd moone, non would work upon it, the pagons upon their ordinary superstition, and the Christians for fear to be noted to be Christians. Soe noe work was done this day. Yet on the Sonday all will work, both Christians and pagons of Japan, and the papistes in Japon will more strictly observe and keepe any other blind hollyday of fayned saintes (made knowne unto them per Jesuites and friars) than the Sabath day. This is daylie seene per experience." After the mass apostasies forced by the Nagasaki bugyo in 1626–1630, Christianity went "underground" in earnest, and those who persevered in the Faith, did so in secret. The Japanese term for apostasy was *korobu*, "to tumble down," or "fall," whence the missionaries also used the Portuguese verb *cahir* which has the same meaning. Revocation of apostasy was termed *tachi-agaru,* "to rise up," or "rise again."

In the first decade of the persecution, outstanding services were rendered to refugees by the brotherhood of the Misericordia, or Holy House of Mercy, at Nagasaki. This was a charitable institution originally founded at Lisbon in the fifteenth century, which was supported entirely by voluntary contributions, and which maintained hospitals and orphanages throughout the chief cities of Portuguese Asia. A Jesuit at Nagasaki wrote in 1615, "In charitable works on behalf of the exiles and other poor persons, the Brotherhood of the Santa Misericordia is that which takes the lead; for despite these calamitous days, and this year of drought and poor trade, it has spent in the last few months the sum of nearly two thousand ducats in alms, never failing to carry out punctiliously the terms of its charter." The writer adds that refugees and beggars from all over Japan came to Nagasaki attracted by the fame of the Misericordia's generosity, nor were they disappointed when they asked its help.

Other very present helps in time of trouble were the religious confraternities, of which there were several. The Dominican organization of the Rosary became one of the most famous, although the Jesuits had formed some in their own flock long before the persecution of 1614. These existed for both sexes and even for children. The members met periodically for mutual religious help and discussion, held retreats and prayer meetings, organized demonstrations at martyrdoms (down to 1623), and kept the European missionaries advised of safe hiding places, and of those who were in need of their ministrations. To some extent their organization coincided with that of the local *gonin-gumi* or groups of five households which were organized together as a mutually responsible and homogeneous group. This organization, which was presumably of Chinese origin, is the ancestor of the modern *tonari-gumi,* or neighborhood

associations, also called *rinpohan*, which were officially revived in 1940, as a system for corporate responsibility and
control in town and country. The Bakufu also made use of
the gonin-gumi in the opposite sense; that is, they made each
one of every five households responsible for ensuring that
there were no Christians in the other four of its particular
group. This responsibility must have led to some awkward
situations at times. On the occasion of Padre Girolamo de
Angelis' martyrdom at Yedo in 1623, thirteen heathens were
involved along with the crypto-Christian members of the
gonin-gumi who had sheltered the missionaries.

When the European missionaries could no longer mas-
querade as foreign merchants, it was through this organization that they traveled in disguise throughout the length and
breadth of Japan, usually at night, being passed on from one
group to another. On occasion, the missionaries even disguised themselves as Japanese women, and it was in this way
that the Augustinian friar, Francisco de Jesus, escaped from
Nagasaki one night in 1626. It was through the gonin-gumi
that the Christian "underground" circulated its news, letters,
and dispatches, some of their reports even going to the Pope.
It was the local gonin-gumi which were entrusted with the
task of bribing the jailors to provide extra food for captive
missionaries. Letters were also frequently smuggled in and out
of prison, judging by the number which were written in
jail, often by martyrs on the eve of their execution, and which
survived to be printed in Europe, as may be seen by those
reproduced in the second volume of Léon Pagés' *Histoire,* or
still preserved in the archives at Rome. On two separate occasions, Zuñiga and Flores escaped from their imprisonment
at Hirado with the aid of the local gonin-gumi, only to be
recaptured each time by a stroke of bad luck. It was this
organization which was the means of preserving Christianity
in secret for more than two centuries in southwest Kyushu,
without the presence of any foreign missionaries, and cut
off from all communication with the outer world.

Because of the increasing severity of the persecution, the

missionaries and their converts were distributed throughout
the length and breadth of Japan in 1623. Whereas in the
halcyon days of the mission, the Christian communities and
their pastors had been virtually confined to Kyushu, the
Gokinai, and Yedo district, they were spread far and wide
at the date of Iemitsu's accession. Six years later, Fray Diego
de San Francisco claimed that the virtual extinction of Nagasaki's once flourishing Christian community had been largely
offset by a gain of 26,000 Christians in the northeast provinces, where there had not been as many as a hundred converts fifteen years previously. He adds that in those comparatively peaceful times, the Church maintained many
dojuku to study the Buddhist scriptures (buppo) with a
view to confuting the bonzes, "and despite all our troubles
and expense only one or two graduated who were any good,
whereas nowadays, without being taught, they learn and
preach much better."

A Jesuit report of 1623, states that there were then
twenty-eight Jesuits in Japan besides a dozen friars and one
Japanese cleric. Twelve of the Jesuits were in the Nagasaki
district and the remainder were distributed throughout the
provinces. The majority were Japanese, and it is not often
realized that out of two to five thousand martyrs who died
for the Faith in 1614–1643, there were less than seventy
European religious all told. The way in which the missionaries traveled around despite all difficulties, is shown by the
fact that in August, 1622, the Dominican, Pedro Vazquez,
disguised as a Japanese official, succeeded in bluffing his way
into Nagasaki prison where his coreligionists lay awaiting the
"Great Martyrdom," and heard their confessions before
leaving unrecognized. The ubiquitous Franciscan, Diego de
San Francisco, traveled throughout Japan disguised as a
samurai, although he had more than once a hairbreadth escape. There are very few Europeans who could pass themselves off as an Oriental, but this sublime audacity was typical of the Japan missionaries of those days.

A contemporary Dutch account (1629) notes that "the

priests are usually concealed in holes in the earth under the floor boards of the rooms of the houses wherein they lie, which holes are covered over with planks and mats; others stand all day long in a small space behind the privy, in dirt and filth, wherein one would not expect to find a beast, let alone a man; others conceal themselves between two partitions or behind the wainscoating which appears to be thinner than it really is." As the pursuit grew hotter, lepers' huts became a favorite hiding place; "for the lepers, of whom there are many in Japan, are greatly abhorred; and nobody will be easily persuaded to enter into their huts or hovels, which are very miserable and merely slight things of straw, put up to keep off the rain at night, since they go abroad to beg in the daytime." Fray Juan Pobre, O.F.M., who died in 1615, did not live to see this justification of the "poxy lepers" cherished by the Franciscans at Kyoto to the disgust of the more worldly-wise Jesuits.

Although relations between the Jesuits and the friars had improved since the days of Valignano and Bishop Cerqueira, dissensions between the Society and the mendicant orders did interfere with the smooth functioning of the Christian "underground" from time to time. At the height of the persecution in 1627, the Jesuits objected to the Franciscans confirming their own converts without having obtained leave to do so from the absentee bishop of Japan. Diego de San Francisco was forced to make a dangerous trip to Waka-matsu and Sendai, for the sole purpose of reassuring the local Christians of the validity of their conversion. One of the certificates which he gave on this occasion, drawn up in Spanish and Japanese, is preserved in the Franciscan archives at Pastrana, Spain. He also complained of the uncoöperative attitude of the Jesuits toward the Franciscans working in Kyushu; by reason of which the latter transferred most of their efforts to the less-cultivated but more promising mission field in the northeast. The reports of the Franciscan, Luis Sotelo, and the Dominican, Collado, are likewise filled with complaints against the allegedly noncoöperative attitude of the Jesuits, nor were the later backward in retorting in kind. There is no need to retail these disputes here, and it will suffice to mention that one of the chief mutual accusations (as later in the China mission) was that the Jesuits were reluctant to hear the confessions of the friars' converts and vice versa. There was also a certain amount of sectarian jealousy between the religious confraternities organized by the Jesuits and those sponsored by the friars.[19]

It is not easy to gauge the precise numbers of Christians at any time after 1614, but a careful scrutiny of the primary sources (as distinct from the later works of Church historians) indicates that the vast majority of native Christians eventually apostatized, either under torture or the threat thereof, in the course of the persecution. By all accounts— including those of the hostile English and Dutch—apostasies were relatively few before 1626, and the real change came in the ensuing decade. Later Japanese sources speak vaguely of 280,000 martyrs, but the contemporary missionary records make no such claim. This figure seems to have originated from misreading a passage in the *Seiyo-kibun* of Arai Hakuseki which refers to the *punishment* of that number of Christians during 1614–1640. Since the contemporary Catholic martyrology of Cardim (1650) gives less than 1,500 deaths for this period, and the Jesuit letters of 1614, give the total number of converts as slightly under 300,000, it is obvious that the figure given by Arai Hakuseki includes apostates as well as martyrs.

In point of fact, the real number of martyrs was probably more than double the figure given by Cardim. A letter of Manuel Ramos, the crown factor at Macao in 1635, reports a discussion among the roju, or elders of the Bakufu cabinet, on the advisability of expelling the Portuguese from Japan, as aiders and abettors of the missionaries. In the course of the discussion, it transpired that out of an average yearly total of between 250 and 300 people who were sentenced to death in Japan, only some fifteen or twenty were condemned as common criminals, the remainder being Christians. This would indicate a maximum figure of between 5,000 and 6,-000 martyrs for the period 1614–1640.

It should not be forgotten that a large proportion of the apostasies after 1614, were only "from the teeth out," and induced solely by the pain or the fear of torture. Fray Juan Pobre, writing in 1605, stated that the Jesuits in Japan had told him that more than 30,000 of their converts had apostatized in 1587–1597, as a result of Hideyoshi's relatively mild persecution of Christianity. This is confirmed by Valignano's "Advertencias" of 1592, which admit a decline of 40,000 Christians in Bungo alone, including those who perished in the Satsuma war and resulting pestilence. Nor is this surprising, for a large number of these Kyushu converts were made at the behest of local Christian daimyo, and had no real feeling for the Faith. These conditions did not hold good after 1614; because the Christian daimyo were dead and gone, and the Tokugawa government had made it crystal clear for some years that it regarded Christianity and its adherents with aversion. Consequently, it is obvious that the majority who apostatized after that date, did not do so voluntarily (as did those of 1587–1597) but only under duress. The final proof of this, if further proof be needed, was the reappearance of about 37,000 Christians during the Shimabara rebellion of 1637–1638, and the discovery of crypto-Christian communties in all save eight of the sixty-six Japanese provinces during the ensuing two decades.

Not being versed in the niceties of canon law, I do not profess to know whether the many thousands of outward apostates were regarded as lost souls by the Church from which they had been formally (and forcibly) separated. But even if the number of martyrs who endured to the end was only about two per cent of the total, the figure nevertheless constitutes a truly remarkable record when all the circumstances are considered. It is no wonder that the exiled English Jesuits of Douai, searching for examples wherewith to inspire their coreligionists in England, selected the Japanese Catholics as bearers of *The Palm of Christian Fortitude*.[20]

Chapter VIII. SAKOKU, OR THE CLOSED COUNTRY

IN a study of the reasons for the adoption of the Sakoku or "closed-country" policy by the Tokugawa dictatorship in 1633–1640, a consideration of the character of the Shogun Iemitsu is of the first importance. Professor Murdoch considers that his accession in 1623 made no great difference, since his father, Hidetada, continued to wield the real authority down to his death nine years later. This assertion is contradicted by the evidence of contemporary Jesuit chroniclers, at least in so far as his attitude to Christianity was concerned. They expressly state that Hidetada left the decision on the punishments to be meted out to the recalcitrant Christians entirely to his son; and it is clear from Japanese records that Iemitsu took a personal if sadistic interest in the interrogation of captured missionaries and apostates which neither his father nor his successors ever evinced. The discovery of a relatively thriving Christian community, complete with foreign bateren, in the shadow of his castle at Yedo came as a severe shock to him in 1623. As a tyrannical megalomaniac he was particularly infuriated to find that whereas the daimyo and leading samurai obeyed the anti-Christian edicts, humble peasants and wandering ronin obstinately declined to conform. "It must have been quite inconceivable to him how these people without power and wealth could resist the ruler's will, unless they were mysteriously seduced and supported by a foreign power. They were clearly traitors who deserved the sternest punishment," says the Japanese authority, Anesaki.

Sansom has pointed out, in another connection, that the early Tokugawa edicts often open with the preamble "since peasants are stupid people," or "since peasants are people without sense or forethought." The same authority likewise

362

observes that the Bakufu thought highly of agriculture but not of agriculturists. It paid lip service to the ideal that a sturdy peasantry was its country's pride, but in practice "regarded the peasantry as a machine to produce rice for the samurai to swallow." Consequently, it must have been all the more annoying for a feudal despot to find the worm turning in this unprecedented fashion. Some inkling of the Bakufu's bewilderment may be gained from the following re-action of a Protestant Dutch eyewitness to the steadfastness of the humble Christian converts. "Their resolution is all the more to be admired, since they knew so little of God's word; so that one might term it stubbornness rather than steadfastness; because (so far as Holy Writ is concerned) they know but little, and can only read a Pater Noster and an Ave Maria, besides a few prayers to Saints; the Romish priests exhorted them not to recant, upon pain of the loss of their salvation, accompanied with many dire threats. It is indeed extraordinary that among them are so many who re-main steadfast to the end, and endure so many insufferable torments, in despite of their scanty knowledge of the Holy Scriptures."

Contemporary Roman Catholic accounts of the charac-ter of the third Tokugawa Shogun may be regarded as prejudiced; but it is worth noting that François Caron and other Protestant Hollanders who had personal knowledge of him, likewise label Iemitsu as vain, capricious, and neu-rotic, apart from his notorious addiction to drunkenness, lechery, and pederasty. The drunkenness may perhaps be dis-counted somewhat when the accounts read that he was ac-customed to drinking sixty cups of saké during a convivial evening. Since a cup of saké is roughly the equivalent of a thimbleful of liquor, it is obvious that Iemitsu would have made a poor showing beside such Bacchanalian figures as King Christian IV of Denmark, who was accustomed to drain thirty or forty goblets of wine at a sitting before being carried off to bed unconscious. The evidence on his sadism is better attested, for he not only derived considerable pleas-

ure from cross-examining Christians under torture, but even
his admirers do not deny that he indulged (incognito) in
nocturnal street excursions with the object of trying out
the edge of his sword on the corpses of criminals (*tameshi-
giri*). His detractors further allege that he did not necessarily
confine himself to the bodies of the dead on these occasions.

On the other hand, contemporary Dutch sources affirm
that he evinced an intelligent interest in the outer world, to
the extent that he studied a number of European globes,
maps, and charts, with the object of obtaining some idea of
the relative size and importance of foreign countries, and
commented on the comparative insignificance of Japan. It
is also worth remembering that his accession coincided
roughly with the return to Japan of Ibi Masayoshi, whom
Hidetada had sent aboard to study foreign countries about
1615. I feel rather doubtful that Ibi ever went to Europe as
is often alleged. An itinerant Japanese would have been such
a *rara avis* in the Western World, that I feel sure his alleged
visits to European courts would have attracted some notice
in contemporary Western records, had he really got that
far. But even if he confined his itinerary to Portuguese Asia
and the Philippines, as seems more probable, he must have
seen enough of the close connection between Church and
State in the dominions of the Most Catholic King, to have
further inflamed the suspicions of the Bakufu on this point.
Granted the intimacy of this connection, it inevitably followed that the Iberian traders from Macao and Manila,
theoretically operating under a crown monopoly, were likewise deeply involved in the propagation of the hated faith,
as indeed they were.[1]

During all this time, the Macao trade was still the temporal
rock and stay of the persecuted Church in Japan. Valignano
had written at the turn of the century in his usual trenchant
style to some colleagues at Goa, after the loss of a Macao junk
carrying supplies for the Japan mission:

[1] For notes to chapter viii, see pages 496–499.

So long as Our Lord God gives us no other help, I do not see why the capital which is normally sent to Japan should not be invested in India, in the years when this voyage is not made, for Japan has no other resource. This is all the easier if we can find some gold or silk through some reliable friend of ours, in such wise that nobody knows of it in India; and without doubt if none of our own people will make a fuss about it, nobody else is likely to object thereto. By the grace of God I was not born the son of a merchant, nor was I ever one, but I am glad to have done what I did for the sake of Japan, and I believe that Our Lord also regards it as well done and that he gives and will give me many rewards therefor. Because if His Divine Majesty had not stung me into doing what I have done for Japan, it might very well be that Japan would now be in the throes of a worse crisis beyond hope of remedy. Wherefore I believe that he who is not here but in a place where he wants for nothing, cannot be a good judge of the difficulties which beset those who are dying of hunger in great want. And if any one of your Reverencies could come here and see these Provinces at close quarters with their vast expenses, and their miserably small income and capital, and this latter derived from such dangerous and uncertain means, I can assure you that you would not peacefully sleep away your time, but that you would do the same as did Padre Francisco Cabral when he was here, wherefore your Reverence and the Father-Visitor should favor us in this matter, and not argue against us before Our Paternity.

If this could be done in the green tree, what would be done in the dry? Although this particular effort of Valignano's to evade both the spirit and the letter of the law forbidding the participation of the religious orders in trade was frowned on, both at Goa and Rome, he and his successors in the Far East had perforce to continue their mercantile operations, whether clandestine or otherwise, in order to pay for the expenses of the Japan mission. The papal and crown contributions were hopelessly in arrears as usual, and the danger of the Dutch and English intercepting Iberian vessels at sea grew yearly worse. In these circumstances, the saintly Jesuit, Father Carlo Spinola, leader of the Great Martyrdom of 1622, acted as Valignano had forecast that anyone would act in his place. A document in the Ajuda Library at Lisbon entitled "List of the cargo belonging to the Jesuits of Macao laden in the six galliots commanded by the Captain-Major Antonio de Oliveira Moraes in July, 1618," discloses that on this particular Japan voyage, the Jesuits embarked silk and textile piece goods to a total value of 11,573 taels. This was probably slightly above their average yearly investment in the following two decades, but it is clear that the Jesuits were as deeply concerned in the annual galliots' cargoes as they had been in those of the Great Ship hitherto, and that their exile made no difference in this respect.

From this list and other documents in the archives at Lisbon and Macao, it is also clear that the Jesuits, like the secular merchants through whom they ostensibly traded, took up considerable quantities of silver for investment in the China silk market. Many other instances could be adduced to show how the laymen of Macao and Manila supported the undercover activities of the missionaries in Japan. In 1617 the Macao Captain-Major, Lopo Sarmento de Carvalho, requested the permission of Hidetada for the construction of a customhouse under Portuguese control at Nagasaki, ostensibly to facilitate the storage of their unsold goods after the ships' departure in the northeast monsoon, but in reality to facilitate the smuggling of padres into Nagasaki in the guise of employees. The request was rejected, probably because the Bakufu suspected its real purpose, but the Portuguese continued to bring in the missionaries disguised as traders or soldiers.

Padre Miguel de Carvalho, "by appointment of his superiors, shipped in secular attire for *Japonia,* in company of some other *Portugueses,* and he was permitted to pass under title of an *Indian* soldier. Being arrived at *Nangasachi,* they were all strictly examined, he only excepted. So that coming to land he procured to find a certaine *Portuguese,* in whose house he made his abode till such time as he was sent into the Island of *Amacusa,* to learn the language." This was the usual way in which missionaries were smuggled into Japan at this time; and so long as the new arrivals could lodge with those of their countrymen who were married and settled at Nagasaki, pending arrangements to send them into the interior, access to Japan although dangerous was not insuperably difficult. About twenty missionaries entered the country by this means in 1615–1618.[2]

In the nature of things, this route became increasingly dangerous to use, and had finally to be abandoned altogether for fear of fatally compromising the Macao trade. The Japanese were suspicious from the first, but the missionaries were lucky in that the responsible local authority, Hasegawa Gonroku, turned a blind eye to their movements whenever it was humanly possible for him to do so. But the discovery that the captain-major, Jeronimo de Macedo, was concerned in the attempts to rescue Flores and Zuñiga from their prison at Hirado in 1621–1622, resulted in him and four other Iberians being "empresoned and condemned and all their goodes confiscat, and looke hourly when they shall be executed." Cocks' forebodings fortunately proved exaggerated, but Macedo remained in Omura jail until his death there ten years later. In the meantime he seems to have had some of his property restored to him and even been allowed to trade to Macao through a Nagasaki agent.

The incriminating papers found on Flores and Zuñiga when their Japanese-chartered ship was taken by the *Elizabeth,* although for months discounted by Hasegawa Gonroku, must have eventually convinced the Bakufu that the Manila authorities would never withdraw their active support of the friars. At any rate no sooner were the two monks identified and burned at the stake, than the decision was taken to sever all intercourse with Manila. This was the easier to do, since it had been languishing ever since the failure of Ieyasu's efforts to open up trade with Mexico a decade earlier. It was at this unpropitious moment that a Spanish embassy arrived from Luzon with the ostensible purpose of placing diplomatic and commercial relations on a more cordial footing. Accounts differ on whether the Spaniards were turned back at Satsuma, at Nagasaki, or on their way to Kyoto, but there is more unanimity about the tenor of the Bakufu's reply, which a contemporary chronicler summarized as follows.

. . . that such Embassages came not of themselves, but procured by Religious men, dwelling in those [Philippine] Islands; and that the Xogun Lord of Iaponia would receive no Embassages from places broaching a law most false, diabolicall and seditious, turning the state upside downe and deceiving the subjects. That already he had been deceived in that kind, and that under cover of traffick and merchandize this pernicious law and the Authors thereof had been brought in, whom he now had banished under rigorous paines and would receive no more.

Apparently the Macao-Nagasaki trade was still regarded as too important for such drastic measures to be enforced against the Portuguese, but the conditions under which their trade was permitted became increasingly onerous. Richard Cocks wrote to his superiors in September, 1622, "It is also said the Emperour will banish all Spaniardes and Portingall howseholders out of Japon, and suffer non to stay but such as com and goe in their shiping, to prevent entertayning of padres." The Spaniards (save for a few local renegades who had adopted Buddhism) were officially forbidden the country in 1624, but the Portuguese residents were not expelled until some years later. During Mizuno Kawachi's governorship of Nagasaki (1626–1629), Japanese Christians were forbidden to lodge foreigners in their houses; this regulation stopped one of the smuggling channels. The Macao traders were likewise no longer allowed to lodge in the houses of their compatriots domiciled at Nagasaki, even before these people were finally expelled from Japan, but had to stay with Buddhist householders—though many of the latter were in reality crypto-Christians. The inexorable tightening-up of this process involved the deportation of all Eurasian children to Macao in 1636, and the construction of the artificial islet of Deshima, connected by a bridge with the water front, whereon the traders and sailors from Macao were rigidly guarded after being closely searched on their arrival from China. Meanwhile the Hollanders at Hirado had freedom of movement within the little fishing town and its immediate environment, but were otherwise scarcely better treated than the Portuguese. The Chinese were now (1636) confined to trading at the port of Nagasaki, whereas hitherto their junks had utilized a number of other Kyushu ports as well.

All these measures rendered it more difficult than ever for the missionaries, whether European or Japanese, to enter Japan from Manila and Macao; but the most effective deterrent to their passage was the increasing reluctance of the Macao authorities to facilitate their transportation for fear of economic reprisals by the Japanese. These had been threatened often enough and were actually imposed for a couple of years in 1628–1630, when the Portuguese trade was placed under an embargo because a Spanish galleon had plundered a Red-seal ship in the Gulf of Siam, thus affronting the shogunal passport. Luckily for the Portuguese, their rivals the Hollanders likewise had an embargo placed on their trade during the same period, because of the quarrels between Japanese adventurers and Dutch colonists in Formosa, culminating in the audacious kidnapping of the governor, Pieter Nuyts, in castle Zeelandia. This last imbroglio had an additional advantage for the Portuguese, in that it made Suetsugu Heizo, the apostate Nagasaki daikwan, a bitter enemy of the Hollanders, since his men were those who were involved on the Japanese side.

Barely had the embargo on the Macao trade been lifted, when a greater peril arose through the discovery of a letter left behind by a Portuguese friar who just had time to leave his host's house by a back door as the sheriff's raiding party broke in the front. The letter clearly revealed that the Macao merchants had been aiding and abetting the concealment of missionaries. At one time it looked as if the whole Portuguese community of Nagasaki would suffer capital punishment, but Jeronimo de Macedo arranged for a colossal bribe to be paid to the local bugyo, Takenaka Uneme. The affair was hushed up, probably because a number of the governor's own minions were involved, but the Macao authorities were seriously alarmed. They fully realized that the Bakufu was in no mood to be trifled with, and that any more such incidents would involve not merely the cessation of the Macao-

Nagasaki trade, but the death in one unpleasant form or other of all their compatriots in Nagasaki. They accordingly asked the local ecclesiastical authorities to prohibit the passage of missionaries to Japan in Portuguese galliots, on pain of excommunication, at least until the persecution abated. The higher Macao clergy saw the point of this reasoning and gave the required assurance; but the Manila authorities when asked for a similar guarantee, either proved more obstinate or less able to control their zealous subordinates.

Although the Macao-Japan trade was gradually changing its scope, in that the Portuguese were increasingly dependent on Chinese and Japanese merchant-princes for their capital, it was still a source of great profit to the tottering Iberian Asiatic empire. A disgruntled colonist writing from Macao in 1622, stated that the average price of the captaincy-major of the Japan voyage on the open market at Goa was less than 20,000 cruzados. He added that the said captain-majors usually made a clear profit of 150,000 cruzados on the voyage, "since their expences are few and small." João Serrão da Cunha, still in the throes of his lawsuit with the crown, certainly would not have agreed with him; but allowing for some natural exaggeration it is evident that the captaincy was still exceedingly profitable, judging by the eagerness with which it was sought after. Even if the crown made no very large direct profit from these voyages, they were of considerable indirect benefit thereto; for they helped to finance the fortification of colonial cities (Macao, Malacca, and Cochin) which would otherwise have been a direct charge on the crown.

In 1621 the Macao senate wrote to Doi Toshikatsu Oi-no-suké, complaining that the piratical activities of the Anglo-Dutch "Fleet of Defense" were making the China Sea unsafe for the Great Ship from Macao, whence the Portuguese had been compelled to use small galliots instead. The senate further complained that the ito-wappu (pancada) system was going from bad to worse and that the Macao merchants could not get a fair price for their silk imports at Nagasaki. Doi Toshikatsu replied to these representations by stating that the shogun had forbidden the Dutch to indulge in their piratical activities in or near Japanese waters; he felt assured that there was nobody so cruel in Japan as to deprive the Macaonese of their rightful share of the profits of the silk trade. "Oyen-dono," as Cocks called him, presumably had his tongue in his cheek when he dictated this reply; but the available evidence goes to show that the Portuguese still continued to reap a handsome profit from their Nagasaki trade, all discouragements and difficulties notwithstanding.

The embargo of 1628–1630 on both Dutch and Portuguese trade, though imposed for different reasons in the case of each nation, had the natural effect of greatly increasing the scope and extent of the Red-seal ships' trade to Indo-China, which received a great if temporary stimulus. Nevertheless it is interesting to note that the Japanese mercantile houses of Kyushu still invested as much money in the Macao trade as they did in their own bottoms. Indeed, it is probable that the Portuguese could not have carried on their commerce in the China Sea for so long as they did, without the capital advanced them yearly by the Nakano, Suetsugu, and other families of the great Hakata trading houses. These sums in silver bullion were advanced at what would seem nowadays the excessive rate of interest of between 35 per cent to 80 per cent per voyage, with an additional 10 per cent on each year's delay in repayment of the capital. This arrangement enabled the Portuguese of Macao to get their working capital from Japan without the necessity of recourse to Goa, contact with which was virtually severed since the Hollanders were the unchallenged masters of the eastern seas.[3]

The stimulus given to the Red-seal ships by the 1628–1630 embargo was short-lived. Despite deep distrust of the Macao merchants as aiders and abettors of the foreign missionaries, the Bakufu was even more neurotically nervous of the potential menace of the ronin. The antecedents of the Red-seal trade had indeed been contaminated by association with the Wako, and it is probable that there were a number of ronin or ex-ronin employed by the Chaya, Suetsugu, Araki, and

other mercantile houses which traded abroad. It is difficult to
see how these few men, scattered throughout southeast Asia
could have seemed dangerous to any government which was as
firmly established as that of the third Tokugawa Shogun. But
from a morbid fear of the overseas ronin using the Red-seal
ships as a means of communication with Japan, the Bakufu
looked increasingly askance at the growing activities of these
vessels. In this respect its foreign policy became directly opposed to its avowed support of Japanese traders against their
foreign competitors at home. The following report of an
interview between some Hollanders at Nagasaki and Heizo
Hiyetsugu, who had succeeded his father as daikwan on the
latter's death in 1630, is worth noting. Rebutting Dutch complaints that the Nagasaki bugyo did not give them a fair deal,
Heizo observed:

These officials are usually sent to Nagasaki against their inclination, and
are only longing for the moment when they will be released from the dangerous task of dealing with the foreign traders. Their object is solely to avoid
compromising themselves; they are thus extremely cautious in their dealings,
and above all things are anxious to avoid doing anything which may be
subsequently misconstrued, or cast in their teeth at Yedo. Their duty is to
guard the interests of their compatriots and to place these above those of
foreigners; the one cannot be favored except at the expense of the other;
more profit for the Hollander is less profit for the Japanese, and whosoever
favors the former injures the latter. A request to the governors to forward
your interests, is therefore equivalent to asking them to do something
which will harm them at court and in the eyes of their own countrymen.

This fine speech about subordinating foreigner's interests
to those of Japanese reads oddly in the light of the measures
actually taken by the Bakufu to first hamstring and then destroy the functioning of the Red-seal ships in 1633–1636. A
series of edicts promulgated during those years effectively leg-
islated the Japanese overseas mercantile marine out of existence, by prohibiting the construction of sea-going junks of
large tonnage, banning the return to Japan of Japanese nationals, and forbidding ships to leave for foreign countries
under any pretext. Japan's overseas trade was thus entirely

abandoned to the Portuguese, Dutch, and Chinese merchants who frequented Nagasaki and Hirado.

Moreover, shortly before these words were spoken, the Hollanders were officially notified (in 1634) that Japanese were forbidden to go to Formosa, and that the Dutch could deal as they pleased with any who did so. This ruling was a complete reversal of the Bakufu's stand on the Nuyts affair six years earlier.

Even now, the Tokugawa shogunate did not feel itself secure from its nightmare of an alliance between Catholic Spain and the disgruntled ronin. With singular shortsighted-ness, in view of their experience of the Japanese as "lambs in their own country but well-nigh devils outside of it," the Hollanders did all they could to encourage the Bakufu to at-tack Macao and Manila, either alone or in conjunction with a Dutch fleet. With a fatuity worthy of Richard Cocks twenty years earlier, they supplied the Japanese with the relevant charts and maps, and suggested ways and means of carrying out the attack. The matter was discussed more than once in the meetings of the roju or great council in 1635–1636; but although upon one occasion a majority of three to two voted in favor of accepting the Dutch proposal, Iemitsu still ap-peared to be hesitant. Matsukura Shigemasa, daimyo of Shima-bara since 1615, had also suggested an invasion of Luzon in 1630, as the sole means of scotching the Christian menace once and for all. He obtained Iemitsu's leave to send a pseudo-embassy to Manila in order to spy out the land. The shogun finally decided to act on these suggestions toward the end of 1637,—possibly goaded by the arrival of the Jesuit, Padre Marcello Mastrilli, and some other missionaries from Manila that year.

Nicholas Couckebacker, the Dutch factor at Hirado, was officially notified in November that the Bakufu had resolved to send an expeditionary force to attack Luzon. The Dutch were requested to supply some ships to protect the transports against any Spanish galleons which might be stationed at

Cavite in Manila Bay. The Dutch assented and promised to supply four ships and two yachts to convoy the Japanese transport junks to their destination. The roju apparently envisaged an expeditionary force of about 10,000 men, which, in conjunction with the Dutch ships, should have been more than sufficient to overwhelm the Spanish garrison comprising a few hundred ill-paid and half-starved if courageous men.

This was not the first time that a Japanese conquest of the Philippines had been projected. Hideyoshi toyed with the idea in 1590, and Archbishop Benavides wrote five years later that the disgruntled Tagalogs had actually asked the Japanese to come and drive out their white oppressors, promising to aid them in dong so. Fortunately for the Spaniards, the Taiko Hideyoshi was too deeply committed in his costly Korean campaign to avail himself of this offer. Two decades later Richard Cocks was urging his scheme for a Japanese conquest of the Philippines on a somewhat reluctant great council. Shortage of shipping was the ostensible reason given for the roju's refusal; but it is more likely that war weariness after the Korean campaign, and doubt whether the Tokugawa could control their vassals at such a distance, were the principal deterring factors. This last consideration was obviously not without weight in 1637, but the overmastering hatred of Christianity proved stronger. The project for attacking Macao seems to have been shelved, either because it was considered to be too strongly fortified or because it would have involved an attack on China,—although the decaying Ming empire, hard pressed by the Manchus in the north and torn by widespread rebellion within, was no longer the formidable opponent of 1592–1598. In any event, conditions for a large-scale Japanese invasion of Luzon in the northeast monsoon of 1637–1638, could hardly have been more propitious, when an entirely unforeseen event occurred which shook the morale of the Bakufu and probably changed the whole course of Far Eastern history.[4]

II

Some writers have expressed surprise that the brutal anti-Christian persecutions did not provoke the victims into taking up arms in self-defense before the end of 1637. The ingrained habit of obedience to feudal superiors was doubtless one reason for the docility which the majority displayed; for the Christians perhaps felt that the mere profession of Christianity in defiance of the shogunal edicts was something unprecedented. Moreover, the missionaries had expressly taught their converts that only passive resistance could ensure them a martyr's crown. Death in battle, even against a wanton oppressor, could not gain them this coveted honor. Other reasons were that the natural leaders of such a revolt, the Christian daimyo and higher samurai, were either dead or had recanted for the most part; whereas few of the peasants and farmers, who constituted the majority of the converts, possessed any weapons.

It is true that there were a number of samurai and ronin who had formerly been in the service of Konishi, Arima, and other Christian daimyo, scattered throughout southwestern Kyushu, who had apostatized only outwardly. After the death of their feudal lords and the proscription of Christianity, they had been absorbed in the farming communities of Shimabara and Amakusa, where some of them were still alive and active in Iemitsu's time. The majority of the bolder spirits had taken refuge with Hideyori in Osaka castle, where they perished in the general massacre which followed on the fall of the fortress. The Bakufu was for decades very nervous of the underground activities of the remaining anti-Tokugawa ronin whom it imagined as nursing their hatred for the ruling house throughout the length and breadth of Japan. These fears were undoubtedly exaggerated, but that they were not entirely baseless was dramatically proved by the Shimabara rebellion of 1637–1638.

Christianity's roots in this corner of Kyushu were deep. The

Shimabara Peninsula had originally formed a part of Arima's fief, and it was here that the Jesuit seminary, printing press, and the bulk of the missionaries had found a secure refuge in the time of Hideyoshi's persecution. Amakusa then formed part of Konishi's domains and most of the islands' inhabitants were converted in that difficult period; and here the seminary and printing press had also found a temporary refuge. After Konishi's defeat and death, the island group was given in fief to Terazawa Hirotaka, bugyo of Nagasaki from 1592 to 1602.

So strongly was Christianity entrenched at this time, that Terazawa met with scant success in his efforts to wean his new vassals from their faith. "He did not try to expel all the Christians, because since they are all peasants and there are more than 10,000 of them, most of the islands would have been depopulated," the Jesuit vice-provincial noted in 1604. Terazawa had to content himself with closing a few churches and telling the peasantry that it was a waste of time for them to become Christians, since the practice of this religion led to a slackening of their work in the rice fields. It was a different story after the persecution began in earnest ten years later, above all during the reign of terror organized by Mizuno and Takenaka in 1626–1632; but although virtually all the peasantry in this area had outwardly apostatized before 1637, the majority were still Christians at heart. Terazawa Hirotaka died in 1633, and was succeeded in his Amakusa fief by his son Katataka, a worthless profligate whose merciless taxation in money and kind left his peasants with little else than their eyes to weep with.

The sufferings of the Amakusa islanders were rivaled by those of their Shimabara neighbors across the water who had been under the heel of the Matsukura daimyo since 1615. The elder, Shigemasa, had apparently been an unwilling persecutor of his Christian vassals to begin with. He showed great kindness to a captured Italian Jesuit in 1622, listening patiently to his exposition of Christian dogma and to his distinction between the "pacific" conquests of the Portuguese in Asia, as against the Spanish occupation of the Philippines.

The same padre says that Matsukura knew very well the exact whereabouts of more than ten missionaries who were hiding in his fief, but he made no effort to seize them. Shigemasa changed his attitude a few years later, since he was the foremost advocate of an attack on Luzon and the prime helper of Mizuno in torturing recalcitrant Christians at Unzen. His son Shigeharu was a still more evil character, for in addition to being an ardent persecutor of Christians, he was a merciless suzerain and landlord, stopping at nothing to exact the last grain of rice from his tenantry. Both father and son are credited (or rather discredited) with originating the *Mino-Odori* or Mino dance,—a form of torture whereby the peasants were dressed in their straw raincoats which were set on fire after their hands had been tied behind them. Another favorite device was to seize the wives and daughters of those who could not pay their taxes. These women were ostensibly held in arrest until the required contributions were forthcoming from their menfolk, but they often died under the torturer's hands before the money to ransom them could be found.

The spark which set off the rebellion was occasioned by one of these incidents, when an outraged father killed the daimyo's stewards who were torturing his daughter before his eyes. The whole village promptly rose en masse, and the rest of the district followed this example as soon as news of the outrage spread. Such at least is the version given by Duarte Correa, a Portuguese who, during these eventful months, was lying in Omura jail, waiting to be burned at the stake. Since all of his informants were Japanese and none of them Christians (so far as is known), there seems no reason to doubt the truth of his assertion that the immediate cause of the revolt was the unbearable cruelty of the local daimyo's methods of tax collection. He further relates that when the roju asked one of Omura's leading retainers whether in his opinion the outbreak was due to religious or to economic causes, "he replied that the rebellion could not be due to the rebels being Christians, since in times when there were many such, including famous captains, they never had rebelled." [5]

Japanese traditional accounts, on the other hand, are unanimous in ascribing a religious origin to the rising, which they regard as deliberately fomented by discontented ronin, formerly in the service of Konishi and other Christian daimyo, who found the prevailing agrarian discontent a fertile soil for the spread of pro-Christian propaganda. Typical of this propaganda was the "Divine Revelation" which was surreptitiously circulated throughout the countryside, and ascribed to one of the Japanese Jesuits exiled in 1614.

> When five years shall have passed five times,
> all the dead trees shall bloom;
> crimson clouds shall shine brightly in the Western sky,
> and a boy of divine power shall make his appearance.
> These things shall usher in a Christian revival in Japan.

Although there were still a couple of years to run if 1614 be taken as the starting point of this prophecy, yet the winter of 1637 was an exceptionally dry one, with crimson clouds in the sunset skies at evening, and the cherry trees flowering out of season in the late autumn. These things caused great excitement among the crypto-Christians; and when some of the daimyo's officials seized and burned a sacred oil painting which had been brought out of its hiding place in a certain village, they were promptly lynched by an infuriated mob.

Whatever the real or ostensible cause of the rising, it speedily assumed a religious character once it had taken hold. The insurgents used banners with Portuguese inscriptions such as "Louvado seia o Santissimo Sacramento" (Praised be the most Holy Sacrament), and shouted the names of Iesus, Maria and Santiago in their attacks. They announced their open adherence to the Christian Faith and proclaimed their intention to live and die in it. The revolt spread so quickly from Shimabara to Amakusa that there seems to be every likelihood that it was a concerted affair. The insurgents elected a young man named Masuda Shiro, popularly known as Amakusa Shiro, the eighteen-year-old son of one of Konishi's old samurai, as their commander. The real leadership, however, seems to have lain with a group of five or six hard-bitten ronin who were the original ringleaders. A few of the rebels had weapons concealed in their farm houses when the revolt began; but most of them were without arms until the annihilation of a couple of samurai punitive columns gave the insurgents a few thousand weapons, apart from their original scythes, sickles, and improvised spears. The Amakusa rebels after some preliminary successes were defeated early in January; but the survivors crossed the water to join forces with their friends at Shimabara. The Arima insurgents had narrowly failed to take the castle of Shimabara, but had occupied two other old castles and seized a number of stockpiles of rice and provisions.

It is rather curious that they made no effort to march on nearby Nagasaki, which was not a garrison or castle town, and whose population (Christian at heart if not in name) would probably have given them a warm welcome. But they made no move in this direction, possibly because they did not wish to antagonize the Bakufu further. Whatever the reason, they were content after their first preliminary successes to concentrate themselves, their wives, and children, together with such supplies as they could find, in the old castle of Hara (Haranojo), standing in a strong position surrounded on three sides by the sea. Estimates of their numbers range from 20,000 to 37,000, apart from women and children. Takekoshi, who for once seems to have coördinated his data rather carefully, gives the total as 37,000, including 15,000 men of fighting age and about 200 ronin. These figures agree almost exactly with those given by some of Duarte Correa's informants, if the women and children are included.

The first news of the rising reached the Bakufu on or about December 17, which was the day on which the unwitting Nagasaki bugyo (there were now two of them, Sakakibara and Baba) arrived at Yedo to make their annual report. Matsukura was dispatched to his fief next day, but he evidently was not in undue haste since he only reached his castle at Shimabara on January 15, 1638, which was the day on which the rebels had completed digging themselves in at Hara castle. Owing to the Bakufu's standing order that no daimyo could move any of his forces outside of his fief without explicit orders from the shogunate, the forces of the neighboring Kyushu daimyo, although partly mobilized, had not moved beyond their own borders. As successive reports poured into Yedo of the religious rather than the economic origin of the revolt, the government became seriously alarmed. The two bugyo speedily returned in their tracks from Yedo to Nagasaki, where they were surprised and relieved to find all quiet and no threat of attack by the insurgents. They lost no time in garrisoning the city and its immediate approaches with a force of 40,000 men drawn from the neighboring fiefs. The bugyo then left with a contingent of 500 men to join the government forces at Shimabara, which they reached on January 20.

As soon as the shogun realized the gravity of the rebellion Itakura Shigemasa, son of old Itakura who had been so friendly to the Jesuits as *shoshidai* or governor of Kyoto in 1602–1614, was appointed special commissioner with full powers to coordinate the forces of the Kyushu daimyo against the rebels. Despite the fact that the feudal levies from the cream of the Kyushu samurai eventually totaled more than 50,000 men under his command, the besiegers were invariably worsted in all the encounters which they had with their despised opponents. The Christians had a few hundred matchlock men among their number, and so long as their ammunition lasted they proved vastly superior to any of their samurai opponents, whether in attack or defense.

When the Bakufu heard that the siege was making no progress, a new commander, Matsudaira Idzu-no-kami Nobutsuna, one of the great council, was nominated to succeed Itakura, and further reinforcements were dispatched to the scene. News of his supersession reached Itakura before Matsudaira's arrival, and he decided to forestall his successor by making an attempt to storm the castle on the traditonally auspicious (Japanese) New Year's Day. In accordance with tradition, Itakura composed a poem before the battle began, his composition being of a decidedly melancholy tinge.

On New Year's Day, last year in Yedo I tied on a court-dress hat;
today before the Castle of Hara I tie on a helmet, and go out to battle.
Thus the world and all things in it change.
When the name only remains of the flower which bloomed at the advent of the New Year,
remember it as leader of the van.

The attack was repulsed with great slaughter; Itakura was killed while trying to rally his men. Matsudaira, who was a notoriously foxy character, whether as a statesman or a tactician, preferred to let hunger do its inevitable work, and although blockading the castle closely he made no attempt to carry it by storm. Through the bugyo of Nagasaki, help in the form of ships and artillery was demanded from both the Dutch at Hirado and the Chinese at Nagasaki. Couckebacker complied by sending the Dutch ship *De Ryp*, which bombarded the castle from seaward. The Hollanders were politely dismissed after the besieged had shot arrows into the Tokugawa forces' encampment which bore pasquils jeering at the samurai for being masters of the abacus rather than of arms, and for being compelled to rely on foreigners in order to suppress a handful of peasants. The Dutch collaboration was probably unavoidable under the circumstances, but it did them no good in Europe, where invidious comparisons were made with their actions against their Huguenot co-religionists at La Rochelle in the previous decade.

Although the besieged had hitherto been almost uniformly successful in their sorties, provisions and munitions had never been abundant from the beginning, and both were virtually gone by the beginning of April. A desperate sally on the night of April 4–5, with the object of seizing some of the besiegers' magazines, miscarried in the darkness and confusion, although the government forces suffered even heavier losses as they continued fighting among themselves after the attackers had withdrawn. Deserters now began to come into the besiegers' lines in increasing numbers. From them Matsudaira learned, what was self-evident from examining the bodies of the slain rebels, that the besieged were in an advanced state of malnutrition, and that their gunpowder stocks were completely exhausted. More by accident than design, a general assault was made on April 12, and although the first attack was repulsed, a second surprise assault a few minutes later was successful, and the outer of the three defense circuits was carried by storm. Two days of fighting and massacre were necessary to dispose of the last-ditch defenders of the *honnomaru* or citadel, who fell wielding iron cauldrons and cooking pots in default of anything more lethal. All the remainder, including women and children, were massacred on April 15, the only recorded survivor being Yamada Emonsaku, an ex-Jesuit dojuku painter, who had apostatized some years previously and was an apparently unwilling participant in the rebellion. He had been discovered in the act of traitorously communicating with the besiegers, and was imprisoned in a dungeon awaiting execution when the castle was stormed.

The attackers by no means came off scatheless in this blood bath; their total losses during the three-month siege are conservatively estimated at 13,000 men. They seem to have numbered more than 100,000 men at their peak, so their casualty rate was a surprisingly high one, especially in view of their numerical and material superiority and the fact that they made only two general assaults in the whole time of the siege. All contemporary evidence goes to show that the Bakufu was surprised and dismayed at the relatively poor showing made by supposedly trained samurai against raw Christian peasants, led by a couple hundred ronin who had not handled arms in twenty years. The best testimony on this point is afforded by the abandonment of the projected Luzon invasion, which the Nagasaki bugyo told the Hollanders had been cancelled as a result of the experiences of the Shimabara campaign. Whereas the Bakufu had considered early in 1637, that 10,000 men would suffice for this expedition, the great council now calculated that 100,000 samurai would probably be needed to take Manila, which was no mere earthwork held by peasants but a heavily fortified city with a veteran garrison.[6]

III

The Shimabara rebellion sounded the death knell of the ninety-five-year old Portuguese trade with Japan. The shogun and his councilors had more than once long and earnestly debated not merely the expulsion of the Macao merchants but an attack on the City of the Name of God in China itself. So far as the Bakufu was concerned, it was difficult for a man of Iemitsu's mentality to believe that the doltish peasantry of southwestern Kyushu would dare to rise in rebellion without being encouraged in some mysterious way from abroad. Intercourse with Manila having been prohibited nearly a quarter of a century previously, and the Red-seal ships suppressed recently, it only remained to close the Macao-Nagasaki route, since the Chinese and Dutch were not seriously suspected of coöperating with the ronin or of diffusing Christian propaganda.

No padres had been found in Hara castle, in contrast to the Osaka siege of 1615, wherein seven religious had participated, but the shogunate suspected that the bateren and iruman were still being smuggled into Japan on board the galliots. This supposition was wrong, since the senate of Macao (with the support of the local ecclesiastical hierarchy) was moving heaven and earth to satisfy the Japanese authorities of their innocence in this respect. Not only had they written to Manila and Goa, imploring the authorities there to forbid the embarkation of missionaries for Japan, but they had written to King Felipe of Spain and Pope Urban VIII in the same sense.

The roju's decision was not reached until 1639, and the Portuguese were still allowed to trade under restrictions at Deshima in the autumn of 1638. Judging by the freedom with which they borrowed money at comparatively low rates of interest from Japanese capitalists that year (the city of

Macao alone borrowed 97,000 taels) the local Japanese themselves did not expect a severance of relations in the predictable future. But when Captain-Major Vasco Palha de Almeida reached Nagasaki with two ships in 1639, he was not allowed to trade, nor would the bugyo accept delivery of goods in payment of the sums borrowed the previous year. The captain-major was handed a copy of the decree signed by the roju on July 5, 1639, ordering the immediate and permanent cessation of the Macao-Nagasaki trade on the following grounds.

1) The galliots were used for smuggling missionaries in defiance of the anti-Christian edicts.

2) The galliots afforded a means of sending supplies and provisions to the missionaries.

3) The men and money smuggled in the galliots were responsible for fomenting the Shimabara rebellion.

The captain-major was ordered to leave with the first fair wind, nobody being allowed to land while the galliots lay at anchor in the harbor, awaiting the arrival of the northeast monsoon. The Portuguese were informed, both verbally and in writing, that their nationals were banished from Japan on pain of death, and were told that this fact should be officially promulgated at Goa and Macao.

Great was the consternation in the City of the Name of God when Palha returned with the fatal news. In spite of the categorical nature of the Japanese decision and the indications that the Bakufu meant what it said, the city fathers thought that they would make one last attempt to induce the shogun to change his mind. They were encouraged in this hope, although they realized that it was a slender one, by the fact that they owed so much money in Japan that the government might be disposed to permit some trade after all, if only for the purpose of eventually paying off these debts. A specially selected mission of four of the leading citizens was organized for the venture. All the participants down to the meanest slave boy in the crew, confessed and took communion before embarking, since it was realized that they had less than an even chance of returning alive.

The ship reached Nagasaki in July, and the passengers and crew were at once placed under arrest in Deshima, pending the decision of the roju on their petition for the reopening of trade which the government had transmitted to Yedo. Nor was the answer long delayed. On August 1, the shogunal commissioners came with the answer, together with as many executioners as there were individuals in the Macaonese party. Next day the Portuguese were summoned to the audience chamber, whither they went dressed in their gala clothes. The presiding official then addressed them as follows: "You villains! you have been forbidden ever to return to Japan on pain of death, and you have disobeyed the command. The former year you were guilty of death but were mercifully granted your lives. Hence you have earned this time nothing but the most painful death; but since you have come without merchandise and only to beg for something, this will be commuted to an easy death."

The envoys and their suite were then seized and trussed like turkeys. One account states that those who would recant were offered their lives, but they all spurned the offer. Thirteen of the native members of the crew were reprieved at the last moment in order to carry the news of the embassy's fate to Macao. The remaining sixty-one were executed (August 4) on Martyr's Mount where they all died bravely. The survivors witnessed the execution, as also the burning of their ship with all the cargo still on board. The lucky thirteen were embarked in a crazy little vessel a few weeks later and given an edict couched in more categorical terms than that of 1639. In this screed the Macaonese were warned that even if "King Felipe himself, or even the very God of the Christians, or the great Buddha contravened this prohibition, they shall pay for it with their heads!" [7]

Pertinacity was a quality which had stood the Portuguese in good stead ever since they had started out on their national career of "conquest, navigation, and commerce" two and a quarter centuries before, nor were the Macaonese less dogged than their forefathers. Any immediate reaction was impossible, in view of the colony's critical situation; but not long after Portugal's successful revolt from Spain and the acclamation of the Duke of Braganza as King João IV in December, 1640, the project of reopening relations with Japan was mooted at Goa and Lisbon. The moving spirit in this audacious proposal was the Jesuit, Francisco Antonio Cardim, procurator of the Japan province and ex-missionary in Indo-China, together with the adventurous Antonio Fialho Ferreira, one of the leading (and most unpopular) men in Macao. King João was induced to find two royal galleons and the wherewithal to equip an embassy on this wild-goose chase to the other side of the world, at a time when every man, ship, and red cent was needed at home or in Brazil to keep his shaky throne from collapsing under the pressure of Spanish land and Dutch sea power. No clearer indication could be given that the Japan trade was still regarded as an El Dorado.

The first duly accredited European ambassador to Japan "from King to King" (previous envoys having been sent by viceroys of India or Mexico) was an elderly and impecunious fidalgo named Gonçalo de Siqueira de Souza, who had seen much service in the East from the Philippines to the Persian Gulf. After a propitious start, his voyage became a chapter of accidents, and he only reached Macao with one galleon at the end of May, 1645. Although the senate had asked for the dispatch of an ambassador to Japan after hearing the news of King João's accession, it had been with the proviso that the envoy should be authorized to promise the Bakufu that under no circumstances whatever would missionaries be permitted to proceed to Japan for so long as the anti-Christian penal laws were in force. Unfortunately, Siqueira's instructions as drafted at Lisbon forbade him to commit himself on this point; and the senate felt that to send the solitary galleon to Nagasaki under these circumstances was to court a repetition of the tragedy of 1640.

The ambassador saw the force of this argument, but being a stubborn old gentleman with a high sense of duty, he sailed for Goa at the end of the year to take council with the viceroy at Goa. A ten-year truce having been concluded with the Dutch recently, Dom Felipe Mascarenhas was able to provide him with an additional and stronger galleon, the *São João Baptista,* together with some ready money. More important still, a high ecclesiastical junta, meeting at Goa in April, 1646, endorsed by a majority vote the suggestion of the Macao senate as against the crown's uncompromising stand. Siqueira now returned with his two vessels to Macao, whence, after one abortive voyage as far as the Ryukyu Islands, he eventually reached Nagasaki in July, 1647.

The Japanese, who had been informed of the intended embassy by the Dutch a couple of years earlier, were nevertheless greatly surprised when it made its belated appearance; but they did not dare to inflict on the two well-gunned galleons the drastic punishment meted out to the ill-fated Macao envoys. Having failed to induce the Portuguese to surrender their arms and ammunition, the galleons were blockaded in the harbor by a stout pontoon bridge erected on the night of August 14–15. Pending a decision on the Portuguese request by the court of Yedo, more than 50,000 men and 2,000 craft of various kinds from neighboring fiefs were ostentatiously concentrated in Nagasaki with the avowed object of staging a repetition of the destruction of André Pessoa's carrack in 1610. If the account of the resident Dutch factor at Deshima (whither the Hollanders had been transferred from Hirado in 1641) is to be believed, the local samurai had no stomach for the expected fight. For all their outward display of bravado, many of them openly wished that the Portuguese would be allowed to leave unmolested.

Toward the end of August, the shogun's answer was received from Yedo in the form of a decree signed by all the members of the great council. It repeated the stereotyped allegation that the missionaries were but the vanguard of temporal conquistadores, quoting the evidence of apostate padres in support of this contention. It further pointed out that the ambassador's written credentials contained no specific promise that Christianity would never again be propogated in Japan by the Portuguese, and that this omission alone made it impossible for the shogun to consider receiving him. Only the fact that Siqueira had entered the harbor in good faith, and the notification of the change of regime in Portugal, saved him from the fate of the Macaonese envoys. The blockade was accordingly raised and the galleons allowed to leave on September 4.

When the Japanese reply eventually reached Lisbon in the *São João Baptista* three years later, King João IV reluctantly yielded, as he was to yield subsequently to Cromwell's demands for the toleration of English Protestants in Portugal. In 1651, a letter was drafted in the royal chancery giving the most explicit assurance that no missionaries would be permitted to leave for Japan in Portuguese vessels or with Portuguese connivance. It was forwarded to the viceroy at Goa for transmission to Japan if ever an opportunity occurred, but it was now too late. If Gonçalo de Siqueira had been able to give a written instead of merely a verbal assurance, it is possible, though scarcely probable, that the shogun might have been induced to relax the sakoku policy somewhat, since a few members of the great council were by no means without liberal views. But the discovery of a great ronin conspiracy and of hundreds of crypto-Christians in Kyushu during the years 1657–1658, gave the Bakufu two successive shocks which hardened its determination.

The Portuguese made a final attempt in 1685, when thirteen castaways from an Isé junk which had been driven by a typhoon to Macao, were sent back to Nagasaki in a Macaonese ship. On this occasion, the Portuguese were thanked for their trouble but warned that the anti-Christian edicts were still in force and that they should not attempt to repeat the experiment. Nor did they venture to do so, for they realized that Japan no longer needed the Macao trade as it had done a century previously. National silk production and textile manufacture were improving rapidly under the stimulus of the luxurious age of Genroku. Trade with China had been placed on an official basis for the first time in centuries with the fall of the Ming dynasty and the accession of the Manchus (1644). A yearly average of fifty Chinese junks and four or five Dutch ships from Batavia provided the port of Nagasaki with all the foreign goods necessary for the island empire. The Southern Barbarian chapter of Japanese history was closed.[8]

IV

The savage persecutions of 1626–1633 had driven the adherents of Christianity completely underground, and after the massacre of the defenders of Hara castle, no trace of its profession remained on the surface. The transplanted Christianity in the northeast had gone the same way as the deeply rooted variety in southwestern Japan, and all Christians outside of jail were either dead, had apostatized, or else professed their faith in secret. An inquisition for the detection and suppression of crypto-Christians had been established about 1640, headed by Inouye Chikugo-no-kami Masashige, who, following in the footsteps of Mizuno and Takenaka, used all his ingenuity to obtain apostates rather than martyrs. Naturally enough, the persecutors had always sought above all to obtain formal recantation from the missionaries, particularly the Europeans, but it was a long time before they met with any success.

The high standard and heroic constancy of both Jesuits, friars, and their respective dojuku are worthy of the greatest admiration. Earlier, Padre Rodriguez Tçuzzu complained of several apostacies among the Japanese iruman and dojuku before 1598, but these weaklings in the Faith, like Fabian and others in later years, left it through personal pique, thwarted ambition, or spiritual disillusionment, and not from *force majeure*. The same thing apparently applied to Thomas Araki, a Japanese priest ordained at Rome, who had been excommunicated and defrocked after his return, and whose apostasy at Omura in 1619, was evidently a voluntary one. It was only in 1633 that the first European padre, the aged and ailing Christovão Ferreira apostatized after a five-hour suspension in the pit (*ana-tsurushi*), but the fact that he was the vice-provincial and acknowledged head of the mission in Japan, rendered this belated triumph all the more welcome to the persecutors.

In 1633 alone, more than thirty missionaries including Padre Julião Nakaura, one of the envoys to Rome in 1593, gave up their lives for the Faith at the stake, in the pit, or in some other painful form of martyrdom. It was now exceedingly difficult to reinforce their depleted ranks, since the Macao galliots would no longer bring missionaries for fear of an embargo on their trade; and those who came from Manila in Chinese junks—virtually the only way left—were generally captured as soon as they set foot on shore. None but those who knew the language exceptionally well had any hope of evading arrest for long. One of the last of these, the courageous Jesuit, Vice-Provincial Sebastião Vieira, was taken in a small boat at Osaka after baffling his pursuers for more than a year. He redeemed his predecessor's fall from grace by dying unflinchingly in the pit (June, 1634). The last surviving members of the original mission seem to have been a party of five (two Japanese and one Italian Jesuit, and two Franciscan friars) who were taken in northeastern Japan in 1638–1639. The Italian (Porro) and one of the Japanese Jesuits (Shikimi) apostatized under torture; but the other Japanese and the two friars triumphantly endured the worst that Inouye's minions could do. Pedro Kasui, S.J., died in the pit and the two Spaniards at the stake, having shown a resolution which confounded their tormentors, as is evident from the wording of the references to them in the *Kirishito-ki*. Besides the two Franciscans martyred on this occasion, there are three others unaccounted for, who must have died or been martyred subsequently.

It has been possible by a careful comparison of Dutch and Japanese sources to ascertain the fate of the majority of those missionaries who tried to penetrate into the "closed country" after 1640. One party, known as the first Rubino group, from the name of the organizer of this and the next expedition, landed at Satsuma on August 11, 1642. It numbered five European Jesuits and three native catechists. They were seized forthwith and sent to Nagasaki where they were subjected to rigorous torture. European accounts are unanimous in stating that they all died martyrs' deaths, but a Japanese official document implies that two of the Europeans apostatized, since one died in 1665 and another in 1690. The fate of the second group, which was captured off the coast of Chikuzen in 1643, is better attested. This party was made up of four European and one Japanese Jesuit, together with five Chinese and Japanese catechists, or ten persons in all. The whole group apostatized after long and severe tortures had been inflicted on them, but one of their number (Alonso de Arroyo) immediately revoked his formal apostasy and died soon afterwards in prison. The *Kirishito-ki* explains that Christians were forbidden to kill themselves, but that Arroyo overcame this religious commandment by taking less food each day until he died of malnutrition,—no very prolonged feat in a Japanese prison.

The Japanese attitude toward the apostates is clearly set forth in the *Kirishito-ki*, which, being written in the form of a secret and confidential memorandum from one inquisitor to his successor, can be trusted in this respect. The apostates were made to join either the Zen or the Jodo sect, Europeans being given a rice ration equal to that for ten men and a *kwamme* of silver, whereas Asiatics were given rations equal to that for seven men. Some (but not all apparently) were given "wives," the marriage ceremony being duly celebrated by the ritual exchange of saké cups. It is not recorded that any of them had children, although Chiara evidently lived with his "wife" up to his death in 1685. They were naturally given Japanese names, Christovão Ferreira being known as Sawano Chuan and Giuseppe Chiara as Okamoto Sanuemon, whose swords and widow he had inherited. The majority were interned in the Kirishitan-yashiki, a prison built specially for the purpose within the grounds of Inouye's estate, although Ferreira seems to have spent much of his life not in Yedo but at Nagasaki. The prison's official title was *Shumon aratame yaku* or Inquisition Office.

Although the pit was the favorite device for inducing apostasy, the *Kirishito-ki* refers to another method evidently widely used after 1640, which is not mentioned in the European records. This was the *mokuba,* or wooden horse, presumably some sort of a contrivance on which the victim was straddled with weights attached to his feet. Inouye warned his successor that an excess of torture usually defeated its own object, since the victim often died under it, thus becoming a martyr instead of an apostate. He advised that when a sufferer on the wooden horse asked to be allowed to perform his natural functions or to be given a whiff of tobacco, that his request should be granted. He also warned that the outcast *Eta,* who were invariably the torturers employed to handle the victims hung in the pit, sometimes killed them accidentally. He therefore advocated that the *tsurushi* should be regulated in accordance with the physical strength of the sufferer. He further warned his successor that padres and Christians under torture were likely to see visions and proclaim "Lo! a miracle!" Inouye advised him against being deceived by any such pretense. Another admonition was that if the tortured Christian thought that the presiding judge was a merciful man, he would try and impose on his good nature, so that undue laxity was to be as much guarded against as undue severity. Finally, Christians who revoked their apostasy should not be treated as Christians, that is, killed in the pit or burned at the stake, but should be decapitated as thieves and robbers. He added that two or three European missionaries had been executed in this way in the Kirishitan-yashiki between 1643 and 1658, and that about fifty or sixty native dojuku and others had suffered in prison for the same reason.[9]

This last observation fits in very well with what can only

be guessed at from other sources; namely, that the majority, if not all of these spiritual outcasts, revoked their apostasy in the end and returned to the Faith in the evening of their days. That their original recantation was solely extorted by torture is obvious from the Dutch eyewitness accounts of the four European padres of the second Rubino group at Yedo in September, 1643. The Hollanders saw them in Hotta's mansion, where they "looked exceeding pitifully, their eyes and cheeks strangely fallen in; their hands black and blue, and their whole bodies sadly misused and macerated by torture. These, though they had apostatized from the Faith, yet declared publicly to the interpreters that they did not freely apostatize, but the insufferable torments which had been inflicted upon them forced them to it." In the cross-examination conducted by the commissioners, which some of the Hollanders could understand since it was conducted in Portuguese, the self-styled apostates boldly refuted the taunts of the inquisitors and of Ferreira that God was unable to deliver them from the shogun's clutches, even had he wished to do so. One of the Jesuits retorted "it is true that these poor miserable bodies are in the shogun's power, which he would not have were it not granted him from God. Also all human authority ceases over man when the soul is departed out of the body." Another ended his reply with the words "without the true God there is no salvation; and without His will and permission, nothing either good or bad can be done."

Apart from extorting these palpably false confessions of apostasy, another prime object of the Japanese Inquisition's procedure was to force the missionaries to admit that they were merely the forerunners of a temporal conquest by the Pope or the King of Spain. Inouye lays great stress on this point in his memoranda, adding that the padres must be tortured again if they do not admit the truth of this statement whenever they were questioned about it. In this connection some of them were forced to sign a statement that the Jesuits in Manila and Macao were busy training Japanese dojuku who had sought refuge there, in order that they might the easier enter Japan in disguise. They further admitted (and this was true enough) that during the Keicho period the Jesuits had placed disguised iruman and dojuku in Buddhist temples with the sole object of studying Buddhist and Shinto texts. They added (which was not true) that copies of these texts were later printed in Europe by papal command and distributed throughout the seminaries for potential missionaries to study. The progress of the Jesuits at the court of Peking alarmed the Bakufu considerably. Chinese junks were strictly searched for any evidence of connection with Christianity, and large numbers of Chinese books were placed on the government's index merely because they contained (or were thought to contain) some passing reference to Christianity.

The apostates were also frequently cross-examined with a view to extorting an admission that killing was no murder where the slayer was a Christian and the victim a heathen. Such an admission of course provided the Bakufu with its crowning argument that Christianity was a subversive and immoral religion. One such admission, extorted from Christovão Ferreira and Martinho Schizayemon (Shikimi) in the first place, was endorsed by Giuseppe Chiara.

> According to a precept of God, it is no sin to kill a heathen who is hostile to the Creator, even when he is a master or parent; but on the contrary it is a service rendered to Heaven. Thus spake the Creator. The Bateren Chuan [Christovão Ferreira] and Martinho Ichizayemon stated this as a fact, as you yourself know. Therefore you now ask me likewise whether this is really a precept of God. It most certainly is so, as the two above-mentioned have said. I hereby affirm that it is so.
>
> On the twelfth day of the eighth month of the fourth Year of Meirki in the Year of the Dog [June 12, 1658]
>   (Signed) Giuseppe Chiara alias Okamoto Sanuemon [seal].

The Shogun Iemitsu was particularly interested in obtaining these admissions so destructive of filial piety and feudal loyalty, and he personally attended the examination of Christians and apostates many times during 1643–1646.

The apostate padres of the second Rubino group confessed under torture, in October, 1643, that they "had also been told that a Namban bateren was to cross over to Japan in the following year. They had likewise heard that twelve Japanese were to be educated as bateren at Macao and five or six in Luzon, in order to be sent over to Japan. It was commonly reported that in this way a large number of bateren were to be brought up in various countries, to be sent to Japan in a continuous stream." Dread of the Jesuits' plan to reënter Japan, "cost what it would in money or blood," became a sort of nightmare with him, but the practical chances of anything of the kind happening were remote. The veterans of the old Japan mission were dead and gone, and nobody else knew the language well enough to make good his escape after being set ashore. The fate of the two Rubino groups proved that; and the native catechists were too few in numbers and yearly decreasing. It was virtually impossible to get a ship, since no owner was ready to take the risk involved. Finally, the apostasy of so many of the Rubino group may have induced the higher ecclesiastical authorities to frown on any more such forlorn hopes.

Cut off from their spiritual pastors and from all communication with Rome, Christianity yet survived "underground" in the most astonishing way, bearing witness to the care with which it had been planted. In 1657–1658, some six hundred Christians were arrested in the rural district of Kori near Nagasaki, in consequence of a visiting farmer's loose talk about a wonderful boy of thirteen, endowed with greater miraculous powers than the leader of the Shimabara rebellion. Of these, 411 were executed, 77 died in prison, and 99 were released on taking the oath of apostasy. The last survivor, who was a girl of eleven at the time she was arrested, died in Omura prison in 1722. The number incriminated was apparently much larger, but the Omura clan officials collected and burned most of the relevant documents in order to prevent further scandal. The next few years list only a few isolated arrests and executions in the Inquisition records, but in 1664–1667 more than 2,000 Christians were arrested, many of whom were killed, and hundreds of others were deported from their homes and detained in segregated communities. The scene of these mass arrests was Owari and Mino in central Japan, which provinces do not figure as Christian strongholds in the missionary records, nor even in those of the Japanese Inquisition before 1664.

When all is said and done though, it was in the districts where Christianity first took firm root that it lasted longest, as might have been expected. In some remote villages and hamlets of Omura and the countryside around Nagasaki, the heads of the gonin-gumi or five-family group contrived to hand down the Faith in secret from generation to generation. Perhaps some forgotten but long-lived Japanese Jesuit or dojuku instructed them originally but this is pure supposition. Emigrants from this area transplanted their *onando-buppo,* or back-room Buddhism as it was euphemistically known, to the Goto Islands (where possibly some former Christians were still living) in the 1680's. The creed was handed down to adults as they came of age, and the duties of catechizing, preaching, baptizing, and so on were distributed among a regular lay hierarchy, each rank of which had its allotted tasks. Naturally certain superstitious habits accumulated in the course of centuries, and there was a tendency to identify St. John the Baptist with the water god, St. Lawrence and St. Francis as wind gods, and so on. Nevertheless in many respects there were no material differences, and the discoverer of the crypto-Christians at Urakami in 1865, could write after interrogating one of the catechists, "Let me first say that his formula for baptism does not differ at all from ours, and that he pronounces it very distinctly." Moreover, they were fully aware of Roman Catholic insistence on the celibacy of the clergy.

This romantic story has often been told, and in any event lies outside the scope of our work. The same can be said of the story of the Abbáte Sidotti, the last European missionary to penetrate the darkness of the "closed country," which he did in 1708. He was imprisoned in the Kirishitan-yashiki and interrogated by no less a person than the famous Confucian scholar, Arai Hakuseki, who was incidentally the first Tokugawa statesman to reject the idea that Christian missionary propaganda was inevitably a forerunner of European temporal conquest. After six years' imprisonment, he secretly converted an elderly married couple who acted as his servants and who at one time had come under the influence of the apostate Cantonese catechist Juan (died, 1700). When this was discovered, he was placed in a punishment cell, that is, a "hole about four or five feet deep, which had only a small opening, through which a little food could be passed to him. Here he lived until he died from suffocation through the horrible stench and stink of his own filth." Doubt has been cast on this contemporary Dutch account, but its absolute accuracy and the tragic end of the Abbáte Sidotti were finally confirmed by the unexpected discovery of the underground death cells on the site of the Kirishitan-yashiki in September, 1940.[10]

That somewhat sententious but otherwise admirable Stoic, Marcus Aurelius Antoninus, wrote in his *Meditations*:

What is wickedness? It is that which many times and often thou hast already seen and known in the world. And so, as anything doth happen that might otherwise trouble thee, let this memento presently come to thy mind, that it is that which thou hast already often seen and known. Generally, above and below, thou shalt find but the same things. The very same things whereof ancient stories, middle age stories, and fresh stories are full. There is nothing that is new. All things that are, are both usual and of little continuance.

So it is with the story of the suppression of Christianity in Tokugawa Japan; for the sickening cruelties and incredible heroism which marked its course have been reënacted on a far vaster scale in our own day and generation. If only for this reason, the history of the Christian Century may perhaps be regarded as a "tract for the times," and one from which the reader can draw his own moral.

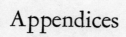

Appendices

APPENDIX I

EXTRACTS FROM A LETTER WRITTEN BY
FRANCIS XAVIER, S.J., TO THE JESUITS AT GOA
DATED KAGOSHIMA, NOVEMBER 5, 1549 [1]

By the experience which we have of this land of Japan, I can inform you
thereof as follows. Firstly, the people whom we have met so far, are the best
who have yet been discovered, and it seems to me that we shall never find
among heathens another race to equal the Japanese. It is a people of very good
manners, good in general, and not malicious; they are men of honor to a
marvel, and prize honor above all else in the world. They are a poor people
in general; but their poverty, whether among the gentry or those who are
not so, is not considered as a shame. They have one quality which I cannot
recall in any people of Christendom; this is that their gentry howsoever
poor they may be, and the commoners howsoever rich they may be, render as
much honor to a poor gentleman as if he were passing rich. On no account
would a poverty-stricken gentleman marry with someone outside the gentry, even if he were given great sums to do so; and this they do because
they consider that they would lose their honor by marrying into a lower
class. Whence it can clearly be seen that they esteem honor more than riches.
They are very courteous in their dealings one with another; they highly
regard arms and trust much in them; always carrying sword and dagger,
both high and low alike, from the age of fourteen onwards. They are a
people who will not submit to any insults or contemptuous words. Those
who are not of gentle birth give much honor to the gentry, who in their
turn pride themselves on faithfully serving their feudal lord, to whom they
are very obedient. It seems to me that they act thus rather because they
think that they would lose their honor if they acted contrarily, than for
fear of the punishment they would receive if disobedient. They are small
eaters albeit somewhat heavy drinkers, and they drink rice wine since there
are no ordinary wines in these parts. They are men who never gamble, because they consider it a great dishonor, since those who gamble desire what
is not theirs and hence tend to become thieves. They swear but little, and
when they do it is by the Sun. There are many persons who can read and
write, which is a great help to their learning quickly prayers and religious
matters. It is a land where there are but few thieves in some kingdoms, and
this by the strict justice which is executed against those that are, for their
lives are never spared. They abhor beyond measure this vice of theft. They
are a people of very good will, very sociable and very desirous of knowledge;
they are very fond of hearing about things of God, chiefly when they understand them. Of all the lands which I have seen in my life, whether those of

---

[1] *Cartas que os Padres e Irmãos da Companhia de Jesus escreverão dos Reynos de Iapão e
China aos da mesma Companhia da India, e Europa, desdo anno de 1549 ate o de 1580*
(Evora, 1598), I, fols. 7ᵛ–15.

Christians or of heathens, never yet did I see a people so honest in not thieving. Most of them believe in the men of old, who were (so far as I understand) persons who lived like philosophers; many of them adore the Sun and others the Moon. They like to hear things propounded according to reason; and granted that there are sins and vices among them, when one reasons with them pointing out that what they do is evil, they are convinced by this reasoning. I discerned fewer sins in the laity and found them more obedient to reason, than those whom they regard as fathers and priests, whom they call Bonzes.

Two things have astonished me greatly about this country. The first, to see how lightly they regard great sins; and the reason is because their forebears were accustomed to live in them, from whom those of the present generation take their example; see how continuation in vices which are against nature corrupts the people, in the same manner as continual disregard of imperfections undermines and destroys perfection. The second point is to see that the laity live better in their state than the Bonzes in theirs; and withal this is so manifest, it is astonishing in what esteem the former hold the latter. There are many other errors and evils among these Bonzes, and the more learned are the worst sinners. I spoke many times with some of the wiser, chiefly with one who is highly regarded by all in these parts, both for his letters, life, and dignity, as for his great age, he being eighty years old, and called Ningit [Ninjitsu], which is to say in Japanese "truthful heart"; he is as a bishop amongst them, and if the term could be applied to him, might well be called "blessed." In many talks which I had with him, I found him doubtful, and unable to decide whether our soul is immortal, or whether it dies with the body; sometimes he told me yes, at others no, and I fear that the other learned are alike. This Ningit is so great a friend of mine, that it is a marvel to see. All, both laity and Bonzes like us very much, and are greatly astonished to see how we have come from such distant lands as from Portugal to Japan, which is more than six thousand leagues, only to speak of the things of God, and how people can save their souls by belief in Jesus Christ; saying that our coming to these lands is the work of God. One thing I tell you, for which you may give many thanks to God Our Lord, that this land of Japan is very fit for our holy faith greatly to increase therein; and if we knew how to speak the language, I have no doubt whatsoever that we would make many Christians. May it please Our Lord that we may learn it soon, for already we begin to appreciate it, and we learned to repeat the ten commandments in the space of forty days which we applied ourselves thereto.

In the place of Paulo de Santa Fé, our good and true friend, we were received by the local Captain and by the Alcayde, with much benignity and love, and likewise by all the people; everyone marvelling to see Fathers from the land of the Portuguese. They were not in the least surprised at Paul having become a Christian, but rather are pleased and delighted thereat, both his relatives as those who are not so, since he has been in India and seen things which they here have never seen. And the Duke [Daimyo] of this land is well affected to him, and renders him much honor, and asked many questions concerning the customs, worth, and authority of the Portuguese and of their Empire in India; and Paulo gave him a very full account of everything, whereat the Duke was greatly contented.

Here they are not now surprised at people becoming Christians, and as a great part of them can read and write, they very soon learn the prayers; may it please God to give us tongue whereby we can speak to them of the things of God, for then we would reap much more fruit with His aid, grace, and favor. Now we are like so many statues among them, for they speak and talk to us about many things, whilst we, not understanding the language, hold our peace. And now we have to be like little children learning the language; God grant that we may likewise imitate them in true simplicity and purity of soul, striving by all means to become like them, both as regards learning the language as in showing the simplicity of children devoid of malice. And in this did God grant us great and notable favors in bringing us to these infidel lands, so that we should not neglect ourselves, since this land is wholly of idolaters and enemies of Christ, and we have none in whom we can confide or trust, save only in God, for here we have neither relatives nor friends nor acquaintances, nor even some Christian piety, but only foes of Him who made the heaven and earth; and for this cause are we forced to place all our faith, hope, and trust in Christ Our Lord, and not in any living creature, since, through unbelief, all are enemies of God.

Likewise it is necessary that we should give you an account of other favors which God hath granted us, teaching us through His mercy, so that you may help us in rendering thanks to God always for them. This is, that elsewhere the abundance of bodily provisions is often the reason whereby disordered appetites are given free rein, frequently despising the virtue of abstinence, which leads to the no little detriment of men's souls and bodies. This is the origin of the majority of corporal ills, and even spiritual, and men have much difficulty in finding a means of relief, and many find that the days of their life are shortened before obtaining it, suffering all kinds of bodily pains and torments, taking physic to cure themselves which gives them more distaste to swallow than enjoyment they received from the dainties which they ate and drank. God granted us a signal favor in bringing us to these lands which lack such abundancies, so that even if we wished to minister to our bodies with these superfluities, the country does not allow of it. They neither kill nor eat anything which they rear. Sometimes they eat fish; there is rice and corn, albeit little; there are numerous herbs, on which they live, and some fruit but not much. This people live wonderfully healthy lives and there are many aged. The Japanese are a convincing proof of how our nature can subsist on little, even if it is not a pleasing sustenance. We live in this land very healthy in body, God grant that we may be likewise in our souls. A great part of the Japanese are Bonzes, and these are strictly obeyed in the places where they are, even if their sins are manifest to all; and it seems to me that the reason why they are held in such esteem is because of their rigorous abstinence, for they never eat meat, nor fish, but only herbs, fruit, and rice, and this once a day and very strictly, and they are never given wine. There are many Bonzes and their temples are of but little revenue. By reason of their continual abstinence and because they have no intercourse with women (especially those who go dressed in black like clergy) on pain of death, and because they know how to relate some histories or rather fables of the things in which they believe, it seems to me they are held in great veneration. And it may well happen that since they and we feel so differently about God and the method of salvation, that we may be persecuted by them with something stronger than words. What we in these parts endeavor to do, is to bring people to the knowledge of their Creator and Saviour, Jesus Christ Our Lord. We live with great hope and trust in him to give us strength, grace, help, and favor to prosecute this work. It does not seem to me that the laity will oppose or persecute us of their own volition, but only if they are importuned by the Bonzes. We do not seek to quarrel with them, neither for fear of them will we cease to speak of the glory of God, and of the salvation of souls. They cannot do us more harm than God permits, and what harm comes to us through them is a mercy of God; if through them for His love, service, and zeal for souls, He sees good to shorten the days of our life, in order to end this continual death in which we live, our desires will be speedily fulfilled and we will go to reign forever with Christ. Our intentions are to proclaim and maintain the truth, however much they may contradict us, since God compels us to seek rather the salvation of our future than the safety of our present lives; we endeavoring with the grace and favor of Our Lord to fulfil this precept, He giving us internal strength to manifest the same before the innumerable idolatries which there are in Japan.

It is well that we should give you an account of our stay in Cangoxima [Kagoshima]. We arrived here at a season when the winds were contrary for going to Miaco, [Kyoto] which is the chief city of Japan, where the King and the greatest lords of the Kingdom reside. And there is no wind that will serve us to go thither, save only five months from now, and then we will go with the help of Our Lord. It is three hundred leagues from here to Miaco, according to what they tell us, and we are likewise told great things of that city, which is said to contain more than ninety thousand houses; there is also a great university frequented by students therein, which has six principal colleges and more than two hundred houses of Bonzes, and of others like friars who are called Ieguixu [Zen-shu], and of nuns who are called Hamacata [Amakata]. Besides this university of Miaco, there are five other chief universities whose names are these, Coya [Koya], Nenguru [Negoro], Feizan [Hieizan], Taninomine [Tamu no mine]. These are in the neighborhood of Miaco, and it is said that there are more than 3,500 students in each one of them. There is another university, a great way off, which is called Bandou [Bando, the Ashikaga Gakko] which is the best and biggest in Japan, and more frequented by students than any other. Bandou is a great lordship where there are six dukes, and a chief one among them, whom the others obey. This chief owes allegiance to the King of Japan who is the great King of Miaco. They tell us such things of the greatness of these lands and universities, that we would prefer to see them before affirming and writing them; and if things be as they tell us, then we will write of our experiences in detail. In addition to these principal universities, they say that there are many other smaller ones throughout the kingdom. During the year 1551, we hope to write you at length concerning the disposition that there is in Miaco and its universities for the knowledge of Jesus Christ Our Lord to be spread therein. This year two Bronzes are going to India who have studied in the universities of Bandou and Miaco, and with them many other Japanese to learn the things of our law.

On St. Michael's day we spoke with the duke of this land, who gave us great honor, saying that we should keep well the books in which was written the law of the Christians, and that if it was the true and good law of Jesus Christ, it would be troublesome to the Devil. A few days afterwards he gave leave to all his vassals that those who might wish to become Christians could do so. This good news I write at the end of the letter for your consolation, and that you may give thanks unto God our Lord. It seems to me that this winter we must occupy ourselves in making a declaration concerning the Articles of Faith in Japanese, somewhat copiously, for it to be printed (because all the principal persons here know how to read and write) so that our holy faith may be understood and spread throughout many parts, since we cannot go to all. Our dearest brother Paulo will translate faithfully into his own tongue everything which is necessary for the salvation of souls.

From Cangoxima, fifth of November of the year 1549.

Your most loving brother wholly in Christ,

FRANCISCO

APPENDIX II

THE RUTTER OF THE *Santa Cruz*
JULY 5, 1585–MARCH 30, 1586 [1]

A voyage made from Macau in China to the haven of Langasaque or Nagasaki in the Island of Japan in the ship called the *Santa Cruz*, the Captain being a Portingall called Francisco Pais, and the Gunner Dirck Gerritszoon of Enchuisen, in the Year of Our Lord 1585, written by the Pilot of the same ship.

5.vii.1585. The fifth of July Anno 1585 upon a Friday in the morning we set sail from the point that lyeth right against the Cloister of St. Francis minding to run to loofward [windward] from a round island or cliff, lying East-Southeast from thence; but because the wind was so scant we could not do it, so that we were forced to drive so to get through the channel of Lanton [Lantao] as we did. The depth that we found therein was from five to six fathoms of water, and that was close by the round island that lieth to seaward from the island of Lanton; and from thence forward it beginneth to be deeper being 18 to 20 fathom, and that depth we found until we were without the island called *A Ilha de Leme* [Lema Islands] that is the island of the arquebus [really, "rudder" or "helm"].

This island of Lanton, as you make towards it, hath a point, where the wind fell very scarce in such a manner that we could hardly keep off an island lying on the left hand of the channel if the stream had not been so strong, that it drave the ship overthwart it loofward, otherwise we had endured great labour and trouble to pass through the channel, because that towards night we were about 4 miles from the island Ilha do Leme; the course we held that night was East and East by South, because we had a sharp wind, having 25 and 20 fathom deep muddy ground; about sunrising we saw right before us the island of Branco, or the white cliff; and because of the depths aforesaid we guessed that we were about half a mile beyond it.

6.vii. The sixth of July being Saturday, we could not take the height of the sun because it was right over our heads, having a Southeast and South-Southeast wind, with very hot weather by day, but by night it was somewhat colder, we held our course East-Northeast, East, and East and by North, as the wind blew, and about noon we found 25–27 fathom water with small black sandy ground, being in sight of land, and at sun rising we saw the land of Lamon [Namoa], which is a long flat land like a table of plain field; on the East-Northeast side having a thin point of land reaching inward to the sea, and on the West-Southwest side there runneth out another thin point of sand into the sea, and hard by against the thickest part thereof, you see the form of a white place which is the island Lamon, to

---

[1] *Iohn Huighen Van Linschoten his Discours of Voyages unto ye Easte and West Indies* (London, 1598), chap. 36, pp. 392–396. I have modernized the spelling of other than place names, and have made a few changes in the punctuation where these appeared to be called for.

seaward whereof lieth three cliffs, lying at the end of the reef of the island of Lamon; there we cast forth our lead, and found 27 fathom water, with small, white and some black sand with small shells among it, being about 7 or 8 miles from the land.

7.vii. The seven of July being Sunday, we had a calm, and sometimes (but not much) Southeast and South-Southeast winds, holding our course East-Northeast, Northeast, and Northeast and by North, at 24 and 26 fathom water; and as soon as we had passed the island of Lamon, we presently had small thin white sand upon the ground with some shells, being in the morning about 7 miles from the land of Chincheo [Fukien], and saw the island that is like the island called Ilha dos Lymoins, that is the island of Lemons, lying by Malacca, and somewhat further we saw a thin land, with a large point standing upon it, which is said to be the Varella do Chinchon, that is the mark or rock of Chinchon [presumably the nan-t'ai-wu Tower near Amoy]. [*8.vii*] being upon the eighth day which was Monday, the next night following we had a calm, wherein the wind came North, being somewhat cold, with some showers of rain, but with a Southeast wind we had no rain, yet in the night time we had two claps of thunder out of the Southeast with lightning out of the Southeast and North parts.

9.vii. The ninth being Tuesday, we had the height of the sun at 23½ degrees, in the night having had the wind East-Southeast with a good gale, and all night we lay driving without sails, with an East and East-Southeast winds, and a good gale casting out our lead, and found 20 and 24 fathom deep, once having 18 fathom, where we found small white sand with some shells.

10.vii. In the morning very early we had a north wind, wherewith we wound eastward having nothing but the foresail and mizzen up, until evening, and at the depths aforesaid we took in our sails, minding to drive; the next day we saw land, which we had seen the day before, and it lay northwards from us, and half a point North and by West.

11.vii. The eleventh being Thursday we took not the height of the sun, because we lay driving without sails, with an East and East-Southeast winds, the waves coming Southeast, our shipping winding Northeast. This was by night but by day we had a Northeast and North-Northeast wind, in such manner, that sometimes we kept on the one side, and sometimes on the other, as wind and weather served, at 24 and 25 fathom deep, small white sand, and sometimes 18 fathom; the night before we had much lightning out of the West and South parts, being the thirteen day of the new moon, and the day before we had the height of the sun at 23½ degrees. The land we saw we could hardly discern, but we supposed it to be the land we had seen the other day.

12.vii. The twelfth day being Friday, we took not the height of the sun because we lay driving without sails, with an East-Southeast wind in the night time, and in the day we had it Northeast, at 24 and 20 fathom deep, and sometimes 18 fathom, with small thin white sand, the ground at 24 fathom, being somewhat greater sand, with some shells; when it began to be day, we were as we thought about 5 or 6 miles from land, and the night before we had much lightning round us, and in the morning some showers of rain without wind, the sky being thick and close, whereby it seemed the weather would change. About evening we had a Southeast wind, presently changing South-Southeast, whereupon we let fall our sails, holding our course Northeast and by East, and also East-Northeast, but most part Northeast, so that the depths began to be greater, and were 35 fathom, with small white sand, the moon as then being at the full, and the waves always running out of the Southeast, and with that wind we sailed for the space of five days together.

13.vii. The 13th being Saturday, we took the height of the sun at 24 degrees, that night running East-Northeast till morning, then sailing East and East by North, and found we had sailed 20 miles, being 8 miles from the coast of China, and in the morning we saw land upon the other side; the ground on that side was white, thin and some black sand, and about sun setting we cast out our lead, and found 35 fathom deep, with very fine black sand.

14.vii. The 14th being Sunday, we took the height of the sun, being scarce 25 degrees, having a Southwest wind with very good weather, holding our course Northeast, and Northeast and by North, all that night at 37 fathom deep, with very thin sand, some black muddy ground; and at the last watch in the morning we found muddy ground at the same depth of 37 fathom, mixed with black sand; and when day began to appear, we saw land, being part of the coast of China, being about 4, 5 or 6 miles from it, and we discovered the Lagarto with the two sisters, that is the Crocodile islands so called; and so we cast out our lead, and found 42 fathom deep muddy ground, and somewhat sandy, and the same day also we saw the island Formosa lying by Lequeo Pequeno, or little Liu Kiu, and then the wind seemed as though it would have blown fuller.

15.vii. The 15th day being Monday, we took the height of the sun at 25½ degrees, and in the night we had the wind North, with very good weather, running about to the Northwest, and we ran East-Northeast, Northeast, and Northeast to East, and when it began to be day, we saw land, being the end of the island Formosa, or the Fair Island, which is a long and low land, broken or rent in the middle, which seemeth to be a breach, but it is nothing else but as I said before; and presently after eastward we saw another higher land, which is islands called Ilhas dos Reis Magos [nowadays called Pinnacle, Crag, and Agincourt off northeast coast of Formosa], that is, the islands of the three Kings; we passed along by about 7 or 8 miles from them, and that night we had 34 fathom deep, and desiring to know what depth we found, being in sight of the land aforesaid, we found above 40 fathom, the aforesaid land lying East-Southeast, from us, being muddy ground; that day we had a sharp wind of the monsoon, but it held no longer than till evening, and then it was calm again, and so held till morning, and then we had it Northwest, so running about from the West till it came Southwest, and continued till night, and then it was calm, being Tuesday.

16.vii. The 16th being in sight of the islands aforesaid, the same day we had the height of the sun at 26 degrees less ⅙ degree, and the end of the great island lay East, and East and by South from us, and the little island East-Southeast. This little island is higher on the South-Southwest side than on the Southwest side, and the point or hook of the Southwest part, hath a breach or rent, to the which, the nearer you approach, the greater it seemeth.

This island is very high in the middle, and descendeth downward towards the end. The Northeast point is lower than the Southeast, so that it maketh as it were a tongue sticking out, which is very low. From thence East-Northeastward are certain islands showing like cliffs. The depth in that place is 25 fathom muddy ground.

17.vii. Wednesday being the 17th, we had a North-Northeast wind, and then it came Northeast, and began to blow so stiff, that we were forced to strike all our sails, letting the ship drive all that day Southeastward, and by night we willed the man at the helm to steer Northwest, [*18.vii.*] and about morning the wind began to blow so stiff with so great waves, that we were forced to go with half our foresail, with all our cords well bound and made fast, and the storm or typhoon was so great, that we were forced to bind all that we had on board, else it was presently stricken in pieces. This tempest began first North-Northeast, and so ran about till it was North-Northwest. At the departure whereof it was so boisterous, that the waves seemed to touch the clouds. This was upon Thursday, being the 22nd day of the new moon; the next night following the wind came west, but because as then the sea ran very high, we let not our sails fall, but in the morning we had the wind Southwest; and then we let fall our sails, minding to follow on our course with great joy throughout our ship, thinking certainly we had the winds of the monsoon, but towards night it was calm again, and then we had a North wind, holding our course Eastward, but not long after it was altogether calm, notwithstanding the waves ran out of the South, so that about two of the clock we had the winds Southeast, wherewith we hoisted sails, running Northeast, and Northeast and by North, and when it began to be day, we saw the island called Dos Reis Magos (that is, the three Kings) lying south about 10 or 12 miles from us, [*21.vii.*] and there I found the height of the sun to be 26– ⅔ degrees being the one and twenty day of the month.

The day before we saw the island Formosa, which is a very high land, and seemeth to reach into the clouds, and there we had 45 and 50 fathom water, muddy ground. On Friday at sunrise we cast out our lead, and found 21 fathom with black sand. The first token that we had of the aforesaid tempest, was a small rainbow close by the horizon on the sea side, being a fair russet colour, with two other greater rainbows; whereof the point or end showed almost like the cloud called Olhos de Bois (that is, cats eyes) [ox eyes in reality] which are small clouds, which at the first show, seem no greater than a man's fist; about the Cape De bona Speranza, which by the sailors that sail in the East Indian Seas are much marked, for they are tokens of sudden falling tempests and cruel storms, as in the voyage from India to Portugal is already declared; wherefor it is good to be advertised thereof, the better to look unto it, and to watch for them, to the which end I thought it not from the matter to speak of them in this place. But returning unto our matter,—I advertise you that when you are come into those countries, as long as the wind cometh out of the north, and so Southwest, you are to make no account thereof, for it will presently be North-Northeast and East, but when it is calm, then you shall have a Southeast wind, and then South and Southwest, which are the monsoon and winds of that time, but if it begin again to be calm, it may so fall out that it will be East-Southeast, but it will presently be Southeast again, with fair weather, which we also found in this monsoon of July, Anno 1585.

22.vii. Monday the 22nd day, we took the height of the Sun at 27½ degrees having a Southeast and South-Southeast wind, with good weather, and held our course Northeast, and as I guessed we had run (after we had fair weather and wind) about 22 miles, being from the land of China from the Cape called Sumbor [Sungmen, northeast of Wenchow in Chekiang province] about 12 miles, being yet about an hundred miles from the island of Meaxuma [Meshima] and that day we cast out the lead and found 55 and 57 fathom water, and saw many black and white sea fowls that hide thereabout, the black birds by the Portingales being called Alcatrases.

23.vii. The 23rd being Tuesday, we had very good weather, in such manner, that at that mealtide we sailed about 15 miles, being about 12 miles from the firm land and found 51 fathom, with white and black sand.

24.vii. Wednesday being the 24th day, we had the height of the sun at 29 degrees, with an East-Southeast and Southeast wind and good weather, holding our course Northeast, and Northeast and by North, and sometimes (but not much) Northeast and by East. I made my account to have holden Northeast, and by North, and so to have sailed 16 miles, being yet from the island of Meaxuma about 70 miles, lying Northeast from us, and there we cast out our lead and found 49 fathom deep, sandy and muddy ground.

25.vii. Thursday the 25 of July, we took not the height of the sun, because we lay driving without sails with an East wind, winding Southward, and so held till the 26 day, and drave westwards, finding two fathom less in our depth.

26.vii. The 26 we wound Northward without sails, yet not long after we let our foresail fall, (but wholly against my mind) but only at the importunate desire of the Chinese pilot, saying that the same day we should have the wind larger, which was not so, but clean contrary, so that all the way we made in that sort was more troublesome unto us; wherefore it is better for such as find themselves in those countries of 29 degrees, to stay for Southeast winds, and then to run North-Northeast, Northeast and Northeast and by North, because the waters and streams run very strong towards Liampo [Ningpo], and when you are under 30 and 31 degrees, having a South-Southeast wind, then you shall have great labour and much pain to get the island Meaxuma, for so it happened unto us, because the wind was so strong that we could bear but our foresail, and half the main topsail, as also because the sea ran very high and hollow, and put our ship out of course, and that the stream ran Southeast. This is about 25 or 30 miles from the island Meaxuma.

But as soon as the wind came full, whereby we ran East, East and by North, and East-Northeast, at 40 and 34 fathom water, the ground being very small sand, holding as much eastward as possibly we might, and sometimes East and by South, whereby we began to have more depth, yet very slowly that it would have wearied us if the ship had gone hardly forward, but because the water ran very hollow, whereby the ship was not very well steered (wherein we only put our trust) at the last we had 50 and 60 fathom deep muddy ground, and then 70 and 75 fathom with small thin sand, and a little after that we had 80 fathom deep, but I believe that chanced because the lead hung somewhat backward. At that casting, the ground was somewhat greater sand, and because (as we made account) we were near unto the island Meaxuma, I presently took in the main top and mizzen in, contrary to the opinion of some pilots, every quarter or watch in the night, cast the lead continually out, and presently in the morning we hoisted the main topsail up again, and sailing so a little time we saw land, which was part of the island Meaxuma, although other pilots that were in the ship said it was the island of Guoto [Goto], but therein they were as perfect as in all the rest of their judgements.

This island of Meaxuma, in the first discovery had a high slope land, lying lowest to the Southwest, and when you are right against it, at the end thereof you find a cliff which showeth like a Fortress; it was told us, that not far from that cliff there lieth a cliff [reef] under the water, whereupon the water breaketh.

31.*vii.* This island of Meaxuma showeth like three or four islands, whereof the first on the Southwest side showeth as I said before, having on the top or uttermost part thereof two round hills like women's breasts, or like a saddle; the other two islands or likeness thereof, in the middle way, are like great cliffs, with many rocks and crags sticking out like organ pipes, and the other island or likeness of an island lying Northeast, showeth like a very long, but not over high cliff; we ran along by the island holding our course Northeast, about two miles beyond it, and when we left Meaxuma because the wind ran Southeast, then we ran Northeast, Northeast and by East, and East-Northeast, and in the morning they said that we had the length of the land of Amacusa [Amakusa], and being to leeward we espied a great thick land, lying close by the island Cabexuma [Kabashima]. This island *Cabexuma* is long flat land, very smooth, on the north side having a cliff; this was the last of July, and the same day we entered into the haven of Langasaque [Nagasaki], which is the haven and place where at this day the Portingales have their most traffic.

Another voyage made out of the Haven of Nagasaki from the island of Japan to Macau in China, in the *Santa Cruz*, the Gunner being Dirck Gerritszoon of Enchuisen, in Anno 1586.[2]

20.iii.   The 20 of March we departed out of the haven of Nagasaki, it being the first of the new moon, upon a Thursday with a Northeast and North-Northeast wind, and by nine of the clock in the morning, we were as far as the island Dos Cavallos [Iwojima], running West-Southwest; and being two miles beyond the island Dos Cavallos, we had a calm, and then the wind came Northwest, in such sort, that we ran Southwest, and Southwest and by West and sometimes half a strike with a slack wind. The next day [*21.iii.*] in the morning we saw the islands of Corequyn [?] and Goto, and about 8 of the clock in the forenoon, we saw the island Meaxuma, so that we saw those three islands all at once, and about twilight, we were East-Southeast and West-Southwest, with the island of Meaxuma and so held our course Southwest, having a hard Northeast wind with rain, the air being very dark and close, yet the clouds came out of the Southwest. [*23.iii.*] Upon Sunday we cast out the lead, and found somewhat more than 40 fathom water, muddy ground, and was about 40 miles from Meaxuma. This depth is a bank lying in the middle way betweene the island Meaxima and the Cape of Sumbor in the firm land of China.

24.iii.   Upon Monday the 24th day we took not the height of the sun, because we saw it not, having so small a wind, that the ship might steer upright, and because we made little way, we cast out the lead and found forty fathom muddy ground; this was at noon, and at night about sun setting we cast it out again, and found five and fifty fathom, whereby we perceived that we began to pass over a bank; at that time we had all one wind being Northeast, and North-Northeast, with a good blast, and yet the clouds came Southwest and South-Southeast, so strong that they put us in fear, doubting the wind would be there, but we had certain men in our ship that had seen and found it so in that place, and yet no alteration, whereby they put us in some comfort, in such sort that we followed on our course with that wind. [*25.iii.*] Upon Tuesday at noon, we took the height of the sun, not full 29 degrees, having not long before as I guessed, marked one point in the card, and esteemed we had sailed a hundred miles from the haven of Langasaque, but by the sun it was not so.

26.iii.   The 26th being Wednesday, we took not the height of the sun,

---

[2] *Ibid.,* chap. 41, pp. 400–402.

because it was a close day, but we had a good Northeast wind, and made good way, so that we seemed to make 30 miles in any one mealtide, but I made account but of 25 miles, because we thought the ship sailed not over-fast; that day we saw many cuttle bones driving upon the water, and held our course Southwest, till morning; and because the wind began to be stiff, I thought it good to make towards the land to know it, therefore as day appeared we ran West till it was evening without knowing Land, by reason of the mistiness of the air, but by the depths of our guessing, we thought we were about 5 or 6 miles from the land, our depth was 37 fathom; and being towards night with cloudy weather, we ran Southwest, and Southwest and by South, all that night, and when day came being Thursday we guessed to be over against the Lagarto or Crocodile (a cliff so called) about five or six miles to seaward from it, but we found it to be somewhat more.

27.iii.   Thursday being the 27th, as soon as day appeared we ran West towards the land, and about four of the clock in the afternoon, we saw the land, being the islands Dos Camaroins (that is, the islands of Granata) [should be *prawns*] those islands are not too high; as soon as we saw them, we held our course South-Southwest, and having sailed a little way, we saw another round island called Ilha de Baboxyn [unidentified] which lay right before us; as soon as we saw it, we presently ran South to shun it, because we were not above a quarter of a mile from it; there we found so strong a stream and course of water which ran with us, that in short time we were two or three miles from the aforesaid island, in such manner, that all that night we ran South, and South and by West, and South-Southwest, and when the moon rose we held our course Southwest.

28.iii.   The 28th being Friday, about morning we began to run West-Southwest, West, and West and by South, and at noon thereabouts we cast out the lead, and found 29 fathoms muddy ground, and running so with that course for a little time, we saw land, but it was so close and misty, that we could not know it; but about two or three of the clock in the afternoon it began to clear up and then we knew it to be the island of Chinchon [Amoy] being North from us, and there we cast out the lead, and found 19 fathom water, sandy ground, and not long after we saw the whole coast and firm land of China; and so we ran all night at the depths of 19, 20 and 22 fathom with so clear and bright a sky, that almost all the night we saw the coast, and when day began to appear, we were somewhat beyond the islands called Ruy Lobo, and presently thereupon we saw the island of Lamon, there we began to have certain storms; as I guess it is from Ilhas de Ruy Lobo, to the island of Lamon ten miles; by the island of Lamon we saw the water shine and burn to seaward, in such sort that we passed close by the reef; those that come from Japan must first pass by the island, and then by the reef; this reef lieth Northeast and Southwest, and is danger-ous for those that sail from Macau to Japan; we ran about three miles from it with a strong Northeast, and East-Northeast wind, so that we made good way, whereby it seemed we made 50 miles in one mealtide. This strong stream and stiff water cometh (as we were informed) out of the river of Tancoan, and continueth till you be past the island Branco, and being past it, the stream runneth presently towards the island Ilha de Leme, which lieth close by Macau; from Lamon we ran West-Southwest, and in truth we found the way from Lamon to Ilha Branco very short, for by night we stroke all our sails, and so lay driving without sails, winding Southwest, always at the depth of five and twenty and six and twenty fathom water; and at the midnight watch we began to hoist up our mainsail and our foresail, in that manner running West to get to 20 fathom deep, which is the middle of the channel where we must pass through, and in the morning we saw the island Do Leme, (that is the island of the arquebus [sic for rudder or helm] lying somewhat on the larboard of us. This island Do Leme, if you go East and West upon it, seemeth very small, and the deeper you are within the channel, the bigger it sheweth, in the entry whereof on the right hand it hath two islands or cliffs, and from thence forward, the islands begin to lie on a row till you come to Macau, as I said in another place.

APPENDIX III

I, Ruy Mendez de Figueiredo, certify that in July, 1596, I went to Japan
as captain-major, taking with me in my ship, Bishop Dom Pedro Martins,
with another six padres and a brother of the Company of Jesus. We reached
the port of Nagasaki where the local padres and Christians received the said
bishop with much love and joy. All the time that I was in Japan, which
was more than seven months, I saw that the fathers and brothers of the
Company who dwell in those parts were living unmolested in the lands of
Omura, Arima, and Amakusa, where they had over twenty houses among
which the padres were distributed, supervizing all that Christianity. They
had a college with more than fifty persons of the Company in Amakusa,
and a seminary in the fief of Arima, wherein they educated more than a
hundred youths in the study of diverse sciences and good habits. I went
to see it with the bishop, and we were received both by the inmates and by
the local Christians with great entertainment and hospitality, and I returned
highly pleased with that seminary and with all that Christianity, having seen
the great fruit made therein; and the bishop was equally pleased, for he
told me that he had never expected to find such a thing in Japan. I also
learned that in the Kyoto district there were other padres who were making
many conversions and who had a flourishing Christianity under their charge.
The bishop of Japan went thither during my stay, and he returned very
pleased with it, judging from what he told me of the people and Christianity
of that region. Both there, as in all other parts whither he went to visit the
Christians, there were always great gatherings of them who received him
with much love and joy, and he confirmed as many thousands of them as he
could under the circumstances. Although Taikosama, Lord of Japan, had
forbidden that any converts should be made or that any padres should stay
in Japan, save only a few in Nagasaki to help the Portuguese, withal they
not only stay continuously cultivating the whole Christianity, but they have
even made fresh converts of many thousands of souls. During the time that
I was in Japan, news came that many had been converted in the Kyoto

---

[1] British Museum, Add. MSS 9858, fols. 4–5. This is not the original but a contemporary
copy, and is unpublished so far as I know. I have selected this affidavit for reproduction since
it is slightly less prolix than that of the Bishop of Japan, Dom Pedro Martins, the signed
original of which (dated Macao, November 17, 1597) will be found in British Museum,
Add. MSS 9860, fols. 55–56, and a contemporary copy in MS 9858 fols. 1–4. A third copy
was reproduced by Colin-Pastells, in *Labor Evangélica*, Vol. II, 697–698. The Bishop's
testimony is substantially the same, but he blames Fray Juan Pobre, O.F.M., for dissuading
Landecho from trying to bring the battered *San Felipe* round to Nagasaki. Incidentally,
Mendez de Figueiredo was evidently anxious to keep in with both sides, since he gave the
Franciscans an affidavit affirming the genuineness of the miracles wrought through their
martyrs, which the Jesuits had dismissed as spurious (*AIA*, Vol. XIX [1923], pp. 166–169).

district, including some great lords, through the fathers of the Company. All this was done with great caution, divine services not being celebrated publicly, but secretly in the Churches, whilst they carried out all their other religious functions in the same way, preaching, administering the sacraments, and indoctrinating the Christians with great diligence and profit. They also adapted their clothing when it was necessary, in order to avoid annoying Taikosama and his governors, who would otherwise have further imperilled Christianity. This method seemed to me very sound and good, and in close conformity with prudence and the necessities of the time; because they went about amongst the Christians, and did not fail them in anything in spite of these precautions; and although Taikosama and his minions knew it, yet they were satisfied with the show of respect for their orders. I further knew that the barefooted friars of St. Francis, who had first come from Manila to Japan two or three years before, proceeded in another manner, holding their services very publicly and preaching openly in their Church at Kyoto. Both the local Christians and the fathers of the Company took this ill, owing to the danger in which it would place them if it came to Taikosama's knowledge. I spoke with some of the friars who were in Nagasaki, and I found them always very fixed in their ways; and so delighted at being in Japan that one of them told me that even if His Holiness should again order them to leave Japan they were determined not to do so, but to stay in Japan in any event until His Majesty should ordain otherwise. I did not like to hear them say this, and if they had proceeded differently and behaved in the same way as the fathers of this Company, probably neither would some have been killed and others deported from Japan, nor would the Christian community and the fathers of the Company be in such trouble and peril as they are now.

At this time, a Castilian ship which was bound from Manila to New Spain was driven by a storm to a kingdom of Japan called Tosa, which lies over a hundred leagues away from the port of Nagasaki where we were. When it tried to enter a port to refit, it grounded on a sandbank whereon it was wrecked, and the lord of the soil [Chosokabe] would not allow any of the cargo to be touched until he had given news of the event to Taikosama. The captain-major of the said ship thereupon sent some men to Kyoto to the friars of St. Francis in order to negotiate with Taikosama for the salvage of their goods and ship. He did not write either to me, or to the bishop, or to the fathers of the Company, whether in these southern regions or in Kyoto, on this matter. However, the bishop who was then there, knowing what had happened, and being desirous of helping the Castilians, summoned the friars' superior and those who had come as envoys, telling them that he and the padres were ready to help in so far as they could, outlining some methods which seemed suitable to him. The [Franciscan] Commissary answered that neither his lordship nor any of the padres should intervene in the business, since he had everything virtually arranged. All this was told me by the said bishop when he returned to Nagasaki. But the friars did not negotiate properly, and covetousness gradually took hold of Taikosama, together with some distrust he conceived from the pilot-major of the same ship saying something very thoughtless to one of Taikosama's governors whom he had sent there, concerning the conquests of the Castilians and their method of proceeding therein, adding that they sent religious ahead to make Christian converts who afterwards joined with the invading Castilian forces. He therefore ordered all the ship's cargo to be confiscated, which was done even to the very clothes which the men wore. When the said Governor [Masuda] returned from Tosa to Kyoto and gave Taikosama an account of what the Pilot had said about the conquests and the sending of religious abroad, the friars were likewise accused of having been sent for this purpose and of having built a Church in Kyoto against his edict, and of preaching and converting Christians publicly,—Taikosama at once said that they should all be killed. Guards were placed forthwith both on the friar's houses as on those of the fathers of the Company who were in Kyoto and Osaka. It was common knowledge and report that he had originally ordered all the padres to be killed, but he subsequently stated that he only wished to punish the Castilian friars from the Philippines and their Christian converts. He finally ordered the crucifixion of six friars, and three Japanese brothers of the Company along with them, besides another seventeen Japanese Christians. All of these were ordered to be sent from Kyoto to Nagasaki to be crucified there, as we all saw. His governors handed over to me another four friars who were in Nagasaki, with orders to deport them to China, as I did in my ship, since Taikosama did not wish them to stay in Japan. He again issued an edict that nobody was to dare to preach our law nor to make Christians under pain of death. Since that time, it has been necessary for the fathers of the Company to retire themselves much more than they had done hitherto. I left them in this condition when I sailed for China, when all those who were crucified were still on their crosses, since Taikosama's governors allowed nobody to take them down. And whilst I am now in this city of Macao, a sea-going junk came from Japan with some of the Castilians who had been wrecked in the aforesaid ship, from whom we learnt that the fathers of the Company are now in dire peril, and were forced to dismantle the college and the seminary, as Taikosama had ordered his governors to embark the fathers of the Company in the ship, since he did not want any to remain, save only a few in Nagasaki on account of the said ship. As this message came just when the ship was on the point of sailing, it was not carried out, but the fathers and all the Christians were left in a sorry plight. And forasmuch as part of all these things aforesaid I saw with my own eyes, and part I knew for certain, since they were publicly and notoriously known throughout all Japan, and since the Father-

Procurator of the Company who resides in Macao asked me for this affidavit, I witnessed it and swear on the Holy Evangelists that everything which I have said truly happened. In Macao on the 14th November of the year 1597.

RUY MENDEZ DE FIGUEIREDO

AFFIDAVIT OF PAULO HITOMI, 1596 [2]

To the Padres of the Companhia.

We are unquestionably Kirishitans belonging to the Companhia. Hence we shall never participate in any other Order, even though Bateren of other Orders may come here. This is our Oath.

On the third day of the last month of the year of
Our Lord 1595 [corresponds to January 2, 1596].

PAULO HITOMI

[Paulo Hitomi also noted on the Japanese date corresponding to October 5, 1596: "In view of the unlawful acts committed since recent times by the Bateren of the Orders other than the Companhia, an admonition is proclaimed not to listen to their words." The "admonition" was of course proclaimed by the Jesuits.]

BISHOP PEDRO MARTINS' ATTITUDE TOWARD FRIARS, 1593 [3]

I, Fray Francisco de Vellerino, religious of this Province of San Gregorio, state that concerning what is asked of me by my prelate in fullfilment of the obedience which is obligatory to me, what I know is as follows . . . Besides this, [Bishop Martins] discussing with me sometimes the things of Japan, he asked me why Padre Fray Juan Cobos of the Order of St. Dominic had gone to Japan, not having done anything there, neither had his visit been of the slightest use. He further asked what was the object of four religious of our Order in going to Japan, and who had sent them into another's household? I gave him some reasons therefore, and reminded his lordship that Our Lord when He sent forth his apostles to preach, told them "Go ye into all the world and preach the Gospel unto every creature," nor did he except Japan from this injunction, but said "Go ye into all the world." I added that all the religious acted thus. To this he retorted that they had gone without

---

[2] Masaharu Anesaki, "Two Kirishitan Documents Discovered at Takatsuki," in *PIA*, Vol. IX (1933), pp. 285–288. There is no question of the genuineness of this revealing document, a photographic reproduction of which will be found in Professor Anesaki's article whence the English translation is taken. The date is in a curious mixture of the Japanese lunar calendar and the Christian era. Paulo Hitomi was probably the father (or some other relation) of that Pedro Hitomi who emigrated from Fushimi to Semboku *ca.* 1610 and founded a Christian community in the northeast (cf. above, p. 335). This affidavit proves conclusively the truth of the Franciscans' oft-repeated accusation that the Jesuits would not allow their converts to have any truck with the friars from the Philippines. The original was dictated by Padre Organtino, S.J.

[3] Bishop Martins, S. J., reached Nagasaki on August 14, 1596, and lost no time in trying to put into effect his threats to expel the friars from Japan. Cf. the documents printed in *AIA*, Vol. XIII (1920), pp. 40–60, whence the above extract is translated (pp. 43–44).

licenses. I answered that on the contrary they had enough and to spare, since they took a Brief of Sixtus V, and many other Briefs and opinions of learned men, adding that the Brief which the Company had obtained concerning Japan was not valid, since it had not been endorsed by the Council of the Indies. He replied that the [Jesuits] possession was an old one and was sufficient for them, adding that he would go to Japan and would not allow a single friar to stay there, and so forth and so on. Whence I inferred that he would go to Japan with the intention of creating some disturbance.

FRAY GONÇALO GARCIA, O.F.M., ON JESUIT INTRIGUES 1593–1596 [4]

Item. The said Governor [Maeda Genni Hoin Munehisa, governor or Shoshidai of Kyoto] having said that he would give us a patent authorizing us to stay in Nagasaki, a port for Manila and the headquarters of the Portuguese in this kingdom, when he was asked for it again, he said that if the governor who was in charge of the district wherein Nagasaki was situated, put obstacles in our way, as indeed he did, he did not do it of his own volition but because others whispered in his ear, asking him not to allow the religious of St. Francis to settle there; that if we were to be allowed there, it should only be in the house and convent of the Company and as its guests. He further said that our own compatriots were inimical to us and not the Japanese . . . Some days later I saw him again, and he repeated that our own compatriots were our enemies and more opposed to us than the natives; and it was they who crossed us, frustrated us, and tied his hands with documents and bribes; adding that they had many who spoke for them and who acted as their advocates, whilst we had nobody. They said that we were despicable people who had come by a route which was of no advantage to the Japanese, whereas the padres brought the Macao ship where they listed. Moreover, he said that they had asked him not to allow us to stay for more than four years in Japan; adding that it was an affront to the king when we who were ostensibly ambassadors maintained hospitals and washed lepers' feet. He said that in order to state this they had taken as intermediaries the Japanese, Harada and Hasegawa, to whom we had been entrusted by order of the King, and that we should [not?] carry on with the hospitals.

HIDEYOSHI'S ATTITUDE TO THE FRIARS, ca. 1595 [5]

Maeda Genni Hoin, the Shoshidai of Kyoto is said to have told the Franciscan Commissary, Fray Pedro Bautista, that Hideyoshi "when he pro-

---

[4] *AIA*, Vol. VI (1916), pp. 246–247 and *ibid.*, Vol. XIII (1920), pp. 39–40. Fray Gonçalo Garcia was a Eurasian Franciscan, born at Bassein in Portuguese India. He joined the Order after spending many years as a trader in Japan, and was their best linguist. He was one of those martyred in February, 1597.

[5] Extract from the *Relación* of Fray Jeronimo de Jesus O.F.M., as printed in *AIA*, Vol. XIII (1920), p. 30. The allegation is repeated in anonymous "Breve Relación de todo lo suc-

hibited the padres of the Company from making Christians, it was not from
hatred which he bore to the religion, because that seemed good to him; but
it was because the padres of the Company were only trying to make converts amongst the great lords, and he was afraid that by this means they
would become masters of the kingdom, and this was the reason why he
ordered their expulsion. Wherefore, since we did not make converts save
only among the poor people, we had nothing to fear, and the King would
not mind in the least; confining himself to prohibiting the conversion of
the nobility, samurai and merchants."

EXTRACT FROM ANDRES DE CUAÇOLA'S AFFIDAVIT OF JUNE 25, 1598 [6]

He heard the interpreter tell the General [Landecho] and this witness
and the other Spaniards, that in the kingdom of Miaco [Kyoto] where the
emperor of that land resides, that two Theatines and three Portuguese had
told the said emperor that the Spaniards who had been cast away in Tosa,
had come in fraudulent and malicious wise to seize the land, and that they
were not vassals of the Portuguese king, and that they had used this same
deceit in Peru, New Spain, and the Philippines. And this witness saw that
on this account the Japanese seized the cargo which the Spaniards had in the
said ship. And to say that the martyrs of Japan were to blame for the loss of
the said cargo is flat contrary to the truth, and a false version of what really
transpired. On the contrary, it was for defending the rights of the vassals of
their king and liege lord that they were crucified; because at the time when
this witness and the other Spaniards reached the said kingdom, the blessed
martyrs were living very quietly and peaceably in the court city of the said
emperor who allowed them to preach the Gospel and who gave them a yearly
allowance of rice.

FRAY JUAN POBRE'S TESTIMONY ON THE PILOT-MAJOR OF THE SAN FELIPE [7]

It will now be right, Christian and fond reader, as I stated in Chapter XXIV,
folio 106 verso, to seek to clarify the matter for our good or ill since the

cedido acerca de los Frailes de San Francisco en Jappon," summarized in Maggs Bros., *Cata-
logue, No. 515* (1929), pp. 12–20, which is one of the best contemporary accounts of the
Franciscan mission in 1593–1597. Maeda was guilty of exaggeration if he really said that
Hideyoshi did not actively dislike Christianity. It is worth noting that, unlike Ieyasu, the
Taiko did *not* encourage the conversion of merchants.

[6] Andres de Cuaçola was a Philippine crown treasury official who was the *escribano*
(purser) on board the *San Felipe*, and thus an eyewitness of what he relates. Another extensive narrative by him, bitterly hostile to the Jesuits (whom he calls Theatines) and
Portuguese, is summarized in English translation in Maggs Bros., *Catalogue No. 515* (1929),
pp. 5–11. The present extract is taken from his deposition as printed in *AIA*, Vol. VI (1916),
p. 293. The original manuscript is in the Archives at Seville (AIS, 68-1-42).

[7] Fray Juan Pobre, O.F.M., "Istoria de la pérdida y descubrimiento del galeón San Phelipe
con el glorioso martirio y gloriosos Mártires del Japón," MS of 431 leaves, most of it

galleon was already lost and the cargo was confiscated. You will surely remember that it was related in this true history how when Fray Juan Pobre departed from the oratory of Belem [at Osaka], where the holy martyrs Fray Martin and Fray Felipe then were, he had written a letter to the holy Fray Pedro at Kyoto, in which he said,—"Brother, you will have realized that the suspicions which we had there have been verified. Brother Fray Martin has told me how the governor is going to confiscate the Spaniards' property. If this is true, you will agree that you should do all you could in the matter, and especially try to reveal the truth to Taikosama, since we have no other witness in our favor." The holy Commissary with his beloved Fray Gonçalo [Garcia] did all he could; so that although nobody would venture to speak or remonstrate with Taikosama, yet the friars of St. Francis did so, and going to him once they said, "Sire, have pity on the Spaniards at Urado." The holy Brother Gonçalo went with João Rodriguez and said to [Maeda] Genni-Hoin that he should remember that Portuguese and Spaniards alike were subjects of the same king. The governor replied "Why didn't you tell me that before?" The holy Fray Pedro Bautista gave him a gift of 100 pesos which a good Christian named Cosme Joya had lent him, so that Maeda might do something for the Spaniards at Urado. He did write a letter to Masuda at Urado, but they immediately arrested the friars as stated previously. This letter reached Urado after the tyrant had confiscated the cargo and the gold, which was about eight or ten days before. When he [Masuda] received the letter, he summoned the general, who was accompanied by the Ensign Cotelo and by two or three others, and said to him:—"One of the governors of Kyoto has just written me a letter, in which he tells me that we should not harm you, since you are not the sort of people that they said you were." "And what did they say?" asked Cotelo.

---

written in Pobre's own hand. Cf. Lorenzo Pérez, O.F.M., "Fray Juan Pobre de Zamora su relación sobre la pérdida del Galeón San Felipe y martyrio de San Pedro Bautista y compañeros," *Erudición Ibero-Ultramarino*, Vol. II (1931), pp. 217–235. The relevant passages are transcribed on pages 219–223 of Perez' article under the subtitle "Origen de la Leyenda de Urado." Both Fray Pobre and his editor overlook the fact that the pilot's statement of the close connection between Church and State in colonial Spain, irrespective of when it was made, did much to inflame Hideyoshi's suspicions, whether or not these were originally awakened by the Portuguese, as the Franciscans state and the Jesuits deny. I have modernized the spelling of Japanese personal and place names.

Just as the Portuguese and Jesuits blamed the Spaniards and friars for the loss of the *San Felipe*'s cargo and the execution of the Franciscans in February, 1597, so the latter were equally emphatic in blaming the former as the real, if to some extent involuntary, culprits. Fray Diego de Guevara, O.S.A., Fray Marcelo de Ribadeneira, O.F.M., and Fray Juan Pobre, O.F.M., all of whom had been in Japan at that time, swore on oath at Manila, that all efforts to expel the friars from Japan "were undoubtedly owing to the intrigues and efforts of the padres of the Company, who are working for the same end to this day; adding that although the Jesuits wanted all the other religious to leave Japan, they did not think that the tyrant [Hideyoshi] would go so far as to inflict the death penalty on them as he did do, but would be contented with their mere expulsion from Japan." ("Relacion del martyrio que padecieron en el Japon y en la ciudad de Nangasaque el ano de 1597, seis frayles de San Francisco y otros 20 Cristianos Japones," in *AIA*, Vol. XIII [1920], p. 174.) This seems to me to be as near the truth as we shall get.

"They told Taikosama that you were pirates who came to spy out his ports." He said no more then. The Spaniards asked him,—"Who told you this?" He replied that two fathers of the Company and three Portuguese or three fathers of the Company and two Portuguese, adding "but take care; with all this, you must still give me all the gold, because another will come after me, who will treat you worse than I." To which they answered that they had already given him all the gold and silver, amounting to about 30,000 pesos, more or less. Ten days later, he ordered half of the goods to be laden on board fifty big fune and sent to Kyoto. Meanwhile another fifty were being loaded, and by way of diverting himself in his work, he liked to meet our people, and summoned some Spaniards to play checkers or cards with him and to teach him to play chess. He also liked to watch them fence. Some banjoes and guitars had been found, and he sent for someone who could play and sing to them. Fray Juan Pobre said "sing 'By the Waters of Babylon We Sat Down and Wept,' " etc.

He then summoned the pilot and asked him how the ship had come thither and how it was steered at sea. He was told, by the sea-card and astrolabe. He ordered them to be brought, and as he asked questions about the chart the pilot replied, showing him the way from Spain to Mexico, from Mexico to Luzon and from Luzon to Japan. When he saw Japan so small on the chart, that is smaller than a thumb, he was astonished at seeing it so small and could not believe it. And as the other lands and seas which he saw were almost all those of our Catholic King, he asked how he owned so much, and the pilot told him that he had much more still. Masuda, astonished, asked "Why do they take padres with them?" The pilot replied that they took them to hear their confessions and such things like shriving the dying, adding that they also took them so that if they reached some lands where they wanted to make Christians, they could make them by means of these padres.

Now it seems that either the interpreter did not translate this properly, or else the tyrant misunderstood it, and the pilot has been greatly blamed for it ever since; but in truth he was not to blame, and if he was a little careless it was because he was thoughtless, but he was well-intentioned. However, whether he was well or ill-intentioned made no difference, since the harm was already done, both as regards the cargo of the ship wrecked at Urado, as in what the bishop had said at Kyoto. There is therefore no reason to blame the pilot, who was blameless. As the pilot continued his explanation of the chart, Masuda asked whose were the Portuguese Indies? The pilot replied, "Our King's." The governor retorted, "Have not you got three Emperors?" The pilot answered, "No, only one." Masuda said "You lie, there are three." He then asked who was Don Antonio, where was England, and why did our King wage war on England and the Great Turk, together with other questions whose drift the pilot did not understand, but it seemed to him they were ominous questions. With this the pilot took his leave and went to the general and told him in my hearing exactly what the governor had said to him, adding, "I did not understand what he was getting at, but it seemed bad to me." The general summoned the Ensign Cotelo, because he understood more Japanese than anybody, since he was very clever and had picked up some words and phrases in the short time that we had been at Urado. He told him to take our interpreter, Antonio, with him, and warned him to stick close to the truth. Cotelo went to the godowns and found Masuda within, who, divining the object of his visit, repeated to him what he had asked the pilot, "What lands did our King possess?" And the ensign told him, Spain, Mexico, and all the East and West Indies. Then the governor said to him "Your Emperor is also Emperor of the Portuguese?," and Cotelo answered "Yes." "That is not true," retorted Masuda, "because I know that you have three Emperors, and that the Portuguese one is the greatest of all." Cotelo replied, "How is it possible, sir, that anyone told you this? Because Portuguese and Spaniards have no other monarch than our own King." Masuda answered, "I know what I told you, from a letter which I got from Kyoto, wherein it was written that the Portuguese had told Taikosama that you have three Emperors. One is the Portuguese, who is the greatest of all, another is yours, and I don't remember what the third is"; moreover, the said Portuguese had asked Taikosama, "How is it possible that your grandeur who is so powerful should allow one or two ships to pass your coasts yearly without having your passport or paying respect to your exalted person; and this ship that has put into Urado is one of these, which are richly laden with gold, scarlet cloth, and other things of great price?" Cotelo replied, "Sir, you now know that this is an evil thing, since you have seen what we carried; and as regards what the Portuguese told Taikosama, you can disillusion yourself by asking those Portuguese who came hither with us, and who as vassals of the same king serve in his ships and fleets, being natives of the same land and kingdom as are the Portuguese who came to Nagasaki. You can also inform yourself from the captain who comes from Macao, and you will see that both the one and the other come with titles conferred by our King." He adduced other reasons and concluded, "all these are indications that our King is likewise that of the Portuguese." The governor, seeing the force of those arguments, was at a loss what to say, and turned the topic by asking, "Well then, who is Don Antonio, and why did King Felipe turn him out of the kingdom, and why does he [Felipe] make war against England and the Grand Turk?" The ensign was surprised to hear such peculiar questions, since it seemed to him that Masuda could not possibly have any knowledge of such things unless he had really been told them by the Portuguese, but he answered as best he could, saying:—"Don Antonio is the bastard son of a Prince of Portugal, and he cannot inherit the kingdom because he is a bastard. With the death of King Don Sebastião, the kingdom passed to Don Henrique, and with the death of Don Henrique, our King Felipe became the legitimate heir. There were many Portuguese who were traitors to him and it was therefore necessary for our king to enter Portugal by force of arms in order to take possession of his kingdom. Don Antonio, seeing this, fled with some of his followers to England. There are many reasons why we have war with England,—firstly, because whereas they were formerly Christians, they are now Lutherans; secondly, because they do much harm to our King by sea, taking his ships and killing his vassals; and lastly, for having given refuge to Don Antonio and his followers, because any one of these reasons in Europe is sufficient to justify a war." The governor seemed to be fairly satisfied with what Cotelo told him, and the ensign added that he was prepared to repeat in front of Taikosama everything that he had just said. He further suggested that he and some other Spaniards should be sent for an investigation into the truth of the matter before the Emperor, and that if they could not prove they were right, they should all be killed as pirates, since this was what they were accused of being with the design of spying out Taikosama's ports,—whilst on the other hand, if the Portuguese and the Jesuit padres were proved to be liars, that they should suffer the death penalty as perjurers. The governor said,— "Either today or tomorrow some news will come from Kyoto, and we will know whether the Portuguese who spoke to Taikosama are still there or if they have returned to Nagasaki; and regarding your suggestion that some of you should go to Kyoto, I will consult with the local daimyo and decide what is best. However, whether you lie, or whether the Portuguese and the padres lie, nobody will be killed for it; since although you ask me to kill them, yet they did not ask Taikosama to kill you, but only to confiscate your cargo and send you away." With this he dismissed Cotelo, who thereupon returned to where the general and his men were.

APPENDIX IV

PEDRO DE BAEZA ON THE CHINA-JAPAN TRADE, ca. 1609 [1]

. . . like the Portuguese do who live in Malacca and China, who do not
depend on Portugal or East India for their livelihood, but on those [Far
Eastern] regions whither they trade, and the same could be done by the
citizens and inhabitants of Manila and the Philippines . . . and it will be
essential for His Majesty to give them leave to enter the port of Macao in
China, a port wherein dwell the Portuguese who go thither by way of East
India, where there are more than twelve hundred households of married
Portuguese, and where I lived for six years. The Spaniards who live in the
Philippines do not communicate with them, although both Spaniards and
Portuguese communicate with all the other nations and provinces in those
parts. This greatly scandalizes the natives of those regions, seeing that only
Spaniards and Portuguese do not deal or communicate with each other as
would be expected of fellow-Christians and vassals of the same king. For
the Portuguese cannot enter the Philippines, nor can the Spaniards trade at
Malacca and Macao, which last place is where the Portuguese live at 18
leagues distance from the great city of Canton. And it often happens that
through a storm or chance event, some Spanish ships are wrecked or forced
into Portuguese ports, and they immediately have their cargoes confiscated, and their men are imprisoned and very badly treated, whence many
deaths and feuds ensue, as is well known and notorious to all, having been
often seen. Time has shown that this is the reason why all the barbarous
nations of those parts are astounded and amazed at seeing these Christian
peoples indulge in such mutual hate and enmity. It is therefore essential

---

[1] Pedro de Baeza, *Este memorial me mando el Conde de Lemos que hiziesse, que es la
resolucion destas materias, y de todos los mas que le tengo dado a su Excelencia, para que se
diesse a Su Magestad* [Madrid, 1609]. The writer had served the crown for thirty years
in the Moluccas, Philippines, Macao, and Japan, in various financial and administrative
posts. From the context, it is clear that he was writing about conditions in Canton during
the last decade of the sixteenth century. After badgering the Count of Lemos and the Consejo
de Indias at Madrid for many years to reward his services, he eventually had to be satisfied
with being appointed crown factor at Ternate in 1617, but he seems to have died before
he could reach his post. Apropos of his observations on the relative value of gold and silver
in China and Japan at the turn of the sixteenth century, Saris, writing on the same topic
fourteen years later, notes "that the Chinese will commonly truck for your silver and give
you gold of 23 carats from 15 to 20 the ounce silver; but sometimes there commeth much
and other some times little." (Saris' *Voyage*, Hakluyt Society ed., p. 230.) The same
authority also states that in Japan "rialls do lose 20 per cent; for a riall of 8 stands you in
four shillings and sixpence, which will yield there but three shillings and sixpence, which
is seven mace that is 25 per cent loss; but they may allow 5 per cent for the finest rialls."
(*Ibid.*, p. 208.) The position seems to have altered in the next twenty years, for Peter
Mundy, writing on the relative value of Spanish and Japanese silver at Macao in 1637–1638,
observes, "If you are to pay 100 taels of Japan plate and you will give him rialls of eight,
then every riall is accounted 8 Mace 4 candareen 3 cash, or 8 Mace, 5 candareens, but if
you owe rialls of eight and would pay it in Japan plate, for every riall which is 7 Mace 4
candareens, you must give 8 Mace 5 candareens in Japan silver, there being 15 per cent
difference in ordinary payments between Spanish and Japan silver, the former the better,
called *Plata corriente* or current silver." (Mundy's *Travels*, Hakluyt Society ed., Vol. III,
Pt. I, p. 311.)

and advantageous for a general settlement of these differences, that His Majesty should allow the Portuguese and Spaniards who live in those parts to communicate with each other, since the sole reason which now prevents them is the selfish interest of private individuals. These say that the Portuguese of Macao would lose if the Spaniards went to trade at Canton like the Portuguese do, since the former would take so much silver to Canton and give higher prices for the goods than the Portuguese can afford to pay. But since God has been pleased to join these two crowns in one, he would likewise approve of the two nationals communicating in those parts. And since he has placed Your Excellency [Conde de Lemos] at the head of all those great realms in the New World, in order that you might remedy these disorders and feuds (for so I may term them) with your great prudence and Christianity, let Him likewise be served that in your time this wrong in those parts may be righted, and that you may induce His Majesty to give them permission to trade and communicate with each other in Christian faith and charity as they should, allowing mutual intercourse without risk of either party being molested or losing their goods. If they are united, they can help each other in time of necessity in the service of the crown, and they will have more strength wherewith to oppose the enemy if he goes to those regions . . .

. . . Forasmuch as throughout all the kingdom of China there is an enormous quantity of fine gold of more than twenty-two carats touch; if this was brought to New Spain, or to Castile, a profit of 75 or 80 per cent would be made on the price as between one region and the other. It is regarded in China as a commodity which rises and falls in accordance with the supply and demand, and it does not have a fixed value there as here in Castile. A peso of gold in China is often worth 5½ pesos of silver, and if there is a shortage thereof and a demand for it from elsewhere, the rate may rise to six or 6½ silver pesos for one of gold. The dearest at which I have ever bought it or seen it sold in the city of Canton in China, was 7½ silver pesos for one of gold, and I never saw it go higher, nor has it done so hitherto. Whereas here in Spain a peso of gold is usually worth 12½ silver pesos, whereby it can be seen how more than 75 per cent or 80 per cent is gained on the gold which is exported from China. Wherefore it ought to be allowed, in consideration of the great benefit that would result to these kingdoms of Spain in exporting gold from China in exchange for silver, that His Majesty should freely give permission to anyone to take silver from New Spain to the Philippines, on condition that they should invest half thereof in Chinese goods and the other half in gold at the market price. For assuming that there is no gold in the Philippines, when the Cantonese and the Sangleys learn that they can exchange their gold for silver in the Philippines, they will bring so much that it will suffice to offset the wealth they take away from New Spain through the silver which they export thence. For in China an enormous quantity of gold is taken from the mines there, whilst the Chinese prefer silver to gold, and this is the reason why they value silver so highly and not gold. And the Portuguese who take silver from the city of Lisbon in the ships which leave thence for the Orient, take it all to China to be invested in their markets, and they gain thereon when they exchange it for Chinese merchandise more than 70 per cent. By this, we can see how much silver is valued there and how little gold.

APPENDIX V

Japanese State Papers on the Macao-Nagasaki Trade, 1611–1621

LETTER FROM HONDA MASAZUMI TO DOM DIOGO DE VASCONCELOS, 1611 [1]

Kozuke-no-suké Fujiwara Masazumi, the Minister of Nippon, respectfully writes this letter to Dom Diogo de Vasconcelos, Admiral of Portugal.

The envoy, Dom Nuno Soutomaior, has come here crossing over the vast sea. He was duly received, and I met him to discuss the destruction by fire of the Black Ship last year.

It seems to me that you are trying to excuse the guilty party. Our countries being widely separated, mutual communication of opinion is very difficult. The facts having been distorted in transmission, we cannot recognize the truth. How can you explain the murder of our innocent people at Macao? Your people behaved arbitrarily and were unfair to ours. Conflict thus occurred between the two sides, and our innocent men were cut down and killed. This matter was eventually reported to our ruler who on the one hand grieved at his vassals being sent to the realm of the shades without cause, and on the other hand resented the foreign barbarians having plotted against and ambushed our nationals. It so happened that a Black Ship entered Nagasaki harbor, and common report accused the captain of that ship as the ringleader in the murder of our people. The Bugyo of the harbor reported as much to our ruler who wanted the captain to be interrogated about the affair. The Bugyo was therefore told to invite the captain ashore but the latter refused to land, and when the request was repeated, he did not even deign to reply. This happened time and time again, so it was clear that the captain was the guilty party. The Ruler of Nippon expressly stated that only the captain was to be summoned and all the others to be left in peace. The fact that many are to be spared for one man is a truly saintly deed. The Bugyo of Nagasaki was ordered to send officials on board the Black Ship to interrogate the captain, whereupon the latter forcibly resisted, firing his cannon and burning some of our ships. He then weighed anchor and set sail. Our men, fearing lest this infringement of our national laws should go unpunished, attacked the ship. The captain then set fire to the ship of his own free will and blew it up with all the treasure on board. The ship then sank under the waves.

Our intention was to seize the captain's person only, which was the reason we summoned him. Why should we want to kill the others? How much less did we mean to burn the ship!

The facts are as stated above. You can reflect and ponder on them at length. Do not doubt the truth of this.

[1] From the *Ikoku Nikki-sho* (Murakami ed., 1929), pp. 57–58. The original was probably from the brush of the celebrated Confucianist scholar, Hayashi Razan, and is to be found in some editions of his collected works.

Now when Dom Nuno Soutomaior came from afar, I received him and his present was accepted and the matter thus regarded as settled. This was certainly a friendly act on my part. My lord likewise does not blame you personally for the previous offense. He will allow the resumption of trade and equable profits to both countries. He will not prohibit the arrival and departure of ships. Therefore, let the Black Ship come to Nagasaki next summer as it did of yore. We earnestly hope for an early resumption of trade on a mutually satisfactory and profitable basis.

If there be any disorders among our officials or merchants, they will be investigated. Strong measures will be taken under the terms of the edict. Do not hesitate. Since the details cannot be fully expressed in this letter, they will be verbally explained by Dom Nuno Soutomaior.

LETTER FROM HONDA MASAZUMI TO THE AUTHORITIES OF MACAO, 1611 [2]

Kozuke-no-suké Fujiwara Masazumi, the Minister of Nippon, respectfully greets the Governor and Elders of Macao.

You sent me a letter which I could understand as well as if we had been talking face to face.

The destruction by fire of the Black Ship last year was exactly as recounted in your letter. Although the captain-major died through his own fault, I am pleased to take notice of your regretful apologies. His crime was minutely described in my letter to Dom Diogo de Vasconcelos, therefore I shall not refer to it again in this letter. Now, repenting of your former misdeeds, you have asked us to restore our old friendship and to be allowed to send your ships to this country again in order to continue the trade forever. Your wish is acknowledged as proper and rightful. We shall never stop you coming nor prevent you leaving. We will not be found wanting in generosity in receiving proposals from foreigners of far distant lands. Your petition was therefore submitted to my liege lord who answered affirmatively. Is not this a fortunate thing for your country? You have been trading here for several decades, and we therefore have a latent wish for mutual intercourse. This is exemplified by my lord's goodwill and desire for friendship with foreign countries. I am therefore anxious to see the Black Ship return to Nagasaki harbor as of old. Do not break your promise. Trade will flourish and be profitable as in days gone by. I hope that you will feel reassured by this.

Fifteenth day of the seventh month in the autumn season of the sixteenth year of Keicho.

---

[2] *Ikoku Nikki-sho* (Murakami ed., 1929), pp. 58–59. The writer of these letters, Honda Kozuke-no-suké Masazumi, who enlivens the pages of Cocks' *Diary* in the guise of Codskin or Codskin-dono, should not be confused with his father, Honda Sado-no-kami Masanobu. They were both lifelong retainers and trusted advisers of Tokugawa Ieyasu, but Hidetada treated them scurvily later on.

LETTER FROM GOTO SHOZABURO TO THE AUTHORITIES AT MACAO, 1611 [3]

Goto Shozaburo Fujiwara Mitsutsugu, a retainer of Nippon, respectfully presents this letter to the Elders of Macao.

I received with thanks a letter from Dom Diogo de Vasconcelos, the captain-major of Macao, and I felt still more pleased at meeting Dom Nuno Soutomaior, the envoy.

The Black Ship was destroyed by fire the other year, because her captain-major murdered our people at Macao when he was acting as governor there, and he denied the fact when he came here, saying that he was not concerned in it. After the ship's arrival at Nagasaki, the true facts were revealed. My lord was told and he ordered the local officials to interrogate the captain-major of the ship. Arima Shuri-no-Taiyu was appointed in connection with this, and he wanted to secure the captain-major alone and leave the ship safe and sound. The former was ordered to come ashore to justify himself but he refused to do so. He opened fire on our shipping and burned and damaged a number of vessels. He then weighed anchor and unfurled his sails, intending to escape from the harbor. Fearing lest this would nullify and thus disgrace the order of his liege lord, Arima constructed a special ship. The captain-major continued firing his heavy cannon and then blew up the Black Ship which sank as a result. You will see that a single person's guilt was responsible for the loss of many lives and much treasure and cargo. This was probably not the intention of the crew as a whole, but Chinese and lascars were on board, and friends and foes alike all shared in the common fate. This is sincerely to be regreted. The fire destroyed trash and precious things alike. Yet many of the survivors were saved and sent back. You know this to be a fact and why should we deceive you?

You have asked me to restore our old-time friendship and to be allowed to send the Black Ship next year. Sympathizing with your request, I made a petition to my lord who was pleased to condescend to it. I am therefore anxious to see the Black Ship's arrival at Nagasaki. Nagasaki is an excellent harbor in the "Western Sea Circuit" in our country and a highly prosperous trading mart. Your letter informs me that the harbor commissioners, Hasegawa Sahioye and Murayama Toan were covetous individuals who had extorted bribes from your people and made them sign certain documents.

This must be only a rumour, and anyway I doubt the truth of this report. The two will be summoned here within the next few days and they

---

[3] *Ikoku Nikki-sho* (Murakami ed., 1929), pp. 59–61. Goto Shozaburo was at this time, among other things, the master of the mint. He was one of Ieyasu's protégés, and was popularly believed to have been a millionaire. Vizcaíno contrasts his greed for money and bribes with the austerity of old Honda who always refused to accept any reward for many favors to foreigners.

will be closely interrogated. The truth will then appear; but I cannot give an interim decision until I hear from both parties. I shall then submit my verbal opinion on the matter to my lord, and our national laws will be strictly enforced. When the time comes for the Black Ship to enter Nagasaki harbor next year, I shall advise the two commissioners not to cause trouble between your people and ours, but to facilitate matters for the Black Ship and enable the trade to be carried on smoothly. You can rest assured of this. Moreover, one or two of your officials will be invited to Shidzuoka, where I will endeavor to satisfy their requests. Shidzuoka is the seat of my lord's august palace; and therefore the Nagasaki commissioners standing in awe of my lord, will not dare to commit any irregularities.

The envoy, Dom Nuno Soutomaior, being a scion of your nobility, was received by my lord in audience. Was this not an honor for Dom Nuno Soutomaior? I had the privilege of being consulted by my lord when the affairs of the Black Ship were discussed. Some of our officials were unfavorably disposed to your country, but I always took your side and pleaded on your behalf. My only reason for this is the friendship I feel for your port. I would be glad if you Elders would inform the local captain-major of this. I felt that I must write this letter and I shall give it to Dom Nuno Soutomaior to take with him when he returns.

LETTER FROM MIGUEL DE SOUSA PIMENTEL TO THE SHOGUN, 1612 [4]

Miguel de Sousa Pimentel, His Majesty's Captain-Major of the galleons of the China Guard, after purifying and prostrating himself a hundred times, respectfully addresses His Imperial Majesty the Emperor [*sic*] of Great Japan.

The Viceroy of Goa on hearing of the burning of the Black Ship, stopped communication between the two countries, and it is said that my country is to blame on this account. Dom Diogo [de Vasconcelos] was therefore dispatched to Macao, and on his arrival there he investigated the responsibility of our people for that affair and punished them. Accordingly, I dispatched Dom Nuno Soutomaior with a letter of explanation to your Imperial Majesty's ministers, in order to explain the attitude of our country. Whether we decide to send a ship in the future depends on whether permission to renew our intercourse on its former footing is granted, as also on whether your Majesty sends us a reply. On my way here, I met Dom Nuno on his homeward voyage at Malacca, and he showed me a splendid sword

---

[4] *Ikoku Nikki-sho* (Murakami ed., 1929), pp. 87–90. A letter couched in a very similar strain from the Viceroy of Goa, Rui Lourenço de Tavora, will be found in *ibid.*, pp. 82–84. Although ostensibly written at Goa, it was probably drafted at Macao like Pimentel's letter. Another letter to the shogun, this time written by the senate of Macao, will be found in *ibid.*, pp. 92–93. The Portuguese originals are no longer extant, but their gist is clear even from these rather peculiar Sino-Japanese versions.

and some letters which he had received from two or three of Your Majesty's ministers, by which I realized for the first time the great generosity you bestowed on my country. Your Imperial favor may be compared with the greatness of the Universe. Evidently that matter [loss of *Nossa Senhora da Graça*] turned out differently from Your Majesty's real intentions, and Your Majesty has been misrepresented.

However, as Your Majesty's former letter is not stamped with the Imperial Seal, we are in some doubt whether we ought to place credence in it.

I have just reached Macao and seen Your Majesty's letter together with that of Hasegawa Sahioye, which I have respectfully perused. I realized the benevolence of Your Majesty and his ministers. Moreover, the letter of the bishop [of Japan] and the favorable report of the father-visitor, proved your ever-increasing benevolence to our country. I can assure you that we will obey your orders.

Subsequently the ship arrived with a full cargo under the Captain-Major Pero Moniz [Gaio] and the Envoy Horatio Nerete, who is a scion of our ruling house [*sic*]. The latter has known Your Majesty's country for a long time, and is a person of exceptional intelligence and merit. He will explain the policy of our government and endeavor to secure your favor. He has a secret request to make.

On previous voyages we had your imperial seal, but this was destroyed when the ship was burnt the other year. However, a copy is still left and this can be proved to you and your officials. If you condescend to comply with our request, please affix your seal to the accompanying two copies thereof. One of these will be retained in this harbor and the other kept on board the ship. If this is done, the ship will come yearly and we shall have no trouble with renewals.

We hear that the Red-hairs have come to your country. They are merely pirates on the high seas and probably of no advantage to you. Therefore we will fit out a warship to convoy the merchant ship, thus ensuring peaceful and speedy trade. If we receive a promise by the favorable winds of this autumn, we will certainly send a merchant ship early next summer, to the mutual advantage of both countries. With deep respect.

Sixth and summer month of the fortieth year of Wanli of the Great Ming [1612].

LETTER OF THANKS FROM DOM NUNO SOUTOMAIOR, 1612 [5]

I thank you very much for the hospitality which I enjoyed in your country last year. My eyes saw with amazement the greatness of Japan, and particu-

[5] *Ikoku Nikki-sho* (Murakami ed., 1929), pp. 100–101. This particular letter seems to have been addressed to Honda Kodzuke-no-suké Masazumi who had remained at Shidzuoka as Ieyasu's confidential secretary and adviser, while his father, Honda Sado-no-kami Masanobu, was attached in a similar capacity to Hidetada at Yedo, after the latter had become the titular shogun in 1605. The Portuguese original has not been preserved.

larly the vast size of Yedo. I told the people in Goa about this on my return. You are one of the leading officials in Japan, and you entertained the stranger magnificently. Words really fail to express my thanks.

When I was at Shidzuoka, you were kind enough to send an envoy to ask after my welfare. Honda Sado-no-kami was also very kind to me at Yedo. I told everyone at Goa about this.

However, the letter to the shogun from the viceroy of Goa was put into Sado-no-kami's pocket and never shown to the former at all. I am sorry about this, but I shall not complain to Sado-no-kami about it, but only inform you. Anyway, I thank you very much for your goodwill. If there is anything I can do for you at Goa, please command me. I am sending a captain to Yedo to express my gratitude.

The second general at Goa.

DOM NUNO SOUTOMAIOR

LETTER FROM HONDA MASAZUMI TO THE CAPTAIN-MAJOR OF MACAO, 1612 [6]

Your letter was opened and read several times. I have never met you, but I felt as though we were sitting and talking on the same floor. No sincerity can be greater than this.

Last year, the envoy Dom Nuno came to this land and was received in audience by Prince Minamoto [Tokugawa Ieyasu], the Ruler of Nippon, to whom he offered a present. At his earnest request, the trading ship was allowed to come again. The Imperial red-seal and letters-patent were given to him, and he sailed away soon after. He must have reached your harbor some time ago.

This year the Black Ship came again to Nagasaki, and the chief envoy, Oratio Nerete, came to Shidzuoka castle, where he was received in audience by Prince Minamoto. Everything went smoothly, the cargo was disposed of, and the commercial negotiations were managed without a hitch and in the way that the captain-major wanted.

I told Nerete about the permission to come and trade freely. No complications occurred, and ships can come in future to exchange the treasures of both countries. What better policy can there possibly be than this?

I am grateful for the viceroy of Goa's presents. I send in return a trifling present of ten garments. You would do well to present them to the viceroy. The details will be explained by the captain-major of the Japan voyage.

Ninth month of the seventeenth year of Keicho [1612].

[6] *Ikoku Nikki-sho* (Murakami ed., 1929), pp. 116–117.

LETTER FROM SHIMADZU IEHISA TO THE SENATE OF
MACAO, 1612 [7]

The answer to the letter of the Four Elders of Namban. Separated far beyond the clouds we have not been able to communicate with each other
hitherto. Unexpectedly, I received your letter of several lines written in
strange characters, whose meaning cannot be clearly understood.

By the efforts of various interpreters, about a tenth or two of the letter
was puzzled out, but eight or nine tenths of it remain beyond our understanding. Therefore, I cannot find suitable words wherewith to return
thanks.

Last spring a merchant ship from my country met a black wind on its
course to Annam and drifted to the land of Kwangtung. Fortunately, the
crew was saved by the great kindness of the Four Elders, and they returned
last month to the Goto Islands in Hizen Province. I am profoundly grateful
for the kindness of the Four Elders.

I here by a report borne on the wind that in your country high and low
alike fulfill their due station in life. In my country, too, the four classes of
warriors, farmers, artisans, and tradesmen are in sound condition. I would
like to explain things more precisely but I am not acquainted with your language. I hope you can guess my meaning.

The eighth month of the year of the Rat and seventeenth year of Keicho.

MAJOR-GENERAL SHIMADZU IEHISA

CORRESPONDENCE BETWEEN DOI TOSHIKATSU AND THE
SENATE OF MACAO, 1621 [8]

The Senate to Doi Oi-no-suké Toshikatsu.

We respectfully offer you a letter.

As we sent a letter of thanks to you last year, you were kind enough to
recommend us to the shogun, and the shogun honored us by a gift of garments for which we feel most grateful.

Moreover, you wrote us a courteous letter for which we, too, express our
thanks.

Again we send you a letter this year. Up till recently we sent the Black

7 *Ikoku Nikki-sho* (Murakami ed., 1929), p. 267. A letter from Shimadzu Iehisa to the
captain of the Macao ship, dated in the same month and year, and couched in a very similar
strain is printed in *ibid.*, pp. 266–267. The Macao records make no mention of the arrival
of this stray Satsuma junk, but the incident is confirmed from other sources. The title of
major-general did not denote an active military rank but was a court title.

8 *Ikoku Nikki-sho* (Murakami ed., 1929), pp. 213–215. Doi Oi-no-suké Toshikatsu (the
Oyendono of Cocks' *Diary*) was one of the favorite councillors of the first three Tokugawa
shoguns, and successively daimyo of Shimosa (10,000 koku), Sakura (30,000 koku), and
Koga (132,000).

Ships, but lately the thirteen pirate ships of Holland are infesting the high seas, so that we cannot use the big Black Ships, but only small ships [*galiotas*]. This is a great nuisance for us. We would be very grateful if you would order the Hollanders to leave Hirado. Since they are nothing but pirates, no other country allows their ships to anchor in their ports; consequently they only gather at Hirado.

We have another complaint. Commodities such as the white silk yarn are now purchased under duress for a very small sum.

Macao submits its petitions on the above-mentioned matters and we bow respectfully.

Twenty-fifth day of the sixth month of the seventh year of Genna

Doi's Reply to the Senate.

Your letter was opened and read. I understood that you feel grateful because last year's envoy was received by the Minamoto shogun, the ruler of Nippon, and received a gift of garments. This year, also, the envoy has arrived and been received in audience by the shogun after we, the several ministers, held a consultation.

I likewise understood that the voyages of the Black Ship had been safe until the recent appearance of pirate ships on the high seas; and also that there were some unreasonable buyers of white silk yarn among our people.

As regards the pirates, they are strictly forbidden by order of the ruler of Nippon to commit piracy in the adjacent sea. As regards the trading profits, it has been ordained likewise that trade shall be carried on in the way desired by your commercial factor. There is nobody who is so cruel as to make unconscionable profits in our country. Please do not feel uneasy. Other details will be explained by the envoy.

Twenty-third day, ninth month of the seventh year of Genna [1621].

APPENDIX VI

The Martyrdom at Omura, August 25, 1624
THE DEATH OF FATHER MIGUEL CARVALHO OF THE SOCIETY OF JESUS AND OF FOURE OTHER RELIGIOUS MEN OF THE HOLY ORDERS OF SAINT DOMINICKE, AND SAINT FRANCIS, WHO SUFFERED FOR PREACHING OF THE HOLY GHOSPELL [1]

. . . "finally order came from Nagasaki, that all the Religious should be put to death, who so soone as they had understood the certainty thereof, shewed extraordinary signes of joy. Upon the 25 of August they were led forth of prison all five, fast bound, with ropes about their necks, and accompanied with a band of soldiers. The Priests went each bearing a crosse in his hand, and continually fixed in prayers till such time as they came to shippe, whither they entered with some few of the officers, the rest continuing their journey by land. They arrived at the place appointed for their death, a field called Hokonohara, when giving thanks unto those who had conducted them, for the pains they had taken they went to land, and the Priests lifting on high the crosses which they bare in their hands, they began to recite psalms with a loud voice; when Father *Carvalho* perceiving now a great multitude to be assembled, turning unto them, *you must understand,* said he, *that we are Christians, and that we die of our free and voluntary accord, for the faith of Christ our Lord.* The admirable serenity of their countenances put their joy so clearly in view of the beholders, that amazed thereat they said, *these men seemed to go rather to some feast or banquet, than unto death.* Finally, their desired end approaching, the first who was tied unto a stake, was Father Miguel Carvalho, of our *Society,* the second Father Peter *Vasquez,* of the Order of Saint *Dominicke,* the third, Father *Luis Sotelo,* the fourth Father *Luis Sasada* both of the same Order of *Saint Francis.* The fifth, Brother *Luis,* Observant of the third Order, a *Japanese;* Being ranked in this order, they were bound in such sort that after the cords should be burned, they might yet be able to stirre themselves, to the end their troubled action and disordered motion, might incite the people to laughter. Every one was attired in his own habit, with his eyes fixed upon heaven. When the fire was kindled, which in regard of the small quantity of wood, burned very slowly, so that, the rope wherewith Brother *Luis* the Japanese was bound, being consumed, he might have departed at his pleasure. The rest of his valorous associates were jointly with loud voice reciting a

[1] *The Palme of Christian Fortitude. Or the Glorious Combats of Christians in Iaponia* (Douai, 1630), pp. 146–150. The fifth victim, whose name is not given here, was Fray Luis Baba, a Japanese Franciscan. I have retained the punctuation and spelling of the original, save for proper names which have been modernized to facilitate identification. It is interesting to note how closely the behavior of the martyrs corresponded to the advice given in the *Exhortation to Martyrdom* as transcribed above, pp. 340–341.

436

certain devote prayer, and the fire grew to advance itselfe; when he departing from his stake, with noble contempt of those raging flames, made haste to do reverence, and kiss submissively the hands of the Priests his companions; then exhorting with a loud voice the standers by to embrace the faith of *Christ* in which alone is true safety and salvation, he returned generously unto the stake again, and leaning himself unto it, without any further tying (for he was already sufficiently bound in the bands of charity to *Christ* our Lord) he endured, without ever moving himself, the fury of those flames, until at length he rendered his invincible soul to God. The others were already so oppressed with the smoke and fire which had now taken possession of their mouths, that they could not as they wished, express themselves; yet should you hear them now and then break forth into those sovereigne names of *Iesus* and *Maria* whose aid the servants of God implored in their torments. Father *Miguel Carvalho,* for as much as there had been more wood, and a more vehement fire about him, was the second who died, after he had given diverse arguments of his stout courage and extraordinary constancy. Father *Luis Sasada,* a Japanese of the Order of Saint *Francis* died in the third place. He, observing that the cordes wherewith he had been tied, were now consumed by the fire, was desirous before he breathed forth his holy soul, to go and do reverence unto the Priests his companions; but making assay, and not being able to move himself, his feet being already burned, he remained at his own stake; from whence doing reverence with profound inclination unto those two his companions, who yet were alive, he died with constancy worthy a Religious man adorned with so remarkable vertue as himself. The other two remained, the fire not well approaching to them, and in particular to Father *Luis Sotelo.* The executers of this cruelty resolved to take some quantity of straw and other dry litter, and setting it on fire, they devided it into two parts, and yet for all this their piles not burning very violently, gave matter of more irkesome torment to these servants of God. They remained therefore 3 hours in the fire, ever immovable, consuming away in lingering slow flames; after which space of time they ended the course of a combat so much more glorious, as it was produced longer, upon the twenty-fifth of August 1624, by order of the Governors of *Omura* and *Nagasaki.*

The glorious champions of *Christ* being dead, that the *Christians* might not enjoy their blessed bodies, they burned them even to cinders; then putting the ashes into a sack, and advancing themselves into a wide sea, there did those impious officers cast them abroad; yea they set some to watch the place where they had suffered, lest any bone or small relic which might be left, should be taken away. Yet it hath pleased God, notwithstanding all the diligence of the *Paynims,* that the *Christians* found certain bones, and pieces of stakes to which they had been bound, which were taken up, and are conserved. A man cannot explicate how great the admiration of some renegados, who found themselves present at the spectacle. And they confessed all that the ordinary heat which the season itself brought with it being unsupportable, they could not understand by what forces the servants of God were able to resist so immovably the lingering flames of the slow fire."

APPENDIX VII

TEXT OF THE SAKOKU, OR CLOSED COUNTRY EDICT OF JUNE, 1636 [1]

1. No Japanese ships may leave for foreign countries.

2. No Japanese may go abroad secretly. If anybody tries to do this, he will be killed, and the ship and owner(s) will be placed under arrest whilst higher authority is informed.

3. Any Japanese now living abroad who tries to return to Japan will be put to death.

4. If any Kirishitan believer is discovered, you two [Nagasaki bugyo] will make a full investigation.

5. Any informer(s) revealing the whereabouts of a bateren will be paid 200 or 300 pieces of silver. If any other categories of Kirishitans are discovered, the informer(s) will be paid at your discretion as hitherto.

6. On the arrival of foreign ships, arrangements will be made to have them guarded by ships provided by the Omura clan whilst report is being made to Yedo, as hitherto.

7. Any foreigners who help the bateren or other criminal foreigners will be imprisoned at Omura as hitherto.

8. Strict search will be made for bateren on all incoming ships.

9. No offspring of Southern Barbarians will be allowed to remain. Anyone violating this order will be killed, and all relatives punished according to the gravity of the offence.

10. If any Japanese have adopted the offspring of Southern Barbarians they deserve to die. Nevertheless, such adopted children and their foster-parents will be handed over to the Southern Barbarians for deportation.

11. If any deportees should try to return or to communicate with Japan by letter or otherwise, they will of course be killed if they are caught, whilst

---

[1] Translated from the Japanese text in I. Tokutomi's *Kinsei Nihon Kokumin-shi*, Vol. XIV (1935), pp. 287–289. Comparison with the version given by Valentyn, which he dates as received at Hirado on December 7, 1635, discloses a few differences besides the date, but evidently the same decree is intended. The most important difference is that Valentyn's ninth paragraph has nothing about the Macaonese offspring, but merely states that merchandise should be sold not to one merchant but to several. Pagés and other writers in his footsteps (Murdoch among them) have mistranslated Valentyn's fourteenth paragraph which states "you will not be so exacting with the Chinese as with the Portuguese," which these historians have wrongly rendered as "you will not be too rigorous with the Chinese or the Portuguese,"—precisely the opposite of the real meaning. (Cf. Valentyn, *Beschryvinge van Japan*, pp. 98–99). The first decree limiting the freedom of Japan's foreign trade was that of 1616, by which European ships were confined to the ports of Nagasaki and Hirado, while the movements of European merchants inland were restricted. The next step was the severance of relations with Spain, Mexico, and the Philippines in 1624–1625. The third was the decrees of 1633–1634 forbidding the navigation of even the Red-seal ships without a special license, and prohibiting the return to Japan of Japanese settled abroad, save those who could prove that they had only recently left the country with intention to return. The fourth and decisive step was this decree of 1636, the final act being taken with the formal expulsion of the Portuguese in 1639.

their relatives will be severely dealt with, according to the gravity of the offence.

12. Samurai are not allowed to have direct commercial dealings with either foreign or Chinese shipping at Nagasaki.

13. Nobody other than those of the five places (Yedo, Kyoto, Osaka, Sakai and Nagasaki) is allowed to participate in the allocation of *ito-wappu* and the fixing of silk import prices.

14. Purchases can only be made after the *ito-wappu* is fixed. However, as the Chinese ships are small, you will not be too rigorous with them. Only twenty days are allowed for the sale.

15. The twentieth day of the ninth month is the deadline for the return of foreign ships, but latecomers will be allowed fifty days grace from the date of their arrival. Chinese ships will be allowed to leave a little after the departure of the [Portuguese] galliots.

16. Unsold goods cannot be left in charge of Japanese for storage or safekeeping.

17. Representatives of the five [shogunal] cities should arrive at Nagasaki not later than the fifth day of the long month. Late arrivals will not be allowed to participate in the silk allocation and purchase.

18. Ships arriving at Hirado will not be allowed to transact business until after the price allocations have been fixed at Nagasaki.

Nineteenth day of the fifth month of the thirteenth year of Kwanei [June 22, 1636].

Addressed to Sakakibara Hida-no-kami and Baba Saburozayemon, the joint bugyo of Nagasaki, and signed by Hotta Kaga-no-kami, Abe Bungo-no-kami, Sakai Sanuki-no-kami and Doi Oi-no-suké, the four great councillors or Go-roju.

APPENDIX VIII

OATH OF APOSTASY, 1645 [1]

We have been Christian believers for many years. Yet we have found out that the Christian religion is an evil religion. It regards the next life as the most important. The threat of excommunication is held over those who disobey the padres' orders, whilst they are likewise kept from associating with the rest of humanity in the present world and doomed to be cast into Hell in the next. It further teaches that there is no salvation in the next life unless sinners confess their faults to the padres and receive their absolution. In this way, the people were led to place their trust in the padres. Yet all this was done with the design of taking the lands of others. When we learned this, I became an adherent of the Hokke sect and my wife of the Ikko sect.

We hereby witness this statement in writing before you, worshipful magistrate. Hereafter we shall never revoke our apostasy, not even in the secret places of the heart. Should we even entertain the slightest thought thereof, then let us be punished by God the Father, God the Son, and God the Holy Ghost, St. Mary, and all Angels and Saints. Let us forfeit all God's mercy, and all hope like Judas Iscariot, becoming a laughing-stock to all men, without thereby arousing the slightest pity, and finally die a violent death and suffer the torments of Hell without hope of salvation. This is our Christian Oath.

We tell you frankly that we have no belief whatsoever in Christianity in our hearts. Should we be guilty of any falsehood in this respect, now or in the future, then let each and both of us be divinely punished by Bonten, Taishaku, Shiten-daijo, the great and small deities of the sixty and more provinces of Japan, particularly Gongen and Mishima-daimyojin of the two regions of Idzu and Hakone, Hachiman-daibosatsu, Tenman-daijizai-Tenjin, especially our own tutelary deity Suwa-daimyojin, and all the minor deities. This is our formal oath.

Second year of Shoho [1645]

KYUSUKE, HIS WIFE

[ENDORSEMENT]

The custom of recanting the Christian religion by such a formal oath, and of stamping on a holy image and so forth, has never yet been applied against the Christians in any other land. How can anyone who is troubled by their apostasy revoke it under these circumstances! Moreover, a true revocation

---

[1] From the *Kirishito-ki* (cf. Voss-Cieslik ed. 1940, pp. 165-166, and Takekoshi, *Economic Aspects*, Vol. II, pp. 88–89). A similar oath of apostasy dated 1635, will be found in "Ein Dokument aus der japanischen Inquisition" *MDGfNVO*, Vol. XII (1909). The identification of Chuan with the apostate Christovão Ferreira is well authenticated, that of Ryojun with the renegade Thomas Araki is probable, and that of Ryohaku is uncertain.

of apostasy is quite impossible without the mediation of a padre. A secret revocation is not possible.

The apostate foreign padre—CHUAN [Christovão Ferreira]

The apostate Japanese padres—RYOJUN [Thomas Araki?]

RYOHAKU [uncertain]

COUNTERSIGNED

We hereby certify that the above-mentioned Kyusuke and his wife have become members of the Ikko sect.

Saishoji Temple
Head Priest, SHUSAN

APPENDIX IX

List of Japanese Nengo or Year Periods 1532–1652 [1]

Tembun	February 6, 1532–January 22, 1555
Koji	January 23, 1555–January 19, 1558
Eiroku	January 20, 1558–February 4, 1570
Genki	February 5, 1570–February 2, 1573
Tensho	February 3, 1573–February 12, 1592
Bunroku	February 13, 1592–January 29, 1596
Keicho	January 30, 1596–January 28, 1615
Genna	January 29, 1615–February 18, 1624
Kwanei	February 19, 1624–February 7, 1644
Shoho	February 8, 1644–January 24, 1648
Keian	January 25, 1648–February 9, 1652

[1] Based on W. Bramsen, *Japanese Chronological Tables*. The change from the Julian to the Gregorian calendar in Italy, Spain, and Portugal took place on October 5–15, 1582. Dates before that change are given according to the Julian calendar, and those subsequently in the Gregorian.

APPENDIX X

LIST OF NAGASAKI BUGYO, 1587–1650

Terazawa Shinano-no-kami Hirotaka and Todo Sado-no-kami Takatora as temporary Commissioners in 1587–1588.

Terazawa Shinano-no-kami Hirotaka	resident bugyo 1592–1602
Ogasawara Ichian	visiting bugyo 1603–1605
Hasegawa Sahioye Fujihiro	resident bugyo 1606–1615
Hasegawa Gonroku	resident bugyo 1615–1625
Mizuno Kawachi-no-kami	resident bugyo 1626–1629
Takenaka Uneme-no-sho	resident bugyo 1629–1632
Soga Matazayemon Imamura Denshiro	coördinate bugyo, 1633
Sakakibara Hida-no-kami Kamio Naiki	coördinate bugyo, 1634
Sakakibara Hida-no-kami Sengoku Yamato-no-kami	coördinate bugyo, 1635
Sakakibara Hida-no-kami Baba Saburozayeman	coördinate bugyo, 1636–1638
Baba Saburozayemon Okawachi Zenbei	coördinate bugyo, 1639
Baba Saburozayeman Tsuge Heiyemon	coördinate bugyo, 1640–1641
Baba Saburozayemon Yamazaki Gompachiro	coördinate bugyo, 1642–1649
Baba Saburozayemon Kurokawa Yohei Masanao	coördinate bugyo, 1650

444

APPENDIX XI

HEADS OF THE JESUIT MISSION IN JAPAN, 1549–1643 [1]

Francisco Xavier, Superior	1549–1551
Cosme de Torres, Superior	1551–1570
Francisco Cabral, Superior	1570–1581
Gaspar Coelho, Superior	1581
Gaspar Coelho, Vice-Provincial	1581–1590
Pedro Gomes, Vice-Provincial	1590–1600
Francisco Pasio, Vice-Provincial	1600–1611
Valentim de Carvalho, Provincial	1611–1617 (from 1614, in Macao)
Jeronimo Rodrigues, Vice-Provincial	1614–1617 (in Nagasaki)
Mateus de Couros, Provincial	1617–1621
Francisco Pacheco, Provincial	1621–1626 (martyred)
Mateus de Couros, Vice-Provincial	1626–1632 (died in Japan 1633)
Christovão Ferreira, Vice-Provincial	1632–1633 (apostatized)
Sebastião Vieira, Vice-Provincial	1633–1634 (martyred)
Giovanni Batista Porro, Vice-Provincial	1634–1638 (apostatized)
Gaspar Luis, Vice-Provincial	1638–1641 (in Macao)
Gaspar do Amaral, Vice-Provincial	1641–1645 (in Macao)
Pedro Marques, Provincial	1643 (apostatized)

[1] Based on the list in Francisco Rodrigues, S.J., *A Companhia de Jesus em Portugal e nas missões, 1540–1934*, p. 35. Xavier and Torres were Spaniards, Pasio and Porro Italians; the remainder were Portuguese.

APPENDIX XII

VISITORS OF THE JESUIT PROVINCE OF JAPAN AND VICE-PROVINCE OF CHINA, 1568–1643 [1]

Gonçalo Alvares	1568–1573
Alexander Valignano	1574–1606
Francisco Pasio	1611–1612
Francisco Vieira	1615–1619
Jeronimo Rodrigues	1619–1621 (in Macao)
Gabriel de Matos	1621–1622 (in Macao)
Jeronimo Rodrigues	1622–1626 (in Macao)
André Palmeiro	1626–1635 (in Macao)
Manuel Dias	1635–1639 (in Macao)
Antonio Rubino	1639–1643 (to Japan, 1642)

[1] Based on the list in Francisco Rodrigues, S.J., *A Companhia de Jesus em Portugal e nas missões, 1540–1934*, p. 45.

APPENDIX XIII

THE APOSTATE FATHERS, 1633–1643 [1]

1. Christovão Ferreira (Portuguese). Apostatized, 1633. Died after 1652 in uncertain circumstances.

2. Giovanni Batista Porro (Italian). Apostatized, 1638. Died after 1643 in jail, probably having revoked his apostasy.

3. Martinho Shikimi or Martinho Ichizayemon (Japanese). Apostatized 1638. Died after 1643 in jail, probably having revoked his apostasy.

4. Alonso de Arroyo (Spaniard). Apostatized, 1643. Revoked his apostasy almost immediately and died of malnutrition in jail soon afterwards.

5. Pedro Marques (Portuguese). Apostatized, 1643. Died in 1657 in uncertain circumstances.

6. Giuseppe Chiara (Italian). Apostatized, 1643. Died in 1685, apparently after having stated that he was still a Christian.

7. Francisco Cassola (Italian). Apostatized, 1643. Died before November, 1644, in uncertain circumstances.

---

[1]Compiled mainly from data in the *Kirishito-ki* (ed. Voss and Cieslik). The Omura document of 1690, quoted by Anesaki (*PIA*, Vol. II, 1926, p. 194) implies that three of the first Rubino group who landed at Satsuma in 1642 apostatized, but the Japanese information on this point is as vague as the European accounts of martyrdom are suspect.

It is worth noting that not a single European friar of the mendicant orders ever apostatized, whether under torture or otherwise.

APPENDIX XIV

Summary Martyrology, 1614–1650 [1]

YEAR	TOTAL OF MARTYRS	INCLUDING EUROPEANS
1614	63	—
1615	13	—
1616	13	—
1617	20	4
1618	68	1
1619	88	2
1620	17	—
1621	20	—
1622	132	13
1623	76	2
1624	198	4
1625	7	—
1626	22	4
1627	120	4
1628	62	2
1629	79	—
1630	316	—
1631	46	—
1632	120	5
1633	88	11
1634	100	5
1635	?	—
1636	18	1
1637	129	4
1638	90	—
1639	5	
1640	63	3 (including 61 of the multi-racial embassy from Macao)
1641–1642	?	
1643	54	6 (?)
1644	?	—
1645	9	—
1646–1648	?	—
1649	23 (doubtful)	—
1650	74 (doubtful)	—
In 36 years about	2,128 martyrs, of whom	71 Europeans

[1] Based on the *Elogios* of Cardim (1650), The *Concordance* of Anesaki (1930), checked by reference to other sources where available, such as the *Diario do Conde de Linhares*, which gives the figure of 120 for the year 1632, as based on the nominal rolls submitted by Padres Ferreira and Porro. Ramos' letter of 1635 (p. 360) estimates about 250 martyrs yearly, although the Jesuit records do not give any victims for that particular year. Delplace (*Catholicisme*, Vol. II, pp. 181–195, 263–275) gives a total of 3,125 for the period 1597–1660.

Notes

ABBREVIATIONS USED IN THE NOTES

AAPH	Anais da Academia Portuguesa da História
ABAP	Anais das Bibliotecas e Arquivos de Portugal
AHSI	Archivum Historicum Societatis Iesu
AIA	Archivo Ibero-Americano
BEDM	Boletim Eclesiástico da diocese de Macau
BIPH	Boletim do Instituto Portugues de Hongkong
BSL-J	Boletim da Sociedade Luso-Japonesa
Cartas	Cartas que os Padres e Irmãos da Companhia de Jesus escreuerão dos Reynos de Iapão e China aos da mesma companhia da India, ... e Europa, desdo anno de 1549 ate o de 1580
JRAS	Journal of the Royal Asiatic Society, London
JRAS:M	Journal of the Royal Asiatic Society, Malayan Branch
MDGfNVO	Mittheilungen der Deutschen Gesellschaft für Natur- und Völkerkunde Ostasiens
MN	Monumenta Nipponica
PIA	Proceedings of the Imperial Academy, Tokyo
SNZM	Schriftenreihe der Neue Zeitschrift für Missionswissenschaft
THM	T'ien Hsia Monthly
TP	T'oung Pao
TASJ	Transactions of the Asiatic Society of Japan
TJS	Transactions and Proceedings of the Japan Society, London
TRAS	Transactions of the Royal Asiatic Society, London
TRAS:K	Transactions of the Royal Asiatic Society, Korean Branch

NOTES TO CHAPTER I
From Marco Polo to Mendes Pinto

[1] For Marco Polo and his travels, the fullest and most accessible work for the general reader is still the three-volume edition by Yule and Cordier, *The Book of Ser Marco Polo* (London, 1903–1920). An admirable survey of early Sino-European relations is in G. F. Hudson's *Europe and China*, of which pages 134–168 are particularly relevant here. *Chipangu* is also spelled *Zipangu, Cipango,* and variants thereof in the various versions of Polo's MSS and texts or maps derived therefrom.

[2] G. A. Ballard, *Rulers of the Indian Ocean* (London, 1927), p. 29, Hudson, *op. cit.*, p. 20. For Henry the Navigator and his work, cf. Edgar Prestage, *The Portuguese Pioneers* (London, 1933); Elaine Sanceau, *Henry the Navigator* (New York, 1947).

[3] Hudson, *op. cit.*, pp. 186, 204–228. I accept, as does Hudson, the essential authenticity of the Toscanelli correspondence, denied by Vignaud. See also Armando Cortesão, *Cartografia e cartógrafos portugueses dos séculos XV e XVI*, Vol. I, 226–228, for a discussion of Columbus' identification of Chipangu and Haiti. Cortesão in this work (Vol. I, 225 ff.) takes the view that Columbus was a secret agent of King João II, deliberately distracting the Spaniards from the Cape route to India, but this view is not accepted by Professor Samuel Morison and leading American scholars. Cf. also C. E. Nowell, "The Discovery of the Pacific, A Suggested Change of Approach," *Pacific Historical Review*, XVI (Feb., 1947) pp. 1–10.

[4] Sequeira's instructions are printed in full in *Cartas de Affonso de Albuquerque,* ed. R. Bulhão Pato (Lisbon, 1898), Vol. II, 403–419. Cf. Armando Cortesão, *História da Expansão Portuguesa no Mundo*, Vol. II, chaps. x, xi. For Ibn Mahjid and Vasco da Gama, cf. Gabriel Ferrand, *Introduction à l'astronomie nautique arabe* (Paris, 1928), pp. 183–237, esp., 192–199; and João de Barros, *Decada Primeira*, Bk. IV, chap. vi.

[5] For the Chinese expeditions to the Indian Ocean, see the exhaustive study by Paul Pelliot, "Les Grands voyages maritimes chinois au début de XVᵉ siècle," *TP*, Vol. XXX (1933), pp. 237–452, forming a voluminous work in itself; and Duyvendak's valuable additions in his article "The True Dates of the Chinese Maritime Expeditions in the Early XVth Century," *TP*, Vol. XXXIV (1938), pp. 341–412. *Idem, China's Discovery of Africa* (London, 1949). The references to Ballard and Hudson are from the latter's *Europe and China*, p. 197. Cf. also K. Ishida, *Nankai ni kansuru Shina shiryo,* chap. vi, pp. 239–327, for a recent discussion of the Chinese overseas expeditions of the early Ming period.

[6] The best account of the Wako in a European language is the essay by Father Tschepe, *Japans Beziehungen zu China seit den ältesten Zeit bis zum Jahre 1600,* pp. 200–234. *Faute de mieux,* the reader may fall back on the study by Y. Takekoshi, *The Story of the Wako,* but those who can read Japanese will do better to consult Y. Okamoto, *Juroku Seiki Nichi-O*

kotsu-shi no kenkyu, pp. 99–124; and K. Akiyama's *Nichi-Shi kosho-shi kenkyu,* pp. 121–132, 411–620.

[7] João de Barros, *Decada Segunda,* Bk. VI, chap. ii. Cf. also my article in *THM* (Dec., 1939), pp. 447–450; A. Cortesão, *Historia,* Vol. II, chaps. x, xi, and the sources there quoted. The term *Folangki* was evidently derived by the Chinese from the Arab-Persian *Farangi* or *Firingi* meaning "Franks." Cf. Yule, *Hobson-Jobson, q.v.* "Firinghee," and Paul Pelliot's posthumous study in *TP,* Vol. XXXVIII (1948), esp. pp. 86–87.

[8] A. Cortesão, *The Suma Oriental of Tomé Pires,* Vol. I, 128–131. I refer to the Ryukyu and their inhabitants indiscriminately as Ryukyu and Luchuans. The parallel extract from the *Commentarios* (ed. 1576) is given in translation in my article in *TJS,* Vol. XXXIII (1936), pp. 14–15. Cf. Akiyama, *op. cit.,* pp. 121–132.

[9] Okamoto, *op cit.,* pp. 80–98, 787–791.

[10] Ferrand's sources for Al-Ghur, *apud* Cortesão: *Tomé Pires,* Vol. I, 128, note 2. I think there is no question of Formosa being meant in the present instance, since the island was then inhabited only by savage headhunters who navigated nowhere. It was very seldom visited either by Chinese or by Japanese before the seventeenth century. Chinese accounts do not always clearly distinguish between Formosa and the Ryukyu, but the descriptions given by Pires and Albuquerque were only applicable *ca.* 1510 to the latter group. For the name Japan, cf. Yule, *op. cit.,* who was not, however, aware of Pires' early mention. It may be noted in passing that João de Barros writing his *Decada Segunda* in 1549, alludes to the islands of the Iapões, although his work did not appear in print until three years later. The Perso-Arab geographer, Ibn Khordadzbeh (848–886), evidently refers to Japan under the form *Wa-kuo* or *Wa-kwok,* "country of the Was," transcribed by him as *Wakwak,* and derived from an old Sino-Korean name for Japan, as heard by Moslem traders with the Korean kingdom of Sila. Cf. *AAPH,* 2d ser., Vol. I (1946), pp. 25–31.

[11] The principal Chinese and European references to Portuguese-Chinese-Wako contacts along the China coast in the first half of the sixteenth century are collected in Okamoto, *op. cit.,* pp. 99–139, esp. 113–116 and 122–125; cf. also Akiyama, *op. cit.,* pp. 585–602, and J. M. Braga, "The Western Pioneers and Their Discovery of Macao," *BIPH,* Vol. II (1949), pp. 7–214.

[12] Cf. Pires' report on China *apud* Cortesão, *Tomé Pires,* Vol. I, 116–128.

[13] For the local Chinese accounts of Portuguese doings, cf. F. S. Balfour, "Hong Kong before the British," *THM* (Jan.–May, 1941), pp. 39–42 of the reprint; J. M. Braga, "Tamão of the Portuguese Pioneers," *THM* (May 1939). *Idem,* article in *BIPH,* Vol. II (1949), pp. 7–214. The versions of Barros and Castanheda, together with some Chinese records are given in D. Ferguson, *Letters from Portuguese Captives in Canton,* 1534–36 [1524] (Bombay, 1902), pp. 8–23, which should be read in conjunction with Cortesão, *Tomé Pires,* Vol. I, xxix–liii, to which should be added Damião

de Goes, *Chronica del Rei D. Manoel,* Vol. II, Pt. IV, 56–58, of the Coimbra University reprint edition, 1926. Goes' mention of *Lequeos, Guores,* and *Japangos* is interesting and at first sight implies that the *Guores* were in fact Koreans. But I think the description of their national characteristics by Pires and Albuquerque proves they were rather Japanese, as argued in the text. T'ien-Tsê Chang, *Sino-Portuguese Trade from 1514 to 1644* (Leiden, 1934), pp. 36–68, corrects some of Ferguson's erroneous Chinese identifications but otherwise adds nothing new of any importance. Chang did not know of Goes' account. Cf. also Okamoto, *op. cit.,* pp. 113–139 for Sino-Portuguese contacts along the China coast, which are also discussed by Akiyama, *op. cit.,* pp. 600–602.

[14] *Letters from Dorothy Osborne to Sir William Temple, 1652–1654,* ed. Parry (London, 1888), p. 245. Samuel Purchas had also made an eloquent plea on behalf of Pinto's reliability in his *Pilgrimes* (1625), Vol. III, pp. 251–252.

[15] The literature on Pinto is voluminous, but the following works will suffice. The *advocatus diaboli* is Father Georg Schurhammer, S.J., whose painstaking demolition of Pinto's reliability as a historian will convince most readers of his *Fernão Mendes Pinto und seine "Peregrinaçam,"* and "O descobrimento do Japão pelos Portugueses no ano de 1543," *AAPH,* 2d ser., Vol. I (1946), pp. 1–172. Both of these works contain full bibliographical surveys of everything of importance written on Pinto in European languages and in Japanese up to the time of their respective dates of publication. Dr. Armando Cortesão made an interesting contribution to the question of Pinto's allegedly Jewish origin in *Seara Nova,* No. 842 (Oct., 1943), but his valiant efforts to defend Pinto's fantastic account of his alleged travels in Tartary and China (*Tomé Pires,* Vol. I, xlviii–lx), to my mind at least, carry no conviction against the arguments of Ferguson (*op. cit.,* pp. 35–39) and Schurhammer, save on a very few minor points. The same may be said of the latest patriotic Portuguese effort to rehabilitate Pinto by the Visconde de Lagoa (*A Peregrinação de Fernão Mendes Pinto. Tentativa de reconstituição geográfica,* Lisbon, 1947), who even credits his hero with a trip to Korea which is one of the few places in the Far East that Pinto does not claim to have visited. The two Portuguese savants have a like-minded if rather less ardent colleague in the Japanese historian Y. Okamoto, who labored to prove the comparative reliability of Pinto's version of the discovery of Japan, in a number of studies finally collated in his *Juroku Seiki.* There are modern annotated editions of the Portuguese text of the *Peregrinaçam* by Brito Rebello (1908), Jordão de Freitas (1930), and Costa Pimpão (1944), but one by a qualified Orientalist has yet to appear. Some of Pinto's editors tend to become infected with his credulity. Thus C. D. Ley in *Portuguese Voyages* (London, 1948), accepts Pinto's fantastic tale of the imperial mausoleum on "Calemphuy" Island, girdled three miles round with a wall of jasper twenty-six spans high, on the grounds that so vivid

an account can hardly be second hand. Vivid it certainly is, but vivid in the
same way as the Revelation of St. John the Divine, or Coleridge's dream of
the Xanadu of Kublai Khan. Professor Le Gentil in his *Fernão Mendes Pinto,
un précurseur de l'exotisme au XVIe siécle* (Paris, 1947), and still more
Maurice Collis in *The Grand Peregrination* (London, 1949), bring out the
great value and interest of Pinto's work from the literary point of view,—
something which is much less debatable than its historical or geographical
veracity, but which has been insufficiently appreciated in the past. Collis'
book appeared after my work had been written, but I would add that he
makes out a convincing case for his belief that the Jesuits' antagonism to
Pinto after he left the Society has been exaggerated by many writers, myself included.

[16] G. Schurhammer, S.J., "Um Documento inédito sobre Fernão Mendes
Pinto," *Revista de Historia,* Vol. XIII (1924), pp. 81–88, esp. 87–88. A
German translation is in his *Fernão Mendes Pinto und seine "Peregrinaçain,"*
pp. 34–42. The Portuguese version is reprinted in his article in *AAPH*, 2d
ser., Vol. I (1946), pp. 146–147.

[17] Or in Siam, where he says (chap. 183, ed. 1614) that he traded continuously in 1540–1545.

[18] Diogo do Couto, *Decada Quinta* (ed. 1612), Bk. VIII, chap. xii, 183–
184; Antonio Galvão, *Tractado* (Lisbon, 1563), and Garcia de Escalante's
report of 1548, in English translation after W. E. Dahlgren, "A Contribution to the History of the Discovery of Japan," *TJS*, Vol. XI (1914), pp.
239–260. All reproduced in Schurhammer's essay in *AAPH*, Vol. I (1946).
Father Schurhammer (*ibid.,* p. 129) states that Couto merely embroidered
Lucena's account of 1600, but since Couto sent home the manuscript of
his *Decada Quinta* in 1597 (cf. the preface to his *Decada Setima*) it is obvious that, on the contrary, Lucena merely summarized Couto's account.
Both probably relied on Galvão's version, but both had the opportunity of
checking it.

[19] The Japanese sources are printed and discussed by Okamoto, *op. cit.,*
pp. 156–160, 187–189. There is a German translation of the most relevant
passages in H. Haas, *Geschichte des Christentums in Japan,* Vol. I, 15–49.
English abstracts are available in James Murdoch, *A History of Japan,*
Vol. II, 41–43, and Portuguese, in C. Ayres, *Fernão Mendes Pinto e o Japão,*
pp. 14–17, and Schurhammer's essay in *AAPH*, 2d ser., Vol. I (1946),
pp. 102–104, 112–116.

[20] Passage in full in Ayres, *op. cit.,* pp. 10–11. For the Scots pilot
"Antão Corço," cf. Schurhammer, *Die Zeitgenossischen Quellen zur
Geschichte Portugiesisch-Asiens und seiner Nachbarländer zur zeit des hl.
Franz Xaver,* p. 80, and Okamoto, *op. cit.,* p. 143. Cf. Schurhammer's essay
in *AAPH*, 2d ser., Vol. I (1946), p. 107.

[21] Pinto, *Peregrinaçam* (Lisbon, 1614), fol. 160. Cf. also *TASJ*, 2d ser.,
Vol. VIII (1931), pp. 69–73. Also Schurhammer's article on the Portu-

guese discovery of Japan in *AAPH*, 2d ser., Vol. I (1946), pp. 149–172.

[22] Japanese texts in Okamoto, *op. cit.*, pp. 187–189. German translation in Haas, *op. cit.*, Vol. I, 29–30, Portuguese in Ayres, *op. cit.*, p. 15, and French in Le Gentil, *op. cit.*, p. 152, although the last has not understood the word *Seinamban*. The latest and best version is Schurhammer, *AAPH*, 2d ser., Vol. I (1946), pp. 102–104.

[23] Spanish original in *Colección de documentos inéditos, relativos al descubrimiento ... de las antiguas posesiones Españolas en America y Oceania* (Madrid, 1855), Tomo V, 202–204; whence Dahlgren's English translation *op. cit.*, pp. 242–246. Schurhammer reproduces the Spanish text in *AAPH*, 2d ser., Vol. I (1946), pp. 89–91.

[24] Xavier in his letter, November 5, 1549, quoted p. 401, says fourteen, which is nearer the mark.

[25] A rather curious statement, for the Japanese have taken very kindly to the modern games of chance, betting, horse races, and so on, although it is true that these practices have always been officially frowned on by the government. Gambling, in the form of dice and cards, was then as now a favorite Portuguese pastime, and the Lusitanians took their passion with them to the East, being probably responsible for the introduction of playing cards into Japan.

[26] I have used the version of Alvares' report printed in *O Instituto*, Vol. 54 (Coimbra, 1906). For the various MSS copies of Alvares' report, cf. Schurhammer, *Quellen*, p. 234, no. 3567, and his remarks in *Shin-To the Way of the Gods in Japan*, pp. 161–164. For the Jesuit Lancilotto's report of December, 1548, utilized by Ramusio in 1554, cf. Schurhammer, *Quellen*, pp. 269–270. This report was only hearsay, being derived mostly from Yajiro.

[27] The latest and best survey of Xavier's voyage to and sojourn in Japan, based on a painstaking collation of all the known manuscripts and printed sources, is that by Schurhammer, *Der heilige Franz Xaver in Japan* (1549–1551), reprinted from the *SNZM*, Vol. II (Switzerland, 1946). The same author, who is the world's authority on the Apostle of the Indies, has recently edited in collaboration with Josef Wicki, S.J., the letters of St. Francis Xavier with a wealth of learned detail, under the title *Epistolae S. Francisci Xaverii aliaque eius scripta, 1535–1552*, of which Vol. II, 5–234, contains much relevant material for Xavier's voyage of 1549.

[28] Perhaps the wording of this sentence is intended as an implicit criticism of the Portuguese passion for gambling, like Father Antonio Vieira's remark in one of his sermons, "He who spends less than he has is prudent, he who spends all is a Christian, and he who spends more is a thief."

[29] There are several versions of this letter. I have translated from the Portuguese copy in *Cartas*, Vol. I, fols. 9–15. A fuller and annotated version of the Spanish original is in Schurhammer and Wicki, *op. cit.*, pp. 166–212.

[30] Padre Luis Frois' letter from Kyoto, April 27, 1565, in *Cartas*, fol. 184.

The Japanese likewise formed a high opinion of Xavier, a seventy-year-old convert describing him thus from his personal recollection in 1606: "A man tall of body, a gentleman, who did not understand the Japan tongue, but preached through an interpreter, and when he preached, his face became red and inflamed." (Padre João Rodrigues Girão, *apud* Schurhammer, *Der heilige Franz Xaver* [reprint], p. 20, note 31.)

NOTES TO CHAPTER II
Japan through Jesuit spectacles

[1] For the state of the nation during the *Sengoku-jidai* and the preceding era, cf. G. B. Sansom, *Japan. A Short Cultural History* (ed. 1946), pp. 351–425, containing the best general survey in English. Murdoch, *A History of Japan*, Vol. II, 15–32, has a good succinct account of the purely political scene. For the sale of court titles by the imperial house, cf. Letter of Cosme de Torres, October 8, 1561, in *Cartas*, fol. 74ᵛ. Those who can read Japanese will find additional "background" material in I. Tokutomi's *Kinsei Nihon Kokumin-shi*, Vols. I–III: *Oda-shi jidai*.

[2] They are collected in Schurhammer, *Shin-To, The Way of the Gods in Japan*, with text in German and English translation.

[3] Since it was mainly with Jesuits from the Province of Portugal that the Japan mission was concerned, the chief sources of information on their education and organization are those by Francisco Rodrigues, S.J., *A Formação Intellectual do Jesuita; A Companhia de Jesus em Portugal e nas missões; História da Companhia de Jesus na Assistência de Portugal*, Vols. I–III. Readers unacquainted with Portuguese will find material of interest in R. Fülöp-Miller, *The Power and Secret of the Jesuits* (London, 1930), and Father Brodrick's well-written if at times controversial volumes, *The Origin of the Jesuits* and *The Progress of the Jesuits, 1556–1579*. Littledale's article in the *Encyclopaedia Britannica* (9th ed., London, 1880), Vol. XIII, 645–656, though hostile in tone and often inapplicable to sixteenth-century Portugal, is still worth consulting as a general survey of Jesuit activity. The merits and defects of the Jesuits' educational system in Portugal are discussed by Professor Hernani Cidade in his *Lições na Cultura e Literatura Portuguesa*; the relevant articles in *The Catholic Dictionary* and in the American *Catholic Encyclopedia* will also be found useful as general guides.

[4] T. B. Macaulay, *History of England* (10th ed., London, 1854), Vol. II, 53–54.

[5] Cf. Fülöp-Miller, *op. cit.*, p. 5; M. Casaubon, *Meditations of Marcus Aurelius* (1635 ed.), pp. 75, 140, 163; Legacy of Ieyasu *apud* Sadler, *The Maker of Modern Japan*, p. 393.

[6] Cf. Sansom, *op. cit.*, p. 350 for his amusing rejoinder. Padre Polanco's bitter criticism of Almeida's and Frois' detailed accounts of Nara and Kyoto

is cited by Schurhammer, *Quellen*, p. xxxv, whence a French translation in H. Bernard, *Aux Portes de la Chine. Les Missionaires du seizième siècle, 1514–1588* (Tientsin, 1933), p. xiii. The Jesuit letters of 1549–1589 utilized in the present work are to be found in *Cartas*.

⁷ *Cartas*, fol. 92. It is interesting to compare Vilela's account with that given by Isaac Titsingh of the Bon Festival as he saw it at Nagasaki *ca.* 1780. "The spectator would almost imagine that he beheld a torrent of fire pouring from the hill, owing to the immense number of boats that are carried to the shore to be turned adrift on the sea. In the middle of the night, and when there is a brisk wind, the agitation of the water causing all these lights to dance to and fro, produces an enchanting scene . . . The whole bay seems to be covered with *ignes fatui*" (*Illustrations of Japan* [London, 1822], p. 143). The *O-Bon*, more accurately *Urabon* festival is of Chinese origin and often called by foreigners the "Feast of Lanterns." In country districts of Japan it is usually made the occasion of a primitive community dance on the last night of the three-day festival known as the *Bon-Odori*, of which Wenceslau de Moraes has given a classic account in his *O-Bon Odori em Tokushima* (Oporto, 1916).

⁸ *Cartas*, fol. 63ᵛ. Frois "lifted" this account almost bodily from Almedia's letter and included it in his own *Historia de Japam*. Cf. the German translation of Frois' work by Schurhammer and E. A. Voretzsch, *Die Geschichte Japans, 1549–1578*, pp. 243–244, whence Sadler translated his English version in *Cha-no-yu. The Japanese Tea Ceremony*, pp. 90–92. It will be noticed that Frois correctly substitutes Diogo for Sancho as the name of the Japanese convert. The ceremony is fully explained in Professor Sadler's book. The term *Chado*, "way of tea," corresponding to *Kendo*, "way of the sword," *Bushido*, "way of the Bushi," etc., is more correct.

⁹ *Cartas*, fol. 165. Frois likewise embodied Almeida's account in his *Historia* (Schurhammer-Voretzsch, *op. cit.*, p. 248). Annotated Japanese extracts from these letters of 1561–1565, together with others of the same period were printed by N. Murakami and S. Watanabe in *Yasokai-shi Nihon Tsushin* (Tokyo, 1927), Vol. I, 23–48, 126–175.

¹⁰ B. H. Chamberlain, "Basho and the Japanese Poetical Epigram," *TASJ*, Vol. XXX, Pt. II (1902), p. 305.

¹¹ The extracts which follow are taken from the collected *Cartas* of 1598 checked by reference to Professor Murakami's annotated selection in Japanese, *op. cit.* Background material may be obtained by consulting Murdoch, *op. cit.*, Vol. II, chap. vii, pp. 144–188, and Sansom, *op. cit.*, pp. 404–422. The material in the *Cartas* is amplified in some particulars in the German translation of Frois' *Historia* (Schurhammer-Voretzsch, *op. cit.*), which may be consulted by those who can read German but not Portuguese. Readers who can grapple with Japanese will find interesting material from Japanese sources in the series of historical essays on the period entitled *Adzuchi-Momoyama jidai shiron* published by the Nihon Rekishi Chiri Gakkai

[Japan Historical and Geographical Society] (Tokyo, 1914). Cf. also M. Anesaki, *Kirishitan dendo no kohai*, pp. 138–158.

¹² *Cartas*, fols. 257–268; Schurhammer-Voretzsch, *op. cit.*, pp. 372–373. Murdoch gives a lengthy account of this interview and what followed therefrom (*op. cit.*, pp. 153–160), but has mistaken the date of these events which occurred in 1569, not 1568. Professor Murakami remarks that Frois' account of the building of Nijo castle complements the traditional version as given in the *Nobunaga-ki*. The later Japanese accounts of Nobunaga and the Jesuits contain the merest modicum of truth among a mass of fairy tales more resembling Sinbad the Sailor, than serious history, but may be read for amusement's sake in the English translation by Paske-Smith and Inouye, *Japanese Traditions of Christianity*, pp. 6–48.

¹³ *Cartas*, fols. 261–262, 270, 313; Schurhammer-Voretzsch, *op. cit.*, p. 375, where the date of Nobunaga's patent is given as April 25, 1569, and that of the shogun as May 2. The trouble with the Tenno and Nichijo is related at great length by Frois (Schurhammer-Voretzsch, *op. cit.*, pp. 377–404). Shorter but substantially accurate (save for the date) is Murdoch, *op. cit.*, 158–162.

¹⁴ *Cartas*, fols. 272–276; Schurhammer-Voretzsch, *op. cit.*, pp. 397–398. Frois' descriptions of Nijo, Gifu, and Adzuchiyama in the *Cartas* may be read in conjunction with McClatchie's paper on the castle and feudal mansions of Yedo in *TASJ*, 1st ser., Vols. VI–VII. Despite the difference in taste between the Adzuchi and Yedo periods, the architectural essentials were the same. Cf. also *The Castles of Japan*, Japanese Government Tourist Library Series, No. 9 (Tokyo, 1936), which contains some excellent photographs of the then-surviving structures.

¹⁵ The following extracts are from *Cartas*, fols. 319–330, checked with the Japanese identifications of Murakami, *op. cit.*, Vol. II, 164–220. Cf. also Schurhammer-Voretzsch, *op. cit.*, pp. 234–241, and Schurhammer, "Das Stadtbild Kyotos zur zeit des heiligen Franz Xavier," *Anthropos*, Bd. 14–17 (1919–1922), *passim*.

¹⁶ *Cartas*, fol. 320. For a good description of the style of these byobu which both Frois and Vilela admired so much, cf. Sansom, *op. cit.*, p. 440. Undoubtedly some of those Vilela saw were by masters of the Kano school.

¹⁷ *Cartas*, fol. 325; cf. also Schurhammer, *Shin-To*, p. 63. Red and green, not gold, are nowadays the most prominent colors in the decoration of the Kasuga Jinja, and the lamps referred to by Vilela as lighted nightly are now lighted annually on the Festival of *Setsubun*. Otherwise the description virtually holds good today, the "mitered" men being the Shinto priests, the sorceresses the sacred dancing girls or *Miko*, who perform the ritual dance known as *Kagura* for a nominal fee. The shrine was founded by the Fujiwara family in 768 as their tutelary shrine, the grounds covered an extent of 213 acres (in 1931) wherein roamed about a thousand deer.

¹⁸ *Cartas*, fols. 326–327. Cf. Murdoch, *op. cit.*, pp. 163–166, and Sansom,

op. cit., pp. 408–410, for the militant Monto or Ikko monks. They may perhaps be compared to a mixture of the fanatical Anabaptist and mercenary *landsknecht* who caused such trouble in contemporary western Germany, although Vilela, temporarily forgetful (I presume) of his unbridled denunciation of their alleged addiction to sodomy, compares them to the Knights of Rhodes! For the prevalence of pederasty in feudal Japan, cf. Yoshi S. Kuno, *Japanese Expansion on the Asiatic Continent*, Vol. II, 368–369.

[19] Frois' letter dated October 4, 1571, in *Cartas*, fols. 330–333. For the Sanno (wrongly transcribed in *Cartas* as Canon, which has misled many Western writers into mistakenly identifying the Shinto deity with the Buddhist goddess Kwannon) cult on Hieizan and at Kyoto, cf. Schurhammer, *Shinto*, pp. 67–70.

[20] Nobunaga's character and death are described in great detail by Frois in his letter of November 5, 1582 (*Cartas*, Vol. II, fols. 61–82) and more succinctly in the second part of his *Historia de Japam*, ed. Pinto and Okamoto, pp. 323–331). For a more detailed discussion of Nobunaga's attitude toward Christianity, cf. the recent studies in Japanese and German by J. Laures, S.J., *Oda Nobunaga to Kirisuto-kyo* (1947), and *Nobunaga und das Christentum* (Tokyo, 1949).

[21] For details of Valignano and his work in Japan, cf. the articles by Voss, Bernard, Braga, and others in *MN*, Vol. I, 70–98, 378–385; Vol. V, 244–245, 523–535; Vol. VI, 391–403 (1938–1943). Father Bernard has proved that Valignano is a more correct orthography than the usually accepted Valignani. MSS copies of his "Sumario" and related reports are to be found at Rome, Evora, Lisbon, and London, of which I have used the British Museum, Additional MSS 9852. Cf. also Valignano's *Historia del principio y progresso de la Compañia de Jesús en las Indias Orientales* (1542–1564), edited with true Jesuit erudition and Teutonic thoroughness by Josef Wicki, S.J., in the Bibliotheca Instituti Historici Societatis Iesu, Vol. II. Pages 126–163 of this work contain the equivalent of chapters i–iii of the 1583 "Sumario" which are in themselves merely an expanded version of chapters xv–xvii of the original draft of August, 1580. Much of this material is likewise included in the highly interesting treatise on Japanese manners and customs compiled by Valignano's orders under the title: *Advertimentos e avisos acerca dos costumes e catangues de Jappão*, printed from the original Portuguese draft of November, 1583–February, 1584, with an Italian translation, notes, and commentary by Joseph Schütte, S.J., *Il ceremoniale per i missionari del Giappone*. There is also a good biographical sketch of Valignano and a modern portrait of him in Father Pasquale d'Elia's *Fonti Ricciane*, Vol. I, 144–146.

[22] British Museum, Add. MSS 9852, pp. 24–25. Valignano compiled an expanded version of the Japan section of the "Sumario" at Cochin in October, 1583 (Brit. Mus., Add. MSS 9852, fols. 71–96), the first three chapters

of which are printed in *Monumenta Xavierana,* Vol. I, 158–188, and again in Father Wicki's edition of the *Historia,* pp. 126–163, as explained in the previous note.

²³ Summary of Valignano's comparison in Portuguese *apud* Francisco de Sousa, S.J., *Oriente Conquistado,* Vol. II, 548–549. The full version, too long for reproduction here, will be found in Father Wicki's annotated edition of the original Spanish *Historia del principio,* pp. 142–150.

²⁴ Valignano, "Sumarios" of 1580 and 1582 (Brit. Mus., Add. MSS 9852), the gist of which is extracted in Sousa, *op. cit.,* Vol. II, 533–553. Cf. also Wicki's edition of Valignano's *Historia del principio,* pp. 126–163.

²⁵ Valignano's attitude is set forth at length in chapter xxvi of the 1580 "Sumario" (Brit. Mus., Add. MSS 9852, pp. 46–48). Cf. also Vieira's "Obediencias" of 1619 in Biblioteca da Ajuda, Lisbon, Codex "Jesuitas na Asia," 49-iv-56. This codex is hereinafter cited as Ajuda Codex "Jesuitas na Asia." The Jesuit attitude toward the crypto-Jews had noticeably hardened since the days of St. Ignatius de Loyola who showed himself much more tolerant, as Father Brodrick explains in *The Progress of the Jesuits* (1556–1579), pp. 116–120, 310–316. This change for the worse was probably induced by the great pressure brought to bear at Rome by the Portuguese and Spaniards in the Society. Cf. Ajuda Codex "Jesuitas na Asia," 49-iv-56, pp. 343–344 (Del modo de hazer las informaciones de la limpieza a los q̃ piden la Compañia).

²⁶ Cf. Father Jean de Fontaney's letter from London dated January 15, 1704, in Lockman, *Travels of the Jesuits into Various Parts of the World; Compiled from Their Letters* (London, 1743), Vol. II, 233. With the substitution of "Japanese" for "Chinese," the rest of Fontaney's letter could easily be taken for an extract from Valignano's "Sumario" (Oct., 1583), chaps. xxii–xxiii. Cf. also Schütte, *op. cit.,* p. 290.

The Jesuit Fernão de Queiroz alleged that the Japanese converts behaved with so much more reverence and decorum in church than did their Portuguese coreligionists that the Jesuits of the Japan mission often celebrated separate Masses for both races on this account (*Conquista temporal e espiritual de Ceylão,* 1687 [Colombo, 1916], p. 932).

²⁷ Sousa, *op. cit.,* Vol. II, 550; Valignano, "Sumario" (1583), chaps. xiii, xvi, "especialmente a los Portugueses que estan acostumbrados a chamar negros aun a los Chinas y Japones"; Diogo do Couto, *Dialogo do Soldado Pratico Portuguez* (ed. 1790), p. 36, "... de geração limpa Portugueza, e não de filhos que tem mais parentes em Cambaya, que de Tra-los Montes": *Diario do Conde de Linhares, Visorei da India, passim;* The Conde de São Vicente wrote the king in 1666 that a rajah of Cochin had once tried to improve his breed of horses by importing European stud mares, but they either aborted or produced weakling foals fit for nothing. The viceroy drew the obvious parallel with the Goanese *mestiços* and Eurasians. Professor G. Freyre (*Brazil, An Interpretation; Casa Grande e Senzala,* and other

works) has adduced powerful arguments to show that the alleged physical inferiority of half-castes was due to their insufficient alimentation and bad up-bringing in unhygienic surroundings. Given proper food and healthy surroundings, there is no reason why they should be physically or mentally inferior to the general run of sinful man.

[28] Valignano's "Sumarios" of 1580 and 1583 (Brit. Mus., Add. MSS 9852); Ajuda Codex "Jesuitas na Asia," 49-iv-56; Sousa, *op. cit.*, II, 533–553; *MN*, Vol. V (1942), 244. For the functioning of these seminaries when they were established, cf., D. Schilling, O.F.M., *Das Schulwesen der Jesuiten in Japan* (1551–1614). Schütte, *op. cit.*, likewise contains valuable relevant material.

[29] The Dojuku and their functions are described at length in chapter xv of the 1583 "Sumario" (de los Dogicos, y sus qualidades, y como no se puedan escusar en Japan). Cf. also the "Addiciones" of 1592; the "Obediencias" as revised by Pasio in 1612 and Vieira in 1619, in Ajuda Codex "Jesuitas na Asia," 49-iv-56; and the *Advertimentos e avisos dos costumes e catangues de Jappão* (Schütte, *op. cit.*, pp. 21–22; and the index thereto, *q.v.* "dojuku").

[30] Ajuda Codex "Jesuitas na Asia," 49-v-56 contains the relevant material for the period 1590–1614. The most detailed (although inevitably incomplete) martyrology is in M. Anesaki, *A Concordance to the History of the Kirishitan Missions*, pp. 25–80. Delplace, *Le Catholicisme au Japon*, Vol. I, 201, states that of a total of eighty Jesuit martyrs during the period 1597–1640, fifty-three were Japanese. For short biographies of these, cf. Antonio Francisco Cardim, S.J., *Elogios e Ramalhete de flores ... Com o catalogo de todos os Religiosos e seculares que por odio da mesma Fé forão mortos naquelle Imperio até o anno de 1640.*

NOTES TO CHAPTER III
Christianity and the Kurofune

[1] The best review of Portuguese trade on the China coast in the first half of the sixteenth century is still that by D. Ferguson, *Letters from Portuguese Captives in Canton 1534–36* [1524], which has not been superseded by the later work of T'ien-Tsê Chang, *Sino-Portuguese Trade from 1514 to 1644*, nor by A. Kammerer's *La Découverte de la Chine par les portugais au XVIème siècle et la cartographie des portulans*, which may, however, be consulted to rectify Ferguson's work on a few minor points. The fullest account of the Sino-Portuguese agreement of 1557, and of the events leading up to it will be found in J. Braga, "O primeiro accordo Luso-Chines," reprinted from *BEDM*, Vol. XXXVI (1940), pp. 376–392 and in *BIPH*, Vol. II (1949), pp. 7–214. These authoritative articles embody many more Chinese sources than those used in T'ien-Tsê Chang's pretentious but un-

satisfactory work, besides utilizing unpublished or little-known Portuguese material from the archives of Ajuda and elsewhere. Cf. also Dr. Yano's article in *BSL-J*, Vol. I (1929), pp. 70–77, and T. Fujita's essay, "Porutogaru-jin Macao senryo ni itaru made no sho mondai," in his *To-Sei kosho-shi no kenkyu (Nankai-hen)* (Tokyo, 1932), pp. 417–491.

² Gago's letter in *Cartas*, Part I (1598), fols. 38–41. The "Sumario" quotations are from British Museum, Add. MSS 9852. Cf. also J. Laures, S.J., *Kinki Shoki Christokyo-shi*.

³ The best Japanese source on the Luso-Japanese trade in the sixteenth century is Y. Okamoto's *Juroku Seiki Nichi-O kotsu-shi no kenkyu*. Readers unable to cope with this language, may be referred to the English translation of Y. Takekoshi's *The Economic Aspects of the History of the Civilization of Japan;* but the greatest caution is necessary in using this work, which is full of misprints, mistranslations, and misapprehensions. Nevertheless, despite its innumerable faults, it contains a great deal of Japanese material which will be quite new to the average Western reader. It is when Takekoshi turns to European sources to check or complement his Japanese records that he and his mistranslator fall flat on their faces. What he has to say about Nobunaga's financial policy and methods of amassing gold (*op. cit.*, Vol. I, 352–354, 363–364, 377–384 and Vol. II, 373–374) is for the most part both relevant and interesting, and is borne out by the observations of Vilela and Frois in their *Cartas*. Cf. also Delmer M. Brown, "The Importation of Gold into Japan by the Portuguese during the Sixteenth Century," *Pacific Historical Review*, Vol. XVI, No. 2 (May, 1947), pp. 125–133, for a clear and concise presentation of the problem.

⁴ It has often been reproduced. There is a good photograph of it in Henri Bernard, S.J., *Les Premiers rapports de la culture européene avec la civilisation japonaise*, which, though small, is perfectly legible. An English translation will be found in R. Hildreth's *Japan as It Was and Is*.

⁵ "Sumario" (1583), chap. xi (Brit. Mus. Add. MSS 9852, fol. 54); Melchior Carneiro, S.J., Bishop of Nicaea and coadjutor of the Patriarch of Ethiopia (1555–1566) was, properly speaking, episcopal delegate and not Bishop of China and Japan at Macao from 1568 till his death there in 1583. His successor, to whom Valignano alludes, was Dom Leonardo de Sá, who was no Jesuit and hence unlikely to agree with their viewpoint. Valignano still pressed for this brief in 1592, instancing the behavior of Captain-Major Domingos Monteiro who insisted on taking his ship into Hirado, despite the opposition of the Jesuits, in 1586–1588. The result was that the anti-Christian daimyo, Matsura, who was on the point of being totally defeated by the Catholic convert, Omura, not only received a new lease of life but forced the latter to sue for peace on disadvantageous terms. In extenuation of Monteiro's conduct it may be pointed out that, in 1586, Nagasaki was occupied by Shimadzu of Satsuma, who was every bit as hostile to the Faith as was Matsura of Hirado.

⁶ Shimadzu Takahisa's letter of Eiroku 4 (1561–1562) in *Cartas* (1598) Vol. I, fol. 112; Japanese translation and comment in Y. Okamoto's *Nagasaki kaiko izen O-hakurai oko*, pp. 253–263. For the attitude of the Kyushu daimyo in general, cf. Takekoshi, *op. cit.*, Vol. I, 283–315, but many of his statements require careful checking. In May, 1581, the daimyo of Kaga, Shibata Katsuie, pressed Frois to arrange for the Macao carrack to visit his fief in western Honshu, offering to loan the Portuguese merchants from ten to twenty thousand taels to start business there. This is a striking instance of the importance of the Kurofune. See *Cartas* (1598), Part. II, 11ᵛ. In 1582, the Jesuits were toying with a scheme to secure Yamagawa in Satsuma as a terminal port for the Great Ship, since Christianity was making great strides there. (Frois, *Segunda Parte da Historia de Japam*, 1582, ed. Pinto-Okamoto, p. 296.)

⁷ *Cartas* (1598) Part I, fol. 100ᵛ; Valignano's second (and better) thoughts on preserving strict neutrality in Japanese internecine disputes are embodied in chapter ii ("Das Cousas da Guerra") of his "Obediencias" (Ajuda Codex "Jesuitas na Asia," 49-iv-56). The comedy of Jesuit interference in the Omura-Arima dispute is related in the 1592 "Addiciones" to the 1583 "Sumario" (Ajuda Codex "Jesuitas na Asia"). Cf. also Father Schütte, *Il Ceremoniale per i missionari del Giappone*, pp. 148–152.

⁸ British Museum, Add. MSS 9852, p. 31. The best Japanese printed sources for the origin of Nagasaki are Okamoto, *Juroku Seiki*, and T. Nagayama's article (in Japanese) on the founding of Nagasaki in *BSL-J*, Vol. I, No. 1 (1939), pp. 143–149. Takekoshi's account (*op. cit.*, Vol. I, 308) is, as usual, a rather garbled one, but does not differ in essence from Valignano's version. Cf. also the Schurhammer-Voretsch translation of Luis Frois' *Historia de Japam*, *Die Geschichte Japans*, p. 404, and Delplace, *Le Catholicisme au Japon*, Vol. I, 176–180.

⁹ The attitude of "killing no murder" implicit in Valignano's complaint that the Jesuits could not summarily execute their converts in 1583, is revealed still more frankly in chapter xxi of this same "Sumario," which deals with the powers that should be conferred on the Jesuit superior in Japan. He puts up a strong plea for allowing local Jesuits to advise Christian daimyo to kill anyone they might think necessary, if the safety of the local Christian community would seem to demand it, "not only generally but in specific cases, since there is no living in Japan without so doing, and killing and enforcing justice here cannot be done after the fashion of European laws." Second thoughts, however, proved better, or else his superiors at Rome did not approve, for the "Addiciones" of 1592, and the "Obediencias" of 1612, both contain the strictest injunctions against doing anything of the kind, or trying to interfere with local politics in any way. (Ajuda Codex "Jesuitas na Asia," 49-iv-56). Cf. also Schütte, *op. cit.*, pp. 148–152. In extenuation of Valignano's viewpoint, it can be said that this was shared by the heretic Hollanders and English who visited Japan in

the next century. The English factor, Richard Cocks, after describing how he saw a crucified murderer and the heads of ten decapitated criminals exposed at Fushimi in August, 1616, adds, "Yf it were not for this strict justice, it were no liveing amongst them, they are so villanouse desperate" (*Diary of Richard Cocks*, ed. N. Murakami [Tokyo, 1899], Vol. I, 161).

[10] The foregoing is from the "Sumario" of 1583 (Brit. Mus. Add MSS 9852) and the "Addiciones" of 1592 (Ajuda Codex "Jesuitas na Asia," 49-iv-56). The standard Japanese work for the importance of foreign trade during this period is Okamoto, *Juroku Seiki Nichi-O kotsu-shi no kenkyu* which is a careful and conscientious synthesis of both Portuguese and Japanese sources. Takekoshi, *op. cit.*, contains a wealth of material, but, as already noted, it is so uncoördinated, ill-digested, and mistranslated into "English as she is Japped," that only the student with a good working knowledge of the period can consult it with safety. Professor M. Anesaki discusses the connection of trade and Christianity in the foundation of Nagasaki in his *Kirishitan dendo no kohai*, pp. 107–113.

[11] Valignano, "Sumario" (1583), chap. xxix (Brit. Mus. Add. MSS 9852). For the captain-major's position and privileges, cf. C. R. Boxer, *Fidalgos in the Far East*, pp. 4–7, 9, 15–18, 29 ff., 269–271; *idem, As Viagens de Japão e os seus Capitães-Mores, 1550–1640.*

[12] Cf. the two anonymous Spanish reports on Portuguese trade in the Far East (Archivo de Indias, Seville, 1–2, 1/13) printed in F. Colin and P. Pastells, *Labor Evangélica de los obreros de la Compañia de Jesus en las islas Filipinas*, Vol. III, 218–221; Pedro de Baeza, *Memorial ...*, fols. 6–8; Boxer, *Fidalgos in the Far East*, pp. 15–17; J. H. Van Linschoten, *Discours of Voyages*, chap. xxv, 42–44, and the Linschoten Vereeniging's annotated reprint of the Dutch original of 1596, edited by Professor Kern, Vol. I, 99–103. It is interesting to compare the anonymous Spanish lists of *ca.* 1600, with the price lists for the same commodities given by Saris in 1613. Cf. E. M. Satow, *Voyage of Captain John Saris to Japan, 1613*, pp. 203–211, 224–230. I am inclined to attribute either or both of the above-mentioned Spanish reports to Pedro de Baeza, who was the crown factor at Macao and who had been in Japan.

[13] Takekoshi, *op. cit.*, is, as usual, almost as much a hindrance as a help, when dealing with this complicated problem of the fluctuating ratio of value between gold and silver in Asia and Europe during the second half of the sixteenth century. But as the only Japanese source available in English dress, the student must be referred (with due caution) to what Takekoshi says in *op. cit.*, Vol. I, 311, 334; Vol. II, 32, 368–369, 405. He gives the value of gold to silver as 1 to 14 in Spain, 1 to 12 or 13 in Japan, and 1 to 11 in China. More specifically, we know from Saris' *Journal*, that the ratio of gold to silver in Japan in his day (1613) was 1 to 13, and in Europe 1 to 12. Pedro de Baeza, in his *Memorial* of 1609, alluding to conditions of the previous decade, states that the highest rate he had ever exchanged gold for

silver at Canton was 7 silver pesos for one of gold, whereas the corresponding rate in Spain was 12½ to one. (Cf. the extracts from his *Memorial* of January 15, 1609, printed in Appendix IV, pp. 425–427, below.) According to the Maeda document of 1592, Hideyoshi fixed the ratio of gold to silver as 1 to 10 at the beginning of his Korean campaign. (Y. Kuno, *Japanese Expansion on the Asiatic Continent,* Vol. I, 315.)

[14] Valignano, "Addiciones" 1592 (Ajuda Codex "Jesuitas na Asia," 49-iv-56); Takekoshi, *op. cit.,* Vol. II, 32–39, 374–377, 400–407. The above was written before the appearance of Delmer M. Brown's interesting essay on "The Importation of Gold into Japan by the Portuguese during the Sixteenth Century," *op. cit.,* pp. 125 ff., which should be consulted by all those interested in the subject.

[15] Valignano, "Sumario," 1583 (Brit. Mus. Add. MSS 9852); "Addiciones," 1592 (Ajuda Codex "Jesuitas na Asia," 49-iv-56); *Apologia* (1598); this last *apud* Colin-Pastells, *op. cit.,* Vol. II, 689–692.

[16] Valignano, "Sumario" (1583), chaps. xxvii–xxxiii; Sousa, *Oriente Conquistado,* Vol. II, 552–553. Colin-Pastells, *op. cit.,* Vol. II, 689–692.

[17] Valignano, "Sumario" (1580), chap. xvii; *ibid.* (1583), chaps. xxvii–xxix; "Apologia" *apud* Colin-Pastells, *op. cit.,* pp. 689–692; Sousa, *op. cit.,* pp. 552–553; D. Schilling, *Das Schulwesen der Jesuiten in Japan 1551–1614,* pp. 13–26 and sources there quoted. Valignano admitted that these high expenses were offset to some extent by the relative cheapness of the cost of living in Japan, where the annual cost of maintaining a European Jesuit was twenty ducats; a dojuku eight; and a servant four and a half; which sums were further drastically cut if the annual Nao miscarried ("Apologia," in Brit. Mus. Add. MSS 9856, chap. xvi, para. 50). His old friend, Otomo Sorin, likewise twitted the Jesuits with spending more money in a year on their establishments than he did in six months on the five provinces under his control during his prime ("Addiciones," 1592, Ajuda Codex "Jesuitas na Asia," 49-iv-56).

[18] Valignano, "Sumario" (1580), p. 32; *ibid.* (1583), chaps. xxvii–xxix; "Apologia," chap. xxvi, 38–44; Report of the Jesuit Visitor of the Japan Province, Padre Luis da Gama, on the trade of his province from 1567 to 1664, drawn up at Macao on December 15, 1664 (Ajuda Codex "Jesuitas na Asia," 49-iv-56; pp. 397–410). This last report is particularly valuable, for it gives a chronological survey of this knotty question, derived from a perusal of the original correspondence between Rome, Goa, Macao, and Nagasaki, preserved in the archives of the Macao College of Madre de Deus. Gama's report corrects and supplements Valignano's version. Cf. also Okamoto's article in the Luso-Japanese Society's *Nichi-Ho kotsu,* Vol. II (1943), pp. 173–214, which reproduces some of the original documents in Portuguese and Spanish.

[19] Gama's report of December 15, 1664, quoting Aquaviva's letter of April 10, 1597. Despite this warning, the Far Eastern Jesuits *did* trade in

commodities other than silk, and elsewhere than in Japan, as they were indeed obliged to do owing to force of circumstances. General Vitelleschi repeated the injunctions against *mercancias secretas* in his letter of January 15, 1619, to Father-Visitor Francisco Vieira (*loc. cit.*). The Macao fathers salved their consciences by declaring at their Congregation of 1623, that this business "non erat mercatura sed opus charitatis," and consequently could be expanded to meet all essential expenses; nor need the trading be limited to the silk formally licensed in 1582, but any suitable alternative could be substituted.

[20] Ajuda Codex "Jesuitas na Asia," 49-iv-56, pp. 400–410 *passim; Brotéria*, Vol. XLV, fasc. 5 (1947), p. 21; *Travels of Peter Mundy*, Vol. III, 164. For later criticisms of the Jesuit trade in China and Indo-China, cf. my article in *JRAS* (April, 1947), pp. 96–97; and *Fidalgos in the Far East*, esp. pp. 169–173.

[21] For the Portuguese carracks and their tonnage, cf. *The Mariner's Mirror*, Vol. XXVI (1940), pp. 388–406; Boxer, *Fidalgos in the Far East*, pp. 12–15; Organtino's letter on Nobunaga's shipping in *Cartas* (1598), Vol. I, fol. 415. Details of sixteenth-century Korean shipping are in H. H. Underwood's article, "Korean Boats and Ships," in *TRAS:K*, Vol. XXIII (1934). Chinese shipping tonnages from Takekoshi, *op. cit.*, and also from Okamoto's *Juroku Seiki*, pp. 197–198, 791–793. For the Spanish ships on the Manila-Mexico run, cf. W. L. Schurz, *The Manila Galleon* (New York, 1939), pp. 193–215.

[22] Cf. C. R. Boxer, "Portuguese Roteiros, 1500–1700," in *The Mariner's Mirror*, Vol. XX, No. 2 (April, 1934), pp. 171–185; A. Fontoura da Costa, *A marinharia dos Descobrimentos* (Lisbon, 1933; reprinted 1940); Gabriel Ferrand, *Relations de voyages et textes géographiques Arabes, Persans et Turks relatifs a l'Extrême-Orient du VII au XVII siècles* (2 vols; Paris, 1913–1914), and his *Introduction à l'astronomie nautique Arabe* (Paris, 1928); J. V. Mills, "Malaya in the Wu-pei-chih Charts," in *JRAS:M*, Vol. XV, Pt. III (Dec., 1937), pp. 1–48; J. L. Duyvendak, "Sailing Directions of Chinese Voyages" (from a Ming Sea Manual in the Bodleian Library) in *TP*, Vol. XXIV (1939), pp. 230–237.

[23] What follows is based on the English translation of the *Reysgeschrift* in Linschoten's *Itinerario* of 1595–1596, published as the third book to the *Discours of Voyages* by John Wolfe at London, 1598. The extracts have been checked by reference to the Linschoten Vereeniging's annotated reprint of the original Dutch edition in five volumes, of which Vols. 4 and 5 contain the relevant material. For my appraisal of the nautical value of this book I have relied heavily on the introduction of the learned Dutch editor of Vols. 4 and 5, the late J. C. M. Warnsinck, who, in addition to his numerous other qualifications, was captain of the naval surveying vessel *Eridanus* in the Netherlands East Indies from 1923 to 1925. I have, however, ventured to correct a few of his identifications of Japanese place names, which are

occasionally open to dispute. A. Kammerer's ambitious work on the China coast section of Linschoten's *Itinerario,* published as *La Découverte de la Chine par les portugais au XVIième siècle et la cartographie des portulans,* suffers from the inclusion of too much irrelevant material. It contains suggestive passages, although some of his identifications have been contested by critics better acquainted with the China coast than is the erudite French diplomat. After this chapter had gone to press, I received a copy of an interesting article by L. Bourdon, "Les Routes des marchands Portugais entre Chine et Japon au milieu du XVIe siècle," reprinted from an unspecified magazine published in Lisbon, 1949.

[24] Cf. Fontoura da Costa, "La Lieue marine des portugais au XVe et XVIe siècles," *Comptes Rendus du Congrès International de Géographie* (Amsterdam, 1938), Tome II, sect. iv, pp. 3–12; and J. C. M. Warnsinck, *Inleiding* to Deel IV of the *Itinerario* (Lin. Ver. ed.), Vol. XLIII, pp. lxiv–lxvii. Padre João Rodriguez, S.J., in his Japanese Grammar of 1608, gives the Kyushu maritime *Ri* or sea-mile as 18 *Cho;* one *cho* being nowadays the equivalent of 109 meters.

[25] *Discours* (1598), Book III, chap. xxxii, p. 385. I have corrected it from the Dutch original where necessary, for example, in the substitution of "hill" for "hovel" which the Elizabethan translator mistook for the Dutch *Heuvel.*

[26] Yule and Burnell, *Hobson-Jobson* (ed. 1903), pp. 947–950. Linschoten's evidence is one of the rare omissions from this work and from the complementary *Glossario Luso-Asiatico* of Dalgado.

[27] Warnsinck, *op. cit.,* p. xiv. For the calculation of tides during the sixteenth century, cf. the article by A. E. Stephens in *Imago Mundi,* Vol. II (1937), pp. 55–59.

[28] The standard work on this subject is still essentially W. E. Dahlgren's essay on *Les Débuts de la cartographie du Japon,* when read, as it is meant to be, in conjunction with P. Teleki's *Atlas zur Geschichte der Kartographie der japanischen Inseln* (Budapest, 1909), and B. Gezelius, *Japan i västerländsk framställning till omkring år 1700* (Upsala, 1910). The later studies of O. Nachod, *Zur Kartographie Japans* (Berlin, 1910), and *Die Älteste Abendländische Manuskript-Spezialkarte von Japan von Fernão Vas Dourado, 1568,* in *Proceedings of the X. Congresso Internazionale di Geografia,* and A. Cortesão, *Cartografia e Cartógrafos Portugueses dos séculos XV e XVI,* brought additional valuable material. Some of the conclusions of these European savants require revision in the light of the Japanese material adducted by the native authors quoted in M. Ramming's article on "The Evolution of Cartography in Japan," *Imago Mundi,* Vol. II (1937), pp. 17–21, to which should be added the notable article of Professor H. Nakamura, "Les Cartes du Japon qui servaient de modèle aux cartographes européens au début des relations de l'Occident avec le Japon," *MN,* Vol. II (1939), pp. 100–123. The perennial fascination exercised by this topic is evidenced by the latest contributions, which have just come my way as I write these lines,

George Kiss, "The Cartography of Japan during the Middle Tokugawa Era; A Study in Cross-Cultural Influences," *Annals of the Association of American Geographers,* Vol. 37, No. 2 (June, 1947), pp. 101–119, and *idem,* "Some Aspects of the Missionary Cartography of Japan during the Sixteenth Century," *Imago Mundi,* Vol. VI (1949), pp. 39–47. The standard work in Japanese for the period is Okamoto's *Juroku Seiki sekai chizu-jo no Nihon,* which is based mainly on the material in Cortesão (*op. cit.*) but does not neglect Japanese sources.

²⁹ Nakamura, *op. cit.,* pp. 117–118. For the Iwami silver mines, cf. Takekoshi, *op. cit.,* Vol. I, 298–299, 455; Vol. II, 34, 38.

³⁰ Cf. *MN,* Vol. II, 119, 123, and fig. 8; *ibid.,* Vol. VI, 391–403. I. Ashida, "Sekai-zu byobu-ko," in *Rekishi-Chiri* (June, 1932), pp. 541–567. For João de Barros (1496–1570), and his interest in China, see my article in *THM,* Vol. IX (1939), pp. 447–468. For Matteo Ricci and his influence on the cartography of China and Japan, cf. the studies of Father Henri Bernard, S.J., in *Monumenta Serica,* Vol. I (1935–1936), pp. 432–446; Father Humbertclaude, S.M., in *MN,* Vol. III (1940), pp. 643–647; Pasquale d'Elia, *Il Mappamondo cinese del P. Matteo Ricci* (Vatican City, 1938); K. Ch'en, in *TP,* Vol. 34 (1938), pp. 179–190. The Gold and Silver Islands are the subject of a lengthy essay by M. Chassigneux "Rica de Oro et Rica de Plata" in *TP,* Vol. XXX (1933), pp. 37–84, but the last word on this fascinating cartographical by-path has not yet been said. I notice that these islands appear under their Japanese designation on the Hangchow draft sketch of a Portuguese map reproduced in Professor H. Nakamura's essay (*op. cit.,* Vol. II, 122, fig. 8). The gist of Valignano's account of Monteiro's (or Moreira) cosmographical and cartographical work in Japan, is given in Cortesão, *op. cit.,* Vol. II, 361–363. Saris' praise of Linschoten's *Itinerario* is to be found in the Hakluyt Society edition of *The Voyage of Captain John Saris,* p. 188.

NOTES TO CHAPTER IV
Jesuits and friars

¹ Valignano, "Sumario" (1583), chap. xxiv (Brit. Mus., Add. MSS 9852). The variety of Hideyoshi's names is confusing. Kinoshita Tokichiro Hideyoshi was born *ca.* 1535 in Owari. He later (1562) took the name of Hashiba Hideyoshi, and from 1574 used the title of Hashiba Chikuzen-no-kami. In 1586 he changed his name to Toyotomi Hideyoshi, having received three years previously the court title of Kwambaku or Kwampaku, which he surrendered to his nephew Hidetsugu in 1592, receiving in exchange that of Taiko, by which he was commonly known until his death in 1598. He rings the changes on all these names in the Jesuit letters of 1560–1598, and, for the sake of simplification, I normally refer to him in

this chapter as Hideyoshi or the Kwambaku. Cf. also *Cartas* (1598), Part
II, fol. 181, and Valignano's "Addiciones" of 1592 (Ajuda Codex "Jesuitas
na Asia," 49-iv-56), for Hideyoshi's attitude toward Christianity and
Buddhism. Those who can read Japanese will find a wealth of detail on
Hideyoshi's Japan in I. Tokutomi's *Kinsei Nihon Kokumin-shi,* Vols. IV–X.

² *Cartas* (1598), Part II, 174–180; Murdoch, *A History of Japan,* Vol.
II, 214–218. None of the printed sources concerning Coelho's momentous
interview with Hideyoshi at Osaka in 1586, contain any hint of the Vice-
Provincial's reactions to the Kwambaku's overtures. These are related in
Valignano's letter dated Nagasaki, October 14, 1590, preserved in the
Jesuit Archives at Rome ("Japsin," 11, fols. 233–236ᵛ). Father Schurhammer kindly sent me a translation of the relevant parts of this interesting
letter which throws a new light on Hideyoshi's reactions to Christianity. The
outline of his scheme for the conquest of China, as given by him in a letter
to Hidetsugu dated May 18, 1592, will be found in Y. Kuno, *Japanese Expansion on the Asiatic Continent,* Vol. I, 314–318. Cf. also Y. Okamoto,
Momoyama-jidai Kirisuto-kyo Bunka, pp. 117–152.

³ *Cartas* (1598), Part II, fols. 174–180. Cf. Murdoch, *op. cit.,* Vol. II,
216–217. A good description of Osaka castle will be found in Brinkley's
Japan. Its History, Arts and Literature (Author's ed., Boston-Tokyo, 1901),
Vol. II, 69–75.

⁴ *Cartas* (1598), Vol. II, fols. 191, 199, for details about the temporary
Satsuma occupation of Nagasaki. Hideyoshi's conquest of Kyushu is well
described in Murdoch, *op. cit.,* Vol. II, 222–236. Hosokawa Fujitaka wrote
a classic account of this campaign. For Otomo's reception by Hideyoshi in
1586, cf. Sadler, *Cha-no-yu,* pp. 126–128, and Takekoshi, *op. cit.,* Vol. I,
395–396, which is interesting to compare with Coelho's reception.

⁵ *Cartas* (1598), Part II, fols. 199–225; Murdoch, *op. cit.,* Vol. II, 236–
253. Delplace, *Le Catholicisme au Japon,* Vol. I, 238–248.

⁶ *Cartas* (1598), Part II, fols. 207–208. This differs slightly from Murdoch's account (*op. cit.,* Vol. II, 241–242), but the latter has used some
second-hand French or Italian version of Frois' letter of February 20, 1588,
whereas I have used the Portuguese original as printed in the 1598 *Cartas,*
Part II, fols. 187–225. Cf. also Y. Okamoto's essay "Nagasaki no fusuta-
sen," in his *Momoyama-jidai Kirisuto-kyo Bunka,* pp. 77–114.

⁷ Valignano's letter of October 14, 1590 (Jesuit Archives, Rome,
"Japsin," 11, fols. 233–236ᵛ). See Frois' long letter of February 20, 1588,
in *Cartas* (1598) Part II, esp. fols. 205, 208–209, 214–215. The text of the
Expulsion Edict as given by Frois is fuller than the version given by Murdoch
(*op. cit.,* pp. 242–243) and those who follow him. It reads rather oddly to
Western ears, but Frois explicitly states that it was translated *ad verbum*
from the original, and indeed the Oriental flavor is obvious. Further details
of Hideyoshi's seizure of Nagasaki in *MN,* Vol. I (1938), pp. 78–79, 123–
137; and *ibid.,* Vol. II (1939), pp. 634–637; *ibid.,* Vol. III (1940), pp.

657–664. Cf. also Colin-Pastells, ed., *Labor Evangelica de los obreros de la Companhia de Iesus en las islas Filipinas*, Vol. II, 55–59, 73, 703–704; Vol. III, 461, for evidence on Hideyoshi's attitude toward Christianity; and Delplace, *op. cit.*, Vol. I, 238–248, for the Catholic point of view, which is less temperately expressed by the Abbé Steichen in his *Les Daimios chrétiens*. For the Japanese viewpoint, cf. M. Anesaki, *Kirishitan dendo no kohai*, pp. 191–200, 215–229, and Okamoto's essay in his *Momoyama-jidai*, etc.

[8] *Cartas* (1598), Part II, fols. 218, 223–224, 234–236, 258. Murdoch, *op. cit.*, Vol. II, 243–253, and most modern non-Catholic writers, take the view that the outburst of July 24 was merely stage-managed by Hideyoshi as the deliberate climax of a deeply-laid design of long standing; but this explanation seems to me as far-fetched as the alternative Jesuit one that the whole thing was a drunken whim, precipitated by his annoyance at the Portuguese refusal to bring the Great Ship round from Hirado to Hakata, and the repulse of his official pimp by some Christian damsels of Arima. It would seem that Hideyoshi had in fact for some time had his doubts about the Jesuits, but that the actual explosion was unpremeditated. His megalomania induced him to take some drastic measures in the heat of anger, which he subsequently regretted and did not enforce, but could not repeal without loss of "face."

[9] A full account of Gracia's conversion is given in my essay, "Hosokawa Tadaoki and the Jesuits 1587–1645," in *TJS*, Vol. XXXII (1935), pp. 79–119. Statistical details on the Jesuit mission in Japan, 1587–1592, in *Cartas* (1598), Part II, fols. 187, 223–224; Delplace, *op. cit.*, Vol. I, 198, 215–218, 276–279. In addition to 113 European and Japanese Jesuits in Japan in 1587, there were about 150 dojuku or catechists, and a community of nearly 200,000 converts. Backsliders from the Faith as a result of Hideyoshi's edict were soon atoned for by fresh conversions, principally in Konishi's fief of Higo (Udo).

[10] Hideyoshi's reception of Valignano's embassy in his "Palace of Pleasures" at Kyoto is briefly described in Murdoch, *op. cit.*, Vol. II, 263–264, and in more detail by R. Kleiser in *MN*, Vol. I (1938), pp. 82–88.

[11] Valignano's and Cerqueira's letters and reports, covering the years 1580–1606 are to be found among the Marsden MSS in the British Museum; those codices particularly germane to the Jesuit-Franciscan dispute are Additional MSS 9852, 9856, 9858, and 9860. Many of these are the original drafts on sixteenth-century Japanese paper, and others are contemporary certified copies; all were taken from the Jesuit Archives at Goa on their seizure by the minions of Pombal in 1759. How Marsden acquired them, I do not know, but there is no doubt about their genuineness. The literature on this thorny topic is legion, and the reader avid for details thereof is referred to Streit and Dindinger, *Bibliotheca Missionum*, Vols. IV–V (1928–1929), where he will find a bellyful. If he is still anxious for more, a perusal of the relevant articles in *MN* (1938–1943) will bring him up to date on

the Jesuit viewpoint; the articles of L. Pérez and others in the Madrid Franciscan review, *Archivo Ibero-Americano*, Vols. IV–XIX (1915–1923), give the Franciscan standpoint. Those who have neither time nor patience to cope with these original printed sources, may be satisfied by reading Murdoch *op. cit.*, Vol. II, chap. xi, or Bernard's *Les Iles Philippines du grand archipel de la Chine*. Fr. Lorenzo Pérez reprinted the documents from the *AIA* in three volumes published separately under the combined title *Cartas y Relaciones del Japón*. They cover the years 1593–1600 and form an invaluable check on the Jesuit sources.

¹² The standard work on the Portuguese Crown patronage in the Far East is that of A. Jann, *Die Katholischen Missionen in Indien, China und Japan*, but it is vitiated by a strong anti-Portuguese bias, and should be corrected in the light of my article "The Portuguese Padroado in East Asia and the Problem of the Chinese Rites, 1576–1773," *BIPH*, Vol. I (1948), pp. 199–226, or Padre A. de Silva Rego's *O Padroado Portugues no Oriente*, for the Portuguese viewpoint. The contemporary Spanish view was well expressed by Fr. Diego Aduarte, O.P., who, advocating the conquest of Cambodia by the Spaniards in 1596, added "and it is certain that neither the Faith nor the Royal Crown will increase much through the Portuguese, since they are satisfied with merely the ports which they have, to ensure the use of the rest for their trade" (*AIA*, Vol. XXXVIII, pp. 455–458).

¹³ British Museum, Add. MSS 9852, pp. 101–105, for Valignano's viewpoint summarized hereinafter. Cf. also Sousa, *Oriente Conquistado*, Vol. II, pp. 535 for a printed summary.

¹⁴ Ajuda Codex "Jesuitas na Asia," 49-iv-56, pp. 48–50. Valignano's references to the *Capuchos* are a trifle cryptic, and perhaps refer to expected arrivals from Macao, Malacca, and Portuguese India, rather than to Franciscans from Manila. In either case, they were clearly unwelcome. It may be noted in passing that the Jesuits usually claimed that Otomo Sorin took his baptismal name from Francis Xavier, whose beatification and canonization he so warmly advocated, rather than from the saintly founder of the Friars Minor. The rivalry between Jesuits and friars is discussed from the Japanese viewpoint in Anesaki's *Kirishitan dendo no kohai*, pp. 203–264, and, more recently, in Okamoto's essay in *Kirishitan Kenkyu*, Vol. III, 225–319.

¹⁵ Fresh light on the well-worn theme of Cobo's embassy and the Franciscan missions which followed it, can be gained from the articles of Père Bernard, S.J., Gregorio Arnaiz, O.P., and J. S. Alvarez, in *MN*, Vol. I (1938), pp. 122 ff.; *ibid.*, Vol. II (1939), pp. 634 ff.; and above all, *ibid.*, Vol. III (1940), pp. 657–664 (*Dos Notas sobre la embajada del padre Juan Cobo*), which contains Spanish, Portuguese, and Japanese original sources for Cobo's embassy. Cobo's linguistic attainments are summarized by Edwin Wolf in *Doctrina Christiana. The First Book Printed in the Philippines, Manila 1593* (Washington D.C., 1947), pp. 31–35. Cf. also the original

Franciscan reports and letters edited by Fr. Lorenzo Pérez in the *AIA*, Vols. IV–XIX (1915–1923).

[16] See Henri Bernard, "Méthodes missionaires du Méxique au Japon," in his *Les Iles Philippines*, pp. 111–127 for a more detailed discussion of these widely differing missionary viewpoints. Cf. also the documents printed by Lewis Hanke in *Cuerpo de Documentos del siglo XVI sobre los derechos de España en las Indias y las Filipinas*, pp. 65–270. For a modern Chinese viewpoint on the attitude of the Roman Catholic missionaries, cf. C. S. Ch'ien, "Critical Notice" of Father Bernard's work on Ricci and the Chinese society of his time in *Philobiblon*, Vol. I (1946), pp. 13–19.

[17] British Museum, Add. MSS 9858, fols. 1–10, 9860, fols. 13–22, contain the evidence of Bishop Pedro Martins, S.J., the Captain-Major of the Japan Voyage of 1596, Ruy Mendes de Figueiredo, and other witnesses' testimonies on oath. I have relied mainly on them for my summary of the *San Felipe* affair, but these primary authorities do not differ essentially from the secondary printed sources (Frois and Charlevoix) used by later historians, such as Murdoch (*op. cit.*, Vol. II, chap. xi). The Spanish version is available in all the standard mission histories of the mendicant orders in the Philippines. These different reports are catalogued in Streit, *Bibliotheca Missionum*, Vol. IV (1928), particularly the items listed on pp. 489–499 of that work. The most temperate expression of the Franciscan viewpoint is probably that by P. Fray Francisco de Santa Inés in his *Crónica* written in 1676, and printed at Manila in 1892; cf. Vol. 3 of this edition. Cf. also *AIA*, Vols. IV–XIX (1915–1923), for the reports of Fray Juan Pobre and other eyewitnesses, likewise reprinted in the *Cartas y Relaciones del Japón*.

[18] Andres de Cuaçola, "Relacion de la arivada del Galeon S. Felipe al Xapon y lo demas que subcedio de su arivada es como sigue." Autograph letter, signed, on Japanese paper (cf. Maggs Bros., *Catalogue No. 515* [1929], item no. 3, pp. 5–11, for extensive summary in English). Among the mass of anti-Jesuit material listed by Streit in *Bibliotheca Missionum* (Vol. IV, pp. 484–511), on the Franciscan-Jesuit controversy in Japan in 1596–1599, the following may be taken as typical: "Certificación de las amenazas que el Obispo de Japon [D. Pedro Martins, S.J.] hizo contra los Frayles Franciscanos que estavan en los mismos reynos, aún estando en Macao." Items 1, 4, and 9 of Maggs Bros., *Catalogue No. 515* (1929), are also relevant. Fray Juan Pobre's version of the Spanish pilot's innocence and of Portuguese and Jesuit complicity in stirring up Hideyoshi against the Spaniards will be found in Fr. L. Pérez's article on "Fray Juan Pobre de Zamora" in *Erudición Ibero-Ultramarino*, Vol. II (1931), pp. 219–223 ("Origen de la leyenda de Urado"), reproduced in part above, Appendix III, pp. 420–424. Although this party was later canonized by the Church, the contemporary Jesuits in Japan unanimously asserted that the Franciscans' wanton rashness was the principal if not the sole cause of their death. They likewise scornfully rejected the suggestion that miracles had occurred at the

crucifixion, drawing up a scathing denunciation of these pseudo-wonders, which was endorsed in due form by Bishop Luis Cerqueira on February 3, 1599 (Brit. Mus., Add. MSS 9860, fols. 63–65). Other aspects of Luso-Spanish rivalry in the Far East are mentioned in my essay on this topic in *TRAS* (Dec. 1946), pp. 150–164. The Franciscan viewpoint is set forth at great length in the documents printed by Fr. Lorenzo Pérez in *AIA*, Vols. IV–XIX (1915–1923). Cf. also the extracts above in Appendix III, pp. 415–424.

[19] The original drafts of Bishop Luis Cerqueira's proposals for the application of Portuguese economic sanctions against Japan with a view to bringing Hideyoshi to heel (or to his ruin) dated February 1597, are to be found in British Museum, Add. MSS 9860, fols. 23–32. An interesting and scholarly discussion concerning the two schools of theological opinion on the justification of crusades against unbelieving states (such as China) is to be found *apud* Father Henri Bernard, S.J., "La Théorie du protectorat civil des Missions en pays infidèle," in *La Nouvelle Revue Théologique*, Vol. 64 (1937), pp. 261–283. Cf. Valignano's letter of October 14, 1590, and *MN*, Vol. I (1938), pp. 78–79, 113, for the efforts (fortunately abortive) of the Jesuit Superior, Gaspar Coelho, to obtain official sanction and support for his schemes of fortifying Nagasaki and supplying the Christian daimyo of Kyushu with arms and ammunition. Hideyoshi's correspondence with Tello, the governor of the Philippines, will be found in Colin-Pastells, *op. cit.*, Vol. II, 703–704. Sánchez' fantastic schemes for the conquest of China (with the aid of a Japanese auxiliary force, be it noted) are dealt with in chapter vi of the present work. Cf. also Fernão Guerreiro, S.J., *Relação Anual, 1602–1603*, Bk. III, chap. xxiii (ed. 1930), pp. 370–372, for proof that the Jesuits took credit for extending the temporal power of Portuguese India by their missionary activities. The title is sufficiently indicative of the contents: "Of the service which the Company renders in all the aforesaid parts of the Orient, not only to God, but to His Majesty and the Crown of this Kingdom." This explicitly supports the theory that the Jesuits were active promoters of a Christian "fifth column," as alleged by their Buddhist opponents,—"Because as many heathen as are converted to Christ, just so many friends and vassals does His Majesty's service acquire, because they later fight for the State [of India] and Christians against the heathen." The writer was not thinking of Japanese, but the moral is obvious. As for Portuguese government policy, the following quotation from Diogo do Couto, the official chronicler of Portuguese India (*Decada Sexta*, Livro IV, cap. vii), is decisive; "The Kings of Portugal always aimed in this conquest of the East, at so uniting the two powers, spiritual and temporal, that the one should never be exercised without the other." ("Porque os Reys de Portugal sempre pretenderão nesta Conquista do Oriente unir tanto os dous poderes, espiritual, e temporal, que em nenhum tempo se exercitasse um sem o outro.")

[20] Cf. Bishop Luis Cerqueira's correspondence with the Archbishop of Goa, in British Museum, Add. MSS 9860, esp. fols. 91–97. Cf. also the "Apologia" of Padre Valentim Carvalho, S.J., Rector of the College at Macao in 1612, in Add. MSS 9856, fols. 1–114. One of the Franciscans crucified at Nagasaki in 1597 (Fray Martín de la Ascensión) had actually suggested to the governor of the Philippines in the previous year that Nagasaki should be seized and held for the Crown of Spain, while the Portuguese padroado east of Ceylon should be turned over to the Spanish patronazgo at Manila. Cf. documents printed in Colin-Pastells, *op. cit.,* Vol. II, 85–87. About 1605, the leaders of the three mendicant orders at Manila wrote to the King, stressing the importance of the Philippines as a base for the "conquest and conversion of many and very excellent Kingdoms, such as China, Japan, Siam, Cambodia and Cochinchina" (*AIA,* Vol. X (1918), pp. 467–468). These examples of combined spiritual and temporal aggression could easily be multiplied.

[21] Cf. Frois' letter of February 20, 1588 in *Cartas* (1598), Pt. II, fols. 187–225; Gaspar Coelho's letter of February 24, 1589 in *ibid.,* fols. 258–262; and Valignano's "Obediencias" of 1592 (Ajuda Codex "Jesuitas na Asia," 49-iv-56). Takekoshi, *op. cit.,* Vol. I, 396–440, and Sansom, *Japan,* pp. 432–441, provide confirmatory material from Japanese sources. Background material for this period will be found in the standard works of Murdoch and Sansom, and (for those who can read Japanese) in Tokutomi, *Kinsei Nihon Kokumin-shi,* Vols. 10–13.

[22] Valignano, "Obediencias," 1592 (Ajuda Codex "Jesuitas na Asia," 49-iv-56). I cannot recall having seen elsewhere anything about the legal stipulation that a samurai could not lead a bachelor's life, nor does it sound inherently probable, but Valignano was usually well-informed. The Father-Visitor's request for permission to solemnize mixed marriages originally received a reluctant verbal consent from the Pope, when the Jesuit General Aquaviva broached the matter to him; but the pontiff subsequently reversed his tentative decision, and specifically forbade the practice as too dangerous an innovation. Apparently, however, papal sanction was given to such marriages between Christians and heathens as had already been contracted. ("Das Cousas que pertencem à Vice-Provincia de Japão" anonymous MS, *ca.* 1600 in the British Museum, Add. MSS 9860, fol. 267.)

[23] Coelho's letter of February 24, 1589 in *Cartas* (1598), Part II, fol. 262.

[24] Cf. chapter 55 of Frois' "Apparatos" (Ajuda Codex "Jesuitas na Asia," 49-iv-57) as printed in extract by J. L. Alvarez in his article on Cobo's embassy in *MN,* Vol. III (1940), pp. 657–662.

[25] Guerreiro, *op. cit.* (ed. 1930), Vol. I, 55–164. For the extremely complicated series of comings and goings of various commissioners (Nabeshima, Kato, Todo, Terazawa, and others) in the years 1587–1592 at Nagasaki, cf. Ozawa's *Nagasaki Nempyo* (Tokyo, 1935), pp. 26–33, and Okamoto, *op. cit.,* pp. 627–656.

[26] Valignano's letters of October 10, 1599 and February 24, 1600 (Brit. Mus., Add. MSS 9860, fols. 68–86). Guerreiro, *op. cit.* (ed. 1930), Vol. I, 55–164, is also relevant. It is amusing to note that Ieyasu told Fray Jeronimo de Jesús, O.F.M., in his interview with the friar toward the end of 1598, that the Spaniards could rely on his protecting the Manila traders in Japan, since "he gave them the word of a gentleman, which he was from his mother's womb, and not that of a stable lad like Taicosama" (Pérez' article in *Erudición Ibero-Ultramarino*, Vol. II, 228).

[27] British Museum, Add. MSS 9860, fols. 84–87; Guerreiro, *op. cit.* (ed. 1930), Vol. I, 154–155. An exhaustive Japanese account of the Sekigahara campaign will be found in Tokutomi's monumental history of Japan, entitled *Sekigahara-Eki* (Tokyo, 1932), Vol. XI. Murdoch and Sadler's books contain concise accounts in English, Murdoch being the better of the two.

[28] British Museum, Add. MSS 9860, fols. 87–88, 123–126; Guerreiro, *op. cit.* (ed. 1931), Vol. II, 7–8, 217; A. Baião, *Carta Anua da Vice-Provincia do Japão do ano de 1604 do Padre João Rodrigues Giram* (Coimbra, 1933), pp. 1–9, 41–42; Anesaki, *Kirishitan dendo no kohai*, pp. 265–284.

[29] Cf. the vice-provincial's reports dated October 14, 1607 (Brit. Mus., Add. MSS 9860, fols. 127–128); October 18, 1606, *ibid.*, fols. 123–126; and Guerreiro, *op. cit.* (ed. 1931), Vol. II, 63–65, 278; *ibid.*, Vol. III (1942), 115–146. Cf. Murdoch, *op. cit.*, Vol. II, 474–478.

[30] "Certidão do Bispo do Jappão acerca do caso de Omuradono," Nagasaki, March 6, 1606 (Brit. Mus., Add. MSS 9860, fols. 107–110). Original document with the bishop's autograph signature. Cf. also *ibid.*, fols. 89–90, 123–128; F. Guerreiro, *op. cit.* (ed. 1942), pp. 115–117, 146–147. It is interesting to note that the contemporary Portuguese chronicler, Antonio Bocarro, in his account of this incident expressly states that the proposal *was* made at the instigation of the Jesuits, and that Ieyasu told Omura as much. But Bocarro's account of events in Japan at this period is rather garbled on the whole (*Decada XIII da História da India* [ed. 1876], chap. clxxxiv, pp. 746–747).

NOTES TO CHAPTER V
Christian culture and missionary life

[1] Valignano, "Sumario," chap. xiii, 1583 (Brit. Mus., Add. MSS 9852); *Monumenta Xaveriana*, Vol. I (1900), pp. 109–110.

[2] Letter of Padre Valignano, Goa, December 1, 1587, in *Cartas*, Pt. II, fol. 233.

[3] The literature on the Jesuit mission press and its publications is extensive, but the following works will suffice for the average student, since most of them contain ample bibliographies and references. E. M. Satow, *The Jesuit Mission Press in Japan* (1591–1610), privately printed in 1888,

which all subsequent studies have merely amplified or corrected in a relatively minor degree; Jordão de Freitas, "A imprensa de tipos móveis em Macau e no Japão nos fins do século XVI," in *ABAP*, Vol. I (1915); D. Schilling, "Christliche Druckereien in Japan," in the *Gutenberg-Jahrbuch*, Vol. XV (1940), pp. 356–395; S. Koda, "Notes sur la presse Jésuite au Japon at plus spécialment sur les livres imprimés en caractères Japonais," in *MN*, Vol. II (1939), pp. 374–385; T. Doi, "Das Sprachstudium der Gesellschaft Jesu in Japan im 16. und 17. Jahrhundert," *ibid.*, pp. 437–465; J. Laures, S.J., *Kirishitan Bunko*, Vol. I, and *Supplement*; Joseph Schütte, S.J., articles in *AHSI*, Vol. VIII (1939), pp. 225–256, and *ibid.*, Vol. IX (1940), pp. 226–280.

⁴ Cf. M. Anesaki, "The Writings of Fabian, the Apostate Irman," *PIA*, Vol. V (1929), pp. 307–310; and *idem, TASJ* (1930), pp. 1–5. A list of the *Monogatari* edited by or for the use of Jesuit language students is given by Professor Doi in his article in *MN*, Vol. II, 448. For the fragments of printed *mai* see Humbertclaude's article in *BEDM*, Vol. XXXIX (1941), pp. 147–161.

⁵ C. R. Boxer, "Padre João Rodriguez Tçuzzu, S.J., and his Japanese Grammars of 1604 and 1620," in *Miscelânea de filologia, literatura e história cultural à memória de Francisco Adolfo Coelho*, Vol. II (Lisbon, 1950), pp. 338–363, and the sources there quoted. Professors Shimmura and Hamada have the following interesting observation on the way in which Christianity indirectly contributed to the popularization of the *hiragana* script. Apropos of its widespread use on tombstones of the Keicho period, they add, "here the *kana*, even the *hiragana* style of characters appeared as monumental inscriptions on the Christian gravestones, mixed with Chinese letters, because the latter are inadequate to transcribe the Christian names of terms. Moreover, in consequence of this, the Chinese characters themselves were often inscribed in a cursive style to be more in keeping with the *kana* characters. This is an epoch-making phenomenon in the history of our epigraphy and it is very curious to notice that the introduction of our national *kana* characters, giving them an independent or prominent part, in the field of Japanese epigraphy, was the result of the propagation of Christianity, of a religion considered to be anti-national by most of the people." (Shimmura and Hamada, *Christian Relics at Takatsuki* [Kyoto, 1923], pp. 16–17.)

⁶ British Museum, Add. MSS 9860, fols. 8–12, 36; Laures, S.J., *op. cit.*; Schilling, *op. cit.*; Boxer, "Padre João Rodriguez Tçuzzu, S.J., and his Japanese Grammars of 1604 and 1620," *loc. cit*. Dom Luis de Cerqueira's embarrassment about Padre João Rodriguez' deep involvement in commercial and municipal business at Nagasaki, is evident from his letter of March 1, 1607, wherein he writes that these affairs were "negocios em si considerados não serem tão proprios de nossa profissão e de sua natureza occasionados a se murmurar, parte pollo modo que o dito padre tem de os tratar,

metendo-se mais nelles, e com menos resguardo e prudencia religiosa do que convem, posto que se não pode negar ser esperto e intelligente nestes negocios." (Rome, Jesuit Archives, "Japsin," 21, fols. 135–137ᵛ. The relevant extracts from this letter were kindly sent me by Father G. Schurhammer, S.J.)

⁷ C. R. Boxer, "Some Aspects of Portuguese Influence in Japan, 1542–1640," in *TJS*, Vol. XXXIII (1936), pp. 13–64; G. Schurhammer, S.J., "Die Jesuitenmissionare des 16. und 17. Jahrhunderts und ihr Einfluss auf die Japanische Malerei," in the *Jubilaumsband* of the *DGfNVD*, Teil 1 (1933), pp. 116–126; Pasquale M. D'Elia, S.J., *Le Origini dell' Arte Christiana Cinese* (1583-1640), and *Fonti Ricciane*, Vol. I (1942), p. 231; Vol. II (1949), pp. 258 note. The best and most thorough study is that by J. E. McCall, "Early Jesuit Art in the Far East," a series of articles in *Artibus Asiae*, Vols. X-XI (1947-1948).

⁸ Boxer, "Some Aspects of Portuguese Influence in Japan, 1542–1640," *TJS*, Vol. XXXIII (1936), pp. 28–36; *idem*, article in the *Connoisseur* (August, 1936); *idem, Fidalgos in the Far East*, pp. 20–26, 126–127; Valignano's instructions for Padre Mesquita, cicerone of the Kyushu envoys to Rome, dated Goa, December 12, 1583, and printed by Abranches Pinto and Henri Bernard, S.J., in *MN*, Vol. VI (1943), pp. 392–403; Frei Antonio de Gouvea, *Relaçam em que se tratam das guerras do Xa Abbas* (Lisbon, 1611), fol. 176ᵛ; F. Pasio, "Obediencias," 1612 (Ajuda Codex "Jesuitas na Asia," 49-iv-56). The trouble over Pedro Kano and his colleagues is related by Bishop Dom Luis de Cerqueira in a letter written from Nagasaki to the Archbishop of Goa, dated November 20, 1604 (Brit. Mus., Add. MSS 9860, fols. 91–97).

⁹ Boxer, *TJS*, Vol. XXXII (1936), pp. 48–50; Schilling, *Os Portugueses e a introdução da medicina no Japão; idem*, "Gründung der Hospitäler St. Joseph und St. Anna in Myako (1594–1595)," "Erschwerte Finanzierung der Hospitaler der Franziskaner in Miyako (1594–1597)," in *NZM*, Vol. I (1949), pp. 1–18, 98–110, 189–202, 258–275; Valignano, "Sumario" (1583), chap. xxx (Brit. Mus., Add. MSS 9852); Certificate of Bishop Cerqueira on the Jesuit hospital, leprosarium, and the Misericordia at Nagasaki, dated January, 1603 (Brit. Mus., Add. MSS 9860, fol. 37); *Carta Anua de Japão de 1604*, ed. A. Baião (Coimbra, 1932), p. 9; "Extracto das Obediencias dos Visitadores," by Padre Francisco Pasio (Nagasaki, 1612), *apud* Ajuda Codex "Jesuitas na Asia," 49-iv-56, Vol. III, fol. 69. Fray Juan Pobre's report of 1595, printed by L. Pérez in *AIA*, Ano. 5. num. 28, Vol. X (July–August, 1918), with the title: "Cartas y Relaciones del Japon. Cartas, Memoriales y Relación de Fr. Juan Pobre."

¹⁰ Brit. Mus., Add. MSS 9860 (Pasio's letter of September 16, 1594); Valignano's "Sumarios" of 1580 and 1583, *passim* (Brit. Mus., Add. MSS 9852); Gaspar Coelho's letter of February 15, 1582, in *Cartas*, Pt. II, fol. 20ᵛ (Evora, 1598); Valignano wrote later ". . . Aprenden con más fa-

cilidad a pintar y a escrivir nuestra letra de lo que hazen commúnmente los Europeos, y puede ser que escriviéndose de los niños de Japón que aprendían más fácilmente a escrivir nuestras letras latinas que los Europeos, por no entenderse esto bien, se tomase ocasión para dizir-se que aprendían las letras latinas y las artes más de priessa que los de Europa." (Quoted by I. Wicki, S.J., in his edition of Valignano's *Historia*, p. 127, note 6.) The standard work on the Jesuit's educational system in Japan is that by D. Schilling, O.F.M., *Das Schulwesen der Jesuiten in Japan, 1551–1614.* For naval and military influence, cf. my article "Notes on Early European Military Influence in Japan (1543–1853)," in *TASJ*, 2d ser. Vol. VIII (1931), pp. 68–93, and Delmar M. Brown, "The Impact of Firearms on Japanese Warfare, 1543–98" in *The Far Eastern Quarterly*, Vol. VII, No. 3 (May, 1948), pp. 236–253. Professor Brown credits the introduction of firearms into Japan with far-reaching economic and social consequences. His carefully documented essay will repay reading even for those who do not go the whole way with him in his conclusions. Various aspects of Kirishitan culture in Japan are discussed in M. Anesaki's *Kirishitan dendo no kohai*, pp. 374–412 and 422–433, and the social significance of the missionaries' work is dealt with from the Japanese viewpoint in A. Ebizawa's *Kirishitan no shakai katsudo oyobi Namban igaku.*

[11] What follows is taken from the following sources, except where otherwise explicitly stated. Valignano's "Sumarios" of 1580 and 1583 (Brit. Mus., Add. MSS 9852); *Advertimentos e Avisos acerca dos costumes e catangues de Jappão,* drawn up by Valignano's direction at Goa in 1583–1584, and printed from the original in the Jesuit Archives at Rome with an introduction, notes and appendices, by Joseph Schütte, S.J., under the title of *Il Ceremoniale per i Missionari del Giappone;* Valignano's "Addiciones" and "Obediencias" of 1592, and Pasio's revised version of the "Obediencias" in 1612, all of which are taken from the eighteenth-century Macao transcripts in the Biblioteca de Ajuda, Lisbon (Codex "Jesuitas na Asia," 49-iv-56); Valentim Carvalho's "Apologia" of 1617 (Brit. Mus., Add. MSS 9856).

[12] Padre João Rodriguez Tçuzzu's remarkably frank letter of February 28, 1598, was printed by Y. Okamoto in the *Nichi-Ho kotsu*, Vol. II (1943), pp. 153–158. For other quotations from this letter and a biographical sketch of Padre Rodriguez, cf. my essay, "Padre João Rodriguez Tçuzzu and his Japanese Grammars of 1604 and 1620," *loc. cit.*

[13] Pasio's revised "Obediencias" of 1612, especially chapter ix: "Da Limpeza nas nossas casas, comer, e vestir," (Ajuda Codex "Jesuitas na Asia," 49-iv-56). Typical allegations of Jesuit good cheer in Japan and China are contained in the anonymous Spanish MSS of *ca.* 1606, entitled "Dudase si conbiene que los Padres Dominicos, Franciscanos y Augustinos entren libremente con licencia de Su Sanctidad y Majestad a predicar el Santo Evangelio en los reynos del Japon y China por la via de las Filipinas"

(Maggs Bros., *Catalogue No.* 515, pp. 33–34), and the *Tratados* of Domingo Fernandez Navarrete, O.P. (Madrid, 1676, 1679). They find some confirmation in Padre Luis da Gama's letter written from Macao, December 15, 1664 (Ajuda Codex "Jesuitas na Asia" 49-iv-56). In this, the father-visitor of the China mission complains that the padres of the Macao college grumbled at being deprived of luxuries ("se no Refeitorio lhes falta, não digo o necessario mas o mimoso não ha quem se entende com elles"). From the accounts of Peter Mundy, Gemelli Carreri, and other seventeenth-century travelers, it is clear that the Jesuits kept a good table at Goa and Macao.

[14] Padre João Rodriguez' letter of February 28, 1598, quoted above, note 12. This is a pretty close echo of Cabral's views at the missionary conference of 1580. Cf. also the views of Ricci, Longobardi, and Trigault on the respective merits of Chinese and Japanese brothers as printed in the documents quoted in d'Elia's *Fonti Ricciane*, Vol. I, pp. cxxx, note 5, and 289–293.

[15] British Museum, Add. MSS 9852, 9856, 9858, and 9860, *passim*.

[16] "Obediencias" of 1592 and 1612 (Ajuda Codex "Jesuitas na Asia," 49-iv-56); "Sumario" of 1583 (Brit. Mus., Add. MSS 9852). After their expulsion from Japan in 1614, the Jesuits continued to train some Japanese dojuku at Macao. There was considerable correspondence with the Crown authorities at Lisbon and Goa over their petition for financial assistance for this work, which seems to have been finally turned down in 1619, at the suggestion of the chancellor at Goa, Goncalo Pinto da Fonseca. (*Documentos Remettidos da India ou Livros das Monções*, for the years 1614–1619, *passim*.)

[17] "Rol dos Dogicos que estão nos Casas de Japão com outra gente de serviço" (1592), in British Museum, Add. MSS 9860, fol. 3. Cf. also Schilling, *op. cit.*, pp. 73–74, and Schütte, *op. cit.*; Pasio's revised "Obediencias" of 1612, chap. vi, "Dos Dogicos" (Ajuda Codex "Jesuitas na Asia," 49-iv-56, fols. 57–58); and the annual letters for 1600–1607 printed in Fernão Guerreiro's *Relação Anual*. The Nagasaki schism of 1614, and the desertion of the Jesuits by their erstwhile pupils, is related more in sorrow than in anger by Padre Valentim Carvalho in his "Apologia" of 1617 (Brit. Mus., Add. MSS 9856, fols. 52–56). The dojuku system was also adopted by the mendicant orders when they came to Japan. The Jesuits complained that what few concrete results the Franciscans did achieve were due to their employment of Jesuit-trained dojuku. For Bocarro's criticism of Jesuit hauteur, cf. his *Decada XIII da História da India*, pp. 745–750. His stories were evidently common gossip in Portuguese Asia, since some of them reappear, with suitable embellishments, in Kaempfer's *History of Japan* and similar works.

[18] The foregoing from Pasio's "Obediencias" of 1612. (Ajuda Codex "Jesuitas na Asia," 49-iv-56). For the Jesuit attitude toward the slave trade

driven by the Portuguese in Japan and China, cf. my *Fidalgos in the Far East*, 1550–1770, pp. 222–241, and the sources there quoted.

[19] The foregoing from the "Obediencias" of 1592 and 1612 (Ajuda Codex "Jesuitas na Asia," 49-iv-56). Guerreiro's *Relação Anual* of 1600–1601, describes how the Jesuit prelate had introduced the Feast of Nossa Senhora da Protecção at the beginning of the Lunar New Year, on the same principle as the popes of the primitive Church had introduced the feast of St. Peter ad Vincula on August 1, with the object of gradually driving into oblivion recollection of the fact that the original festival of that day was in honor of Caesar Augustus.

[20] "Obediencias" of 1592 and 1612 (Ajuda Codex "Jesuitas na Asia," 49-iv-56); letter of Bishop Luis de Cerqueira, S.J., dated Nagasaki, March 5, 1612, in Victor Ribeiro's *Bispos Portugueses Jesuitas no Japão*, pp. 46–56. The figure of 300,000 Christians in 1614 is taken from Carvalho's "Apologia" of 1617 (Brit. Mus., Add. MSS 9856). Although much lower than that usually given, it can be taken as correct, since Carvalho was in charge in 1614, and had been in Japan for many years. The position and policy of the Church in Japan during the Keicho period is discussed in M. Anesaki's *Kirishitan dendo no kohai*, pp. 314–347. A. Ebizawa's *Kirishitan no shakai katsudo oyobi Namban igaku*, may also be recommended to those who can read Japanese, but the sources he utilizes are almost exclusively European.

[21] The chief sources for the Jesuit methods of evangelization in Japan are the manuscript "Obediencias" of 1592 and 1612 in the Ajuda Library, Lisbon (Ajuda Codex "Jesuitas na Asia," 49-iv-56), and Valignano's "Sumarios" of 1580 and 1583 (Brit. Mus., Add. MSS 9852). These manuscripts, and the *Advertimentos*, edited by Father Schütte in 1946, are the sources utilized in this chapter for the Jesuit viewpoint, except where otherwise explicitly stated. The most recent account of the Chinese rites controversy in English is A. H. Rowbotham's *Missionary and Mandarin* (Berkeley, 1942). The quarrel over the *Contas de Santa Jeronima* in 1614, is related at length in the Jesuit correspondence for 1614–1615 in British Museum, Add. MSS 9860, fols. 210–232, and in Carvalho's "Apologia" of 1617 (Add. MSS 9856). For the Franciscan sources, see note 22, below.

[22] Fray Juan Pobre of Zamora (so called to distinguish him from Fray Juan Pobre of San Lucar de Barrameda who was his contemporary as a missionary in the Far East) was a truly remarkable man of well-nigh limitless activity. One of Alva's veterans in Flanders, he subsequently became a Franciscan lay brother and came out to the Philippines in 1594. He inspected the Franciscan mission stations in Japan in 1595–1596, and, after returning to Manila, embarked for Mexico in the great galleon *San Felipe*, which was wrecked off Tosa in October. He narrowly escaped being involved in the martyrdom of February, 1597, and was deported in the Portuguese carrack *Santo Antonio* to Macao, whence he made his way to Manila in January, 1598. He was sent to Spain next year, and returned

with a band of missionaries in 1602, but "jumped ship" at Guam en route, where he remained for seven months (not a year, as is usually stated) before being picked up by the Manila-bound galleon *Jesús María* (October, 1602). He returned to Spain in 1603–1604, and spent the next three years between Valladolid and Rome, battling for the revocation of Gregory XIII's pro-Jesuit Brief of 1585, which was eventually achieved, largely through his efforts, in 1608. He returned to the Philippines in this last year, and thence for the third time back to Europe in 1611, but by way of Portuguese India, the Persian Gulf, and Mesopotamia. The peripatetic friar died at Madrid five years later, on the eve of his intended fourth departure for the Philippines. King Felipe III was so impressed with Pobre and his peregrinations, that he ordered his portrait to be painted after his death. His namesake, who was likewise originally a soldier, was one of Legaspi's *conquistadores* in his youth, and died the next year at Manila, aged one hundred and two. Their careers coincided so closely that most biographers invariably confuse the two. Juan Pobre the older served as captain of a Japanese contingent in the bloody suppression of the Chinese (Sangley) rebellion at Manila in October, 1603, despite the fact that he was then nearly ninety years old. The one frequently cited in this chapter is Fray Juan Pobre of Zamora, and all quotations are taken from one or other of the following sources: an undated autograph letter (of the end of 1604 or early 1605 from internal evidence) in the present writer's collection; "Memorial dado al Rey N.S. en Razón de que entren Religiosos de la horden de S. Francisco a la conversión de Japón y China" (Brit. Mus., Harleian MS 3570, fol. 330-336); "Cartas, Memoriales y Relación de Fr. Juna Pobre," edited by Pérez, O.F.M., in *AIA*, Ano 5, num. 28, Tomo X (1918), pp. 26–70; *idem*, "Fray Juan Pobre de Zamora," in *Erudición Ibero-Ultramarino*, Vol. II (1931), pp. 217–235. Jesuit refutations of Franciscan allegations will be found in Padre Valentim de Carvalho's "Apologia" written at Macao in May, 1617. (Brit. Mus., Add. MSS 9856.) The latest work on the Franciscan hospitals at Kyoto is Schilling's article, "Gründung der Hospitaler St. Joseph und St. Anna in Myako (1594–1595)," *NZM*, Vol. I (1949), pp. 1–18, 98–110, 189–202, 258–275.

[23] The foregoing from Fray Juan Pobre, autograph letter, signed, of 1605, and documents printed in *AIA*, Vol. X (1918); Carvalho, "Apologia" (1617) (Brit. Mus., Add. MSS 9856); and Bishop Cerqueira's letter of November 20, 1604, to the Archbishop of Goa (Brit. Mus., Add. MSS 9860, fols. 91–97). This confirms the contemporary Dutch and English accounts of Fray Juan de Madrid's *gaffe*. Cf. Cocks' letter of October 10, 1614, quoted in *TJS* Vol. XIII, Pt. II (1915), pp. 159–166 where Cocks slyly adds "others cannot forget so notable a miracle monger."

[24] Fray Juan Pobre, autograph letter, signed, of 1605, in the writer's collection. For Luso-Spanish rivalry in the Far East at this time, cf. also C. R. Boxer, "Portuguese and Spanish Rivalry in the Far East during the Seventeenth Century" (in *TRAS*, Dec., 1946, April, 1947); the Spanish docu-

ments listed in Maggs Bros., *Catalogue 515;* and Henri Bernard, S.J., *Les Iles Philippines du grand archipel de la Chine.* Full details of the relevant sources will be found in Boxer and Bernard.

[25] Bishop Cerqueira's letter of November 20, 1604 (Brit. Mus., Add. MSS 9860, fols. 91–97) ; Fray Juan Pobre, autograph letter, signed, "Cartas" and report cited in note 22 above; autograph letter, signed, of Fray Diego Aduarte, O.P., countersigned by Fray Gabriel de San Antonio, O.P., dated Valladolid, February, 1605, in the author's collection. Both Aduarte and San Antonio had worked in Cambodia and the Philippines; the former had participated in Luis Pérez Dasmariñas' ill-fated expedition to the Kwangtung coast in 1599. Aduarte had been tortured by the Chinese at Canton, convalesced at Macao and Malacca, been wounded in a fight with Malay pirates off Singapore, and generally led an adventurous missionary life in the Far East before returning to Spain via Portuguese India in 1601–1603. He was later appointed Bishop of Nueva Segovia, and died in the Philippines in 1636, having completed the first part of his *Historia de la Provincia del Sancto Rosario de la Orden de Predicadores en Philippinas, Iapon, y China,* which was printed posthumously at Manila in 1640, after its publication had been held up for some years owing to its outspoken criticism of the Jesuits.

[26] Bishop Cerqueira's letter, November 20, 1604, in British Museum, Add. MSS 9860, fols. 91–97. An English translation of the proposals of Aduarte and Los Rios Coronel concerning Macao, Manila, and Japan will be found in Blair and Robertson, *The Philippine Islands,* Vols. XVIII–XIX, which likewise contain much information on Manila's trade with Japan.

[27] The friars' allegations from Pobre's autograph letter, signed, of 1605, and Aduarte's of 1605, in the writer's collection. Cf. Maggs Bros., *Catalogue 515,* pp. 28–44. Valignano's "Apologia" of 1598 (Brit. Mus., Add. MSS 9858) and Valentim de Carvalho's "Apologia" of 1617 (Brit. Mus., Add. MSS 9856) give the Jesuit defense and retort against their rivals in the mendicant orders. The relevant passage from Vitelleschi's letter concerning the transfer of the Jesuits' warehouse at Macao, will be found in Padre Luis da Gama's report of December 15, 1664 (Ajuda Codex "Jesuitas na Asia," 49-iv-56).

[28] Same sources as those quoted in note 27, particularly Carvalho and da Gama.

[29] Carvalho, "Apologia" (Brit. Mus., Add. MSS 9856); a copy of Cerqueira's letter of March 1, 1607, in the Jesuit Archives at Rome ("Japsin" 21, 135–137), was kindly sent me by Father Georg Schurhammer, at my request.

[30] Bishop Cerqueira's letter of November 20, 1604 (Brit. Mus., Add. MSS 9860, fols. 91–97) ; Carvalho's "Apologia" of 1617 *(ibid.,* 9856); Domingo Fernandez Navarrete, *Controversias Antiguas y Modernas de la Mission de la Gran China.* This highly controversial work, a continuation of Navarrete's *Tratados* of 1676, was suppressed by the Inquisition after the death of his

patron, Don Juan de Austria, but there is a copy in the British Museum and another in the New York Public Library, Lenox Collection. I made copious extracts from the latter copy in 1946, which I have used in this present work. A collection of printed and manuscript Spanish memorials by various Spanish clerics and government officials during the first quarter of the seventeenth century in the British Museum Library (Press-Mark C. 62-i-18) contains a manuscript draft entitled "Rasones que presenta a su Mage-stad el Padre Gabriel de Mattos de la Compañia de Jesus procurador de Japon, por las quales se muestra no ser de provecho, antes de daño la ida de los Religiosos por Nueva España y Filipinas a Japon." It is unsigned and undated, but, from the context, was written in 1616. It recapitulates the Jesuits' arguments for the exclusion of the friars, and frankly admits that the discord between the missionaries of the Society and those of the mendi-cant orders, was worse and more harmful than the ill-feeling between their respective converts.

NOTES TO CHAPTER VI
Pirates and traders

[1] The principal European source for the Wako raids on China is P. A. Tschepe, S.J., *Japans Beziehungen zu China seit den ältesten Zeit bis zum Jahre 1600*, esp. pp. 162–307. Unfortunately, Father Tschepe, although relying entirely on Chinese chronicles for his essay, in no single instance gives the names of his sources or indicates their degree of reliability. It is, however, the only serious work in a European language on the subject, although an-other provided with proper critical apparatus and a bibliography is long overdue. So far as possible, I have checked Tschepe's statements from the following: Y. Takekoshi, *Economic Aspects of the History of Japan*, Vol. I., chap. xvii, pp. 211–229; and chap. xxiv, pp. 336–348; T. T. Chang, *Sino-Portuguese Trade from 1514 to 1644* (Leiden, 1934): Y. Okamoto, *Juroku Seiki Nichi-O kotsu-shi no kenkyu;* Y. S. Kuno, *Japanese Expansion on the Asiatic Continent*. The latest and best Japanese work on the subject which has come my way is K. Akiyama's *Nichi-Shi kosho-shi kenkyu*, which con-tains much documentary material from Chinese, Luchuan, and Korean sources; pages 411–620 give an excellent account of the Wako activities from the Kamakura to the Muromachi periods inclusive.

[2] For the Tenryuji-bune, cf. Takekoshi, *op. cit.*, Vol. I, 211–229, and for the doings of Japanese envoys and pirates in China, Tschepe, *op. cit.*, pp. 153–222 *passim;* Kuno, *op. cit.*, Vol. I, 89–100, 266–297.

[3] Takekoshi, *op. cit.*, Vol. I, 211–229; Tschepe, *op. cit.*, pp. 262–273, 286–293, for the checkered career of Wangchi; Akiyama, *op. cit.*, pp. 585–620.

[4] Tschepe, *op. cit.*, pp. 216–245, and Chang, *op. cit.*, pp. 81–84, for

Chuhuan's viceroyalty and his tragic death. Ricci's and Valignano's remarks on Chinese soldiery and the Wako, are taken from the documents printed in Wicki's edition of Valignano's *Historia*, pp. 247–248. A striking Japanese tribute to the bravery of their Chinese opponents in Korea, as related to the Dutch factor at Hirado, Cornelis Nieuwenroode, will be found in my *Fidalgos in the Far East*, pp. 90–91. Portuguese translations of the Chinese edicts of 1613 and 1616, forbidding Japanese to live at Macao, are to be found in Manuel Murias' *Instruccão para o Bispo de Pequim*, pp. 115–116. The text of Hideyoshi's edict for the suppression of piracy is given in Kuno, *op. cit.*, Vol. I, 296–297, from the original copy in the archives of the Honpoji, Kyoto.

[5] Cf. the English translation of the documents in the Spanish archives printed by Blair and Robertson, *The Philippine Islands* (1583–1588), Vol. VI, 197–233, 258–310; eds., Colin-Pastells, *Labor Evangelica de los oberos de la Compañia de Jesús en las islas Filipinas*, Vol. I, 438–455; Henri Bernard, S.J., *Les Iles Philippines du grand archipel de la Chine. Un Essai de conquête spirituelle de l'extrême Orient*, pp. 48–51, and *idem, La Théorie du protectorat civil des missions en pays infidèle* (Louvain, 1937), pp. 263–274.

[6] For the Japanese in the Philippines and Indo-China, and their relations with the Spaniards in those regions, cf. Fray Diego Aduarte, O.P., *Historia de la provincia del Sancto Rosario de la Orden de Predicadores en Philippinas, Iapon, y China;* Fray Gabriel de San Antonio, O.P., *Breve y verdadera relacion de los successos del Reyno de Camboxa*, originally printed at Valladolid in 1604, and reprinted with a French translation, introduction and notes by A. Cabaton, under the title *Brève et véridique relation des événements du Cambodoge par Gabriel Quiroga de San Antonio;* W. E. Retana's edition of Anotonio de Morga, *Sucesos de las islas Filipinas;* Colin-Pastells, *op. cit.;* M. Paske-Smith's essay on "Japanese Trade and Residence in the Philippines before and during the Spanish occupation," *TASJ*, Vol. XLII (1914), pp. 685–710, may be consulted as a secondary source. Blair and Robertson, *op. cit.*, Vols. V–XX, may be consulted with profit, as also the numerous contemporary reports, documents, and letters reproduced by Fr. Lorenzo Pérez, O.F.M., in the two Madrid Franciscan historical reviews, *Archivo Ibero-Americano* and *Erudición Ibero-Ultramarino*. Japanese works dealing with this subject, of which S. Iwao's *Nanyo Nihon-machi no kenkyu* is the best and latest known to me, are compelled to rely almost entirely on Western sources, such as those quoted above, and afford no additional information worthy of mention.

[7] G. Kawajima, *Shuin-sen boeki-shi* is the best Japanese book on the subject. Largely based on this work, but with a good deal of additional material is Noël Peri's excellent *Essai sur les relations du Japon et de l'Indochine aux XVIe et XVIIe siècles*, reprinted from *Bulletin de l'Ecole Française d'Extrême Orient*, Vol. XXIII (1923). Takekoshi, *op. cit.*, Vol. I, chap. xxxiv, pp. 480–503, may be consulted with due caution. Cf. also E. M.

Satow, "Notes on the Intercourse between Japan and Siam in the Seventeenth Century," in *TASJ*, Vol. XIII (1885), pp. 139–210; see also K.
Gunji, *Tokugawa Jidai no Nichi-Sha*, and *Jushichi Seiki ni okeru Nichi-Thai
kankei* for an exhaustive synthesis of Japanese and Occidental sources.

[8] An outline of Thomas Araki's career was given me in a private letter
from Father Georg Schurhammer, S.J., based on the relevant documents in
the Jesuit Archives at Rome. The facts and figures concerning the *shuinsen*
in the text are taken from a comparison of those given by Kawajima, *op. cit.*,
pp. 74–94, 121–149, and Peri, *op. cit.*, pp. 23–36. Trade with the Philippines
is dealt with in the sources quoted in note 6 above.

[9] Kawajima, *op. cit.*, pp. 101–120; C. R. Boxer, "Some Aspects of Portuguese Influence in Japan, 1542–1640," *TJS*, Vol. XXXIII (1936), pp. 24–
26. The subject merits further study by a competent seaman.

[10] Peri, *op. cit.*, pp. 105–114, although the learned Orientalist did not
realize that the Japanese word *fusuta*, which he transcribes on p. 105, is
merely the *kana* transliteration of the Portuguese word *fusta*, "a foist."
The Portuguese galiot-type ship was likewise naturalized in Japanese under
the form of *kareuta*. For Spanish fears of Fray Luis Sotelo, O.F.M., teaching
the Japanese ship building, cf. Blair and Robertson, *op. cit.*, Vol. XVIII,
295. English sources taken from N. Murakami's edition of the *Diary of
Richard Cocks, Cape-Merchant in the English Factory in Japan 1615–1622*,
Vol. I, 177–178. Cf. also Y. Okamoto, "Nagasaki no fusuta-sen," in his
Momoyama-jidai no Kirisuto-kyo Bunka, pp. 77–114.

[11] Don Pedro de Acuña's quotation from his letter of July 7, 1605, printed
in Colin-Pastells, *op. cit.*, Vol. II, 342, note; Michelbourne's account of the
fight of the *Tiger* and *Tiger's Whelp* with the Wako, in *Purchas His Pilgrimes* (London, 1625), Book I, 137; Cornelis Matelief's account of the
Wako is in *Begin ende Voortgangh* (Amsterdam, 1646), Deel II, 91; I
cannot remember the exact source of the other Dutch quotation, but I
believe it to be attributable to Jacques Specx, and the wording was
"Het is een ruwe ende ontzinige volk, lammeren in hunne eigen land maar
bijna duivelen daarbuiten," or something very like it. The Kwangtung invasion scare of 1606, which was closely connected with Padre Lazaro Cat-
taneo, S.J., is related at length in Guerreiro, *Relação Anual* for 1606 and
1607, chap. xx, fol. 83–86, and in Tomo II, 298–302 of the reprint
(Coimbra, 1931). Cf. also *Fonti Ricciane*, Vol. II (1949), pp. 372–390.

[12] The foregoing is based on the original manuscript report of Padre
Rodriguez Girão, dated Nagasaki, March, 1610 (Brit. Mus., Add. MSS 9860,
fols. 129–135), entitled "Relação da queima da náo Nossa Senhora da Graça
de que foi Capitão-Mòr André Pessoa no ano de 1610"; an English summary
will be found in my *Fidalgos in the Far East*, pp. 52–62. Antonio de Morga
(*Sucesos*, p. 103) relates that Ieyasu crucified 400 (other contemporary
writers state 200) Satsuma Wako who had pirated Manila-bound Chinese
junks in 1600, as an earnest of his desire for peaceful trade with the Philip-

pines. The shuinjo of 1609 is translated from the revised edition of the *Ikoku Nikki* edited by Professor N. Murakami (Tokyo, 1929), p. 40.

[13] The foregoing is mainly from the 1610 "Relação" (Brit. Mus., Add. MSS 9860, fols. 129–135). For Murayama's career, cf. Peri, *op. cit.*, pp. 55–58, and sources there quoted.

[14] Padre João Rodriguez Girão, "Relação," 1610 (Brit. Mus., Add. MSS 9860, *passim*). It is interesting to note that Japanese complaints that the Spaniards were too hard on their compatriots at Manila, are counterbalanced by Spanish allegations that the colonial authorities were too lenient. Thus D. Juan Cevicos, referring to the Macao imbroglio of 1608, declares that the Manila authorities spared rebellious Japanese owing to the intercession of the clergy on more than one occasion, "En Manila algunas vezes muy pocos y muy viles Japones sin mais ocazion que su indomito natural, ayudando a ello el poco castigo que con ellos respeto del de su tierra se uza, y en las jntersesiones que en Religiozos Allan," *AAPH*, Vol. VIII (1944), p. 312. Cf. also *MN*, Vol. II (1939), p. 502, note 34.

[15] Padre João Rodriguez Girão, "Relação," 1610 (Brit. Mus., Add. MSS 9860, fol 132). This assertion is flatly contrary to what Señor J. L. Alvarez writes about the friendly feeling between Spaniards and Portuguese in his article entitled, "Don Rodrigo de Vivero et la destruction de la Nao Madre de Deos 1609," in *MN*, Vol. II, No. 2 (1939), pp. 479–511. But Alvarez, like myself and other writers on this affair up to that date, did not realize that João Rodriguez had made his categorical assertions about Luso-Spanish enmity in Japan as early as 1610, and Alvarez considered them to be a later interpolation by Charlevoix. In this he erred, but his article is nevertheless of permanent value for its frequent citation of Japanese sources and their careful collation with the European versions which were available to him at the time he wrote. An English summary of Don Rodrigo Vivero y Velasco's account of his stay in Japan will be found in Murakami and Murakawa, *Letters Written by the English Residents in Japan, 1611–1623* (Tokyo, 1900), pp. 59–72. Cf. also Murdoch, *History of Japan*, Vol. II, 479–482.

[16] Padre João Rodriguez Girão, "Relação" 1610 (Brit. Mus., Add MSS 9860); figures of tonnage, armament, and crew of a typical *Nao da Viagem do Japão* are taken from the "Processo" of João Serrão da Cunha, captain-major of the 1614 voyage, in the Arquivo Historico Colonial at Lisbon (Papeis da India; Avulsos; Caixa 9; January 29, 1629). This was published in part by Frazão de Vasconcelos in *AAPH*, Vol. VIII (1944), pp. 316–325. Two of Arima's samurai tried to board the carrack in disguise and kill Pessoa, but not being allowed alongside the ship, they had to return empty-handed. This incident recalls a similarly abortive plan of the late Admiral Togo and others to kill the admiral of the English squadron which bombarded Kagoshima in 1863.

[17] Foregoing from Padre João Rodriguez Girão, "Relação," 1610 (Brit. Mus., Add. MSS 9860).

[18] Foregoing from Padre João Rodriguez Girão, "Relação," 1610, collated with the account given by Fray Gaspar de San Agustín, O.S.A. in his *Conquistas de las islas Filipinas* (ed. Casimiro Díaz, 1890), Vol. II, 84–85; cf. also "Relación del Reino de Nippon por Bernardino de Avila Girón," chap. iv, of a contemporary Spanish account on which Gaspar de San Agustín evidently based his version, as edited by D. Schilling, O.F.M., and Fidel de Lejarza in *AIA*, Año XXII, tomo 38 (1935), pp. 120–127. Rodriguez tells us in his "Relação" of March, 1610, that Pessoa's last words were "Blessed be thou, Oh Lord, since thou willest that all this should end." The Augustinian friar, Juan Damorin, was the only Catholic religious on board, although Murdoch and other historians throw in six, twelve, or twenty Jesuits for good measure. For the articles recovered by divers from the wreck of the *Nossa Senhora da Graça* during the last three centuries, cf. the article by Professor C. Muto in the *BSL-J*, Vol. I (1929), pp. 101–142, and my article, "The Affair of the Madre de Deus," *TJS*, Vol. XXVI (1929), pp. 63 and 86. Cf. also my *Fidalgos in the Far East*, pp. 60–62.

[19] Padre João Rodriguez, "Relação," 1610 (Brit. Mus., Add. MSS 9860, fols. 134–135).

[20] The Japanese version of the correspondence between the authorities at Goa and Macao on the one hand and the Bakufu on the other, is taken from the documents printed in the revised version of the *Ikoku Nikki* (ed. Murakami), pp. 40–121 *passim*. For the Portuguese version of Soutomaior's embassy in 1611, cf. Antonio Bocarro, *Década XIII da Historia da India*, chap. xxii, p. 97, and my essay "The Affairs of the Madre de Deus," *TJS*, Vol. XXVI (1929), pp. 55–58) and sources there quoted. *The Madre de Deus* was identical with the *Nossa Senhora da Graça*, and it is still not absolutely clear by which name the carrack was really called. The fullest Japanese account of the affair is to be found in the *Kurofune hanchin-ki*, but neither this nor the numerous traditional accounts (*Keicho Nikki, Nagasaki Yawagusa, Todaiki*, etc., etc.) are worthy of much credence. They are discussed in Professor C. Muto's article in *BSL-J*, Vol. I (1929), pp. 101–142, and a typical specimen will be found in Kaempfer's *History of Japan*, Book IV, chap. v. The *Ikoku Nikki* also contains (Murakami, *op. cit.*, pp. 266–267) two letters from Shimadzu Iehisa to the Macao senate over the safe return of a Red-seal Satsuma ship which had been forced into Macao by stress of weather, in 1611, and whose crew was befriended by the Portuguese. See below, Appendix V.

[21] For the voyage of the *Liefde* and the *Trouw*, cf. F. C. Wieder, *De Reis van Mahu en de Cordes door de Straat van Magalhães naar Zuid-Amerika en Japan, 1598–1600* (Linschoten Vereeniging edition, 3 vols.; The Hague, 1923–1925); the letters of Will Adams as printed in *Purchas,*

his Pilgrimes (London, 1625), and reprinted in numerous versions since; Fernão Guerreiro, *Relação Anual* ... 1600–1601 (ed., 1930), pp. 107–108; Diogo do Couto, *Cinco Livros da Decada Doze,* Livro v, cap. ii. For the voyage of Oliver Van Noort and the loss of one of his ships in Manila Bay, cf. the Linschoten Vereeniging edition of his work (2 vols.; The Hague, 1926), and W. E. Retana's annotated reprint (1909) of Antonio Morga's *Sucesos de las islas Filipinas,* pp. 103–119, 279–310. For the capture of Van Neck's men at Macao in 1601, cf. the account of his voyage in the *Begin ende Voortgangh van de Vereenighde Nederlantsche Geoctroyeerde Oost-Indische Compagnie,* and the affidavit of the principal survivor, Martinus Ape (or Apius), as taken in 1604, and reprinted in the *Bijdragen ende Mededeelingen van het Historisch genootschap gevestigd te Utrecht,* Deel VI (1883), pp. 228–242. In contrast to their attitude toward the crew of the *Liefde* in Japan, the Macao Jesuits (or some of them) made every effort to save the lives of Van Neck's men, although they were only successful with Ape and two youths. Ape blames the local merchants and the Ouvidor for urging the execution of the remainder on the youthful Captain-Major, Dom Paulo de Portugal. This incident acquired a widespread notoriety a few years later, through the publicity given it in Grotius' classic *Mare Liberum* (Leiden, 1609).

[22] For the establishment of the Dutch factory at Hirado and Matelief's cruise in Far Eastern waters, cf. my "The Affair of the Madre de Deus," *TJS,* Vol. XXVI (1929), and the sources there quoted.

[23] Cf. the following extracts from Adams' correspondence regarding his standing with Ieyasu. "I pleased him so, that what I said he would not contrarie. At which my former ennemies did wonder; and at this time must intreat me to do them a friendship, which to both Spaniards and Portingals have I doen; recompencing them good for evill . . ." (October 22, 1611). "This yeere 1612 the Spaynnards and Portingalles hav ussed me as an instrument to gett there liberty in the manner of the Hollanders, but uppon consideration of farther inconvenience I hav not sought it for them. It hath pleased God to bring things to pass, so as in ye eyes of ye world [must seem] strange; for the Spaynnard and Portingall hath bin my bitter ennemis, to death; and now they must seek to me an unworth wretch; so the Spaynard as well as the Portingall must hav all their negosshes go through my hand. God hav ye prayse for it . . ." (January 12, 1613). The dates given are old style. (Murakami, *Letters Written by the English Residents in Japan, 1611–1623,* pp. 12, 27–28.)

[24] The history of the English factory at Hirado is fully documented, the principal sources being the following: L. Riess, "History of the English Factory at Hirado (1613–1623)" in *TASJ,* Vol. XXVI (1898); Murakami's annotated reprint of the Hakluyt Society's edition of the *Diary of Richard Cocks, 1615–1622;* Murakami, *Letters;* E. M. Satow, *The Voyage of Captain John Saris to Japan, 1613* (Hakluyt Society ed., 2d ser., Vol. 5);

C. J. Purnell, "The Log Book of William Adams, 1614–1619, and Related Documents," *TJS*, Vol. XIII, Pt. II (1915), pp. 156–302; Paske-Smith, *Western Barbarians in Japan and Formosa in Tokugawa Days, 1603–1868.* All quotations in the text are taken from one or another of the first five works. Saris' Voyage has been recently (1948) reprinted in Japan, but I have not had access to this new and annotated edition.

[25] The foregoing is based on Peri, *op. cit.*, pp. 60–63, 76–98, 127–130; and M. Kawajima, *Shuin-sen boeki-shi*; S. Iwao, *Nanyo Nihon-machi no kenkyu*, pp. 15–116; K. Gunji, *Jushichi seiki ni okeru Nichi-Thai kankei.*

[26] Murakami, *Letters*, pp. 180–181, 184; *Diary of Richard Cocks*, Vol. I, 35, 131, 149, 219, 251, 277; Vol. II, 10, 356; *Documentos Remettidos da India ou Livros das Monções*, Vol. I, 335. Bocarro, *op. cit.*, pp. 725. Chang, *op. cit.*, p. 120 quoting the *Ming-shih*, chap. 325, p. 102. *THM*, Vol. XI (1941), pp. 401–439, and sources there quoted. The Chinese merchants living in Japan did not bring their wives with them but lived with local women. Valignano had a lot of trouble with those who married Catholic Japanese, and then abandoned them and their children, since the Christian marriage ceremony meant nothing to them ("Obediencias," 1592. Ajuda Codex "Jesuitas na Asia," 49-iv-56). For Ieyasu's futile efforts to secure official trade with China, cf. Kuno, *op. cit.*, II, 282–295.

[27] The Spaniards, like the English in the early days of the Anglo-Japanese alliance, were fond of comparing the Japanese with themselves, and, unlike Valignano, rated them higher than the Chinese. "Los Japoneses, que son, como doctamente dijo Gracián, los Españoles del Asia, y los Chinos, que con la cultura de la politica y amor á las letras, parecen diversos, aunque tocados á la piedra de la experiencia, son lo mismo que los Indios." (Fr. Gaspar de San Agustín, O.S.A., *Conquistas de las islas Filipinas*, Vol. II, 57.) About one third of the soldiers whom Don Juan de Silva raised for his abortive expedition to Malacca in 1615 were Japanese, and they were formed into a separate unit under a Spanish captain. For Japanese in the Philippines in general during this period, cf. W. L. Schurz, *The Manila Galleon* (New York, 1939), pp. 99–128, and Paske-Smith's article in *TASJ*, Vol. XLII, Pt. II (1914), pp. 683–710. For the expansion of the silk trade at Manila to the detriment of Macao, cf. Duarte Gomes de Solis, *Discvrsos sobre los comercios de las dos Indias* (Madrid, 1622), fols. 118–119. The best review in Japanese is that by S. Iwao, *Nanyo Nihon-machi no kenkyu*, pp. 215–338, but it is based entirely on European sources.

[28] A full account of Serrão's voyage is contained in the papers relating to his lengthy lawsuit in the Arquivo Historico Colonial at Lisbon (Papeis da India, Caixa 9, 1629), part of which have been printed by Frazão de Vasconcelos in *AAPH*, Vol. VIII (1944), pp. 316–325. Some of the information about current prices is interesting. The ship's officers and the European sailors each got a picul of rice a month in addition to their pay. A picul was

the equivalent of 100 catties and this amount of rice cost one *pardáo de reales* at Macao in those years. We learn from Coppindale's correspondence that the price of rice in Japan in October, 1615, was 2 taels, 6 mace per *koku*, but this was double the normal price in consequence of the Osaka summer campaign. (Cf. Riess, "History of the English Factory at Hirado," *TASJ,* Vol. XXVI [1898], p. 60.) Cocks in a letter dated December 23, 1617, states ". . . they reckon in Japan the ryal of eight at eight *mas* Japan, or four shillings sterling" (Murakami, *Letters,* p. 214). The pardáo de reales was another name for the ryal of eight, and ten *mas* (mace) went to the tael (Chinese, *liang*). The pardáo de reales or ryal of eight was worth 436 Portuguese *reis* at Goa on first arrival from Europe in Linschoten's time (1580), whereas the *xerafim* was an Indo-Portuguese coin nominally worth about 4 shillings in English Elizabethan money. Padre João Rodriguez Tçuzzu in his Japanese Grammar of 1604–1608, equates 10 Japanese *momme* with one Chinese silver tael, or one Portuguese *cruzado* of 400 reis. This would be roughly the equivalent of four English shillings or a little less at that time.

²⁹ In 1617, Hasegawa Gonroku likewise sent to tell the Dutch at Hirado that they would be allowed to send their ships "to lay wait for thamakan shipp, as they gave it out they would doe, as also to command the Hollandes Capt. in themperours name that he should see it performed" (Cock's *Diary,* Vol. I, 263). As regards Serrão, his peregrinations were by no means over with the sale of his ship in 1616. He somehow found the wherewithal to pay for an overland trip to Europe from Goa, and spent five years kicking his heels at the court of Madrid before returning to India. The lawsuit dragged on until 1629 at least, and the matter was finally settled by his appointment as governor of the Cape Verde Islands about 1644, by way of compensation for his losses. He had previously been granted a share in the Crown cinnamon monopoly in Ceylon, which the viceroy refused to honor (Biblioteca da Universidade de Coimbra, MSS 460, fols. 69–73).

³⁰ *Diary of Richard Cocks* (ed. Murakami), Vol. I, 33, 106, 257, 261–263; Vol. II, 264, 313–314; Saris' *Journal* (ed. Satow), p. 83; and Murakami, *Letters,* pp. 76–77.

NOTES TO CHAPTER VII
The palm of Christian fortitude

¹ Carvalho in his "Apologia" of 1617 (Brit. Mus., Add. MSS 9856, fol. 22) makes special mention of a Portuguese merchant named Vicente Rodriguez who spoke fluent Japanese and was well versed in the national customs. He was involved in a lawsuit over some goods lost in the *Nossa Senhora da Graça,* against one of the Funamoto family, famous as traders

to Indo-China. This Rodriguez is also mentioned in the contemporary Macaonese documents as a merchant of importance. Other leading traders who spoke good Japanese at this period include Domingos Jorge (martyred in 1619) and Duarte Correa (martyred in 1639), apart from the Goanese, Jorge Durões, who figures prominently in Cock's *Diary* and Bocarro's *Decada XIII da Historia da India*. There were also a number of banishees from Manila and Macao who were settled (somewhat disreputably) at Hirado and Nagasaki, where both sides made use of them. Frequent mention of these waifs and strays will be found in Cocks' correspondence. Alvaro Muñoz, one of the most prominent, was working for the Portuguese in 1635.

² Cf. Cocks' *Diary* (ed. Murakami), Vol. I, 173, 175, 246; Vol. II, 280–283; *Letters, 1611–1623* (ed. Murakami), pp. 159, 195–197. The complementary Spanish and Portuguese sources will be found in Colin-Pastells, *Labor Evangelica de los obreros de la Compañia de Jesús en las islas Filipinas*, Vol. III, 379–380, 484–485, and Carvalho, "Apologia" (Brit. Mus., Add. MSS 9856, fols. 93–94). The act of Elizabeth (reg. 27) which condemned Catholic priests to death for coming to England received the royal assent in March, 1585.

³ Vizcaíno's original report was printed in *Colección de documentos inéditos relativos al descubrimiento, conquista y organizacion de las antiguas posesiones Españoles de America y Oceania* (Madrid, 1867), Vol. VIII, 101–199. An English summary of this and other related documents will be found in Zelia Nuttall's study, *The Earliest Historical Relations between Mexico and Japan* (University of California Publications in American Archaeology and Ethnology, Vol. 4, no. 1, pp. 1–47). The author's commentary, as distinct from her translation, is by no means free from errors—such as the statement that there were then 15,000 Japanese settled at Manila, whereas 1,500 would be nearer the mark. Another version of Ieyasu's reply to the Viceroy of Mexico, stressing the incompatability of Buddhism and Christianity will be found in Kuno, *Japanese Expansion on the Asiatic Continent*, Vol. II, 27, 303–305. Cf. also Murdoch, *History of Japan*, Vol. II, 600–615. The fullest account of Date Masamune's embassy of 1613–1620, is still that by G. Meriweather, "A Sketch of the Life of Date Masamune and An Account of His Embassy to Rome," in *TASJ*, Vol. XXI (1893), which contains much material from both Japanese and European sources. Additional material will be found in the documents printed by Angel Nuñez Ortega, *Noticia Historica de las Relaciones Politicas y Comerciales entre México y el Japón durante el siglo XVII* (México, 1933), and Lorenzo Pérez, O.F.M., *Apostalado y Martirio del Beato Luis Sotelo en el Japón*.

⁴ For the Arima-Daihachi affair, cf. [Morejon] *A Briefe Relation of the Persecution Lately Made Against the Catholic Christians in the Kingdome of Iaponia*, pp. 58–63 (being a translation of the Annual Letter for 1614, printed at Mexico in 1616, and intended for circulation among the Catholics in England); Carvalho's "Apologia" (Brit. Mus., Add. MSS 9856, fols.

86–90), and Colin-Pastells, *op. cit.*, Vol. III, 381, 411–414. For the Okubo scandal, cf. Y. Takekoshi, *The Economic Aspects of the History of the Civilization of Japan*, Vol. II, 73–75. Murdoch appears to place too much credence on the legendary Japanese version which he reproduces (*op. cit.*, Vol. II, 492–494). There is nothing in the European sources to indicate that Okubo was a Christian, still less to implicate the missionaries in treasonable correspondence with him. The memory of Julia Ota, Ieyasu's real or alleged Korean mistress who was exiled to Oshima (Idzu), was revered as a divinity by the islanders down to 1926 at least (*PIA*, Vol. II [1926], p. 301).

[5] For the crucifixion of Jirobioyei, and Hasegawa's attitude, cf. Colin-Pastells, *op. cit.*, Vol. III, 376–381; *A Briefe Relation* (1619), pp. 134–135.

[6] The foregoing is chiefly based on Satow's translation of Ieyasu's Expulsion Edict, printed in *TASJ*, Vol. VI (1878), pp. 46–48. Another version of Soden's draft will be found in Kuno, *op. cit.*, Vol. II, 47–48. Cf. also M. Anesaki, *Kirishitan dendo no kokai*, pp. 449–465.

[7] *A Briefe Relation* (1619), pp. 130–132. For Takayama Ukon, see *MN*, Vol. V (1942), pp. 86–112 and *ibid.*, Vol. VI (1943), pp. 233–244; P. Y. Kataoka, *Takayama Ukon Taiyu Nagafusa den*; Johannes Laures, S.J., *Takayama Ukon no shogai*.

[8] The statistics for the Christian missions in the years 1612–1614 are taken from British Museum, Add. MSS 9860, fols. 218–219 ("De como por derradeiro foi a Companhia desterrada de Japam," dated Nagasaki, November 8, 1614, that is, on the day of the ships' departure); "Catalogo dos Padres e Irmãos e Casas desta Provincia, e ministros da Christandade de Japão antes de perseguição, feito no anno de 1612," in Colin-Pastells, *op. cit.*, Vol. III, 383–384; Carvalho's "Apologia" (Brit. Mus., Add. MSS 9856, fols. 15–16); *A Briefe Relation* (1619), pp. 71, 284–285, 301–302, and Fray Diego Aduarte, *Historia de la Provincia del Santo Rosario.* ... In the few instances where the Portuguese and Spanish accounts differ, I have followed the former as being better informed. For a discussion on the population of Japan in the Tokugawa period, cf. Kuno, *op. cit.*, Vol. II, 359–379.

[9] *A Briefe Relation* (1619), pp. 288–289, 305–306; letter dated Nagasaki, November 7, 1614, in British Museum, Add. MSS 9860, fols. 228–230; Colin-Pastells, *op. cit.*, Vol. III, 397. The exceptional courtesy shown to Serrão da Cunha on Ieyasu's orders, even made the Jesuits think for a time that there was a chance of the latter relenting—"Porque Safioye que es el Governador de Nangasaqui, hauia mostrado extraordinario gusto con su venida y hazia al Capitan y Portugueses muy differente acogida de lo que hasta alli hauia hecho, y procedia con tan nuevas Cortesias y cumplimientos que a todos daua esperanças de grande bonança." They might have guessed that this exceptional friendliness was merely to induce the Portuguese merchants to continue trading irrespective of what happened to the padres.

[10] *A Briefe Relation* (1619), pp. 296–349; Adams' letter to Specx is in *TJS*, Vol. XIII, Pt. II (1915), pp. 88. Cf. also *Letters, 1611–1623* (ed. Murakami), pp. 52, 192; Cocks, *Diary* (ed. Murakami), Vol. I, 3–6. "I thought it good to note downe that a padre or Jesuit came to the English howse and said his name was Tomas and a Bisken by nation, and gave it out he was a merchant; and others gave him the name of Captain" (June 3, 1615). "After dyner came a Franciskan frire, called Padre Appolinario, whom I had seene 2 or 3 tymes in Firando heretofore. He was in the fortress of Osaka when it was taken, and yet had the good happ to escape" (June 7, 1615). This last individual was Fray Apolinario Franco, O.F.M., martyred at Omura in September, 1622. Cf. also Colin-Pastells, *op. cit.*, Vol. III, 400–401. For the Nagasaki schism of October, 1614, cf. Carvalho, "Apologia" (Brit. Mus., Add. MSS 9856, fols. 52–60, and 9860, fols. 231–232) as also the documents printed in Colin-Pastells, *op. cit.*, Vol. III, 385–395.

[11] The Arima martyrdom of October, 1613, is fully described in *A Briefe Relation* (1619), pp. 122–129. Other accounts will be found in any of the standard mission histories of Japan. The quotations from Padre João Rodriguez Girão's letter of March 15, 1616, are taken from the contemporary MS copy in the British Museum (Add. MSS 9859, fols. 270–293). A good account of the Osaka campaign will be found in Murdoch, *op. cit.*, Vol. II, chap. xvii, and a less coherent one in Sadler, *The Maker of Modern Japan*, pp. 277–294. The most exhaustive Japanese account is that by I. Tokutomi in his *Kinsei Nihon Kokumin-shi*, Vol. XII: *Osaka Eki*.

[12] A letter compiled by the Jesuit visitor in November, 1614, states that although the Japanese suspected in some areas, and knew for certain in others, that padres were lying concealed in Nagasaki and elsewhere, "yet because they behaved with more tact and prudence, the Japanese dissembled with them, as they often do when they see that their laws and edicts are treated with due respect" (Brit. Mus., Add. MSS 9860, fols. 233–237). For the Suetsugu-Murayama quarrel, cf. Casimiro Díaz, *Conquistas de las islas Filipinas*, Vol. II, 143–144; Jesuit Annual Letter for 1618, *apud* Baião, *Carta Anua* (Coimbra, 1933), p. xi, and Cocks' *Diary* (ed. Murakami), Vol. II, 39–69. Heizo's wife remained a Christian even after her husband's apostasy, judging by Cocks' interview with this lady during March 19–29, 1618: ". . . she being a Christian, who urged me much to know our principles of religion, and whether we had churches in our countrey. Unto all which I answered in particular that we had both archbushopps, bushops, and other sortes of church men, but not mas priests which said service in Lattin, but in our owne language, . . . " (*ibid.*, pp. 24–25).

[13] Foregoing from *Letters, 1611–1623* (ed. Murakami), p. 240; British Museum, Add. MSS 9859, fols. 270–293, and MS 9860, fols. 239–242; Takekoshi, *op. cit.*, Vol. II, 88; Satow's article in *TASJ*, Vol. VI (1878), pp. 51; *Kirishito-ki und Sayo-yoroku, Japanische dokumente zur Missions-*

geschichte des 17. Jahrhunderts (ed. Voss and Cieslik, 1940), pp. 47–49; M. Anesaki, *Concordance to the History of the Kirishitan Missions*, pp. 31– 46. For Pedro Hitomi, cf. also my article in *TJS*, Vol. XXXIII (1936), pp. 54–55, although Professor R. Tsunoda has since informed me that Bensai is a better reading of his given name than Sansai.

¹⁴ For the foregoing, cf. *Kirishito-ki* (ed. Voss and Cieslik, 1940), esp. pp. 14–109 *passim;* M. Anesaki, "Japanese Refutations of Christianity in the Seventeenth Century," *TASJ*, 2d ser., Vol. VII (Dec., 1930), pp. 1–15; *idem,* "Writings on Martyrdom in Kirishitan Literature," *ibid.,* Vol. VIII (Dec., 1931), pp. 20–65; *idem,* "Psychological Observations on the Persecution of Catholics in Seventeenth Century Japan," in *Harvard Journal of Asiatic Studies,* Vol. I (1936), pp. 13–27, 1936; A. Ebisawa, "Relation between the Ethics of Bushido and Christianity" (from the English translation of the Japanese original in the *Shigaku Zasshi*) in *Cultural Nippon,* Vol. VII, nos. 3, 4 (Nov.–Dec., 1939); *A Briefe Relation* (1619), pp. 126, 239, 243–246, 340; C. R. Boxer, "Hosokawa Takaoki and the Jesuits, 1587– 1645," in *TJS*, Vol. XXXII (1935), pp. 79–119; Dias, *op. cit.,* Vol. II, 190–200; *The Palme of Christian Fortitude* (ed. 1630), pp. 13–21. François Caron, *A True Description of the Mighty Kingdoms of Japan and Siam* (ed. Boxer, 1935), p. 46. Although crucifixion was early abandoned in favor of burning alive when European missionaries were sentenced, Japanese converts were often executed by the former method. A particularly cruel form of this was the "water crucifixion." Seventy victims were crucified upside down at low tide in Shinagawa (Yedo), being drowned when the tide arose. The torture was so great that the faces of the dead were unrecognizable. (Takekoshi, *op. cit.,* Vol. II, 100, where date is given as 1640.)

¹⁵ British Museum, Add. MSS 9860, fols. 239–253; Richard Cocks, *Diary* (ed. Murakami), Vol. II, 207, 250; Diaz, *op. cit.,* Vol. II, 142; Anesaki in *Harvard Journal of Asiatic Studies,* Vol. I (1936), pp. 13–27. Full details of the martyrdoms of the 1620's will be found in the contemporary reports and letters listed in Streit-Dindinger, *Bibliotheca Missionum,* Vol. V, 458–531.

¹⁶ See Fr. Domingo Martinez, O.F.M., *Compendio Historico,* pp. 169–172, for the original Spanish account of Fr. Diego de San Francisco's imprisonment. An English version, based on the French translation of Pagés will be found in Murdoch, *op. cit.,* Vol. II, 604–605, note. Cf. also *AIA*, Vol. I (1914), pp. 333–354, 515–537, and Vol. II (1915), pp. 68–98, 241–255, for this courageous friar's later career in Japan. Yatsushiro jail is described in British Museum, Add. MSS 9860, fols. 162. Cf. the account of Nagasaki jail in *AIA*, Vol. XIV (1920), pp. 46–47, and of Omura jail in Pagés, *Histoire de la religion chrétienne au Japon,* Vol. II: *Annexes,* p. 327.

¹⁷ *Letters, 1611–1623* (ed. Murakami), p. 239; Caron, *op. cit.,* (ed. Boxer, 1935), pp. 44–46, 173–188. It need hardly be added that the Japanese had no monopoly in roasting people alive, as may be seen from the following

extracts of an eyewitness report of an *auto da fé* at Lisbon in the same century. "The execution was very cruel . . . the woman was alive in the flames above half an hour, and the man above an hour . . . the fire being recruited as it wasted to keep him at just the same degree of heat . . . but all his entreaties could not procure him a larger allowance of wood to shorten his misery . . . as he turned himself about his ribs opened before he had left speaking" (Bishop Burnet's correspondent as quoted by Mary Brearley, *Hugo Gurgeny, Prisoner of the Lisbon Inquisition* [London, 1947], pp. 149–150). Anyone who imagines that Anglo-Saxons did not indulge in such barbarous proceedings may be referred to the ghastly episode, described without the least sign of guilt or regret, in *The Voyage of Sir Henry Middleton to the Moluccas* (Hakluyt Society ed.; London, 1943), pp. 121–122. Murdoch's remark is taken from his *History*, Vol. II, 628, note.

[18] The water torture is described in British Museum, Add. MSS 9860, fol. 255 (account of Mastrilli's martyrdom), and Aduarte, *op. cit.*, Book II, chap. xix (English translation in Blair and Robertson, *The Philippine Islands*, Vol. 32, p. 243). The Dutch applied it to Flores and Zuñiga in 1621 (cf. Diaz, *op. cit.*, Vol. II, 136 ff.), and to the English at Amboyna a few years later. It was widely used the world over, and is not an invention of the Japanese *Kempeitai* in recent years, as many people erroneously imagine. For Kawachi and Takenaka's persecution in 1626–1632, cf. Fr. Diego de San Francisco's correspondence printed in the *AIA*, Vol. I (1914), pp. 514–537; Caron, *op. cit.* (ed. Boxer, 1935), pp. 78–88. Further details on Unzen in the letter of Padre Christovão Ferreira, S.J., dated March 22, 1632, in Pagés, *op. cit.*, Vol. II: *Annexes*, pp. 369–374. For one of the many eyewitness accounts of the suspension in the pit which completely contradict Professor Anesaki's mistaken theories on the method of this torture, cf. the report on Mastrilli's martyrdom in British Museum, Add. MSS 9860, fols. 253–257. Caron, *op. cit.*, (ed. Boxer, 1935), pp. 44–45 are also relevant. Fr. Diego Aduarte, O.P., states that the record for anyone living under this torture was thirteen and a half days (*op. cit.*, Book II, chap. 52) which agrees with Caron's observation that a young woman lived fourteen days in the pit and died without recanting. The concluding exhortation on martyrdom is taken from Anesaki's translation in his *Concordance*, p. 186.

[19] Material in this section is taken from Anesaki's articles in *TASJ* (see note 14, above); Cocks, *Diary* (ed. Murakami), Vol. II, 156, British Museum, Add. MSS 9869, fols. 278; *A Briefe Relation* (1619), pp. 91, 106–107, 230–237; *AHSI*, Vol. IX (1940), pp. 40–49; Pagés, *op. cit.*, Vol. II: *Annexes*, pp. 108–197, 204–263, 397; *Kirishito-ki* (ed. Voss and Cieslik), pp. 15–16; Murdoch, *op. cit.*, Vol. II, 499, note; and Caron, *op. cit.* (ed. Boxer, 1935), pp. 83–84. For Luso-Spanish rivalry in Japan and China at this period, cf. my article in *TRAS* (Dec., 1946, April, 1947), and sources there quoted. Jesuits and friars were still wrangling over the authenticity of the 1597 martyrs at the height of the persecution at Nagasaki in 1622.

The waspish Dominican, Diego Collado, excommunicated some of the local Portuguese in September of that year (and month of the Great Martyrdom) because they declined to testify in the process (*AIA*, Vol. XIX [1922], pp. 145–173, esp. p. 170 and note 1).

[20] Cardim's figures are from his *Elogios*, pp. 266–331. As can be seen from the official Martyrology in Delplace, *Le Catholicisme au Japon*, Vol. II, 181–195, 263–278, and Anesaki's *Concordance*, pp. 25–80, something between two and four thousand martyrs is the total accepted by reputable historians who have taken the trouble to check their sources, and not (like others who shall be nameless) inflated the figures to a couple of million without the slightest justification. Ramos' letter has been generally overlooked, and if his average figure be taken as applicable to the years 1614–1630 (as I suggest it is), this would about double the estimates of Cardim, Delplace, and Anesaki. A translation of his letter will be found in *TJS*, Vol. XXVII (1930), pp. 4–11. Fr. Juan Pobre's figure of apostates in 1587–1597 is taken from an unpublished autograph letter in my collection, and Valignano's admission from the "Advertencias" of 1592 (Ajuda Codex "Jesuitas na Asia," 49-iv-56).

NOTES TO CHAPTER VIII
Sakoku, or the closed country

[1] For the study of Iemitsu's character and the attitude of the Bakufu to Christianity about this time, cf. M. Anesaki's article in the *Harvard Journal of Asiatic Studies*, Vol. I (1936), pp. 16–19; G. B. Sansom, *Japan* (ed. 1931), pp. 438–457; I. Tokutomi, *Kinsei Nihon Kokumin-shi*, Vol. XIV (ed. 1935), pp. 121–122, and the sources there quoted. Other details are taken from Murdoch, *History of Japan*, Vol. II, 624–635, and *The Palme of Christian Fortitude*, pp. 13–14; *MN*, Vol. I (1938), pp. 293–300.

[2] Valignano's remarks from the original copy with his autograph signature in British Museum, Add. MSS 9860 fols. 66–67, being the draft of a letter written at Shiki, October 12, 1599. The *Rol do fato* of Jesuit-owned cargo in 1618, is in the Biblioteca de Adjuda, Codex "Jesuitas na Asia," 59-v-11, fol. 139ᵛ. For Lopo Sarmento's embassy, cf. *Documentos Remettidos da India ou Livros das Monções*, Vol. V, 197–198. Carvalho's clandestine arrival is described in *The Palme of Christian Fortitude*, p. 151. The entry of the Visitor Francisco Vieira, S.J., in a similar fashion is narrated in Padre João Rodriguez Girão's letter of November 12, 1618, *apud* Baião, *Carta Anua* (Coimbra, 1933), p. xi.

[3] The foregoing from Cocks' *Diary* (ed. Murakami), Vol. II, 334–336; *The Palme of Christian Fortitude*, p. 82; Casimiro Díaz, *Conquistas de las islas Filipinas*, Vol. II, 255–256; Colin-Pastells, eds., *Labor Evangelica de los obreros de la Compañia de Jesús en las islas Filipinas*, Vol. III, 517;

Diario do Conde de Linhares, pp. 26, 95–100; the name of the Augustinian priest concerned is not given but he was in all probability Fr. Francisco da Graça, O.S.A., martyred at Nagasaki on August 19, 1633, since he seems to have been the only Portuguese of his order in Japan at the time; C. R. Boxer, articles in *TJS,* Vol. XXVII (1930), pp. 4–11 and Vol. XXXI (1934); *idem, Fidalgos in the Far East,* pp. 100–121, and *Azia Sinica e Japonica,* Vol. I, 223–236. For the Macao-Japan voyages, cf. also Lourenço de Lis Velho's letter in the Arquivo Torre do Tombo, Lisbon, "Colecção de São Vicente," XIV, fol. 162; *Ikoku Nikki* (ed. Murakami) *passim;* and Noël Peri, *Essai sur les relations de Japon et de l'Indochine aux XVIe et XVIIe siècles,* pp. 115–118, for a discussion of the interest rates.

[4] Caron, *A True Description* (ed. Boxer, 1935), pp. xliii and source described in Manuel Ramos' letter translated in *TJS,* Vol. XXVII (1930), pp. 4–11. The various edicts of 1633–1636 on the navigation of the Shuinsen are given in part in Y. Kuno, *Japanese Expansion on the Asiatic Continent,* Vol. II, 310–317, and Y. Takekoshi, *The Economic Aspects of the History of the Civilization of Japan,* Vol. II, 127 ff. The original Japanese texts will be found in I. Tokutomi, *Kinsei Nihon Kokumin-shi,* Vol. XIV: *Sakoku-hen,* pp. 280–290. Cf. also, L. Riess, "Die ursachen der vertreibung der Portugiesen aus Japan 1614–1639," in *MDGfNVD,* Vol. VII, Teil 1 (1898); Murdoch, *op. cit.,* Vol. II, 636–641, and Sansom, *op. cit.* (ed. 1938), pp. 433–437, for a general discussion. The danger of a Japanese expedition in aid of discontented Filipinos, is taken from Archbishop Benavides' memorial in L. Hanke, *Cuerpo de Documentos,* p. 211. Most historians state that the reason for the cancellation of the intended Japanese invasion of Luzon in 1638 was the death of Matsukura Shigemasa, who was the moving spirit therein. But he died in 1630, and it is crystal clear from the Dutch documents quoted in my edition of Caron's *True Description* (cf. pp. xliv–xlvi) that the matter was frequently discussed in the ensuing decade, and a definite decision to attack Manila was taken in 1637.

[5] The foregoing from British Museum, Add. MSS 9860, fols. 89–90; Fernão Guerreiro, *Relação Anual,* I (ed. Coimbra, 1930), pp. 177–178; Anesaki's article in *PIA,* Vol. III (1927), pp. 637–638; L. Pagés, *Histoire de la religion Chretiénne au Japon,* Vol. II: *Annexes,* pp. 280–283; Duarte Correa's account of the Shimabara rebellion is reprinted in Pagés, *ibid.,* pp. 403–411. Those who are intrigued by life's little ironies may care to know that the original draft, when printed in 1643, was dedicated to the Inquisitor-General of Portugal, Dom Francisco de Castro, a notorious Jew-baiter and burner, Correa himself having been roasted to death over a slow fire in August, 1639.

[6] Accounts of the Shimabara rebellion are numerous and the following have all been utilized in these pages; L. Riess, "Der Aufstand von Shimabara" in *MDGfNVD,* Vol. 5, Heft 45 (1891), pp. 191–214; Murdoch, *op. cit.,* Vol. II, chap. xxii, pp. 642–662; Takekoshi, *op. cit.,* Vol. II, 91–103; Kuno,

op. cit., Vol. II, 72–81; Paske-Smith, *Japanese Traditions of Christianity*, pp. 49–100; I. Tokutomi, *op. cit.*, Vol. XIV *Sakoku-hen*, pp. 322–448, with a wealth of documentary material. Assertions that Yamada Emonsaku lived and died a practicing Christian seem rather dubious in view of the many traditional Japanese accounts that he was a renegade; though there is no necessity to credit him with the invention of the *efumi* (*fumie*) or picture-treading ceremony, as some Japanese writers have done—and I in their footsteps in my time. For the abandonment of the projected combined attack on Manila, cf. my edition of Caron's *True Description*, pp. xlv–xlvi.

[7] For the foregoing, cf. my edition of *Azia Sinica e Japonica*, Vol. I, 236–247; Kuno, *op. cit.*, Vol. II, 84; Caron, *A True Description* (ed. Boxer, 1935), pp. lv–lvi and sources from the Deshima *Dagh-Register* there quoted. The fullest contemporary narrative of the Macaonese embassy of 1640, based on the account printed at Manila in 1641, is by the present writer: "Embaixada de Macau ao Japão em 1640," in *Anais do Club Militar Naval*, Vol. LXII (1940). For the Japanese version, cf. Tokutomi, *op. cit.*, Vol. XIV, 269–273.

[8] The embassy of 1644–1647 has been dealt with by the present writer *per longum et latum* in his work *The Embassy of Captain Gonçalo de Siqueira de Souza to Japan in 1644–47* (1938). Cf. also *MN*, Vol. II, 512–517, for textual reproduction of some of the Japanese documents. Tokutomi, *op. cit.*, pp. 273–279, has a brief account from the Japanese side. The attempt of 1685 is narrated *in extenso* by the original documents relating thereto printed in the *Arquivos de Macau*, Vol. I (1929), pp. 177–234. Kaempfer has a concise and reasonably accurate account in his *History* (ed. 1728), Vol. I, 2–3.

[9] For the foregoing, cf. Caron, *A True Description* (ed. Boxer, 1935), pp. xxx–xxxiii (Vieira's martyrdom and Dutch efforts to capitalize thereon); Anesaki, *A Concordance to the History of the Kirishitan Missions*, esp. pp. 63–77; *Kirishito-ki und Sayo-yoroku* (ed. Voss and Cieslik), pp. 41–109 *passim;* Satow's article in *TASJ*, Vol. VI (1878), pp. 56–62. Apropos of Mastrilli's martyrdom in the pit (October, 1637), Inouye scoffs at the stories of his miraculous death which were circulated at Macao, Manila, and in Europe, to the effect that he lived several days in the pit and when finally taken out to be executed, the sword could not cut his neck at the first and second attempts. Inouye states that on the contrary Mastrilli died "an agonizing death, yammering and screaming in the pit," although he does *not* insinuate that he apostatized. He states that the members of the second Rubino group who landed at Chikuzen in June, 1643, were the stupidest and most ignorant missionaries he had ever seen. They had come to Japan desirous of emulating Mastrilli's miraculous martyrdom and were sadly disillusioned when they learned that he had died in the pit. Inouye was writing confidentially for his successor's eye only, so his assertion cannot be dismissed as mere baseless propaganda; but, on the other

hand, the affidavits of Mastrilli's martyrdom which were drawn up at Macao appear to be quite trustworthy save for the sword episode, which reminds one of the similar Japanese legend about Nichiren.

[10] The foregoing from *Kirishito-ki und Sayo-yoroku* (ed. Voss and Cieslik), *passim*. This carefully annotated edition supersedes the earlier extracts given by Satow in *TASJ*, Vol. VI (1878), pp. 51–62, and other writers, both Japanese and European, in any works published before 1940. The articles of Father Thurston, S.J., in *The Month* (May–August, 1905), though still eminently readable, also require revision in the light of the recent research which has been utilized here. One result of this latter has been to show to what a remarkable extent the Dutch at Deshima were kept informed by the Nagasaki interpreters. Several assertions by Montanus, Valentyn, and other Dutch historians who used the original Deshima records have recently been fully verified after having been regarded dubiously for centuries. The fate of the second Rubino group and of the Abbáte Sidotti are typical instances. Cf. also Montanus, *Atlas Japannensis*, pp. 357 ff.; Takekoshi, *op. cit.*, Vol. II, 85–102; Ebizawa's articles in *Cultural Nippon* (Nov.–Dec., 1939); Anesaki, *Concordance, passim*, and *idem*, *PIA*, Vol. IV (1928), pp. 319–321; *MN*, Vol. V (1942), pp. 246–253, for the end of Abbáte Sidotti, and the subterranean death cells of the Kirishitan-yashiki discovered in 1940. For Iemitsu's interrogations of the apostate Jesuits, cf. *MN*, Vol. I, 293–300. For an account of the Kirishitan-yashiki, cf. *ibid.*, pp. 592–596, and *Kirishito-ki* (ed. Voss and Vieslik), pp. 191–202. As noted previously, the fate of the three European Franciscan friars who were still in hiding in Japan as late as 1640, has never been ascertained. It is quite possible that they survived to die natural deaths in the remote northeast, and that Fr. Diego de San Francisco, "el preso y mártir en vida," was one of them. The last missionary reports smuggled out of Japan were those of 1632.

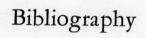

Bibliography

BIBLIOGRAPHY

NOTE.—*This bibliography is limited to classifying the principal material according to the way in which it was used in this book. The bibliography is not, of course, exhaustive, as seekers after knowledge in the standard bibliographies of Cordier, Nachod, Streit, and Laures will discover. But it does cover the ground adequately and indicates to the general reader where he should look for further information. The inclusion of so much material relating to Macao and the Philippines is deliberate, since these places were so closely connected with Japan in the Christian century. Chapter and verse for the various sources used in this book appear in the notes.*

Manuscripts

Arquivo Histórico Colonial, Lisbon. Macau, Caixa I; Papeis da India, Caixa IX: Janeiro, 1629.

Arquivo da Torre do Tombo, Lisbon. MSS de São Vicente, Tomo XIX.

Author's Collection MSS. Autograph reports of Fray Juan Pobre, O.F.M., and Fray Diego Aduarte, O.P., Valladolid, 1604–1605.

Biblioteca da Ajuda, Lisbon. Codices 49-v-71, 49-v-11, 49-iv-56; "Jesuitas na Asia."

Biblioteca Geral da Universidade de Coimbra. MSS 459, 460.

British Museum, Additional MSS.

3570: Fray Juan Pobre's Memorial. Other Franciscan MSS.

9852: Missionary conferences of 1580–1591. Padre Alessandro Valignano's "Sumarios" of 1580, 1583.

9856: Eighteenth-century transcript of Padre Valentim Carvalho's "Apologia" of 1617.

9858: Documents of the *San Felipe* affair. The martyrdom of 1597. Padre Valignano's "Apologia."

9859: Jesuit letters and reports, 1585–1625.

9860: Jesuit letters and reports of 1593–1686. The Japan documents end with Mastrilli's martyrdom, 1637.

18287: Eighteenth-century transcript of Don Rodrigo Vivero y Velasco's narrative.

British Museum Library. Codex C.62-i-18: Padre Gabriel de Mattos' report of 1616.

Jesuit Archives, Rome. MS 11: "Japsin," fols. 233–236; MS 21: fols. 135–137. (Extracts from these materials were furnished by Father Georg Schurhammer, S.J.)

Printed Archival and Source Material
and Learned Periodicals

Archivo del Bibliófilo Filipino. 5 vols. Madrid, 1895–1905.

Archivo Ibero-Americano. Estudios Históricos sobre la Orden Franciscana en España y sus Misiones. Madrid, 1914–1948.

Archivo Portuguez-Oriental. 8 vols. Nova Goa, 1857–1876.

Arquivos de Macau. 4 vols. Macao, 1929–1941.

Archivum Franciscanum Historicum. 35 vols. Florence, 1908–1942.

Archivum Historicum Societatis Iesu. 13 vols. Rome, 1932–1945.

BLAIR, E. H., and J. A. ROBERTSON, EDS. *The Philippine Islands, 1493–1898.* 55 vols. Cleveland, Ohio, 1903–1905.

(The first thirty-five volumes are relevant to the present book; they contain many translations of Spanish documents from Spanish archives.)

Boletim Eclesiástico da diocese de Macau. Macao, 1904–1941.

(The volumes for 1937–1941 are the only ones which contain relevant material.)

Catálogo de los documentos relativos á las islas Filipinas existentes en el Archivo de Indias de Sevilla por D. Pedro Torres y Lanzas, edited by Padre Pablo Pastells, S.J. Barcelona, 1925–1936.

(Volumes 1–9 contain relevant material.)

Documentos remettidos da India ou Livros das Monções. 5 vols. Lisbon, 1880–1935. (Volumes 1–4 edited by R. Bulhão Pato.)

Erudición Ibero-Ultramarino. Madrid, 1930–1935.

(Volume 2 [1931] contains valuable material on Fray Juan Pobre and the *San Felipe.*)

HANKE, LEWIS, AND A. N. CARLO, EDS. *Cuerpo de documentos del siglo XVI sobre los derechos de España en las Indias y las Filipinas.* Mexico, 1943.

Harvard Journal of Asiatic Studies. Cambridge, Mass., 1936 to date.

Imago Mundi. A Periodical Review of Early Cartography. 6 vols. Berlin, London, Stockholm, 1935–1949.

Mittheilungen der Deutschen Gesellschaft für Natur- und Völkerkunde Ostasiens. Tokyo, 1873–1940. *Jubilaumsband.* 2 vols. Tokyo, 1933.

Monumenta Nipponica. 6 vols. Tokyo, 1938–1943.

Monumenta Serica. 10 vols. Peking, 1936–1946.

Monumenta Xaveriana. Madrid, 1899–1900. Vols. I, II.

Sinica Franciscana. Florence, 1933–1936. Vols. II, III.

The T'ien Hsia Monthly. 11 vols. Shanghai, 1935–1941.

T'oung Pao. Archives concernant l'histoire, les langues, la géographie l'ethnographie et les arts de l'Asie Orientale. Leiden, 1890 to date.

Transactions of the Asiatic Society of Japan. Yokohama, Tokyo, 1872–1940.

Transactions and Proceedings of the Japan Society. London, 1896–1940.

(Volumes 31–33 are particularly relevant.)

GENERAL WORKS

AZEVEDO, JOÃO LUCIO. *Historia dos Christãos-Novos Portugueses.* Lisbon, 1922.

———. *Épocas de Portugal Económico.* Lisbon, 1929.

BARROS, JOÃO DE. *Terceira Decada da Asia.* 1st ed. Lisbon, 1563.

———. *Decada Segunda da Asia.* 2d ed. Lisbon, 1628.

———. *Decada Primeira da Asia.* 2d ed. Lisbon, 1628.

Begin ende Voortgangh van de Vereenighde Nederlantsche Geoctroyeerde Oost-Indische Compagnie. 2 vols. Amsterdam, 1646.

BOCARRO, ANTONIO. *Decada XIII da Historia da India.* 2 vols. Lisbon, 1876.

BRINKLEY, F. *Japan and China, Their History, Arts and Literature.* 12 vols. Boston, 1901–1902.

BRODRICK, JAMES. *The Origin of the Jesuits.* London, 1940.

———. *The Progress of the Jesuits.* London, 1946.

CIDADE, HERNANI. *Liçoes na Cultura e Literatura Portuguesa.* 2 vols. Coimbra, 1940–1943.

CORTESÃO, ARMANDO. *Cartografia e Cartógrafos Portugueses dos séculos XV e XVI.* 2 vols. Lisbon, 1935.

———. "O descobrimento da Australasia e a 'Questão das Molucas,'" Cap. X; and "A expansão portuguesa atraves do Pacífico (Australásia, Macau, Japão)," Cap. XI, in Vol. II of *Historia da Expansão Portuguesa no Mundo,* 3ª Parte: A Expansão Atraves do Oriente. Lisbon, 1937. Fasciculo 17.

———. *The Suma Oriental of Tomé Pires and the Book of Francisco Rodrigues,* Hakluyt Society, 2d ser., vols 89–90. London, 1944.

COUTO, DIOGO DO. *Decada Quinta da Asia.* Lisbon, 1612.

———. *Decada Setima da Asia.* Lisbon, 1616.

———. *Cinco Livros da Decada Doze.* Paris, 1645.

———. *Dialogo do Soldado Pratico.* Lisbon, 1790; new edition, Lisbon, 1937, edited by Professor Rodrigues Lapa.

FÜLÖP-MILLER, RENÉ. *The Power and Secret of the Jesuits.* London, 1930.

GOES, DAMIÃO DE. *Chronica do Rei Dom Manuel.* 2 vols. ed. Coimbra, 1926.

HILDRETH, R. *Japan as It Was and Is.* Tokyo, 1905.

HUDSON, G. F. *Europe and China.* Oxford, 1931.

JANN, A. O. M. CAP. *Die katholischen Missionen in Indien, China und Japan. Ihre organisation und das portugiesische Patronat vom 15. bis ins 18. Jahrhundert.* Paderborn, 1915.

KUNO, YOSHI S. *Japanese Expansion on the Asiatic Continent: A Study in the History of Japan with Special Reference to Her International Relations with China, Korea, and Russia.* 2 vols. Berkeley, 1937–1940.

MARNAS, F. *La "Religion de Jésus" (Iaso ja-kyo) ressucitée au Japon dans la seconde moitié du XIX siècle.* 2 vols. Paris, 1897.

MUNSTERBERG, OSKAR. *Japans auswärtiger Handel von 1542 bis 1854.* Stuttgart, 1896.

MURIAS, MANUEL. *Instrucção para o Bispo de Pequim.* Lisbon, 1943.

NAGAYAMA, TOKIHIDE. *An Album of Historical Materials Connected with Foreign Intercourse.* Nagasaki, 1918.

RODRIGUES, FRANCISCO, S.J. *A Formação Intellectual do Jesuita*. Oporto, 1917.

———. *História da Companhia de Jesus na Assistência de Portugal*. 6 vols. Oporto, 1931–1944.

———. *A Companhia de Jesus em Portugal e nas missões*. Oporto, 1935.

SANSOM, G. B. *Japan, A Short Cultural History*. London, 1938 and 1946.

———. *The Western World and Japan*. New York, 1950.

SILVA REGO, A. *O Padroado Portugues no Oriente*. Lisbon, 1940.

TAKEKOSHI, YOSABURO. *The Economic Aspects of the History of the Civilization of Japan*. 3 vols. London, 1930.

TEIXEIRA, MANUEL. *Macau e a sua diocese*. 2 vols. Macao, 1940.

WORKS DEALING WITH THE CHRISTIAN CENTURY OR CLOSELY RELATED SUBJECTS

ADUARTE, DIEGO, O.P. *Historia de la Provincia del Sancto Rosario de la Orden de Predicadores en Philippinas, Iapon, y China*. Manila, 1640.
(English translation in part in Blair and Robertson, *see above*.)

ANESAKI, MASAHARU. *A Concordance to the History of Kirishitan Missions*. Tokyo, 1930.

———. *Proceedings of the Imperial Academy*. Vols. 2–9 (1926–1933). Tokyo.

———. *Transactions of the Asiatic Society of Japan*, 2d ser. Vols. 7, 8 (1930–1931). Tokyo.

———. *Harvard Journal of Asiatic Studies*. Vol. I (1936). Cambridge, Mass.

AYRES, CHRISTOVÃO. *Fernão Mendes Pinto, Subsidios para a sua biografia e para o estudo da sua obra*. Lisbon, 1905.

———. *Fernão Mendes Pinto e o Japão. Pontos controversos-Discussão-Informações novas*. Lisbon, 1906.

BAEZA, PEDRO DE. *Este Memorial me mando el Conde de Lemos que hiziesse, que es la resolucion destas materias, y de todos los mas que le tengo dado a su Excelencia, para que se diesse a su Magestad*. Madrid, 1609.

BERNARD, HENRI, S.J. *Les Iles Philippines du grand archipel de la Chine. Un essai de conquête spirituelle de l'Extrême Orient* (1571–1641). Tientsin, 1936.

———. *Les Premiers rapports de la culture Européene avec la civilisation Japonaise*. Tokyo. 1938.

———. *La Première ambassade du Japon en Europe, 1582–1592*. Monumenta Nipponica Monographs, Nr. 6. Tokyo, 1942.

BOURDON, LÉON. "Luis de Almeida, chirurgien et marchand avant son entrée dans la Compagnie de Jésus au Japon 1525 (?)–1556," in *Mélanges d'études portugaises offerts à M. Georges Le Gentil*. Lisbon, 1949. Pp. 69–85.

————. "Les Routes des marchands Portugais entre Chine et Japon au milieu du XVI⁰ siècle," Lisbon, 1949. [Reprinted from an unspecified magazine.]

————. "Rites et jeux sacrés de la mission japonaise des Jésuites vers 1560–1565," in *Miscelânea de filologia, literatura e história cultural à memória de Francisco Adolfo Coelho*. Lisbon, 1950. Vol. II, pp. 320–337.

BOXER, C. R. *The Affair of the Madre de Deus. A Chapter in the History of the Portuguese in Japan*. London, 1929. Reprinted from the article of the same title in *Transactions of the Japan Society*. Vol. XXVI (1929), pp. 4–94. London.

————. "Notes on Early European Military Influence in Japan (1543–1853)," *Transactions of the Asiatic Society of Japan*. Vol. VIII, 2d ser. (1931), pp. 68–93. Tokyo.

————. "The Swan-song of the Portuguese in Japan, 1635–1639," *Transactions of the Japan Society*. Vol. XXVII (1930), pp. 3–11. London.

————. "European Influence on Japanese Sword-fittings, 1543–1853," *Transactions of the Japan Society*. Vol. XXVIII (1931), pp. 151–178. London.

————. "Embaixada de Macau ao Japão em 1640," *Anais do Club Militar-Naval*. Vol. 53 (1933). Lisbon.

————. "Portuguese Roteiros, 1500–1700," *The Mariner's Mirror*. Vol. XX, No. 2 (April, 1934), pp. 171–186.

————. "Hosokawa Tadaoki and the Jesuits, 1587–1645," *Transactions of the Japan Society*. Vol. XXXII (1935), pp. 79–119. London.

————. "Some Aspects of Portuguese Influence in Japan, 1542–1640," *Transactions of the Japan Society*. Vol. XXXIII (1936), pp. 13–64. London.

————. "More about the Marsden Manuscripts in the British Museum," *Transactions of the Royal Asiatic Society* (April, 1949), pp. 63–86. London.

————. "Padre João Rodriguez Tçuzzu, S.J., and His Japanese Grammars of 1604 and 1620," in *Miscelânea de filologia, literatura e história cultural à memória de Francisco Adolfo Coelho*. Lisbon, 1950. Vol. II, pp. 338–363.

————. *The Embassy of Captain Gonçalo de Siqueira de Souza to Japan in 1644–1647*. Macao, 1938.

————. "Fresh Light on the Embassy of Gonçalo de Siqueira de Souza to Japan in 1644–1647," *Transactions of the Japan Society*. Vol. XXXV (1938), pp. 13–62. London.

————. "Notes on Chinese Abroad in the Late Ming and Early Manchu Periods. Compiled from Contemporary European Sources," *T'ien Hsia Monthly*. Vol. IX (1939), pp. 447–468.

————. *As Viagens de Japão e os seus Capitães-Mores (1550–1640)*. Macao,

1941. Reprinted from *Boletim Eclesiástico de diocese de Macau*. Ano 39, nr. 448 and Ano 39, nr. 449 (July-October, 1941).

BOXER, C. R. *Azia Sinica e Japonica. Obra póstuma e inédita do frade Arrabido José de Jesus Maria*, edited by Major C. R. Boxer. Vol. I, Macao, 1941; Vol. II, Macao, 1950.

——. *Macau na época da Restauração. Macau 300 Years Ago*. Macao, 1942.

——. "Portuguese and Spanish Rivalry in the Far East during the Seventeenth Century," *Transactions of the Royal Asiatic Society*. (Dec., 1946 and April, 1947). London.

——. *Fidalgos in the Far East, 1550-1770. Fact and Fancy in the History of Macao*. The Hague, 1948.

——. "The Portuguese Padroado in East Asia and the Problem of the Chinese Rites, 1576-1773," *Boletim do Instituto Português de Hongkong*. Vol. I (1948), pp. 199-226. Macao.

BRAGA, J. M. *O Tamão dos Pioneiros Portugueses*. Macao, 1939.

——. *O Primeiro accordo Luso-Chines de 1554*. Macao, 1939.

——. "The 'Tamão' of the Portuguese Pioneers," *T'ien Hsia Monthly*. Vol. VIII (May, 1939), pp. 420-432.

——. "The Western Pioneers and Their Discovery of Macao," *Boletim do Instituto Português de Hongkong*. Vol. II (1949), pp. 7-214. Macao.

——. "The Panegyric of Alexander Valignano S.J. (Reproduced from an old Portuguese codex)," *Monumenta Nipponica*. Vol. V (1942), pp. 523-535. Tokyo.

BROWN, DELMER M. "The Importation of Gold into Japan by the Portuguese during the Sixteenth Century," *The Pacific Historical Review*. Vol. XVI (May, 1947), pp. 125-133. Berkeley, California.

——. "The Impact of Firearms on Japanese Warfare (1543-1598)," *The Far Eastern Quarterly*. Vol. VII, No. 3 (May, 1948), pp. 236-253.

CABATON, A., ED. *Brève et véridique relation des événements du Cambodge, par Gabriel Quiroga de San Antonio, de l'Ordre de Saint Dominique*. Nouvelle édition du texte espagnol avec une traduction et des notes. Paris, 1914.

CAMARA MANOEL, J.P.A. *Missões dos Jesuitas no Oriente nos seculos XVI e XVII*. Lisbon, 1894.

CARDIM, ANTONIO FRANCISCO, S.J. *Elogios e Ramalhete de flores borrifado com o sangue dos Religiosos da Companhia de Jesu, a quem os tyranos do Imperio de Jappão tiraram as vidas por odio da Fé Catholica. Com o catalogo de todos os Religiosos e seculares, que por odio da mesma Fé forão mortos naquelle Imperio, até o anno de 1640*. Lisbon, 1650.

——. *Batalhas da Companhia de Jesus na sua gloriosa Provincia do Japão*. Lisbon, 1894.

CARON, FRANÇOIS AND JOOST SCHOUTEN. *A True Description of the Mighty Kingdoms of Japan and Siam*, reprinted from the English edition of 1663, edited with an introduction, notes, and appendices by C. R. Boxer. London, 1935.

Cartas que os Padres e Irmãos da Companhia de Jesus escreverão dos Reynos de Iapão e China aos da mesma Companhia da India, e Europa, desdo anno de 1549 ate o de 1580. Evora, 1598.

(Despite the title the letters cover the period 1549–1589.)

CHAMBERLAIN, BASIL HALL. *Transactions of the Asiatic Society of Japan.* Vols. XVI–XVII (1889). Yokohama, Tokyo.

CHANG, T. T. *Sino-Portuguese Trade from 1514 to 1644.* Leiden, 1934.

COCKS, R. *The Diary of Richard Cocks, Cape-Merchant in the English Factory in Japan, 1615–1622,* edited by N. Murakami. 2 vols. Tokyo, 1899.

(This edition is preferable to the original Hakluyt Society version edited by E. Maunde Thompson.)

COLIN, F., AND P. PASTELLS, S.J. *Labor Evangélica de los obreros de la Compañía de Jesús en las islas Filipinas.* 3 vols. Barcelona, 1903–1904.

COLLIS, M. *The Grand Peregrination. Being the Life and Adventures of Fernão Mendes Pinto.* London, 1949.

DAHLGREN, W. E. *Les Débuts de la cartographie du Japon.* Upsala, 1911.

———. *Transactions of the Japan Society.* Vol. XI (1914). London.

DELPLACE, L., S.J. *Le Catholicisme au Japon.* 2 vols. Brussels, 1909–1910.

DENING, W. *The Life of Toyotomi Hideyoshi.* London, 1930.

DÍAZ, CASIMIRO, O.S.A. *Conquistas de las islas Filipinas: La Temporal por las armas de nuestros Católicos Reyes de España, y la espiritual por los religiosos de la Orden de San Agustín.* Valladolid, 1890. Vol. II.

(For the first volume of this work, *see* below, San Agustín.)

ELIA, PASQUALE M. D', S.J. *Le Origini dell'Arte Cristiana Cinese, 1583–1640.* Rome, 1939.

———. *Fonti Ricciane.* 3 vols. Rome, 1942–1949.

FERGUSON, DONALD. *Letters from Portuguese Captives in Canton, 1534–36.* Bombay, 1902.

———. *The Travels of Pedro Teixeira.* Hakluyt Society, 2d ser. Vol. IX. London, 1902.

FREITAS, JORDÃO DE. *Subsidios para a Bibliographia portugueza relativa ao estudo da Lingua Japoneza e para a biographia de Fernão Mendes Pinto.* Coimbra, 1905.

———. "A imprensa de tipos móveis em Macau e no Japão nos fins do século XVI," *Anais das Bibliotecas e Arquivos de Portugal.* Vol. I, no. 5 (1915), pp. 209–221. Coimbra.

FROIS, LUIS, S.J. [*Historia de Japam*] *Die Geschichte Japans, 1549–1578* [translated from Portuguese into German by G. Schurhammer and E. A. Voretzsch]. Leipzig, 1926.

FROIS, LUIS, S.J. *Segunda Parte da Historia de Japam* (1578–1582), edited by J. A. Abranches Pinto and Y. Okamoto. Tokyo, 1938.

GROENEVELDT, W. P. *De Nederlanders in China*. The Hague, 1898.

GUERREIRO, FERNÃO, S.J. *Relacão Anual das coisas que fizeram os Padres da Companhia de Jesus nas suas Missões ... nos annos de 1600 a 1609.* Edited by Artur Viegas [António Antunes Vieira, S.J.]. 3 vols. Coimbra, 1930–1942.
(Some of the quotations from the second volume are taken from the original edition of 1605.)

HAAS, HANS. *Geschichte des Christentums in Japan*. 2 vols. Tokyo, 1902–1904.

KAMMERER, A. *La Découverte de la Chine par les Portugais au XVIième siècle et la cartographie des portulans*. Leiden, 1944.

Kirishito-ki und Sayo-yoroku. Japanische Dokumente zur Missionsgeschichte des 17. Jahrhunderts, by Gustav Voss, S.J., and Hubert Cieslik, S.J., Monumenta Nipponica Monographs, Nr. 1. Tokyo, 1940.

LAURES, JOHANNES, S.J. *Nobunaga und das Christentum*, Monumenta Nipponica Monographs, Nr. 10. Tokyo, 1950.

LE GENTIL, GEORGES. *Fernão Mendez Pinto. Un Précurseur de l'exotisme au XVIᵉ siècle*. Paris, 1947.

LINSCHOTEN, J. H. [*Itinerario and Reys-gheschrift*, 1595–1596] *John Huighen Van Linschoten His Discovrs of Voyages into Ye Easte and West Indies*, translated by John Wolfe. London, 1598.

———. *Itinerario*, 1579–1592, annotated reprint of original Dutch edition of 1596. 5 vols., edited by J. C. M. Warnsinck [vols. 4 and 5]. The Hague, Linschoten Vereeniging, 1910–1939.

MCCALL, J. E. "Early Jesuit Art in the Far East," *Artibus Asiae*. Vols. X–XI (1947–1948).

MAGGS BROS., LTD. *Catalogue No. 515. Bibliotheca Asiatica. Part III: Manuscripts of the Sixteenth and Seventeenth Centuries on the Spanish and Portuguese Catholic Missions and Martyrdoms in India, China, Japan.* London, 1929.

MANÇANO, MELCHIOR, O.P. *Relacion verdadera del insigne y excelente Martyrio, que diez Religiosos de la sagrada Orden de Predicadores, padecieron en el populoso Imperio de Iapon, por Christo nuestro Señor, el año pasado de 1622, i de otro Religioso de la mesma Orden que padecio el año de 1618, en el dicho Reino*. Binondoc, 1623.

MARTINEZ, DOMINGO, O.F.M. *Compendio Histórico de la Apostolica Provincia de San Gregorio de Philipinas, de Religiosos descalzos de N. P. San Francisco*. Madrid, 1756.

MONTANUS, ARNOLDUS. *Atlas Japannensis: Being Remarkable Addresses by way of Embassy from the East-India Company of the United Provinces to the Emperor of Japan*, translated by John Ogilby. London, 1670.

MOREJON, PEDRO, S.J. *A Briefe Relation of the Persecution Lately Made Against the Catholike Christians in the Kingdome of Iaponia. Divided into two Bookes. Taken out of the Annuall Letters of the Fathers of the Society of Jesus and other Authenticall Informations. Written in Spanish, and printed first at Mexico in the West Indies, the yeare of Christ MDCXVI. And Newly translated into English by W. W. Gent.* Printed at the English Jesuit College of Saint-Omer, 1619.

(This translation into English from the Spanish was by W. Wright, S.J. A second part was announced but never published.)

MORGA, ANTONIO DE. *Sucesos de las islas Filipinas,* por el Dr. Antonio de Morga. Nueva edición, enriquecida con los escritos inéditos del mismo autor, ilustrada con numerosas notas que amplían el texto y prologada extensamente por W. E. Retana. Madrid, 1909.

MUNDY, PETER. *The Travels of Peter Mundy in Europe and Asia, 1608–1667.* Vol. III, Pt. I: *Travels in England, Western India, Achin, Macao and the Canton River, 1634–1637,* edited by R. C. Temple and L. Anstey. Hakluyt Society, 2d ser. Vol. XLV. London, 1919.

MURAKAMI, NAOJIRO. *Letters Written by English Residents in Japan, 1611–1623.* Tokyo, 1900.

MURDOCH, JAMES, AND ISOH YAMAGATA. *A History of Japan during the Century of Early Foreign Intercourse, 1542–1651.* Kobe, 1903.

NAGAYAMA, TOKIHIDE. *Collection of Historical Materials Connected with the Roman Catholic Religion in Japan (Kirishitan Shiryo-shu).* Nagasaki, 1924. Text in English and Japanese.

NAVARRETE, DOMINGO FERNANDEZ, O.P. *Controversias Antiguas y Modernas de la Mission de la Gran China.* Madrid, 1679.

NORONHA, MIGUEL DE. *Diário do 3° Conde de Linhares, Vicerei da India,* Vol. I [no more published]. Lisbon, 1937.

NUTTALL, ZELIA M. *The Earliest Historical Relations between Mexico and Japan,* University of California Publications in American Archaeology and Ethnology, Vol. 4, no. 1. Berkeley, California, 1906.

PAGÉS, LÉON. *Histoire de la religion Chrétienne au Japon depuis 1598 jusqu'a 1651.* 2 vols. Paris, 1869–1870.

PASKE-SMITH, MONTAGUE. *Japanese Traditions of Christianity.* Kobe, 1929.

———. "Japanese Trade and Residence in the Philippines before and during the Spanish Occupation," *Transactions of the Asiatic Society of Japan.* Vol. XLII (Nov., 1914), pp. 685–710. Tokyo.

PÉREZ, LORENZO, O.F.M. *Cartas y Relaciones del Japón.* 3 vols. Madrid, 1916–1923.

———. *Relaciones de Fr. Diego de San Francisco sobre las persecuciones del cristianismo en el Japón, 1625–1632.* Madrid, 1914.

———. *Apostolado y Martirio del Beato Luis Sotelo en el Japón.* Madrid, 1924.

Pérez, Lorenzo, O.F.M. *Fr. Jerónimo de Jesús Restaurador de las Misiones del Japon, sus cartas y relaciones, 1595–1604.* Florence, 1929.

Peri, Noël. *Essai sur les relations du Japon et de l'Indochine aux XVIᵉ et XVIIᵉ siècles.* Hanoi, 1923.

Ribadeneira, Marcelo de, O.F.M. *Historia de las islas del archipiélago Filipino y reinos de la Gran China, Tartaria, Cochinchina, Malaca, Siam, Cambodge y Japón.* [Barcelona, 1601]. Edicion, prologo, y notas, por el P. Juan R. de Legísima, O.F.M. Madrid, 1947.

Ribeiro, Vitor. *Bispos Portugueses e Jesuitas no Japão. Cartas de D. Luiz Cerqueira.* Lisbon, 1936.

Riess, Ludwig. "History of the English Factory at Hirado," *Transactions of the Asiatic Society of Japan.* Vol. XXVI (1898), pp. 1–114, 163–218. Yokohama.

———. "Der Aufstand von Shimabara, 1637–1638," *Mittheilungen der Deutschen Gesellschaft für Natur- und Völkerkunde Ostasiens.* Vol. V, Heft XLV (1890), pp. 191–214.

———. "Die Ursachen der Vertreibung der Portugiesen aus Japan (1614–1639)," *Mittheilungen der Deutschen Gesellschaft für Natur- und Völkerkunde Ostasiens,* Vol. VII (1898), pp. 1–52.

Rodriguez, João, S.J. (Tçuzzu). *Arte da lingoa de Iapam composto pello Padre Ioão Rodriguez Portugues da Companhia de Iesu.* Nagasaki, 1604.

———. *Arte Breve da lingoa Iapoa tirada da Arte Grande da mesma lingoa.* Macao, 1620.

Rodriguez Girão, João, S.J. *Carta anua da Vice-Província do Japão do ano de 1604,* ed. by Antonio Baião. Coimbra, 1932.

Sadler, L. *The Maker of Modern Japan. The Life of Tokugawa Ieyasu.* London, 1937.

———. *Cha-no-yu. The Japanese Tea Ceremony.* Kobe, 1934.

San Agustín, Gaspar de, O.S.A. *Conquistas de las islas Philippinas la temporal por las armas del Señor Don Philipe Segundo El Prudente; y la espiritual por los religiosos del orden de San Agustín.* Madrid, 1698. (For the second part of this work, *see* above, Diaz.)

Santa Inés, Francisco de, O.F.M. *Crónica de la Provincia de San Gregorio Magno de Religiosos descalzos de N. S. P. San Francisco en las islas Filipinas, China, y Japón en 1676.* Manila, 1892.

Saris, John. *The Voyage of Captain John Saris to Japan, 1613,* edited by Sir E. M. Satow. Hakluyt Society, 2d ser. Vol. V. London, 1900.

Schilling, Dorotheus, O.F.M. *Das Schulwesen der Jesuiten in Japan 1551–1614.* Münster, 1931.

———. *Os Portugueses e a introdução da medicina no Japão.* Coimbra, 1937.

———. "Christliche Druckereien in Japan (1590–1614)," *Gutenberg-Jahrbuch.* Vol. XV (1940), pp. 356–395.

————. "Der erste Tabak in Japan," *Monumenta Nipponica.* Vol. V (1942), pp. 113–143. Tokyo.

————. "Was des Franziskaner Odorich von Pardenone in 14. Jahrhundert in Japan?" *Monumenta Nipponica.* Vol. VI (1943), pp. 86–109. Tokyo.

————. "Cattura e prigionia dei Santi Martiri di Nagasaki, *Antonianum.* Vol. XXII (1947), pp. 201–242. Rome.

————. "Zwei unveröffentlichte Briefe des seligen Ludwig Sotelo, O.F.M.," *Antonianum.* Vol. XX (1948), pp. 127–148. Rome.

SCHURHAMMER, GEORG, S.J. *Shin-To the Way of the Gods in Japan According to the Printed and Unprinted Reports of the Jesuit Missionaries in the Sixteenth and Seventeenth Centuries.* Leipzig, 1923.

————. *Fernão Mendes Pinto und seine "Peregrinaçam."* Leipzig, 1927.

————. *Das Kirchliche sprachproblem in der Japanischen Jesuiten-mission des 16. und 17. Jahrhunderts.* Tokyo, 1928.

————. *Die disputationen des P. Cosme de Torres, S.J., mit den Buddhisten in Yamaguchi im jahre 1551.* Tokyo, 1929.

————. *Die Zeitgenössischen Quellen zur Geschichte Portugiesisch-Asiens und seiner Nachbarländer zur zeit des hl. Franz Xaver.* Leipzig, 1932.

————, with J. Wicki, S.J. *Epistolae S. Francisci Xaverii aliaque eius scripta 1535–1552.* 2 vols. Rome, 1944–1945.

————. "Das Stadbild Kyotos zur Zeit des hl. Franz Xaver, 1551," *Anthropos.* Vols. XIV–XV (1919–1920), pp. 821–856; Vols. XVI–XVII (1921–1922), pp. 147–182. St. Gabriel-Mödling, Vienna.

————. "P. Johann Rodriguez Tçuzzu als Geschichtschreiber Japans," *Archivum Historicum Societatis Iesu,* Vol. I, fasc. 1 (1932), pp. 23–40. Rome.

————. "Die Jesuiten missionare des 16. und 17. Jahrhunderts und ihr Einfluss auf die japanische Malerei," *Jubilaümsband der Deutschen Gesellschaft für Natur- und Völkerkunde Ostasiens.* Teil II (1933), pp. 116–126. Tokyo.

————. "O Descobrimento do Japão pelos Portugueses no ano de 1543," *Anais da Academia Portuguesa da História.* 2ª ser. Vol. I (1946), pp. 1–172. Lisbon.

————. "Der hl. Franz Xaver in Japan, 1549–1551," *Schriftenreihe der Neuen Zeitschrift für Missionswissenschaft.* Vol. II, pp. 165–186, 255–273. Reprint, Beckenreid, 1947.

SCHÜTTE, JOSEPH, S.J. "Drei Unterrichtsbüches für Japanische Jesuitenprediger aus dem XVI. Jahrhundert," *Archivum Historicum Societatis Iesu.* Vol. VIII (1939), pp. 223–256. Rome.

————. "Christliche Japanische Literatur, bilder und druckblätter in einem unbekannten Vatikanischen codex aus dem Jahre 1591," *Archivum Historicum Societatis Iesu.* Vol. IX (1940), pp. 226–280. Rome.

————. *Il ceremoniale per i Missionari del Giappone.* Rome, 1946.

SHIMMURA, I. *Studies on the Christian Relics in Japan Found Near Takatsuki and in Kyoto.* Tokyo, 1926.

SICARDO, JOSEPH, O.S.A. *Christiandad del Japon y dilatada persecucion que padeció. Memorias Sacras de los martyres de las ilustres Religiones de Santo Domingo, San Francisco, Compañia de Jesus, y crecido numero de Seglares; y con especialidad de los Religiosos del Orden de N. P. S. Augustin.* Madrid, 1698.

SOUSA, FRANCISCO DE, S.J. *Oriente Conquistado,* 2 vols. Lisbon, 1710.

STEICHEN, M. *Les Daimyos Chrétiens ou un siècle de l'histoire et politique du Japon, 1549–1650.* Hongkong, 1904.

TACCHI-VENTURÍ, PIETRO, S.J. "Tre Lettere inedité di quatro *Beati* Martiri del Giappone," *Archivum Historicum Societatis Iesu.* Vol. IX (1940), pp. 40–49. Rome.

TAKEKOSHI, YOSABURO. *The Story of the Wako.* Tokyo, 1940.

TEIXEIRA, PADRE MANUEL. *Macau e a sua diocese.* 2 vols. Macao, 1940.

———. *Camões em Macau.* Macao, 1940.

———. *A Fachada de São Paulo.* Macao, 1940.

The Palme of Christian Fortitude or the Glorious Combats of Christians in Iaponia. Taken out of letters of the Society of Jesus from thence Anno 1624, translation ascribed to Edmund Neville. Douai or Saint-Omer, 1630.

THURSTON, HERBERT, S.J. "Japan and Christianity," *The Month, A Catholic Magazine* (1905). London.

TSCHEPE, ALBERT, S.J. *Japans Beziehungen zu China seit den altesten Zeit bis zum Jahre 1600.* Yenchoufou, 1907.

VALIGNANO, ALESSANDRO, S.J. *Historia del principio y progresso de la compañia de Jesús en las Indias Orientales, 1542–1564,* edited by Josef Wicki, S.J. Rome, 1944.

———. *Advertimentos y avisos acerca dos costumes e catangues de Jappão.* See above, Schütte, *Il ceremoniale.*

VASCONCELLOS, FRAZÃO DE. "Accão heróica de André Pessoa, Capitão da nau 'Madre de Deus' em Nagasaqui no ano de 1610. Relação contemporânea e outros documentos inéditos publicados por F. de V.," *Anais da Academia Portuguesa da História.* Vol. VIII (1944), pp. 301–325. Lisbon.

JAPANESE LANGUAGE WORKS

AKIYAMA, KENZO. *Nichi-Shi kosho-shi kenkyu.* Tokyo, 1939.

Adzuchi-Momoyama jidai Shiron. Tokyo, 1914.

ANESAKI, MASAHARU. *Kirishitan shumon no hakugai to sempuku.* Tokyo, 1925.

———. *Kirishitan dendo no kohai.* Tokyo, 1930.

EBIZAWA, ARIMICHI. *Kirishitan-shi no kenkyu.* Tokyo, 1942.

———. *Kirishitan tenseki soko.* Tokyo, 1943.

———. *Kirishitan no shakai katsudo oyobi Namban igaku.* Tokyo, 1944.

FUJITA, TOYOHACHI. *To-Sei kosho-shi no kenkyu (Nankai-hen)*. Tokyo, 1932.

GUNJI, KIICHI. *Tokugawa Jidai no Nichi-Sha*. Tokyo, 1940. New ed. entitled: *Jushichi Seiki ni okeru Nichi-Thai kankei*. Tokyo, 1942.

ISHIDA, MIKINOSUKE. *Nankai ni kansuru Shina Shiryo*. Tokyo, 1945.

IWAO, SEIICHI. *Nanyo Nihon-machi no kenkyu*. Tokyo, 1944.

KATAOKA, P. Y. *Takayama Ukon Taiyu Nagafusa den*. Tokyo, 1936.

KAWAJIMA, MOTOJIRO. *Shuin-sen boeki-shi*. Kyoto, 1921.

KODA, SHIGETOMO. *Oranda Zatsuwa*. Tokyo, 1934.

———. *Oranda Yawa*. Tokyo, 1931.

LAURES, JOHANNES, S.J. *Oda Nobunaga to Kirisuto-kyo*. Tokyo, 1947.

———. *Kinki shoki Christokyo-shi*. Tokyo, 1948.

———. *Takayama Ukon no shogai*. Tokyo, 1948.

MURAKAMI, NAOJIRO. *Ikoku ofuku shokan-shu. Sotei Ikoku Nikki-sho*. Tokyo, 1929.

———. *Yasokai-shi Nihon Tsushin*. 4 vols. Tokyo, 1926–1936.

Nichi-Ho kotsu. Vol. I. Tokyo, 1929; Vol. I has Portuguese subtitle *Boletim da Sociedade Luso-Japonesa*. Vol. II (1943). Tokyo.

OKAMOTO, YOSHITOMO (OR RYOCHI). *Nagasaki kaiko izen O-hakurai oko*. Tokyo, 1931.

———. *Juroku Seiki Nichi-O kotsu-shi no kenkyu*. Tokyo, 1936.

———. *Juroku Seiki sekai chizu-jo no Nihon*. Tokyo, 1938.

———. *Momoyama jidai Kirisuto-kyo Bunka*. Tokyo, 1947.

———. *Kirishitan kenkyu*. Vol. III (1947), 225–319. Tokyo.

———. *Kyushu sanko ken-O shisetsu koki*. Tokyo, 1949.

SHIMMURA, IDZURU. *Nihon Kirishitan Bunka-shi*. Tokyo, 1941.

———. *Namban Koki*. Tokyo, 1929.

———. *Zoku Namban Koki*. Tokyo, 1929.

TOKUTOMI, IICHIRO. *Kinsei Nihon Kokumin-shi*. Vols. 1–14; rev. ed. Tokyo, 1934–1945.

TOYAMA, USABURO. *Namban-sen boeki-shi*. Tokyo, 1943.

REFERENCE WORKS AND BIBLIOGRAPHIES

ADDIS, W. E. *Catholic Dictionary*. London, 1917.

ANESAKI, MASAHARU. *A Concordance to the History of Kirishitan Missions (Catholic Missions in Japan in the Sixteenth and Seventeenth Centuries)*. Tokyo, 1930.

BRAMSEN, WILLIAM. *Japanese Chronological Tables*. Tokyo, 1880.

CHAMBERLAIN, B. H. *Things Japanese*. New ed. Kobe, 1927; reprinted, 1938.

CORDIER, HENRI. *Bibliotheca Japonica*. Paris, 1912.

DALGADO, S. R. *Glossário Luso-Asiático*. 2 vols. Coimbra, 1919–1921.

LAURES, JOHANNES, S.J. *Kirishitan Bunko. A Manual of Books and Docu-*

ments on the Early Christian Missions in Japan. Monumenta Nipponica Monographs, Nr. 5. Tokyo, 1940.

————. *Supplement to Kirishitan Bunko.* Monumenta Nipponica Monographs, Nr. 5a. Tokyo, 1941.

STREIT, ROBERT, O.M.I., AND P. JOHANNES DINDINGER, O.M.I. *Bibliotheca Missionum.* Vols. IV–V, Aachen, 1928–1929.

PAPINOT, E. *Historical and Geographical Dictionary of Japan.* Yokohama, 1909; Ann Arbor, Mich., 1947.

PFISTER, LOUIS, S.J. *Notices biographiques et bibliographiques sur les Jésuites de l'ancienne Mission de Chine* (1552–1773). 2 vols. Shanghai, 1932–1934.

YULE, SIR HENRY AND A. C. BURNELL. *Hobson-Jobson. A Glossary of Anglo-Indian Words and Phrases.* London, 1903.

ADDENDA TO THE BIBLIOGRAPHY

The following are the principal works in this field which have been published between 1950 and 1966. They all contain adequate bibliographies which list other relevant books and articles.

BOXER, C.R. *The Great Ship from Amacon; Annals of Macao and the Old Japan Trade, 1555-1640.* Lisbon, 1959; reprinted, 1963.

BOXER, C.R., and J. S. CUMMINS. "The Dominican Mission in Japan (1602-1622) and Lope de Vega," *Archivum Fratrum Praedicatorum*, Vol. XXXIII (1963), pp. 5-88. Rome.

CIESLIK, HUMBERT, S.J. *Hoku-ho Tanken-ki.* Tokyo, 1961.

COOPER, MICHAEL, S.J. *They Came to Japan; An Anthology of European Reports on Japan, 1543-1640.* Berkeley and Los Angeles, 1965.

FERNÁNDEZ, PABLO, O.P. *Domínicos donde nace el Sol.* Barcelona, 1958.

HARTMANN, ARNULF, O.S.A. *The Augustinians in Seventeenth Century Japan.* King City, Ontario, 1965.

LAURES, JOHANNES, S.J. *Kirishitan Bunko.* 3d ed., revised and enlarged, Tokyo, 1957.

————. *The Catholic Church in Japan; A Short History.* Tokyo, 1954.

LOPE DE VEGA, FELIX CARPIO. *Triunfo de la Fee en los Reynos del Japon.* Ed. by J. S. Cummins, London, 1965.

LOPEZ GAY, JESÚS, S.J. *El Matrimonio de los Japoneses; Problema, y soluciones según un ms. inédito de Gil de la Mata, S.J. 1547-1599* Rome, 1964.

————. *El Catecumenado en la mision del Japon del siglo XVI.* Rome, 1966.

SCHURHAMMER, GEORG, S.J. *Gesammelte Studien.* 4 vols., in 5, Rome, 1962-65. Especially useful are Vols. I (a new and revised edition of the *Zeitgenössischen Quellen*), II (*Orientalia*), and III (*Xaveriana*).

————. *Franz Xaver, Sein Leben und seine Zeit.* II Band, *Asien, 1541-1552,* Erster Halbband, *Indien und Indonesien, 1541-1547,* Freiburg, 1963. The concluding volume, covering Xavier's stay in Japan, is in press.

SCHÜTTE, JOSEF FRANZ, J.S. *Valignano's Missionsgrundsätze für Japan.* 2 vols., Rome, 1951-58. Further volumes in progress.

————. *El "Archivo del Japon." Vicisitudes del Archivo Jesuítico del Extremo Oriente. Descripción del fondo existente en la Real Academia de la Historia de Madrid.* Madrid, 1964.

UYTTENBROECK, THOMAS, O.F.M. *Early Franciscans in Japan.* Himeiji, 1958.

VALIGNANO ALEJANDRO, S.J. *Sumario de las cosas de Japon (1583). Adiciones del sumario de Japon (1592).* Ed. by S.L. Alvarez-Taladriz. Vol. I, Tokyo, 1954. Vol. II, in press.

There is now a Japanese historical review, entitled *Kirishitan Kenkyu* and published at Tokyo, which is devoted to the study of Christianity in feudal Japan. This periodical and the older review edited at Sophia University (Jochi-Daigaku), *Monumenta Nipponica*, contain contributions by leading Japanese, European, and American authorities.

INDEX AND GLOSSARY